Dictionary of Literary Biography

Documentary Series

1 *Sherwood Anderson, Willa Cather, John Dos Passos, Theodore Dreiser, F. Scott Fitzgerald, Ernest Hemingway, Sinclair Lewis,* edited by Margaret A. Van Antwerp (1982)

2 *James Gould Cozzens, James T. Farrell, William Faulkner, John O'Hara, John Steinbeck, Thomas Wolfe, Richard Wright,* edited by Margaret A. Van Antwerp (1982)

3 *Saul Bellow, Jack Kerouac, Norman Mailer, Vladimir Nabokov, John Updike, Kurt Vonnegut,* edited by Mary Bruccoli (1983)

4 *Tennessee Williams,* edited by Margaret A. Van Antwerp and Sally Johns (1984)

5 *American Transcendentalists,* edited by Joel Myerson (1988)

6 *Hardboiled Mystery Writers: Raymond Chandler, Dashiell Hammett, Ross Macdonald,* edited by Matthew J. Bruccoli and Richard Layman (1989)

7 *Modern American Poets: James Dickey, Robert Frost, Marianne Moore,* edited by Karen L. Rood (1989)

8 *The Black Aesthetic Movement,* edited by Jeffrey Louis Decker (1991)

9 *American Writers of the Vietnam War: W. D. Ehrhart, Larry Heinemann, Tim O'Brien, Walter McDonald, John M. Del Vecchio,* edited by Ronald Baughman (1991)

10 *The Bloomsbury Group,* edited by Edward L. Bishop (1992)

11 *American Proletarian Culture: The Twenties and The Thirties,* edited by Jon Christian Suggs (1993)

12 *Southern Women Writers: Flannery O'Connor, Katherine Anne Porter, Eudora Welty,* edited by Mary Ann Wimsatt and Karen L. Rood (1994)

13 *The House of Scribner, 1846–1904,* edited by John Delaney (1996)

14 *Four Women Writers for Children, 1868–1918,* edited by Caroline C. Hunt (1996)

Yearbooks

1980 edited by Karen L. Rood, Jean W. Ross, and Richard Ziegfeld (1981)

1981 edited by Karen L. Rood, Jean W. Ross, and Richard Ziegfeld (1982)

1982 edited by Richard Ziegfeld; associate editors: Jean W. Ross and Lynne C. Zeigler (1983)

1983 edited by Mary Bruccoli and Jean W. Ross; associate editor: Richard Ziegfeld (1984)

1984 edited by Jean W. Ross (1985)

1985 edited by Jean W. Ross (1986)

1986 edited by J. M. Brook (1987)

1987 edited by J. M. Brook (1988)

1988 edited by J. M. Brook (1989)

1989 edited by J. M. Brook (1990)

1990 edited by James W. Hipp (1991)

1991 edited by James W. Hipp (1992)

1992 edited by James W. Hipp (1993)

1993 edited by James W. Hipp, contributing editor George Garrett (1994)

1994 edited by James W. Hipp, contributing editor George Garrett (1995)

1995 edited by James W. Hipp, contributing editor George Garrett (1996)

Concise Series

Concise Dictionary of American Literary Biography, 6 volumes (1988-1989): *The New Consciousness, 1941-1968; Colonization to the American Renaissance, 1640-1865; Realism, Naturalism, and Local Color, 1865-1917; The Twenties, 1917-1929; The Age of Maturity, 1929-1941; Broadening Views, 1968-1988.*

Concise Dictionary of British Literary Biography, 8 volumes (1991-1992): *Writers of the Middle Ages and Renaissance Before 1660; Writers of the Restoration and Eighteenth Century, 1660-1789; Writers of the Romantic Period, 1789-1832; Victorian Writers, 1832-1890; Late Victorian and Edwardian Writers, 1890-1914; Modern Writers, 1914-1945; Writers After World War II, 1945-1960; Contemporary Writers, 1960 to Present.*

Dictionary of Literary Biography® • Volume One Hundred Seventy-Seven

Italian Novelists Since World War II

Dictionary of Literary Biography® • Volume One Hundred Seventy-Seven

Italian Novelists Since World War II

Edited by
Augustus Pallotta
Syracuse University

A Bruccoli Clark Layman Book
Gale Research
Detroit, Washington, D.C., London

The paper used in this publication meets the minimum requirements
of American National Standard for Information Sciences—Permanence
Paper for Printed Library Materials, ANSI Z39.48-1984.♾ ™

Library of Congress Cataloging-in-Publication Data

Italian novelists since World War II / edited by Augustus Pallotta.
p. c.m.–(Dictionary of literary biography; v. 177)
"A Bruccoli Clark Layman book."
Includes bibliographical references and index.
ISBN 0-8103-9940-7 (alk. paper)
1. Authors, Italian–20th century–Biography. 2. Italy–Civilization–1945- . I. Pallotta, Augustus.
II. Series.
PQ 4057.I73 1997
853' .91409–dc21   97-6993
[B]   CIP

10 9 8 7 6 5 4 3 2 1

To my brother Ernie with love

Contents

Plan of the Series

. . . Almost the most prodigious asset of a country, and perhaps its most precious possession, is its native literary product — when that product is fine and noble and enduring.

Mark Twain*

The advisory board, the editors, and the publisher of the *Dictionary of Literary Biography* are joined in endorsing Mark Twain's declaration. The literature of a nation provides an inexhaustible resource of permanent worth. We intend to make literature and its creators better understood and more accessible to students and the reading public, while satisfying the standards of teachers and scholars.

To meet these requirements, *literary biography* has been construed in terms of the author's achievement. The most important thing about a writer is his writing. Accordingly, the entries in *DLB* are career biographies, tracing the development of the author's canon and the evolution of his reputation.

The purpose of *DLB* is not only to provide reliable information in a convenient format but also to place the figures in the larger perspective of literary history and to offer appraisals of their accomplishments by qualified scholars.

The publication plan for *DLB* resulted from two years of preparation. The project was proposed to Bruccoli Clark by Frederick C. Ruffner, president of the Gale Research Company, in November 1975. After specimen entries were prepared and typeset, an advisory board was formed to refine the entry format and develop the series rationale. In meetings held during 1976, the publisher, series editors, and advisory board approved the scheme for a comprehensive biographical dictionary of persons who contributed to North American literature. Editorial work on the first volume began in January 1977, and it was published in 1978. In order to make *DLB* more than a reference tool and to compile volumes that individually have claim to status as literary history, it was decided to organize volumes by topic, period, or genre. Each of these freestanding volumes provides a biographical-bibliographical guide and overview for a particular area of literature. We are convinced that this organization — as opposed to a single alphabet method — constitutes a valuable innovation in the presentation of reference material. The volume plan necessarily requires many decisions for the placement and treatment of authors who might properly be included in two or three volumes. In some instances a major figure will be included in separate volumes, but with different entries emphasizing the aspect of his career appropriate to each volume. Ernest Hemingway, for example, is represented in *American Writers in Paris, 1920–1939* by an entry focusing on his expatriate apprenticeship; he is also in *American Novelists, 1910–1945* with an entry surveying his entire career. Each volume includes a cumulative index of the subject authors and articles. Comprehensive indexes to the entire series are planned.

The series has been further augmented by the *DLB Yearbooks* (since 1981) which update published entries and add new entries to keep the *DLB* current with contemporary activity. There have also been *DLB Documentary Series* volumes which provide biographical and critical source materials for figures whose work is judged to have particular interest for students. One of these companion volumes is entirely devoted to Tennessee Williams.

We define literature as the *intellectual commerce of a nation:* not merely as belles lettres but as that ample and complex process by which ideas are generated, shaped, and transmitted. *DLB* entries are not limited to "creative writers" but extend to other figures who in their time and in their way influenced the mind of a people. Thus the series encompasses historians, journalists, publishers, bibliographers, and screenwriters. By this means readers of *DLB* may be aided to perceive literature not as cult scripture in the keeping of intellectual high priests but firmly positioned at the center of a nation's life.

DLB includes the major writers appropriate to each volume and those standing in the ranks behind them. Scholarly and critical counsel has been sought in deciding which minor figures to include and how full their entries should be. Wherever possible, useful references are made to figures who do not warrant separate entries.

Each *DLB* volume has an expert volume editor responsible for planning the volume, selecting the figures for inclusion, and assigning the entries. Volume editors are also responsible for preparing, where appropriate, appendices surveying the major periodicals and literary and intellectual movements for their volumes, as well as lists of further readings. Work on the series as a whole is coordinated at the Bruccoli Clark Layman editorial center in Columbia, South Carolina, where the editorial staff is responsible for accuracy and utility of the published volumes.

One feature that distinguishes *DLB* is the illustration policy – its concern with the iconography of literature. Just as an author is influenced by his surroundings, so is the reader's understanding of the author enhanced by a knowledge of his environment. Therefore *DLB* volumes include not only drawings, paintings, and photographs of authors, often depicting them at various stages in their careers, but also illustrations of their families and places where they lived. Title pages are regularly reproduced in facsimile along with dust jackets for modern authors. The dust jackets are a special feature of *DLB* because they often document better than anything else the way in which an author's work was perceived in its own time. Specimens of the writers' manuscripts and letters are included when feasible.

Samuel Johnson rightly decreed that ''The chief glory of every people arises from its authors.'' The purpose of the *Dictionary of Literary Biography* is to compile literary history in the surest way available to us – by accurate and comprehensive treatment of the lives and work of those who contributed to it.

The *DLB* Advisory Board

Introduction

World War II represents a watershed in the social and cultural history of Italy: the end of the war coincided with the beginning of a process of social transformation that would continue, essentially uninterrupted, for the next fifty years. The novel, historically the most socially conscious literary form, is a witness to and an accurate mirror of this transformation. The novelists treated in this volume convey, through various modes of narration and often contrasting viewpoints and ideologies, the social and political realities they lived; and they often identify the war as the cause of those realities.

The most important vehicle of social expression in the second half of the twentieth century, the novel has replaced poetry as the dominant literary genre in Italy. Like the cinema, the novel sought to renew itself following two decades of caution and apprehension under the repressive Fascist regime. Fascist censorship was harsh but did not suppress all creative activity. Established authors who had little sympathy for the government, such as Carlo Bernari, Alberto Moravia, and Elio Vittorini, continued to publish; indeed, looking back, one is surprised by the amount of literature obliquely critical of Fascism that was cleared by the censors. Even so, the damage wrought by censorship was considerable. It was, above all, psychological: it stifled creativity by reminding artists of the risks they incurred.

The fall of Fascism afforded writers and filmmakers freedom of expression but also made them cognizant of the challenge posed by the new realities of national life: political pluralism, a democratic government, and a vast array of social and economic problems. From 1945 to 1955 the cinema, more than the novel, conveyed a genuine picture of Italian life. The term *Neorealism,* first used by the film critic Antonio Pietrangeli in his review of Luchino Visconti's *Ossessione* (Obsession, 1942) in *Cinema,* soon began to be widely applied to the novel as well. Pietrangeli pointed out that Visconti's film conveyed a sense of authenticity that contrasted sharply with the artificial atmosphere of the films produced under the Fascist regime. Cesare Zavattini, a writer of screenplays who collaborated with the director Vittorio De Sica, remarked in the December 1952 issue of the *Rivista del cinema italiano* that the main objective of filmmaking is not to entertain but to urge the spectator to think and that cinema has a moral responsibility "to represent reality and avoid fantasy."

Italian Neorealism was heavily influenced by Marxism, which would prove to be the most incisive force in Italian culture for the first three decades following the war. Most Italian writers emerged from the struggle against Fascism as committed Marxists who viewed the Communist Party as the most effective vehicle for effecting a social, political, and cultural renewal of Italian society. The party boasted its own cultural organs, the daily *L'Unità* and the review *Rinascita;* in addition such journals as *Politecnico* and *Il menabò della letteratura* were openly receptive to Marxism.

The principal apostle of Italian Marxism was Antonio Gramsci, a Sardinian intellectual who in 1924 became general secretary of the Communist Party. He was arrested by the Fascist regime in 1926, and died a week after being released from prison in 1937 at the age of forty-six. His works, including *Letteratura e vita nazionale* (Literature and National Life, 1950), advocated the creation of a national literature that would identify the needs and the aspirations of the lower classes. Along with the suffering and destitution caused by the war, Gramsci's works heightened the social consciousness of Italian writers.

The relationship between leftist writers and the Italian Communist Party was strained in 1956 when Soviet tanks rolled into Hungary to quell a revolt against the Communist regime. Moravia, Vittorini, and Italo Calvino were among the prominent writers who publicly dissociated themselves from the party. But separation from the party did not mean estrangement from Communism: many of the writers who opposed Soviet foreign policy did not lose faith in Marxism, and they continued to call attention to the plight of the economically deprived. For example, Moravia, the most popular postwar Italian writer and one with a large international readership, displayed in his novels a strong and relentless animosity toward the middle class, whose values and outlook he deemed superficial, egotistical, and degenerate.

Since its birth with Alessandro Manzoni's *I promessi sposi* (1827; translated as *The Betrothed,* 1828), the modern Italian novel has had to confront the thorny questions of regionalism and language—two sides of the same coin, inasmuch as virtually every region in Italy has its own dialect. Benito Mussolini had sought, with marginal success, to eliminate regional dialects; after World War II Neorealism rekindled the problems of language and regional identity. Following the linguistic experimentation pioneered by Carlo Emilio Gadda, the novelist Beppe Fenoglio, who was strongly attached to the Langhe region of his native Piedmont, recast the language of his people in standard Italian, although in some works, such as *La malora* (1954; translated as *Ruin,* 1992), he mixed standard Italian and local speech. A more radical position was taken by Pier Paolo Pasolini, whose early poetry was written in the dialect of Friuli, the region of northern Italy where he and his family spent their summers during his childhood. Pasolini saw the elevation of dialects to full literary legitimacy as a means of recognizing the "otherness" of the underclasses who spoke them. In 1950 he moved to Rome; five years later he published the novel *Ragazzi di vita* (translated as *The Ragazzi,* 1968), featuring the dialect spoken by the Roman working class.

The first subject postwar novelists and filmmakers confronted was the war itself. Almost all of the writers treated in this volume were affected by the war and the scars it left on Italian society. Many novels published between 1945 and 1955 depict the disruption of family life and civic activity, the loss of loved ones, economic deprivation, and the indignity of occupation by foreign troops. Among the novelists who experienced the war as soldiers, as partisans fighting Nazi and Fascist troops, or as victims of displacement are Fenoglio, Cesare Pavese, Giose Rimanelli, and Vasco Pratolini.

Much of Fenoglio's work carries the mark of his experiences during the turbulent months (September 1943 to April 1945) of militant struggle against Fascism. The Resistance—as it came to be known—is depicted in Fenoglio's narratives in memorable episodes of individual sacrifice and commitment to freedom, juxtaposed to vivid sketches of rural life in the Langhe hills of Piedmont. Fenoglio's works depict the full range of human conduct, from selflessness and idealism to brutality.

Pavese's *La luna e i falò* (1950; translated as *The Moon and the Bonfires,* 1952) deals only marginally with the war, but it is important because it bridges, within the socioeconomic setting of the peasant class, the Fascist and postwar periods. No less important, the American experiences of Pavese's protagonist, reflecting the novelist's attraction to American literature that matured in the 1930s, foreshadows the American influence in Italy that would leave deep traces in the novels of the late 1950s and subsequent years.

In 1953 the publisher Mondadori brought out a novel by an unknown writer that caused considerable commotion in the literary world. Rimanelli's *Tiro al piccione* (Pigeon Shoot; translated as *The Day of the Lion,* 1954) was, in part, an autobiographical account by a young man who fought on the "wrong side" in the war—with the Blackshirts of Mussolini's army. This feature, in itself, was a novelty in an atmosphere dominated by stories depicting the heroics of the Resistance. The novel was widely read because it offered a compelling, eyewitness account of the tragic absurdity of war: a politically naive youngster killing and maiming equally naive young men on the other side. In his *Storia della letteratura italiana contemporanea, 1940–1965* (History of Contemporary Italian Literature, 1967) the critic Giuliano Manacorda—no lover of Fascism—called *Tiro al piccione* "forse la più vivace testimonianza della guerra in Italia vista dall'altra parte" (perhaps the most vivid firsthand account of the war seen from "the other side").

Among these writers it is Pratolini whose works most clearly exemplify Neorealism. Born in a working-class section of Florence, he moved from youthful adherence to Fascism to involvement in the Resistance. A Marxist, he used his personal experience to portray the plight of the urban underclass. His early works, such as *Il quartiere* (1944; translated as *The Naked Streets,* 1952) and *Cronache di poveri amanti* (1947; translated as *A Tale of Poor Lovers,* 1949), deal with ordinary people in working-class neighborhoods of Florence who develop a sense of social consciousness and solidarity amid poverty and the struggles of daily life during the Fascist period. These novels brought the author substantial recognition, especially in leftist literary circles. In 1955, however, Pratolini published the novel *Metello* (translated as *Metello,* 1968), in which he sought to move beyond Neorealism. Such an evolution was seen as a sign of growth and maturity by the Marxist critic Carlo Salinari, but most of his colleagues—including Franco Fortini and Carlo Muscetta—attacked the work because Pratolini's view of history and treatment of character did not conform to Marxist doctrine. The same sort of criticism was leveled at Pasolini's *Ragazzi di vita,* whose youthful characters were seen as lacking in class consciousness. A committed Communist, Pasolini dutifully rectified this "flaw" in his next novel, *Una vita violenta* (1959; translated as *A Violent Life,* 1968), in which the protagonist displays an awareness of his social identity.

The polemics surrounding *Metello* mark the end of Neorealism, a short-lived, liberating reaction to Fascism. Neorealism in literature produced novels and short stories worthy of note, but it did not reach the heights of characterization and ideological expression achieved by such neorealist films as Roberto Rossellini's *Roma città aperta* (1945; released in English as *Open City,* 1945), De Sica's *Ladri di biciclette* (1947; released in English as *The Bicycle Thief,* 1947), and Federico Fellini's *La Strada* (1954).

The most successful Italian novel of the 1950s was Giuseppe Tomasi di Lampedusa's *Il Gattopardo* (1958; translated as *The Leopard,* 1960). An international best-seller, the work depicts the tensions between the aristocracy and the rising petite bourgeoisie in late-nineteenth-century Sicily. The success of *Il Gattopardo* disturbed Marxist writers such as Vittorini, Moravia, and Pratolini, who interpreted it as conveying a conservative bourgeois ideology. The work was popular in Italy because middle-class readers had grown tired of being reminded of the horrors of World War II, of their complicity in the rise of Fascism (the explicit theme of Pratolini's novel *Lo scialo* [The Waste, 1960]), and of their alleged exploitation of the working class. Many Italians were yearning for a novel that appealed to their intellect and aesthetic sense rather than to their social conscience, and they found it in Lampedusa's *Il Gattopardo.*

From 1958 to 1963 Italy experienced remarkable economic growth: worker productivity was among the highest in Europe; industrial output more than doubled; purchasing power increased threefold; and the standard of living rose significantly. But the growth was uneven: rapid industrial expansion took place in northern Italy, mostly in the cities that make up the so-called industrial triangle–Milan, Turin, and Genoa–while the central and southern parts of the country remained virtually unchanged. The demand of industry for labor, combined with the desire of the poor for a better life, resulted in the migration of tens of thousands of unskilled laborers, artisans, and poorly educated farmers to northern cities.

The rapid industrialization and emigration left their mark on the novels of the time. Provincial life, which had been the primary setting for fiction under Fascism, was replaced by the city and the factory. Vittorini was among the first to sense the social changes and to prepare the ground–through *Politecnico* and another journal he edited, *Il menabò*–for what he correctly saw as the inevitable shift from a humanistic to a technological culture–that is, from a traditional culture centered in ethical and spiritual concerns to a functional, pragmatic, and materialistic view of human existence. In 1961, under the full impact of industrialization, Agostino Pirella pointed out in the fourth issue of *Il menabò* that most Italian novelists were victims of "un vizio antico e minaccioso" (an old and dangerous habit) of fashioning a fictitious reality gleaned from other books. He urged them to be cognizant of a changing society and to look at the factory as a positive force: "La letteratura non ha da rifiutare nulla dell'esperienza umana, tanto più di quella che si attua nel lavoro" (Literature must not refuse anything dealing with human experience, least of all the experience of work).

During the 1960s an important subgenre of Italian narrative, called *letteratura e industria* (literature and industry), did focus on the phenomenon of industrial expansion. The writers–including Lucio Mastronardi, Goffredo Parise, Ottiero Ottieri, and Paolo Volponi–who contributed to this literature did not share Pirella's optimism, however. They saw the factory as a place of profound alienation and as the main cause of the psychological ailments that were beginning to manifest themselves on a wide scale in Italian society. The main themes of literature and industry narratives are the compulsive pursuit of material enrichment, on the one hand, and spiritual impoverishment, on the other. In this regard Mastronardi's novels about the shoe industry in his hometown of Vigevano, not far from Milan, offer a disquieting view of materialism in a provincial town enjoying the fruits of the postwar economic boom. Parise's *Il padrone* (1965; translated as *The Boss,* 1966) uses parody and satire to underscore the protagonist's estrangement in a setting dominated by industry. Ottieri kept a diary for nearly ten years while employed in the human relations department of a large company; the diary served as the basis for his *Donnarumma all'assalto* (1959; translated as *Men at the Gate,* 1962), which deals with the disruption and violence that ensue when a Milanese firm opens a plant in the South and scores of people flock to the factory gates looking for work. Based, like Ottieri's, on personal experience, Volponi's novels offer absorbing psychological portraits of confused, alienated, and disturbed individuals whose exposure to factory life leads them to revealing reflections on Italian society in the 1960s.

Most industry-inspired novels of this period reflect some form of linguistic innovation, but Mastronardi was the writer who dwelled most extensively on the interplay between language and character. In his novella *Il calzolaio di Vigevano* (The Shoemaker of Vigevano, 1962) the characters express themselves exactly as such people would speak to one another in the street. In introducing the work when it was first published, in *Il menabò* in 1959, Vittorini pointed out that Mastronardi "concentra sul piano del linguaggio tutt'intero il peso delle proprie responsabilità" (places on language the full weight of its responsibilities). A year later in comments on *Il giorno della fiera* (The Day of the Fair), a short novel by Stefano D'Arrigo in which Sicilian dialect is used, Vittorini expressed a strong dislike for the dialects of southern Italy:

> Io non ho nessuna simpatia né pazienza per i dialetti meridionali.... Ricordiamo che essi sono tutti legati a una civiltà di base contadina e tutti impregnati di una morale tra contadina e mercantile, tutti portatori di inerzia, di rassegnazione, di scetticismo, di disponibilità agli adattamenti corrotti, e di furberia cinica.

> (I have no sympathy nor patience for southern dialects.... Let us remember that they are all tied to a basic peasant culture, they are all permeated with a morality spanning the peasant and the mercantile classes, they are all carriers of inertia, resignation, skepticism, suitability to corrupt arrangements, and cynical shrewdness.)

Vittorini goes on to say that the dialects that ought to be used in socially conscious novels are those of the northern industrial cities; he argues that language should become a force capable of lifting former peasants out of their southern inertia so that they might lead emancipated lives as factory workers in the North. The Marxist writers Mastronardi, Parise, Ottieri, and Volponi viewed the factory as a place of alienation; Pirella and Vittorini saw it as a progressive setting in which the working class could rise above the servile condition of the southern peasantry.

In Giorgio Bassani's novella *Gli ultimi anni di Clelia Trotti* (1955; translated as *The Final Years of Clelia Trotti,* 1971) there is a scene that vividly reveals the decisive turn Italian culture was taking in the mid 1950s. In a square in Ferrara the Socialist mayor is delivering a eulogy for Clelia Trotti, a courageous woman who defended socialist ideals under Fascism. During the speech a teenager, totally indifferent to the ceremony, drives past the crowd on her noisy motor scooter on the way to meet her date. The narrator wonders: "Possibile che dovunque, in Italia, gli adolescenti fossero ormai cosí: come se uscissero ignari di tutto, dalle pagine di una rivista americana?" (Was it possible that everywhere in Italy adolescents were now like ignorant teenagers that had come out of an American magazine?). In literary works and in such films as Fellini's *La dolce vita* (1960) it was becoming clear that America was making deep inroads into the fabric of Italian life. From

1958 to 1965, while the "economic miracle" was in full force, the Marxist intellectual elite spoke on behalf of the Italian proletariat in abstruse dialectical terms intelligible only to themselves; meanwhile, factory workers, in movie theaters and in front of television sets, were looking enviously at the expanding American middle class with its swimming pools, sparkling new automobiles, and increased leisure time. In time Italian Marxists would realize that they had failed miserably in their avowed aim of developing a proletarian consciousness. Infatuated with their own rhetorical abstractions, they failed to understand that Italian "communist" workers shared the same values as American "capitalist" workers—indeed, the same values as the much-scorned bourgeoisie: the values exemplified by the "American way of life."

The penetration of American influence into virtually all aspects of Italian society was facilitated by the Italians' perception of themselves as second-rate Europeans, citizens of a country discredited by Fascism and military defeat, with a stagnant culture unable to break out of its stifling provincialism. This perception manifested itself in a downgrading of nearly everything Italian. To the leaders of the leftist parties, the practice of self-denigration proved to be a double-edged sword: on the one hand, the notion of a traditional, socially conservative society steeped in Catholicism (epitomized in literature and film by the recurrent image of the priest in black robes) drew much of the intellectual class to the communist and the socialist camps. On the other hand, the notion of lagging behind that was reinforced by books, film, and television—products of the intellectual class that was permeated by Marxist ideology—moved the dissatisfied working class to look to the United States, not the Marxists' beloved Soviet Union, as the land of prosperity.

Postwar Italian culture is, then, characterized by a steady affirmation of the American way of life. On various occasions in the 1960s, Pasolini complained loudly that Italian workers were being seduced by the siren of consumerism. With a good deal of foresight, he wrote that class struggle, the bedrock of Marxism, would eventually wane. By the mid 1960s it was apparent that the two historical contestants for primacy in Italian society, Catholicism and Marxism, had both lost out to America, the land of free enterprise and "rugged individualism." In *A History of Contemporary Italy* (1990) Paul Ginsborg says:

> The "economic miracle," by linking rising living standards with accentuated individualism, seemed to fulfill the American dream. It had introduced a new model of

social integration to Italy.... The Catholic family was under dire attack. The American model of a consumer society had revealed itself as the Trojan horse within the citadel of Catholic values.

Illustrations of fulfilling "the American dream" are offered by Mastronardi's novellas, whose provincial characters are so taken by the pursuit of material prosperity that money becomes the center of their lives, so much so that greed becomes a form of social pathology that ends up destroying psychological well-being.

While these social and economic changes unfolded primarily in northern Italy, the South was experiencing a different reality, one marked by continuing poverty, emigration, and a mistrust of government. Michele Prisco's collection of short stories, *La provincia addormentata* (The Sleepy Province, 1949), set in a cluster of towns in the vicinity of Naples, depicts the intellectual lethargy and cultural disinterest of the middle class; the family as a values-shaping institution threatened by internal conflicts and dissension; and social interactions marked by hypocrisy and self-interest. *Il mare non bagna Napoli* (1953; translated as *The Bay Is Not Naples,* 1955), a collection of short stories by Anna Maria Ortese, deals with life in districts of Naples afflicted by unemployment, violence, and despair, enclaves of abject poverty where survival is a daily struggle and the only escape is through fantasy. Ortese's quiet realism is as compelling in its implicit call for drastic change as are the Marxist narratives of Pratolini. Another southern writer is Leonardo Sciascia, whose novels confront the complexities of Sicilian society and its intricate connections with the Mafia. Yet as the title of Marcelle Padovani's book of interviews with Sciascia, *La Sicilia come metafora* (Sicily as Metaphor, 1979), indicates, in his incessant probing of *sicilitudine* (the quality of being Sicilian) Sciascia is actually seeking to understand Italian culture in general and, ultimately, the human condition.

After World War II the wide acceptance of psychoanalysis led novelists to use Freudian notions to explore their characters' inner lives in greater depth and with greater technical sophistication than had been the case before the war. In *Menzogna e sortilegio* (1948; translated as *The House of Liars,* 1950), Elsa Morante draws superb portraits of people caught in a world of fantasies, lies, and invented stories; the characters' inability or unwillingness to deal with reality leads not to the love and self-assurance they so desperately seek but to suffering and mental disorder. Moravia has pointed out that the two essential points of reference in his work are Karl Marx and Sigmund Freud. In most of his novels, the systematic probing of the inner lives of alienated characters centers on their futile efforts to find meaning and authenticity in a materialistic society dehumanized by the forces of capitalism. The protagonist of Volponi's *Memoriale* (1962; translated as *My Trouble Began,* 1964) is a neurotic and alienated individual who writes a memorandum as a means of self-therapy. Rather than combating his neuroses, however, he seeks to preserve them because he believes that they help him to assess the dehumanizing experience of working on the assembly line. In Volponi's next novel, *La macchina mondiale* (1965; translated as *The Worldwide Machine,* 1967), the main character uses a diary to understand his fears and anxieties. Feeling persecuted, he seeks out friends only to find the scorn and ridicule that drive him to suicide. Giuseppe Berto's *Il male oscuro* (1964; translated as *Incubus,* 1966) had its genesis in a diary the novelist was asked to write by a psychiatrist as part of therapy. An absorbing account of a man's journey into his subconscious in a desperate attempt to find the cause of his physical and mental ailments, the novel is patterned on the Freudian technique of free association; hence the text is free of punctuation and logical relationships. Berto probes his narrator's search for identity as well as his fear of death and disease.

Working in a different psychological key, Dino Buzzati, Tommaso Landolfi, and Guido Morselli explore the fantastic and surreal facets of human consciousness. In *Il deserto dei Tartari* (1940; translated as *The Tartar Steppe,* 1952) Buzzati fashions a tale in which distant desert lands and idealized characters are powerful symbols of the dashed hopes, fears, and alienations of contemporary life. Landolfi's characters move in a suspended reality where the incongruous, the irrational, and the grotesque dominate; in this terrifying world of metamorphoses and monstrous beings the reader discerns disturbing metaphors for twentieth-century life. Morselli's works were deemed to be so far outside the mainstream of Italian culture that publishers repeatedly rejected his manuscripts; most of his works appeared after his suicide in 1973—a suicide that some claim was prompted by his unsuccessful efforts to see his novels published. His *Dissipatio H.G.* (The Dissolution of the Human Race, 1977) depicts a deserted and haunting landscape after a cataclysm has nearly eliminated all human life. Animal and plant life continue to flourish, but what is left of man is the bare outline of human figures. Morselli's caustic irony shows that excessive emphasis on materialism results in beings without substance.

The postwar years also saw the continuance of a literary form called *il romanzo della memoria* (the novel of remembrance), which had flourished in the 1930s despite Fascist constraints on literary expression because it avoided the problematic present. The use of memory, of course, is a common strategy in fiction and can be found in the works of nearly all of the novelists treated in this volume, but the writers in whose novels this mnemonic vein is especially strong include Bassani, Pavese, Giuseppe Dessì, Natalia Ginzburg, Gianna Manzini, and Lalla Romano. These novelists share the Proustian quest to recapture past experiences, especially those associated with childhood, which assume mythical dimensions.

Bassani refused to follow the tenets of Neorealism and chose instead to renew the traditional novel, relying on memory as the chief vehicle of narration. His popular novel *Il giardino dei Finzi-Contini* (1962; translated as *The Garden of the Finzi-Contini*, 1965), the story of unrequited love between two Italian Jewish youths of different social backgrounds, is a multilayered novel that deals with the problems of social stratification, Fascism and its persecution of Italian Jews, and such timeless elements as historical pessimism, solitude, and death—all fashioned by a writer who, through the narrator, becomes the conscience of his time. Pavese's protagonists seek to recapture a mythical quality of life identified with their childhood. Memories of childhood experiences are tied in Dessì's narratives to a few familiar towns of his native Sardinia, evoking a sheltered and carefree adolescence but also the struggle for survival in a harsh environment. Several of Ginzburg's novels carry the imprint of painful memories of the three years (1940 to 1943) she spent in the remote village of Abruzzo, where her husband was confined because of his opposition to Fascism. In her *Tutti i nostri ieri* (1952; translated as *Dead Yesterdays,* 1956) recollections of the abusive behavior of German soldiers are juxtaposed to the exploitation of the peasants by the ruling class. In some works by Manzini and Romano the use of memory is tied to adolescent family experiences. In Manzini's *Ritratto in piedi* (A Standing Portrait, 1971) the focus is on the narrator's relationship with her father, an exceptional man who shuns family wealth and privelege to devote his life to further the ideals of a just and egalitarian society. The difficulty to communicate, a recurrent theme in postwar narrative, is treated with unusual skill and sensitivity in Romano's *Le parole tra noi leggere* (Light Words Between Us, 1969)—the study of a mother's complex and painful rapport with her son.

The rich legacy of Italian Catholic writing, which in the nineteenth century found its highest expression in the works of Manzoni, barely survived in the second half of the twentieth century. Only a small share of postwar fiction can be identified as religious in nature, and Catholic writers such as Rodolfo Doni and Mario Pomilio have found themselves isolated in a tacitly hostile, Marxist literary environment. This sense of isolation is found in Doni's *Le strade della città* (City Streets, 1973), in which the protagonist—inspired by Giorgio La Pira, the popular mayor of Florence of the late 1960s who was known as "il santo politico" (the saintly politician)—is unappreciated by the members of his own party and ignored by a dominant secular culture that is uninterested in his words of love and compassion. Doni's main characters, who hold strong moral and religious convictions, are nonetheless tested by the lure of individual gain through questionable means. The effort to free oneself from the bondage of sin takes the form of painful self-scrutiny in Pomilio's first novel, *L'uccello nella cupola* (The Bird in the Cupola, 1954), which attests to the author's religious crisis following his disenchantment with the Socialist Party he joined after World War II. Pomilio is best known for *Il quinto evangelio* (The Fifth Gospel, 1975), about the search for a presumably lost fifth Gospel, which can be read as a quest for eternal life and a modern allegory of a medieval pilgrimage. In his *Scritti cristiani* (Christian Writings, 1979) Pomilio says that World War II taught him "la differenza fondamentale tra il bene e il male" (the fundamental difference between good and evil), the exploration of which he believes ought to be one of literature's central concerns.

Such, in broad strokes, are the principal lines of the Italian narrative from 1945 to 1965. In the rest of the volume the reader will find a more detailed and comprehensive study of individual novelists.

—*Augustus Pallotta*

ACKNOWLEDGMENTS

This book was produced by Bruccoli Clark Layman, Inc. George P. Anderson was the in-house editor. He was assisted by Philip B. Dematteis. The publisher thanks Rosalind and Aldo Nesticó for their help in illustrating the volume.

Administrative support was provided by Ann M. Cheschi and Brenda A. Gillie.

Bookkeeper is Joyce Fowler.

Copyediting supervisor is Laurel M. Gladden Gillespie. The copyediting staff includes Phyllis A. Avant, Patricia Coate, Jeff Miller, William L. Thomas Jr., and Allison Trussell.

L. Kay Webster and Jane M. J. Williamson are editorial associates.

Layout and graphics supervisor is Pamela D. Norton.

Office manager is Kathy Lawler Merlette.

Photography editors are Julie E. Frick and Margaret Meriwether. Photographic copy work was performed by Joseph M. Bruccoli.

Production manager is Samuel W. Bruce.

Software specialist is Marie Parker.

Systems manager is Chris Elmore.

Typesetting supervisor is Kathleen M. Flanagan. The typesetting staff includes Stephanie L. Capes, Melody W. Clegg, Delores Plastow, and Patricia Flanagan Salisbury.

Walter W. Ross, Steven Gross, and Mark McEwan did library research. They were assisted by the following librarians at the Thomas Cooper Library of the University of South Carolina: Linda Holderfield and the interlibrary-loan staff; reference-department head Virginia Weathers; reference librarians Marilee Birchfield, Stefanie Buck, Stefanie DuBose, Rebecca Feind, Karen Joseph, Donna Lehman, Charlene Loope, Anthony McKissick, Jean Rhyne, Kwamine Simpson, and Virginia Weathers; circulation-department head Caroline Taylor; and acquisitions-searching supervisor David Haggard.

Dictionary of Literary Biography® • Volume One Hundred Seventy-Seven

Italian Novelists Since World War II, 1945–1965

Edited by
Augustus Pallotta
Syracuse University

A Bruccoli Clark Layman Book
Gale Research
Detroit, Washington, D.C., London

Dictionary of Literary Biography

Giovanni Arpino
(27 January 1927 – 10 December 1987)

Claudio Mazzola
The College of the Holy Cross

BOOKS: *Sei stato felice, Giovanni* (Turin: Einaudi, 1952);

Barbaresco (Milan: Edizioni della Meridiana, 1954);

Il prezzo dell'oro (Milan: Mondadori, 1957);

Gli anni del giudizio (Turin: Einaudi, 1958);

Rafée Micropiede (Turin: Einaudi, 1959);

La suora giovane (Turin: Einaudi, 1959); translated by Peter Green as *The Novice* (London: Hodder & Stoughton, 1961; New York: G. Braziller, 1962);

Le mille e un'Italia (Turin: Einaudi, 1960);

Un delitto d'onore (Milan: Mondadori, 1961); translated by Raymond Rosenthal as *A Crime of Honour* (London: Weidenfeld & Nicolson, 1963; New York: G. Braziller, 1963);

Una nuvola d'ira (Milan: Mondadori, 1962);

L'ombra delle colline (Milan: Mondadori, 1964);

Testi di Arpino e Frisia (Milan: Bassoli Fotoincisioni, 1964);

L'assalto al treno e altre storie (Turin: Einaudi, 1966);

Un'anima persa (Milan: Mondadori, 1966);

La babbuina e altre storie (Milan: Mondadori, 1967);

I ventisette racconti (Milan: Mondadori, 1968);

Il buio e il miele (Milan: Rizzoli, 1969);

Fuorigioco (Milan: Rizzoli, 1970);

Randagio è l'eroe (Milan: Mondadori, 1972);

Racconti di vent'anni (Milan: Rizzoli, 1974);

Domingo il favoloso (Turin: Einaudi, 1975);

Il primo quarto di luna (Turin: Einaudi, 1976);

Azzurro tenebra (Milan: Rizzoli, 1977);

Lune piemontesi, by Arpino and Guido Jannon (Ivrea: Priuli & Verlucca, 1978);

Area di rigore, by Arpino and Alfio Caruso (Turin: Società editrice internazionale, 1979);

Calcio nero, by Arpino and Caruso (Milan: Feltrinelli, 1980);

Il fratello italiano (Milan: Rizzoli, 1980);

Giovanni Arpino

Vino e osterie, by Arpino and Gian Paolo Cavallero (Ivrea: Priuli & Verlucca, 1980);

Un gran mare di gente (Milan: Rizzoli, 1981);

Bocce ferme (Turin: D. Piazza, 1982);

Fiabe piemontesi (Milan: Mondadori, 1982);

Raccontami una storia (Milan: Rizzoli, 1982);

Vita, tempeste, sciagure di Salgari, il padre degli eroi (Milan: Rizzoli, 1982);

La sposa segreta (Milan: Garzanti, 1983);

Torino, by Arpino and Marcello Bertinetti (Vercelli: White Star, 1984);

Passo d'addio (Turin: Einaudi, 1986);

Fogli segreti, 1984–1987 (Lugano: Gaggini-Bizzozero, 1987);

La trappola amorosa (Milan: Rusconi, 1988);

Stile Arpino (Turin: Società editrice internazionale, 1989);

Storie dell'Italia minore (Milan: Mondadori, 1990).

Giovanni Arpino is one of the most puzzling authors in contemporary Italian literature because he defies a neat classification within the major narrative trends of the past decades. A distinctive stylist whose novels varied in theme throughout his more than thirty-year career, Arpino can be seen as an exception to the axiom that every great author writes the same book over and over. Yet, beyond the variety of his writing, it is possible to note certain attitudes and approaches common to his body of work.

Arpino was born in Pola in 1927 but studied and grew up in the Langhe region of Piedmont, the area south of Turin that also appears in the novels of Cesare Pavese and Beppe Fenoglio, two important Piedmontese writers who were Alpino's contemporaries. His first works of fiction were published in 1947 in the famous literary magazine *900.* He was the editor of many newspapers, among them *Il Giorno* and *La Stampa;* he was also codirector of the magazine *Tempo* between 1954 and 1956.

Alpino's first novel, *Sei stato felice, Giovanni* (You Were Happy, John), was published in 1952 at a time when both cinema and fiction were dominated by Neorealism. Artists felt free to express what for many years had been censored by the Fascist regime, and Arpino began a period of self-discovery. His novel was originally published in the prestigious Gettoni series of new fiction that Elio Vittorini edited for the publisher Einaudi. Vittorini's support was important because it encouraged Arpino and other young writers to experiment with new narrative forms. The neorealist character of the novel is evident in the dry tone and the milieu. The novel is set in the slums of Genoa, populated by prostitutes, sailors, and simple workers — all struggling in the wake of the post–World War II poverty. The everyday problem of surviving hunger makes Giovanni a typical picaresque hero, but he also has an unstoppable desire for freedom. He enjoys being without social obligations and constrictions, even if that means the lack of any security for the future. "A me piaceva vivere cosí, alzarmi a sonno finito,

essere legato solo al sole o al freddo, andare al porto, passeggiare. Piaceva sedere nei giardini del quartiere coi vecchi artritici nel sole pieno di vento e la schiena fredda" (I liked to live like that, getting up when I had enough sleep, being tied only to the sun and to the cold; I liked to go to the docks, to walk. I liked to sit in the city parks with old, arthritic people in the sun, with the wind and a cold back).

The realistic tone of *Sei stato felice, Giovanni* has often been compared to the writings of Ernest Hemingway and Pavese. The abundance of fast-paced dialogue is also reminiscent of many American films of the 1940s and 1950s, which were popular in Italy after the war. Giovanni resembles some of the outcasts Fenoglio portrays in another neorealist novel, *La paga del sabato* (Saturday's Paycheck, 1969). The evident presence in *Sei stato felice, Giovanni* of the influences of Marxist ideology as well as American films and literature attests to a mode of derivative writing that was common in Italy in the early 1950s.

Although Arpino shows a penchant for realistic writing, especially in his early work, in his novels he rarely uses dialect, so dear to many neorealist writers. Many of his protagonists come from rural areas, yet they hardly ever resort to the use of their dialect as a form of expression. Even in writing dialogue, his principal means of communicating the characters' inner tension, Arpino eshews the use of dialect. The reason can be traced to his belief that dialect does not really enhance the narrative. Parting ways with Pavese, he felt that using Piedmontese dialect would result in a strained and artificial style.

Soon after his first novel came out Arpino turned to poetry, publishing two volumes of verse: *Barbaresco* (1954) and *Il prezzo dell' oro* (The Price of Gold, 1958). Closely connected to his fiction, Arpino's poetry often elaborates themes and situations found in his prose. In 1958 Arpino returned to fiction, beginning what is generally described as his first intense creative phase. From 1958 to 1969 he wrote seven novels: *Gli anni del giudizio* (The Years of Maturity, 1958), *La suora giovane* (The Young Nun, 1959), *Un delitto d'enore* (1961; translated as *A Crime of Honor,* 1963), *Una nuvola d'ira* (An Angry Cloud, 1962), *L'ombra delle colline* (The Shadows of the Hills, 1964), *Un'anima persa* (The Lost Soul, 1966), and *Il buio e il miele* (Darkness and Honey, 1969). These works show Arpino's neorealist tendency to present characters ideologically, as involved in rebuilding Italy after World War II, while also exploring the themes of solitude and isolation, typical of a neurotic and alienating society.

The city plays an important role in Arpino's novels and is usually portrayed as malignant and hostile. He often juxtaposes the urban environment to the countryside, in particular the Langhe region in Piedmont. But Arpino does not romanticize the country. The rural landscape and people are devoid of the mythical aura they acquire in Pavese's work. Arpino chooses instead a more realistic representation of the peasants, though the reader feels a sense of calm and peace through the observation of the cycles of nature. There is a nostalgic aura to Arpino's vision of the country because it is a world he lost when he moved to the big city. He describes Turin, the city he knew best, in a particularly depressing fashion and seems to associate Turin, Genoa, and Milan with the important decisions of adulthood.

Arpino's city is a place with no friends and many enemies. The white- and blue-collar workers struggle to achieve a bourgeois status, while the political class has lost its social consciousness. The large cities trap those inhabiting them. The dichotomy between urban and countryside is present for the first time in *Gli anni del giudizio,* in which one finds the lyrical evocation of the countryside through a rich, emotive style consisting of adjectives and metaphors that conjure up vivid images of nature. The representation of the urban environment is tied to problematic and anomalous situations, such as those present in *La suora giovane* and the novels that follow it.

The autobiographical nature of the protagonist in *Sei stato felice, Giovanni* gradually disappears in subsequent novels as Arpino strives for a more objective approach to character and reality. His characters are not defined by psychological traits and are not shaped by a logic of cause and effect but instead exist, especially in the early novels, as part of a cultural and social system. Choosing not to impose an authorial view, Arpino encourages readers to provide their own interpretations of his characters. It is common for Arpino's characters to display an illuministic belief in reason as they seek to discover the world through firsthand experience. They realize that the process of learning can be costly because they pay for the mistakes they make. Yet, they never give up, showing a strong faith in their efforts to understand themselves and others. Arpino's focus on his protagonist's individual struggle underscores his concept of the hero: an imposing, often physically large character who is capable of facing any adversity. In *Randagio è l'eroe* (Vagabond Is the Hero, 1972), for example, the tall, strong Giuan, a man of great wisdom and intelligence, feels that his mission is to save the world from the forces of evil.

The dramatic situation Arpino's characters face does not typically arise from the conflict between good and evil; instead, he generally explores the consequences of the abnormality hidden behind every day's reassuring banality. His heroes are unique and often unpredictable; their value systems do not allow the reader to identify with them easily. Even when the protagonist's behavior appears normal, as is the case with the accountant Antonio Mathis in *La suora giovane,* Arpino introduces a surprising complication by having him begin a relationship with a nun. *La suora giovane* is a representative work in the sense that the daily routine governing the life of the protagonist is disrupted by an external element.

The salient point that sets *La suora giovane* in motion is the monotony afflicting Antonio, a middle-aged accountant who has received nearly everything he wanted from life. Suddenly he realizes that what he has is not what counts: "Non ricordo un amore da ragazzo. . . . Non ho mai fatto politica, non sono sportivo. . . . Non so niente. I giorni mi sono scappati via" (I don't remember falling in love as a youngster. . . . I was never involved in politics, I am not a sports fan. . . . I don't know anything. The days have passed me by). This sense of desolation begins to wane when he becomes involved with a nun whom he meets regularly on a streetcar. The experience enables him to escape the monotony of his existence. It is unclear whether Antonio rejects his previous life simply because he discovers that he is restless inside the walls of a typical bourgeois home, or whether he is simply exploring alternatives. At times he seems to obey an inexplicable desire for the unexpected and the unstable. At other times, as he does at the end of the novel, he appears to be searching for a new existence, for he keeps following the woman even after she has lost the initial attraction of being a nun and has been transferred to another convent.

The young nun, Serena, is an exceptional female character for Arpino. Usually Arpino's women are strong but completely dedicated to their men. They find harmony within themselves and with the world surrounding them only through relationships with men, embracing their men's causes without ever questioning their own needs. To Arpino love means harmony, reciprocal understanding, and respect. His women find personal happiness, even if it is almost always through the male point of view that love reaches some form of fulfillment. Serena, however, not only tries to run away from the monastery but seeks independence from her family.

Antonio's search for self-reliance begins when he is attracted to the nun, whom he meets regularly at a bus stop, and follows her through the streets of Turin. He is attracted to her not only because her habit represents that which is forbidden and supposedly out of reach but because his interest in her enables him to break away from his boring middle-class life and boring fiancée. Arpino's women bring with them positive values, but it can also be said that they are important only because they give men a sense of hope and security.

In *Gli anni del giudizio* and *Una nuvola d'ira,* both of which are concerned with political ideology, Arpino introduces women as first-person narrators. Even so, he does not give particular importance to their points of view. The choice seems a technical solution that allows him to distance himself from his characters and to discuss more freely the political ideas of the male protagonists. Sperata, the narrator of *Una nuvola d'ira,* is not really allowed her individual views on what takes place as she and her husband become involved in a political love triangle. She is merely the focal point as the men attempt to break with the old bourgeois perception of love. The husband, Matteo, however, does not accept the situation and gives in to a series of violent acts against his wife and against himself. Nevertheless, though women are forced to conform to their partners' dominant order, they bring a sensitivity into the male world that sometimes contributes to change, at least in part, the men's points of view.

Un'anima persa is a fast-paced novel that relies on the structures of a mystery. The novel begins with a boy joining his uncle's family in Turin to take his school's exams. Slowly he learns that his uncle lives a double life, pretending to be a successful engineer while he spends his days gambling his wife's money. The boy discovers that the supposed existence of the uncle's sick brother (kept in a secluded room of the big mansion) is an invention of the uncle. The mysterious and dark atmosphere that surrounds the boy's surprising discoveries is reminiscent of the Gothic tradition. All the characters the boy meets are described as belonging to a strange, fantastic world. The boy lives a nightmare in which the sense of the abnormal is even more powerful because it is hidden behind the reassuring walls of a wealthy family in the industrial city of Turin.

Un'anima persa and *Il buio e il miele* signal a major change in Arpino's fiction. No longer content to depict a rational process of familiarization with reality, Arpino chooses to enrich his work with symbolism. Rather than a realistic background, he gives his story a fantastic dimension that makes his heroes more unpredictable than ever. Both novels deal with people who are alienated and detached from reality, but the focus is no longer on the individual's effort to feel part of society, as was the case in *Sei stato felice, Giovanni.* The nihilism of the protagonists

turns in part against them and in part against the people that surround them.

In *Il buio e il miele* Arpino explores a completely unpredictable side of the human mind. The protagonist is an blind man, Fausto, whose isolated bitterness goes beyond that caused by his handicap alone. His tension is eased through his violent attacks against the world. Arpino's characterizations of those who surround the protagonist are weak. Each has only a specific function in terms of their relationship to the blind man and otherwise lack individual identity. Despite such weaknesses, *Il buio e il miele* proved to be Arpino's most successful novel. It was made into a movie produced by Dino Risi in 1973 as *Profumo di donna* (Scent of a Woman); in 1992 an American adaptation titled *Scent of a Woman* was made with Al Pacino playing the leading role.

Representative of Arpino's usual female characters, Sara, the woman who loves Fausto and is fully devoted to him, is one-dimensional. She sacrifices everything to stay next to the blind man who accepts her reluctantly and treats her with utter contempt. She says of herself: "Dicono che sono innamorata di lui. Lo dicono tutti, persino mia madre. . . . Ma non è lo stupido amore, lo svenimento . . . Io solo ho deciso. Io ho scelto, come un cane che s'incammina dietro un tizio per strada" (They say I am in love with him. Everybody says that, even my mother. . . . But it is not the stupid love, the fainting . . . I alone decided. I made the choice, like a dog that walks behind someone on the street). Sara gains Fausto's love only after giving up everything for him, and in the end she is destined to become his caretaker.

Il buio e il miele brings to light one of the recurring themes in Arpino's work: travel. The protagonist of the novel travels from Turin to Naples to meet a friend. On one hand, travel affords the opportunity to distance oneself from pressing everyday reality. In Arpino's fiction the trip is often a return to what has been left behind, the country, and life there is juxtaposed to urban life. On the other hand, traveling can provide one with a new identity, conferring the status of a wanderer with no particular goal beyond the pure pleasure of enjoying the environment. The traveler in Arpino's work often has a peasant's state of mind and sees life as having a natural rhythm, in which there is time for pleasure even in small things, such as a talk with a friend at the local espresso bar.

Arpino has always been active as a journalist. In the years following 1953 his name was associated with a large variety of newpapers and magazines, including *Paese Sera, Il Giorno, La Stampa,* and, in the last years of his career, *Il Giornale.* He wrote for famous as well as far less known newspapers without regard to their political orientation. Arpino never perceived his journalism as a secondary activity. He believed his articles served the purpose of promoting the opportunity to reflect on reality. He wrote about life in the country and in the big city: he wrote about famous artists, including Fellini and Montale, and he wrote about soccer. His decision to become a soccer reporter can be regarded as a rejection of politics after Italy's turbulent student movement in the late 1960s. Arpino feared the political upheavals in Italian society, in particular during the early 1970s when terrorist bombings and political kidnapping threatened to undermine the country's political system. Arpino did not view his new career as detracting from his novels. He always liked to point out that he was a storyteller, that his inspiration was everyday life. In this sense, dividing his time between fiction and journalism (a solution that Italo Calvino thought to be impossible because, according to him, one cannot use language in such different ways as fiction and journalism demand) was the only logical solution for a writer who needed to be inside reality to exercise his vocation.

In *Randagio è l'eroe* Arpino again explores an absurd situation against the backdrop of everyday life. The new element here is the role of the protagonist, the imposing Giuan, who becomes a missionary carrying a message of hope. Although Giuan and his wife seem to lead a normal and quiet life, soon it becomes apparent that they are up to something rather peculiar. They wander through the streets of Milan on a bicycle, stopping every time they see graffiti on the walls to transform offensive messages into the humanitarian words of Christ. Giuan strives for an ideal brotherhood in the mainstream of a modern society in decay. He does not analyze the situation but attacks it with slogans that sound rather empty.

The mixture of realism and fantasy in Arpino's fiction tends to disorient the reader. This is particularly evident at the end of the novel, when Giuan abandons his faithful wife to search for a truth that he feels must be sought in the streets of Milan among marginalized people. The novel takes a sudden metaphorical turn when Giuan meets a priest and decides to kidnap him because he feels the Catholic Church is not doing enough for the poor. The episode with the priest allows Giuan to express his religious feelings and culminates in a type of epiphany when Giuan performs a miracle by making a giant tree grow out of a small sage tree and then dies from exhaustion.

Arpino's watchful distance from the political world surfaces in *Azzurro tenebra* (Dark Blue, 1977), a

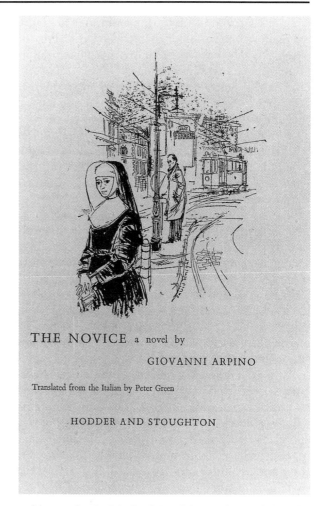

THE NOVICE a novel by

GIOVANNI ARPINO

Translated from the Italian by Peter Green

HODDER AND STOUGHTON

Title page for the British edition of the translation of Arpino's 1959 novel La suora giovane, *in which a middle-aged man falls in love with a young nun*

novel in which a journalist named Arp is sent to Germany to cover the World Soccer Cup. When Arp complains about his role, the Italian team's coach replies that he could be somewhere in Vietnam reporting on the war or in Rome interviewing boring ministers. Although Arpino's move to sports as a subject may be viewed as a conservative retreat from the world, his connection with sportswriting certainly did not weaken his prose style. He finds new possibilities of expression through the metaphors of sports using the soccer world as a microcosm for the outside world.

The protagonists of *Il fratello italiano* (The Italian Brother, 1980) are two old men who can be thought of as aged versions of Arpino's typical character. They share some moments of mutual understanding when they spend some hot summer days dealing with the troubles that their respective daughters leave behind. One of the daughters is completely indifferent to her father's problems. She is only concerned with her life and wants her father to protect her from her former husband. For this reason she leaves a gun for her perplexed father. The other daughter moved north from the south and has become a drug addict and a prostitute. Her inability to communicate with her father goes well beyond the generation gap.

The two fathers come from completely different backgrounds, one from the north and the other from the south. Both are failures as fathers in a society that at the time was facing dramatic changes. Unlike most of Arpino's previous works, *Il fratello italiano* is a dramatic novel entirely focused on the presence of evil in contemporary society. Even the bond established between the two fathers cannot be taken as positive because it does not have a future. One of the two does not want the address of the other one who is leaving for Germany.

Arpino continued to write until his death. In his next novel, *La sposa segreta* (1983), Arpino describes the parallel love stories of a mother who finds the perfect woman for her son and, unexpectedly, a caring man for herself. In this novel Arpino stresses the fundamental theme of his fiction: there is no life outside a human relationship. With *Passo d'addio* (1986) Arpino returns to the pessimistic view of reality of *Il fratello italiano*. Two professors make a pact that the younger should kill the older when he becomes unable to care for himself. It is a novel rich with pessimistic reflections on death and God.

Arpino's last novel, *La trappola amorosa* (1988), was published posthumously. It tells the story of an old actor whose boring life suddenly becomes exciting because of some messages he receives from an unknown woman. The protagonist feels trapped in a world that gives him a false sense of freedom: "Il mondo intero è uno zoo. Ti lascia circolare, ti lascia l'idea di crederti padrone del tuo spazio, ma sempre zoo rimane" (The entire world is a zoo. You think you can roam around, you think you own your own life, nevertheless it is still a zoo). The woman represents something that the man never had: "Non sono le donne . . . sono quello che ti manca (It is not women . . . it is what you don't have). The protagonist knows that this could be a trap (the trap of the title) but he openly says that this temptation is worth giving in to. There is, in this last novel, a positive sense of being available to experience, whatever it may be, even death.

Although Arpino was awarded two important literary prizes during his lifetime – the Strega in 1964 for *L'ombra delle colline* and the Campiello in 1980 for *Il fratello italiano* – he has not received the posthumous regard he deserves from Italian critics. Part of the reason for his limited reputation can be traced to the uniqueness of his achievement and the fact that his work cannot be clearly identified with the significant trends in postwar Italian literature. Arpino, though, is not less important for standing alone.

References:

Giorgio Bàrberi-Squarotti, *La narrativa italiana del dopoguerra* (Bologna: Cappelli, 1965);

Bàrberi-Squarotti, *Poesia e narrativa del secondo Novecento* (Milan: Mursia, 1961);

Giuseppe Costanzo, "L'ultimo Arpino," *Il Ponte*, 16 (July 1964);

Marco Forti, "Romanzo e antiromanzo," *Aut Aut* (January 1962);

Olga Lombardi, *La narrativa italiana nella crisi del Novecento* (Caltanisetta: Sciascia, 1971);

Giuliano Manacorda, *Storia della letteratura italiana contemporanea* (Rome: Editori Riuniti, 1967);

Gaetano Mariani, *La giovane narrativa italiana tra documento e poesia* (Florence: Le Monnier, 1962);

Eugenio Montale, "Arpino. La Suora Giovane," *Il Corriere della sera*, 25 March 1960;

Giorgio Pullini, *Il romanzo italiano del dopoguerra* (Milan: Schwarz, 1961);

Pullini, *Volti e risvolti del romanzo italiano contemporaneo* (Milan: Mursia, 1971);

Bruno Quaranta, *Stile Arpino. Una vita torinese.* (Turin: SEI, 1989);

Massimo Romano, *Invito alla lettura di Arpino* (Milan: Mursia, 1974);

Riccardo Scrivano, *Giovanni Arpino* (Florence: La Nuova Italia, 1979);

Giovanni Tesio, "Frammenti per un ritratto critico di Giovanni Arpino," *Studi Piemontesi* (17 November 1988);

Tesio, *Piemonte letterario dell'Otto-Novecento* (Roma: Bulzoni, 1992);

Gian Mario Veneziano, *Giovanni Arpino* (Milan: Mursia, 1994);

Giancarlo Vigorelli, "I due versanti del naturalismo moderno," *La fiera letteraria*, 31 October 1954;

Ferdinando Virdia, "Venti giorni in un inverno," *La fiera letteraria*, 29 November 1959.

Anna Banti
(27 June 1895 – 25 September 1985)

Olga Ragusa
Columbia University

BOOKS: *Itinerario di Paolina* (Rome: Augustea, 1937);

Il coraggio delle donne (Florence: Le Monnier, 1940); revised edition (Milan: La Tartaruga, 1983); one story translated by Martha King as "The Courage of Women," in *New Italian Women: A Collection of Short Stories,* edited by King (New York: Italica Press, 1989);

Sette lune (Milan: Bompiani, 1941);

Le monache cantano (Rome: Tumminelli, 1942);

Artemisia (Florence: Sansoni, 1947); translated by Shirley D'Ardia Caracciolo as *Artemisia* (Lincoln & London: University of Nebraska Press, 1988); excerpts translated by Joan Borelli in *Longman Anthology of World Literature by Women, 1875–1975* (New York & London: Longman, 1989), pp. 340–343;

Le donne muoiono (Milan: Mondadori, 1951);

Il bastardo (Florence: Sansoni, 1953); republished as *La casa piccola* (Milan: Mondadori, 1961);

Lorenzo Lotto (Florence: Sansoni, 1953); republished as *Rivelazione di Lorenzo Lotto* (Florence: Sansoni, 1981);

Allarme sul lago (Milan: Mondadori, 1954);

La monaca di Sciangai e altri racconti (Milan: Mondadori, 1957);

Corte Savella (Milan: Mondadori, 1960);

Opinioni (Milan: Il Saggiatore, 1961);

Le mosche d'oro (Milan: Mondadori, 1962);

Campi elisi (Milan: Mondadori, 1963);

Matilde Serao (Turin: Unione tipografico-editrice torinese, 1965);

Noi credevamo (Milan: Mondadori, 1967);

Je vous écris d'un pays lointain (Milan: Mondadori, 1971);

La camicia bruciata (Milan: Mondadori, 1973);

Tele e cenere (Pistoia: Tip. Pacinotti, 1974);

Da un paese vicino (Milan: Mondadori, 1975);

Giovanni da San Giovanni, pittore della contraddizione (Florence: Sansoni, 1977);

Un grido lacerante (Milan: Rizzoli, 1981);

Quando anche le donne si misero a dipingere (Milan: La Tartaruga, 1982).

Portrait of Anna Banti by Adriana Pincherle, circa 1956 (Anna Banti Collection)

OTHER: Bernardo Bizoni, *Europa milleseicentosei,* edited by Banti (Milan & Rome: Rizzoli, 1942);

Fra Angelico, text by Banti (Milan: Sidera, 1953);

Diego Velasquez, text by Banti (Milan: Gazzanti, 1955);

Claude Monet, text by Banti (Milan: Garzanti, 1956);

Autobiographical sketch, in *Ritratti su misura di scrittori italiani,* edited by Elio Filippo Accrocca (Venice: Sodalizio del libro, 1960), pp. 43–44;

Daniel Defoe, *Opere,* edited by Banti and G. G. Castorina, with an introductory essay by Banti (Milan: Mondadori, 1980);

Roberto Longhi, *Breve ma veridica storia della pittura italiana,* edited by Banti (Florence: Sansoni, 1980).

TRANSLATIONS: William Makepeace Thackeray, *La fiera delle vanità* (Milan: Longanesi, 1948);

Virginia Woolf, *La camera di Jacobbe* (Milan & Verona: Mondadori, 1950); republished as *La camera di Jacob* (Milan: Mondadori, 1980);

Francis Carco, *L'amico dei pittori* (Milan: Martello, 1955);

André Chastel, *L'arte italiana,* 2 volumes (Florence: Sansoni, 1957–1958);

Henri Alain Fournier, *Il grande amico* (Milan: Mondadori, 1971); republished as *Il gran Meaulnes* (Milan: Mondadori, 1977);

Colette, *La vagabonda* (Milan: Mondadori, 1977);

Jane Austen, *Caterina* (Florence: Giunti-Marzocco, 1978).

About midway in her literary career, in an autobiographical sketch published in *Ritratti su misura di scrittori italiani* (Portraits Made to Measure of Italian Writers, 1960), Anna Banti described her fiction as having moved away from introspection to subjects outside herself without, however, having abandoned the particular point of view on the world that her largely female protagonists express: "Questo punto di vista che io credo onesto (ciascuno deve parlare di quel che sa) e anche utile (non sempre gli uomini capiscono le donne, e viceversa) ha una sua morale che non è moralismo, ma profonda attenzione verso i più chiusi problemi umani" (This point of view, which I consider honest [one must speak of what one knows] and also useful [men do not always understand women, and vice versa], has a moral, not a moralistic dimension: an attentive concentration on the most hidden human problems). In a later self-assessment, which appeared in an interview published in *Le signore della scrittura* (Women Who Write, 1984), Banti responded to the question as to why the designation of feminist writer had always irritated her: "Perchè il mio è più una forma di umanesimo che vero e proprio femminismo" (Because mine is more a kind of humanism than real and proper feminism). Banti believed that novels grow out of the capacity to understand human beings and that writers understand best what they know most intimately.

Banti's interest in the fate of women predated the later vogue of political, militant feminism. Although the majority of her works were published after World War II, her intellectual and literary roots lay in the years between the world wars, and her style owed more to the fiction written at that time than to Neorealism. In some respects her literary career was anomalous, for she came to writing, if not unwillingly, at least reluctantly, her first vocation having been the study of art history. In the transparently autobiographical novel *Un grido lacerante* (A Piercing Cry, 1981), written toward the end of her life, Banti conveys through the protagonist Agnese Lanzi a sense of regret for having failed to develop her potential as an art historian because her husband's reputation in the same field had relegated her professional interests to a subsidiary role. Yet there can be little doubt that as the wife of Roberto Longhi (1890–1970), renowned art critic and connoisseur, the maestro she admired and probably stood in awe of ever since she had been his student at a *liceo* (secondary school) in Rome, Banti enjoyed a privileged position that distinguished her from other women writers of the 1930s and 1940s and contributed to her recognition on a par with the most prestigious male writers of her time.

Anna Banti was born Lucia Lopresti in Florence to a family of Calabrian and Piedmontese backgrounds. The Calabrian side is memorialized in her 1967 novel, *Noi credevamo* (We Believed), in the figure of Domenico Lopresti, Risorgimento patriot and fighter for Italian unity, who ended his days as a civil servant in the new government of the kingdom of Italy. She claims to have been a precocious child who began writing stories at the age of five. By the time she married Longhi in 1924, she had begun to publish in art journals; her 1919 article "Marco Boschini scrittore d'arte del secolo XVII" (Marco Boschini, Writer on Art of the 17th Century) was favorably reviewed by Benedetto Croce, the leading Italian intellectual of the first half of the twentieth century. As Lucia Lopresti and later as Lucia Longhi Lopresti, she continued to write on art until 1934 when her first short story, "Cortile" (Courtyard), was published under the name of Anna Banti. The pseudonym by which she would henceforth be known, suggested by the name of a relative on her mother's side, was chosen to keep her professional identity separate from her husband's.

In the 1930s and 1940s Banti wrote both fiction and nonfiction for literary journals, newspapers, and magazines. To this period also belong her first full-length works: *Itinerario di Paolina* (Paolina's Itinerary, 1937), an evocation of childhood; *Il coraggio delle donne* (The Courage of Women, 1940), a collection of five long stories, the narrative form (*racconto lungo,* to use the Italian designation) for which she later expressed her preference; *Sette lune* (Seven Moons, 1941), her first straightforward third-person novel; and a second collection of stories, *Le monache cantano* (Nuns Are Singing, 1942), which introduced the theme of the cloistered life of Christian women she was to treat repeatedly. In 1944 she began to work on *Artemisia* (1947; translated, 1988), the historical *Künstlerroman* (novel of an artist) with which she remained preeminently identified.

The most important event in Banti's literary career was no doubt Longhi's appointment in 1949 at the University of Florence and his founding the following year of the monthly *Paragone*. Alternate issues of the journal were devoted to the figurative arts and to literature. Banti became the editor of *Paragone-Letteratura* while Longhi edited *Paragone-Arte;* at his death in 1970 she became the editor of both parts. The journal aimed at bringing the best in creative and critical writing, by both established and beginning writers, to the attention of readers united by their passion for literature and art: "a chi legge per istinto" (to those who read by instinct).

Although Banti did not cease publishing elsewhere—film criticism in *L'Approdo,* for instance, between 1952 and 1977—the bulk of her occasional writings, such as reviews of current French, English, and Italian works, appeared in *Paragone*. Her fiction came to reflect her widened cultural horizons. At the head of a select group of collaborators and disciples, Banti earned the reputation of being "impersonal," "distant," "unapproachable," and "haughty" but also inspired awe. To Cesare Garboli she was "an idol of unattainable perfection"; to Giovanni Testori, "a woman larger than life"; and to Grazia Livi, "a writer disdainful of what is perishable."

In the international pantheon of women writers Banti is perhaps closest to Virginia Woolf, whose *Jacob's Room* (1922) she translated in 1950. In the context of Italian literature, the critic Gianfranco Contini places her with the writers of poetic prose associated with the review *Solaria* (1926–1934), to which she did not contribute. Her fiction includes narratives of various length, some of which she reworked over considerable lapses of time. She throws light on the condition of women both in the past and the present, choosing as her protagonists figures from pre-Roman times as well as ordinary members of anonymous families in the Italy of her lifetime. The collection of her essays titled *Opinioni* (Opinions, 1961) is indispensable auxiliary reading, for in her discussion of general problems of literature and criticism and in her examination of other writers, from Alessandro Manzoni to Katherine Mansfield, she reveals much that is pertinent to her own writing as well.

Artemisia is Banti's best-known novel, perhaps her only well-known work outside the circle of initiates. American critic James Gardner wrote of the fig-

ARTEMISIA
Anna Banti

Translated by Shirley D'Ardia Caracciolo

Dust jacket for the translation of Banti's 1947 novel, whose subject is the seventeenth-century painter Artemisia Gentileschi

ure of Artemisia Gentileschi in his 1989 review of both the translation of the novel into English and Mary Garrard's coincident monograph, *Artemisia Gentileschi: The Image of the Female Artist in Italian Baroque Art:* "For many feminists, Artemisia Gentileschi (1593–1652) is a fully contemporary champion of their interests . . . she appeals as a thoroughly independent woman who . . . triumphantly overcame the prejudices and intrigues of jealous male rivals. . . . Above all, her rape at the age of 16 and the dramatic lawsuit that followed have turned her into a kind of feminist proto-martyr." The critic was quick to add that "It is her art that has made plausible her present prestige."

Only at an elementary level of description can *Artemisia* be defined reductively as a novel by a twentieth-century woman writer about a seventeenth-century woman painter. It is not any woman painter who is its subject; it is one whose aesthetic significance for Banti is at least equal—if not superior—to the qualification of her sex. Moreover, the work is an example of the use of self-conscious narrative strategies in which three separate conceptions of the painter are invoked. In *Artemisia,* as Emilio Cecchi noted in his 1948 review, "sono originalmente contesti motivi ed aspetti di biografia, di romanzo, ed a tratti quasi di autobiografia" (are innovatively interwoven motifs and aspects of biography, the novel, and at times almost of autobiography). Cecchi's perception was corroborated forty years later in the 4 January 1989 *New York Times* by a commentator who saw the novel as belonging to a new type of fiction in which the biography of a historical figure is "invented."

The historical Artemisia was born in Rome, the daughter of Orazio Gentileschi, a painter from Pisa who became famous enough to be called to the court of Maria de' Medici in France and later to that of Charles I of England, to which his daughter followed him. The significance of her achievement and the essence of her career is epitomized toward the end of the book in a passage that recalls some of the crucial experiences of her life—her years of apprenticeship to her father in Rome, the rape she endured when she was not much more than a child, the resulting trial and public loss of reputation, her short-lived marriage, and her later full-fledged acceptance into the fellowship of artists. Banti concludes, "Non c'è piú dubbi, un pittore ha avuto nome: Artemisia Gentileschi" (There is no longer any doubt, a new painter has been born: Artemisia Gentileschi) —where the operative word is *pittore,* the masculine form of *painter.*

The historical Artemisia is joined in the novel by a ghostly literary Artemisia, who owes her existence to the circumstance of Banti's having had her original manuscript destroyed in a fire during the occupation of Florence in 1944. This second Artemisia, in the first part of the novel, is looking for her "author" so that she may live again. In a move reminiscent of the daughter's action in Luigi Pirandello's *Six Characters in Search of an Author* (1921), she pushes herself forward, replaying scenes from her childhood and adolescence amid the give-and-take of a varied cast of characters from the teeming life of baroque Rome—the "characters" Banti had first encountered through Longhi's studies of Caravaggio and his circle and through her reading of the legal records of the rape trial. Banti's later play, *Corte Savella* (The Savella Court of Justice, 1960), is a further elaboration in dramatic form of this same subject matter.

Finally, there is a third Artemisia, the protagonist of the novel, in which Banti fleshes out the relatively little that is known about Artemisia Gentileschi as a historical personage. Banti demonstrates a special kind of imagination, the capacity of identifying with, or, as Alessandro Manzoni describes the faculty needed for historical fiction, the ability to integrate the plausible (what could have been) with the facts (what actually was). The three Artemisias, superimposed upon one another and yet one, entice the reader to follow the narrator in the blurring between past and present as the aspiration of a long-dead woman intermingles with the same impulse of her modern-day re-creator to become emblematic of the search for personal identity through, as Banti writes in the foreword, "the right to congenial work and the equality of spirit between the sexes."

Ranked immediately after *Artemisia* in Banti's canon is the short story "Lavinia fuggita" (Lavinia Has Fled), written in 1950 and published as the fourth story in *Le donne muoiono* (Women Are Dying, 1951), the collection that won the Viareggio Prize in 1952. In her introduction to *La monaca di Sciangai e altri racconti* (The Nun of Shanghai and Other Stories, 1957) Banti wrote that in the short-story form it is possible to recapitulate all the elements found in the novel but one must do so in perspective, "as it were, on the crest of the wave." Thus, "Lavinia fuggita," unlike *Artemisia,* is not the continuous narrative of a life, however episodic and elliptical, but the retrospective illumination of a decisive moment. A rupture—Lavinia's flight—stands at its center and continues to puzzle the two companions who witnessed it as they go over it again and again in memory.

The story's forward-moving tension or suspense lies in the unveiling of the mystery at its core. Like Artemisia, Lavinia is an artist, a musician, one of the orphans raised at the Venetian Ospedale della Pietà (Charity Hospital), famous throughout Europe for its all-girl orchestra and choir in the years when the great composer Antonio Vivaldi was active there. She is the choir-mistress, a position assigned to her not as a mark of distinction but to curb and humiliate her imperious self-confidence by subjecting her to the numbing routine of serving the work of others. One day on a summer outing—the story's principal scene—Lavinia disappears. Has she followed the Turk, with his "red and yellow turban" and "enormous coal-black moustache," whose insistent gaze, according to her companions, she had returned with a look of recognition? She, too, like the other foundlings, had her amulet, a piece of oriental cloth in which she was wrapped when brought to the Pietà as an infant. For a fleeting moment the Ali

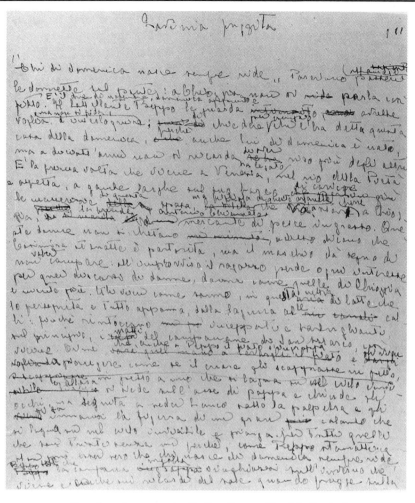

Page from the manuscript for Banti's story "Lavinia fuggita"

Baba motif emerges from the shimmering waters of the lagoon and points back in passing to the oriental source of all storytelling in the West.

But Banti's focus—in the case of Artemisia as rape victim or in that of Lavinia as foundling—is not on situations overworked in popular fiction. Lavinia's difference, her otherness, is not connected to her origin but to her musical gift. Her practice of music has gone beyond execution to composition, and during one of Vivaldi's absences she has substituted her own oratorio, *Ester,* for one of his. This "crime" or "mania," "trick" or "prank"—all terms by which her transgression is from different points of view judged—is the "scandal" that has ostracized her, even though one of her old companions remembers with unsuppressed admiration that it had proved that "anche una ragazza può comporre in musica, se vuole" (a girl too can compose music, if she wants to). Lavinia's self-justification, by contrast to this feminist statement, claims not the hollow right to legal, statistical equality but the proud

right to self-expression, to a public forum for her art: "Non avevo altro mezzo, mai mi prenderebbero sul serio, mai mi permetteranno di comporre. La musica degli altri è come un discorso rivolto a me, io devo rispondere e sentire il suono della mia voce" (I had no choice, they would never take me seriously, never allow me to compose. The music of others is like words addressed to me, I must reply and hear the sound of my own voice).

Two other short stories—"I porci" (The Pigs) and "Joveta di Betania" (Yvette of Bethany)—as well as a second novel, *La camicia bruciata* (The Burned Shirt, 1973), further illustrate Banti's emphasis on exceptional female figures in historical settings. The setting, however attentively reconstructed, is not an end in itself, a touch of local color to give variety, but the matrix out of which a sociological and psychological understanding of the characters springs, completing the intuition that first drew Banti to the character. For Banti, a character's presence imposes itself before his or her actions and motivations are fully known, whether that character corresponds to the actual existence of a documented person, as in the case of Artemisia, or, as is more frequent, it is completely "invented." The process of writing is, as Banti indicates in the preface to *La camicia bruciata,* akin to that of Freudian analysis.

Set in the remote past, "I porci," written in 1946 and included in *Le donne muoiono,* has enjoyed some of the same critical success as "Lavinia fuggita." No monuments and few documents survive to bear testimony of life in the Po valley in the period that was long known as the Dark Ages. The story's main setting of a degraded villa, located somewhere in the vicinity of what is today Modena, could as easily be from myth as from history. Lucilio and Priscilla, brother and sister from a patrician Roman family fleeing from the invading Vandals, have little in common except their origin and their brutalization as refugees. When they reach the villa, they find that it is not only an empty shell, but also is being used as a pigsty by the primitive local population who are expert pork butchers and sausage makers.

The different reaction of the two siblings is significant in terms of Banti's recurrent portrayal of what can be seen as distinctly female. Lucilio, lacking Priscilla's deeply felt sense of loss and her determination to reclaim what she can of her former life, sinks into the way of the local inhabitants and becomes the husband of one of the twenty-seven daughters of the Barbarian chieftain. Priscilla, instead, holds ever more strongly to her Roman origins, clinging to the pure Latin of her childhood and treasuring the few volumes of the classics she brought with her. She succeeds in rebuilding part of the villa into a cloister or sanctuary, a place of worship where she surrounds herself with the daughters of the invaders who choose to follow her and abandon their rough ways.

Priscilla, in overcoming her initial despair, becomes the dominant character, for whom the story might well have been named and in whom Banti invests the bulk of her empathy. She is the one who acts rather than being acted upon; if she finds refuge in a cloister, it is a cloister of her own making. Sustained by the faded memory of the religion of her childhood, she is inspired even more by the memory of the women in her family: "L'ava, la madre, la zia; e la cugina partita in Africa e fin le schiave più pie" (Her grandmother, her mother, her aunt, the cousin who left for Africa, and even the most devoted and pious of the household slaves). In rituals that hover between the Christian and the pagan, she and her attendants conserve the tenor of life of a gentler, more civilized existence.

The mingling of faiths as revealed by a sufficiently long historical perspective is also a theme in "Joveta di Betania," written about twenty years after "I porci" and published in *Je vous écris d'un pays lointain* (I am Writing You from a Distant Country, 1971). This *racconto lungo* is set in feudal Palestine at the time of the Latin Kingdom of Jerusalem, and its protagonist is the youngest daughter of King Baldwin II, left unprovided for at her father's death. She is forced to fashion a fulfilling existence for herself on her own, caught in the midst of the medieval fighting man's world on the shores of the Mediterranean, where East and West, past and future, Christian, Jew, and Moslem meet.

A pictorial representation of the deep split in Joveta's identity opens the story. She is shown cross-dressed, a slender knight wearing a white silk turban in place of a helmet, standing up in her stirrups to look down into a barren valley. The valley had once been a "paradise," the site of the Syrian prince's harem, where the child Joveta was held as a Christian hostage. It is that memory that colors the revolutionary new Rule she devises for the convent whose abbess she eventually becomes—a program in which prayer, fasting, and the mortification of the flesh go hand in hand with pleasurable pursuits such as picnics, games, songs, and the playing of the lute—all in a setting of luxuriant gardens surrounding a delightful dwelling. The attractive aspects of convent life—the convent being in many respects the best possible choice for an unmarried woman in a patriarchal society—have perhaps never been more appreciatively stated than in the sly, perhaps ironic, question Banti puts into Joveta's mouth: "Ma in fondo, cos'è un convento se non un harem senza letto coniugale?" (But after all, what is a convent if not a harem without the marriage bed?).

There is a stubborn, intellectual side to Joveta as well, something she shares with many of Banti's other women. She insists on the most rigorous religious instruction prior to taking her vows and precipitates "tempestuous" theological discussions. While rebuilding the monastery and cultivating its land, she endows a library rich enough to rival those found in bishoprics, where she had spent long hours studying Greek, Latin, and Arabic texts, anxious to be the equal of her most learned contemporaries. In time, like other feudal lords, she puts her fiefdom to practical use: the convent becomes a boarding school for the princesses of the Overseas Kingdom, and in educating them Joveta passes on the example of her overbearing and independent will that her students will exercise in the secular world of political power.

Many of Banti's critics—notably Enza Biagini and Anna Nozzoli—consider *La camicia bruciata,* winner of the D'Annunzio Prize in 1973, her most successful historical novel, the one in which she finally solved the problem of point of view, avoiding the intrusions of autobiography that from the beginning had beset her fiction. The figure of Marguerite Louise, "Fille de France" (daughter of the Royal House of France), cousin of Louis XIV, whom she had been groomed to marry, and wife of Cosimo III, the penultimate of the Medici grand dukes of Tuscany, aroused Banti's curiosity because she appeared to have been, if not maligned, then certainly mis- or insufficiently understood by historians.

In spite of her birth and status, Marguerite Louise was for Banti an ordinary woman, a victim like Alessandro Manzoni's nun of Monza in *I promessi sposi* (The Betrothed, 1825–1827), "non del tutto innocente mai, mai del tutto colpevole; infelice nel pianto nascosto e bruciata nell'orgoglio" (never completely innocent, never completely guilty; unhappy in her secret tears and stung in her pride). In the first part of the novel she is shown as a teenage bride in an incompatible marriage who burns her belaced and embroidered wedding nightgown the day before it is supposed to be used; a rebel for thirteen years against court life in Florence, who shocks people by her outlandish behavior; and an eccentric, mature woman in the convent of Montmatre, where she had been sent after her separation from Cosimo. In Banti's view Marguerite Louise would have been more at home in the world of the twentieth century than in that of the seventeenth.

In fleshing out the figure of Marguerite Louise, in retracing and often inventing the events of the monotonous days that history has not recorded, Banti ends up producing "un drappo istoriato," the crowded tapestry that serves as backdrop in historical fiction. In the second part of the novel Banti deals with the generation of Cosimo's and Marguerite Louise's children: Ferdinand, the heir who predeceased his father; Gian Gastone, almost ten years younger than his brother, who came to power too late to check the precipitous decline in Medici power and prestige; and Anna Maria Ludovica, her father's favorite, anxious to discredit her brothers and govern in their stead. The absent mother, whom official memory has suppressed to the point of having her portraits removed from the grand-ducal galleries, continues to act, half-remembered and half-forgotten, as a conditioning force on her husband and children but especially on Ferdinand's wife, Violante.

Beatrice Violante of Bavaria, trapped for dynastic reasons in a marriage almost as difficult as that of her mother-in-law, develops in the last part of the book into Marguerite Louise's opposite: a dignified, mature woman ruled by reason and reasonableness instead of by rebellious self-assertion. "Il ritratto della principessa tedesca . . . si configura così come un *unicum* nella narrativa bantiana una meta di consapevole e rasserenata lucidità nella quale trovano requie le multiformi tensioni delle sue eroine" (Thus the portrait of the German princess . . . forms a unique example in Banti's narrative, a target of self-aware and recovered serenity and lucidity in which the multiform tensions of her heroines find peace)—to cite Nozzoli's words in the conclusion to her 1978 essay on Banti's historical fiction.

"Vocazioni indistinte" (Confused Vocations), a short story first published in *Il coraggio delle donne,* is one of the early examples of Banti's treatment of women in a twentieth-century context. It belongs to a group of stories probably originally intended as a cycle devoted to the tenor of pre–World War I life in several emblematic provincial towns that figured in Banti's life prior to her university studies. Its protagonist is not an aspiring or triumphant woman but a defeated one. Banti's approach in the story is an example of what Contini calls her "harshness, even dismissive harshness" that at times replaces the "deep sympathy" with which she handles her fundamental theme, the condition of women. For Banti, that condition is not an abstraction; there are as many different conditions as there are individual women.

Ofelia, the principal character in the story, first appears as an awkward, unimaginative adolescent who is expected eventually to marry and is meanwhile studying the piano. Her family subscribes to the practical wisdom of the day and considers teaching the piano to be a preferable vocation to secretarial work: "Una donna deve bastare a se stessa" (A woman should be self-sufficient) and "L'insegnamento del piano è una professione più gentile" (Teaching the piano is a more ladylike profession). Ofelia spends years at the piano, but her relationship to music has nothing in common with Lavinia's nor with Artemisia's artistic vision. She is egged on by the challenge of technical perfection but has no understanding for questions of interpretation, taste, or style.

Forced by her teacher finally to *listen* to music, Ofelia amazes him by being able to reproduce note for note a famous pianist's concert. But Banti's authorial voice is merciless: "Non si divertiva né godeva in alcun modo, stando attenta come un cane e lavorando poi d'imitazione come un castoro" (She felt no diversion, no pleasure whatsoever, paying attention like a [trained] dog and imitating like an [eager] beaver). Only once does Banti show Ofelia experiencing something like fulfillment in her music. During her stay in Rome the invigorating presence of Giulia, her cousin, brings her to the point that "le sue dita miracolose si rincorrevano, giocavano con ritmi diversi, godevano delle pause, scoprivano insomma una specie di ginnastica festosa, di danza esilirata" (her miraculous fingers chased one another over the keyboard, toyed with different rhythms, paused rejoicing, in brief, discovered a kind of gymnastics, an exhilarating dance). But it is a moment of brief duration.

In her self-possession, easy teasing manner, and vivacity Giulia sets off the drabness and unattractiveness of Ofelia, just as in the first part of the story the breath of fresh air she brings from Rome relieves the gloom of her cousin's cramped small-town environment. A more conventional writer than Banti might have been kinder to her than to Ofelia, if only to extend the contrast of the paired characters. But Banti is as pitiless in her portrayal of the silly, superficial city-girl Giulia as she is of the inhibited, provincial Ofelia: neither is endowed with any redeeming qualities or talents. Whether through her authorial voice or through Ofelia's point of view, Banti heaps ridicule on Giulia by undercutting her reputation of precocious intelligence and emphasizing the irreconcilable attitudes plain in her speech and mannerisms: "orgoglio, intransigenze, arroganze, indulgenze e vanità, tutto annaffiato di buffonerie e di risate insopportabili" (pride, intransigence, arrogance, self-indulgence and vanity, all sprinkled with buffooneries and unbearable bursts of laughter). Banti's most damning indictment concerns Giulia's human insensitivity, for in her championship of Ofelia as a great concert artist Giulia is unaware of the psychological damage she inflicts upon a weak and suggestible personality. Her rediscovery of Ofelia many years later as a harassed, impoverished, and unbalanced wife and mother is a veritable "descent into Hell."

Il bastardo (The Bastard, 1953), later republished in a slightly revised version with a new title, *La casa piccola* (The Other Family, 1961), depicts a more complex descent into hell than that of "Vocazioni indistinte" and Banti's other early stories of family life. Its first reviewers noted its affinity with Sicilian *Verismo* (realism), especially as exemplified in the work of Federico De Roberto. *Il bastardo,* set sixty years after the ruling Bourbon aristocracy had lost its political raison d'être, is a story of Italy's South.

The blunt 1953 title and the more allusive 1961 title–from the local Neapolitan expression "tiene una casa piccola" (he has a second illicit family)–both point to the same situation: Baron Gug-

lielmo de Gregorio, whom Donna Elisa Infantado married when she was in her thirties and well-known for her eccentricities, already had a mistress and a son he recognized as his own. Donna Elisa refused to admit this son to the regular family, and shortly after an angry quarrel he was found drowned in a well. Exactly what happened on that fateful 7 October is never made clear, but the tragedy (crime or accident) leaves its mark on all the members of the family. Donna Elisa's mental balance becomes more and more precarious; de Gregorio withdraws into the administrative responsibilities of his estate; their only son turns to the priesthood; and Cecilia, the older daughter, rejects the prospects of marriage and family for the single-minded pursuit of her studies and career.

Cecilia, the novel's protagonist, was suggested by a woman Banti mentions in her 20 October 1945 article for *Il mondo,* "Dedicato alle ragazze" (Dedicated to Girls): "Morí nel '42, a Roma, una donna ancor giovane, ancor bella, ricca di nascita, che la passione del lavoro e degli studi aveva portato a rinunzie monacali: essa era ingegnere elettrotecnico e capo di una azienda importante" (There died in Rome, in 1942, a woman, still young, still beautiful, rich by birth, brought by the passion for work and learning to monastic renunciations: she was an electrical engineer and head of an important firm). In the article this anonymous woman figures as one of the "worker bees," self-effacing, childless, single women of the generation born between 1910 and 1920, who under Fascism had represented not the dominant ideal of motherhood but the earlier, "pioneering" model of productive, independent, and personally rewarding work outside the home.

The Cecilia of the novel is a conflicted, complex character. While she carries her author's feminist message, she is also the product of the novelist's psychological probing and representational skills in narrative form. Cecilia is part of a family: daughter of her mother *mamma;* niece of her married, childless aunt (*mammina*) who is only slightly less eccentric than her sister, Elisa; sister to Annella, whose feeling of sibling rivalry ends in her siding with the rest of the family in ostracizing Cecilia; and half sister of "the bastard," for whose death she continues to feel mysteriously and hopelessly responsible. Her feeling of guilt never exorcised, Cecilia never succeeds in making up to her family for the loss they suffered. While on one hand she exemplifies Banti's female characters who have succeeded in making their ambition acceptable in the outside world, on the other she fails at achieving what some would consider the quintessential feminine goal, that of creating an environment of mutual understanding and love.

In 1955 Banti won her second literary prize with *Allarme sul lago* (Alarm on the Lake, 1954), a novel composed of three complementary stories linked by their similar subject matter and by the frame within which their telling takes place. The threat of an unspecified cataclysm, perhaps the explosion of an atom bomb, has blocked four women, strangers to one another, in an abandoned hotel on the shores of a lake. Three of the women–Katrina, Ottorina, and Adele–each in their turn take the occasion to speak of marital experiences in order, as one of them says, to "mettere in chiaro molte cose" (make many things intelligible). An early reviewer used the adjective "wintry" to describe the harsh, desolate atmosphere created by the three stories. Each one analyzes a marriage, making no concessions to the reserve that usually shields intimate family life. The effect is cumulative and essentially impersonal, such as a sociological study might achieve, but the particular circumstances of each marriage are different and observed in pitiless detail.

Katrina and Ottavio married by choice; Ottorina's marriage to Giuseppe was arranged by their respective families; Adele and Corrado were forced to marry after he had seduced her. All three wives learn to know their husbands only after they are married. Indeed, getting to know them–or trying to get to know them–becomes their principal occupation, for the wife's position in each marriage is one of utter dependence. Katrina, who had come to Italy from an unidentified northern country as a student of modern dance, is drawn into a morass in which she plays a subordinate role to her husband's artist friends, to his business partners, and finally to the mistresses who come to share their ménage. Ottorina's marriage at first seems normal: two daughters are born. But it is not long before her husband asks of her a strange "service" indeed: she is to feign a pregnancy to cover for the real pregnancy of a young girl for which her husband is responsible. Adele's husband, like Ottavio, is a failed artist, but he also turns out to be a sex fiend, bent on punishing his wife for having given in to him. He drives her into an affair with a friend of his and insists that she visit brothels so that she can learn the trade. In addition to psychological abuse, the three wives are also kept in economic subjection, variously forced to account for every penny they spend in spite of the fact that these are financially stable households.

The fourth woman at the hotel, Eugenia, caps the "confessions" of the other three with a conciliatory, humanist message. She has never married, she says, but she does not hate men nor does she fear them: "Vivo lavorando in mezzo a loro" (I live,

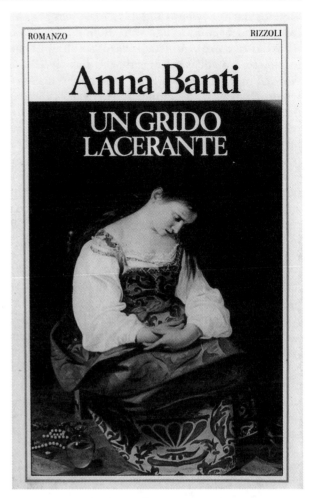

Dust jacket for Banti's 1981 novel, in which she explores her life through the protagonist, Agnese Lanzi

working among them). She has learned that "gli uomini non sono diversi da noi . . . e la colpa è nostra se, per difetto di carità fraterna, li lasciamo oppressi dal nostro destino" (men are not different from us . . . and it is our fault if for lack of brotherly charity we permit them to be oppressed by the weight of our fate). Thus, Eugenia reverses the perspective of the three stories that critic Enza Biagini would later summarize tersely if rather indiscriminately as "marriage is always a losing proposition for a woman." These are not simply stories of the oppression of women by men within marriage. More significantly, the stories show women who are unable to free themselves from feelings of subjection to men and fail in finding a way for setting both sexes on the road to the mutually satisfying interdependence that marriage can provide.

Le mosche d'oro (Golden Wasps, 1962) is the most ambitious of Banti's novels of modern life, a *roman de moeurs* (novel of manners) of the 1950s. The title derives from a Tuscan proverb, according to which even the beautiful golden wasp ends up by falling and becoming mired in the mud. *Le mosche d'oro* has two protagonists: Libero, a young Italian intellectual of peasant origin who has lived and worked in Paris for two years; and his French girlfriend Denise, who belongs to the wealthy upper bourgeoisie. After the birth of a child, their affair, which had played itself out against the Bohemian background of the Left Bank, comes to an end. The first chapter describes Libero's train trip back from Paris to Florence; the second depicts Denise's return home after a day of aimless wandering through the streets of St. Germain. Thus, these chapters present the protagonists not so much in their psychology as in their contrasting social conditions, and in good realist fashion their stories, together and apart, are tied to their milieus. Libero and Denise meet again only in the last chapter of the book when they are brought together by chance in Venice; they have become strangers to one another in their apathy and sense of failure, which the gray tones of an autumnal Venice can do little to lighten.

Critics have disagreed in their comparative evaluations of the two blocks of material that constitute this novel. Some have found the "provincial" pages that describe Libero's return home with his infant son, Dantino, to his family's tenant farm in Tuscany the more successful. Others have pointed out how the broadening of cultural horizons that accompanied Banti's first ten years with *Paragone* resulted in her exploration of the Paris of Jean-Paul Sartre and Simone de Beauvoir, whose *Les Mandarins* (1954; translated as *The Mandarins*, 1956) Banti reviewed in April 1955.

Le mosche d'oro is as well researched as Banti's historical fiction and its sociological settings are representative and accurate. But the characters—Libero, the son of farmers, becoming an art student in the postwar years; Denise and the women around her variously victimized by irresponsible, unstructured living—are so familiar that they lack the fascination of Banti's historical re-creations. The portrayal of Libero's political education has all the earmarks of a Marxist "lesson." Denise's instability and the instances of sexual dysfunctions in her circle are neither sympathetically nor objectively presented but engender feelings of revulsion akin to those produced by Elsa Morante's *Aracoeli* (1982; translated, 1985).

There is, however, one extraordinary sequence in *Le mosche d'oro:* Libero's attempt to look after Dantino himself. As he says to his sister, who has an illegitimate child she is raising: "Che c'è di strano se io mi occupo del mio bastardino? Tu mi dovresti capire meglio degli altri, siamo nelle stesse condizi-

oni e io non faccio differenza fra un uomo e una donna, hanno gli stessi doveri e gli stessi diritti" (What's so strange about my taking care of my little bastard? You should understand me better than anyone else. We're in the same situation and there's no difference, as far as I'm concerned, between men and women: they have the same duties and the same rights). But Libero's attempt to fill a woman's role fails. He is defeated by the mind-numbing routine of keeping a household going, even if it is only a furnished room, and taking care of a small, unhappy child. But in the process of constructing this episode—one more example of Libero's fundamental ineptitude—Banti writes some unforgettable pages, more powerful than any direct description of a woman's daily grind would have been. With this unusual reversal of roles, Banti calls attention to one of her many male characters that have unjustly been overshadowed in critical commentary. Despite her own repeated statements that seem somewhat to justify an exclusively ideological reading of her work, Banti's fiction is fundamentally humanistic and deserves broader critical attention.

Interviews:

L. P., "Sedici domande ad Anna Banti," *La Fiera letteraria,* 5 (3 February 1957);

Enzo Siciliano, "Strappare il velo che oscura la verità," *Corriere della sera,* 12 August 1981;

Nico Orengo, "Banti: la mia scrittura è donna ma non per i critici," *Tuttolibri,* 5 September 1981;

"Ls sfortuna di essere seri," in *Le signore della scrittura. Interviste,* edited by Sandra Petrignani (Milan: La Tartaruga, 1984), pp. 101–109.

Bibliographies:

Enza Biagini, "Nota bibliografica," in her *Anna Banti* (Milan: Mursia, 1978), pp. 185–197;

Laura Desideri, "Bibliografia degli scritti di Anna Banti," *Paragone-Letteratura,* 41 (December 1990): 73–123.

References:

Enza Biagini, *Anna Banti* (Milan: Mursia, 1978);

Paola Blelloch, "Anna Banti da *Il coraggio delle donne* a *Le donne muoiono*," *NEMLA Italian Studies,* 11–12 (1987/1988): 97–103;

Vanni Bramanti, "Ritratto di Anna Banti (1937–1975)," in *Saggi novecenteschi* (Ravenna: Edizioni Essegi, 1988), pp. 33–54;

JoAnn Cannon, "Artemisia and the Life Story the Exceptional Woman," *Forum Italicum,* 28 (Fall 1994): 322–341;

Giulio Cattaneo, "I quarant'anni di *Paragone*-Letteratura," *Nuova Antologia,* 2175 (July–September 1990): 233–240;

Emilio Cecchi, "Artemisia Gentileschi," in his *Di giorno in giorno* (Milan: Garzanti, 1954), pp. 19–22;

Gianfranco Contini, "Anna Banti," in *Letteratura dell'Italia unita 1861–1968* (Florence: Sansoni, 1968), p. 867;

Contini, "Parere ritardato su *Artemisia*" (1949), in his *Altri esercizi (1942–1971)* (Turin: Einaudi, 1972), pp. 173–178;

Giuseppe De Robertis, "Anna Banti (tra Artemisia e Lavinia, 1954)," in his *Altro novecento* (Florence: Le Monnier, 1962), pp. 282–287;

Valeria Finucci, " 'A Portrait of the Artist as a Female Painter': The Kunstlerroman Tradition in A. Banti's *Artemisia,*" *Quaderni d'italianistica,* 8, no. 2 (1987): 167–193;

Cesare Garboli, *Anna Banti e il tempo* (Florence: Pananti, 1992);

Garboli, "Breve storia del giovane Longhi," in *Scritti servili* (Turin: Einaudi, 1989), pp. 165–207;

James Gardner, "A Star is Reborn," *National Review* (4 August 1989): 44–45;

Margherita Ghilardi, "Il quaderno salvato. Anna Banti e Leonetta Cecchi Pieraccini," *Il Vieusseux,* 5 (September–December 1992): 83–110;

Nella Giannetto, "Anna Banti, (1895–1985)," in *Dizionario critico della letteratura italiana,* edited by Vittore Branca (Turin: UTET, 1986), pp. 188–191;

Mina Gregori, "Gli scritti di critica d'arte di Anna Banti," *Paragone-Letteratura,* 42 (August 1991): 17–22;

Rita Guerricchio, "I racconti di Anna Banti," *Paragone-Letteratura,* 41 (December 1990): 22–55;

Deborah Haller, "Remembering Artemisia: Anna Banti and Artemisia Gentileschi," in *Donna: Women in Italian Culture,* edited by Ada Testaferri (Toronto: Dovehouse, 1989), pp. 99–108;

Grazia Livi, "Anna Banti: Il modello," in her *Le lettere del mio nome* (Milan: La Tartaruga, 1991), pp. 135–142;

Benedetta Montagni, "Donna in grigio. Anna Banti scrittrice di costume," *Paragone-Letteratura,* 42 (October 1991): 17–22;

Montagni, "Quando Anna Banti firmava Lucia Lopresti. 1919–1929, Un decennio di scritti d'arte," *Studi Italiani,* 6, no, 1 (1994): 95–106;

Anna Nozzoli, "Anna Banti: La scelta del romanzo," in her *Tabù e coscienza. La condizione femminile nella letteratura italiana del Novecento* (Florence: La Nuova Italia, 1978), pp. 85–111;

G. A. Peritore, "Anna Banti," in *Letteratura italiana. I contemporanei,* 3 (1975): 211–234;

Pier Paolo Pasolini, "Anna Banti, *La camicia bruciata,*" in his *Descrizioni di descrizioni* (Turin: Einaudi, 1979), pp. 85–89;

Thomas Peterson, "The 'Feminine' Writing of Anna Banti: *Un grido lacerante,*" *NEMLA Italian Studies,* 11–12 (1987/1988): 87–96;

Giovanni Previtali, ed., *L'arte di scrivere sull'arte. Roberto Longhi nella cultura del suo tempo* (Rome: Editori Riuniti, 1982);

Olga Ragusa, "Figures of Women in Anna Banti's Fiction," in *Perspectives on Italy,* edited by Borden W. Painter Jr., special issue of *The Cesare Barbieri Courier* (Hartford, Conn.: Trinity College, 1992), pp. 64–91;

Giovanni Testori, "Ritratto di Anna Banti," *Paragone-Letteratura,* 41 (December 1990): 13–21.

Papers:

The Banti papers are held at the Longhis' eighteenth-century villa on the outskirts of Florence, the seat of the Fondazione di Studi di Storia dell'Arte Roberto Longhi, a research center.

Giorgio Bassani

(4 March 1916 –   )

Augustus Pallotta
Syracuse University

See also the Bassani entry in *DLB 128: Twentieth-Century Italian Poets.*

BOOKS: *Una città di pianura,* as Giacomo Marchi (Milan: Arte Grafica Lucini, 1940);

Storie di poveri amanti e altri versi (Rome: Astrolabio, 1945; enlarged, 1946);

Te lucis ante (Rome: Ubaldini, 1947);

Un'altrà liberta (Milan: Mondadori, 1952);

La passeggiata prima di cena (Florence: Sansoni, 1953);

Gli ultimi anni di Clelia Trotti (Pisa: Nistri-Lischi, 1955);

Cinque storie ferraresi (Turin: Einaudi, 1956); republished as *Le storie ferraresi* (Turin: Einaudi, 1960); revised as *Dentro le mura* (Milan: Mondadori, 1973); translated by Isabel Quigley as *A Prospect of Ferrara* (London: Faber & Faber, 1962); translated by William Weaver as *Five Stories of Ferrara* (New York: Harcourt Brace Jovanovich, 1971);

Gli occhiali d'oro (Turin: Einaudi, 1958); translated by Quigley as *The Gold-Rimmed Spectacles* (London: Faber & Faber, 1960; New York: Atheneum, 1960);

Una notte del '43 (Turin: Einaudi, 1960);

Il giardino dei Finzi-Contini (Turin: Einaudi, 1962; revised edition, Milan: Mondadori, 1974); translated by Quigley as *The Garden of the Finzi-Continis* (New York: Atheneum, 1965; London: Faber & Faber, 1965); translated by Weaver as *The Garden of the Finzi-Continis* (New York: Harcourt Brace Jovanovich, 1977);

L'alba ai vetri: poesie 1942–'50 (Turin: Einaudi, 1963);

Dietro la porta (Turin: Einaudi, 1964); translated by Weaver as *Behind the Door* (New York: Harcourt Brace Jovanovich, 1972; London: Weidenfeld & Nicolson, 1973);

Le parole preparate, e altri scritti di letteratura (Turin: Einaudi, 1966); revised and enlarged as *Di là dal cuore* (Milan: Mondadori, 1984);

L'airone (Milan: Mondadori, 1968); translated by Weaver as *The Heron* (New York: Harcourt

Giorgio Bassani

Brace Jovanovich, 1970; London: Weidenfeld & Nicolson/Panther Books, 1970);

L'odore del fieno (Milan: Mondadori, 1972); translated by Weaver as *The Smell of Hay* (New York: Harcourt Brace Jovanovich, 1975; London: Weidenfeld & Nicolson, 1975);

Epitaffio (Milan: Mondadori, 1974);

Il romanzo di Ferrara (Milan: Mondadori, 1974; revised, 1980);

20

In gran segreto (Milan: Mondadori, 1978);
In rima e senza: 1939–1981 (Milan: Mondadori, 1982).

Edition in English: *Rolls Royce and Other Poems,* translated by Francesca Valente (Toronto: Aya Press, 1982).

UNCOLLECTED PERIODICAL PUBLICATION:
"Risposte a nove domande sul romanzo," *Nuovi argomenti,* 38–39 (1959): 1–5.

What sets Giorgio Bassani apart from other Italian writers of the period following World War II is above all his individualism. This quality, which he shares with only a few of his contemporaries, can be defined as confidence in his ability to deal free from any subordination to literary trends or ideologies with complex human relationships. His work is identified with the vicissitudes of Italian Jews under Fascist rule from 1922 to 1942. Yet Bassani's interest in the Jewish community of Ferrara, which constitutes the spirit and substance of his work, is not strictly ethnic and is hardly provincial in nature; it is an interest of a higher order that transcends ethnic and national boundaries. Although Bassani proudly affirms his Jewish identity, he is not a religious man and associates his Jewishness with the cultural, rather than the religious, aspect of his ethnicity. At the same time, while Bassani's Jewish identity is important to the understanding of his work, as a writer and an intellectual, he has consistently been at the center, not at the margins, of postwar Italian culture.

Bassani's individualism is reflected as well in a steadfast faith in his poetics, which has entailed a rejection of various forms of experimentation that emerged in Italy following World War II. The most prominent, though short-lived, of such movements was Neorealism, which was dominant from 1945 to 1955. Opposed to the vacuous rhetoric of the Fascist era, neorealists stressed a simple, essential, popular idiom as they sought to portray the struggles of everyday life among the lower classes during the bleak days that followed the end of the war. Bassani's interest in the less fortunate groups of society is rooted in his Jewish experience, and he distanced himself from neorealism because from the start it was identified with the Marxist ideology espoused by the political parties of the Left. Bassani has always maintained that literature should not advance the interests of any social or political cause; it should serve only truth and humanity to the extent that it can.

Cognizant that he was running against the ideological grain of his time by exhibiting indifference to neorealism and other forms of experimentation, Bassani looked to the aesthetic tenets of Benedetto Croce, the Neapolitan philosopher, critic, and historian who exerted a strong influence on Italian intellectual life during the first half of the twentieth century. In a 1988 interview with Walter Mauro, Bassani referred to Croce in explaining his identification with Italian Jews on the basis of ethnicity rather than religion: "La mia religione era quella della libertà. Credevo nella libertà come religione: seguace anche in questo di Benedetto Croce" (My religion was freedom. I believed in freedom as a religion, and in this too I was a disciple of Benedetto Croce). He was attracted to Croce's view of history as an intellectual activity guided by precise philosophical and moral concerns. The forces of cultural renewal released by the defeat of fascism and by World War II were to erode Croce's influence, but this did not deter Bassani from treating history in his work in ways that affirmed Croce's views.

A second major influence on Bassani was Alessandro Manzoni, the father of the modern Italian novel who structured his work in accordance with three basic tenets: the pursuit of truth, the intrinsic interest of literature, and the usefulness of literature to society. Bassani was drawn as well to the texture of Manzoni's narrative that emphasizes clarity and everyday usage. Equally important, he admired Manzoni's credibility as a writer. As he explained in 1977, "Da Manzoni credo di aver imparato soprattutto la lezione circa la credibilità del poeta, che non si considera un privilegiato, che è quello che è, che esercita il massimo sforzo di sincerità" (From Manzoni I believe I learned, above all, the lesson relative to the credibility of a writer who does not see himself as privileged, but sees himself for what he is, who exercises the utmost effort of sincerity).

Bassani was born in Bologna to Dora and Enrico Bassani, a surgeon, on 4 March 1916, six years before the advent of Fascism and the one-party rule instituted by Benito Mussolini. An important university town, Bologna played a large part in his intellectual development. But it is Ferrara, the city in the plains of Emilia-Romagna where Bassani was raised and spent much of his youth, that serves as the primary setting of his novels. His opposition to Fascism began when he was a student at the University of Bologna, where he enrolled in 1934, and it was strengthened by the enactment in 1938 of anti-Semitic laws that severely restricted the participation of Jewish citizens in Italian society. Bassani graduated from the university in 1939 and soon began his literary career.

A youthful reaction to Fascism transpires in Bassani's first book, *Una città di pianura* (A City in

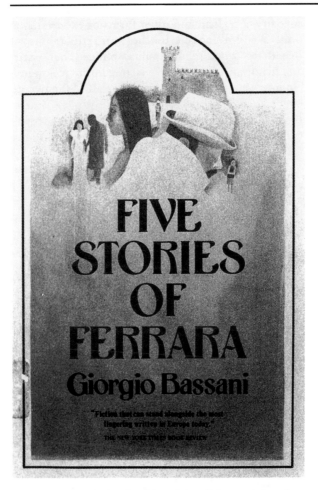

Dust jacket for the American edition of the translation of Bassani's 1956 collection of interconnected stories

the Plains, 1940), a collection of short stories that appeared under the pseudonym Giacomo Marchi. Bassani adopted the pseudonym because the new laws prevented Jews from publishing; yet, in choosing Marchi, the last name of his Catholic grandmother, he managed to keep his family identity. *Una città di pianura* offers descriptions and situations betraying a state of spiritual weariness one can identify with everyday life under Fascism. In one story the psychological disposition of the narrator is captured by a short sentence that is as terse and suggestive as a line of poetry: "Le ore passano, cresce col sonno una malinconia che è stanchezza dell'anima" (The hours pass, with sleep there grows a melancholy which is tiredness of the soul).

During World War II Bassani took an active part in the Resistance, a coalition of political forces of different ideological convictions – socialists, Catholics, communists – that shared the objective of overthrowing Fascism. Bassani was one of a small group of foes of Fascism who founded the Partito

d'Azione (Action Party). This and other acts of opposition led to his arrest in May 1943; he was released from prison after two months when the Fascist Party was outlawed. In August 1943 he married Valeria Sinigallia and decided to move to Florence with his wife and parents. The ensuing outbreak of the civil war, in which Nazi and Fascist forces fought the Resistance, forced Bassani to go into hiding and to assume a false name. When the war ended in April 1945, he settled in Rome permanently.

While earning a living by writing film scripts and contributing articles to newspapers, Bassani published two volumes of poetry, *Storie di poveri amanti* (Stories of Poor Lovers, 1945) and *Te lucis ante* (Before the Day Ends, 1945), that attracted favorable notice in literary circles. The psychological impact of Fascism on Bassani would prove to be deep and pervasive, and many of the poems in the second volume echo the mental anguish he experienced in prison during the spring of 1943. Forty years later he called the Fascist prison "a terrible experience." In a 27 October 1968 interview with Grazia Livi, Bassani described his youthful disposition as a writer: "Come scrittore, a quell'epoca mi trovavo ancora involto nella presunzione giovanile dell'ineffabilità. Scrivendo, non mi impegnavo solitamente a 'tirar fuori' tutto quello che avevo dentro, convinto come ero che ciò che avevo, o credevo di avere, dentro non poteva, e quindi non doveva esser tirato fuori" (At that time, as a writer, I was still affected by a youthful proclivity toward the ineffable. When I wrote, I did not, as a rule, try hard to "pull out" everything that was within me, convinced, as I was, that what I had, or I thought I had, within me could not and, therefore, was not to be pulled out).

Between 1949 and 1955 four of Bassani's short stories appeared in the literary review *Botteghe oscure,* two of which, *La passeggiata prima di cena* (1953) and *Gli ultimi anni di Clelia Trotti* (1955), were published separately. These and a fifth story, "Una notte del '43," were collected in *Cinque storie ferraresi* (1956; translated as *A Prospect of Ferrara,* 1962, and *Five Stories of Ferrara,* 1971), which was republished as *Le storie ferraresi* (Stories of Ferrara, 1960). The stories strongly suggested that prose fiction, not his somewhat hermetic poetry, would prove to be the vehicle best suited to Bassani's talent. Early in his career he had achieved depth and maturity as a writer; indeed, some critics regard *Cinque storie ferraresi* as the high point of his work. The representation of the walled city of Ferrara and its prosperous middle class as a web of human interactions woven by diverse and contrasting social forces lends structural unity and cohesiveness to the collection. The unity of the work is reinforced by allusions to or appearances of a few characters in more than one story.

Though linked, the stories are quite distinct, differing in narrative strategies, in the fusing of history and fiction, and in the portrayal of characters, particularly in the interaction between Jews and gentiles. Moreover, Bassani creates a personal authorial voice, one that convinces the reader he is a witness to the fictive and historical events described. Bassani underscored the importance of this narrative strategy in an 8 October 1960 interview published in *Il punto:* "Chi ha letto le *Storie ferraresi,* si sarà reso certamente conto che il personaggio più importante, forse di tutto il libro, è proprio la figura, dissimulata è vero ma per questo non meno presente, dell'io narratore, poeta, giudice e storico" (Those who have read the *Storie ferraresi* must have realized that perhaps the most important character in the book is precisely the disguised but nonetheless very real figure of the narrating I, who functions as writer, judge, and historian).

History, social consciousness, and Jewish identity are three of the most important themes of *Cinque storie ferraresi.* With few exceptions, these themes are treated not separately but as dependent and mutually enriching. Such is the case with "Lida Mantovani," the first story in the collection, and *La passeggiata prima di cena* (A Stroll Before Supper), both of which focus on the marriage between a Jew and a Catholic and on the lives of poor people. "Lida Mantovani," published initially as "Storia di Debora," was revised four times before it achieved a definitive form. Lida, a young Catholic woman born out of wedlock who, like her mother, is a seamstress, falls in love with David, an indolent, noncomformist youth who enjoys the financial security of his upper-class Jewish family. When Lida has a child, David, who views marriage as "a bourgeois farce," leaves her. Left alone with their child, Lida eventually marries a kind neighbor, thirty years her senior. Similarly, in *La passeggiata prima di cena* Gemma Brondi, a young Catholic of peasant background, marries Elia Corcos, a doctor from a prosperous Jewish family.

In both stories social and religious disparities are compounded by the problem of communication, a popular theme in postwar existentialist narrative. David and Lida share a physical attraction and little else. After their marriage, Elia and Gemma are hardly seen doing anything together; indeed, the reader is led to suspect that, emotionally, they have grown far apart. Likewise, several years after her separation from David, Lida thinks of him as a total stranger: "Chi era David? Che cosa cercava? Che cosa voleva? Perché?" (Who was David? What was he looking for? What did he want? Why?). In *La passeggiata prima di cena* Elia becomes isolated: "Neppure a Gemma, benché moglie, e padrona, era mai riuscito di oltrepassare il muro invisibile dietro il quale Elia si estraniava" (Not even Gemma, his wife and lady of the house, had managed to cross the invisible wall which protected Elia's reserve).

The sense of isolation, whether self-imposed or not, is identified in these stories and elsewhere with the Jewish persona. Between Jewish and Catholic Italians a social barrier exists even when intermarriage is accepted. When David and Lida have a date, he chooses to wait for her at the door, refusing to set foot in her modest home: "Mai aveva voluto entrare, mai aveva sentito il dovere di presentarsi" (He always refused to come in; he never felt the obligation to introduce himself). Similarly, Gemma's mother refuses to visit her daughter after she marries Elia: "In quella casa si era sempre rifiutata di venirci" (She had always refused to enter that house).

Gli ultimi anni di Clelia Trotti (The Last Years of Clelia Trotti), one of the most successful of the Ferrara stories, is the only work that explores political ideology, personified by the protagonist, in a sustained fashion. Clelia Trotti is a strong-willed, uncompromising political activist who has remained loyal to Socialist ideas even under Fascist rule in the 1930s. The story begins in the autumn of 1946 with a ceremony honoring Clelia's memory. Among those present is Bruno Lattes, a Ferrarese Jew who lost his parents in the concentration camps and now lives in the United States. The veneer of attributes extolling Clelia as "martire del socialismo e guida eroica della classe operaia" (a martyr of socialism and heroic leader of the working class) can barely conceal Bassani's disturbing pessimism toward ideology, human beings, and institutions that permeates the texture of this work. This pessimism spares no one, not even the protagonist.

Prejudice, intolerance, cynicism – partly congenital in the human psyche and partly fostered by a repressive regime – are perceived as the forces fraying Italian society. The real, perhaps subconscious reason for Clelia's funeral is conveyed by the skeptical narrator: "Sembrava di essere stati chiamati ad assistere a uno di quegli esami di coscienza attraverso i quali una società vecchia e colpevole cercava di rinnovarsi" (One had the feeling of being invited to witness a collective scrutiny of conscience through which an old and culpable society sought to renew itself). Yet the ideal of social renewal, which necessarily entails optimism and a collective effort, is nowhere in sight.

Clelia Trotti, who as a political prisoner "sognava la rinascita del socialismo italiano" (dreamed the rebirth of Italian socialism), has become only a

Cover for the 1977 American edition of the translation of Bassani's 1962 novel, which examines a wealthy, isolated Jewish family in Fascist Italy

cherished memory. To those, such as Bruno Lattes, who knew and admired her, the funeral stands as a symbolic act of closure. The point Bassani makes through the title of the story is that Clelia's socialism never moved beyond the stage of a utopian dream: "ll mondo migliore, la società giusta e civile di cui Clelia Trotti rappresentava, insieme, la prova vivente e il relitto, sarebbero tornati mai più?" (A better world, a more just society, of which Clelia Trotti represented both the living proof and the residue, would they ever return?).

Bassani's pessimism is not limited to the experience of Fascism alone. The narrator remarks that beginning in 1915 — seven years before Mussolini seized power — and through the 1930s, the country had experienced "la progressiva degenerazione di ogni valore" (the progressive degeneration of all values). Before immigrating to America, Bruno Lattes feels "rabbia e disgusto" (anger and disgust) at what

Italian society has become under Fascism. The better world of socialism that Trotti dreamed would be brought about by idealistic youths such as Lattes never materialized. The reality of postwar Italy is marked by the empty rhetoric of a politician and the intrusive presence of a young woman who, showing total indifference to the funeral, disturbs the ceremony with her noisy scooter. The cultural model for postwar youth is not that envisioned by Clelia but the United States:

> Possibile che la guerra, gli anni nei quali lui era stato ragazzo, e lei bambina, non le avessero lasciato addosso la minima traccia? Possibile che dovunque, in Italia, gli adolescenti fossero ormai cosí: come se uscissero teenagers ignari di tutto, dalle pagine di una rivista americana?

> (Was it possible that the war, the years in which he had been a youngster and she [the girl on the scooter] a child, had no effect on her? Was it possible that everywhere in Italy adolescents were now like ignorant teenagers that had come out of an American magazine?)

Bassani draws from his experiences and knowledge of World War II in two other stories, "Una notte del '43" (A Night in '43) and "Una lapide in Via Mazzini" (A Plaque in Via Mazzini"). "Una notte del '43" re-creates the execution by Fascist thugs of eleven Ferrarese men the night of 15 November 1943 as a reprisal for the assassination of a high-ranking Fascist official in Ferrara. In the postwar trial the only witness who can identify the murderers lies to the court to prevent the disclosure of his wife's adulterous conduct. "Una lapide in Via Mazzini" is dominated by the eerie presence of Geo Josz, a Ferrarese Jew who was sent to a concentration camp in Germany with eighty-six of his coreligionists. Two years later he reappears unexpectedly in Ferrara while a plaque is being affixed to the wall of the synagogue in Via Mazzini to honor the Jews of Ferrara deported to Germany.

In "Una notte del '43" Bassani examines setting and characters with a cold, impassioned clarity that brings to mind the work of the historical novelist Alessandro Manzoni. The analogies between "Una notte del '43" and Manzoni's *Storia della colonna infame* (1842; translated as *The Column of Infamy,* 1964), in which two men are unjustly accused of spreading the bubonic plague in seventeenth-century Milan, center on a heinous crime committed against innocent individuals. More important, what links Bassani to Manzoni is the rational dimension of the story, in the sense that events are not simply described or reported but are brought under scrutiny by an ethically conscious author. Commenting on his relationship to Manzoni in a 1977 interview, Bassani remarked: "Se c'è uno scrittore dell'Otto-cento che mi abbia attirato ancor più, molto di più di Leopardi, è Manzoni. Il suo sforzo, in tutti i sensi, e politico e morale, e soprattutto letterario, sta all'o-rigine della società in cui viviamo. E in qualche modo io ho cercato di riprenderlo, di farlo mio." (If there is a nineteenth-century writer who attracted me more, much more than Leopardi, that writer is Manzoni. In every sense, his effort – political, moral, and, above all, literary – forms the base of the society in which we live. And in some ways, I tried to imitate him, to appropriate him).

What Bassani sought to appropriate from Manzoni's work is a distinctive treatment of histori-cal narrative not found in postwar Italian realistic fiction, namely a rational, morally informed analy-sis of individual conduct under strenuous circum-stances. Bassani found rational analysis attractive because it helped him, ethically and narratively, to resolve complex ideological questions posited by World War II. His examination of history takes the shape of a painful search for truth, an investigation of individual and collective responsibility not unlike that pursued by Manzoni in *I promessi sposi* (The Be-trothed, 1825–1827). Bassani's translation of his-torical consciousness into a moral imperative is more immediate and compelling than Manzoni's.

In "Una lapide in Via Mazzini" Geo Josz, his humanity degraded by the experience of deporta-tion, finds a redeeming function to justify his sur-vival and thus truly honor the death of his coreli-gionists: he decides to become a living emblem of the atrocities committed against the Jews during the war. For several months, from 1946 to 1947, he dons the clothes he was made to wear in the concen-tration camp and reappears "nelle vie, nelle piazze, nei cinema, nei teatri, alle cerimonie pubbliche" (in the streets, in the squares, in the movie houses, in the theaters, at public functions), haunting the con-sciences of those who through their acquiescence were morally responsible for the Holocaust. To the people of Ferrara, including the Jews who had es-caped deportation, Josz became a nuisance, a "faccia di malaugurio" (a face of ill omen) who interfered with their desires to forget the war and return to a normal life. Too soon and too conveniently, insinu-ates the author, the community had forgotten or wanted to forget the horrors of Auschwitz and Buchenwald. With resigned pessimism, the narrator includes himself in his general indictment: "Anche noi ritornavamo quelli di una volta, quelli di prima della guerra e di sempre" (We too had become our former selves, what we were before the war and shall always be).

The novella *Gli occhiali d'oro* (1958; translated as *The Gold-Rimmed Spectacles*, 1960) can be seen as an extension of the Ferrara stories, for the setting re-mains for the most part the city of Ferrara, and the main character is again an Italian Jew. Yet signs of innovation, as regards narrative form and thematic focus, are also in evidence. In the autobiographical account, "Laggiù, in fondo al corridoio" (Down There, at the End of the Corridor), found in *Il ro-manzo di Ferrara* (The Romance of Ferrara, 1974) Bassani looks back to this period of his life:

Non appena ultimata la stesura di *Una notte del '43*, avevo cominciato a sentire di aver esaurito un ciclo. Or-mai Ferrara c'era. A forza di accarezzarla e indagarla da tutte le parti, mi pareva d'esser riuscito a metterla in piedi, a farne a grado a grado qualcosa di concreto, di oggettivamente esistente. Era molto, pensavo. Ma an-che poco. E, in ogni caso, non bastevole.

(As soon as I completed the final draft of "Una notte del '43" I started to feel that I had come to the end of a cy-cle. Now Ferrara could stand on her own. By dint of stroking and investigating her from every angle, it seemed to me I had succeeded in making her stand up, to turn her gradually into something concrete, alive, and objective. It was a lot, I thought. But also little. And, in any event, not enough.)

Bassani's main change in *Gli occhiali d'oro* from his earlier work is his adoption of a first-person nar-rator. His narrator tells the story of a respected phy-sician who, with the gradual disclosure of his homo-sexuality, is shunned, scorned, and eventually ostra-cized from the community. As Douglas Radcliff-Humstead points out, the narrator cautiously ap-proaches Dr. Fadigati until he is able to comprehend "the depth and desolation that an individual suffers when rejected by society." The fact that both men are Jewish at a time of increasing anti-Semitism in Ferrara only intensifies their mutual empathy as so-cial outcasts.

While offering a sympathetic portrait of Dr. Fadigati at a time when homosexuality was widely condemned, Bassani also examines the moral codes of a bourgeois society intent on maintaining at all costs external decorum and respectability. The so-cial perception of Dr. Fadigati undergoes, within the ten years of his medical practice in Ferrara, a grad-ual but profound change – from unconditional es-teem for his professional expertise, to doubts ex-pressed about his sexuality when he does not ac-tively look for a wife, to feigned indifference when his homosexuality is known, to condemnation and ostracism when he appears in public with his lover, a handsome university student half his age. It is his open disdain for public decorum, more than his

Bassani at the 1962 awards reception for the Premio Vireggio, which he won for his novel Il giardino dei Finzi-Contini

sexuality, that dooms the doctor, precipitating a traumatic crisis which ultimately leads to his suicide.

In his most successful novel, *Il giardino dei Finzi-Contini* (1962; translated as *The Garden of the Finzi-Continis,* 1965), Bassani again re-creates the past, combining history and memory as inseparable structural elements. Attention to history validates and dignifies the act of writing as a worthy pursuit; memory lends texture, color, lyricism, and enduring meaning to the narrative. Bassani's fascination with the past, coupled with his remarkable capacity to draw from his youthful experiences and ethnic background, has led some critics to speak insistently of a "Proustian memory" in *Il giardino.* Bassani acknowledged a qualified debt to Marcel Proust, the author of *A la recherche du temps perdu* (1913–1927; translated as *Remembrance of Things Past,* 1922–1932), in a 1977 interview:

> Quanto a Proust la *Recherche* è stata una delle letture che hanno occupato di più i miei anni giovanili. Mi sono in qualche modo formato lí, però sia ben chiaro che all'origine della mia piccola *Recherche* non c'è nessuna Madeleine, cioè lo scatto irrazionale.

(As far as Proust is concerned, *Recherche* is one of the works that more than others occupied my youth. My literary formation can be traced, to some extent, to that book; but let me be unequivocal about the fact that at the heart of my own *Recherche* there is no Madeleine, that is to say, there is no irrational impulse.)

In other words, memory in *Il giardino,* as well as in the *Cinque storie ferraresi,* is part of a rational consciousness that selects and judges, with unsentimental clarity and often with caustic irony, the people and events that inhabit his fictional microcosm.

The setting that Bassani re-creates in *Il giardino* is again Ferrara under Fascist rule. However, the narrative and symbolic epicenter of the book is not the city but the mansion of an aristocratic Jewish family, the Finzi-Continis, who live physically and ideologically isolated both from the city and the Jewish community of Ferrara. The physical distance marking such isolation is paralleled by the social distance that separates the main figures of the novel: Micòl Finzi-Contini, mysterious and unreachable; and the narrator, a shy university student who comes from a middle-class Jewish family. Their relationship is the book's narrative catalyst as well as its focus, but it is the family mansion and its grounds that stand out as the novel's most significant metaphors. Much like the Prince's villa in Tomasi di Lampedusa's *Il Gattopardo* (1958; translated as *The Leopard,* 1960), the Finzi-Contini mansion and the family inhabiting it represent a privileged class — the wealth coming from huge tracts of land in the fertile plains of Emilia-Romagna — that will be swept away by the forces of change brought about by World War II.

The signs of deterioration are carried by nearly all the members of the Finzi-Contini family: Micòl's senile grandmother; her aging parents, Ermanno and Olga; and her brother Alberto, the introverted, taciturn, and reclusive young man who will die from an incurable disease. Micòl is the only character who radiates life, energy, and freedom; she looks fondly to the past but lives in the present, and she is the only family member who maintains a functional contact with the outside world. Without wishing to abandon her Jewish identity, she feels a strong need to go beyond the confines of her ethnic culture represented by the walls and the mansion and partake of the larger reality of Italian society.

Death is the leitmotiv of the novel. It appears in the prologue, as the narrator — who bears more than a casual resemblance to the author — recalls his adolescent years in Ferrara through a seemingly unrelated visit to an Etruscan necropolis outside of Rome. As a situs of remembrance, the ancient tombs remind the narrator of the Jewish cemetery in Via Montebello in Ferrara and the mausoleum built therein by Moisè Finzi-Contini, Micòl's grandfather. The hovering presence of death follows the narrative to the end, when the reader learns of the deportation of Micòl and her family to the extermination camps in Germany.

Bassani's historical consciousness is also reflected in the depiction of the ethnic community. Taken together, his Ferrara stories and *Il giardino dei Finzi-Contini* delineate the experience of Italian Jews from the time of Italy's political unification in 1860 to the end of World War II. Bassani's work brings to light the cherished memories of ancestral heritage, customs, and traditions but also undermines age-old generalizations regarding Jews, such as the belief in the community's social and political unity. Readers learn of the great diversity that exists within a Jewish community, stemming from such factors as differences in national origin, language, religious rites, and social and professional status—all of which can create considerable strains to the unifying core of a common faith.

A rich cultural legacy is evident in the Finzi-Continis' use of many foreign words — Latin, Hebrew, Spanish, and German — which attests to both the diverse background and the sophistication of the family. For example, Olga Herrera, Micòl's mother, was raised in a "famiglia sefardita ponentina molto buona" (very good Sephardic family), her Hispanic background being thus tied to the estimated two thousand Sephardic Jews who settled in Ferrara following their expulsion from Spain in 1492. In that spirit, Micòl's father decides to finance the badly needed restoration of the Spanish synagogue in Ferrara. The narrator, cognizant of the cultural diversity among Ferrarese Jews, speaks of "una sinagoga italiana distinta da una tedesca, con quanto di particolare tale distinzione implicava sul piano sociale e sul piano psicologico" (an Italian synagogue distinguished from a German synagogue, with the characteristics that such a distinction entailed on a social and psychological plane).

Although the structure of *Il giardino* is Proustian, it is also connected to a facet of Italian postwar fiction called *memorialista,* which employs sentiment and rational reflection to reconstruct the past and includes such well-known novelists as Carlo Cassola and Cesare Pavese. Critics have largely neglected to point out how Bassani uses memory innovatively to restructure and refine traditional narrative. The salient elements in *Il giardino* clearly arise from the classic novel, foremost among them the socioeconomic differences that separate Micòl and the narrator; the unrequited love that in part is a result of their class differences; and the elusive character of Micol, an attractive expression of her femininity, which is juxtaposed to the emotional transparency of the narrator — a transparency rendered more apparent by the first-person and the quasi-confessional form of the work.

Although Bassani is attentive to the differences between Catholics and Jews and to the presence of some prejudice on both sides, what stands out in his stories and in *Il giardino* is the integration of Jews into Italian society. Since the presence of Jews on the Italian peninsula can be traced to the early Middle Ages and even farther back to the Roman Empire, historians regard the resulting social assimilation as a natural evolution. Consequently, the last phase of Italian Fascism — marked by Italy's closer relationship to Germany, the anti-Jewish laws of 1938, and the deportation of Jews to the concentration camps — inflicted a deep wound on the psyche of Italian Jews. It should be noted, though, that Mussolini enjoyed strong and widespread support among Italian Jews during his early years of power. Bassani pointed this out, with little hesitation, in 1988: "Anche gli ebrei, che erano quasi tutti borghesi, commercianti, proprietari di terre eccetera, anche gli ebrei erano quasi tutti fascisti" (Italian Jews too, who were predominantly middle class, merchants, landowners, etc., they too were predominantly fascists).

Bassani was so affected by his experience of Fascism that each of his literary efforts may be regarded as a controlled attempt to understand, through the quasi-therapeutic exercise of writing, what happened to Italy during the first half of this century. While his resentment and barely suppressed anger (often through the character of Bruno Lattes) about Fascism are evident in the stories of Ferrara, his reaction in *Il giardino* is apparent in the narrator's plaintive, grieving tone and in the concealed despair of the narrator's father, who sees himself as a proud Italian.

Some believe that living in the past or reliving intensely a particular experience is a sign of weakness or an act of self-indulgence. Bassani would maintain that the adage "Time heals all wounds" does not hold true for everyone. His novella *Dietro la porta* (1964; translated as *Behind the Door,* 1972) retrospectively explores the difficulties of an adolescence never wholly left behind. The topos of adolescence, coupled with the pervasive attention devoted to it in the field of psychology in the postwar years, was the focus of such popular works as Alberto Moravia's *Agostino* (1944) and *La disubbidienza* (1948; translated as *Disobedience,* 1950).

To the first-person Jewish protagonist of *Dietro la porta,* the years that have passed since his adolescence "non sono riusciti a medicare un dolore che è rimasto là, intatto, come una ferita segreta, sanguinante in segreto" (have not been able to soothe a pain that has remained there, intact, like a secret wound bleeding secretly). He is left wondering: "Guarirne? Liberarmene? Non so se sarà mai possibile" (Will it heal? Will I be free from it? I don't know whether it will ever be possible). The narrator, now in his forties, effectively explores the consciousness of being perceived as different and not belonging fully to his society. The feeling of exclusion, whether real or perceived, marks what the narrator calls "l'eterno bisogno che gli altri mi volessero bene" (the eternal need to feel loved). Accentuated by the adjective *eternal,* such human need transcends the narrator's predicament and symbolizes the collective yearning of the Jewish persona, historically excluded, persecuted, and marginalized.

The novel depicts the narrator's relationship with a group of five or six boys in his class during the academic year beginning in 1929, when he was sixteen years old. A good share of the narrative focuses on the passage from adolescence to adulthood and the psychological difficulties associated with this experience, marked as it is by deep insecurity about one's identity, the dominant presence of the mother, and the problematic issue of parental authority. The narrator suffers from deep alienation and repressed anxiety. His Jewish identity prompts the alienation he feels from his classmates and leads to withdrawal and defensive behavior. Driven not only to succeed but to be the first in his class, the narrator's anxiety is heightened by his inability to compete with the confident, handsome, and highly intelligent Carlo Cattolica.

The narrator's most painful psychological wound originates in a scene of sexual initiation. Asked to stand alone behind a door in a room of Cattolica's house, the narrator eavesdrops as his best friend, Luciano Pulga, makes sexual references to the narrator's mother in the presence of Cattolica and two other classmates. As a result, Marilyn Schneider points out, the boy "can no longer look upon his mother except in sexual terms." The wound is deepened by the narrator's repeated assessment through the years of his cowardly reaction to the incident, his failure to push the door wide open and confront Luciano Pulga. His feeling of impotence is rendered more painful by the recollection that a few weeks after the incident, the narrator found himself face-to-face with Pulga but was again unable to stand up to him: "La porta, dietro la quale ancora una volta stavo nascosto, non avrei mai potuto trovare, in me, la forza e il coraggio necessari a spalancarla" (Once again, I was hiding behind a door, incapable of finding the necessary courage and the strength to open it).

The psychological scar borne by the narrator is also the mark of a profound, absolute, and unredemptive pessimism toward human beings. In retrospect, what the narrator resents most is the entrapment devised by his classmates that caused him to lose his innocence. He recalls how cherished values and ideals were not only tainted and defiled but transformed into their antitheses: friendship into cynicism; loyalty into betrayal; maternal love into a youngster's perception of his mother as an object of incestuous desire. In this sense, the loss of innocence marked by sexual knowledge points not to initiation to life and hence to prospective maturity but, as Giusi Oddo De Stefanis observes, "una iniziazione al male" (an initiation into evil) — a disturbing realization of the devious and deceptive ways in which individuals often fashion human relationships.

Bassani began to work on his last novel, *L'airone* (1968; translated as *The Heron,* 1970), three years after the publication of *Il giardino dei Finzi-Contini,* the novel that confirmed his reputation as one of Italy's most important contemporary writers. However, for Bassani, approaching fifty at the time, this was a difficult period, as he indicated in a 27 October 1968 interview, published soon after the appearance of *L'airone:*

> Quando cominciai a scriverlo mi trovavo in uno stato particolare. Ero amareggiato, stanco; ogni rapporto con le persone e con la vita era diventato arido, non aveva più ragione. Mi pareva di vivere in una specie di vuoto, mi mancavano gli interessi.

> (When I started writing [this novel] I found myself in a particular frame of mind. I was bitter, tired; every relationship with people and with life had become arid, made no sense. I had the feeling of living in a void, and I had no personal interests.)

Bassani's psychological state sheds some light on *L'airone,* which, like *Gli occhiali d'oro,* features a deeply alienated middle-aged man. The forty-five-year-old protagonist has become estranged from his wife, his material possessions, his city, and his Jewish identity. But above all he is alienated from himself, to the point that he succumbs to prostration and abulia.

Although only six years separate *L'airone* from *Il giardino,* the differences in the two novels are significant and reflect a profound change in Bassani's work. With *L'airone* the novelist moves outside the city walls of Ferrara, essentially abandoning the problems of the Jewish community, which brought him recognition and enriched Italian literature. While authors often feel the need for change and innovation, Bassani's bold abandonment of the literary core of his previous narrative, which reflects the guiding tenets of Croce and Manzoni, results in a puzzling and uneven work.

Structured with a clear appreciation for the brevity and directness of a stage play, *L'airone* covers twenty-four hours in the life of a wealthy landowner from Ferrara, Edgardo Limentani, who is unhappy with his married life and his diminished social status. One morning he forces himself to go through a planned hunting trip to the marshlands of the Adriatic. The introspective assessment of his life, carried out in the course of the day, leads him to choose suicide as the only viable alternative to a meaningless existence.

In terms of form, the shift in this work from the first-person narration in *Il giardino* and *Dietro la porta* to a third-person, omniscient narration is explained by Bassani as an effort to create a distance between the author and the protagonist and to lend greater objectivity to the narration. However, the distance sought by the author creates instead a dis-

Dust jacket for the American edition of the translation of Bassani's L'airone *(1968), which focuses on the alienation of a middle-aged, wealthy man*

tance between the reader and the protagonist, resulting in the reader's inability to comprehend fully his inner anguish. The reader is also distanced from the protagonist by Bassani's sketchy characterization. The reader learns little about Limentani's family, his upbringing, his youth, and his life during the fifteen years that have led to the crisis.

Limentani's life is reported from the outside. From his parents he inherited about a thousand acres of land in the fertile plains of Emilia. When the anti-Jewish laws of 1938 were to take effect, the property was placed in the name of his wife, a Catholic woman of lower social status. The titular loss of his property, the marriage to a woman he does not love, and his escape to Switzerland during World War II to avoid deportation to Germany no doubt contribute to Limentani's prostration. But these experiences are not given the psychological force that would justify, given the distance in time, his crisis. As a result, Limentani can be seen as an estranged Sartrean character of the 1960s, depicted with a narrative treatment more akin to that of Alain Robbe-Grillet and his "new novel" than to the intense, rational method of Bassani's earlier work.

The turning point in Limentani's life occurs in the hunting trip, the structural and allegorical center of the novel. Throughout the incessant shooting and the mechanical slaughter of the fowl in the marshes of Codigoro, Limentani remains a spectator hidden in the hogshead, having delegated the shooting to his guide, Gavino. Highlighting the scene is a long, superb description of the heron, the symbolic analogue of Limentani who circles above Gavino. After first being missed by Gavino's shots, the heron, one of its wings badly wounded, returns a few minutes later and is downed by the hunter. In eloquent prose Bassani describes the humanized figure of the heron, bleeding slowly to death as it searches for a safe place; the bird approaches Limentani, stares at him, then swims clumsily away in a last, hopeless effort to survive:

E la terraferma a portata di gamba avrebbe significato una possibilità ulteriore di fuga, forse addirittura la salvezza. Ma come si illudeva.... Si allontanava sempre più, nel frattempo, tirandosi dietro con fatica l'ala spezzata; e lui credeva di poter leggere sulla sua piccola, stretta nuca ostinata, tutti questi ragionamenti. Ma come s'illudeva ... s'illudeva a un punto tale, era chiaro, povero stupido, che se a pensare di sparargli non gli fosse sembrato, a lui, di stare sparando in un certo senso a sè stesso, gli avrebbe tirato immediatamente.

(And the mainland within a short distance would mean a further opportunity to escape, perhaps even salvation. But [the heron] was mistaken.... In the meantime, it got farther and farther, dragging painfully its broken wing; and he [Limentani] thought he could read in its small, narrow, and obstinate neck all these thoughts. But, clearly, the poor, stupid animal was mistaken ... so much so that if he had not sensed that shooting at the heron would be, in a way, like shooting at himself, he would have fired at once.)

That evening, looking through a taxidermist's shop in the nearby town of Codigoro, Limentani is struck by the lifelike appearance of the stuffed animals in the display window. The sight affords him the discovery of a life preserved from decay, as a result of which he experiences "un'onda improvvisa di felicità" (a sudden rush of happiness) that can be sealed only through death. On the road home he plans his suicide, which he carries out in his house with meticulous precision.

In his 20 October 1968 review for *Il corriere della sera,* Geno Pampaloni characterized *L'airone* as "la storia di una conversione alla morte" (the story of a conversion to death) – an observation that has been accepted and elaborated by other critics. It seems strange, if not paradoxical, that the religious term *conversion* is used to characterize the exaltation of death through suicide, an act condemned by nearly all religions. By its very nature suicide is a negation of life, a negation of the spiritual force that sustains life. Yet some critics rationalize the act of suicide as a conversion to a higher domain of life. In 1988 Bassani remarked that "l'originalita di Limentani sta soprattutto nell'aver capito che l'unico modo, per lui, di sopravvivere, è quello di uccidersi" (Limentani's originality lies, above all, in his realization that the only way for him to survive is to take his life).

Bassani's assertion is surprising because his characterization of suicide as a dignified expression of free will runs against the grain of his Holocaust-based work, which is deeply grounded in the affirmation of life. Although some critics have suggested parallels between Limentani and Fadigati of *Gli occhiali d'oro,* the cases of the two characters are profoundly different. In *Gli occhiali d'oro* suicide is treated as a tragic and desperate act by an individual who has lost his good name, his professional activity, and his dignity. The analogies between Limentani and Fadigati are tenuous because of the substantial disparity in introspective treatment. To put it plainly, Limentani's quest for personal dignity through suicide is unconvincing. At best, it can be seen as an act of selfish courage by a mediocre and sterile survivor of the Holocaust, who stagnates in self-indulgence and is unable to rescue himself from a situation which, unlike Fadigati's, is difficult but by no means desperate. Bassani's treatment of suicide is also contrary to its traditional treatment in Western literature, where, as a rule – for example, Dante's portrait of Cato in *Purgatorio* – taking one's life is done for a cause higher than the individual being. Traditionally, such individuals are called heroes or martyrs. Yet, as Radcliff-Humstead points out, "rather than a novel of victorious martyrdom, this work becomes a study of retreat into nihilism."

Despite the disturbing turn of *L'airone,* Giorgio Bassani is clearly one of the foremost Italian writers of this century. His work endures because of his essentially traditional conception of the novel, rooted in realism, history, and characterization. Mindful of these tenets, Bassani has fashioned memorable characters and re-created tragic historical episodes that are bound to remain eloquent documents of twentieth-century Italian life.

Interviews:

Il punto, 8 October 1960;

Grazia Livi, "Bassani: come nasce un romanzo," *Epoca,* 27 October 1968, pp. 120–124;

Manlio Cancogni, *La fiera letteraria,* 14 November 1968, p. 11;

Ferdinando Camon, "Giorgio Bassani," in his *La moglie del tiranno* (Rome: Lerici, 1969), pp. 85–91;

Camon, "Intervista con Bassani," in his *Il mestiere di scrittore* (Milan: Garzanti, 1973), pp. 54–71;

Stelio Cro, "Intervista con Giorgio Bassani," *Canadian Journal of Italian Studies,* 1 (1977): 37–45;

Anna Dolfi, *Le forme del sentimento: Prosa e poesia in Giorgio Bassani* (Padua: Liviana, 1981), pp. 79–115;

Carla Stampa, "Per scrivere ho bisogno del mare," *Epoca,* 25 April 1981, pp. 84–89;

Lietta Tornabuoni, *La Stampa: Tuttolibri,* 17 April 1982, p. 1;

Walter Mauro, "Intervista a Bassani," in *Giorgio Bassani. Lo scrittore e i suoi testi,* edited by Antonio Gagliardi (Rome: La Nuova Italia Scientifica, 1988), pp. 61–72.

References:

Ignazio Baldelli, "La riscrittura totale di un'opera: Da *Le storie ferraresi* a *Dentro le mura* di Bassani," *Lettere italiane,* 26 (1974): 180–197;

Renato Bertacchini, "Giorgio Bassani," in *Letteratura italiana. I contemporanei,* volume 3 (Milan: Marzorati, 1969), pp. 797–816;

Adriano Bon, *Come leggere "Il giardino dei Finzi-Contini" di Giorgio Bassani* (Milan: Mursia, 1979);

Canadian Journal of Italian Studies, special issue on Bassani, edited by Stelio Cro, 1 (Fall 1977–Winter 1978);

Alessandra Chiappini and Gianni Venturi, eds., *Bassani e Ferrara: le intermettenze del cuore* (Ferrara: Gabriele Gorbo, 1995);

Giusi Oddo De Stefanis, *Bassani entro il cerchio delle sue mura* (Ravenna: Longo, 1981);

Anna Dolfi, *Le forme del pessimismo: Prosa e poesia in Giorgio Bassani* (Padua: Liviana, 1981);

Gian Carlo Ferretti, *Letteratura e ideologia: Bassani Cassola Pasolini* (Rome: Editori Riuniti, 1964);

Anna Folli, *Vent'anni di cultura ferrarese: 1925–1945,* 2 volumes (Bologna: Patron, 1978);

Antonio Gagliardi, ed., *Giorgio Bassani. Lo scrittore e i suoi testi* (Rome: La Nuova Italia Scientifica, 1988);

Massimo Grillandi, *Invito alla lettura di Bassani* (Milan: Mursia, 1972);

Pier Paolo Pasolini, *Passione e ideologia* (Milan: Garzanti, 1960), pp. 415–419;

Douglas Radcliff-Humstead, *The Exile into Eternity: A Study of the Writings of Giorgio Bassani* (Rutherford, N.J.: Fairleigh Dickinson University Press, 1987);

Marilyn Schneider, *Vengeance of the Victim: History and Symbol in Giorgio Bassani's Fiction* (Minneapolis: University of Minnesota Press, 1986);

Marianne Shapiro, "The *Storie ferraresi* of Giorgio Bassani," *Italica,* 49 (1972): 30–48;

Giorgio Varanini, *Bassani* (Florence: La Nuova Italia, 1970).

Carlo Bernari
(13 October 1909 – 22 October 1992)

Rocco Capozzi
University of Toronto

BOOKS: *Tre operai* (Milan: Rizzoli, 1934);

Quasi un secolo (Milan: Mondadori, 1940);

Il pedaggio si paga all'altra sponda (Rome: Edizioni di Lettere d'Oggi, 1943);

Napoli pace e guerra (Rome: Sandron, 1946);

Tre casi sospetti (Milan: Mondadori, 1946);

Prologo alle tenebre (Milan: Mondadori, 1947);

Speranzella (Milan: Mondadori, 1949);

Siamo tutti bambini (Florence: Vallecchi, 1951);

Vesuvio e pane (Florence: Vallecchi, 1952);

Domani e poi domani (Florence: Vallecchi, 1957);

Il gigante Cina (Milan: Feltrinelli, 1957);

Amore amaro (Florence: Vallecchi, 1958);

Bibbia napoletana (Florence: Vallecchi, 1960);

L'effetto corporeo della sacra unzione degli infermi nella dottrina dei teologi (Rome, 1962);

Era l'anno del sole quieto (Milan: Mondadori, 1964);

Per cause imprecisate (Milan: Mondadori, 1965);

Le radiose giornate (Milan: Mondadori, 1969);

Alberone eroe, e altri racconti non esemplari (Milan: Bietti, 1971);

Un foro nel parabrezza (Milan: Mondadori, 1971);

Non gettate via la scala (Milan: Mondadori, 1973);

Tanto la rivoluzione non scoppierà (Milan: Mondadori, 1976);

Napoli, silenzio e grida (Rome: Editori Riuniti, 1977);

26 cose in versi (Milan: Schweiller, 1977);

Dall'Etna al Vesuvio (Rome: Gremese, 1978);

Il cronista giudizioso (Rome: Quaderni di Piazza Navona, 1979);

Dal Tevere al Po (Rome: Gremese, 1980);

Il giorno degli assassinii (Milan: Mondadori, 1980);

Via Raselli non passa per Via Fano (Rome: E&A, 1987);

Il grande letto (Milan: Mondadori, 1989);

Non invidiate la loro sorte (Turin: Nuova ERI, 1992);

L'ombra del suicidio: Lo strano Conserti (Rome: Newton Compton, 1993).

OTHER: *Inchiesta sul neorealismo,* edited by Carlo Bo (Turin: Radio Italiana, 1951);

Omaggio a Corrado Alvaro, edited by Bernari (Rome, 1957);

Carlo Bernari

Giandomenico Giagni, *Il confine,* edited by Bernari and Vasco Pratolini (Rome: Basilicata, 1976).

In the 1950s, during the debates on Neorealism, Carlo Bernari saw his name associated with the main forerunners of the movement: Alberto Moravia, Cesare Pavese, and Elio Vittorini. In Carlo Bo's *Inchiesta sul neorealismo* (An Inquiry on Neorealism, 1951), Bernari clarified how and why his neorealism was "*ante litteram*" and different from the post-war memorialistic current.

Despite Bernari's reservations about being associated with the movement, most critics now agree with the poet Eugenio Montale, who was among the first to consider *Tre operai,* an incunabula of Neorealism. As critics reexamine the origins and the development of Neorealism as a literary and artistic trend, they are paying closer attention to its different components, exploring its connections to neorealistic cinema, the works written during the Fascist era from the early 1920s to 1945, the postwar novels that reconstructed the war period and the underground resistance to Fascism, and to the heterogeneous body of literature that focused on the socioeconomic reality of the Italian South, the so-called *letteratura meridionale* (southern literature). As a result of this reevaluation, the critical consensus holds that Bernari's *Tre operai,* along with Corrado Alvaro's early works and Francesco Jovine's *Un uomo provvisorio* (A Provisional Man, 1934), exemplifies the first stylistic and thematic traits of the cultural movement that was dominant in Italy from the 1930s to the mid 1950s.

Bernari's work shows a deep sense of civic and moral responsibility that he considered an essential element of literature. However, he was always careful not to link social engagement with party politics, even when his works were clearly anti-Fascist. His social commitment can best be understood as what Marxist critic Georgy G. Lukás has called "critical realism"—a dialectical examination of the reality being scrutinized. For over fifty years Bernari elaborated his own critical realism in novels, short stories, poems, a play, several essays, and many newspaper articles written from the 1930s to the day before he was paralyzed by a cerebral hemorrhage in the fall of 1988. From *Tre operai* on, Bernari pursued what he called a search for "the reality of reality" by focusing on the conflicts between individuals and social institutions. While most of his protagonists are forced to live in a general state of "attesa" (waiting), Bernari never ceased to denounce the contradictions, injustices, and absurdities that prevent social changes from taking place.

Bernari was born as Carlo Bernard in Naples on 13 October 1909. His ancestors arrived from France with the Napoleonic army around 1806. The previous two generations of his family were involved in a fabric-dying and dry-cleaning business. In *Tre operai* and other works, Bernari makes references to this family trade and to the environment in which he grew up. In a 1975 interview he said that the colors that appear so frequently in his works are some of the colors he experienced, as a child, in his family's shop.

At thirteen, Bernari was expelled from school (under Fascism his expulsion meant that he was automatically expelled from all Italian public schools) because he had participated in a stone-throwing protest against his teacher. This led to Bernari's self-education and to the first of various jobs, including a position in which he bought and sold rare books. From his teens to his early twenties, Bernari spent much of his time in the company of his cousin Guglielmo Peirce, an architect, and his inseparable, lifelong friend Paolo Ricci, a painter and art critic. The trio, recognizable in the main characters of Bernari's short story "Bettina ritrovata" (Bettina Turns Up) and his novel *Prologo alle tenebre* (Prologue to Darkness, 1947), enriched their education by studying Francesco Flora and Benedetto Croce and by taking part in Neapolitan cultural circles during the early years of Fascism. Bernari's politics, which he characterized as "Hegelian left," influenced his intellectual activities. Together with Peirce and Ricci, Bernari published the futurist, avant-garde pamphlet *Manifesto U.D.A.: Unione Distruttivisti Attivisti* (The Manifesto of the Union of Destructive Activists, 1929), in which, responding in part to the Futurist manifestos of Filippo Tommaso Marinetti, he endorsed the end of traditional art in favor of new scientific and technological expressions.

Bernari's artistic and literary interests continued to grow as he immersed himself in literature, cinema, and journalism. In Milan, while employed by the publisher Mondadori, he and Cesare Zavattini started the magazine *Tempo;* he also began to contribute regularly to newspapers such as the *Milano sera*. In the early 1930s he moved to Rome, settling there permanently with his wife, Marcella, and his three sons. Bernari and Vasco Pratolini launched the weekly magazine *La settimana.* For thirty years Bernari wrote for several newspapers; he chose *Il Mattino,* Naples's daily newspaper, as the forum for his social and cultural views.

While he was working on *Tre operai* and before he was drafted into the army, Bernari spent about four months in Paris (1930–1931), where he met André Breton and other writers and artists associated with Surrealism and Dadaism. Bernari recalled this Parisian sojourn in the "Nota 65," a note about the genesis of the novel written for the 1965 edition. Moreover, as is evident in *Non invidiate la loro sorte* (Do Not Envy Their Fate, 1992), Bernari's early

Cover for Bernari's first novel, which is considered an important early example of Neorealism

journalistic activities acquainted him with many Italian poets and novelists. From the late 1930s to the end of the 1950s, in Milan, Rome, and Florence, Bernari met and interviewed many authors, including Giuseppe Ungaretti, Salvatore Quasimodo, Luigi Pirandello, Massimo Bontempelli, Vasco Pratolini, and Moravia, at a time when most of them were seeking recognition with their first publications.

In 1934 Zavattini, who at the time worked for the publisher Rizzoli, selected *Tre operai*—a novel that details the misfortunes of three workers, Teodoro, Anna, and Marco, looking for jobs in the midst of strikes, a failing economy, and political unrest—to open a new series devoted to young writers. Zavattini knew that Bernari's unusual treatment of themes, ambience, and characters deserved attention, but he did not foresee that the novel would be censored by the Fascist regime. Indeed, some contemporary reviews of *Tre operai* were never published because the novel was taken off the shelves shortly after its appearance.

Now regarded as a courageous attempt to deal with the lack of social awareness among workers and the difficult conditions they and intellectuals had to face after World War I, *Tre operai* originally received both praise and criticism. While he angered the Fascist regime with his attention to proletarian life, Bernari surprised Italian critics not only with his style but also with unfamiliar scenes of daily life in Naples, a widely stereotyped and misunderstood city. Bernari could understand why Fascists would object to his unflattering picture of working conditions, but he did not anticipate that many nonfascist readers would not appreciate his interest in workers and in his native city.

The gray, industrial, polluted Naples that forms the background of *Tre operai* was shocking to readers accustomed to picturesque images of a sunny city on a blue sea with people singing in the streets, the Naples fashioned by literary tradition and the popular lyrics associated with Salvatore Di Giacomo. Bernari replaces the postcard picture with a real city where people cannot find work, where workers live in shacks near industrial plants, where the sun does not shine every day, where children live and die in miserable conditions, and where people are preoccupied with survival and with making ends meet. Some readers found it even more disturbing that a "decadent" Teodoro first moves in with two sisters, Anna and Maria, and later cohabits with Anna and Marco.

Bernari's main targets were the disorganization of the working class, the misguided labor unions, and the shortsightedness of socialist and communist leaders. Historic, social, political, and personal factors all combine in defeating the three workers: Teodoro Barrin, a restless dreamer whose ambition is to become something more than a worker; Anna, a saintly figure who sacrifices herself to please others; and Marco, a selfish individual who relies on recommendations, labor unions, and political associations to find himself a job. Whereas Anna is shown as a victim of socioeconomic forces, Teodoro and Marco are painted mainly as victims of political structures.

Partly to avoid censorship and partly because of Bernari's artistic interests, *Tre operai* does not appear to have been written by a critical realist. Bernari depicts the physical settings of the novel—Naples, Taranto, Cotrone, and Rome—mostly through impressionist, expressionist, and surrealist techniques. However, Bernari's utilization of literary, cinematic, and artistic techniques is not limited to descriptions of factories, buildings, streets, and the sea; he is also sophisticated in his treatment of the difficult love relationships between the main characters, especially in depicting Teodoro's private thoughts and dreams. *Tre operai* was not an experiment; it was the first of many subsequent examples of Bernari's remarkable linguistic and narrative skills. Unfortunately, such skills proved to be so heterogeneous that some frustrated critics assigned to Bernari the label of neorealist writer.

Quasi un secolo (Almost a Century, 1940) is Bernari's most ambitious attempt to realize characters against a backdrop of large-scale sociohistorical events. The calamities that befall Giovanni Pinna and his son Giustino are at the center of this saga about three generations of the Pinna and the Zenobbi families. Set first in Naples and then in Rome, the novel spans the years from Italian unification in 1861 to the early days of Fascism, as Bernari recreates the historical roots of the social and existential conditions that afflict the protagonists of *Tre operai*.

Quasi un secolo deals mainly with the social injustices and abuses of power that pave the road for the Fascist regime. The novel at first centers on Fausto Zenobbi, a powerful Neapolitan shipbuilder who murders his feared competitor, Cannolicchio. After seducing Anna, the wife of his ship officer, Giovanni Pinna, Fausto succeeds in covering up his actions by letting the defenseless Pinna accept the blame for the homicide. The boy Giustino Pinna grows up without knowing his real father. However, when Giovanni is released from prison, Giustino, whose name alludes to the sense of justice he pursues, moves with his real father to Rome, where he happens to fall in love with Zenobbi's granddaughter, Clelia, the daughter of Giulia Zenobbi. At the end of the novel Giovanni Pinna dies at the outskirts of Rome in a shack that is about to be demolished; Clelia leaves Giustino to return to her bourgeois world.

Il pedaggio si paga all'altra sponda (The Toll Is Paid on the Other Side) is the least known of Bernari's works, primarily because its first publication in 1943 and its reprint in *Siamo tutti bambini* (We Are All Children, 1951) saw a limited distribution. This story of about fifty pages was written shortly after *Tre operai* and contains the symbolic, allegoric, and surrealistic descriptions prevalent in Bernari's early narratives. His many pictorial techniques reinforce the suspense in a simple love story narrated by the author, who knows personally his characters and who intervenes in the story to bring it to an end.

The touching tale of Giovannina—better known by her nickname, Micella (little kitten), because of her pitiful condition—and Meuccio unfolds in a fusion of naturalistic and dreamlike, surrealistic descriptions. The story is about two poor children who overcome difficult economic problems, grow up, marry at an early age, and die while still young. The story ends abruptly as Bernari, the narrator, appears in propria persona (as himself), an expedient that reappears in *Vesuvio e pane* (Vesuvius and Bread, 1952). Bernari explains to the parents of the young couple that the sad story of Meuccio and Micella is a fiction: that the two lovers never had a chance to grow up because they died when they were little children. This metanarrative strategy provides the aesthetic and critical distance needed to set aside the love story and to focus instead on the miserable economic conditions which, Bernari suggests, cannot yield a happy ending.

The three stories that make up *Tre casi sospetti* (Three Suspicious Subjects, 1946) again show Bernari's skillful use of pictorial techniques that bring to mind French surrealism, German expressionism, and the paintings by such Italian artists as Mario Sironi, Carlo Carrà, and Giorgio De Chirico. Written between 1939 and 1943, during the most oppressive days of Fascism, *Tre casi sospetti* is saturated with light-and-shadow effects that accentuate the leitmotivs of fear and suspicion. In many instances the work echoes Lautréamont's spectral realism and Bontempelli's magical realism. Using allegory and symbolism to avoid the censors, Bernari in *Tre casi sospetti* offers a Kafkaesque critique of a society that reduces life to a nightmare. Bernari, however, did not wish to limit his criticism solely to the Fascist regime: he wanted to denounce the dangers of all oppressive institutions.

Each story of *Tre casi*—"Il Pugliese," "Cupris," and "Minutolo"—is titled after an individual who succumbs to the fear and paranoia caused by his oppressive environment. "Il Pugliese" is a southern worker who buys with gold the silence of those who know that he is wanted by the police. Pugliese works by day in a steel factory; at night he looks for gold along the River Ticino, where he lives in a wooden shack. A young woman named Mara and her father, a factory manager tired of his work, decide to join the solitary Pugliese. Unfortunately their presence leads to Pugliese's arrest when Mara's father dies in the shack and draws the attention of police informers, who are called, ironically, *fratelli* (brothers) by the authorities.

Of the three stories, "Cupris" is the most intense and suspenseful as an allegorical attack of an oppressive society. Cupris is an honest clerk who does not know that he is the object of a practical joke planned by his fellow workers. He becomes obsessed with the fear that the authorities will arrest him if they discover that he owns a weapon, a cane with a hidden blade. Cupris ends up dying of fear while he hides, without food, in a secluded house.

Minutolo is a bricklayer who meets his death after he is drawn into a ridiculous struggle on the island of Procida involving powerful people who build high walls on their property line just to antagonize their neighbors. Readers learn from Minutolo's long correspondence with a local priest about his not wanting to be coerced and his concern for justice. Minutolo, Pugliese, and Cupris are all victims of despotic institutions; it is hardly a surprise that they share the same desire to be free.

Bernari's sociological writings about Naples, together with autobiographically related stories and anecdotes, were first collected in *Napoli pace e guerra* (Naples in Peace and at War, 1946). Most of the stories were revised in the magnificently illustrated volume *Bibbia napoletana* (Neapolitan Bible, 1960) and later in *Napoli, silenzio e grida* (Naples: Silence and Outcries, 1977). These writings, passages of which appear verbatim in some of his novels, help the reader to develop a deeper understanding of Bernari's portrait of Naples, a culturally rich city marked by contradictions. Bernari republished these works because he wanted to share with his readers some of his experiences in the city he calls "una nazione nella nazione" (a unique nation within a nation). At this time Bernari regarded Naples as a microcosm for the complex realities of southern Italy. He believed that the image Italians had of Naples and the Italian South coincided with the perception of Italy held by people around the world. Thus, in Bernari's work Naples and southern Italy are used to unmask myths, legends, clichés, and superficial first impressions about Italy as a whole.

Bernari's love-hate relationship toward Naples deepened even after he left his native city as he continued to study its history and culture. Beginning with *Tre operai,* Bernari tried to erase the stereotype that identified Naples with a large stage where people behave like actors performing for the public. He claimed that Neapolitan writers such as E. De Filippo promoted such stereotypes by depicting Neapolitans as people who enjoy playing "the role of Neapolitans." Bernari showed that, far from enjoying the theatrical flavor of life, many Neopolitans suffer from psychological and existential anguish rooted in their socioeconomic condition. To epitomize the spirit of Naples, Bernari in the novel *Vesuvio e pane* uses the clown Pulcinella, who combines farce and tragedy in acting the role of a clown while masking his misery and despair. Bernari's Pulcinella is an emblematic figure of the *homo neapolitanus,* protagonist and spectator of his own life.

Bernari deals with some of the complexities of his city in three historical works: *Prologo alle tenebre* (Prelude to Darkness, 1947) is concerned with the Resistance to Fascism; *Speranzella* (Little Hope, 1949) with the days of the national referendum; and *Vesuvio e pane* with the postwar period when opportunists and powerful individuals rebuild the city. But whether Naples appears as the main focus as in *Speranzella* or *Vesuvio e pane* or as a backdrop as in *Tre operai* and later in *Era l'anno del sole quieto* (It Was the Year of the Quiet Sun, 1964) and *Il giorno degli assassinii,* (The Day of the Murders, 1980) Bernari never describes the city with nostalgia or sentimentalism.

Written around 1945, *Prologo alle tenebre* focuses on the opposition between Communists and Fascists in a city being torn apart by the war. The novel is divided into five parts, and each part unveils the "secrets" and fears shared by the central protagonists. It is mainly through Eugenio, the first-person narrator of the novel, and through his cousin Andrea, Eugenio's alter ego, that the events, characters, and ideas of the five episodes are linked. In a city terrorized by fascist spies and periodic bombings, Eugenio chases after Andrea, partly for personal reasons and partly because he would like to be involved in his cousin's secrets and in his presumed underground political activities. Bianca, who has had a relationship with both cousins; the fascist "Marchese Grafuni," who entertains the Neapolitan intelligentsia in his house; and the old waiter Don Placido, who invents the fiction of his missing son, are the other characters whose secrets are slowly revealed as the story unfolds. Bianca becomes Eugenio's excuse for neglecting his responsibilities as he begins to mix sex and politics and becomes preoccupied more with his private self and less with the antiFascist cause.

Bernari reduced the 435-page *Prologo alle tenebre* to 285 pages when he revised the novel as *Le radiose giornate* (The Radiant Days, 1969). It is not a shorter version of the original work but a new novel with a fresh message, focused on Eugenio twenty years later as he looks back on the main events of his time. The change in tone is indicated by the new title, which evokes ironically the less than "radiant days" that preceded the end of World War II. In *Prologo alle tenebre* Eugenio dwells primarily on the protagonists and the secrets they hold; in *Le radiose giornate* Eugenio, in the course of confessions, self-analysis, and hindsight, admits that he was no different from Andrea, Bianca, Don Placido, and even the fascist Grafuni. They were all guilty of wearing masks, of fabricating lies, living with contradictions, following selfish personal interests, and making serious mistakes. Making full use of the aesthetic and temporal distance that separates his two Eugenios, Bernari reexamines the closing days of the Resistance and faces up to the truth that some of the actions of the opponents of Fascism were just as absurd as the political climate in which t. .y lived. Eugenio's narcissism, his readiness to become a protagonist of his own fiction, will be echoed in other novels such as *Un foro nel parabrezza,* (1971), *Tanto la rivoluzione non scoppierà* (1976), and *Il grande letto* (1989).

Winner of the 1950 Viareggio Prize, *Speranzella* is probably Bernari's most neorealistic as well as his most successful work. The title refers to Via Speranzella, a well-known main street, that divides Naples in two. It is mainly in the surrounding neighborhoods that Bernari sets the story of Nannina, an abandoned girl who contracts syphilis from an Allied soldier and who is cared for by Elvira, nicknamed "La Caffettera" for the illegal coffee shop she runs in a back room, and by her husband, Ciccillo. Michele, who also comes to the rescue, falls in love with Nannina while he helps Signor Mele, Elvira, and Ciccillo to get some hard-to-find penicillin. The main characters are surrounded by a large chorus of Neapolitans who are heard mainly through the words of the "street-philosopher" Don Vincenzo and through the gossip of ladies such as Pizzicatella and Pachichia. As the story comes to a close, it becomes clear that the title of the novel also alludes to the various little hopes that slowly disappear, because several characters, including a little boy named Pascalotto, meet a bitter fate. Perhaps the only hope kept alive belongs to Nannina and Michele, who at the end of the novel move to Milan to look for work.

The story of Nannina and Elvira unfolds in a chaotic city that is experiencing a letdown after the initial euphoria brought by American soldiers, who were supposed to bring wealth and happiness. The upcoming national referendum in 1946 divides Neapolitans into two groups: those who, like Elvira, remain faithful to the spirit of the monarchy and those who support the republic. Elvira, a strong woman who dominates her husband Ciccillo, campaigns for the monarchy and attracts people from different walks of life with her espresso bar and her mysterious power as a seer. However, even Elvira is defeated by the new social forces that are beyond anyone's control.

In *Speranzella* critics singled out Bernari's outstanding linguistic skills. More than in his other novels, the characters express themselves through colorful language that betrays their psychological and socioeconomic realities. *Speranzella* shows that Bernari's close attention to language, in the tradition of the Sicilian writer Giovanni Verga, preceded

Cover for Bassani's 1957 novel, in which a love affair is complicated by the conservative culture of southern Italy

both Carlo Emilio Gadda's and Pier Paolo Pasolini's experiments in combining dialect with standard Italian.

Bernari's deep understanding of Naples is found to a greater degree in *Vesuvio e pane,* a work in which a fablelike atmosphere surrounds characters and events. The novel begins as Esposito, the "Viandante" (wayfarer), returns to Naples as profiteers, crooks, and the *magliari* (a term Bernari coins that might be approximated by the word *carpetbaggers*) are fighting for the control of the city, "che si vende per due soldi" (which is being sold for two cents). In the closing pages the "Viandante" leaves Naples on a truck; rather than looking back he stares at a painted scene of the picturesque bay of Naples with a smoking Mount Vesuvius, preferring the mythical to the real. Some of Bernari's most unforgettable characters appear in the colorful scenes of salvaging the sunken ships in the bay of Naples and in several other episodes unrelated to Esposito's misfortunes. Nanda's suicide, the appearance of Pulcinella, and the old lady Kerton stand out among many superb scenes and characterizations that appear suspended between reality and make-believe.

In *Vesuvio e pane* Bernari used several pages from *Napoli pace e guerra* as he combined autobiographical experiences with history, sociology, century-old injustices, dreams, laughter, and death. He capitalizes nouns such as *il Sogno* (dream), *la Fame* (hunger), *il Debito* (debt), and *la Famiglia* (family). Among so much symbolism and allegory, Pulcinella's appearance in a sketch showing statues and monuments coming to life seems quite natural. In the closing pages Bernari briefly appears as himself, as a Neapolitan writer who lives in Rome and is willing to help Kerton find a home for the stray cats and dogs she used to feed every night before being evicted from her apartment.

Domani e poi domani (Tomorrow and the Day After, 1957) combines historical realism with excellent psychological characterizations and lyrical descriptions. Against the background of a conservative southern mentality that holds on to prejudices, outdated traditions, and external appearances, Bernari fashions a fascinating love story between a middle-aged southern lawyer, Nicola Monaco, and a young northern manicurist, Virginia. Monaco's brief joy soon turns into rebellion against his relatives and the townspeople who criticize his falling in love soon after his wife's death. An analogous difficult love story develops between the peasants Vito Minguzzo and Concettina. They too have to fight prejudices and social customs, but their problems are viewed from the perspective of poor peasants.

While the novella *Amore amaro* (Bitter Love, 1958) was published shortly after *Domani e poi domani,* it was written in the late 1930s. It is a psychological love story set in Rome between Ugo, a young man who works in a dry-cleaning store, and Renata, a middle-aged widow who has a young, sick child, Vittorio. Ugo's bitter experience is both sentimental and ideological. Through Renata, a Fascist sympathizer who neither trusts nor likes the good-looking, persistent Ugo, Bernari stresses the political undertone of the affair. Ugo becomes a close friend of Renata's young son, and after helping the boy gain confidence in himself he learns that Renata has decided not to see him any more. A few years later, Vittorio runs into Ugo and tells him that his mother, pressured by his grandmother, married a much older man. It is Vittorio then who must encourage Ugo to go on living without losing confidence in himself, in others, and in life.

During Italy's industrial and economic boom years from 1958 to 1963, Bernari wrote an intriguing and revealing story about the problems of industrializing the South. *Era l'anno del sole quieto* highlights the frustrations of an idealistic professor from the North, Orlando Rughi, who invests time and money in an industry that will help a community not far from Naples. The unfolding events underscore the failures of a society victimized by bureaucracy, corruption at all levels of government, Mafia-style protectionism, and political favoritism. Before the onset of industrialization in southern Italy, a corrupt system had established itself with the help of priests, lawyers, banks, government officials, and loan agencies. The same obstacles that prevent Rughi's neocapitalistic dream from becoming a reality also preclude many from finding work. Among the several symbolic figures who appear in this labyrinth of corruption, the most intriguing is Puntillo (a little dot), a character in some ways reminiscent of Samuel Beckett's Godot. Puntillo's control is felt by everyone everywhere, but he cannot be found by anyone. At the end of the novel, Rughi returns to his teaching job convinced that his defeat was unavoidable in such "un mare di negativita" (a sea of negativity). This conclusion is reinforced by Ciro Domenica, one of the last artisans in town, who is forced to immigrate to Germany to find work.

With *Era l'anno del sole quieto* and in subsequent books, Bernari begins to explore the idea of "narrative lies in search of truth" and creates narrators who prolong their stories so to extend their experiences as protagonists of their own fiction. Novels such as *Un foro nel parabrezza* (A Hole in the Windshield, 1971), *Tanto la rivoluzione non scoppierà* (After All, the Revolution Will Not Break Out, 1976), and *Il giorno degli assassinii* also suggest a theme that from the 1960s onward becomes an integral part of Bernari's fiction: the exploitation of intellectuals by a consumeristic and technological society that attempts to recycle everything, including people and culture.

Un foro nel parabrezza centers on the dilemma of a journalist, Eugenio. He purports to be in love with a mysterious woman, Rossana, who keeps taking his reserved parking space. When Eugenio discovers a bullet hole in the windshield of Rossana's blue sports car, he decides to play detective and to investigate the matter. Like all of Bernari's bitter love stories, Eugenio's affair ends unhappily. Rossana tells him that she has no intention of leaving her paralyzed husband. Eugenio's experience, however, is much more than a brief love affair. Rossana may indeed be a means of escape into a world of fiction that at times appears to be more real than the absurd world in which he works. Yet solving the mystery of the "hole in the windshield" is for Eugenio also an experience that forces him to reexamine his relationship with his family, problems with his employer,

Dust jacket for Bernari's last novel, which includes episodes based on his childhood in Naples and his experiences in Rome during the 1940s

and most of all his dissatisfaction with his unauthentic self. What at first appears to be a relatively simple detective story actually unfolds on aesthetic, psychological, and sociopolitical levels.

The historical background of *Tanto la rivoluzione non scoppierà* is the terrorist years of the 1970s, when the Italian Communist Party under the leadership of Enrico Berlinguer could have won a majority in Congress. The novel tells the story of a writer who feels exploited by a society that follows primarily the laws of maximum profit. Denito Elia decides to stand up to his employer, the publisher Rocchi, who uses people in the same fashion that the second-hand dealer Calabò recycles used objects. When Rocchi discovers that Denito is writing a novel about his rebellion, he begins to write his own fiction, which is Denito's story narrated from an opposite viewpoint. The two novels offer a mirror reflection of a master-slave relationship. Unfortunately Denito's rebellion deteriorates into a game of trying to outwit his employer after Rocchi begins to use Denito's secretary, Leda, to get more information

about his project. As a reaction Denito seduces Rocchi's wife, Sara, just to get back at him, but in the process he begins to resemble a clown paid to entertain his boss.

The story ends as Rocchi dies in an explosion and Denito a short while later dies of burns after a prostitute sets him on fire. Two accidents? The real reasons for the deaths will be determined by the ongoing and possibly neverending investigation. The title of the novel, with its assurance of the failure of real change, refers specifically to Denito's protest against the consumeristic society represented by Rocchi. But it also refers to the Italian reality illustrated so masterfully in Tomasi di Lampedusa's *Il Gattopardo* (1958; translated as *The Leopard*, 1960)—things are allowed to change only so far as they help things to remain the same. Denito is in fact well aware that those in power make sure that a real revolution will never take place.

Bernari's art in taking individuals and events from daily life and transforming them into fiction reaches a peak in *Il giorno degli assassinii*. Set like

Tanto la rivoluzione non scoppierà in the 1970s which in Italy were the years of terrorist activities, *Il giorno degli assassinii* is more concerned with daily acts of violence than with political violence. The first-person narrator takes on the role of a detective, thinking and behaving like the killer as he tries to prove the innocence of Dino Rabella, a man who in the nonfiction world of Naples had been convicted for the murder of three people. The structure of the novel is complex as the story moves back and forth between the notes found in a manuscript, long monologues, frequent discussions on terrorism and on violent crimes, and a recording of a legal prosecution.

In the best tradition of Leonardo Sciascia, Bernari wrote a murder story that examines the contradictions of a society that confuses political terrorism with violent crimes. Bernari's understanding of the real murder case was so effective in unveiling certain hidden truths that Rabella was retried and freed. *Il giorno degli assassinii* made the news in major Italian newspapers because a work of fiction was able to change the life of a real man. The incident certainly answered Bernari's desire that literature should have a social as well as an intellectual function.

Il grande letto (The Big Bed, 1989), the last and the most autobiographical of Bernari's novels, reprises many of Bernari's familiar themes and motifs. The most interesting pages are unquestionably the accounts of his life in Naples: his youth, his family, his activities with Peirce and Ricci, and his writing of *Tre operai* and *Le radiose giornate*. He also dwells on his political and cultural experiences in Rome, mainly during the 1940s. Under the big bed is where the narrator Dario and his cousin Adelmo used to hide when they were children. But the big bed is also a metaphor for the beginning and the end of life. The content and the characters suggest that Bernari may have had a premonition that this would be his last novel. In any case, he apparently wrote *Il grande letto* to encourage the examination of his previous works and to promote the full appreciation of his critical views of contemporary Italian society.

Few contemporary critics neglect to mention the importance of *Tre operai* as a forerunner of Neorealism, yet they usually limit their comments about Bernari's other works to just a few lines. When the literary journal *La fiera letteraria*—after the success of *Domani e poi domani* and *Amore amaro*—dedicated its 2 February 1958 issue to Bernari, writers and critics joined to praise his work. For the next three decades writers such as Domenico Rea, Michele Prisco, and Raffaele La Capria looked to Bernari as a major figure among contemporary Italian novelists.

Bernari's art has always been appreciated by well-known critics such as Bo, Bàrberi Squarotti, Pampaloni, Walter Mauro, and Pedullà. Most who have written on his work agree that Bernari's "coherent incoherence," his mixture of different styles and traditions, attests to the rich repertoire of his narrative skills. Giacinto Spagnoletti, Enzo Golino, Giuliano Manacorda, Nicola Tanda, Emilio Pesce, Lombardi, Eugenio Ragni, Rocco Capozzi, and Claudio Toscani are among the critics who have been the most attentive to Bernari's works. They have singled out his talent for juxtaposing fiction, fantasy, and reality and for fusing the private stories of his characters with sociohistorical settings. Giuseppe Amoroso is the only critic who has carefully analyzed Bernari's revisions of *Tre operai* and *Domani e poi domani*. The revision of *Prologo* into *Le radiose giornate* awaits a similar examination. Unfortunately, too little criticism has appeared on Bernari's use of expressionistic and surrealistic descriptions.

In the volume of essays and interviews *Non gettate via la scala* (Do Not Throw Away the Ladder, 1973), Bernari stated that he preferred to extract from real life the material for his novels because for him daily reality was in itself incredible and fantastic. Life under Fascism, the daily theater in the streets of Naples, the industrial boom of the 1960s, and the days of terrorism in the 1970s as well as other real-life sources proved to be a gold mine from which he drew the subject matter for his narratives. His work has attracted the interest of movie producers—*Tre operai, Amore amaro,* and *Un foro nel parabrezza* have been adapted for motion pictures—while some of his novels have been translated into Spanish, French, German, and Russian. Since Bernari's death in 1992, reprints of his earlier works have begun to appear. As his works are republished there is no question that Bernari will gain increasing recognition as one of Italy's major contemporary novelists.

Interviews:

G. A. Cibotto, "Bernari invita Pulcinella a togliersi la maschera," *La fiera letteraria,* 30 November 1952;

Rocco Capozzi, "Intervista a Carlo Bernari," *Italianistica,* 4, no. 1 (1975): 142–168;

Eugenio Ragni, "Dialogo con Bernari," *Studi romani,* 24 (1976): 206–218;

Claudio Toscani, "Incontro con Bernari," *Il lettore di provincia,* 7 (1976): 48–54;

Gianni Infusino, *Napoli da lontano* (Napoli: Società Editrice Napolentana, 1981);

Toscani, "Colloquio con C. Bernari," in *La voce e il testo* (Milan: Istituto Propaganda Libraria, 1987), pp. 20–57.

References:

Giuseppe Amoroso, "Officina di Bernari," *Letteratura italiana contemporanea,* 2 (1981): 31–55;

Amoroso, *Sull'elaborazione dei romanzi contemporanei* (Milan: Mursia, 1970), pp. 123–163;

Salvatore Battaglia, "*Tre operai* di C. Bernari," *Filologia e letteratura,* 11 (1965): 337–342;

Rocco Capozzi, *Bernari tra fantasia e realtà* (Naples: SEN, 1984);

Capozzi, "Naples: Myth, Reality and Theatricality in Carlo Bernari," *Forum Italicum,* 13 (1979): 231–248;

Capozzi, "The Narrator-Protagonist and the Creative Process in Bernari's *Un foro nel parabrezza,*" *Romance Notes,* 17 (1977): 230–235;

Capozzi, "Time and Aesthetic Distance in Bernari's *Le radiose giornate,*" *International Fiction Review,* 2 (1975): 153–156;

Carmine Di Biase, *L'altra Napoli* (Naples: SEN, 1978), pp. 83–94;

La fiera letteraria, special issue on Bernari (2 February 1958);

Enzo Golino, *Cultura e mutamento sociale* (Milan: Ediz. Comunità, 1969), pp. 268–275, 312–315;

Giuliano Manacorda, "Carlo Bernari," in *Novecento* (Milan: Marzorati, 1979), pp. 7256–7287;

Walter Mauro, "Carlo Bernari," *I contemporanei,* volume 2 (Milan: Marzorati, 1963), pp. 1587–1600;

Mauro, *Cultura e società nella narrativa meridionale* (Rome: Edizioni dell'Ateneo, 1965), pp. 77–82, 133–139, 174–178, 278–282;

Angelo Mele, "Bernari," *Sei narratori del Novecento* (Naples: Istituto del Mezzogiorno, 1972), pp. 179–234;

Eugenio Montale, "Carlo Bernari: *Domani e poi domani,*" *Corriere della sera,* 29 May 1957;

Emilio Pesce, *Bernari* (Florence: La Nuova Italia, 1970);

Eugenio Ragni, "Carlo Bernari," in *Letteratura italiana contemporanea,* edited by G. Mariani and M. Petrucciani (Rome: Lucarini, 1980), pp. 647–657;

Ragni, *Invito alla lettura di Bernari* (Milan: Mursia, 1978);

Giacinto Spagnoletti, "Bernari," *Scrittori di un secolo* (Milan: Marzorati, 1974), pp. 648–658;

Spagnoletti, "Ritratti critici: Bernari," *Belfagor* (March 1980): 175–184;

Nicola Tanda, "La crisi dell'oggettività nell'opera di Bernari," *Incontri,* 7 (1972): 113–123.

Giuseppe Berto

(27 December 1914 – 1 November 1978)

Giacomo Striuli
Providence College

BOOKS: *Il cielo è rosso* (Milan: Longanesi, 1947); translated by Angus Davidson as *The Sky is Red* (New York: New Directions, 1948; Aylesbury, U.K.: Shire Publications / Leeds: Dunn & Wilson, 1973);

Le opere di Dio (Rome: Macchia, 1948); translated by Davidson as *The Works of God, and Other Stories* (London: Secker & Warburg, 1949; Norfolk, Conn.: New Directions, 1950);

Il brigante (Turin: Einaudi, 1951); translated by Davidson as *The Brigand* (London: Secker & Warburg, 1951; New York: New Directions, 1951);

Guerra in camicia nera (Milan: Garzanti, 1955);

Un po' di successo (Milan: Longanesi, 1963);

L'uomo e la sua morte (Brescia: Morcelliana, 1964);

Il male oscuro (Milan: Rizzoli, 1964); translated by William Weaver as *Incubus* (New York: Knopf, 1966; London: Hodder & Stoughton, 1966);

La fantarca (Milan: Rizzoli, 1965);

La cosa buffa (Milan: Rizzoli, 1966); translated by Weaver as *Antonio in Love* (New York: Knopf, 1968; London: Hodder & Stoughton, 1969);

Modesta proposta per prevenire (Milan: Rizzoli, 1971);

Anonimo veneziano (Milan: Rizzoli, 1971); translated by Valerie Southorn as *Anonymous Venetian* (London: Hodder & Stoughton, 1973);

La Passione secondo noi stessi (Milan: Rizzoli, 1972);

Oh, Serafina! (Milan: Rusconi, 1973);

È forse amore (Milan: Rusconi, 1975);

La gloria (Milan: Mondadori, 1978);

La colonna Feletti: i racconti di guerra e di prigionia (Venice: Marsilio, 1987).

Giuseppe Berto was a novelist, a film critic, and a playwright. His writings express a compassionate concern for the human condition as he sought to find causes for such universal evils as injustice, poverty, war, and personal despair. The uneasiness of his protagonists mirrors a society afflicted by a pervasive universal evil—"il male universale," as Berto calls it. In this regard he can be linked to Italo Svevo, Carlo Emilio Gadda, Alberto Moravia, and other Italian writers who have focused on existential and psychoanalytic themes. A religious longing is a cohesive element in Berto's seemingly uneven literary production. His tormented quest for God, which can move us to laughter and sadness and from exuberant hope to the deepest despair, is apparent in many of his works. At once humorous and compassionate, Berto's descriptions of people unfold in simple yet lyrical prose that often has biblical overtones. Berto had visions of himself as a writer-prophet and believed in warning people about the threats posed by the political class and by technology. Ultimately, he lived in exile in his own land, an anarchist who believed in literature as a means to cope with adverse personal and social realities.

Berto's literary career is divided into three phases that correspond to the main expressions of postwar Italian literature. In his neorealistic first phase, which lasted from the 1940s into the 1960s, he produced such novels as *Il cielo è rosso* (1947), *Le opere di Dio* (1948), and *Il brigante* (1951), which are written in a documentary style and deal with the human suffering caused by World War II. In his second phase, beginning in the 1960s and stretching into the 1970s, Berto established an avant-garde reputation at home and abroad with such works as *Il male oscuro* (1964) and *La cosa buffa* (1966), in which he relies on humor as a means of reflecting on human despair. Berto's third phase, the years before his death in 1978, is characterized by a transcendental yearning evident in such works as *Anonimo veneziano* (1971), *Oh, Serafina!* (1973), and *La gloria* (1978). In his last books Berto revisited earlier themes in an effort to find solutions to unresolved problems: a lifelong struggle with his father and the quests for God and literary glory.

Berto has arguably attracted more attention in the United States than in his native Italy. American critics seem particularly interested in what they regard as Berto's contradictory mixture of Marxist and Catholic ideas. Once an ardent Fascist, Berto shifted to a Marxist position after World War II be-

Giuseppe Berto and Leonida Répaci at the Premio Viareggio awards reception in 1964

fore returning in the mid 1960s to a more conservative political stance. Of his rejection of Marxism he wrote in his preface to *Il brigante:*

> Motivo di disperazione del nostro tempo, il sospetto che neppure dal marxismo l'uomo possa aspettarsi felicità e giustizia, la supposizione angosciante che tra marxismo e composizione psicologica umana ci sia una incompatibilità che costringe il potere alla violenza e alla crudeltà.

> (A reason for despair in our times is the suspicion that not even Marxism can bring happiness and justice, a fearful assumption that the incompatibility between Marxism and the human psyche generates violence and cruelty in those who have power.)

Berto's novels alienated those who admired the commitment of such writers as Ignazio Silone, Elio Vittorini, and Primo Levi to the indictment of social injustices. Berto made no attempt to treat historical or political matters, and little factual information can be gleaned from his books. Instead, his novels are characterized by his penchant for dark com-

edy as a stratagem to observe and magnify his characters' foibles. As Berto explained in a 1968 interview with Claudio Toscani, his humor was an innovative stylistic element that broke with postwar Neorealism, and more important, provided a mirror in which both characters and readers could catch a glimpse of their inner selves:

> Non essendo più possibile avere quella fiducia nella realtà, negli ordinamenti sociali, nella missione dello scrittore, che si poteva avere negli ultimi anni della guerra e nel dopoguerra, ora uno scrittore deve guardare il mondo con maggior distacco, riflessione, senso critico, umorismo.

> (Since it is no longer possible to have faith in reality, in social institutions, in the writer's mission, a faith one could still have during and immediately after World War II, now a writer has to look at the world with greater detachment, reflection, critical awareness, and a sense of humor.)

Berto has contributed to a greater understanding of his life and artistic work through his lengthy interviews and prefaces and has unabashedly placed himself at the center of his writings. He states in this regard: "Uno scrittore è davvero utile alla società solo quando realizza se stesso nel modo più completo possibile: anche narrando la vita umana, e questa dovrebbe essere l'aspirazione più giusta per uno che scrive" (A writer can be truly useful to society only when he can be completely true to himself: even when telling a human story, and this should be the most appropriate aim for someone who writes).

Berto was born on 27 December 1914 in Momigliano Veneto, a small town north of Venice. This rural, predominantly Catholic region has frequently served as the setting for his novels. In works such as *Oh, Serafina!* the Veneto is seen as a land of poverty that has forced millions of its inhabitants to immigrate to Argentina and Brazil. In "L'inconsapevole approccio" (The Unconscious Approach), a long introductory essay printed in the 1965 edition of *Le opere di Dio,* Berto, then at the midpoint of his career, offers a frank evaluation of his works and reflects on his life. Writing in the third person with his usual irony, he evokes painful memories, observing that the year of his birth coincided with the outbreak of World War I and thus was an appropriate prelude to a series of tragic events that would adversely affect his life. Berto also attributes his existential misfortunes to the unfavorable Zodiac sign of Capricorn, which, he is quick to point out, also prescribed the tragic destinies of two equally star-crossed men: Joseph Stalin and Paul Cézanne.

Berto's family was dominated by an authoritarian father, a retired military man. The second eldest of five siblings, Berto felt unloved as a child. From the age of eight until he turned fifteen, he studied in a boarding school run by Salesian priests who believed in corporal punishment and at times forced him to eat stale bread and to study day and night. He made use of this painful past in the portrait of the young protagonist of *Il cielo è rosso.* Despite his understandable dislike for formal schooling, Berto successfully earned his diploma from a *liceo* (high school) in Treviso. After graduation he served two years of military duty while studying at the University of Padua. He chose the Faculty of Letters simply because—as he later admitted with a touch of sarcasm—it was the most affordable.

Wishing to distinguish himself not as a scholar but as a man of action, the twenty-one-year-old Berto began a four-year hitch in Ethiopia in 1935, serving as second lieutenant of a racially mixed platoon of the Italian army. While on combat duty in eastern Africa in 1939, he was wounded in the right foot and awarded a silver and a bronze medal. Having returned to Italy on 10 June 1940, Berto went to Padua to take his final examinations. He passed with little effort and graduated with a degree in art history. As Italy was about to enter World War II, Berto was eager to return to Africa.

In 1940 Berto made his literary debut with the publication of "La colonna Feletti" (The Feletti Column), a story about his war experiences in Ethiopia that appeared in the *Gazzettino sera,* a Venetian newspaper. The story honors the memory of four comrades-in-arms who died in combat. While it is stylistically rough and little more than a journalistic effort, "La colonna Feletti" also reveals Berto's talent for realistic portrayal of human relationships. By his own observation, his simple style contrasted with the "letteratura nazionale acclamata in quegli anni" (the national literature acclaimed at the time).

Berto's request for assignment to the front was not immediately approved. For two years he taught Latin and history in a teacher's college and literature in a technical school. He so disliked the experience that he vowed never to teach again. In 1942 Berto volunteered for the front line in northern Africa and took part in the battle of El Alamein, Egypt, which resulted in the crushing defeat of the Axis powers. Berto's African experience is chronicled in *Guerra in camicia nera* (At War in a Blackshirt, 1955). Blending irony and nostalgia, he depicts the daily life of soldiers who must "act like men" at all costs and uses that axiom as a point of departure for various aspects of his disillusionment with military life.

Death became a daily reality to Berto; the horrors of war led not only to a distorted view of himself but also of life. More than the physical degradation he suffered, Berto's worst pain was caused by the shattering of his beliefs, his pride in "la grandezza della nazione, la potenza militare italiana, l'unione di tutto un popolo intorno al duce, una finale onestà del fascismo" (the nation's greatness, Italy's military power, a people united around Mussolini, the final honesty of Fascism). With masochistic candor, he shoulders the guilt for his role in the war: "Il senso di colpa che come uomo egli genericamente sente per le crudeltà della guerra, e il senso di colpa che come italiano e fascista sente per aver contribuito allo scatenarsi della guerra" (The general sense of guilt that as a man I felt for the cruelties of war, and the personal sense of guilt as an Italian and a fascist for my part in the outbreak of the war).

Berto's adventures in Africa ended when he was captured by the Allied forces on 13 May 1943 and interned at Hereford, Texas, America's second-largest POW camp. During this trying time, religion was one of the factors that afforded comfort to Berto as it brought together captors and captives. His religious leanings become manifest in his early work through the notion of *male universale,* a universal evil

44

beyond human understanding that causes its victims to blame God for their tribulations. The characters of *Il cielo è rosso,* for example, unable to understand the futility, violence, and pain caused by war, can only be angry: "Oppure avevano maledetto Dio, che era la cosa più giusta, perché era un modo di maledire sé stessi e il male di tutti gli uomini" (Or they cursed God, which was the right thing to do, because it was a way to curse themselves and the evils of mankind).

While at Hereford, Berto became an avid reader of American fiction, favoring writers such as Ernest Hemingway, John Steinbeck, and John Dos Passos. At the same time, Berto's disenchantment with Fascism and its repression of the literati became most intense. He wrote: "Sentivo un forte senso di rivolta contro la letteratura rinunciataria del tempo fascista . . . Svevo e Gramsci ci mancarono: il primo nessuno ce lo proponeva e il secondo era proibito" (I felt a sense of revulsion for the defeatist literature of the Fascist era . . . Svevo and Gramsci were not available to us: nobody cared for the former and the latter was banned). Berto recognized Hemingway as his literary mentor: "Cominciò a leggere in inglese, soprattutto per imparare la lingua, e forse fu in questo periodo che conobbe per la prima volta Hemingway: in una raccolta di *Esquire,* ci doveva essere *The Short Happy Life of Francis Macomber* e, probabilmente, anche *The Snows of the Kilimanjaro*" (I began to read in English, especially to learn the language, and it was then that I discovered Hemingway: in a set of collected issues of *Esquire* magazine which I believe included *The Short Happy Life of Francis Macomber* and probably *The Snows of the Kilimanjaro*).

From American authors Berto learned to write in a simple, uncomplicated language, but their most important lesson was a tragic vision of life, in which one found meaning in the contemplation of the struggle against pain, death, and fate:

> Gli americani avevano da offrirci un insegnamento non tanto di stile, quanto di coraggio: coraggio per guardare, senza schemi letterari davanti, la nostra vita, comunque fosse. In altre parole, gli americani, più che "come scrivere," avevano da insegnarci "cosa scrivere."

> (Americans did not offer us a lesson in style, but in courage: the courage to look without literary preconceptions, at life, realistically. In other words, more than anything else, American authors were to teach us "what to write," not "how to write.")

Berto could not have imagined at the time that his imprisonment at Hereford would mark the beginning of his distinguished career. The misfortunes

Dust jacket for the British edition of the translation of Berto's first novel, which depicts the struggles of four children in post–World War II Italy

of war, however, had brought Berto into contact with writers Dante Troisi and Gaetano Tumiati, the painter Alberto Burri, and other artists. Invited to contribute to a newsletter for Italian prisoners, Berto found a situation that afforded him not only a forum to express his ideas and to influence others but also the opportunity to learn his craft. Eventually he wrote several short stories that were collected in the 1963 volume *Un po' di successo* (A Little Success). The strongest stories were "Economia di candele" (A Few Candles), "Gli eucaliptus cresceranno" (The Eucalyptus Will Grow), and "Il seme tra le spine" (The Seed among the Thorns). The last of these especially demonstrates Berto's ability to write an amusing tale that underscores the inevitability of man's loneliness and his search for happiness.

Berto also wrote longer and more substantial tales at Hereford, such as the novella *Le opere di Dio* and the long, poignant novel *Il cielo è rosso,* which, though it was written a few months after *Le opere di Dio,* became his first published book. After the war Berto met with the critic Giovanni Comisso, who recommended the manuscript to the publisher Leo Longanesi. *Il cielo è rosso* introduces thematic ideas and narrative strategies that are developed in later works. Berto's most enduring interest is the portrayal of characters who suffer feelings of guilt for their failure to meet the expectations placed upon them by society or by God.

Il cielo è rosso tells the story of two boys and two girls who must resort to crime to survive in a city ravaged by war. In "Inconsapevole approccio" Berto recalls that the idea for the novel came from pictures in an issue of *Life* magazine that showed Italian children feeding themselves on garbage or begging for food. He was also moved by the reports of newly arrived prisoners from Italy, who related the savage bombing of Treviso, an important city in the Veneto region. Deeply touched by these tragic events in his homeland, Berto feverishly began *Il cielo è rosso,* somehow managing to write it on toilet paper. As Berto explains in his essay, the novel was not about the war but about the trauma of war on the psyche of the main character, Daniele. His alienation from himself, from others, and from God mirrors that of the author, a prisoner in a foreign land. The book opens with the description of a barren wintry landscape, a metaphor for the spiritual void of its inhabitants: "Ognuno era chiuso in sé, e come smarrito, e gli uomini erano divisi, e senza pietà gli uni per gli altri" (Everyone was withdrawn, seemingly lost, the men divided, without a sense of compassion for one another).

Berto's realistic portrait of the devastating effects of the war on innocent children no doubt contributed to the critical consensus that *Il cielo è rosso* ranks among the best novels written about World War II. The picture of suffering children is as piercing and sorrowful as that of the best neorealistic films, such as Roberto Rossellini's *Open City* (1946) and *Paisàn* (1947) and Vittorio de Sica's *Bicycle Thief* (1948). Both the children and the ravaged landscape become symbols of the *male universale,* the unexplainable presence of evil. Berto's ability to blend in his prose realistic dialogue, evocative imagery, and psychological insight contribute to offset what some critics view as a lack of intellectual rigor. In 1948 it received the coveted Firenze Prize in recognition of its compassionate portrayal of human misery.

Le opere di Dio was for the most part ignored by critics and the public alike when it was first published as a book in 1948. A modern odyssey about human responsibility for the crimes and afflictions associated with war, it has come to be considered

Berto's literary gem. Few writers have written about war against children as poignantly as Berto did in this work. The child's perspective of tragic events enhances the emotional appeal of the narration. Stylistically, the novel is written with great beauty, compassion, and realism. Like *Il cielo è rosso,* *Le opere di Dio* is about human despair, loneliness, and the quest for God.

The novel's theme is stated in its title, which is taken from the ninth chapter of the Gospel of John. Asked by the disciples whether a man born blind was punished for his parents' sin or for his own, Christ replied that neither was at fault since the blindness was necessary to manifest "the works of God" and then gave the man sight. Berto thus implies that the tribulations endured by his family of Italian farmers during World War II are manifestations of universal afflictions whose causes are not readily apparent to human reason. In a compressed time span, the story chronicles the ordeals of the Mangano family, displaced by advancing American troops and a retreating German army. The actions of war and the exodus of local inhabitants structure the story and show the characters' inability to cope with adverse circumstances.

Le opere di Dio begins with a quasi-biblical depiction of Filippo Mangano, the grandfather, who, signaled by the blasts of an air raid, interrupts the harvest to lead his family on an aimless journey. At the end of the novel the surviving members of his devastated family seek consolation in an embrace as they continue on a seemingly endless journey. In a land ravaged by war, these characters—the Old Man, the Mother, the Daughter, the Redhead, the Child—become symbols of universal suffering, analogous to the protagonists of *Il cielo è rosso.* As in that novel, the characters are faced with the ineluctability of their tribulations and are estranged from God. Unable to understand their own feelings, they are isolated from each other and mute with guilt. The book ends in sadness, as the daughter embraces her mother, who seems unable to be consoled after the futile and violent death of her spouse: "Ma non ha capito . . . non ha capito" (But he did not understand . . . he did not understand).

With the poor reception of *Le opere di Dio,* Berto was determined to prove wrong the critics who suspected he had already written his one success. He wrote *Il brigante,* another war novel based on his own life, seeking full recognition as a neorealist writer, as he candidly admits in the preface to the 1964 edition: "*Il brigante* rappresenta il mio cosciente e volenteroso tentativo di entrare, di pieno diritto, in un movimento culturale chiamato Neorealismo" (*The Brigand* represents my cognizant and willful attempt to be part of the cultural movement called Neorealism). Unfortunately, Neorealism was fading, and a more personal and psychological approach to art was emerging. While neorealistic commitment to social causes was still respected, many longed for greater artistic freedom. Berto later chose the title "L'inconsapevole approccio" to indicate that his Neorealism was the result of an "unconscious approach"—meaning that his indictment of social injustice in Italy began in America when he was out of touch with the dominant literary movement of his native land.

Il brigante did not fulfill Berto's desire for success. Panned in Italy, the book was nonetheless praised as a short masterpiece in the United States. As a film directed by Renato Castellani *Il Brigand* achieved popular success in 1961. The book tells the story of Michele Rende, a veteran of the war in northern Africa who returns to Italy to bury his father. Inspired by the character of Salvatore Giuliano, a Christ-like Sicilian bandit who fought the rich to help the poor, Rende is part fiction and part Berto's literary persona. He is portrayed as a sensitive, children-loving man whom war gradually turns into a fierce killer.

Similar to his bittersweet approach in *Il brigante*, Berto in *Guerra in camicia nera* shows a compassionate awareness of humanity that elevates what at first may seem a banal and inappropriate depiction of men at war. Tinged with a blend of melancholy and elation, the diary brings into focus the confessional element of Berto's literary personality. Like Jean-Jacques Rousseau, he uses autobiography as a means of self-discovery. Through the disclosure of his most painful and intimate memories, Berto gains a sense of personal worth while making his work individual. The excruciating physical pains that the protagonists attribute to God resemble the sufferings endured by other characters in Berto's books who search for personal salvation from guilt, anxiety, and isolation. *Guerra in camicia nera* has a tone of ambivalence, presenting a dialectical tension between courage and despair that becomes more apparent in Berto's later texts.

During the 1950s and 1960s Berto was in an emotional and professional quandary. Living and working in Rome, he contributed film reviews to *Rotosei* and other newspapers. In 1964, at the brink of suicide and insanity resulting from a bitter divorce, mental disorders, and harsh criticism, Berto turned for help to a psychoanalyst named Nicola Perotti. As part of the therapy, Perotti asked Berto to keep a diary. The revised form of this manuscript is Berto's best-known novel, *Il male oscuro* (1964; translated as *Incubus,* 1966).

An instant success, *Il male oscuro* won the Viareggio and the Campiello prizes in 1964 and was translated into several languages. As Oscar Handlin wrote in his review published in the *Atlantic Monthly,* *Incubus* is hilariously funny and, among the modern novels, most akin to James Joyce's *Ulysses* (1922). There is one difference, according to Handlin: "*Ulysses* ends in the great paean of affirmation, *Incubus* in resignation." A confessional novel that makes use of Freudian psychology and the subconscious, it reveals Berto's affinity for comic and bizarre situations. Berto acknowledges his debt to two famous psychoanalytic works that combine comic episodes with a serious intent: Italo Svevo's *La coscienza di Zeno* (Confessions of Zeno, 1923) and Carlo Emilio Gadda's *La cognizione del dolore* (Acquainted with Grief, 1963).

Like Svevo and Gadda, Berto creates a first-person protagonist who, facing death in his old age, seeks to find a meaning for various dimensions of his past personal life: rebellious son, unfaithful husband, loving father, and struggling artist. The search forces the protagonist to contemplate his hatred for his father, agoraphobia, fear of cancer and disease, sexual inadequacies, and other embarrassing and troublesome truths. With a mixture of melancholy and cheerfulness, the protagonist, Berto's alter ego, recalls his life, especially the episode that broke his emotional equilibrium: the abandonment of his father who was dying of cancer. The ensuing guilt gradually contributes to the development of his "male oscuro," or incubus, the forbidding malaise that will physically and spiritually affect him for the rest of his life.

Il male oscuro can be read as a Dantean journey to the subconscious in its uneasy search for existential meaning. The narrator is explicit in his purpose: "Inizio il lungo viaggio verso l'inconscio alla scoperta delle radici dei miei presenti malanni" (I begin the long journey to the subconscious to discover the causes of my present afflictions). Berto adheres to the dictum that one can find comfort in the contemplation of personal ailments, be they physical or mental, and it is the intensity of the author's honesty that gives the book its underlying strength.

The narration relies on the technique of associative discourse—what the author described as "lo stile psicoanalitico," or psychoanalytic writing. To represent the protagonist's mental disarray, Berto eliminates punctuation and logical association between and within sentences. However, he continues to use the simple, everyday speech of his earlier writings. His stylistic innovation is thus neither unbridled nor iconoclastic and remains faithful to narrative simplicity. Berto's ability to inject humor into

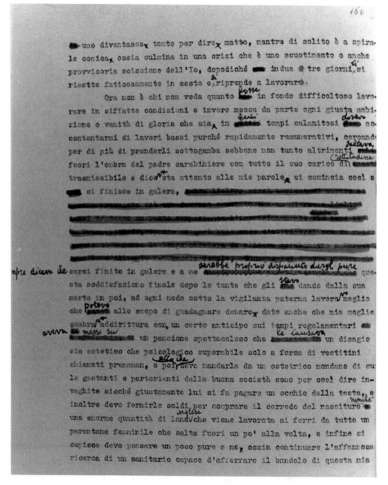

Page from the revised typescript for Il male oscuro *(Collection of Giuseppe Berto)*

his account of the protagonist's disposition toward death, love, and self-identity is noteworthy:

D'altra parte avevo più volte esperimentato che senza di lei le cose andavano molto peggio, sicché ora non appena sentivo caldo alle lombari o sudori freddi o dolori a quel dannato punto del colon che già aveva fregato il padre mio, e per farla breve non appena da qualche regione fisica o metafisica del mio corpo sentivo partire una corrente di malessere caldo o freddo che andava all'assalto del mio Io col proposito di disintegrarlo cercavo lei in una città che pur sovrabbonda di medici e cliniche per ammalati di cervello, ed ecco che lei quando può viene, talvolta anche di notte viene e si sdraia accanto a me sopra le coperte col plaid addosso e mi tiene le mani e mi dice che non sono solo al mondo perché c'è chi non mi abbandonerà mai, e io sento che con lei al mio fianco non mi perderò.

(On the other hand I had often experienced that without her things were a lot worse, so now, whenever I would feel hot spells in my lower back or cold shivers or pains in that same place near the colon that had already

screwed my father, in other words, as soon as I was feeling that a sort a electric shock piercing some physical or metaphysical part of my body was about to attack my Ego with the intent of destroying it, I would look for her in a city overcrowded with doctors and mental hospitals, and then here she comes, whenever she can, sometimes even at night, and she lies next to me under the blankets, and holds my hands and tells me that I am not alone in this world because there is someone who will never leave me, and I feel that with her at my side I will not be lost.)

The novel also contains scathing details about his dealings with producers and filmmakers, many of whom misunderstood his artistic vision and exploited his talent. Despite his dislike of the movie industry, which he would reiterate in the preface to his play *Anonimo veneziano,* Berto was involved with motion pictures for more than thirty years.

At the zenith of his career in 1965, Berto produced two new works, *La fantarca* (The Magical Ship), published in 1965, and *La cosa buffa,* published the following year. *La fantarca,* which he called a "science-fiction fable," is a spoof with episodes reminiscent of Miguel de Cervantes's *Don Quixote* (1615). Set in 2160, the book proposes a final solution for the socio-economic gap between northern and southern Italy: the shipping of the last inhabitants of southern Italy to Saturn aboard a dilapidated spaceship called "Hope No. 5." The description of the battered spaceship evokes Don Quixote's lamentable state after his confrontation with the windmills: "Cosí vecchia, poverina, che era piena di rabberciature e pecette, ma d'altra parte questo era l'ultimo viaggio interplanetario che avrebbe compiuto" (so old, poor thing, so full of patches and glue, but on the other hand this was going to be its final trip).

The narrator, a master of understatement, asserts that the evacuation of the South is sure to be "expensive and difficult." The plot is replete with autobiographical references and double entendre. For example, the spaceship is launched from Capo Vaticano, a name that suggests both Cape Canaveral and Vatican City and satirically implies the church's involvement in a morally questionable effort. There is no end to the southerners' plight, however, as they struggle to reach their ultimate destination, Saturn, one of most remote planets in the universe.

In *La cosa buffa* (1966; translated as *Antonio in Love,* 1968), Berto uses the third-person narrative to relate the unfortunate loves and misguided literary ambitions of Antonio, another mirror image of the author. The novel is ostensibly a sequel to *Il male oscuro,* in which he refers to the plot of *La cosa buffa:*

Eppertanto mettendomi alla scrivania non mi sento cosí in forma come dovrei essere per intraprendere il cominciamento del quarto capitolo che è molto impegnativo e infatti vi deve accadere che il ragazzo il quale è povero si reca a casa di lei che viceversa è ricca per chiederla in sposa e non occorre dire che gli va parecchio male.

(So as I sit at my desk I do not feel as ready as I should be to tackle the beginning of the fourth chapter which is very difficult to write, as a matter of fact it deals with a poor young man who goes to his girlfriend, who is very rich, to ask her to marry him, needless to say he will run into a lot of trouble.)

Joseph Conrad, quoted at the opening of the novel, is the source of the title *La cosa buffa* (A Funny Thing): "What a funny thing is life, such as a mysterious articulation of unforgiving logic leading to a futile purpose." Berto remains faithful to his plan to write a funny work about serious problems, such as the relationship between art and sexuality. Returning to a more traditional style of writing than one

finds in *Il male oscuro,* with proper punctuation and structural coherence, Berto uses third-person narration to attain a critical detachment that nevertheless renders a compassionate view of Antonio's foibles. Whereas *Il male oscuro* brought to mind Italo Svevo and the artist as an old man, *La cosa buffa* is ostensibly reminiscent of James Joyce's *A Portrait of the Artist as a Young Man* (1915).

The novel offers an intimate glimpse into Antonio's provincial background and his lonely life as a university student in Venice. His isolation arises from the hatred he feels for other students who came to his hometown for the holidays and embarrassed him with their money and good looks. For Antonio, as for other male characters in Berto's novels, women are either virtuous creatures or agents of evil. As a result, physical love is a constant source of shame and guilt. He fails in his clumsy attempts at conquering the blond, chaste Maria, the daughter of Cavalier Borghetto, the owner of Venice's most lucrative shipbuilding industries. Later, he is equally inept at loving the dark, lustier Marica. This tension constantly reverberates in the text and can be felt in the physical descriptions of Venice. Seen through Antonio's eyes, the city takes on the somber contours of his inner state:

In quel tempo di mezzo inverno benché si recasse ogni pomeriggio di sole sulla terrazza del Caffè delle Zattere, vale a dire in un luogo per niente spiacevole e anzi rallegrato dalle scarse cose liete che si possono trovare in una città umida qual'è Venezia durante la brutta stagione, Antonio aveva soprattutto voglia di morire. Detto così il suo comportamento potrebbe benissimo apparire un po' scombinato e corrispondente ad uno stato psicologico quantomeno confuso.

(During those midwinter days, though, he would go, every sunny afternoon, on the deck of the Caffè delle Zattere, a rather nice place where one can be cheered up by those pleasant things that are hard to find in a city as wet as Venice during the unpleasant season. Antonio wished above all to be dead. Stated so bluntly, one could say that his behavior was foolish and indicative of a rather confused state of mind.)

After the publication of *La cosa buffa,* Berto's emotional state worsened once again. Unable to hold a permanent position, he found sporadic employment with *Resto del Carlino* and other newspapers. He also wrote a personal column for *Bellezza,* a fashion magazine. Women, Berto believed, were his most loyal readers, the only ones who truly appreciated and understood his writings.

In 1971 Berto published two works: his first play and a collection of essays. His drama *Anonimo veneziano* (translated as *Anonymous Venetian,* 1973) was

*Cover for Berto's 1966 novel, which takes its title from a
remark by Joseph Conrad*

made into a successful 1971 film directed by Enrico
Maria Salerno. It is the romantic story of a musician
stricken with cancer who is in love with a beautiful
woman. Set in Venice, the baroque music of Benedetto Marcello provides the unifying leitmotiv to
the movie. Berto's *Modesta proposta per prevenire* (A
Modest Preventive Proposal, 1971), a collection of
sixty-one satiric essays, deals with contemporary social and political issues. The title pays homage to the
Anglo-Irish master of satire, Jonathan Swift, as
Berto candidly admits: "L'ho copiato di sana pianta
da Swift" (I stole it verbatim from Swift).

Berto's next project was another play, *La Passione secondo noi stessi* (The Passion According to Us,
1972), which took the form of a fictional debate on
the death of Christ. Similar in its psychoanalytic approach and characterization to *Il male oscuro,* the play
was successfully brought to the stage by the director
Arrigo Vezzani in 1975. The figure of Christ manifests the traits that are typical of Berto's antiheroes.

One can imagine him, the author writes, "con
l'aiuto di Freud, come un uomo massacrato da senso
di colpa e da volontà di potenza, uno che volle osti-
natamente e grandiosamente farsi ammazzare per
diventare Dio" (with Freud's help, as a man crushed
by guilt and by willpower, someone who obstinately
and with great pride willed his own death in order to
become God).

Published in 1973 with the subtitle "Fiaba di
ecologia, di manicomio e di amore" (An Ecological
Fable, about Insanity and Love), *Oh, Serafina!* was
well received but less successful than *La cosa buffa.*
Originally written as a story for a film, this bittersweet novel won the Premio Bancarella in 1974 and
was then made into a film. In the preface Berto offers typically self-deprecatory remarks that provide
a useful insight into his life and work:

> Ho scritto questo libro perché avevo bisogno di soldi.
> Mi capita spesso d'aver bisogno di soldi: non guadagno
> poi molto, sono imprevidente nelle spese, e lo stato mi
> fa pagare troppe tasse. Di solito, risolvo questi problemi
> di denaro lavorando per il cinema. Anche questa volta
> volevo far così e in effetti *Oh, Serafina!* sarebbe dovuto
> essere soltanto un soggetto per film.

> (I wrote this book because I needed money. It often
> happens that I need money: I don't make much, but I
> am extravagant with my money, and the Government
> forces me to pay high taxes. I usually solve my financial
> problems working for the film industry. So this time I
> wanted to do the same and in fact *Oh, Serafina* was
> meant to be only a film script.)

The main character, Augusto Valle Jr., is thirty-three
years old when he inherits a small factory in a rural
area outside Milan from his grandfather, Augusto
Valle. Like Saint Francis, Augusto loves and speaks to
birds—which alienates him from his mother, his wife,
and his workers—and like Jesus, he is good, misunderstood, and persecuted. He is forced to enter an insane
asylum where he falls in love with another inmate,
Serafina, a naive and attractive young woman. Beneath
the comic facade of *Oh, Serafina!* lies a satire addressing
the warped values of Italian society in the industrial
age.

In 1975 Berto collected short stories written
between 1944 and 1963 in a volume titled *È forse
amore* (Maybe It's Love). The selection seems to reflect a sense of renewed hope, as it contains some
optimistic tales. However, Berto's literary career
was at a standstill. Having severed contacts with the
cultural world, he was living in the isolation of Capo
Vaticano, a secluded, unspoiled little town on the
Calabrian coast. Away from civilization and feeling
ostracized by other writers, Berto worked on the

novel he hoped would bring him everlasting literary glory. Ten years earlier in *Il male oscuro,* Berto at the height of his career had imagined himself as an old man near death living in the isolation of Capo Vaticano. The glow of the fire that consumes the pages of his books seems to symbolize the light of a glorious new day:

> Ora accendo un fuoco e prendo i tre capitoli del capolavoro e li brucio un foglio alla volta ma senza rammarico perché si sa che ormai la mia gloria non può importare a nessuno, e poi brucio anche le fotografie del padre morto senza guardarle si capisce e anzi voltando la testa . . . eh Domine forse è già tempo.

> (Now I will light a fire, I will take the three chapters of my masterpiece and burn them page by page because it's clear now that nobody cares about my glory. I will also burn the photographs of my dead father without looking at them, in fact diverting my eyes . . . oh Lord maybe it's time.)

La gloria (Glory, 1978) was published posthumously by Mondadori, only a month after the author's death in Rome on 1 November 1978. The novel thus marks the culmination of Berto's work, and as the title indicates, glory is the unifying metaphor. The book is an account of Christ's last days, told in the first person by Judas Iscariot. As critics noted, the novel is a literary testament, the final legacy of Berto's embattled vision of his life. The voice of the author can be clearly heard in the words of the narrator, Judas, the embodiment of guilt and Berto's despised lesser self.

While thematically akin to Berto's earlier concerns with guilt and universal evil, *La gloria* lacks the brilliant humor and monologues that previously underscored Berto's keen insight into human behavior. Not organized into conventional chapters, the story is told by two narrators who intervene to discuss Christ's actions and motives: Judas the Apostle and Judas the narrator who contributes his own thoughts on Christ by pointing out what Sigmund Freud, Carl Jung, Albert Camus, Friedrich Engels, and others had to say about him.

Judas Iscariot, like Daniele and Michele Rende, and other pathetic protagonists in Berto's stories, committed suicide to escape the void of existential despair. The figure of Judas in *La gloria* recalls as well the relationship between Berto and his father in *Il male oscuro,* which is also resolved by death when the son, transcending his hostility for his earthly father, is united with the Heavenly Father. Camus's perception of Christ as an existential hero symbolic of the solitude of modern man, which was apparent in *La Passione secondo noi stessi,* also haunts this novel written six years later. Judas and Jesus embody Berto's dialectics of the self, the ego and the ideal self, as evidenced by Judas's conflicting feelings of love and hatred toward Christ. Although idealized, Jesus is depicted as a guilt-ridden individual who cannot forget Herod's massacre of the innocents.

The Christ of *La gloria* is a familiar character in Berto's fiction. Like Berto, he is an unpredictable man in a love-hate relationship with his father. Judas also manifests psychological traits shown by other men in Berto's novels who are afflicted by persecution and inferiority complexes. Living self-absorbed lives, these men equate love with surrender, as a negation of their sense of self. They seek to evade mediocrity by means of a false and grandiose aggrandizement of self, even an illusion of glory. At the end of the novel, Judas agonizes as he witnesses Christ's loneliness and despair on the cross. Judas seeks to escape suffering and madness, but he is unwilling to surrender through repentance. Like schizophrenic personalities, Judas distrusts Christ and misunderstands his motives; in his eyes, Christ is a man tormented by temptation. Judas believes that he is the anointed one, and he views his act of betrayal as a sacrifice. His own death becomes an act of love so that Jesus might attain glory. According to Berto's interpretation, Judas then is the true instrument of divine will, not Christ.

Giuseppe Berto never subscribed to a political ideology, and he was not welcome in social or academic circles because of his outspoken personality. Like the characters of his novels, Berto defended his individuality against family members and the world. He battled fellow writers, film producers, and literary critics throughout his life. Disenchanted with the literary establishment, he became active in Capo Vaticano's social life. At the end, Berto's life seemed to mirror his fiction. As the protagonist of *Il male oscuro* had imagined, Berto died of cancer, like his father. Ultimately, Berto's tortured quest for the love of both an earthly and a heavenly father seemed, at least in his fiction, to be answered in death. Berto is a representative Italian author who went beyond the social commitment of Neorealism and developed his own experimental stylistics to deal with existential and psychological concerns. The strength of Berto's writings is in his use of biographical experiences as a structuring device. Undoubtedly, his works will continue to interest readers in years to come.

Interview:

Claudio Toscani, *Il ragguaglio librario* (March 1968): 108–110.

References:

Everardo Artico and Laura Lepri, eds., *Giuseppe Berto* (Venice: Marsilio/Olschki, 1989);

Arnaldo Balduino, "Una fiaba di ecologia, di manicomio e d'amore di Giuseppe Berto," in *Messaggi e problemi della letteratura contemporanea* (Venezia: Marsilio, 1976), pp. 133–145;

Rossana Esposito, "Rassegna di studi su Giuseppe Berto," *Critica letteraria,* 1 (Spring 1973): 176–184;

Enzo Fabiani, "Berto," *Gente* (28 September 1978): 173–176;

John Gross, "*The Sky is Red,*" *Christian Science Monitor,* 30 September 1948, pp. 11–12;

Oscar Handlin, "*Incubus,*" *Atlantic Monthly,* 217 (1965): 162–164;

Stephanie Harrington, "Prisoned in the Self," *New York Times Book Review,* 20 October 1968, p. 55;

Alfred Hayes, "The Works of God," *New York Herald Tribune,* 18 June 1950, p. 26;

Donald Heiney, *America in Modern Italian Literature* (New Brunswick, N.J.: Rutgers University Press, 1964), pp. 156–163;

Heiney, "The Final Glory of Giuseppe Berto," *World Literature Today,* 54 (Fall 1980): 238–240;

Aleramo P. Lanapoppi, "Immanenza e trascendenza nell'opera di Giuseppe Berto: la realtà di dentro," *Modern Language Notes,* 87 (January 1972): 78–104;

Lanapoppi, "Immanenza e trascendenza nell'opera di Giuseppe Berto: la trappola del Neorealismo," *Modern Language Notes,* 85 (January 1970): 42–66;

Olga Lombardi, *Invito alla lettura di Berto* (Milan: Mursia, 1974);

Giulia Massari, "La gloria," *Tuttolibri,* 14 October 1978, p. 4;

Ferruccio Monterosso, *Come leggere "Il male oscuro" di Giuseppe Berto* (Milan: Mursia, 1977);

Rossana Ombres, "Sulle tracce di Giuda," *Tuttolibri,* 11 November 1978, p. 4;

Corrado Piancastelli, *Berto* (Florence: Nuova Italia, 1970);

Piancastelli, "Berto," in *Novecento,* volume 9, edited by Gianni Grana (Milan: Marzorati, 1979), pp. 7866–7886;

Giacomo Striuli, *Alienation in Giuseppe Berto's Novels* (Potomac, Md.: Scripta Humanistica, 1987).

Libero Bigiaretti
(16 May 1905 – 3 May 1993)

Gabriele Erasmi
McMaster University

BOOKS: *Ore e stagioni* (Rome: Liberia L.I.C., 1936);

Care ombre (Rome: Augustea, 1940);

Esterina (Rome: Lettere d'oggi, 1942);

Una amicizia difficile (Rome: De Luigi, 1945); republished as *Esterina Un'amicizia difficile* (Milan: Bompiani, 1962);

Incendio a Palèo (Rome: Editrice Cultura Moderna, 1945);

Il villino (Milan: Garzanti, 1946);

Roma borghese (Rome: Organizzazione Editoriale Tipografica, 1947);

Un discorso d'amore (Milan: Garzanti, 1948);

Carlone (Milan: Garzanti, 1950);

La scuola dei ladri: tre romanzi brevi (Milan: Garzanti, 1952);

I figli (Florence: Vallecchi, 1954; revised edition, 1960);

Disamore (Pisa: Nistri-Lischi, 1956);

Lungodora (Rome: De Luca, 1956);

Schedario (Milan: Schweiller, 1956);

Carte romane (Turin: Società Editrice Internazionale, 1957);

Leopolda (Venice: Sodalizio del Libro, 1957);

Uccidi o muori (Florence: Vallecchi, 1958);

I racconti (Florence: Vallecchi, 1961);

Il congresso (Milan: Bompiani, 1963); translated by Joseph Green as *The Convention* (London: Macmillan, 1965); republished as *A Business Convention* (New York: Knopf, 1965);

Cattiva memoria (Milan: Nuova Accademia, 1965);

Le indulgenze (Milan: Bompiani, 1966);

Il dito puntato (Milan: Bompani, 1967);

La controfigura (Milan: Bompiani, 1968);

Il dissenso (Milan: Bompiani, 1969);

Dalla donna alla luna (Milan: Bompiani, 1972);

L'uomo che mangia il leone (Milan: Bompiani, 1974);

Le stanze (Milan: Bompiani, 1976);

Due senza (Milan: Bompiani, 1979);

Questa Roma (Rome: Newton Compton, 1981);

A memoria d'uomo (Ancona: Bagaloni, 1982);

Il viaggiatore (Milan: Rusconi, 1984);

Libero Bigiaretti

Posto di blocco (Bologna: Il Lavoro Editoriale, 1986); translated by Gabriele Erasmi and Gerald Chapple as *Checkpoint: Poems of Death and Old Age* (Lewiston, N.Y.: Edwin Mellen Press, 1992);

Abitare altrove (Milan: Bompiani, 1990);

Con i tempi che corrono: Una conversazione autobiografica con Gilberto Severini (Ancona-Bologna: Transeuropa, 1992);

Un sogno di ferragosto (Fano: Editrice Fortuna, 1993);

Scritture di fabbrica (Turin: Scriptorium, 1994);

Il mio paese (Grottammare: Stamperia Dell'Arancio, 1995).

TRANSLATIONS: Henri Becque, *La parigina* (Rome: Delfino, 1946);

André Gide, *La scuola delle mogli* (Milan: Mondadori, 1949);

Gustave Flaubert, *Madame Bovary* (Turin: Einaudi, 1950);

Guy de Maupassant, *Pietro e Giovanni* (Milan: Universale Economica, 1952);

Jean Giraudoux, *La bugiarda* (Milan: Mondadori, 1970).

Because the events in Libero Bigiaretti's life constitute the background and a point of reference for his fiction, he has often been called an autobiographical writer, with the implication being that his imagination and talent are limited by his experience. He has at times encouraged this perception, as when one of the characters from his last novel, *Il viaggiatore* (The Traveler, 1984), confesses, "Sono privo di immaginazione: non saprei inventare niente, neppure qualche supporto alla memoria. Lo so, e non me ne dolgo" (I have no imagination: I could not invent anything, not even a support for my memory. I know this and do not regret it). However, such an admission from a character should not be read as expressing Bigiaretti's final word on his work.

Bigiaretti's belief in the importance of experience is akin to Protagoras's assertion that man is the measure of all things or Benedetto Croce's implication that all history is present history. For Bigiaretti, autobiography—understood as a set of formative events and life experiences—is the determining factor in one's view of the world in all its dimensions. Although individuals can transcend their social and historical backgrounds and physical limitations, they cannot change them. Within the inevitable limits one's life imposes, however, there are innumerable possibilities for growth and understanding. *Madame Bovary* (1857), a novel shaped but not limited by Gustave Flaubert's experience of life, is the model for Bigiaretti's approach to literature.

Believing that a writer writes best about what he knows best, Bigiaretti through hard artistic discipline has written many different novels and short stories. Bringing out books with singular regularity during his fifty-year career, he has always maintained a high level of craftsmanship and inspiration—a fact literary critics never fail to acknowledge. While Bigiaretti's autobiography provides the basic identity of his protagonists, this identity stems from the author's vantage points that vary with his age, time, place, experience, state of mind, and conditions of health. Even so, his writing is always the projection of a constant point of view that is uniquely his own. His approach is not new, but it is noteworthy by virtue of the seriousness, rigor, and consistency with which Bigiaretti applied it in all his works.

Bigiaretti is no postmodernist writer who looks at his fiction as a verbal game or as a parody of previous literature. His long writing career has taught him about verbal games, has made him aware of his debt to other writers, but has, as he writes in the poem "L'altare" (My Religion), left intact his faith in "l'unico bene nostro essendo il verbo" (words being our only certainty). For Bigiaretti, as for Marcel Proust, the pursuit of literature is a search for and a process of discovery of the self. He often said that he wrote to ascertain who he was, that the act of writing sets in motion a process of exploration and discovery as the self confronts the world outside the self, the *other*, and must come to terms with it.

The unifying thread in Bigiaretti's creative work is his search for a new dimension of the self that his author-protagonist was not aware of at the outset of the novel. In this perspective, "autodidattismo," what critics have called his being self-taught, is the process that leads to the discovery of the self. As Bigiaretti stated in his inaugural lecture at the University of Urbino on 20 August 1986: "Ho detto cose che ho imparato mentre le pensavo e le scrivevo" (I have said things that I learned as I thought and wrote them). For Bigiaretti, a writer is at once a witness to and a participant in his times; he is, as he writes in the poem "Processo" (Trial), an "accuser and an all too willing accomplice." Literature, from his point of view, is a reflection of reality. The novelist is not a detached reporter mechanically registering a series of facts but an individual who, through an act of the imagination under the stimuli of unavoidable circumstances, achieves self-consciousness as the agent in a reality of which the novel serves as a vehicle of discovery.

Libero Bigiaretti was born in Matelica in Le Marche, a central Italian region bordering on the Adriatic Sea, on 16 May 1905. Like the protagonist of *Il congresso* (1963; translated as *The Convention,* 1965), Bigiaretti often declined to reveal his age; as a consequence, many reference works list his year of birth as either 1906 or 1908. His anarchist father, Lucano, gave him the unusual Christian names of Libero (A Free Man), Spartaco (Spartacus), and Ribelle (The Rebel). His parents moved to Rome when he was six, and as a youngster Bigiaretti spent most of his time in the working-class districts of

Rome, though he returned every summer to Matelica, thus maintaining a vital link with his native town. His father worked as a construction foreman and tried to set up his own construction business; when that failed, he became the director of construction cooperatives, which the Fascist government eventually outlawed.

Bigiaretti at first followed in his father's footsteps, working in construction between the ages of sixteen and twenty-four. Later, he was employed as a draftsman and a clerk and also worked as an interior decorator and made ceramics. By attending evening classes, he graduated from the Liceo Artistico in Rome. With an instinctive passion for literature, he read everything that came into his hands when he was young, though later his reading became programmed and systematic. For a time he wanted to become a painter, showing considerable skill. He befriended several painters and through them began to meet men of letters. During his free time in the early 1930s Bigiaretti wrote poems, which appeared in newspapers and magazines, including *Il Messaggero, La Stampa, Il Corriere Padano, L'Ambrosiano, Tribuna, Quadrivio,* and *Augustea.* In 1936 he published his first collection of poetry, *Ore e stagioni.* He married in 1938, and his only child, Valeria, was born the following year.

In the 1940s Bigiaretti succeeded in establishing himself as a man of letters. Leaning politically to the left, he was active in the Resistance during World War II and barely escaped being captured by the Fascists. In 1942 he published his first novel, *Esterina,* a novel that anticipates many of the concerns analyzed in later works. Bigiaretti's protagonist seeks, through the experience of love, the ideal synthesis with the other only to discover that the self cannot be one with the other, that the two halves constitute and inhabit separate and irreconcilable worlds. The success of this work led him, once the war was over, to devote all his time to writing short stories, novels, and essays. After the war he contributed to newspapers and magazines with a wide circulation, such as *Rinascita, L'Avanti, L'Unità,* and *La fiera Letteraria.* He also worked for the National Writers Union, which he founded in 1945 with Corrado Alvaro and Francesco Jovine, and began his distinguished career as a translator.

Bigiaretti has often emphasized his coming late to literature after cultivating painting and drawing and after being trained as a craftsman. Certainly his approach to writing is that of a craftsman: he constantly polished his prose, taking a special pride in the finished product. Indeed, few contemporary writers can match his skill, his meticulous attention to detail, his sense of careful and balanced construc-

Bigiaretti's self-portrait, September 1959

tion that rivals an architect's. At heart Bigiaretti remained a craftsman, never hesitating to remind his readers of his nonliterary origins. Even the fashionable architect in his 1966 novel, *Le indulgenze* (Indulgences), is described as having "un corpo da operaio" (the body of a laborer). But unlike Umberto Saba, whose early works show his limited schooling, nothing in Bigiaretti's writing betrays him as a self-taught, self-made author. *Esterina* may be a youthful work, but it is as accomplished as *Il viaggiatore,* the last expression of Bigiaretti's maturity.

Bigiaretti continued to explore aspects of the dialectical clash between the self and the other in the next two novels he published in the decade. In *Una amicizia difficile* (A Difficult Friendship, 1945) the other is an unfamiliar world into which the protagonists are thrust. The novel shows the process of growing up, and again the attempt of the individual to transcend difference fails while the solitude of the self, the gap between the ideal and reality, is sorrowfully rediscovered and reaffirmed. The third novel, *Il villino* (The Villa, 1946), registers another failure, that of the individual who seeks to improve his social condition.

In his fiction Bigiaretti creates a specific self that in each work, though in different ways, reflects his life. From *Esterina* to *Il viaggiatore,* Bigiaretti's protagonist is always someone from a working-class background who leaves a village to move to the city, is compelled to adapt and adjust, experiences displacement and alienation, and is often divided between the world he left and the world he must inhabit. The city and the village, the focal points of his experiences, are nearly always identified with Rome and his native Matelica. Later, after his twelve years in northern Italy (1952–1963) and his many summers spent in Vallerano, a little town close to Viterbo, where he bought a country home previously owned by Corrado Alvaro, Bigiaretti wrote about these places as well. Ivrea and Milan are contrasted with Rome, but they never replace it.

The specific image of a father involved in construction, often frustrated in his business deals and in his ambition to improve his condition, sometimes in conflict with his son, often accompanies and complements the basic identity of the protagonist. *Carlone* (1950), an idealized biography of Bigiaretti's father, written like *Il villino* in the third person, projects the son's identity onto that of the father. In the novel there is a son who dies shortly after his birth. Bigiaretti apparently felt compelled to confront himself, through the experience of the previous generation symbolized by his father, with the history of twentieth-century Italy, the other that historically defines the contemporary self. With this novel Bigiaretti begins to postulate, for the first time, the encounter with the other in cautiously positive terms.

In 1949 Bigiaretti was sent as a special correspondent to Russia where he and Pablo Neruda were among the first Western reporters to see the ruins of Stalingrad and to witness Russia's reconstruction efforts. In 1952 Adriano Olivetti asked him to manage Olivetti's press office at Ivrea. He worked there with other prominent Italian intellectuals such as Paolo Volponi, Franco Fortini, and Geno Pampaloni until 1964 without, however, interrupting his literary activities. In 1957 his wife, Eugenia, died. In 1961, he met Matilde Crespi, a fashion writer, and married her in 1962.

In 1952, three years before Pier Paolo Pasolini created his "ragazzi di vita" (low-life youngsters), Bigiaretti had already portrayed his "ragazzo del giro" (thieving youngster) in *La scuola dei ladri* (A School for Thieves). Pasolini wrote in the third person, accurately registering the language, the behavior, the scandalous living conditions of the Roman subproletarian youth, but his writing was motivated by and subordinated to political ends. Bigiaretti, as a man of the Left, was as interested as Pasolini in the material and intellectual progress of Italian society, but his young petty thief came into existence as an act of understanding and empathy. Bigiaretti retraced and researched his personal experiences as a youngster in Rome living in the poorer sections of the city, discovering the circumstances, the influences, the psychological elements that could have led him to become like his protagonist.

To find the other in oneself means to discover aspects that are common and universal; making a character real, or believable in fiction, implies identifying the steps that will trigger the transformation or the evolution of the self into another. An unpredictable shift, a moment of insight, perhaps on a subconscious level, must occur to determine the transformation of the writer's self into that of his character. Jacques Monod's essay on natural philosophy, *Le hasard et la nécessité* (Chance and Necessity, 1970) is an important source for understanding the philosophical principles underlying Bigiaretti's process. His novels are usually written in the first person, because any character begins his existence in the concrete self of the writer; then, through "uno scarto improvviso," a sudden shift, the self becomes the reality of the other. In this fashion, Bigiaretti's subjective procedures allow him in *La scuola dei ladri* to produce an objective portrayal of the alienating social conditions that existed in Italy in the 1950s.

Whereas in his early novels Bigiaretti presented the alienation of the self in sentimental terms, he portrayed it objectively as the basic aspect of the human condition beginning in the 1950s. With *I figli* (The Sons, 1954) and *Disamore* (Not Really Love, 1956) Bigiaretti explores in greater depth the ambiguities of feelings, the difference between what one feels and what one thinks one should feel. In contrast to *Carlone*, *I figli* depicts a clash between fathers and sons, suggesting that while the self is a product of history, it is nevertheless alienated from it. With *Disamore* Bigiaretti portrays the alienation that the self seeks to mask through the "comedy or diplomacy of feelings."

Starting in 1963 with *Il congresso,* a novel that reflects his experiences as an intellectual in the business world, and continuing in the subsequent novels, Bigiaretti's protagonists are no longer young men; instead they reflect their aging author. He moves eventually from the successful professional man portrayed in *Il congresso* and in *Le indulgenze* to the retired scholar of *Il viaggiatore,* where Bigiaretti describes the experience of his own progressive isolation. In the latter work one also finds references to Bigiaretti's travels during the 1960s, 1970s, and the early 1980s. Recurring throughout, with different emphasis in each story, one also finds allusions to Bigiaretti's early training as a craftsman and a painter.

Il congresso is the first of a series of novels in which Bigiaretti deals with the other in positive terms. He specifically analyzes the feeling of commitment to society, to one's profession, to one's ideals, and to another person. In each case the self can only be defined through the consciousness it will eventually acquire of its alienation from the other. Unlike Cesare Pavese, Bigiaretti does not see the fundamental reality of the individual self as being tragic. Tragedy for Bigiaretti is the rejection of the human condition as it is, which entails the refusal of life and the negation and annnihilation of the self. Only if one accepts the condition of dissatisfaction and alienation can one begin to come to terms with the other. The secret is simply to accept the gift of life for what it is, to enjoy all the illusions one may wish to entertain and even recognize the necessity of nurturing such illusions, provided one does not confuse illusion with reality.

In *Le indulgenze,* dedicated to Bigiaretti's second wife, Bigiaretti explores the illusion of romantic love, or *disamore.* In spite of its premise of disamore, *Le indulgenze* is, nevertheless, a love story. In it, the other, a city, a society, or a woman emblematically symbolizing them, is initially perceived as extraneous and threatening, to be approached with an attitude of diffidence and self-defense or to be exploited, if possible. At first the protagonist only wishes to take Eva to bed and is wary of any other entanglement; yet, by learning to be tolerant, even compassionate toward her, and by learning to accept her shortcomings, he discovers in the end that, like a mirror, she allows him to see himself and vice versa. Bigiaretti's characters, carefully drawn from Italian life as it evolved in the past fifty years, are endowed with such an extraordinary capacity to penetrate the most subtle psychological motivations that they become universal and timeless. In *Le indulgenze* the acceptance of the other is translated, for the first time, into the acceptance of the self. The condition of disamore in the protagonist's relation to other human beings still obtains, for, while the self reflects itself in the other, it cannot become the other. Yet love is possible because the self loves and justifies in the other his own limitations. Again and again, Bigiaretti is fond of repeating, with typical irony, that we are always prepared to understand and forgive ourselves.

In the two novels that followed, *La controfigura* (The Stunt Double, 1968) and *Dalla donna alla luna* (From the Planet Woman to the Moon, 1972) and later, in *Due senza* (Double Sculls, No Coxswain, 1979), Bigiaretti attempts subtle, experimental analyses of human relations by investigating the myths and taboos that define social behavior. His psychological penetration is increasingly coupled with psychoanalytic observations and intuitions, sometimes resulting in surrealistic effects. Marriage, that most basic of human institutions where the self opts to live in symbiosis with the other, is explored in the context of the new Italian middle class of the 1970s, at a time of economic prosperity.

The male protagonist of *La controfigura* is apparently happily married to a pretty young lady, Lucia, who seems to represent the kind of modern and fashionable wife that a successful young man would want. It is a comfortable marriage like many others, with the usual petty arguments, jealousies, and misunderstandings. The husband, however, is in love not with Lucia but with the ideal that she so imperfectly represents. Nora, the protagonist's mother-in-law, is the complete woman Lucia cannot be, her stunt double. Bigiaretti shows that the marriage bond can exist only when husband and wife accept each other as they are. If the husband seeks the ideal woman rather than the real one, the relationship will be destroyed, for any game works only if the players accept its rules. The point of the novel is that the self's perception of the other is blurred by contradictory desires and expectations. Bigiaretti, who casts his allegory in a contemporary self-indulgent society, elegantly drives the plot to its logical conclusion. The mother-in-law, a beautiful and available forty-year-old, is far from unreachable.

In *Dalla donna alla luna* Bigiaretti narrows the sphere of human action that defines the self to the confines of the alienated mind. The deep uneasiness of the self toward the other displayed for a moment by the husband in *La controfigura* when in a fit of jealousy he wishes to eliminate the putative lover of both his wife and mother-in-law in this novel reaches the pathological level of neurosis, for the self has come to refuse the encounter with the other and has turned inward, to madness. Bigiaretti shows that when the self turns inward, either reality or humanity is abolished. One either ends up in a straightjacket or having a finger on the button of a destructive device. Bigiaretti undertakes this voyage into the diseased mind through one of those sudden shifts that turn the familiar elements of Bigiaretti's life into negative images. For the novelist irony and detachment are the only elements that can exorcise tragedy and madness and enable one to live with the paradoxes of life.

Bigiaretti often explores the point that marriage, as a dimension in which the self seeks permanently to embrace the other, is at best inauthentic

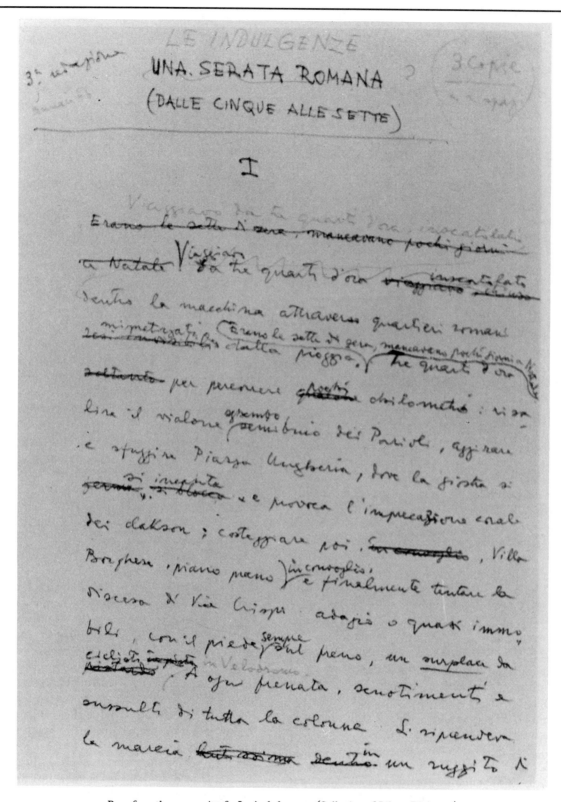

Page from the manuscript for Le indulgenze *(Collection of Libero Bigiaretti)*

and unsatisfactory. In *Due senza,* where the title pointedly comments on the married condition through the language of rowing, the first-person protagonist is a detached observer, an old bachelor sociologist studying an average married couple. Bigiaretti pokes fun at sociological jargon by having his protagonist coin new terms to define the separate components, or halves, of the married couple: *semicoppie* or "demicouples." The amusing investigation eventually establishes that there are many reasons for the two demicouples to go their own separate ways, but oddly enough this does not happen. Moreover, the investigator, having met the unattached mother-in-law of one of the characters in question, loses the little objectivity he has and veers dangerously toward marriage himself.

Between *Dalla donna alla luna* and *Due senza,* Bigiaretti wrote *Le stanze* (The Suite, 1976), his most overtly autobiographical novel. Although Bigiaretti identifies himself as the first-person protagonist, the book is a fascinating work of fiction, not a typical autobiography, for the author does not provide a chronological account of the important events in his life. Bigiaretti as always searches for meaning and definition, but the search is conditioned by memory. The protagonist is what he remembers, for what he cannot remember is not a part of his consciousness. Moreover, consciousness is not linear, follows no chronological order, and is not bound by place. Self-consciousness is not a single act of remembering but many acts activated by external stimuli. Memory makes places and times that are separated in space and time present simultaneously in the consciousness of the self. Bigiaretti calls these places *stanze,* rooms in the home of his psyche. Even in this most personal narrative, he writes for others. The reader, moving through the different rooms of Bigiaretti's self, discovers that he inhabits similar rooms with similar functions. *Le stanze* is the best evidence that his creativity has been dedicated to the proposition that the examined life of one individual encompasses the life of all human beings.

With *Il viaggiatore,* a work rich in allegorical possibilities, Bigiaretti returns for the last time in the novel form to confront the ambivalence of the self toward the other. Here the other is death, or the self stripped of all its illusions and hopes. The spontaneous acceptance of life must have as a corollary the reluctant acceptance of death. The protagonist, a retired historian, obsessively analyzes his casual friendship with another retiree at a summer resort in southern Italy. He sees in his acquaintance all the signs of the same monomania he cannot see in himself. A *scarto improvviso* that jolts the reader as well as the protagonist occurs at the very end of the novel.

After the historian returns home from his vacation, he looks at a photo of himself and the other retiree, the only souvenir of the summer vacation that symbolizes his life. He is shocked to discover that, in the tricky light, in spite of the real physical differences between the two men, one can easily be confused with the other.

Bigiaretti served as the general editor of a series of major literary works in Italian translation called I Classici della Letteratura (Major Literary Writers) published by Curcio. He continued to write poetry and short stories until the end of his life, despite the sudden death of his much-loved daughter in 1988. *Posto di blocco* (1986; translated as *Checkpoint: Poems of Death and Old Age,* 1992) is a collection distinguished by the poignant concision, directness, and deceptively simple language, mark the last phase of Bigiaretti's art. The poems testify equally to his craftsmanship, his continual evolution as a writer, and to the unity of his poetics. Angelo Mundula, reviewing Bigiaretti's last collection of short stories, *Abitare altrove* (Living elsewhere, 1990) in *L'osservatore romano* (1990), praised the insightfulness that had marked the writer's career: "Insomma, il 'vecchio' Bigiaretti la sa lunga. Finge di *abitare altrove* e abita invece, nientemeno che nel cuore stesso dell'uomo e della società in cui vive ed opera" (Old Bigiaretti has yet another tale to spin. He pretends to live elsewhere, but, in fact, he lives in the very heart of man and his society). In 1992 Bigiaretti published the essay *Con i tempi che corrono* (The Times We Live in), a serene reflection on his long literary life. In April 1993 he published his last work, *Un sogno di ferragosto* (A Midsummer Dream), a short story written in August 1992 when his health was rapidly deteriorating. It provides a fitting conclusion to his lifetime work and explicitly presents, with ironic detachment, his agnostic view of life. He died in his Roman apartment, with his wife by his side, on 3 May 1993, two weeks before his eighty-eighth birthday.

Bigiaretti's work, spanning fifty years of Italian culture, has been receptive to different influences without ever being identified with a specific literary trend. Actively involved in Italian intellectual life, he could not avoid absorbing suggestions that came from such movements as *rondismo* (the return to well-crafted poetic forms), Hermeticism, Neorealism, and the "industrial" novel. At times, his work anticipates other writers, as is the case with *La scuola dei ladri* and Pasolini. *Le indulgenze* can be read as a long meditative response to the tragic alienation of Pavese's *Tra donne sole* (1949; translated as *Among Women Only,* 1959), just as *Carlone* addresses the very questions Pavese had agonized over in *La casa in collina* (1948; translated as *The House on the Hill,* 1956).

Bigiaretti's works balance psychological penetration with realistic portraits of society that reflect different stages in the evolution of Italian life in the last half century. In the 1940s and 1950s he described the limited horizons of the provincial world of the Italian proletariat and middle class in the years before and immediately after World War II. In the 1960s he depicted the economic boom with its positive as well as damaging effects, and in the 1970s and 1980s the newly found wealth and the pursuit of pleasure and leisure. His keen eye and ironic detachment in describing ephemeral trends, fashions, and personalities as well as his ability to see through appearances have also earned him the label of moralist. But this and other labels define only some aspects of Bigiaretti's art, which could best be described as allegorical realism.

As a sharp observer of evolving social life in Italy, Bigiaretti has kept a steady eye on Rome, which serves as both the central stage and the background for his stories. His sketches of the eternal city have been gathered in *Questa Roma* (This Rome, 1981). Bigiaretti's thoughts on literature and its role in contemporary society are thoughtfully articulated in several carefully edited and published interviews. Particularly important in this connection is the essay in the form of a letter, *Il dito puntato* (Pointing the Finger, 1967), addressed to Valentino Bompiani.

A modest man, Bigiaretti considered himself a minor writer. Deeply esteemed by many of his colleagues, he enjoyed moments of popularity in the 1960s and 1970s, but the press never accorded him the attention that sustained the careers of some of his contemporaries and virtually ignored his work in the 1980s, when, in spite of the quality of his continuing productivity, he became virtually isolated and forgotten. By identifying him with the generation of Pavese, critics have placed his works within the general framework of Neorealism. The absence of social and political indictments in his narrative, at a time when ideology and political activism dominated Italian letters and criticism, earned him a respected but less important position among his more celebrated contemporaries. Even his best critics, while appreciating the originality of his individual works, failed to see that the unity of his inspiration stemmed from his positive, persistent investigation of the contradictions of the human condition. For this reason they failed to see as well that his art, while rooted in the forms of French realism, is pervaded with the spirit and irony of Italo Svevo and Luigi Pirandello.

The parable described by Bigiaretti's fiction can be said to have a parallel in Svevo's trilogy, as it moves from the sentimental failures of Bigiaretti's early works to a cautious, ironic acceptance of life and death. With the crumbling of the ideological certainties of the old Left, it should be possible to see the continued relevance and interest of Bigiaretti's works. Some recent reviews seem to point in that direction. Upon Bigiaretti's death, long commemorative articles appeared in *Il Corriere della Sera* and in all the main Italian newspapers, and his passing prompted wide national television coverage. Such attention may indicate serious and far-ranging reassessments of his career to come.

References:

Luigi Baldacci, "Libero Bigiaretti: Amore e cultura nella società di massa," in *Novecento,* volume 9, edited by Gianni Grana (Milan: Marzorati, 1979);

Giorgio Baroni, *Libero Bigiaretti* (Florence: La Nuova Italia, 1980);

Gabriele Erasmi, "Autodídaktos d'eimí: Libero Bigiaretti e il rapporto con l'altro ne *Le indulgenze* e ne *Il viaggiatore,*" *Quaderni d'italianistica,* 11 (Spring 1990): 61–71;

Geno Pampaloni, "La nuova letteratura," *Storia della letteratura italiana. Il Novecento* (Milan: Garzanti, 1969);

Ugo Piscopo, *Libero Bigiaretti* (Naples: Editrice Ferraro, 1977);

Piscopo, "Libero Bigiaretti," *Letteratura italiana: Novecento: I contemporanei,* volume 9, edited by Gianni Gravia (Milan: Marzorati, 1979), pp. 8825–8846;

Luigi Silori, *Invito alla lettura di Bigiaretti* (Milan: Mursia, 1977);

Giacinto Spagnoletti, *Scrittori di un secolo,* volume 2 (Milan: Marzorati, 1974);

Ferdinando Virdia, "Libero Bigiaretti," in *Letteratura italiana: I contemporanei,* volume 2 (Milan: Marzorati, 1975), pp. 1371–1394.

Giuseppe Bonaviri

(11 July 1924 –)

Umberto Mariani
Rutgers University

BOOKS: *Il sarto della stradalunga* (Turin: Einaudi, 1954);

La contrada degli ulivi (Venice: Sodalizio del Libro, 1958);

Il fiume di pietra (Turin: Einaudi, 1964);

La divina foresta (Milan: Rizzoli, 1969);

Notti sull'altura (Milan: Rizzoli, 1971); translated by Giovanni R. Bussino as *Nights on the Heights* (New York: Peter Lang, 1990);

Le armi d'oro (Milan: Rizzoli, 1973);

L'isola amorosa (Milan: Rizzoli, 1973);

La Beffària (Milan: Rizzoli, 1975);

L'enorme tempo (Milan: Rizzoli, 1976);

Follia, edited by Georgio Barberi Squarotti (Catania: Società di Storia Patria, 1976);

Martedina e Il dire celeste (Rome: Editori Riuniti, 1976);

Dolcissimo (Milan: Rizzoli, 1978); translated by Umberto Mariani as *Dolcissimo* (New York: Italica Press, 1990);

Il treno blu (Florence: La Nuova Italia, 1978);

Il dire celeste e altre poesie (Milan: Guanda, 1979);

Nel silenzio della luna (Sora: Dioscuri, 1979);

Novelle saracene (Milan: Rizzoli, 1980);

Di fumo cilestrino (Ancona: Dossier Arte, 1981);

Quark (Rome: Edizioni della Cometa, 1982);

O corpo sospiroso (Milan: Rizzoli, 1982);

L'incominciamento (Palermo: Sellerio, 1983);

L'arenario (Milan: Rizzoli, 1984);

L'asprura (Rome: Edizioni della Cometa, 1985);

È un rosseggiar di peschi e d'albicocchi (Milan: Rizzoli, 1986);

Lip to lip (Lecce: Manni, 1988);

Il dormiveglia (Milan: Mondadori, 1988);

Ghigò (Milan: Mondadori, 1990);

Il re bambino (Milan: Mondadori, 1990);

Fiabe siciliane (Milan: Mondadori, 1990);

Apologhetti (Catania: Il Girasole, 1991);

Il dire celeste (Milan: Mondadori, 1993);

Il dottor bilob (Palermo: Sellerio, 1994);

Silvina (Milan: Mondadori, 1996);

Giufà e altre storie della terra di Sicilia (Milan: Mondadori, 1996).

OTHER: Settimo Emanuele Bonaviri, *L'arcano,* edited by Bonaviri (Frosinone: Bianchini Printing Shop, 1975);

"Autobiografia di uno scrittore," *Archivio storico per la Sicilia orientale,* 76 (1980): 313–322.

Giuseppe Bonaviri is one of the foremost Italian writers of the second half of the twentieth century; his opus is so extensive and impressive that in recent years he has often been mentioned as a possible candidate for the Nobel Prize for literature. Primarily a novelist, Bonaviri also writes poetry and short fiction of remarkable originality. He has published a play and a volume of literary criticism and is a frequent contributor to the literary pages of newspapers and magazines; in fact, there is hardly a literary genre that has not engaged this unique writer.

Bonaviri's masterpieces belong to the middle period of his creative activity, beginning with *La divina foresta* (1969) and including *Notti sull'altura* (1971), *Dolcissimo* (1978), and *Novelle saracene* (1980). These works embody a complex and original view of reality, a new cosmology, a new anthropology. It is neither the animistic, pantheistic vision of Bonaviri's Sicilian ancestry nor the scientific worldview of his formal education (he is a practicing physician), but a poetic synthesis of both, "an altogether different poetic intuition," as he describes it, which "attempts to reflect the deeply disturbing way we live now."

Bonaviri's major works express the pain of man's violent passage through the twentieth century. Men and women have suffered the anguish of an age of restlessness and rapid change, losing the certitudes of the past while still longing for some form of salvation from both solitude and mortality. Bonaviri expresses his view of reality through language that fuses his Sicilian and scientific cultures in a prose different from any other, frequently abandoning ordinary logic and making the startling leaps one associates with modern poetry. Often relying on sound, rhythm, and sequences of objective cor-

Giuseppe Bonaviri with his grandson Gianluigi (photograph by Emanuele Bonaviri)

relatives to carry his meaning, he disconcerts the reader's rational expectations, creating his own logic.

Giuseppe Bonaviri was born on 11 July 1924 in Mineo, Sicily, a town built atop one of the hills that form a range rising from the plain of Catania, with magnificent views of Catania and the Ionian Sea as well as of the higher mountains of central Sicily. Bonaviri maintains that Mineo—with its beautiful landscape, flora, deep blue sky, clear firmament, and constant winds that with the changing seasons bring new fragrances, sounds, and flights of birds—exercises a powerful stimulus on the imagination of its inhabitants, so that many simple peasants and artisans took part in the yearly poetic competition once held nearby. Settimo Emanuele, Bonaviri's father, was a tailor and secretly wrote poetry. Bonaviri edited his father's poetry eleven years after his death in a collection titled *L'arcano* (1975). Most of Mineo's poets, however, composed in an exclusively oral tradition and recited their poems at local competitions or at any other suitable festive gathering. Bonaviri's mother, Giuseppina Casaccio, like many of the women of Mineo, was a treasurehouse of old tales and entertained her children on countless winter nights; she had learned many of her stories from old townsfolk and eventually heeded her son's plea to write some of them down, shortly before she died in her eighties.

Bonaviri has repeatedly stated that the beauty of his native town and the nature of its people were influential in shaping his imagination and giving him an inexhaustible fund of memories from which to draw. Mineo is the emotional setting for all of his major works, even when the stories are located in India, as in *È un rosseggiar di peschi e d'albicocchi* (1986), or before the gates of Troy, as in *Le armi d'oro* (1973). He gives Mineo different names—Qalàt Minàw in *Notti sull'altura,* Nanénia in *La Beffària* (1975), Tjmucah in *L'isola amorosa* (1973), and Zebulonia in *Dolcissimo*—but it is always Mineo that haunts his memory, even in outer space, as in *Martedina e Il dire celeste* (1976).

Bonaviri began to write before he was ten. He first wrote poems and short stories and then novels and plays, keeping everything he wrote, finished or unfinished. He continued to write through his high school years in the nearby provincial capital, Catania, where he entered medical school in 1943, receiving his degree in 1949 and a specialization in cardiology in 1955. Some of his youthful works were later published in *Il treno blu* (1978), a collection of short stories, and in two volumes of poems, *Di fumo cilestrino* (1981) and *Quark* (1982). While awaiting his draft notice, he began a novel that he continued to work on at the military academy in Florence and at training camps in Alessandria and Casale in Piedmont; he took the finished manuscript to the Turin publisher Einaudi, where it was accepted by Elio Vittorini, the editor for a series dedicated primarily to new young writers.

The novel *Il sarto della stradalunga* (The Tailor of Main Street, 1954) is largely the story of Bonaviri's childhood. The central figures are the members of his own family, particularly his father, the tailor of the title with the shop on Main Street, although many events, including the crucial death of the mother at the beginning of the story, are invented. It is a story of loss and tragedy as well as nurturing and love, told in a starkly realistic language yet permeated by a powerful imagination so that it reads like a stylized exemplary tale in which the earth and the sky seem to share in the suffering of the Sciré family.

If one considers that the years of the book's composition, from 1949 to 1951, were the peak years of Italian Neorealism, when it was thought almost heretical to write in anything other than a documentary style about the tragedy and suffering of the Fascist period, the war, the German occupation, and the Resistance, the originality of Bonaviri's first published novel is clear. Clear, too, are the signs of his future development, particularly his use of fantasy, as the next works, *La contrada degli ulivi* (The Land of the Olive Trees, 1958), a book of short stories, and *Il fiume di pietra,* (1964), his second novel, were to confirm.

Il fiume di pietra (River of Stone) deals with the end of Fascism as the war front moved through the Mineo region in the summer of 1943. At the time, the nineteen-year-old Bonaviri was soon to enter medical school, but in the novel he makes the dramatic events of that summer coincide with the early adolescent experience of his narrator. Thus, the experiences are lived and related as though they were playful adventures in which the narrator and his band of adolescent friends are participants. Indeed, the boys gradually become the orchestrators of almost every important event: the final depredations of the retreating Fascists, the exploits of the Allied soldiers, and the punishments and celebrations attending the replacement of the local authorities.

The narrator and his friends seem to assume authority for the duration of the transition, subverting all military, political, and social functions and all the rules of ordinary living. Everything is turned into a game with its own rules and rituals. Two bands of boys roam the area, one dedicated to play, the other to necrophilia; the first group is subversive of the adult world, while the second carries its imitation of that world to extremes, specializing particularly in the ritual burial of cats. The two adversarial groups come together when the leader of the first is accidentally killed by a bomb and the leader of the second is designated to provide the proper ritual that will signal the conclusion of their extraordinary summer-long adolescent carnival. Bonaviri also treats significant historical events through the eyes of a group of boys in *Le armi d'oro* (Arms of

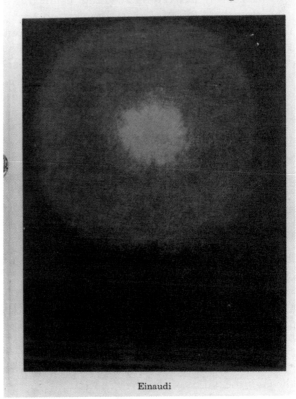

Giuseppe Bonaviri

Il fiume di pietra

Einaudi

Dust jacket for Bonaviri's second novel, in which the end of Fascism is seen through the eyes of a young boy

Gold), a book he wrote for adolescent readers that reconstructs some events of the Trojan War.

As a young doctor Bonaviri worked for a few years in Mineo, part of that time as a public health officer, and was often involved in fruitless struggles with the corrupt, do-nothing provincial and municipal governments. The experience was to become the source of *L'enorme tempo* (A Dreadful Time), written in the early 1950s but not published until 1976. It is the most neorealistic novel Bonaviri ever wrote in being the most biographic and documentary, yet it is richly inventive as well. It is not the diary of a country doctor but a descent into the purgatory of a region still steeped in superstition and pagan rituals, a place of misery for the poor and impotence and indifference for the authorities, of rampant endemic sickness and death regarded with so great a familiarity that the open common grave of the cemetery is a tolerated spectacle. The worst enemy of progress is ignorance, and in the world depicted nothing can move. The newly gained democracy leads to stagnation, because the very people who suffer most from the present conditions are the most opposed to change. The only change taking place is the mass emigration of the young.

In 1955 Bonaviri took an additional degree in cardiology and left Mineo, settling eventually in Frosinone, south of Rome, where he married a local grade-school teacher, Raffaella Osario, in 1957. As a member of the staff of the local hospital, he experienced even greater anguish and frustration than in Mineo. Some of that experience was translated into fiction in the earthbound first half of *Martedina,* written in 1960 but not published until 1976. In 1964 Bonaviri began private practice as a cardiologist, which since has allowed him to dedicate half of his time to writing. Most of Bonaviri's novels are stories of quest, transformation, and maturation. The recurring journey, whether in the familiar territory of Mineo or in the fantastic regions Mineo is transformed into, moves toward the discovery of the self and of one's place within the realm of nature. Yet the quest often appears to be fruitless, when it is not clearly a failure.

Bonaviri's first novel clearly structured on such a journey is *La divina foresta* (The Divine Forest), which signals a new direction in his fiction with the introduction of a cosmological motif. The narrator's story begins when, as a molecule, it is tossed through the winds of space; it finds, in the vicinity of Mineo, the propitious environment for its later metamorphoses and adventures, first as a plant and later as a hawk. The work describes a world in the making, evolving with consciousness of its constituent elements, mostly through encounters, dialogues, and fusions with each other. The elements will their detachment from the formless, nameless, primal matter of the universe and their acquisition of conscious individuality, an act that releases the springs of wonder, curiosity, and knowledge.

In the same year that man landed on the moon to explore an alien and inhospitable environment, Bonaviri's protagonist chooses the earth. While his contemporaries make history through computer calculations and supposedly infallible diagrams, believing everything quantifiable and measurable, Bonaviri decries the human behaviors that are making the earth uninhabitable; he poses the barrenness of modern industry and the metropolis against a world yet uncontaminated by the machinery of man, a world in which evolution toward higher forms of life occurs nonviolently, through mutations obeying natural rhythms, without disturbing nature's fertility, as man does whenever he appears in the novel. When man is not present, the world the novel depicts is a feast of sounds and smells, a rustling and murmuring of forests and streams. The novel thus suggests a restoration of what is being lost by its vision of how things were before man's disturbance and destruction.

The novels that followed all recur to and renew this contrast between the world being lost and the one being made. *Notti sull'altura* (1971; tranlated as *Nights on the Heights,* 1990), a more complex novel than *La divina foresta,* creates an even more magical atmosphere. The story is deceptively simple. At the death of his father, the narrator returns home and, with all the other members of his family and the townsfolk, undertakes a search for the "spiritual remains" of the patriarch, whose body has been given the traditional burial.

While the specific goal proves elusive, the search is rich in discoveries of all sorts: of the universe that surrounds Mineo in all directions, including the sea and the sky; of the wondrous things and the surprising people encountered; and eventually of the fate of the searchers themselves. In Bonaviri's fusion of his ancestral childhood mythologies with his scholarly knowledge of the history of human consciousness from astrology to alchemy to modern science, the novel becomes a journey of collective and individual discovery of both physical and human nature. On a deeper level, the journey symbolizes the search for an understanding of life and death, for consolation in the face of the grim reality of human mortality, for an answer to the ultimate question of human existence—whether beyond biological death man has any place in the cosmos and in what form.

Bonaviri creates an original world of his own that owes little to writers past or contemporary. His work must be approached on its own terms and cannot be understood by referring to Gabriel García Márquez or magical realists, or to the Sicilian writer Elio Vittorini, or to the neorealists or the avant-gardists—the allusions often found in his reviews. His prose is always sinuously moving from realistic to lyrical, from arcane to spellbinding.

L'isola amorosa (The Loving Island) is another story of a journey: this time from the roof of a metropolitan skyscraper to the floating island of Tjmucah, from the dehumanizing and unlivable city of the future to a place and a life of ahistoric, blissful communion with nature and natural rhythms, until an invasion of destructive humans causes another dispersal and exodus. Again, Bonaviri dwells on the meaning and conditions of life in contemporary society. The story line is almost nonexistent, and the meaning of the narrative is entrusted almost exclusively to the flow and the evocative power of its language.

La Beffària (The Big Joke) involves another voyage of discovery but in the opposite direction from that of *L'isola amorosa*. Two explorers, grandfather and grandson, leave hospitable Boozia and Nanenia (the village of tailors, from the nickname of Bonaviri's father, Nané) to travel to Beffària, the inhospitable megalopolis of the present and the future, destined to destruction, from which the two ultimately flee in an air balloon. This novel returns to the satiric-ironic tone found to a lesser extent in the novels *Il fiume di pietra* and *L'enorme tempo* and in the first half of *Martedina*—all works Bonaviri wrote before or around 1960.

In the first half of *Martedina* Bonaviri focuses, often in a satiric vein, on the experience of his protagonist-doctor in a local hospital, a life so alienating and unbearable that he leaves and tries to make a living as a chicken farmer. Woefully unsuccessful, he answers an advertisement for a spaceship physician for a routine space trip that turns into a space odyssey. The portion of *Martedina* that Bonaviri wrote while he was working on *La Beffària* turns into the story of a journey to the scientific and technological world of the future. The inhuman future makes the country-bred astronauts, unlike the city-bred fanatics of science aboard, long for the world they left behind in desperation, a world that in retrospect seems a restful green Eden.

Dolcissimo (translated as *Dolcissimo*) also structured on the journey and the quest, explores death and the possible dimensions of life beyond time. As in *Notti sull'altura,* an initial official inquiry—here soon abandoned, as the searchers are diverted into more meaningful paths of inquiry—is merely a pretext for a whole series of quests. For the narrator the inquiry is also an occasion to return to his birthplace after years of absence. A succinct summation of the geological, archaeological, and historical past of the town is followed by a long and nostalgic re-evocation of the Zebulonia of the narrator's childhood and adolescence.

This journey into what Bonaviri calls the dimension of "ancestral memory" turns the dying town into a garden of delights, rich in spices and perfumes, aromatic herbs, exotic and exquisite fruits, and rare birds—an Eden made richer by the arts of its inhabitants, from the cooking and embroidery of the women to the poetry, music, and crafts of the artisans. The lives of all its inhabitants have been enriched by the extraordinary gifts and deeds of the absent hero of the story, Dolcissimo. The most critical of the townsfolk of Zebulonia, he has disappeared into subterranean regions in search of new dimensions of life.

Dust jacket for Bonaviri's 1978 novel, in which an Italian town is remembered as a culturally rich Eden

In what is probably his finest novel, Bonaviri weaves an adventure of extraordinary resonance, mixing autobiographical detail with rare invention, narrating his story in a style subtly adapted to the richness and strangeness of the worlds it explores. In *Dolcissimo* the poetic language of Bonaviri's prose perfectly harmonizes with its subject. The reader finds it natural when almost an entire chapter is written in verse.

From 1976 to 1985 Bonaviri dedicated much of his time to editing the works of his youth, which included a play, *Follia* (Madness, 1976), the short stories of *Il treno blu* (The Blue Train), and the poems collected in *Nel silenzio della luna* (In the Silence of the Moon, 1979), *Di fumo cilestrino* (Of Bluish Smoke), and *Quark*. In *L'arenario* (The Sandpit, 1984) he gathered some of the literary commentary he had contributed to newspapers and weekly magazines, and in *L'asprura* (Harshness, 1985) he collected the verse he had written shortly after his father's death in 1964.

Bonaviri was also writing new poetry, including *Il dire celeste e altre poesie* (The Language of the Heavens and Other Poems, 1979) and *O corpo sospiroso* (O Sighing Body, 1982), a collection that continues the stylistic experimentation of *Il dire celeste* but focuses on material closer to home, the sensorially rich world of Bonaviri's familiar natural and human landscape. In *L'incominciamento* (Beginnings, 1983) Bonaviri offers poetic versions of narrative pieces on facing pages. The poems gathered in *Il re bambino* (The Baby King, 1990) were written mostly after the birth of his first grandson and are less intense and cerebral, more playful, than his earlier poetry. In the same lighter vein are the prose pieces of *Lip to lip* (1988) and *Apologhetti* (Brief Apologues, 1991).

In *Novelle saracene* Bonaviri transformed the tales his mother used to tell her children, some of which she had written down before she died, into a series of short stories. The Saracen tales have an intensely folk flavor and fit perfectly in the spiritual landscape of the Mineo of memory and myth that Bonaviri had been constructing in his previous work. They derive from the same collective imagination that through the centuries gave Sicily her elaborately ornamented folk carts, her stories recited at country fairs and in marketplaces and the painted scrolls that illustrate them, and her dramatic versions of the clashes between Christian and Moorish warriors in the traditional *pupi* theater. Bonaviri's telling of these Saracen tales makes a remarkable work of art.

È un rosseggiar di peschi e d'albicocchi (Everywhere the Rose of Peach and Apricot Trees) and *Il dormiveglia* (Between Sleep and Waking, 1988) again center on the motif of the quest. In *È un rosseggiar di peschi e d'albicocchi* Bonaviri stresses the meaninglessness, fleetingness, and expendability of human existence through the mystery of his setting, a remote, exotic incarnation of Mineo, and its uncertain place in the cosmos. In *Il dormiveglia* a pair of typical Bonaviri explorers, in the course of a fantastic trip from Sicily to Rome to China to the moon, try to learn about the nature of human consciousness in the state between sleeping and waking. Cut off from the usual awareness and volition of the fully waking state, the consciousness is subjected to involuntary impulses and becomes sublogical, subconscious, perhaps no longer personal but cosmic, under the influence of a universal noosphere. Through the language of the novel Bonaviri attempts to suggest such subconscious mental processes.

Ghigò, published in 1990, is divided into two halves, the first narrated by his mother, the second by Bonaviri. It concerns the events of their lives from her marriage to his arrival in Catania as an adolescent, when he was compelled to leave Mineo for the first time in order to continue his studies in the provincial capital. She stops in the middle of the book, considering that from then on he should have enough memories of the events of his childhood to be able to continue on his own. No previous Bonaviri novel had so closely respected the author's autobiographical data. The charm of the novel lies in the engaging way in which it is told by both narrators and in their ability to charge every detail of their story with wonder and significance, as if it belonged to a fairy tale.

Innovative and outside the mainstream, Bonaviri has often inspired other Italian writers, including some who are widely known. His career has continued into the 1990s and into his eighth decade. Two more collections of Sicilian stories, gathered and retold by the author in his inimitable style, have been published: *Fiabe siciliane* (Sicilian Fables, 1990) and *Giufà e altre storie della terra di Sicilia* (Giufà and Other Stories of Sicily, 1996). In 1993 Mondadori brought out an edition of his complete poems, *Il dire celeste*. Bonaviri has also written two novels that are delicate and whimsical love stories, *Il dottor bilob* (Doctor Bilob, 1994) and *Silvina* (1996). The remarkably productive career of Giuseppe Bonaviri seems to be far from over.

References:

Giuseppe Amoroso, *La narrativa italiana, 1975–1983* (Milan: Mursia, 1983);

Giorgio Barberi Squarotti, *Poesia e narrativa del secondo Novecento* (Milan: Mursia, 1967);

Salvatore Battaglia, "L'arcadia metafisica di Bonaviri," *Il dramma,* 8–9 (August–September 1971): 93–96;

Carmine Di Biase, *Giuseppe Bonaviri: La dimensione dell'oltre* (Naples: Cassitto, 1994);

Rodolfo Di Biasio, *Giuseppe Bonaviri* (Florence: La Nuova Italia, 1978);

La fusta, special issue on Bonaviri, edited by Umberto Mariani, 6 (Spring–Fall 1981);

Emerico Giachery, *Due maestri e cinque amici* (Rome: Argileto, 1974), pp. 27–38;

Antonio Iadanza and Marcellino Carlino, eds., *L'opera di Giuseppe Bonaviri* (Rome: La Nuova Italia Scientifica, 1978);

Mario Landolfi, *Giuseppe Bonaviri: Il romanzo di Mineo* (Naples & Rome: LER, 1990);

Giuliano Manacorda, "Cosmicità e terrestrità di Bonaviri," in *Letteratura nella storia,* volume 2 (Rome: Sciascia, 1989);

Giorgio Manganelli, "Introduzione," in *La divina foresta* (Milan: Rizzoli, 1980);

Carmelo Musumarra, "La favola nuova di Bonaviri," in *Argomenti di letteratura siciliana* (Catania: Giannotta, 1979);

Musumarra, "Ritorno alle radici," *La Sicilia,* 5 October 1990;

Giancarlo Pandini, "L'itinerario nel meraviglioso di Giuseppe Bonaviri," in his *L'oscura devozione* (Milan: Marzorati, 1977), pp. 79–91;

Antonio Ricci, "L'avventura metafisica di Giuseppe Bonaviri," *Italianistica,* 7 (January–April 1978): 205–210;

Gennaro Savarese, "Giuseppe Bonaviri," in *Novecento. I contemporanei,* volume 8, edited by Gianni Grana (Milan: Marzorati, 1979), pp. 7205–7224;

Giuliana Sentella, "Rassegna di studi critici su Bonaviri," *Otto/Novecento,* 4 (September–December 1980): 385–397;

Enzo Siciliano, "Giuseppe Bonaviri: *Novelle saracene,*" *Corriere della sera,* 2 March 1980;

Paolo Mario Sipala, "La lunga strada di Giuseppe Bonaviri," in his *Il romanzo di 'Ntoni Malavoglia e altri saggi sulla narrativa italiana da Verga a Bonaviri* (Bologna: Patron, 1983), pp. 217–227;

Giacinto Spagnoletti, "Allegoria della vita nei romanzi di Bonaviri," in his *Scrittori di un secolo,* volume 2 (Milan: Marzorati, 1974), pp. 1060–1067;

Spagnoletti, "Introduzione," in *O corpo sospiroso* (Milan: Rizzoli, 1982), pp. 5–16;

Franco Zangrilli, *Bonaviri e il mistero cosmico* (Abano Terme: Piovan, 1985);

Zangrilli, *Bonaviri e il tempo* (Catania: Marino, 1986);

Zangrilli, "Giuseppe Bonaviri," in his *La Forza della parola* (Ravenna: Longo, 1992), pp. 87–117;

Zangrilli, *L'immaginario cosmico di Bonaviri* (Catania: La Cantinella, 1996);

Zangrilli, "Pirandello e Bonaviri," in his *Linea pirandelliana nella narrativa contemporanea* (Ravenna: Longo, 1990);

Sarah Zappulla Muscarà, ed., *Giuseppe Bonaviri* (Catania: Maimone, 1991).

Alessandro Bonsanti

(15 November 1904 – 18 February 1984)

Andrea Guiati
State University of New York at Buffalo

BOOKS: *La serva amorosa* (Florence: Solaria, 1929);
I capricci dell'Adriana (Florence: Solaria, 1934);
Racconto militare (Florence: Parenti, 1937);
Dialoghi e altre prose (Florence: Parenti, 1940);
Introduzione al gran viaggio (Rome: Tuminelli, 1944);
La vipera e il toro (Florence: Sansoni, 1955);
Sopra alcuni personaggi eventuali (Sarzana: Carpena, 1956);
I cavalli di bronzo (Florence: Sansoni, 1956);
Racconti lontani (Milan: Mondadori, 1962);
La buca di San Colombano, 3 volumes (Milan: Mondadori, 1964);
La nuova stazione di Firenze (Milan: Mondadori, 1965);
Teatro domestico (Milan: Mondadori, 1968);
Portolani d'agosto, 1971–1974 (Milan: Mondadori, 1978).

Alessandro Bonsanti's writing career spanned fifty years: he published his first work in 1928 and his last in 1978. He was most popular during the 1950s and the 1960s. In those decades Bonsanti was considered the most prolific and best representative of the *prosa dell'arte,* (artistic prose) writers, a literary movement inspired by the neobaroque style of artistic expression, prevalent especially in the seventeenth century, which is marked by extravagant and elaborate forms. Such dynamics are clearly evident in Bonsanti's complex, ingenious, bizarre, and often ambiguous prose.

Alessandro Bonsanti was born on 15 November 1904 in Florence. His family, unable to afford to live in the city, moved to the country, where young Bonsanti spent most of his adolescence. The memories of those years occur frequently in his work; indeed, they are the fulcrum of his regionally based narrative. Bonsanti went back to Florence to attend the university, where he majored in engineering. However, the family's economic conditions prevented him from finishing his studies, and he was forced to find an occupation to support himself and his aging parents. Bonsanti was drafted in 1925 and served in the army for one year. In 1926 he moved

Portrait of Alessandro Bonsanti by Vieri Freccia, circa 1930
(Alessandro Bonsanti Collection)

to Milan, where he found employment as a bank teller. At the same time, he developed a strong interest in Italian writers. The world of finance would never interest him as much as the world of literature. He started to write in 1928.

In addition to writing, Bonsanti devoted his energies to other endeavors. After returning to Florence and publishing his first novel, *La serva amorosa* (The Amorous Maid, 1929), he codirected with Alberto Carocci the review *Solaria* from 1930 to 1932. He taught history of the theater at the Conservatory of Music in Bologna, and in 1937 he founded the journal *Letteratura.* In 1945 he and Eugenio Montale founded the short-lived periodical, *Il mondo,* which ceased publication in 1947. He became the director of the Gabinetto Scientifico-Letterario Viessieux in Florence in 1941, a position he held until 1980. He also served as the curator of the Archivio Contemporaneo from 1979 to 1983, securing from the city of Florence a magnificent historic building, the Palazzo Corsini-Suarez, to house the institution. Shortly before his death in 1984, Bonsanti was elected mayor of his native city.

Bonsanti was twenty-four years old and living in Milan when he published his first work, the short story "Briganti in Maremma" (Outlaws in Maremma), in the cultural review *La fiera letteraria.* Set in the harsh countryside of Maremma in the nineteenth century, it is a story of sensuality involving a Tuscan farmer, Bardozzo. One night Bardozzo is forced to give hospitality to four outlaws, among them Paolo Tecchia and his mistress, Rosa. Bonsanti's skills as a narrator are apparent from the first paragraphs of the story as he captures the reader's interest by intimating that something unusual is going to happen and draws a fine psychological portrait of the protagonist. While the plot is simple and the action limited, Bonsanti capitalizes on the element of suspense, as Bardozzo, at the end of the story, makes love to Rosa outside his old farmhouse.

Bardozzo, who is painted as being anything but bright, finds himself in an awkward situation, makes the best of it, and enjoys an unexpected experience. The reader sympathizes with him. Bonsanti depicts the simple lifestyle of Tuscan farmers and their daily existence, steering clear of the political turmoil of the time. The farmer takes full control of the situation, and the episode of lovemaking becomes the heart of the story. The work remains focused on the relationship between a man and a woman and his erotic memories from adolescence. One of the memories is framed in the form of a story, which he tells to entertain his guests and excite Rosa. The geographical setting is used to shed light on the background of the protagonist. Yet neither Bardozzo nor Rosa stand out as characters: they are ordinary human beings caught in the turmoil of unexpected circumstances.

Similar emotions, though not charged with the same sexual intensity of "Briganti in Maremma," reappear in *La serva amorosa,* also set in the nineteenth century. This also is a sensual story that shows the intricate ways lust affects human beings: Nino, a young Florentine aristocrat with an insatiable appetite for women; and Giulia, the attractive young daughter of a nearby greengrocer, who becomes another of Nino's lovers. Two other important characters in the story are Zi Meco, a retired farmer who serves as the conscience of the story, and Alaide, Nino's maid who has taken care of him since his mother's death. Alaide is responsible for coercing Giulia into accepting the relationship with Nino. Even though she gets a comfortable life Giulia is not happy, and Zi Meco, who tried to save Giulia from falling into Nino's web by involving the local priest, is upset by the turn of events. In contrast to "Briganti in Maremma," in which Bonsanti does not moralize, *La serva amorosa* underscores traditional values while indicating the power the aristocracy exercises over the poor and the clergy's sympathy with the rich rather than with those in need. Yet even here Bonsanti remains largely unconcerned with morality and religion per se, choosing optimism in life as the defining element of his narrative. Bonsanti's conclusion seems to imply that even though Nino's actions were unethical, in the end everyone benefits in some way, except for Zi Meco, who represents the old and wise.

In 1934 Bonsanti published a collection of stories, *I capricci dell'Adriana* (Adriana's Whines). The story is again set in nineteenth-century Italy. As in Bonsanti's earlier work, memory plays an important role in the texture of the narrative. Here it serves as the means through which the protagonist, Adriana del Ponte, seeks to escape her daily existence. Born into a family of farmers and gifted with a beautiful voice, Adriana leaves her happy rural life to become a famous singer who is courted by many theatergoing aristocrats. Bonsanti penetrates Adriana's psychology and reveals her restlessness, as her memories of the past help her to alleviate the difficulties of her present life.

Bonsanti develops the past/present dichotomy with consummate skill. He contrasts Adriana's memories of the past—the idyllic countryside and the simple life of humble people—with the hectic pace of the city. Even so, Adriana is unable to go back to the past, for one day in the country is sufficient to elicit pleasant as well as unpleasant memories of her youth. The hardships of life in the country come back to her in the form of nightmares. Readers are thus left with an ambivalent feeling that in the twentieth century marks the theme of the country and the city.

Based in part on Bonsanti's own military service, the novel *Racconto militare* (A Military Story, 1937) depicts two opposite views of military life represented by a newly drafted soldier in training and his training officer, Pasquale De Luca. Bonsanti focuses on De Luca, a simple, honest young man from a small southern village who has chosen to pursue a career in the military. The privates can look at their present existence as a temporary absence from home and its freedom, but for De Luca the military life has become his entire existence. There are moments when he realizes that life in the military compound is not so different from the life he left behind, with its ups and downs. He is hurt when the newly arrived captain criticizes him and turns down his request to have a single room for himself, but the request is fulfilled later when a fatherly colonel intervenes. De Luca finds that even in the structured military world, he must face and overcome difficulties. In the space of one morning De Luca redefines his relationship with his surroundings and, in so doing, finds himself struggling with the uncertainties of the present and the certainties of the past. Bonsanti's compression of time and space as well as his ironic tone represent a progression in his technique and anticipates his future work.

Dialoghi e altre prose (Dialogues and Other Stories, 1940) contains four dialogues–"Dialogo della Luna Rossa" (Dialogue of the Red Moon), "Dialogo del Signore di Almaviva" (Dialogue of Mister Almaviva), "Dialogo delle Olive di Grecia" (Dialogue of the Olives of Greece), and "Dialogo dei Pescatori d'Anime" (Dialogues of the Fishermen of Souls)–and two short stories, "Un'elegia" (An Elegy) and "Dell'amicizia" (Of Friendship). The four dialogues deal with philosophical and moral issues and are independent of one another; the two short stories are connected and deal with childhood and the development of the human psyche. In "Un'Elegia" the adult Pierino revisits places and experiences of his childhood in an effort to discover what made him the adult he is today. In "Dell'amicizia" Pierino focuses on one of these experiences, remembering how as a child he was forbidden to befriend a boy in a wheelchair, whom he saw every day from the window of his room. Through the character of Pierino, Bonsanti seeks to unveil the meanderings of the mind. Like Giacomo Leopardi, Bonsanti sees childhood as the only time a human being can entertain all possible realities without any constraints. As he looks back at his adolescence, Pierino is convinced that constraints and limitations come with reason and maturity. He also discovers that feelings develop unconsciously during childhood, that he loves or hates because of associations made in childhood, and that in his mind emotion has become just another function of memory.

In *Introduzione al gran viaggio* (Introduction to the Long Trip, 1944) Bonsanti again uses Pierino to explore memory. Divided into two parts, "Introduction to the Long Trip" and "The End of Adolescence," the novel picks up the plot of "An Elegy" and "Of Friendship." The first part deals with Pierino's childhood, the second with his maturity. Through Pierino's recollections readers are led into a series of lengthy descriptions with little action, as when he recalls his house in the country:

> Una lunga fila di case, che a poco a più di un quarto di miglio attraversa la pianura dopo essersi distaccata dalla cerchia della città, di cui si scorgevano tuttavia i bastioni di levante, e si perdeva finalmente tra la campagna già sottratta all'occhio dai grossi alberi del bosco vicino, se al di là delineava, una interminabile fuga di campagne fruttifere verso i monti, non sempre sgombre da nebbie e caligini anche nella buona stagione, al di qua formava il lato più lontano di una figura geometrica, la quale racchiudeva nel suo interno quell'insieme di vasti prati, di frutteti e di orti, che arrivava fin sotto la casa di Pierino ragazzo e adolescente e ne restava separato soltanto dalla stradicciola campestre incassata tra i muri di confine, malandati e qua e la diroccati.

> (A long row of houses crossed the plain for little more than a quarter of a mile, and after they separated from the city walls, whose eastern bastions one could still see, they were finally lost in the countryside, hidden by the large trees of a nearby forest. On one side, the forest offered rapid glimpses of the country with endless lots of fruit-bearing trees pointing towards the mountains, which were not always free of fog and mist even in a good season. On the other side, the land took the shape of the farthest side of a geometrical figure enclosing meadows, orchards, and vegetable gardens which reached all the way to Pierino's house and was separated by a narrow country road, boxed in between the walls that marked the property lines and were in need of repair, in spots falling down.)

This long, refined sentence, combining lyrical descriptions and realistic references, is an example of prosa dell'arte, a prose that elevates form and style over content. While the sense of the sentence is that Pierino lived in a house in the countryside, the emphasis is on the memories Pierino has of his house and its surroundings. It is a subjective description that reflects a consciousness in motion. While Pierino in *Dialoghi e altre prose* had similar memories, Bonsanti in *Introduzione al gran viaggio* broadens the narrative scope to reveal nuances of Pierino's development. Every detail is treated as a piece of a complicated puzzle that Bonsanti arranges before the eyes of his readers.

Bonsanti draws once again from the storehouse of memory to write *La vipera e il toro* (The Viper and the Bull, 1955), a novel notable for detailed flashbacks, little action, and the introduction of an

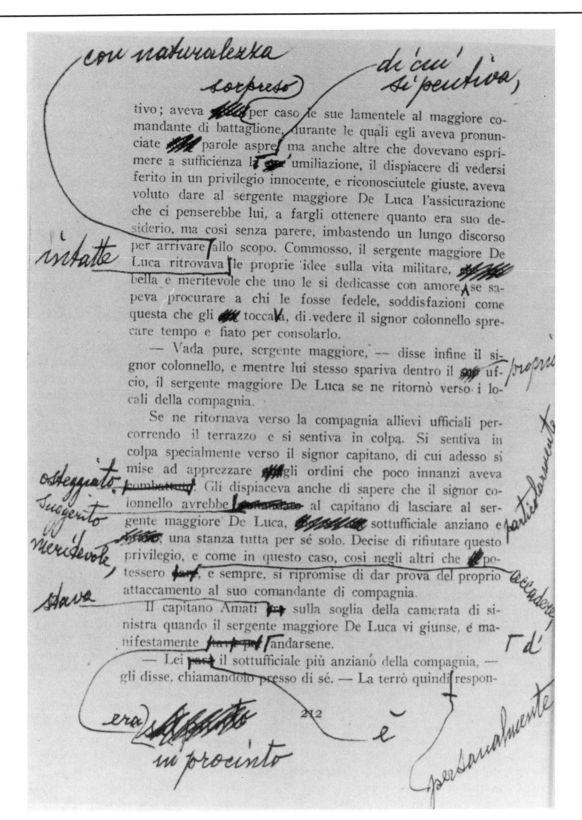

con naturalezza

sorpreso)   *di 'cui'*
                                                              si'pentiva,

tivo; aveva ~~per~~ per caso le sue lamentele al maggiore comandante di battaglione, durante le quali egli aveva pronun-
ciate ~~parole~~ parole aspre, ma anche altre che dovevano esprimere a sufficienza la ~~sua~~ umiliazione, il dispiacere di vedersi
ferito in un privilegio innocente, e riconosciutele giuste, aveva
voluto dare al sergente maggiore De Luca l'assicurazione
che ci penserebbe lui, a fargli ottenere quanto era suo desiderio, ma così senza parere, imbastendo un lungo discorso
per arrivare allo scopo. Commosso, il sergente maggiore De

intatte   Luca ritrovava le proprie idee sulla vita militare, ~~~~
bella e meritevole che uno le si dedicasse con amore, se sapeva procurare a chi le fosse fedele, soddisfazioni come
questa che gli ~~~~ toccava, di vedere il signor colonnello spre-
care tempo e fiato per consolarlo.

— Vada pure, sergente maggiore, — disse infine il si-
gnor colonnello, e mentre lui stesso spariva dentro il ~~suo~~ uf-   *proprio*
cio, il sergente maggiore De Luca se ne ritornò verso i lo-
cali della compagnia.

Se ne ritornava verso la compagnia allievi ufficiali per-
correndo il terrazzo e si sentiva in colpa. Si sentiva in
colpa specialmente verso il signor capitano, di cui adesso si   *particolarmente*
mise ad apprezzare ~~~~ gli ordini che poco innanzi aveva

osteggiato. ~~combattuto~~. Gli dispiaceva anche di sapere che il signor co-
suggerito   lonnello avrebbe ~~~~ al capitano di lasciare al ser-
             gente maggiore De Luca, ~~~~ sottufficiale anziano e
meritevole, ~~~~, una stanza tutta per sé solo. Decise di rifiutare questo
             privilegio, e come in questo caso, così negli altri che ~~~~ po-   *accadere*
dava   tessero ~~darsi~~, e sempre, si ripromise di dar prova del proprio
             attaccamento al suo comandante di compagnia.

Il capitano Amati ~~era~~ sulla soglia della camerata di si-
nistra quando il sergente maggiore De Luca vi giunse, e ma-
nifestamente ~~~~ andarsene.   *d'*

— Lei ~~~~ il sottufficiale più anziano della compagnia, —
gli disse, chiamandolo presso di sé. — La terrò quindi respon-

era) ~~~~ 212 *è*   *personalmente*

in procinto

Page from the revised typescript for Racconto militare *(Alessandro Bonsanti Collection)*

important character, Giovanni Borghini. The reader is not told much about the present life of the main character, except that he is a bank teller with literary ambitions. The narrative is absorbed by Borghini's memories of the past, small adventures, intrigues, sensual imaginings. The constantly indecisive Borghini dwells on events that in his mind are transformed into dreamlike fragments. Past and present are woven into a narrative fabric, distinguished by psychological detail and the elegance of Bonsanti's style.

In structure and character development, *La vipera e il toro* can be compared to Luigi Pirandello's play *Enrico IV* (Henry IV, 1922), as Borghini's daydreaming is not so different in intent from Enrico's fictitious madness. In both cases the characters seek to escape their existential predicaments. In other ways, Bonsanti looks to the *Crepuscolari* (twilight) poets, such as Sergio Corazzini, Guido Gozzano, and particularly Marino Moretti, who found their poetic muse within themselves, in a world of intimate dreams and nostalgic memories. Both Bonsanti and Moretti preferred small towns, rural villages, and quiet countryside to the boisterous life in large industrial cities. Bonsanti's novel, in turn, offers a narrative model based on memory that may have influenced the work of Carlo Cassola two decades later.

In *I cavalli di bronzo* (The Bronze Horses, 1956) Giovanni Borghini, here a dull professor with literary ambitions, is again the protagonist. He is complemented by several secondary characters, including Maria Antonietta; her husband, Tonino; and her young sister, Elena. Elena plans to marry her fiancé in America instead of marrying in her native village of Colbiate, but though Maria Antonietta tries to dissuade her, Tonino and their old friend—Borghini—refuse to help her. The young couple ends up dying in a plane crash. This element of tragedy is a novelty in Bonsanti's work; a second novelty is the setting of Venice, rather than Florence and the Tuscan countryside.

The Borghini of this and other novels can be compared to some of the characters of Pirandello or Italo Svevo, who as victims of society alleviate their suffering through artistic fantasies. Readers begin to feel they are reading a novel by Borghini in the making, as the narration is structured by his memories and detailed physical and psychological descriptions that overshadow the action of the novel. For critic Bortolo Pento, Bonsanti began to deal more effectively with his recollections of adolescent memories in *La vipera e il toro,* whereas in *I cavalli di bronzo* he achieves a balance between lyricism and the realism one expects to find in his prose. On the other hand, Carmine Paolino convincingly argues that

such equilibrium was present in the previous works as well.

Many autobiographical references in *I cavalli di bronzo* link Bonsanti to his character Borghini. He writes that Borghini in his youth had written short stories. In one of them Borghini recalls a dialogue between two priests and the devil but could not remember much more about it, except that he had neglected to talk about the odor of sulphur found in hell. Bonsanti's attitude toward his work is clearly tongue-in-cheek, playfully minimizing his importance as a writer and perhaps the importance of literary fiction in general. In the same vein, Bonsanti acknowledges his affinities with Marcel Proust's use of memory, but he also points out that he avoided sensorial experiences as a conduit to recall and reexperience the past.

Sopra alcuni personaggi eventuali (On Some Potential Characters, 1956) is a collection of thoughts and social commentaries together with sketches of various characters with different behavioral traits and moral consciousnesses. He draws social tableaux, which he follows with reflections and commentary. In structure the work brings to mind Leopardi's *Zibaldone,* but Bonsanti's book is rather superficial compared to Leopardi's tome.

During the 1960s Bonsanti reached the height of his career with his gargantuan and best-known novel, *La buca di San Colombano* (San Colombano's Pit, 1964), published in three volumes. The work is divided into four parts: "Passioni Senili" (Senile Passions), "Caffè concerto" (Concert at a Sidewalk-Cafe), "Gardenia appassita" (Wilted Gardenia), and "Apologia dell'innocenza" (An Apology of Innocence). The subtitles indicate the structure of the book, which starts with the present, when the characters are old, and retrospectively traces their lives to the idyllic age of adolescence, the age of unfulfilled potential and the only time worthy of an apology.

No Italian novelist of the twentieth century has treated the process of aging in such lyrical detail as Bonsanti, and *La buca di San Colombano* is a two-thousand-page account of memories, recounted often in a demented, senilelike fashion. The main characters are the waiters of the Buca (a local cafe), Eustachio and Melchiorre; the owner, Signor Callisto; and the customers Luigi, Guido, and Luisa. The focus is on Eustachio, Melchiorre, and especially Callisto, whose life is described in minute detail through the use of flashbacks. It is a more Proustian work than previous novels: at one point Bonsanti, like Proust in *A la recherche du temps perdu* (1913–1927, translated as *Remembrance of Things Past,*

1922–1931), even uses the aroma of tobacco to evoke past events.

La buca di San Colombano sets a good balance between action and memory. When Eustachio, shaving in front of a mirror, starts to think about his past, Bonsanti uses fifty pages to bring those memories to life, showing that reality is seen through remembered experiences, so much so that often what occurs in the present is nothing more than a pretext to evoke the past. While the representation of time may be said to be nonrealistic—one wonders at fifty pages of memory in the space of a shave—readers can lose themselves in Bonsanti's eloquence. The reality of such representation is also questioned by those who say he largely ignores political and social turmoil in his writing. But Bonsanti, like Pirandello, believed in the subjective perception of reality. He stresses how and not what when Callisto recalls his past life. In other words, he paints reality as Callisto perceived it and remembers it; clearly another character could offer a different view of the same events. This point is perhaps clearest in the relationship between Melchiorre and Eustachio. While Melchiorre loves his friend and co-worker and collects cigar butts for him to stuff in his pipe, the reality, as the reader learns, is that Eustachio actually despises Melchiorre.

Although Bonsanti began working on *La nuova stazione di Firenze* (The New Railroad Station in Florence) in 1954, it was not published until 1965. The well-known Giovanni Borghini is featured in this novel, which is divided into three parts and covers just five hours. In the first part Borghini converses with an architect while riding on a train from Florence to Rome. In the second, and much longer, part Borghini shares with the architect salient aspects of his youthful life. He recounts the Fascist era and his experiences as a young writer when he contributed to the journal *Solaria*. In the third part Borghini listens attentively as his traveling companion speaks about architecture. In the noteworthy second part Bonsanti injects several personal experiences and talks about his love for writing, his political views, and his literary ideas. Through Borghini he tells his readers that what is important in a novel is not objective reality but the many possibilities of interpretation it allows.

In 1968 Bonsanti turned to playwriting with a small volume titled *Teatro domestico* (Domestic Plays). One of the plays, *Don Giovanni* (Don Juan), had originally been published in 1937 in the review *Letteratura*. The new work included two additional plays, *Ottaviano* (Octavian) and *Maria Stuarda* (Mary Stewart). The three plays are constructed in a similar fashion in that Bonsanti uses memory as a dramatic structure supporting the action. *Maria Stuarda* and *Don Giovanni* are marked by long monologues dwelling on the beauty of youth and the sorrows of old age.

Ottaviano is the most interesting of the three because it contains Bonsanti's views on the act of writing. A note of resignation and pessimism marks emperor Octavian's dialogue as he prepares to dictate his autobiography. Certain to be condemned by posterity for the evil deeds he has committed, he is tempted to forgo the effort. But he also realizes that, if he does not recall his life, its important details and events will be misunderstood or neglected by future historians. In the end he decides that communication is preferable to silence. Thus, the play suggests the courage often entailed in the act of writing.

Bonsanti was a conservative writer. Indifferent to experimentation, he was not interested in the literary trends of his time, which stressed formal innovation and immersion in social and political problems. The road he chose to pursue was paved with nostalgia for a past that lacked many of the problems his society endured in his lifetime, but the eloquence of his writing endures.

References:

Elia Filippo Accrocca, "Alessandro Bonsanti," *Ritratti su misura di scrittori italiani* (Venice: Sodalizio del Libro, 1960), pp. 91–92;

Giacomo Antonini "Les tendences du roman italien," *Mercure de France,* 244 (1933): 5–37;

Piero Bigongiari, "Bonsanti, una lontananza vicina," in his *Prosa per il Novecento* (Florence: La Nuova Italia, 1970), pp. 77–84;

Carlo Bo, "Nota su Bonsanti," in his *Nuovi Studi* (Florence: Vallecchi, 1946), pp. 150–156;

Bo, "Romanzo e società nell'Italia degli ultimi dieci anni," *Paragone,* 88 (1957): 3–23;

Gianfranco Contini, "A. Bonsanti o dell'attività pura," in his *Esercizi di lettura sopra autori contemporanei* (Florence: Le Monnier, 1947), pp. 205–227;

Contini, Introduction to Bonsanti's *Racconto militare* (Milan: Mondadori, 1968), pp. 9–19;

Eurialo De Michelis, "Dialoghi di Bonsanti," *Civiltà moderna,* 12 (1940): 398–410;

Giuseppe De Robertis, *Scrittori del Novecento* (Florence: Le Monnier, 1943), pp. 311–316;

Enrico Falqui, "Alessandro Bonsanti: *La vipera e il toro,*" in *Novecento letterario* (Florence: Vallecchi, 1961), pp. 429–434;

Fiera letteraria, special issue on Bonsanti, 22 August 1965;

Eugenio Montale, "La serva amorosa," *Pegaso,* 2 (March 1930): 377–379;

Pietro Pancrazi, "Il clima e il tempo di A. Bonsanti," in his *Scrittori italiani del '900* (Bari: Laterza, 1934), pp. 308–312;

Carmine Paolino, *La narrativa di Alessandro Bonsanti* (Rome: Bulzoni, 1988);

Edilio Rusconi, "Alessandro Bonsanti," in his *Comune solitudine* (Milan: Rizzoli, 1944), pp. 238–246;

Luigi Russo, *I narratori* (Milan: Principato, 1951), p. 298;

Susetta Salucci, *Alessandro Bonsanti* (Florence: La Nuova Italia, 1978);

Natalino Sapegno, "La serva amorosa," *La nuova Italia,* 1 (1930): 166–167;

Giuseppe Trombatore, "Due di Solaria," in his *Scrittori del nostro tempo* (Palermo: Manfredi, 1959), pp. 149–154;

Claudio Varese, "Narrativa di oggi: *La vipera e il toro* e *I cavalli di bronzo,*" *Nuova antologia,* 93 (1958): 554–561;

Ferdinando Virdia, "I cavalli di bronzo," *La fiera letteraria,* 30 December 1956.

Dino Buzzati
(16 October 1906 – 28 January 1972)

Sharon Wood
University of Strathclyde

BOOKS: *Bárnabo delle montagne* (Milan: Garzanti, 1933);

Il segreto del bosco vecchio (Milan: Mondadori, 1935);

Il deserto dei Tartari (Milan: Rizzoli, 1940); translated by Stuart C. Hood as *The Tartar Steppe* (London: Secker & Warburg, 1952; New York: Farrar, Straus & Young, 1952);

I sette messaggeri (Milan: Mondadori, 1942);

La famosa invasione degli orsi in Sicilia (Milan: Rizzoli, 1945); translated by Frances Lobb as *The Bears' Famous Invasion of Sicily* (New York: Pantheon, 1947);

Paura alla Scala (Milan: Mondadori, 1949);

In quel preciso momento (Venice: Pozza, 1950);

Un caso clinico (Milan: Mondadori, 1953); translated by Ursule Molinaro and Lane Dunlop as *Seven Floors, Chelsea*, 8 (1960);

Il crollo della Baliverna (Milan: Mondadori, 1954); translated by Judith Landry and Cynthia Jolly as *Catastrophe: The Strange Stories of Dino Buzzati* (London: Caldar & Boyars, 1966);

Esperimento di magia (Padua: Rebellato, 1958);

Sessanta racconti (Milan: Mondadori, 1958);

Il grande ritratto (Milan: Mondadori, 1960); translated by Henry Reed as *Larger than Life* (London: Secker & Warburg, 1962; New York: Walker, 1962);

Egregio signore, siamo spiacenti di (Milan: Elmo, 1960);

Un amore (Milan: Mondadori, 1963); translated by Joseph Green as *A Love Affair* (New York: Farrar, Straus, 1964; London: Deutsch, 1965);

Il capitano Pic ed altre poesie (Venice: Pozzi, 1965);

Il colombre e altri cinquanta racconti (Milan: Mondadori, 1966);

La boutique del mistero (Milan: Mondadori, 1968);

La fine del borghese (Milan: Bietti, 1968);

L'uomo che andrà in America, due tempi (Milan: Bietti, 1968);

Poema a fumetti (Milan: Mondadori, 1969);

I miracoli di Val Morel (Milan: Garzanti, 1971);

Le notti difficili (Milan: Mondadori, 1971); translated by Lawrence Venuti as *Restless Nights* (San

Dino Buzzati

Francisco: North Point, 1983; Manchester: Carcanet, 1984);

Cronache terrestri, edited by Domenico Porzio (Milan: Mondadori, 1972);

I misteri d'Italia (Milan: Mondadori, 1978);

I dispiaceri del re (Turin: Stampatori, 1980);

Teatro (Milan: Mondadori, 1980);

Le poesie (Vicenza: Pozza, 1982);

180 racconti (Milan: Mondadori, 1982);

Il reggimento parte all'alba (Milan: Frassinelli, 1985);

Bestiario (Milan: Mondadori, 1991);

Il buttafuoco (Milan: Mondadori, 1992).

Editions and collections: *L'uccisione del drago e altri racconti,* edited by Domenico Manzella (Milan: Mondadori, 1958);

Romanzi e racconti, edited by Giuliano Gramigna (Milan: Mondadori, 1975).

PLAY PRODUCTIONS: *Piccola passeggiata,* Milan, 1942;

Un caso clinico, Milan, Piccolo Teatro, 1953;

Drammatica fine di un musivista, Milan, 1955;

La colonna infame, Milan, Piccolo Teatro, 1962;

La famosa invasione degli orsi in Sicilia, Milan, 1965;

La fine del borghese, Milan, 1966.

OTHER: *Ferrovia sopraelevata,* libretto by Buzzati (Bergamo: Edizioni della Rotonda, 1955);

Procedura penale, libretto by Buzzati (Milan: Ricordi, 1959);

Il mantello, libretto by Buzzati (Milan: Ricordi, 1960);

Era proibito, libretto by Buzzati (Milan: Ricordi, 1961);

Battono alla porta, libretto by Buzzati (Milan: Piccola Scala, 1963).

The works of Dino Buzzati have remained as enigmatic, elusive, and open to interpretation as the author himself. With his sense of irony, his refusal to align himself with the political or literary forces of his time, his adoption of the fantastic–a genre that was quite at odds with either the disengaged hermeticism dominant in his youth or the political materialism of the postwar period–Buzzati produced a body of work outside the canon of traditional literary tradition. A novelist, short-story writer, poet, and dramatist as well as a journalist and painter, Buzzati will never be tied to a specific social or historical movement. He explores an anguished sense of anxiety, an ineradicable unease that is existential and moral as well as erotic, in stories that can be interpreted as allegories or parables of states of mind. His fantastic tales encapsulate not Promethean heroics but small moments of trauma in small lives, overpowered by a tragic, ironic sense of destiny and mortality. Buzzati writes of a world beyond human comprehension, and his work has been most frequently compared to the alienating narratives of Franz Kafka.

Dino Buzzati was born into a wealthy bourgeois family near Belluno, in the mountainous northeast region of Italy. The harsh, rugged, majestic landscape of his youth permanently shaped his vision of mankind in relation to the natural world.

On the other hand, the frantic city life of cosmopolitan Milan, where his father was a professor of law at the Bocconi University and where his family lived for long periods, constituted the other pole of his mental geography. Buzzati followed his father and graduated in law, but as a young man he was already writing verse and short stories, reacting against the mediocrity in which he believed most people lived. In the disciplined life of the army he found a sense of order that was congenial to a temperament in search of purpose as well as an environment that was to figure directly in his most successful novel, *Il deserto dei Tartari* (1940; translated as *The Tartar Steppe,* 1952).

His military service completed, Buzzati began work in 1928 as a journalist for *Il Corriere della sera,* a leading national, centrist daily newspaper published in Milan. There he rose from the status of humble reporter to music critic, special envoy, war correspondent, and leading writer and editor. In the reviled trade of journalism, Buzzati, like South American writer Gabriel García Márquez, found an abundance of material to feed his sense of the quirkiness and fundamental absurdity of life.

Buzzati began his career as journalist and writer just a few years after Mussolini came to power. The press was tightly controlled and generally acquiescent in the Fascist era, and writers were subject to rigid though inconsistent censorship. Despite his career, Buzzati remained largely aloof from the political and cultural debates of the day. He cited the influence of foreign rather than native writers, particularly French, British, and American. His artistic disposition was always avowedly Nordic rather than Mediterranean, yet he always remained an acute observer on the margins of Italian literary society. In 1939 he was sent by *Il Corriere della sera* as special envoy to Eritrea, occupied by Italy in its expansionist ambitions, and later to other parts of Africa and Asia. It was the Eritrean desert that was to metamorphose into the empty spaces of the soul in *Il deserto dei Tartari.* During World War II Buzzati continued to report from the front, describing firsthand the horror of battle from aboard a ship.

The ideology and aspirations of the Resistance gave an impetus to post–World War II Italian cultural life. There existed a collective desire to transform and modernize a society that had been politically and intellectually stagnant under Fascism. Buzzati, however, stood aside from the neorealist aesthetic that was rooted in its political ethic and remained uninvolved in the formal linguistic experimentalism of the early 1960s. Only on rare occasions–such as in "Paura alla Scala," the title story of his 1949 collection–could his work be said to be critical of the dominant class, and he always maintained a style of clarity and transparency. In his later years Buzzati published poetry and wrote for the theater; he also agreed, for the first time, to have exhibitions of his paintings. He married in 1966, a few years after the death of his mother, with whom he spent most of his life. Six years later he died of cancer at the age of sixty-five.

Buzzati's first novel, *Bárnabo delle montagne* (Bárnabo and the Mountains, 1933), clearly springs from the author's love for the mountains of his childhood. It also prefigures Buzzati's technique in later works, in which he creates a dualistic landscape, associating the natural world with a moral order that the human world lacks. The novel is set among the deserted woods and mountains of the North, where the young Barnabo is dismissed as a forest ranger when he acts cowardly in the face of an attack by bandits. Years of unhappiness and regret follow, but he is determined to redeem himself by killing the men who caused his fall from grace. He awaits them on the mountainside and has them in the sights of his rifle when he discovers that the faces before him are not those of hardened ruffians but of aged and rather pitiable men.

The preoccupations of Buzzati's career are all touched upon here: the expectation, as in Samuel Beckett's work, of some definitive event that will give purpose to life; the failure of such an event to materialize and the disappointment it inevitably engenders; the unstoppable passage of time; and the futility of existence. The novel has a serenity missing from later works, a lighter note of optimism in which the smallness of man seems redeemable by the poetry of nature. The bandits who haunt Bárnabo are really inner enemies who are overcome by the lonely solitude of the mountains.

While Buzzati always regarded himself as a nonpolitical writer, the choices made by his characters indicate a specific ideological and artistic orientation. By refusing to kill the bandits and play the heroic role of single-handed conqueror, Bárnabo implicitly rejects the myth of heroic action so central to Fascist dogma and the philosophy of the *ubermensch* on which it was predicated. Bárnabo also renounces his desire to tell the tale, to recount his exploits, to produce a narrative out of his deeds, making instead the radical choice of silence and solitude. While Bárnabo's refusal of society may be seen as a rejection of the values of that society and thus an ideological criticism of Fascism, the silencing of his voice may be read as suggesting the acquiescence of intellectuals to the Fascist demand for consent, a refusal to engage in active opposition.

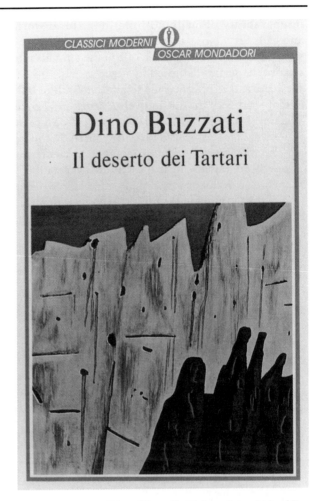

Cover for a 1995 edition of Buzzati's third novel, in which soldiers stationed at a desert outpost endure a meaningless existence

The natural world is similarly at the forefront of Buzzati's second novel, *Il segreto del bosco vecchio* (The Secret of the Old Forest, 1935). In this moral fable the world of men is tightly bound up with the lives of animals, plants, and spirits in a vision of anthropomorphic animism, where nature, exploited by men for gain, risks destruction. Representing the choices that are faced in adolescence, *Il segreto del bosco vecchio* is the story of the young boy, Benvenuto, who is initiated into adulthood, surviving his scheming uncle's designs on his life as he takes possession of his newly inherited property. The novel belongs to a long line of narratives, including works by Aesop, Jean La Fontaine, Kafka, and Julio Cortázar, where an anthropomorphic vision becomes the framework for moral teaching and an assertion of the relationship between man and nature. Buzzati's fantastic world, where animals speak, organize, act, and have both will and conscience, is closely tied to a child's vision, unfettered by crude rationalism. *Il segreto del bosco vecchio*, like *Bárnabo,* emphasizes the inseparability of mankind from the natural world and calls for a moral ethic based in nature. Nature's superiority is averred, as the role of the animals is to restore the order disrupted by men.

Buzzati established his reputation both in Italy and abroad with his third novel, *Il deserto dei Tartari.* The novel was drafted in and inspired by the offices of *Il Corriere della sera,* where Buzzati realized that many of his colleagues, like his protagonist, Lieutenant Drogo, were passing their days in the expectation of some future dramatic event–fame, success, the revelation of the meaning of their lives. In an interview Buzzati's observation of himself and his colleagues takes on a wider existential meaning:

> Era un lavoro piuttosto pesante e monotono, e i mesi passavano, passavano gli anni e io mi chiedevo se sarebbe andata avanti sempre cosí, se le speranze, i sogni inevitabili quando si è giovani, si sarebbero atrofizzati a poco a poco, se la grande occasione sarebbe venuta o no, e intorno a me vedevo uomini, alcuni della mia età altri molto più anziani, i quali andavano, andavano, trasportati dallo stesso lento fiume e mi domandavo se anch'io un giorno non mi sarei trovato nelle stesse condizioni dei colleghi dai capelli bianchi, alla vigilia della pensione, colleghi oscuri che non avrebbero lasciato dietro di sé che un pallido ricordo destinato presto a svanire.

> (It was a rather heavy and monotonous job; months and years passed, and I began to ask myself whether life would continue like that, whether individual hopes and the inevitable dreams of youth would gradually become atrophied, whether the big break would come. Around me I saw men, some of my age, others considerably older, who marched on, carried by the same slow river and I asked myself whether one day I would be on the same boat as my gray-haired colleagues approaching retirement, obscure colleagues who would have left behind but a pale memory of themselves that would soon die.)

Buzzati's tale is set, however, not in the offices of the newspaper but in the military environment of a remote, almost forgotten fortress whose function is to guard against the anticipated invasion of the Tartars across the desert. On the edges of the kingdom, the fortress looks out into the void. It has been inhabited by generations of soldiers whose initial eager expectations of battle and glory become gradually more muted, slipping inexorably into a sense of life as unsalvageable and irredeemable waste.

The transfer of the story into a military context, to the regulations and self-perpetuating routines of army life, offers Buzzati several advantages. Lieutenant Drogo begins his duty at the Fortezza Bastiani in the firm belief that his posting is only temporary. The rigorous discipline and order of military life dramatically and inexorably mark off the passage of time as Drogo's hope of returning to the city fades. Drogo and his fellow soldiers march toward the void in order, obedience, and perfect time: a formal, aesthetic illustration of the inevitable passage of time and its chilling implications. As Drogo rises through the ranks, he and his companions search out reasons to justify their situation and their wasted lives: a suspected invasion by the Tartars turns out to be nothing but a stray horse. In the absence of a real purpose to their lives on this forgotten frontier of time, the means, or military discipline, becomes all-important. When a soldier fails to give the correct password to be readmitted into the fortress after a patrol, he is shot as an enemy in accordance with regulations. If one recalls how Buzzati was inspired to write the novel from his observations of the routine of journalism, the empty, self-serving forms of military life may also be seen as a metaphor for writing.

The empty passage of time is further emphasized on Drogo's few visits back to his native city, where his hope of glory is counterposed to the normal business of people's lives: his fiancée marries another man; his friends find work and set up families; his mother dies. Drogo's abstraction from the minutiae of daily living, from the work and family that lend some sort of coherence to most existences, serves to underline his enthrallment to the relentlessness of time. But, though inexorable, time is seen to be not absolute but relative. When Drogo leaves for the fortress, the rhythm of his horse's hooves appears to be different from that of his friend who accompanies him; as he looks back, he sees his room being cleared, a sign of his entry into another dimension of existence. After his return to the city, time goes even faster as his solitude is emphasized.

The imagined setting of the fortress underlines the allegory of the novel. Lost on a forgotten frontier of both space and time, the fortress, supposedly close to the city, retreats before Drogo as he approaches it for the first time. No one is sure of its location, and messengers or helpers, such as those found in fairy tales, are required to help Drogo find his way. The precise actions and routines of the soldiers are outside orthodox history: their uniforms belong to no identifiable army; their rigorous drills and routines serve no identifiable purpose. Buzzati's use of specific dates and months, as when Drogo is said to leave the fortress in late September, only emphasizes the sense of temporal dislocation.

When the Tartars do, finally, arrive, the fortress swings into action in fulfillment of its purpose.

But for Drogo it is too late: an old man, sick and unsteady on his feet, he is dismissed from the fortress by his superiors as an encumbrance, nullified by the same orders and regulations to which he has given his life. As the fortress becomes engaged in battle, Drogo, now a high-ranking officer, is taken down the mountainside in an elegant coach, the external trappings of his status a poor substitute for the achievement of his ambition. The arrival of the long-awaited Tartar invasion prompts Drogo's recognition that in the distilled, rarefied sphere of the fortress, it is death itself that he has awaited all these years.

Buzzati wrote *Il deserto dei Tartari* in a seven-year period that coincided with the final years of the Fascist dictatorship. It is tempting to read the novel as a parable of time lost under Fascism, of the illusions of glory, of the long wait for some sort of deliverance and liberation, of the desire for a rational underpinning to existence or for a system of values. Yet while the novel clearly could be read as a parable of the fate of the intellectual under the Fascist dictatorship, Buzzati's narrative is more profound. It is a fable of the human condition, of the relentless march of time toward death that makes no allowances for human hopes, illusions, and expectations. Drogo incarnates an entropic and deeply pessimistic vision of life as a headlong rush toward disintegration and decay held only temporarily at bay by frenetic, meaningless activity and willful illusions.

After the publication of his first three novels Buzzati turned his attention to short stories. He found writing stories particularly congenial to his talent and wrote several hundred in the course of his career. As a journalist precision, concision, and the need to attract and maintain the reader's interest from the opening paragraphs were clearly tools of the trade. His spare, unrhetorical style, shorn of embellishment and the lyrical excess that marked the work of many of his contemporaries, was particularly suited to the short story, which typically explores a situation, a mood, or an event. Pace is all-important for Buzzati, who usually begins his stories in medias res. Typically, a situation, frequently bizarre or fantastic, is outlined in the opening lines and is then worked out to its inexorable conclusion. As in the work of Kafka, the initial absurdity or dislocation of reality is subject to iron rules of logical progression. Buzzati's sense of existential unease and strangeness is achieved by disrupting normal perceptions of reality, not with flights of the imagination.

Buzzati published eight volumes of short stories between *I sette messaggeri* (The Seven Messengers) in 1942 and *Le notti difficili* (translated as *Rest-*less Nights,* 1983) in 1971. While there is no significant development in content and structure, there are dominant and recurring themes: an existential preoccupation with sickness and death; the metaphysical province of sin (against man and against nature); guilt and forgiveness which, again as in Kafka, are reducible to no religious system but are expressive of a modern existential and ontological crisis.

In "I sette messaggeri," the title story of his first collection, a prince leaves his family and home to explore his kingdom, sending back seven messengers at intervals to give and receive news. As distances and time expand, the messages he receives are ever more strange, eventually becoming incomprehensible fragments of a time already dead and buried. As up-to-date as the light from dead stars, the messengers' reports concern places that have already disappeared and people now aged or dying. The prince's messages, too, will be read as increasingly strange, irrelevant, and incoherent. The story eloquently dramatizes not only the complexities of communication but the ravages of time on memory and experience. When in Italo Calvino's short work, *Le città invisibili* (Invisible Cities, 1972), Marco Polo sets out to explore the kingdom of the Kubla Khan, the strange and marvelous descriptions he brings back are all, in the final analysis, descriptions of his point of departure, Venice; similarly, Buzzati's story concerns not the exploration of space but the involution of the subject. What the prince explores is not the kingdom but his own life; the final boundary toward which he rides is not the edge of empire but the end of life.

"I sette piani" (The Seven Floors), another story from Buzzati's first collection, demonstrates again an inexorable logic and the same progressive marking of time toward death. The wealthy and successful Giuseppe Corte enters a clinic for what he believes to be just a minor disturbance to his health and is placed on the top floor where patients with only slight ailments are treated. Gradually, for one reason or another—the painting of a ward, the presence of a better-qualified doctor, the shortage of space—he is moved down through the floors to be with other patients suffering ever more serious illnesses, still under the benign illusion that such moves are only temporary. Finally, and inevitably, he finds himself on the lowest floor, now a sick and aged man in the antechamber of death. His belief that he could escape the workings of time is exposed as a fallacy: wealth and status are no protection in the face of the great leveler. "I sette piani" and "I sette messaggeri"—Buzzati's obsession with numbers is only one point of contact with Dante's

Dust jacket for the British edition of the translation of Buzzati's 1954 collection, in which the title story is about a building that collapses

work—and the rigorous marking of time in *Il deserto dei Tartari* function as a reminder of death, the inescapable conclusion to all of our lives.

While Buzzati's tales can effectively skewer the illusions and absurdities by which people live, they also demonstrate a large degree of moral didacticism, as in a third story from *I sette messaggeri* titled "L'uccisione del drago" (The Slaying of the Dragon). The dragon, to whom people of an unnamed village pay homage by bringing gifts of food, is willfully and barbarically slaughtered by those in power, even though the fearsome beast turns out to be a small, harmless creature, female and with young. The dragon's breath that enters the count's lungs and inevitably causes his death is a small revenge for the murder. The tale is a parable warning against the destruction of nature by wanton man.

Buzzati's 1949 story "Paura alla Scala" (Fear at La Scala) is one of his most explicit comments on the social mores and conventions of his day. A gala evening at La Scala attended by the rich and powerful elite of Milan is disrupted by news of the imminent arrival of the dreaded Morzi, an image perhaps of the threatened takeover by the Communists. Behavior, social codes and decorum, dignity, and the trappings of success all rapidly disintegrate in the face of threat; the masks of bourgeois power are stripped away to reveal little more than self-serving hypocrisy and cowardice. The threat does not materialize, but the moment of fear, which, unusually for Buzzati, can be traced to a precise historical moment in the aftermath of World War II, is an unforgiving demystification of a corrupt society determined to maintain its political dominance.

On the other hand "Una goccia" (A Drop), another story from the same collection, remains a tantalizing story in its resistance to interpretation, in its evocation of a fear that has no name and springs from no identifiable—and therefore challengeable—source. In a block of tenement flats a drop of water plops up the stairs each night, past the doors of the terrified residents. As in the drawings of M. C. Escher, the water goes up and not down, defying the law of gravity. The drop of water functions as a symbol that can be endlessly reinterpreted—as an allegory; as a dream of death or imminent, faceless danger; as a metaphysical hypothesis; or even as a joke. "Una goccia" distills Buzzati's expressionist talent for bodying forth fears and anxieties less within political and social realities than within the ludic realm of language. In this sense many of his tales can be seen as the laboratory of the unconscious mind.

Buzzati's ability to evoke a sense of obscure guilt, sin, and blame is clearly illustrated in two stories from *Il crollo della Baliverna* (1954; translated as *Catastrophe,* 1966). In the title story the enormous building known as the Baliverna—a classic Buzzati setting that is part prison, part hospital, and part fortress—collapses one day with everything and everyone still inside, after a passerby casually breaks off an iron rod protruding from its wall. A monstrous progression of effects leads to the catastrophic disintegration of the building, which is pulverized more thoroughly than if it had been bombed. Somebody must be held accountable—the builders, the administrators, or the unfortunate passerby? Guilt and blame are simultaneously elusive, inexplicable, and devastating in their consequences. What is clear is that all are guilty and no one can be held to be innocent, even though the sin can be defined according to no traditional transcendental code and is part of the act of living. In "Una bambina dimenticata" (A Forgotten Child) a moment of maternal distraction again leads to cataclysm: returning home, a mother finds nothing but a pool of blood on the floor in the shape of her daughter. This is not a moral warning to take better care of our children, but a graphic illustration of a malign world in which the slightest action can lead to tragedy, in which guilt and grief are unavoidable.

In his fourth full-length novel, *Il grande ritratto* (The Large Portrait, 1960; translated as *Larger than Life,* 1962), which was published twenty years after his third, Buzzati moves from the fantastic to science fiction; indeed, it is one of the first Italian novels to exploit new technologies such as computers and cybernetics for a literary purpose. While it is generally regarded as the least successful of his novels, *Il grande ritratto* reflects Buzzati's continuing preoccupation with the fate of human desire in time, with the fragility of human constructions against the void, and with the fear and anguish with which people face the world. For the first time in the novel form, Buzzati writes a love story with a female character central to the action, anticipating the explosion of frustrated eroticism unleashed later in *Un amore* (1963; translated as *A Love Affair,* 1964).

Like *Il deserto dei Tartari*, *Il grande ritratto* is set in a military complex surrounded by mountains, and as in the previous novel, the precise descriptions of the complex find no corollary in maps or atlases. At the base scientists are developing a computer capable of independent thought and decision-making powers for use by the military, but Buzzati's interest lies less in the possibilities of artificial intelligence than in human notions of love, desire, fear, and destiny. The narrative draws on contemporary anxieties about the porous dividing line between man and machine and the possible usurpation of human functions and power by computers. The rigid discipline of army life is counterposed by the mysterious murmurings and whisperings that wash over the complex, which turn out to emanate from the computer itself. The architect of the machine called "Number One," Professor Endriade, has endowed the computer with much of the all-too-human frailty and sensuous charm of his deceased wife, Laura. The woman-machine experiences her own jealousies and desire and reaches the point of murdering one of her human rivals. The computer's free will—in the emblematic form of a crystal egg—is destroyed, and Number One returns to being just a machine.

The fear felt by a whole generation unfamiliar with and wary of the awesome potential of computer power is only part of the point here. The relationship of man to nature, signified by the ever-present mountains, is clearly disturbed by the attempt to circumvent mortality and short-circuit human destiny, to merge woman and machine. As in a whole tradition of science-fiction stories, the machine as an object of desire and of science metamorphoses from being elegantly frivolous to being darkly menacing and dangerous. No longer the Beloved, the woman-machine Laura must be destroyed. A feminist reading of this novel might suggest that as long as Laura remains the construction of Endriade's fantasy—gay, flirtatious, and light-hearted—she survives, but when she begins to make demands she becomes threatening and fearsome. In such an interpretation, the novel becomes, as in *Il deserto dei Tartari,* an exploration of the odyssey of male desire.

Un amore is loosely based on Buzzati's own unhappy experiences in love. Despite the apparent divergence in style and genre from his previous stories, Buzzati in *Un amore* continues his preoccupations with time, desire, and death in the realm of the erotic. The author's rebuttal of accusations that he was bowing to the current fashion of Neorealism is vindicated by this fundamental continuity of theme. Neither is his style, essentially, much changed. Always precise, spare, and unadorned—a result of the readability required of high-quality journalism—Buzzati's analytical prose is ideally suited to this clinical investigation of love, not as romance but as pathology à la Émile Zola.

Un amore is set in the Milan of the economic boom in the late 1950s and early 1960s. The hell of the big city is explicitly identified with Laide, the young ballerina–call girl with whom the protagonist, Antonio Dorigo, falls in love. The youthful, enticing, treacherous, and volatile Laide, always unreachable, uncontainable, unpredictable, offers not satisfaction but exacerbated desire. Her intangibility makes her desirable; her refusal to give herself makes her the more wanted.

The emotion of love is dissected in this novel with almost surgical precision. Emblematic of the city corrupted by its own success, Laide is also a construction of Dorigo's desire, just as Laura was the product of a male's fantasy in *Il grande ritratto*. The name *Laide* points to the fundamental psychological mechanisms explored. To the extent that she stands for corrupt desire, the woman as *laida* (ugly) or *laidezza* (ugliness) represents the obscene enslavement to the irrational and the brutely physical; simultaneously, as the object of desire, she is the "ideal" in anagram. Love is neither progressive nor redeeming but a reiterative series of delusions and illusions, as circular as in Dante's Hell.

Buzzati joins a long literary tradition in creating a woman split by male desire into the Beatrice

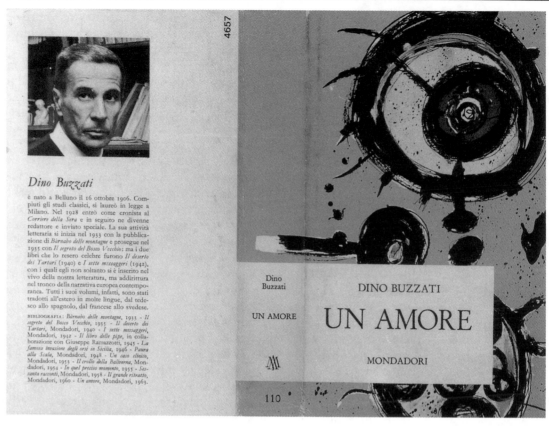

Dust jacket for Buzzati's 1963 novel, which focuses on an obsessive love affair

figure of salvation and the Eve of perdition. The schism of Madonna and whore is reenacted here in the realm not of the religious and teleological but of the psychological. There is no saving grace, and the only end point is death. Like Drogo in *Il deserto dei Tartari,* Dorigo (the similarity of names is striking) searches for the absolute, the culminating, crowning moment that will justify and give value to life, but just as the Tartars come too late, so the charmed reciprocity of love eludes Dorigo. The immobilizing repetition of military maneuvers here gives way to the equally senseless and futile repetition of ever more frenzied raised expectations and dashed hopes as Laide resists becoming enmeshed in Dorigo's idea of her. With Laide's pregnancy at the end of the novel, she is suddenly returned from the realm of the fantasizing and fetishizing psyche to the reality of the body, to the status of just another woman, to be cherished perhaps but no longer the source of disorienting madness. Reality roots itself within female biology, as in a further mystery inaccessible to the male mind.

Un amore was praised by Eugenio Montale for opening up a chink in the armor of bourgeois hypocrisy in the manner of Vladimir Nabokov's *Lolita*

(1955) or Heinrich Mann's novel that was made into the 1929 film *The Blue Angel.* It is the narrative of a compulsive obsession, a painfully honest account of deep and obscure psychic needs. There are no positive female characters to be found in Buzzati, but this is surely beside the point. The eroticism, the rigorous analysis of male desire found in *Un amore,* both complements and illuminates the impulses that lie behind all of Buzzati's best works: how to fill the time between birth and death; how to deceive the passing of time. If *Un amore* recalls *Il grande ritratto* in its portrait of a woman, then it also evokes *Il deserto dei Tartari* in its depiction of life as a brief sojourn on the wasteland where all one can do is wait for death.

Buzzati returned to writing stories after *Un amore.* "Viaggio agli inferni del secolo" (A Voyage to the Hells of the Century, 1966) again recalls Dante in its descent to the infernal city—no longer another world but contemporary Milan. As in Dante, Hell is all the more horrific not for its otherness but for its summoning up of the everyday and the banal. On his journey Dante meets not invented figures but friends, neighbors, and historical figures; Buzzati's Hell, though, is even more familiar and universal and can be easily reached by the new underground system. Buzzati combines the maximum of reality with the maximum of fantasy. Reality is not set aside but inverted, viewed from another angle, made strange but not unfamiliar through the operation of the fantastic narrative.

A painter as well as a writer, Buzzati allowed exhibitions of his work in later years. He combined his talents in his illustrated notebooks and in his remarkable and disturbing *Poema a fumetti* (A Poem in the Form of a Cartoon, 1969), a modern reinvention of the tale of Orpheus and Eurydice that in its juxtaposition of text and image draws knowingly on the increasingly popular tradition in Italy of comic strips and *fotoromanzi* (photo stories) as well as classical myth and legend.

As in "Viaggio agli inferni del secolo," the Hell of *Poema a fumetti* is the most banal of places, accessible through a gate in the wall opposite the house of Orfi, a singer-songwriter, or *cantautore,* in the modern Italian tradition. In one song Orfi sings of what those in Hell no longer have—dreams, pleasure, music, love, scattered leaves, the silence of the mountains. The unfettered eroticism of the images and drawings as well as the text evokes the psychological and sexual anxiety evident in Buzzati's other works such as *Il grande ritratto* and *Un amore.* Bordering at times on sadistic pornography in its vision of women as alternately aggressively dominant and helpless victims of violence, *Poema a fumetti* explores the ancient and modern obsession with love and death. Love becomes merely a prelude to death and can never triumph: in Buzzati's version Eura is lost to Orfi simply because she refuses to leave the realm of the dead, opposing an unbreakable law to his desire.

During his career Buzzati transposed several of his short stories for the theater. "I sette piani" was the source for his most notable play, *Un caso clinico,* which was produced in 1953 at the Piccolo Teatro in Milan. Its dramatic effect was compared to that achieved in Boris Vian's *Les Batisseurs d'Empire. La colonna infame* (The Column of Infamy, 1962) is a reinterpretation of Alessandro Manzoni's eponymous story, while *La famosa invasione degli orsi in Sicilia* (1945; translated as *The Bears' Famous Invasion of Sicily,* 1947), a parable for children, was first performed in 1965 and has been revived several times.

While Buzzati's work has often been linked with that of Kafka, it should also be associated with figures of modern European philosophy such as Martin Heidegger, Søren Kierkegaard, Jean-Paul Sartre, and Albert Camus; indeed, Camus staged some of Buzzati's theatrical productions in France. Buzzati's interest was phenomenology, and his abid-ing preoccupation was the relationship of man to himself in an uncertain, secular, inexplicable world. His characters are not psychological studies, nor are his tales socially and historically informed. His anonymous, almost interchangeable characters inhabit an absurd universe, while the formalism of his narrative only serves to make all the more disquieting the irrational laws by which his characters—and his readers—must all somehow contrive to live.

Interview:

Yves Panafieu, *Dino Buzzati: un autoritratto* (Milan: Mondadori, 1973).

Bibliographies:

Armida Marasco, *Buzzati nella critica dal 1967 ad oggi* (Bari: Adriatica, 1973);

Nella Giannetto, *Il coraggio della fantasia. Studio e ricerche intorno a Dino Buzzati* (Milan: Arcipelago, 1989), pp. 93–151.

References:

Antonia Arslan Veronese, *Invito alla lettura di Buzzati* (Milan: Mursia, 1974);

Elio Bartolini, "Buzzati e la nuova letteratura allegorica," *Il Mulino,* no. 44 (June 1955): 520–534;

Romano Battaglia, ed., *Il mistero in Dino Buzzati* (Milan: Rusconi, 1980);

Renato Bertacchini, "Buzzati e Kafka," *Idea,* 9 (1957): 12–16;

Bertacchini, "Il favoloso Buzzati," *Letterature moderne,* 10 (1960): 321–333;

Gian Paolo Biasin, "The Secret Fears of Men," *Italian Quarterly,* 6 (1962): 78–79;

Mauro Bonifazi, *Il racconto fantastico da Tarchetti a Buzzati* (Urbino: STEU, 1971);

Luigi Borelli, "Osservazioni su Dino Buzzati," *Italica,* 33 (1956): 93–101;

Charles Boulay, "Situation de l'homme dans l'oeuvre de Dino Buzzati," *Etudes Italiannes* (October–December 1959): 295–324;

Marcel Brion, "Trois écrivains italiens nouveaux," *Revue des deux mondes,* 19 (1950): 530–539;

Marcello Carlino, *Come leggere "Il deserto dei Tartari"* (Milan: Mursia, 1976);

Ferdinando Castelli, *Letteratura dell'inquietudine* (Milan: Massimo, 1963);

Pierina Castiglione, "Dino Buzzati," *Italica,* 34 (1957): 195–201;

Emilio Cecchi, "L'evoluzione di Buzzati," in his *Di giorno in giorno* (Milan: Garzanti, 1954);

Ilaria Crotti, *Dino Buzzati* (Florence: La Nuova Italia, 1977);

Alvise Fontanella, ed., *Atti del convegno "Dino Buzzati"* (Florence: Olschki, 1982);

Fausto Gianfranceschi, *Dino Buzzati* (Turin: Borla, 1967);

Nella Giannetto, *Il coraggio della fantasia. Studio e ricerche intorno a Dino Buzzati* (Milan: Arcipelago, 1989);

Giannetto, ed., *Il pianeta Buzzati* (Milan: Mondadori, 1992);

Giovanna Ioli, *Dino Buzzati* (Milan: Mursia, 1988);

François Livi, *"Le désert des Tartares": profil d'une oeuvre* (Paris: Hatier, 1973);

Mario Mignone, *Anormalità e angoscia nella narrativa di Dino Buzzati* (Ravenna: Longo, 1981);

Antonella Montenovesi, *Dino Buzzati* (Paris: Henry Veyrier, 1985);

Luciana Pietrosi, "Dino Buzzati," *Italica,* 42 (1965): 391–402;

Marilyn Schneider, "Beyond the Eroticism of Dino Buzzati's *Un amore,*" *Italica,* 46 (1969): 292–299;

Claudio Toscani, *Guida alla lettura di Buzzati* (Milan: Mondadori, 1987);

Claudio Varese, "Scrittori d'oggi," *Nuova antologia,* 91 (1959): 115–123.

Carlo Cassola
(17 March 1917 – 29 January 1987)

Emanuele Licastro
State University of New York at Buffalo

BOOKS: *Alla periferia* (Florence: Rivoluzione, 1942);

La visita (Florence: Parenti, 1942; enlarged edition, Turin: Einaudi, 1962);

Fausto e Anna (Turin: Einaudi, 1952; revised edition, 1958); translated by Isabel Quigley as *Fausto and Anna* (New York: Pantheon, 1960; London: Collins, 1960);

I vecchi compagni (Turin: Einaudi, 1953);

Il taglio del bosco (Milan: Fabbri, 1954); translated by Raymond Rosenthal as *The Cutting of the Woods, Texas Quarterly,* 4 (Summer 1961): 222–267; reprinted in *Six Modern Italian Novellas,* edited by William Arrowsmith (New York: Pocket Books, 1964);

Viaggio in Cina (Milan: Feltrinelli, 1956);

I minatori della Maremma, by Cassola and Luciano Bianciardi (Bari: Laterza, 1956);

La casa di via Valadier (Turin: Einaudi, 1956);

Un matrimonio del dopoguerra (Turin: Einaudi, 1957);

Il soldato (Milan: Feltrinelli, 1958);

Il taglio del bosco; Racconti lunghi e romanzi brevi (Turin: Einaudi, 1959);

La ragazza di Bube (Turin: Einaudi, 1960); translated by Marguerite Waldman as *Bebo's Girl* (New York: Pantheon, 1962; London: Collins, 1962);

Un cuore arido (Turin: Einaudi, 1961); translated by William Weaver as *An Arid Heart* (New York: Pantheon, 1964);

Il cacciatore (Turin: Einaudi, 1964);

Tempi memorabili (Turin: Einaudi, 1966);

Storia di Ada (Turin: Einaudi, 1967)—includes *La maestra;*

Ferrovia locale (Turin: Einaudi, 1968);

Una relazione (Turin: Einaudi, 1969);

Paura e tristezza (Turin: Einaudi, 1970);

Monte Mario (Milan: Rizzoli, 1973); translated by Sebastian Roberts as *Portrait of Helen* (London: Chatto & Windus, 1975);

Poesia e romanzo, by Cassola and Mario Luzi (Milan: Rizzoli, 1973);

Fogli di diario (Milan: Rizzoli, 1974);

Carlo Cassola

Gisella (Milan: Rizzoli, 1974);

Troppo tardi (Milan: Rizzoli, 1975);

L'antagonista (Milan: Rizzoli, 1976);

Il gigante cieco (Milan: Rizzoli, 1976);

Ultima frontiera (Milan: Rizzoli, 1976);

Conversazione su una cultura compromessa, edited by Antonio Cardella (Palermo: Il Vespro, 1977);

La disavventura (Milan: Rizzoli, 1977);

L'uomo e il cane (Milan: Rizzoli, 1977);

La lezione della storia (Milan: Rizzoli, 1978);

Letteratura e disarmo (Milan: Mondadori, 1978);

Un uomo solo (Milan: Rizzoli, 1978);

Il superstite (Milan: Rizzoli, 1978);

Il paradiso degli animali (Milan: Rizzoli, 1979);

Contro le armi (Marmirolo: Ciminiera, 1980);

Partono i bastimenti (Milan: Mondadori, 1980);

Vita d'artista (Milan: Rizzoli, 1980);

La morale del branco (Milan: Rizzoli, 1980);

Ferragosto di morte (Marmirolo, Reggio Emilla: Ciminiera, 1980);

Il ribelle (Milan: Rizzoli, 1980);

L'amore tanto per fare (Milan: Rizzoli, 1981);

Il romanzo moderno (Milan: Rizzoli, 1981);

Un territorio detto Lunigiana, by Cassola and Basco Bianchi (Milan: Silvan Editoriale, 1981);

La zampa d'oca (Milan: Rizzoli, 1981);

Gli anni passano (Milan: Rizzoli, 1982);

Colloquio con le ombre (Milan: Rizzoli, 1982);

Il mondo senza nessuno (Marmirolo, Reggio Emilia: Ciminiera, 1982);

Mio padre (Milan: Rizzoli, 1983);

La rivoluzione disarmata (Milan: Rizzoli, 1983);

Le persone contano più dei luoghi (Florence: Pananti, 1985);

L'Orologio della paura (Trento: New Magazine, 1989).

OTHER: "Alla ricerca di Thomas Hardy," 4 parts, *La fiera letteraria,* 26 September 1968, pp. 16–19; 3 October 1968, pp. 17–20; 10 October 1968, pp. 16–18; 17 October 1968, pp. 16–17;
"Grandezza e solitudine di Thomas Hardy," Introduction to *I romanzi di Thomas Hardy* (Milan: Mondadori, 1973), pp. XI–LXI.

Novelist and short-story writer Carlo Cassola is recognized as an advocate of the poetics of the subliminal as well as a poet of the everyday who transposes the banality of material appearance into a vision of the transcendental. His intention was not to obtain the sublime but, like William Wordsworth or Wallace Stevens, to redeem the quotidian moment. Cassola's best pages provide singular moments of insight into existence.

Throughout his long career Cassola not only refused to identify himself with the various currents in postwar Italian literature–Neorealism, experimentalism, Marxism, or "Gruppo '63"–but he also willfully criticized and at times peremptorily wrote works to oppose these contemporary trends. Occasionally, he found himself at the center of controversy: during the early 1960s, for instance, he was attacked by old-guard neorealists for having abandoned the tenets of social realism and by young avant-gardists for his old-fashioned narrative discourse.

Carlo Cassola was born on 17 March 1917 in Rome. His family had a long tradition of patriotism, political involvement, and anticlericalism. His grandfather Carlo, an activist for Italy's independence, was forced to live as an exile in Switzerland, and after the Risorgimento became a judge. His father, Garzia, a lawyer, was the editor of the national socialist paper *Avanti!;* following in his footsteps, Cassola would become a militant socialist.

Since his parents were from Volterra–his mother's hometown, where his father had moved from Pavia–Cassola passed his summer vacations in the Tuscan Maremma. He always considered himself more Tuscan than Roman and is thought of as a Tuscan writer. Growing up in Rome, Cassola attended the Liceo Tasso, where as a fifteen-year-old he and other students–including Benito Mussolini's son Vittorio–founded a short-lived antifascist and antifuturist movement, the Movimento Novista Italiano. Their manifesto proclaimed, "Il *Novismo* è nazionale ma non sciovinista: pone, prima del cittadino, l'uomo; prima dell'Italia, l'Umanità" (the *Novismo* is patriotic but not chauvinistic; it places man before the citizen; Humanity before Italy). It was at this time that Cassola and his lifelong friend Manlio Cancogni discovered their vocation as writers.

As a law student in Rome (1935–1939) and as a soldier in Spoleto and Bressanone (1937–1938), Cassola began writing short stories. The year after he finished his university studies, he got married and moved to Grosseto, in southern Tuscany, where he spent his life and where, with few exceptions, his works are set. His first stories were published in two small volumes, *Alla periferia* (On the Outskirts, 1942) and *La visita* (The Visit, 1942).

In his stories Cassola tried to capture moments of epiphany that surface from under the level (*sub limine*) of consciousness–rare moments revelatory of life in its essence–not life experienced consciously and in its practical forms. In a 1966 interview with Rodolfo Macchioni Jodi, Cassola explained: "Il sublimine è l'oggetto spogliato di ogni suo attributo ideologico, etico, psicologico, etc. Coincide cioè con l'esistenza, col nudo fatto dell'esistere; o meglio con l'esistenza e col solo attributo reale che essa comporti, la coesistenza dei sessi" (The subliminal is the object stripped of its attributes, ideological, ethical, psychological, etc. It coincides with existence, with the naked fact of existing; better, with existence and with its only real attribute, the coexistence of the sexes).

In his seminal essay "Il film dell'impossibile" (The Impossible Film), which was written in 1942 and used as the introduction to the 1964 edition of

La visita, Cassola writes of beauty realized through a static visual image:

> Il fondamento della bellezza di un quadro, di una fotografia, è lo stesso: l'immobilità del personaggio. Immobilità apparente piena di moto sostanziale. Perchè il personaggio immobile ha tutte le possibilità di movimento intatte, cioè tutte le possibilità di vita intatte. La sua immobilità allude al movimento, la sua mancanza di vita alla vita, l'assenza del tempo al fluire del tempo. E lo stesso vale per un paesaggio. . . . Animare una stampa, cioè far muovere e vivere i suoi personaggi, è appunto, tentare un film dell'impossibile.

> (The foundation of beauty in a painting, a print, a photograph is the same; the immobility of the character. Apparent immobility full of substantial movement. For the motionless character maintains intact all the possibilities of movement. Its immobility alludes to movement, its lack of life to life, its absence of time to the flux of time. The same holds true for a landscape. . . . In order to animate a print, that is, to make its characters move and live is, exactly, to attempt the impossible film.)

Cassola compares these still moments to characteristic moments in Eugenio Montale's poetry, which "è fatta di barlumi, di segni, di allusioni, di varchi, di occasioni che non possiamo sfruttare . . . [perchè] la vita ci è preclusa" (consist of gleams, signs, allusions, openings, occasions of which we cannot take advantage . . . [since] life precludes us). One can only experience an awareness of being in fleeting moments when one is removed from the events of everyday life. Hence Cassola believed such moments are most powerful when they are relived in memory.

In many of his first stories Cassola registers atmospheres, sensations, and moods by means of fleshless chronicles. Writing in *La letteratura italiana, Otto-Novecento* (1974), Gianfranco Contini remarks: "Il loro fascino, forse non più uguagliato, è nell'assurdo che si sprigiona da referti ordinari e insignificanti" (their charm, perhaps unequaled, resides in the absurd released from ordinary and meaningless references). Cassola's method is to start from a small detail or scene, which he probes in order to find its secret life.

In the story "La visita" Cassola begins by describing the trip that Delfo, a British colonel living in Australia, is making to the Murchison family, who left the United States for Australia in 1790. In his living room Mr. Murchison keeps a painting of George Washington's visit to Philadelphia. The colonel, on the other hand, speaks of Napoleon's recent military campaigns. Only after reading a third

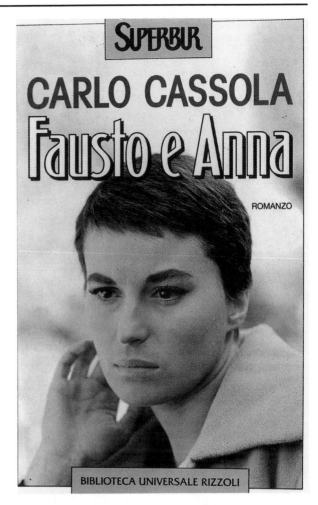

Cover for a 1996 edition of Cassola's 1952 book, which unlike other postwar Italian novels offers a less-than-heroic view of the Resistance

of the narration does the reader learn that he has been reading a description of the events leading up to the scene that inspired a tapestry artist. The tapestry itself depicts two eighteenth-century men near a river and, as it turns out in the story, is hanging in the bedroom of the widow Rosa Boni. Her brother-in-law is resting on her bed after a long trip, and Rosa before leaving the room glances at the tapestry.

The second part of the story is set in an unnamed Tuscan village in the 1930s and recounted in the same tone, rhythm, and style as the first. Rosa, whom the narrator claims he saw on a train some time before, is being visited by her brother-in-law because his wife is about to die and he would like Rosa to take her place and raise his children. Rosa, however, refuses. She is satisfied waiting for her final journey, the passage from this world to the next that will reunite her with her dead husband.

Carlo Cassola

IL TAGLIO DEL BOSCO

FRATELLI FABBRI EDITORI

Cover for Cassola's 1954 novella, in which a woodcutter mourns the death of his wife while continuing his monotonous labor

rativo veniva a mancarmi. Smisi di scrivere" (But wasn't mine a mad, "impossible" endeavor? . . . I had to reduce the weight of facts to a minimum. . . . Narrative breath was failing me. I stopped writing). The dilemma between the need to narrate and the need to eliminate "content" ends the first period of Cassola's literary career.

In 1942 Cassola, then a high-school teacher, joined the Resistance against Fascism; he fought with a group of Communist partisans even though he did not share their ideology and politics. His participation in the Resistance was meaningful not only because he risked his life but because war gave him the opportunity, as he says in the introduction to his 1954 novella *Il taglio del bosco,* "di conoscere da vicino . . . la gente del popolo, gli operai, gli artigiani, i contadini" (of becoming closely acquainted with common people, workers, artisans, farmers). After the war Cassola worked as a newspaperman and became interested in political life.

These experiences—marriage, work, war, journalism, and politics—reshaped Cassola's attitudes and perceptions. Carlo Marabini calls Cassola's second period of creativity (1946–1960) the committed period. In his interview with Macchioni Jodi, he recalls:

> Quando ricominciai a scrivere . . . avevo ancora l'occhio alla mia poetica giovanile, ma non osavo più applicarla in modo rigoroso, perchè sapevo . . . che poteva convertirsi in un'inibizione paralizzante.
>
> (When I started writing again . . . I still looked to my youthful poetics, but I didn't dare apply it strictly, because I knew . . . it could turn into a paralyzing inhibition.)

One evident sign of the change is the length of his works: instead of short and very short stories, Cassola began to write long stories, novellas, and novels. The most telling innovation, though, is Cassola's use of his own experience, as he begins to present Resistance events and to discuss partisan ideology. This period includes both texts that show Cassola's social commitment and those in the lyrical existential vein of his earlier work, such as the stories "Rosa Gagliardi," written in 1946 and first published in 1947 in *Botteghe Oscure,* and "Il soldato" (The Soldier), written between 1953 and 1957 and first published in 1957 in *Nuovi Argomenti.* The stories were published as a book under the title *Il soldato* in 1958.

Instead of providing glimpses of still lifes, Cassola began to let his characters move in the ordinariness of daily routine. In keeping with the author's metaphor of representative art, one could say that

From the image of the tapestry Cassola evokes a past; from the image of Rosa on the train he conjures a future. Each event and character is flattened to the same plane of importance—Washington's trip, Delfo's, the Murchisons', the brother-in-law's, Rosa and the narrator's on the train, and Rosa's after death. The faraway events of the past—resonating with war, revolution, empire, and art—fade into one another and collapse into the inevitability of time. Cassola explores not facts but situations, not psychological designs but moods, not great events but banalities, not history but fantasy, not plots but moments.

Cassola commented on his approach to fiction in his early stories in his 1967 interview with Macchioni Jodi: "Ma non era, il mio, un tentativo pazzesco, un tentativo 'impossibile'? . . . Dover ridurre al minimo il peso dei fatti. . . . Il respiro narhe would animate a bas-relief rather than bring life to a tapestry. However, his stories remain without intricate plots, psychological investigation, or heroic action. Cassola's interest is the plot of personal existence, not the plot of history where the feelings and beliefs of the characters are linked to the larger concerns of their culture and society. His protagonists are not citizens but human beings—a conception that matches the fifteen-year-old Cassola's naive idealism.

Most critics view the existential *Il taglio del bosco* (translated as *The Cutting of the Woods,* 1961) as Cassola's best novella. It was written in 1949 and first published in 1950 in *Paragone*. He discusses its genesis in Ferdinando Camon's *Il mestiere di scrittore* (The Writer's Craft, 1973):

> Era concepito come una vicenda puramente esistenziale.... Cinque tagliatori vanno a tagliare un bosco, durante alcuni mesi fanno ogni giorno lo stesso lavoro, ripetono gli stessi discorsi, etc. Ecco un magnifico tema per una narrazione *negativa:* mi permetteva infatti di raccontare qualcosa e, nello stesso tempo, di non raccontare nulla ... che avesse un significato particolare. Il solo significato ... era puramente esistenziale.

> (It was conceived as a purely existential event.... Five woodcutters go to cut wood; for a few months they do the same work every day, repeat the same things, etc. Here was a magnificent subject for a *negative* narration: in fact it allowed me to narrate something and, at the same time, to narrate nothing ... with a special meaning. Its only meaning ... was purely existential.)

In 1949, as he was halfway through the story, Cassola's wife died. His emotional state was such that he could no longer write, as he intended, a stark and emotionless story. He told Camon how the death affected his approach: "Quando ripresi a scrivere ... conservai la vicenda esistenziale del taglio, ma ne feci il semplice sfondo di un sentimento particolare, il dolore del protagonista per la morte della moglie" (When I restarted writing ... I kept the existential matter of woodcutting, but I made of it the simple background of a particular feeling, the protagonist's grief for his wife's death).

This short novel depicts in a plain, precise style the details of the woodcutters' monotonous labor. Their routine is hardly broken by changes of weather or landscape. Nature itself, neither lyrical nor consoling, is imbued with melancholy and grief. The stillness of time becomes alive with Guglielmo's sorrow, and the book's pessimism is underlined by its haunting conclusion: "E guardò in alto. Ma era tutto buio, non c'era una stella" (And he looked up. But it was all dark, there wasn't a single star). Neither silent nature nor the gods—"stella" is reminis-

cent of the endings of the canticles in Dante's *Divine Comedy*—can alleviate his loneliness. The adversative conjunction *but* underscores a painful cognizance of the human condition.

In 1951 Cassola remarried and fathered a daughter. He continued to teach in high school and to write on social and literary topics for newspapers such as *Corriere della sera* and *Il mondo* as well as professional journals such as *La fiera letteraria, Il ponte,* and *Le ragioni narrative*. With the publication of *Fausto e Anna* his popularity grew to the point that in 1954 *Il taglio del bosco* was published in book form and became a best-seller; the critical response was also quite favorable.

Cassola continued to be active in local and national politics, and these interests are reflected in his creative work: except for two novellas—*Il soldato* and *La maestra* (The Teacher), started in 1957 and published in *Storia di Ada* (Ada's Story, 1967)—all his fictions are based on contemporary Italian history, World War II, and the postwar period. Cassola's writings of social engagement include the novellas *Baba,* which was published in *Il mondo* in 1946, *Esiliati* (Exiled), which first appeared in *Il ponte* in 1953, *La casa di via Valadier* (The House on Valadier Street, 1956), *Un matrimonio del dopoguerra* (A Post-War Marriage, 1957), and the two full-length novels *Fausto e Anna* and *La ragazza di Bube.*

Fausto e Anna (translated as *Fausto and Anna,* 1960) combines existential, socio-ideological, and autobiographical elements. Both protagonists had appeared in preceding novellas: Anna in the existential "Le amiche" (Girl Friends), which was published in *Botleghe Oscure* in 1949, and Fausto, whose story is largely reiterated in the new work, in the political *Baba e Esiliati*. *Fausto e Anna* is noteworthy because, for the first time, Cassola weaves a plot, details a relationship, chronicles linear biographies, and more than once creates suspense. Cassola considered *Fausto e Anna* his only autobiographical novel, and he incorporated his experiences as a student on a summer vacation in southern Tuscany and in the Resistance, his political views, and his ideas of social justice. The same experiences and ideas are also reflected in his critical writings of the time. In the same year the novel was published, Cassola cofounded the political party Unità Popolare (Popular Unity), which later merged with the national Socialist Party.

The main themes of love and war in *Fausto e Anna* do not intersect in a crescendo of suspense but remain almost completely separate. In the first part of the novel Fausto and Anna Mannoni meet, fall in love, and break up. An intellectual with aspirations of being a writer, Fausto is always self-conscious, always judging his actions, even as he kisses Anna for the first time. On the other hand, Anna is unselfconscious, impulsive, optimistic. Perceiving the impossibility of their love, she chooses Miro, Fausto's opposite, a relaxed man, one with nature, whose great enjoyment is hunting. In the second part of the novel Fausto's restlessness causes him to join the Communist partisans who seek to overthrow Fascist rule in Italy. He discusses political ideas with Baba, the Communist leader, but his participation, lacking ideological conviction, is more a sublimation of the libido than the sharing of a sublime struggle for which people are ready to die. No matter how physically involved in the fight, he remains emotionally apart from his comrades. At the end of the war, Fausto and Anna meet by chance and go their separate ways.

Fausto's middle-class values prevent him from sharing the simple enthusiasm of the proletarian partisans, some of whom act stupidly and cruelly, as when they kill helpless Fascists and wounded German prisoners. Nor can he share the political idealism of the educated Marxist leaders. In fact, in spite of its powerful pages on the Resistance, the novel ultimately is not a Resistance book. It differs from the memoirs, pamphlets, chronicles, diaries, and many of the novels based on the Resistance that mushroomed in Italy after the war. It seems as though Cassola chooses to foreground the least appealing aspects of the Resistance movement. Perhaps this was the reason *Fausto e Anna* was rejected by the publishers Mondadori and Bompiani before being accepted by Einaudi.

Only the outer shell of *Fausto e Anna* is that of a committed historical novel; read closely, it proves to be an existential work. Fausto is an egotist who does not want to be restricted by circumstances that would bind him to others, and the social changes he seeks are too abstract to be realized. Anna's actions and feelings, like Fausto's, are also never touched by historical events. She never once expresses concern about the war, except as it disturbs her own life. As Giuliano Manacorda writes in *Invito all lettura di Carlo Cassola* (An Invitation to Read Carlo Cassola, 1973), the book's first line, "Era tutto buio. Non s'udivano rumori di sorta" (It was completely dark. No one heard a sound), and the last, "Era tutto buio. Non c'era nessuno" (It was completely dark. There wasn't anyone), seem to imply that man's actions come from and disappear into the shadows. With this first novel, Cassola won substantial recognition by literary critics and the public alike. However, he was bitterly attacked by Marxist critics for having defiled the heroes and the ideals of the Resistance.

Cassola's success continued with the publication of his second and most famous novel, *La ragazza di Bube* (translated as *Bebo's Girl,* 1962), which was awarded the Strega Prize, the most prestigious in Italy. It sold hundreds of thousands of copies, was translated into more than twenty languages, and was made into a movie. The story, based on a real event, takes place after World War II. Bube, a Communist and former partisan, nicknamed the Avenger for his violence and dedication, pays a visit to his dead comrade's family and meets his half sister, Mara. They fall in love and become engaged. But it is difficult for Bube to adjust to peacetime. In a rage he kills the son of a police officer who had killed one of his friends. While waiting for his Communist friends to drive him to safety in France, he hides with Mara in a solitary hut, where they make love for the first time in their lives. Two years later he is extradited, and in spite of a general political amnesty, he is sentenced to fourteen years in prison. Meanwhile, Mara, who had started a new relationship with Stefano, decides—after the sentence—to wait for Bube, for she is Bube's girl.

The story has the making of a romantic novel: youth, love, faithfulness, unfaithfulness, forced separation, sorrow, hope, political idealism, sacrifice, and the dedication of youth. The fairy-tale enchantment of the book's love story comes from the fated attraction of the two protagonists in spite of their contrasting worlds. Young Bube's violent ways, no less than his ideas and desires, are the result of party indoctrination. When he meets Mara, he is attracted to her, but he is also shy and awkward. To give himself confidence, he shows off his revolver, which, beyond its phallic symbolism, represents all he actually is, a blind tool. As Italo Calvino first pointed out, Bube is "passive and conditioned by circumstances," while Mara is free.

At the beginning Mara is immature, thoughtless, and self-assured, with "una illimitata fiducia nella sua bellezza e nella sua furberia" (a limitless trust in her beauty and in her cunning). She is in control of what she thinks and what she does. In the hut, while waiting for the car to take Bube away, it is she who initiates the lovemaking, just as later she chooses to offer herself to Stefano, who refuses because they are not married. At the end she understands Bube's sadness, and through it she becomes aware of life's sadness. She agrees with Bube that the responsibility for the killing is not only his: "Forse che uno fa quello che veramente si sente di fare? No, uno fa quello che gli altri si aspettano che faccia" (Do you think one does what he really feels like doing? No, one does what others expect him to do).

Once resigned to Bube's fate, Mara becomes aware that everyone has a destiny, and she submits herself to hers, hence her sacrifice. The novel ends with these words by Mara, which echo Cassola's existential views: "Mi sono convinta che la colpa non è stata di nessuno. . . . Nessuno ebbe colpa . . . fu solo un male . . . [i giudici] hanno fatto un altro male" (I am convinced that it was no one's fault. . . . No one was guilty . . . it was only an evil act . . . [the judges] committed another evil act). Cassola portrays both Bube and Mara as victims not of historical events but of life.

Although much praised, *La ragazza di Bube* also became a focus for various criticisms. The political reaction to the novel reiterated the criticism leveled at *Fausto e Anna*. Some attacked it for dwelling on the failure of the idealistic causes espoused by the Resistance: to be sure, no character is heroic and the partisans are stripped of grandeur. Even the most idealistic character, Mara's father, grows disillusioned and morose toward the end of the novel. Cassola's writing also sparked apolitical criticism. In 1963 the Italian avant-garde "Gruppo '63," which held no socio-ideological interests at all, attacked Cassola and other popular writers such as Giorgio Bassani and Alberto Moravia for holding on to traditional narrative structures such as plot and character.

The sharpest attack on the novel was on traditional literary grounds. During the presentation of the Strega Prize, Pier Paolo Pasolini—whose novels deal with the life of the Roman subproletariat and make use of its colloquial speech—recited a verse composition, "In morte del Realismo" (On the Death of Realism), a long harangue against Cassola in the meters and metaphors of Antony's funerary oration in *Julius Caesar*. In effect, he accused Cassola of betraying the social tenets of realism. Cassola's "lyricism of intimate prose" was seen as a symptom of an intellectual looking at society from his ivory tower and was criticized as an aristocratic view of the world. Pasolini called Cassola a neo-purist, a white socialist: "Ecco il colpo / tagliente di Cassola–ch'era amico / . . . / Perchè Cassola, lo sapete, è socialista: / ha agito dentro il cuore dell'idea / realista: e il suo è il colpo più brutale" (Here is the deep / stab of Cassola–who was a friend / . . . / For Cassola, as you know, is a socialist: / he has acted from within the realist / idea: and his stab is the more brutal).

Cassola answered that Pasolini was confusing realism with Neorealism, a literary form conditioned by Marxist ideology. Pasolini, he argued, was no doubt referring to Neorealism in defending "impuro Realismo / sigillato col sangue partigiano e la passione dei marxisti" (impure Realism / sealed with partisan blood and the passion of Marxists).

He also observed that his choice not to write in dialect did not mean he was a neopurist, unless all Tuscans were by definition neopurists.

In 1962, following the success of *La ragazza di Bube,* which allowed him to quit teaching, Cassola's career took a second dramatic turn. Dissatisfied with his long years of committed writing, he returned to the existential poetics of his youth, expanding some of the plots and even repeating some of the titles of his earliest pieces. His third novel and third best-seller, *Un cuore arido* (1961; translated as *An Arid Heart,* 1964), depicts the everyday world of his youthful stories. In the previous two novels the emotional life of the protagonists is not connected to historical events, even if the presence of tumultuous times in the text is substantial. In *Un cuore arido* nothing resembling the dramatic events treated in *Fausto e Anna* or in *La ragazza di Bube* occurs. It has been rightly suggested that the events of the novel could take place in 1933 or 1833 because of its emphasis on the private life of its protagonist.

Un cuore arido introduces a female protagonist, Anna Cavorzio, who is a linear and static character. Whereas Mara in *La ragazza di Bube* undergoes a progression from childlike lack of consciousness through pain to conscious self-sacrifice, Cassola's new protagonist is self-sufficient because she shuns self-sacrifice and refuses to take an active role in ordinary daily life. She desperately strives to prevent unyielding facts from impinging upon her spiritual and emotional life; her ideal is to cultivate and savor her private moods and visions. After rejecting her suitor, Enrico, she falls in love with and steals her sister Bice's fiancé, Mario. She gives herself to him the night before he is to leave for America. With no real interest, she becomes the lover of the superficial and selfish Marcello, who is already engaged; a few months later she abruptly stops seeing him. At the end of the novel, Cassola observes: "Niente, niente avrebbe potuto sconvolgere la sua vita . . . perchè . . . l'essenza vera della vita era qualcosa d'intangibile. Niente poteva intaccarla: i fatti . . . erano in realtà cosa senza importanza, senza significato" (Nothing, nothing could have upset her life . . . because . . . the true essence of life was something intangible. Nothing could corrode it: and facts . . . were really something without importance, without meaning).

Un cuore arido reflects the influence of Thomas Hardy upon Cassola. He believed that Hardy's greatness lay in his vivid representation of the Wessex countryside, which Cassola visited in 1968 and wrote four essays about for *La fiera letteraria.* Cassola also edited and contributed an introduction to Hardy's novels, published by Mondadori. In *Il mestiere di scrittore* he recalls:

Cover for a 1995 edition of Cassola's 1961 novel, which shows
the influence of British novelist Thomas Hardy

In quel tempo io ero sotto l'influenza di Thomas Hardy
e in particoloare di *Tess dei d'Urbervilles* . . . uno scrittore
che va unicamente dietro l'immaginazione: un personaggio di Hardy inizialmente è per l'autore una specie di
nebulosa che si chiarisce poi a poco a poco. . . . *Un cuore
arido* io lo scrissi proprio in questo modo . . . inizialmente non avevo nulla in mente, sono partito da un'immagine, quella della ragazza sulla spiaggia, come appare
appunto nel primo capitolo.

(At the time I was under the influence of Thomas
Hardy and in particular of *Tess of the D'Urbervilles*.
Hardy is a writer who follows only his imagination: a
character of his initially is for the author a kind of nebulous vision which slowly becomes clear. . . . I wrote *Un
cuore arido* exactly in this manner. . . . Initially I had
nothing in mind, I started with an image, the girl on the
beach, precisely as it appears in the first chapter.)

Cassola in *Un cuore arido* seems to be bringing
to life a tapestry, just as he did in his first short

story, "La visita," some twenty-five years earlier.
Like Hardy, he fills his novel with page after page of
quotidian detail, as his protagonist seeks a subliminal level of existence. On the last page, Anna is still
trying to understand the meaning of her life:

La vita quotidiana si componeva di tante cose, piccole e
grandi, rifare i letti e mangiare, fidanzarsi e sposare; ma
la vita vera era come la luce e il calore del sole, qualcosa
di segreto e di inafferrabile.

(Everyday life consisted of so many things, small and
big, like making the beds and eating, getting engaged
and married; but real life was like the light and the
warmth of the sun, something secret and ungraspable.)

Cassola uses the southern Tuscan seaside not
just as a backdrop but as a means of structuring the
story and affecting the emotions of characters and
readers. The moods evoked by the descriptive passages help express and substantiate the protagonist's existential condition. For example, after her
sister's wedding, Anna is alone in the house:

Spalancò la finestra . . . la campagna inondata dalla tie-
pida luce del sole. . . . Anna aveva l'impressione che una
forza luminosa e calda frugasse dappertutto, per in-
fondere vita nelle cose. . . . Frugava anche nel suo animo, e lo inondava della gioia di vivere.

(She opened up the window . . . the countryside was
flooded by the tepid light of the sun. . . . Anna had the
impression that a luminous and warm force was searching everywhere, to instill life into things. . . . It was also
searching in her soul, flooding it with the joy of being
alive.)

While *Un cuore arido* depicts the sense of life's
rapture in the silence of the heart of a young woman
who has renounced even love, the short novel *Il cacciatore* (The Hunter, 1964) expresses life's quiet desperation. The plot is simpler than in Cassola's previous novel as even the few subplots and minor characters that were present in *Un cuore arido* are eliminated. In love with Andrea, who left for military
service in World War I, Nelly is attracted to Alfredo, whose heart ailment exempts him from the
draft. He seduces and abandons her with child. At
the end of the war Andrea returns home and marries Nelly.

Cassola recounts the events in an unemphatic
tone. What would be considered a crucial fact in a
traditional story is presented in the most casual
manner: at the beginning of part 3 Cassola simply
notes that Nelly is pregnant. Little more is said
about the matter. Instead, Cassola focuses attention
on Alfredo's hunting. Although Alfredo only wan-

ders over a few square miles, Cassola scrupulously details the hunt and the varied terrain through the changing of the seasons in a manner reminiscent of *Il taglio del bosco,* making it seem a search through an eternally insoluble maze.

Self-sufficient and hedonistic, Alfredo is transfigured into a quester for meaning. Hunting is a means of overcoming his anguish: "Non era così la vita? Il caso, il caso soltanto ne determinava il corso!" (Wasn't life like that? Chance, only chance determined its course!). It provides him with a reason for excluding himself from any sentimental or social attachment. His father having died of heart failure at forty, Alfredo's stubborn defense of his freedom seems a product of his sense of having limited time: "'Io, quella Nelly, non la voglio sposare. Non ci sento più niente.' Gli pareva, anzi di non averci mai sentito niente" ('That Nelly, I don't want to marry her. I no longer feel anything.' Actually, it seemed to him that he had never felt anything for her). His only gesture of tenderness is nourishing a sick bird back to life.

In *Tempi memorabili* (Memorable Times, 1966) Cassola depicts the passage from childhood to adolescence through the discovery of love. In the first chapter, young Fausto—the character with this name is always somewhat autobiographical in Cassola's work—remembers how as a child he, his mother, and brothers used to leave Rome every summer to spend a month at the seaside in Tuscany. The memory is not very pleasant. In the second chapter he remembers blissfully a summer month which he, alone, and his mother passed at the same place. A memorable summer!

This short novel covers a brief period in Fausto's life. His love for Anna is not a desire for contact or relation and does not even need to be requited; it is an awakening into the existential state of discovering himself alive. He does not need anyone, including his father, whom he subconsciously kills: "Suo padre era vecchio, mentre lui era appena entrato nella vita. D'ora innanzi, che cosa avebbero potuto dirsi?" (His father was old while he had just entered life. From now on what possibly could they say to each other?). Fausto sees only through his feelings: "Fausto guardava tutti con simpatia, perchè erano i compaesani di Anna. Mentre se incontrava qualche villeggiante, nemmeno gli badava" (Fausto looked at everyone with sympathy because they were Anna's fellowvillagers. Whereas if he met some vacationer, he wouldn't bother even looking at him).

His sensation of love is so fulfilling that Fausto does not feel the need to communicate it to anyone. Even if he wanted to, he couldn't find the right words. The effort would be as hard as the artistic expression of it. Says Fausto-Cassola: "Ma se lui stesso . . . fosse diventato uno scrittore: gli sarebbe forse stato possibile esprimere il proprio sentimento?" (But if he himself became . . . a writer: would it be possible for him to express his own feelings?) The experience will remain eternally present and intact: "A Roma pioveva e faceva freddo; a Marina, invece, il tempo s'era fermato. Fausto sorrideva: dentro di lui era sempre estate" (In Rome it was raining and it was cold; in Marina, instead, time had stopped. Fausto was smiling: inside him it was always summer).

With *Ferrovia locale* (Local Railroad, 1968) Cassola comes closest to realizing his artistic goals of abolishing narrative and nullifying facts. His process of rarefaction reaches the limit. The critic Giuliano Manacorda observed that perhaps the term *novel* is not quite appropriate for this book. The unifying frame of the text is a thirty-six-hour round-trip on a freight train from Pisa to Orbetello. The beginning is as arbitrary as the end; it could have been a longer or shorter trip. What is narrated is also arbitrary since it consists of what Dino—a young, low-level employee—supposedly sees; he could have seen anything.

As in Cassola's earliest stories, life is conjured up from images—a girl at a window, the daughter of a railroad employee, the stationmaster's wife. These images expand centrifugally into some thirty vignettes. The book is structured along multiple parallel lines of events. Fragments of these events are arbitrarily cut and substituted for other unrelated fragments. An event just occurs and when it stops occurring there is no resolution, no climax. There are only glimpses of existence. The patchy, partial knowledge the reader gleans is the same as that acquired in everyday life. It is only by imagination that one can give substance to such images.

One of the motifs Cassola employs is couples: Diego, the sickly stationmaster, and Dina, his very healthy wife; an old couple, Mario and Delia, in love and jealous; a young couple, Luigi and Adriana, expecting for the first time; Emilio and his too-young wife, Rina. Other characters include two students, Bruno, who is discovering love, and Riccardo, who takes the same train every day; Cannizzi, a physician; and a Sicilian with an illegitimate daughter. Attitudes vary; the observed girls are both good and bad, both unhappy to leave their village and happy to leave it. People and moments converge into one another. The landscape also flashes by as framed still images moving as swiftly as the train.

Cassola composes these many images—banal, chaotic, inconclusive—into a meaningful mosaic. No tessera sticks out in his impassive tone or in the precise, unadorned language. His syntax is elementary and his paragraphs are short, at times only a line. In presenting his book Cassola declared: "Non si dà alcun giudizio sulla realtà, perchè giudicare la vita è una prevaricazione" (No judgment is given because to judge life is to betray it). He presents objects, people, events as they are perceived subliminally, stripped of conscious design, morality, history, religion, and, above all, of rhetoric. Cassola suggested as an analogy the eternal and untouchable bottles of Giorgio Morandi.

In his fourth and longest full-length novel, *Paura e tristezza* (Fear and Sadness, 1970), Cassola's minute description of daily routine, instead of including dozens of characters, is concentrated only on the protagonist. Six-year-old Anna Dell'Aiuto lives with her unwed mother, a washwoman who is afraid her daughter will end up like herself. The mother's abnormal situation hints at her difficulty of relating to people and the world, hence her fear and sadness. As a teenager Anna is happy only because she is in love with the adolescent Alvise, a refugee who soon must leave the village. The sadness of her loss ends the first part of the novel. Anna eventually goes to nearby Volterra to work as a maid. She accepts Guido's proposal of marriage half-heartedly since she is still in love with Alvise, but then Guido is drafted and has to leave. Her sadness for her mother's death ends part two. Not in love with the gentle Guido, Anna then lets herself be seduced by the vulgar farmer Enrico. Part three also ends in calamity; she is now unwed and pregnant.

Instead of resigning herself to her fate as other Cassolan women do in his previous novels, Anna contemplates the appropriate literary ending of suicide. The steep cliffs she would jump off appear in the book's first line; the father of Anna's childhood friend Pia jumped to his death there, and the cliffs are described as dangerous throughout the text. Cassola, however, found it impossible to retract his conviction that existence is an absolute value. In a 1981 interview with Pietro Poiana, he said: "L'istinto di morte . . . può esserci nell'animo umano ma è soffocato . . . dall'istinto di vita. . . . La letteratura [deve] solo testimoniare l'amore della vita in quanto bene inestimabile, anche quando si riduce ad essere semplice esistenza" (The death wish . . . may exist in the human soul but it is suppressed . . . by the wish for life. . . . Literature [must] be a witness only to love for life in that it is an invaluable good, even when it is reduced to simple existence).

Cassola added a last chapter that brings the novel full circle. Anna, now married to Enrico, is the mother of four. Her oldest girl is six, just as she was at the beginning of the novel. It is apparent that the cycle of fear and sadness will be repeated. As Anna looks at her daughter "le venivano le lacrime agli occhi. Che ne sarebbe stato di lei? Non le poteva aspettare nulla di buono." (tears would come to her eyes. What would become of her? she couldn't expect anything good). After just six years of marriage, Anna suffers from varicose veins and swollen legs. Her hair and teeth have fallen out. The novel's ending suggests that fear and sadness are not necessarily connected to Anna's particular trials. Her unhappiness, according to Natalia Ginzburg, is something that existed before her story began.

A heart attack in 1971 did not stop Cassola's literary activity. In 1973 he published *Monte Mario* (translated as *Portrait of Helen,* 1975). The novel is something of a surprise: for the first time Cassola's protagonists belong to the upper middle class; the setting is not the usual Tuscan village of the past but, nominally at least, Rome of the 1970s; and it is written all in dialogue except for the last few pages. The novel covers the four weeks twenty-six-year-old Elena spends with her former fiancé at his apartment. She keeps rejecting him in spite of her desire; he is attracted to her in spite of her rejections. They are unable to communicate. Through a careful orchestration of the dialogue, Cassola succeeds in revealing their inner worlds.

In the middle 1970s, living alone in the Tuscan Maremma after he had separated from his wife and his only daughter had moved to Florence, Cassola came to a third turning point in his intellectual life. The artist who for fifteen years, since *La ragazza di Bube,* had renounced and denounced the literature of commitment converted to a moral ideology. In 1977 he confessed in "Perchè scrivo storie de cani" (Why I Write Stories About Dogs), an article appearing in the 24 December *Tuttolibri:* "Un tempo . . . tra una letteratura rivolta verso il vero e una . . . rivolta verso il bello non avrei esitato un minuto a scegliere la seconda. Oggi sono per una bellezza che si accordi con la verità" (Once upon a time . . . between a literature inclined towards truth and one towards beauty I wouldn't have hesitated a minute to choose the second. Today I am for a beauty which agrees with truth). In 1981 he told Poiana that he lent more importance to "un'azione con gli altri, un'azione collettiva, un'azione politica più che la rappresentazione letteraria" (an action shared with others, a collective action, a political action rather than its literary representation). At this stage one could call Cassola an anarchist and utopian. Convinced of an impending nuclear and ecological catastrophe, he founded the "League for Italian Unilateral Disarmament" in 1977 and started a campaign against militarism and nationalism.

Cassola's new concerns influenced his works. In his novel *Un uomo solo* (A Man Alone, 1978) Tito is an anarchist who refuses to compromise with both Fascists and antifascists. He is the exact opposite of his childhood friend, Agenore, who befriends Fascist officials but is glad his son will marry Tito's daughter in case the Fascist regime is toppled. Tito is not interested in his daughter's wedding. He prefers to be alone. Cassola was so taken by his ideological commitment that he decided to write animal fables. He explained to Poiana: "Le favole sono il genere in cui i vizi umani si prestano meglio ad essere satireggiati . . . perchè . . . l'animale rimane universale" (Fables are the genre in which human faults are easier to satirize . . . because . . . animals are universal). In *L'uomo e il cane* (The Man and the Dog, 1977) Jack, a dog, wanders through Tuscan valleys and mountains alone, scared to be free. But the master he finally finds leaves him chained to a post to die. Cassola's polemic is against Italian intellectuals—few of whom answered his call to arms against militarism—who right after the defeat of Fascism joined other parties. A dog is also the protagonist of his subsequent novel, *Il superstite* (The Survivor, 1978). The only survivor of a worldwide nuclear holocaust, the dog lets himself die.

During his last period Cassola would still sometimes return to writing on behalf of beauty. Two years before his death he published the novella *Le persone contano più dei luoghi* (People Count More than Places, 1985), a sequel to *Un cuore arido*. In the first novel Anna Cavorzio believes that places are more important than people; they incorporate "il ricordo di Mario come già tutti gli altri, fin dei tempi remoti della sua infanzia" (the memory of Mario as well as all other memories since the remote times of her infancy). In the sequel Anna has changed her mind. When Mario sends a second letter renewing his marriage proposal, Anna accepts and gladly joins him in Chicago. Both, though, feel homesick for Marina, the small Tuscan village a few miles away from Cassola's own residence.

Together with this novella, Cassola published a short essay, "Paura della morte" (Fear of Death), which can be read as a farewell. Cassola writes: "Prendo in mano un libro, ma poco dopo mi stanco e lo lascio cadere. . . . Nelle mie condizioni devo guardare sopratutto alla salute. . . . Ho deciso di vivere per gli altri. . . . Egoisticamente, desidero solo la morte" (I pick up a book, but in a short time I get tired and I let it fall. . . . In my condition I must care about my health above all. . . . I have decided to live for others. . . . Selfishly, I wish only death).

Dust jacket for Cassola's 1968 novel, which describes the events surrounding the journey of a freight train from Pisa to Orbetello

In his best pages, by eschewing the surface and the contingent and by concentrating on the minutiae of everyday life, Cassola's fiction vibrates with an awareness of being, through an impersonal, bare, antirhetorical style. Because of its plainness and subtlety, Cassola's style requires the reader to pay attention and listen carefully. As Montale suggests: "L'arte di Cassola tende sempre . . . ad essere un'arte del silenzio" (Cassola's art tends to be . . . always an art of silence).

Interviews:

Antonio Filippetti, "Incontro con Cassola," *Studi e ricerche,* 4 (April–June 1968): 607–612;

Ferdinando Camon, *Il mestiere di scrittore* (Milan: Garzanti, 1973), pp. 72–93;

Peter N. Pedroni, "Interview with Carlo Cassola," *Italian Quarterly,* 21 (Spring 1980): 103–116;

Pietro Poiana, *Cassola racconta* (Marmirolo, Reggio Emilia: Ciminiera, 1981).

References:

Carlo Annoni, "La narrativa civile di Cassola," *Vita e pensiero,* 51 (July–August 1968): 577–596;

Alberto Asor Rosa, "Cassola," in his *Scrittori e popolo* (Turin: Einaudi, 1988), pp. 233–284;

Giorgio Bàrberi-Squarotti, "Cassada," in his *Poesia e narrativa del secondo Novecento* (Milan: Mursia, 1961), pp. 216–223;

Bàrberi-Squarotti, *La narrativa italiana del dopoguerra* (Bologna: Cappelli, 1966), pp. 161–164;

Renato Barilli, "Regolari e irregolari nella narrativa italiana," *Mulino,* 8 (1958): 216–223;

Renato Bertacchini, *Carlo Cassola* (Florence: Le Monnier, 1979);

Carlo Bo, "Romanzo e società dell'Italia degli ultimi dieci anni," *Paragone,* 8 (April 1957): 483–502;

Italo Calvino, "Due domande su *La ragazza di Bube,*" *Mondo operaio,* 13 (July–August 1960): 87–100;

Ferdinando Camon, "Sul binario morto," in his *Letteratura e classi subalterne* (Venice: Marsilio, 1974), pp. 31–34;

Manlio Cancogni, *Azorin e Miró* (Milan: Rizzoli, 1968);

Giuseppe Cintioli, "Guerra e letteratura di guerra," *Il menabò,* 1 (1959): 240–252;

Gianfranco Contini, "Carlo Cassola," in his *La letteratura italiana, Otto-Novecento* (Florence: Sansoni, 1974), pp. 980–983;

Rossana Esposito, *Come leggere "La ragazza di Bube" di Carlo Cassola* (Milan: Mursia, 1978);

Giovanni Falaschi, ed., *Carlo Cassola, Atti del convegno (Firenze, Palazzo Medici-Riccardi, 3–4 novembre 1989),* (Florence, Becocci, 1993);

Enrico Falqui, "Il nuovo romanzo di Cassola," *Nuova antologia,* 510 (September 1970): 410–416;

Giuseppe Fava, "Il paesaggio in Cassola," *Paragone,* 478 (December 1989): 17–31;

Gian Carlo Ferretti, "Cassola," in his *Letteratura e ideologia: Bassani, Cassola, Pasolini* (Rome: Riuniti, 1964), pp. 64–161;

Ferretti, "Un'ipotesi di ricerca: Cassola," in his *Il mercato delle lettere* (Turin: Einaudi, 1979), pp. 220–232;

Franco Fortini, "Di Cassola," in his *Saggi italiani* (Bari: De Donato, 1974), pp. 203–216;

Natalia Ginzburg, "La felicità è alle spalle," *La stampa,* 8 November 1970, p. 3;

Massimo Grimaldi, "Carlo Cassola," in *Letteratura italiana. I contemporanei* (Milan: Marzorati, 1969), III: 835–862;

Romano Luperini, "Il sentimento della vita in Cassola saggista," *Paragone,* 478 (December 1989): 32–42;

Giorgio Luti, "Piccola antologia critica," *Itinerari,* 2 (December 1954): 368–387;

Rodolfo Macchioni Jodi, *Cassola* (Florence: La Nuova Italia, 1967);

Carlo A. Madrignani, "Il superstite secondo Carlo Cassola," *Belfagor,* 44 (November 1989): 647–658;

Madrignani, "L'ultimo Cassola" (Rome: Riuniti, 1991);

Giuliano Manacorda, *Invito all lettura di Carlo Cassola* (Milan: Mursia, 1973);

Claudio Marabini, "Carlo Cassola," in his *Gli anni sessanta: narrativa e storia* (Milan: Rizzoli, 1970), pp. 37–69;

Marabini, "Ricordo di Carlo Cassola," *Nuova antologia,* 557 (April–June 1987): 181–185;

Eugenio Montale, "Il racconto del silenzio," *Corriere della sera,* 17 April 1966, p. 3;

Howard K. Moss, "The Existentialism of Carlo Cassola," *Italica,* 54 (Fall 1977): 381–398;

Peter N. Pedroni, *Existence as theme in Carlo Cassola's Fiction* (New York: Peter Lang, 1981);

Frank Rosengarten, "The Italian Resistance Novel (1945–1962)," in *From "Verismo" to "Esperimentalismo,"* edited by Sergio Pacifici (Bloomington: Indiana University Press, 1969), pp. 231–234;

Carlo Salinari, "Cassola, la sua illusione, la sua libertà," in his *Preludio e fine del realismo in Italia* (Naples: Morano, 1964), pp. 323–330;

Furio Sampoli, "The Italian Novel of Recent Years," translated by Sandra Gray, *Italian Quarterly,* 7 (Summer 1963): 16–32;

Riccardo Scrivano, "Carlo Cassola and New Italian Fiction," *Italian Quarterly,* 6 (Fall–Winter 1962): 46–63;

Scrivano, "Cassola e il romanzo," *Il ponte,* 16 (August–September 1960): 1245–1260;

Vittorio Spinazzola, *Il realismo esistenziale di Carlo Cassola* (Modena: Mucchi, 1993);

Zina Tillona, "Neorealism revisited: *La ragazza di Bube,*" *Forum Italicum,* 1 (January 1967): 2–10;

Vittirio Spinazzola, *Il realismo esistenziale di Carlo Cassola* (Modena: Mucchi, 1993);

Michele Tondo, "Carlo Cassola," *Letteratura,* 7 (January–April 1959): 133–143;

Claudio Varese, "Carlo Cassola," in his *Occasioni e valori della letteratura contemporanea* (Bologna: Cappelli, 1967), pp. 399–415.

Piero Chiara
(23 March 1913 – 31 December 1986)

Cinzia Donatelli Noble
Brigham Young University

BOOKS: *Incantavi* (Lugano: Poschiavo, 1945);
Itinerario svizzero (Lugano: *Giornale del Popolo,* 1950);
Dolore del tempo (Padua: Rebellato, 1959);
L'opera grafica di Giuseppe Viviani (Padua: Rebellato, 1960);
Il piatto piange (Milan: Mondadori, 1962);
Mi fo coraggio da me (Milan: Scheiwiller, 1963);
La spartizione (Milan: Mondadori, 1964); translated by Julia Martines as *A Man of Parts* (Boston: Little, Brown, 1968; London: Cresset, 1968);
Con la faccia per terra (Florence: Vallecchi, 1965); republished as *Con la faccia per terra e altre storie* (Milan: Mondadori, 1972);
Ti sento, Giuditta (Milan: Scheiwiller, 1965);
Il povero Turati (Verona: Sommaruga, 1966);
I ladri (Milan: Scheiwiller, 1967);
Il balordo (Milan: Mondadori, 1967);
L'uovo al cianuro e altre storie (Milan: Mondadori, 1969);
I giovedì della signora Giulia (Milan: Mondadori, 1970);
Un turco tra noi (Milan: Scheiwiller, 1970);
Ella, signor giudice (Milan: Scheiwiller, 1971);
Il pretore di Cuvio (Milan: Mondadori, 1973);
Sotto la sua mano (Milan: Mondadori, 1974);
La stanza del vescovo (Milan: Mondadori, 1976);
Le corna del diavolo e altri racconti (Milan: Mondadori, 1977);
Il vero Casanova, edited by C. Ravizzoli (Milan: Mursia, 1977);
Il cappotto di astrakan (Milan: Mondadori, 1978);
Vita di Gabriele D'Annunzio (Milan: Mondadori, 1978);
La macchina volante (Teramo: Lisciani e Zampetti, 1978);
Una spina nel cuore (Milan: Mondadori, 1979);
Ora ti conto un fatto (Milan: Mondadori, 1980);
Le avventure di Pierino al mercato di Luino (Milan: Mondadori, 1980);
Helvetia, salve! (Bellinzona: Casagrande, 1980);
Vedrò Singapore? (Milan: Mondadori, 1981);
Viva Migliavacca! e altri 12 racconti (Milan: Mondadori, 1981);

Piero Chiara (photograph by Mario De Biasi)

L'Amorosa notte (Milan: Rizzoli, 1983);
Il Lago di Como descritto e illustrato nell'Ottocento da anonimo autore (Milan: Il Polifilo, 1983);
40 storie negli elzeviri del "Corriere" (Milan: Mondadori, 1983);
L'Adriatico (Florence: Alinari, 1984);
Prato nella vita e nell'arte di Gabriele D'Annunzio (Prato: Edizioni del Palazzo, 1985);
Una storia italiana (Milan: Sperling & Kupfer, 1985);

Il capostazione di Casalino e altri quindici racconti (Milan: Mondadori, 1986);

Saluti notturni dal Passo della Cisa (Milan: Mondadori, 1987);

Sale e tabacchi (Milan: Mondadori, 1989).

MOTION PICTURE: *Venga a predere il caffè da noi,* screenplay cowritten by Chiara, based on his novel *La spartizione* (1964), Mars Film (Rome), 1970.

TV SCRIPT: *I giovedì della signora Giulia,* based on a story by Chiara, R.A.I.-T.V. Italia, 1970.

OTHER: *Quarta generazione: antologia della poesia italiana del dopoguerra,* edited by Chiara and Luciano Erba (Varese: Magenta, 1954);

Luis de Góngora, *I sonetti funebri,* translated by Chiara (Milan: Scheiwiller, 1955); revised and enlarged as *I sonetti funebri e alre composizioni* (Turin: Einaudi, 1970);

Giacomo Casanova, *Lettere a un maggiordomo,* edited by Chiara (Milan: Ferriani, 1960);

Casanova, *Storia della mia vita,* 7 volumes, edited by Chiara (Milan: Mondadori, 1964–1965);

Casanova, *Saggi, libelli e satire,* edited by Chiara (Milan: Longanesi, 1968);

Casanova, *Epistolario,* edited by Chiara (Milan: Longanesi, 1969);

Petronio Arbitro, *Satiricon,* edited by Chiara (Milan: Mondadori, 1969);

Johann Jacob Weitzel, *Viaggio pittoresco al Lago Maggiore e al lago di Lugano,* translated by Chiara (Milan: Il Polifilo, 1973);

Sacro e profano nella pittura di Bernardino Luini, edited by Chiara (Milan: Silvana, 1975);

Casanova, *Storia della mia fuga dai Piombi,* edited by Chiara (Milan: Mondadori, 1976);

Gabriele D'Annunzio, *Quattordici lettere a Barbara Leoni,* edited by Chiara (Milan: Mondadori, 1976);

Giovanni Boccaccio, *Il Decameron,* edited by Chiara (Milan: S. E. E. D., 1976).

Piero Chiara is among the most popular Italian novelists of the post–World War II period. His stories and novels are widely read and have been adapted for television and film. Although Chiara began to write in a society that was struggling to rebuild from the ruins of war and that still remembered the evils of dictatorship, his focus was never on the grand events of history. Instead, Chiara depicts the individual's personal concerns and situations. His readers recognize themselves and their world in his writing and identify with the situations he depicts. Yet his stories of ordinary lives in small towns can capture the whole society. He has won more than a dozen literary prizes, including the Campiello in 1964 and the Bancarella in 1979. In addition to fiction Chiara has worked in cinema, literary criticism, and art history. As a literary critic he has gained an international reputation for his studies on the life and works of Giacomo Casanova. Some critics have noticed a shared taste for adventure in Chiara and Casanova.

Piero Chiara was born in Luino, a small town on the shores of Lake Maggiore on 23 March 1913. His father was originally from a small Sicilian town, Roccalimata, and his mother was born in Comnago, on Lake Maggiore. Theirs was a "mixed" marriage in that husband and wife were from opposite ends of the Italian peninsula. Such marriages were common between men emigrating from the South and the women of the North. By marrying a Lombard woman, a southern man was assured of becoming integrated in his new society and acquired a higher social status. Chiara was raised as a Lombard, and his hometown shaped his character as a man and as a writer.

Luino is in the northernmost part of Italy, adjacent to the Swiss border, an area of Lombardy inhabited by people of varied social classes and ethnic backgrounds. As Maria Clotilde Ottaviani points out in the October 1962 *Paragone*, this atmosphere led Chiara to create works with a peculiar "atmosfera di zona di confine, con quella mescolanza di costumi e linguaggi diversi, con quel tanto di paradossale per cui finanziere e contrabbandiere sono professioni ugualmente riconsciute, e ciò che è lecito qui non lo è a pochi chilometri di distanza" (atmosphere of boundary lines, with a mixture of different customs and languages, a paradox in that both customs officers and smugglers are recognized as legitimate professions; that which is allowed there is not permitted a few kilometers away).

A school setting never agreed with Chiara's nature, and his formal education did not go beyond middle school. He had to repeat third grade twice and moved from one private school to another; finally, in 1927 he dropped out of high school and went to work. He worked in Italy and France, including jobs as an auto mechanic and as a helper to a photographer. He did not abandon books, for reading offered him comfort and diversion from the routine of a boring life.

Chiara started to study on his own, and his literary education was marked by a broad spectrum of Italian and foreign authors that included Giovanni Boccaccio, Alessandro Manzoni, Luigi Pirandello, Robert Louis Stevenson, Herman Melville, Gustave

Flaubert, Honoré de Balzac, and Marcel Proust. After becoming a government clerk in 1931, Chiara resorted to writing to escape boredom. An opponent of Fascism, he experienced persecution and fled to Switzerland, where he taught in a private school from 1936 to 1939; he returned to Italy in 1943. In the meantime his marriage to a Swiss woman, Jula Scherb, had failed. In 1945 he retired from government service to devote full time to writing.

Like his father, Chiara was a natural storyteller. In a 1974 interview with Davide De Camilli, Chiara recalled that as a boy he followed a funeral procession of a stranger all the way to the cemetery. To those who inquired, he said in tears that he was the deceased's son. He claimed he did not intend to deceive but just wanted to tell an interesting story. Chiara told stories as a means of overcoming the monotony of life in a provincial town and cultivated his talent through socializing with his friends, who encouraged him to write down his stories. Initially, Chiara did not like to compose on paper, preferring to dictate his stories to his secretary. This approach allowed him to enjoy his narration, to feel the story coming alive. He wanted, as he told Alfredo Barberis, "stare nell'onda di questa eccitazione narrativa che mi viene solo parlando" (to remain in the midst of a narrative excitement I feel only when I speak).

In his works Chiara represents life as monotonous, predictable, absurd, and, most important, governed by chance. He believes life must be accepted with patience, because it is, as he told Luigi Baldacci in 1969, "una cosa tutta da raccontare, ma difficile da capire" (something that can be narrated, but difficult to understand). Chiara has no interest in tracing the causes of tragedies and human suffering, which can be attributed to a higher agent or simply be seen as the expressions of a mocking and cruel destiny. He is a good-humored observer of reality, looking at life without moral judgments; he believes life cannot be changed or fully understood.

In his first novel, *Il piatto piange* (The Crying Dish, 1962), Chiara centers the action on his birthplace, a town that becomes a universal symbol of provincial life: "Luino non deve essere cercata sulle carte geografiche, o nell'elenco dei comuni d'Italia, ma in quell'altra ideale geografia dove si trovano tutti i luoghi immaginari in cui si svolge la favola della vita" (One should not look for Luino on geographical maps, nor on the list of Italian towns, but in the other, ideal geography where all imaginary places are found and the tale of life unfolds). The center of social life is the café, where townspeople gather every day to talk, to drink, to relive their love adventures, and to play cards. The title alludes

Cover for a 1993 edition of Chiara's first novel, in which a cardplayer tells tales of life in a provincial town

to a common expression among gamblers, signaling the need for a new stake. The empty kitty on the card table, an emptiness that "cries out" for fulfillment, symbolizes that something substantial is missing from provincial life. But the game must continue and the effort to escape the routine must continue also, even though the chances for change are slim. To Chiara, the narrator who tells stories about the people he meets around the card table, such is life, and a different one does not exist.

Even those who do escape are likely to return and bring back only a story—a tale of the "real" world: "Lo aspettiamo di ritorno, un giorno o l'altro, perché ci racconti la sua storia" (We wait for his return, one day or another, so that he may tell us his story). Chiara the storyteller believes that tales are the only way to escape reality, that memory and imagination can serve as a magical means of bettering human existence. Memory enables people to focus on their lives and see more clearly within themselves. In his narrative Chiara often alternates between past and present—a rhetorical device aimed at preventing life from running away so quickly.

More than card games, love and death can facilitate the effort to escape reality. Having inherited the literary tradition of such romantic themes, Chiara depicts how, in any lazy corner of any Italian province, love and death form the circle of life. He tells of difficult or illegitimate loves, of violent and suspicious deaths that haunt apparently peaceful lives. Provincial grayness can be overcome through a new love, a new conquest. A love affair offers escape from routine; it lightens the world with fresh colors and lends life a new purpose. But such escape is temporary. Soon, even unbridled passions no longer satisfy, and ultimate escape can be reached only through total ruin or death. Chiara does not say whether, in such circumstances, death is a form of punishment or an expiation of guilt. He simply suggests that love and death are natural consequences of a natural desire to escape the limitations of life.

In *La spartizione* (1964; translated as *A Man of Parts,* 1968) Chiara relates a story concerning an apparently honest man, Emerenziano Paronzini, who marries one of three stern, mature sisters and becomes the lover of the other two. Each of the three ugly women has only a single attraction: hair (Fortunata), legs (Tarsilla), and hands (Camilla). Until the marriage, they had lived apart from the world, confined in the home and religion. Suddenly they overturn their former behavior, rid themselves of all religious scruples and archaic social conventions, and nourish new desires for exciting adventures. Once she gives way to her passions, the old, bigoted Tarsilla cannot retreat; she can only become more and more involved and is ready for anything at the contact of a man's hand on her shoulder:

> L'essere femminile è un vulcano che non si spegne mai. Può avere lunghi periodi d'inattività e in una notte può squarciare le rocce, travolgere i boschi e le case cresciute tranquillamente sul suo fianco. Fuoco e fiamme, borborigmi profondi e scuotimento di terra sono l'annuncio del vulcano risvegliato.

> (The feminine being is like a volcano that is never extinguished. It can have long periods of inactivity, but in a single night it can tear rocks, and sweep away entire forests and houses quietly risen on its slopes. Fire and flames, deep thunders and shaken earth announce the awakening of the volcano.)

Chiara humorously describes such contradictory behavior. At the end of the story he becomes grotesque in describing the lucky husband's death from a stroke brought on by excessive physical exhaustion. However, even in the most risqué situation, Chiara remains an example of moderation and balance and has been called both a Lombard realist in the tradition of Alessandro Manzoni and a new Ludovico Ariosto endowed with provincial wisdom.

Chiara dedicated his third novel, *Con la faccia per terra* (With the Face on the Ground, 1965), to his father, who had just passed away. More autobiographical than his previous novels, it centers on a man's search for his identity through his origins. Using his own memories as his foundation, Chiara explores an ever-present personal dichotomy: though born in northern Italy, he is a descendant of and is still tied to many Sicilian relatives, toward whom he has ambivalent feelings. He feels superior to them but still part of them. In order to solve this conflict and reach objective clarity, he must travel to Sicily:

> Cosa c'è di meglio del ricordare? Ritornare sui posti della vita passata a compiere verifiche e rievocazioni è sempre un passo sbagliato. Non si aggiunge nulla ai ricordi e anzi si guasta il lavoro della memoria, si confondono le immagini già chiare che il tempo ha composto e si smentisce la pura verità della favola nella quale tutto ancora può vivere. Ma si vuole forse ritornare proprio per farla finita coi ricordi, per rimestarli, appesantirli, metterli in condizione di colare a fondo e di perdersi finalmente nel passato. È col ritorno che si pone per sempre una pietra sugli anni che non ci somigliano più.

> (What is better than remembering? It is always wrong to return to places associated with the past in order to validate the present or evoke the past. In so doing, we add nothing to remembrance; on the contrary, we ruin the function of memory. We confuse images which the passing of time has made clear, and we deny the truth of imagination in which everything can still be alive. And yet we want to go back to the past to do away with memories, to stir them up, to make them weighty, so they can sink to the bottom and get lost in the past. When we return to the past, we finally let go of the years with which we don't share anything anymore.)

Since everything is transfigured by memory, Chiara must return to the South to free himself from an archetypal past and thus belong totally to the North. In this way he pays a debt to his origins and gains a clearer vision of his roots. While his journey leads him toward independence, he at the end comes to recognize his heavy dependence on his heritage.

The setting of *Il balordo* (The Weirdo, 1967) is 1930, when Fascism and traditional bourgeois morality began to come into conflict. The main character, Anselmo Bordigoni, is a schoolteacher, an average person, silent, peace loving, and alien to excitement. He would happily spend his life unnoticed in the background, completely satisfied with his only passion—music. But Bordigoni is a slow, huge man—with rolls and layers of fat and almost two meters tall—who has a considerable musical talent and cannot pass unnoticed. Chiara creates a halo of mystery around Bordigoni. He appears in town as though from nowhere.

Because of Bordigoni's appearance and the mystery surrounding him, gossip and accusations begin to spread. But he does not care and hardly realizes what people say about him. One after another, accusations of immorality are made against the honest Bordigoni. He is banished to confinement in a faraway town. In isolation, his reputation is restored through his musical talent, and he returns triumphantly to the same town where he was slandered. Ironically, the townspeople change their tune: the man they had treated with calumny is now exalted as a hero:

> Tutti, anche quelli che non l'avevano mai visto né sentito nominare, dicevano di aver conosciuto il Bordigoni e magnificavano il suo carattere, la sua fermezza ai tempi del fascismo, e l'importanza della sua partecipazione alla vittoria delle armi alleate.

> (Everyone, even those who had never seen nor heard of him, swore to have met him, and praised his qualities, his steadfastness against Fascism, and the importance of his contribution to the victory of the Allied forces.)

Chiara's novel provides a close study of the provincial mentality. The inhabitants of the little town strive for recognition and self-importance. Wanting to be heard, they spread tales, whether true or false is irrelevant. Bordigoni, however, thinks that patience, a little balance, and minding one's own business will help anyone overcome life's obstacles. Chiara creates in Bordigoni an image of the Italians, who retired to private life to avoid any ties with the Fascist regime and continued to nurture honesty, dignity, and independence.

Chiara's novels in the 1970s included *Il pretore di Cuvio* (1973), *La stanza del vescovo* (1976), and *Il cappotto di astrakan* (1978). In *Una spina nel cuore* (A Thorn in the Heart, 1979) Chiara draws on his own experience to focus again on love and the relationship between man and woman. He treats women here as shady creatures one cannot trust, but who are—precisely for this reason—irresistibly attractive. According to Chiara, women have a twofold nature, and men can never fully understand them. Even though they love, the dialogue between men and women remains shallow. Lovers never really know each other intimately; their relationship remains superficial and fleeting.

The focus of the novel is Caterina, the enigmatic woman who left a thorn in the heart of the unnamed protagonist, a writer, who is the first-person narrator. Even her eyes are of an ambiguous color, between sea green and gray, "volti in basso per pudore oppure girati di un quarto, non per guardare, ma per disperdere nelle lontananze un segreto pensiero" (looking down modestly or turned one-quarter to the side so as not to look, but to chase away a secret). The main character, Caterina's lover, experiences one surprise after another. He discovers that Caterina has a long list of lovers who follow each other to her bedroom. Even so, she remains an innocent creature, chaste and pure, unable to understand the gravity of her actions. She becomes for him the symbol of a woman in her thirties, generously offering her body but retaining within complete integrity:

> Sentivo oscuramente, o ne avevo già avuto indizio, che dovevano esistere delle donne, all'apparenza incontaminate o sottomesse all'amore solo quel tanto che occorre per diventare madri, le quali in un momento della loro vita, per opera di miscele ereditarie divenute esplosive, potevano affondare nel baratro della lussuria. Non coi fidanzati o coi mariti, ignari di tanto fuoco, bensí con il più imprevedibile complice e nel segreto di un rapporto destinato talvolta a restare per sempre nell'ombra.

> (Strangely I felt, or I had perceived, that there were women, apparently uncontaminated and subject to love only long enough to become mothers, who, at a certain moment in their lives, on account of some hereditary mixtures that had become explosive, could sink into the abyss of lust. Not with their fiancés or their husbands, unaware of such a fire, but with the most unsuspecting acquaintance, and in the privacy of a relationship sometimes destined to remain forever in the shadows.)

By giving herself to a man physically, Caterina prevents him from reaching the substance of her soul: "Non è indifferenza–rispose–forse è istinto, abbandono naturale alla propria sorte. Potrebbe anche essere una specie di vendetta verso gli uomini. Una maniera per nasconderla dentro di noi la vera integrità, in un luogo irraggiungibile" ("It is not indifference," she answered, "perhaps it is instinct, letting ourselves go naturally to our destinies. It could also be a sort of revenge against men. A way to hide our true integrity within us, in an unreachable place").

Even though she is a rather simple woman, Caterina can conquer any man, even the most sophisticated *dongiovanni*. The critic Marco Mascardi analyzes Caterina's gift:

Questo accogliere in sé l'uomo, qualsiasi uomo, in Caterina è un gesto materno: proprio per dare all'uomo l'unica occasione di rivelarsi completamente per quel che è. Un essere umano. Caterina sublima l'esigenza amorosa dell'uomo attraverso la sua carne. L'amore è un momento di grande verità.

(This acceptance of man within herself, any man, is a maternal gesture in Caterina: only to give him the opportunity to reveal himself fully as he is—a human being. Caterina sublimates through her flesh man's need for love. Love is a moment of great truth.)

As a mother figure, Caterina gives new life to men through sex, which Chiara sees as the only moment of full truth in life. It is not a coincidence that Caterina's best friend is a midwife, a person who in her work witnesses the miracle of love, birth, and sometimes death, and is therefore better able to understand the essence of life. In *Una spina nel cuore* Chiara does not indict the nature of love but the provincial life that cuts men's wings and does not let them be free to fly or to express themselves fully. This is why Chiara's protagonist is deeply grateful to Caterina: after their relationship, he has a better understanding of himself and life. Love allows him to find fulfillment as both a man and a writer.

Ordinary infatuations and uneventful provincial life are again the main themes of Chiara's *Vedrò Singapore?* (Will I See Singapore?, 1981). For the first time, Chiara moves his narrative from the shores of Lake Maggiore and his native Luino to Friuli. But the environment is the same since both Italian provinces offer similar limitations and lifestyles from which it is impossible to escape. Besides the unnamed main character's story, Chiara relates the vicissitudes of several secondary figures, often grotesque, narrow-minded people who are humiliated and defeated by the lives they lead.

Like the humble people in Giovanni Verga's *I Malavoglia* (1881; translated as *The House by the Medlar Tree*) Chiara's men and women are content with small things, knowing they will never reach life's true substance. They let themselves be driven by destiny, their only true master. Chiara begins his characterizations with accurate physical descriptions, which always reflect a person's character. The unusual names he employs are often distinctive in order to single people out and distinguish them from others. Chiara creates his characters not through the actions of individuals but through their memories and interactions with friends. He shows their limited existence inside a café, around the green table, having a cup of coffee or a glass of liqueur: "Che la vita fosse qualche cosa di molto difficile e che bisognasse ridurla a grande semplicità per

reggerla, cominciava ad apparirmi chiaro" (It began to be clear to me that life was something very difficult, and that it was necessary to turn it into great simplicity in order to govern it). Some cannot endure life and turn to its negation: suicide. Others, however, turn to apathy and superficial living.

Chiara's main character is an officer of justice, a recurring character in his books. The man seems above reproach, yet he harbors secret weaknesses and leads a double life. The townsfolk hold him in high esteem:

Di solito, a partita terminata, i giocatori mi cedevano il posto . . . anche in considerazione della mia qualità di funzionario, di sacerdote o almeno sagrestano nel tempio della giustizia, dentro il quale sapevano per memoria atavica che chiunque, un giorno o l'altro, può trovarsi condotto, a torto o a ragione.

(Usually, when the game was finished, the players would give me their seats at the table . . . out of respect for my position as an officer, a priest or at least a sacristan in the temple of justice, inside which they knew by ancestral memory that anyone, one day or another, might be brought, rightly or wrongly.)

He is respected for his position, not for his character. Since the office has placed him on a pedestal, the townspeople are shocked at his human weaknesses when his true self is revealed. But to Chiara there is no cause for surprise. He knows that chance may make one man successful and ruin another in an instant. It is not important to understand why misfortunes happen, but it is essential to accept that life moves on regardless.

Chiara believes that memory alone can help one focus on life, subduing the pains and joys of life so that they can be analyzed with detachment and objectivity. Memory prevails in *Viva Migliavacca!* (Hurray for Migliavacca!, 1981), one of several collections of short stories Chiara published in his career. The thirteen stories begin in medias res and, of course, are set in the past. The recollection of events seems at first out of focus, and a deep melancholy and sadness pervade the stories.

In the first story, "Con quel naso" (With a Nose Like That), a telescope pointing toward a faraway balcony brings closer that which is distant in space; it symbolizes the vehicle of memory, which brings closer that which is distant in time. The protagonist sees a woman at the window as she waters her geraniums: "La riconobbi, ma senza ricordarne il nome. L'avevo conosciuta in un'epoca lontana" (I recognized her, but could not remember her name. I had met her long ago). Little by little, the narrator's memory focuses on the past, just as one can bring a telescope into focus. He recalls the woman's youth, the love affairs she had, her ironic destiny, and the provincial aspect of her life. Memory brings into sharp focus images of the past that become lucid, detailed, and precise, just as on a movie screen.

These stories are marked by Chiara's characteristic humorous and ironic situations but show a greater melancholy and sadness in regard to the instability of human destiny than in his earlier work, as though Chiara had given free vent to his innermost feelings. Man is never certain of the future, because no one is spared "quelle fatalità che sono nascoste nel corso di vita d'ogni essere umano" (those fatalities that are hidden in the course of life of every human being). Even those who are seemingly secure in their happiness and prosperity have reason to fear: "Appena un grand'uomo sta per raggiungere il vertice, si muove una forza occulta che mira a distruggerlo" (As soon as a successful man nearly reaches the top, a concealed force arises and tries to destroy him).

When Chiara wrote *Saluti notturni dal Passo della Cisa* (Nocturnal Greetings from Passo della Cisa, 1987), his posthumous novel, he was sick and tired in body, but his spirit wanted to flirt once more with the lively, mysterious world. The title is a greeting written on a postcard, idyllically reminiscent of the Italian countryside and its natural beauties. The scene is peacefully deceptive: a mysterious double murder takes place in the little town where no one would expect secret plots of love, personal interest, and gain. While Chiara's small world may seem remote to many, it is recognizable in everyone's experiences and common to all.

Chiara often reminded his readers that his stories are fantastic; there is no connection with real places or people. But his invention is so realistically felt that fantasy and reality always appear seamlessly joined. The ever-present humor and irony derive from a detailed analysis of human weaknesses, of man's intrinsic contradictions. Chiara knew that all human beings have similar faults and cannot escape a common destiny. This is why readers can all recognize themselves in his characters; even if they have never acted similarly, they have had similar desires and aspirations.

Some critics have accused Chiara of having repeated again and again the same themes present in his first novel. But his situations and characters are always different; Chiara describes real, everyday life in its variation and tedium. His stories teach the appreciation of life, the acceptance of its joys and dissappointments. Chiara believes that too often people let go of what is important and lose valuable opportunities. He has been called a comic realist,

Cover for a 1989 edition of Chiara's posthumously published novel, in which a double murder occurs in a seemingly idyllic provincial town

writing in a style in which humor is never self-serving, never solely to generate laughter, but along with melancholy is part of a serious objective. A refined and cordial gentleman, Piero Chiara faced the vicissitudes of life forthrightly in his stories and novels, believing that life was most meaningful when its stories are shared with others.

Interviews:

Alfredo Barberis, "Nascono al caffè le opere del pensionato Piero Chiara," *Il giorno,* 16 September 1964, p. 5;

Davide De Camilli, "Piero Chiara," *Italianistica* (May–August 1974): 385–389.

References:

Luigi Baldacci, "Chiara e Carpi: due autori ai poli opposti," *Epoca,* 7 May 1967, p. 134;

Baldacci, "Per Piero Chiara il mondo è tutto da raccontare," *Epoca,* 4 May 1969, p. 163;

Vanni Bramanti, "I ladri di Piero Chiara," *Antologia Viesseux* (January–March 1968): 45–49;

Vincenzo De Martinis, "Romanzi in vetrina," *La civiltà cattolica* (September 1965): 440;

Enrico Ghidetti, *Invito alla Lettura di Piero Chiara* (Milan: Mursia, 1977);

Olga Lombardi, "L'uovo al cianuro e altre storie," *Nuova antologia* (July 1969): 402–404;

Marco Mascardi, "E adesso, Chiara, parliamo un po' d'amore," *Grazia,* 9 December 1979, pp. 60–63;

Cinzia Donatelli Noble, "Piero Chiara: A Writer Not Yet Discovered In America," *World Literature Today* (Winter 1986): 17–22;

Giovanni Raboni, "Il realismo comico," *Tuttolibri,* 20 March 1976, pp. 12–13;

Sergio Salvi, "*Il Balordo* di Piero Chiara," *Letteratura* (January–June 1967): 279–280;

Salvi, "*La Spartizione* di Piero Chiara," *Letteratura* (January–April 1964): 179–181;

Giovanni Titta Rosa, "*Il piatto piange* di Piero Chiara," *L'Osservatore Politico e Letterario* (June 1962): 109;

Ferdinando Virdia, "Cordiali veleni ma con malinconia," *Fiera letteraria,* 13 October 1974, p. 20;

Virdia, "Piero Chiara e il suo passato," *Fiera letteraria,* 1 October 1972, p. 21.

Giuseppe Dessì

(7 August 1909 – 6 July 1977)

Mario Aste
University of Massachusetts at Lowell

BOOKS: *La sposa in città* (Parma: Guanda, 1938);

San Silvano (Florence: Le Monnier, 1939); translated by Isabel Quigly as *The House at San Silvano* (London: Harvill, 1966);

Michele Boschino (Milan: Mondadori, 1942);

Racconti vecchi e nuovi (Turin: Einaudi, 1945);

Storia del principe Lui (Milan: Mondadori, 1949);

I passeri (Pisa: Nistri-Lischi, 1955);

La ballerina di carta (Bologna: Cappelli, 1957);

Isola dell'Angelo ed altri racconti (Caltanisetta: Sciascia, 1957);

Introduzione alla vita di Giacomo Scarbo (Venice: Il Sodalizio del Libro, 1959);

Racconti drammatici: La giustizia, Qui non c'è guerra (Milan: Feltrinelli, 1959);

Il disertore (Milan: Feltrinelli, 1961); translated by Donata Origo as *The Deserter* (London: Harvill, 1962); translated by Virginia Hathaway Moriconi as *The Deserter* (New York: Harcourt, Brace & World, 1962);

Sardegna, una civiltà pietra, by Dessì, Franco Pinna, and Antonio Pigliaru (Rome: L.E.A., 1961);

Eleonora d'Arborea: racconto drammatico in quattro atti (Milan: Mondadori, 1964);

Drammi e commedie (Turin: E.R.I., 1965);

Lei era l'acqua (Milan: Mondadori, 1966);

Paese d'ombre (Milan: Mondadori, 1972); translated by Frances Frenaye as *The Forests of Norbio* (New York: Harcourt Brace Jovanovich, 1975; London: Gollancz, 1975);

La scelta (Milan: Mondadori, 1972);

La leggenda del sardus pater (Urbino: Stamperia Posterula, 1977);

Un pezzo di luna (Milan: Mondadori, 1979);

Diarii: 1926–1931, edited by Franca Linari (Rome: Jouvence, 1993).

PLAY PRODUCTIONS: *La giustizia,* Turin, Teatro Stabile, January 1959;

Il grido, Rome, Teatro Quirino, March 1959;

Qui non c'è guerra, Turin, Teatro Stabile, March 1960.

Giuseppe Dessì (photograph © Jerry Bauer)

OTHER: Rafael Sabatini, *La congiura di Scaramouche,* translated by Dessì (Sonzogno, 1958);

Narratori di Sardegna, second edition, edited by Dessì and Nicola Tanda (Milan: Mursia, 1965);

Scoperta della Sardegna: Antologia di testi di autori italiani e stranieri, 2 volumes, edited by Dessì (Milan: Il Polifilo, 1966).

Giuseppe Dessì's contribution to Italian literature is marked by impressive narrative works. What stands out, though, is his masterpiece, *Paese d'ombre*

(1972; translated as *The Forests of Norbio,* 1975), which he wrote during seven hard years of physical therapy he endured following a stroke in 1965. During this difficult period he was supported by his wife, Luisa, and the friendship of several writers, among them Giorgio Bassani and Vasco Pratolini. *Paese d'ombre* is the summa of Dessì's literary work, where one encounters the totality of his narrative techniques and his ideology. The novel was the result of a deep internal probing as Dessì faced his mortality and was reminded of those who had preceded him in Villacidro, the place that nurtured him as a writer.

Dessì's philosophy and literary inspiration are born of his personal experiences and keen observations of the physical world and the human condition. *Paese d'ombre* shows his awareness of the modern predicament even though he describes it through his depiction of a bourgeois culture at the turn of the century. His relevance to the modern reader can be found in the solitude of his characters, which eventually leads them to seek to communicate with each other. Their lives become interdependent, linked in a chain of experiences that leads to change without destroying their individual identities. Showing a wisdom and optimism that comes from age and from understanding, Dessì analyzes his characters, probing their lives and minds, frequently progressing in unexpected directions.

Throughout his works Dessì's narrative focus shifts continually to the region of Sardinia, for which the villages of his novels—San Silvano, Cuadu, and Norbio—are metaphors. He explores the poignant historical and political themes that have affected his beloved island without falling into the pitfall of a simplistic consciousness of ethnicity. In Dessì's work the reader is able to find three different conceptions of Sardinia, the first two of ancient origin. The first is a Sardinia of primitive social values inspired by concepts of natural justice. The second is a Sardinia whose life is based on ancient laws that justify the barbarian right to vengeance and the tribal rules of solidarity. Its laws honor the value of *omertà* (silence) and encourage the unity of clan members in order to avoid the acceptance of any form of justice coming from the outside.

Dessì also offers the reader a third view of Sardinia, as a modern autonomous state within a larger nation. This Sardinia looks outside of itself, searching for a dialogue with the world, while still clinging to its ancient history and growing in self-identification and self-determination. In Dessì's vision this process is rooted in the history of the island, beginning with the ferments of an independence movement in the fourteenth century led by Mariano IV's militaristic adventure and by Eleonora d'Arborea's juridical accomplishments. The process extends to the contemporary democratic movements achieved during Dessì's lifetime.

Giuseppe Dessì was born 7 August 1909 in Cagliari. His father was an officer in the Italian army. Dessì grew up in his maternal grandfather's house in Villacidro, a small town near Cagliari where he received his primary education. At a young age he studied in his grandfather's library, which was well stocked with the classics and with books of philosophy. He continued his formal education from 1929 to 1932 at a lyceum in Cagliari, where he developed a friendship with his philosophy professor, Delio Cantimori. Later he became a good friend of the literary critic Claudio Varese, whom he met in Cagliari at Cantimori's house. The two men stimulated Dessì's intellectual interest in literature.

To understand Dessì it is important to realize the impact that his grandfather's library had on his intellectual development. According to Mario Miccinesi, Dessì as a young man probably read works by Voltaire, Denis Diderot, Edmund Spenser, Friedrich Nietzsche. In the 31 May 1967 issue of *Belfagor,* Dessì recalled having read Charles Darwin's *On the Origin of the Species,* Gottfried Wilhelm Leibniz's *The Monadology,* Auguste Comte's *Course on Positive Philosophy,* Benedict de Spinoza's *Ethics,* and Heinrich Heine's *Germany.* This early philosophical grounding was strengthened during his high school years in Cagliari under the guidance of Cantimori, who helped him to focus his thoughts and ideas. Dessì continued to broaden his education in the library of his teacher, where he found books by Plato, Rainer Maria Rilke, Thomas Mann, and Hermann Hesse. Later, in Pisa, in the study of his friend and new mentor Claudio Varese, he was drawn to the *A la Recherche du temps perdu* volumes of Marcel Proust.

During his secondary education in Cagliari, Dessì began to acquire a political consciousness. Emilio Lussu, the organizer of a political party designed to bring together farmers and shepherds in a strong union, was an influence. These efforts led to the foundation of the "Partito Sardo d'Azione" (Sardinian Action Party). No less influential was Antonio Gramsci, the Sardinian intellectual who was instrumental in the early organization of the Italian Communist Party. Both Lussu and Gramsci chartered the hopes of the Sardinian people for a better future through social justice and education. In 1920 Dessì and some fellow students, sympathetic to the plight of Sardinians, started a program to fight illiteracy. But these were also the years of Fascism and its early exercise of power. Keenly aware of this reality, Dessì realized that the "resistenza" (Resistance to Fascism) had begun.

After graduation from secondary school Dessì enrolled at the University of Pisa in 1932. There he had Attilio Momigliano and Luigi Russo as teachers and mentors and renewed his friendship with Varese. In 1936 he earned a degree in education; his thesis on Alessandro Manzoni was suggested to him by Luigi Russo. As a result of subsequent teaching posts and his work as school superintendent, he lived in several cities: Ferrara, Grosseto, Bassano del Grappa, Ravenna, and Sassari. In 1955 he settled in Rome, where he devoted himself to writing novels, short stories, plays, and essays until his death in 1977.

Dessì began his literary career in 1937 by publishing his first short stories in *La stampa, Nuova antologia,* and other publications. Heartened by a favorable critical reaction to his work, Dessì in 1938 published a collection of stories, *La sposa in città* (The Bride Is in Town), some of which he had written while he attended the Liceo Dettori. This volume was followed by the novel *San Silvano* (1939; translated as *The House at San Silvano,* 1966), in which the treatment of past time reminded critics of James Joyce and Marcel Proust and which earned Dessì the sobriquet of "Sardinian Proust." Memory and reality are the pivots around which the action of Dessì's work and its characters rotate.

San Silvano established Dessì as a novelist within the European literary tradition. Like other Sardinian writers before him, Dessì attempted to free himself from the insularity of Sardinian life. More important, he began to look at his native land with a critical eye. Rather than following the example of another Sardinian writer, Grazia Deledda, who chose the filters of folklore, customs, and popular traditions, Dessì analyzes Sardinian life with a fresh perspective. He is able to use the popular elements deftly treated by Deledda to foster a new vision of the island, a vision entailing realistic solutions of age-old problems. His approach to Sardinia's problems is similar to that of Gramsci and Lussu. However, while they were socially and politically involved, Dessì's interests were primarily literary and educational; hence his ideas were expressed mostly through the narrative.

With *San Silvano* Dessì freed himself from the limitations of much postwar literature grounded in the tenets of Neorealism. Many so-called neorealistic novels lacked a critical consideration of the social reality and described a limited world of recollection by sentimentally evoking childhood experiences. In *San Silvano* Dessì is able to transform the past into a series of living movements, creating rich images that

Dust jacket for Dessì's second novel, in which a poor farmer struggles for self-knowledge

lend a lasting appeal to the narrative. At times readers experience the feeling of discovering the narrator's world, but now and then they also feel lost in the meandering of factual details. However, Dessì's search for an individual form of expression brought him closer to Lussu and Gramsci, especially in terms of his comprehension of the political and cultural realities of Sardinia. Thus, *San Silvano* is an autobiographical text in which Dessì's affectionate memories of his region are tied to his effort to seek social progress.

Written while the world around him was at war, Dessì's next novel, *Michele Boschino* (1942), tells the story of an impoverished farmer, first harassed by his family and later by his own lawyer. The novel's two-part structure reflects Dessì's struggle for subjective self-discovery and his need for objective observation of the external world. He believed that presenting the dichotomy between the objective and subjective understandings of reality was necessary in communicating with readers through narrative.

The first part, often identified by critics as an expression of regional naturalism, is narrated in the third person and focuses on the protagonist's education under the watchful eyes of a father figure. The second part, an existential search for the self, is narrated in the first person and offers a reflective autobiographical style akin to Proust's. The switch from third- to first-person narration, however, shows Dessì's preference for subjectivity.

Dessì's description of the "coeur simple" of farmer Boschino and his narrative style in the first part of *Michele Boschino*—its stylistic tensions, short paragraphs, and the silent communication between characters—is reminiscent of Gustave Flaubert, especially of his *Correspondance* (1887–1893). The circularity of Boschino's existence is completed in the second part when the small farmhouse in the middle of the fields becomes the center of Boschino's universe. Consumed by illness he languishes in a solitary bed under the shadow of a crucifix mounted on the wall.

Dessì relies on Sardinian history to frame the biography of old Count Scarbo in *Inroduzione alla vita di Giacomo Scarbo* (Introduction to the Life of Giacomo Scarbo, 1959). The novel tells the story of a middle-class family against a historical background marked by clashes between *prinzipales* (wealthy land tenants) and small landowners in the waning years of World War II. There are three main characters: Count Massimo Scarbo, a widower; his youthful son Giacomo; and Alina Eudes, a woman of simple tastes who becomes the count's second wife. A psychologically complex relationship between Alina and Giacomo is resolved when Giacomo is involved in an accident and is saved by Alina, who then, responding to unfulfilled maternal desire, decides to channel her love for Massimo to his adolescent son. The setting of the novel affords Dessì the opportunity to present the social life and experiences of people familiar to him.

Introduzione alla vita di Giacomo Scarbo anticipates *Paese d'ombre* in its presentation of the symbiosis of Sardinia's primitive and contemporary cultures. Dessì represents Sardinia from the workers' perspective when, perhaps for the first time, they are shown challenging the authority of the bosses and the landowners. Yet the voice given to workers is emphasized less than is Dessì's own perspective and judgment. Much of the narrative is given over to the evocation of images of Sardinia's past, the past of ancient and faraway times joined by recollection of the more recent past.

In the late 1950s Dessì began to work on two plays that he published as *Racconti drammatici* (Dramatic Stories, 1959). *La giustizia* (Justice) shows the corruption of the administration of justice in Sardinia and features an innocent man tried for a crime he did not commit. He is eventually killed in a shoot-out with the police during his escape, after he refuses, for honor, to have a woman testify to his innocence. Dessì followed this with *Qui non c'è guerra* (There Is No War Here), a theatrical adaptation of his novel *I passeri* (The Sparrows, 1955), which continues the story of Massimo Scarbo. Dessì also worked in the theater in the early 1960s, basing *La trincea* (The Trench, 1962) on stories of World War I he heard from his father. In the last of his racconti drammatici, *Eleonora d'Arborea* (1964), Dessì again drew on Sardinian history to shed light on the island's people.

Il disertore (1961; translated as *The Deserter*, 1962) takes place after World War I in the Sardinian village of Cuadu. The key characters are Maria Angela—whose son, Saverio, a criminal as well as a decorated hero, has deserted the army but is presumed dead—and Don Pietro, the local priest, who knows the truth about him. They are contrasting interlocutors who discuss problematic issues such as desertion, personal anguish, moral choices, and the relationship between divine and human laws. Two parallel stories, the secret life of Saverio and the more complex history of the small traditional village, continually interface and interfere with each other. The stories unfold through recollection side by side as the tragic overtones of personal experiences are echoed by the village's sorrowful silence.

Dessì's *Paese d'ombre* is a historical novel set in Sardinia in the latter part of the nineteenth century, whose shadowy characters are based on persons known to the author in his youth. They "visit" him by returning to his memory and making him aware of his mortality and that of others who have preceded him. Throughout the story Dessì struggles against presenting a nostalgic image of his land while using the island's rich legacy. The life of the protagonist, Angelo Uras, provides a window through which to view the community and larger society in which he lives. *Paese d'ombre* is divided into five parts corresponding to the stages in Uras's life.

Uras is first seen as a poor orphan in the service of Francesco Fulgheri, a lawyer who serves as a father figure; the relationship helps Uras to become a rich man. Unfortunately, destiny has chosen a different direction for his future, consistent with an old Sardinian aphorism: "La vita è regolata da leggi irreversibili, alle quali gli uomini sono soggetti come fili di paglia" (Life is ruled by irreversible laws to which men are subject like blades of grass).

While the Sardinian miners and their leader, Sante Follesa, dream of a world without masters, in which the police take orders from the "Camera del Lavoro" (Chamber of Commerce) and not from the local bosses, Uras, who has gained his position as a respected member of the middle class through a long process of adaptations and self-sacrifices, becomes the voice of conservatism. He continues to be adamantly opposed to the forces of change, posing all along as the guardian of Sardinia's patrimony, like the "nuraghi," the prehistoric stone constructions that on the island are seen as the silent observers of time. Between Follesa and Uras there is respect and trust but little understanding for each other's individual position. Follesa advocates change through violence; Uras supports gradual change within the framework of existing social structures and institutions. Follesa views violence as necessary to bring about the changes that free human beings from the yoke of oppression and servitude; Uras believes in the qualities of individual initiative, the same qualities that have enabled him to reach his present station in life.

Follesa shows some understanding for Uras's social ideas; he calls his friend "giusto, equanime, onesto" (just, equitable, honest), but he also points out his attachment to property. On the other hand, Uras respects Follesa unconditionally, but he belongs to a different class now and is conditioned by it. After Uras becomes the mayor of Norbio, he offers his friend passage on a cargo ship to France to avoid persecution for his political activities, and Follesa accepts. In one of the last acts of his administration, Uras purchases forestlands for the benefit of the villagers, a purchase that causes him to forgo considerable personal gain. This action safeguards the common good, and years later the woods stand as a testament to his foresight.

The last part of the novel unfolds under the threat of violence. When World War I breaks out, Francesco Fulgheri, Uras's son-in-law, is called away by an unknown and misunderstood foreign power to fighting at the front. One day Uras and his favorite grandson witness a murder in the course of the Carnevale (Mardi Gras) celebration. Nothing could be more shocking to the old man than this disrespect for human life. His life was spent on improving the quality of life in the community by constantly searching for the ancient purity and beauty of times past. His search for a state of nature before history and the yearning for ancient times of Sardinian prehistory seem to lead Uras toward the incomprehensible, and he accepts the notion that violence is, at times, a manifestation of the sacred. He continues to believe that a new age is possible only because, as he interprets the ruins of the ancient civilization of Sardinia, humanity is always searching for

Dust jacket of the American edition of the translation of Dessì's 1972 novel, which depicts nineteenth-century Sardinian society

understanding, peace, and brotherhood. Uras believes that everyone must work to achieve this end.

In Angelo Uras, Dessì brings together memory and history, the two dimensions of introspection and social involvement. Uras is a complex, solid character, but he is also idealistic in his professed belief in an equilibrium between ideas and actions. His life creates a series of "ombre" (shadows) delineating a world that expands from the microcosm of Norbio to the totality of Sardinia, an island tormented by a history of conquest and exploitation.

Sardinia's agricultural and pastoral civilization is portrayed by Dessì in its darker moments when the "continentali" (the royal house of Savoy and its retinue) came to the island as "padroni" (conquerors and overlords), transforming Sardinia into a de facto colony. In the novel Dessì describes how the Piedmontese government showed no concern for the conservation of the island's forests and, even after the unification, still treated Sardinia as a colony to be exploited. To Dessì Sardinia is the cornerstone of a world that longs to be purified, awaiting the restoration of a golden age. While the innocence of past ages has been replaced by the anguish and the unmeasurable problems of the modern world, the reader finds in the Sardinia of Dessì's memory something that time has neither spoiled nor soiled.

Dessì's representation of ancient Sardinia is not an escape into fantasy, but the quest for a deeper understanding of the historical reality of the island, a reality difficult to perceive in the larger context of Italian history. In *La scelta* (The Choice, 1972), an unfinished novel, Dessì offers some insights into the relationship between Sardinia and Italy while tying up the loose ends of previous novels. Here he gives his readers clear answers to all the symbolic places and themes of *Paese d'ombre*.

La scelta is dominated by the figure of Marco, Uras's grandchild, who is depicted in Dessì's autobiographical sequences. The geographical location of Norbio becomes Dessì's beloved Villacidro. The waterfalls of "Sa Spendula," the house in Via Roma, the pine forest, and the church of San Sisinio—all are places dear to Dessì from his adolescence. Dessì, like Angelo Uras, the *ombra* (shadow) of his grandfather, is the Sardinian boy who grows in the shadows of time and death in the town of Villacidro, a town rich in history and traditions but also lost in the night of past ages. The town, a small, refracted point in the universe, becomes through him a projected point to the whole universe and delivers a message of peace and understanding to all.

References:

Giorgio Bárberi-Squarotti, *Poesia e narrativa del secondo Novecento* (Milan: Mursia, 1967), pp. 248–251;

Giancarlo Contini, "Inaugurazione di uno scrittore," in his *Esercizi di lettura* (Turin: Einaudi, 1974), pp. 175–180;

Giacomo De Benedetti, "Dessì e il golfo mistico," in his *Intermezzo* (Milan: Mondadori, 1963), pp. 190–220;

A. Leone De Castris, *I passeri,* in his *Decadentismo e realismo* (Bari: Adriatica, 1959), pp. 181–186;

Eurialo De Michelis, "Giuseppe Dessì," in his *Narratori al quadrato* (Pisa: Nistri-Lischi, 1962), pp. 69–79;

Pietro De Tommaso, "La narrativa di Dessì," in his *Narratori italiani contemporananei* (Rome: Edizioni dell'Ateneo, 1965), pp. 149–164;

Anna Dolfi, "Le costanti narrative nell'opera di Dessì e l'eccezione ferrarese di *San Silvano*," *Esperienze letterarie,* 1 (1979): 76–88;

Dolfi, *La parola e il tempo. Saggio su Giuseppe Dessì* (Florence: Vallecchi, 1977);

Dolfi, Preface to Dessì's *Il disertore* (Milan: Mondadori, 1976), pp. 5–27;

Dolfi, "Profili di contemporanei: Giuseppe Dessì," *Rivista italiana di drammaturgia,* 13 (1980): 115–125;

Dolfi, *Un romanzo interrotto: La scelta* (Milan: Mondadori, 1978), pp. 129–176;

Enrico Falqui, "Giuseppe Dessì," in his *Novecento letterario* (Firenze: Vallecchi, 1961), pp. 121–146;

Niccolò Gallo, "La narrativa italiana del dopoguerra," in his *Scritti letterari* (Milan: Polifilo, 1975), pp. 324–341;

Romano Luperini and Vanna Gazzola Stacchini, *Letteratura e cultura dell'età presente* (Bari: Laterza, 1980), pp. 36–37;

Giorgio Luti, *Narratori italiani del Secondo Novecento* (Rome: Nuova Italia Scientifica, 1985), pp. 89–91;

Giuliano Manacorda, "Giuseppe Dessì," in *Vent'anni di pazienza. Saggi sulla letteratura italiana contemporanea,* edited by Manacorda (Florence: Nuova Italia, 1972), pp. 87–115;

Manacorda, *Storia della letteratura italiana contemporanea* (Rome: Editori Riuniti, 1972), pp. 492–497;

Mario Miccinesi, *Invito alla lettura di Dessì* (Milan: Mursia, 1976);

Antonio Seroni, "*Racconti* di Dessì," in his *Esperimenti critici sul Novecento letterario* (Milan: Mursia, 1967), pp. 78–81;

Vittorio Stella, "Introspezione e storia nella narrativa di Giuseppe Dessì," *Trimestre,* 3/4 (1974): 359–393; republished in his *L'apparizione sensibile. Analisi e revisioni* (Rome: Bulzoni, 1979), pp. 243–277.

Rodolfo Doni
(20 March 1919 –)

Umberto Mariani
Rutgers University

BOOKS: *Società anonima* (Florence: Landi, 1957);
Sezione Santo Spirito (Florence: Vallecchi, 1959);
Fuori gioco (Florence: Vallecchi, 1962);
Faccia a faccia (Florence: Casini, 1964);
La provocazione (Florence: Vallecchi, 1967);
I numeri (Florence: Vallecchi, 1969);
Passaggio del fronte: diario di un cinquantenne (Florence: Vallecchi, 1971);
Le strade della città: diario di un cinquantenne (Florence: Vallecchi, 1973);
Muro d'ombra (Milan: Rusconi, 1974);
Giorno segreto (Milan: Rusconi, 1976);
Se no, no (Milan: Rusconi, 1978);
Ultimatum della coscienza: diario di un anno sconvolgente (Rome: Logos, 1978);
La doppia vita (Milan: Rusconi, 1980);
Ritratti (Naples: Ferrero, 1980);
Il senatore Mazzoni (Milan: Rusconi, 1981);
Servo inutile (Milan: Rusconi, 1982);
Memoria per un figlio (Milan: Rusconi, 1983);
Legame profondo (Milan: Rusconi, 1984);
Medijugorje (Milan: Rusconi, 1985);
La città sul monte (Milan: Rusconi, 1986);
Le grandi domande (Milan: Rusconi, 1987);
Altare vuoto (Florence: Vallecchi, 1989);
I popolari (Florence: Vallecchi, 1990);
I duelli di Ignazio. I folli. La povera Gemma (Milan: Massimo, 1991);
Colloquio con Lorenzo (Milan: Ares, 1992);
Un filo di voce (Milan: Mondadori, 1993);
Premio Letterario (Milan: Ares, 1994);
Il Presidente e il Filosofo (Milan: San Paolo, 1995);
La Vita Aperta (Turin: S.E.I., 1995);
Dialogo sull'Aldilà con il Figlio Lorenzo (Florence: Giunti, 1977).

Rodolfo Doni (photograph by Alfredo Caruti)

Rodolfo Doni is unique among Italian writers of his generation because of the themes he has pursued from the beginning of his career. Almost all of his major stories are built around the inner struggle of a person who comes to maturity after the crucial experience of the final years of Fascism and World War II. Doni's quintessential character returns to the strong religious beliefs of his youth during a period of hospitalization for a war wound and then attempts to realize his moral and religious convictions in the rough-and-tumble world of politics in the tense, polarized sociopolitical environment of Italy in the thirty years after the war. Doni initiated the genre of the political novel of postwar Italian politics by exploring the position of the discontented insider active in the Catholic party. Before Doni, in the Neorealism of the early postwar years with its many war and resistance novels, other writers had occasionally assayed the political novel, albeit with-

111

out the religious motif—Cesare Pavese's *Il compagno* (1947; translated as *The Comrade,* 1959) is an example—but had soon abandoned it, as if in recognition of their failure.

From his first novel, *Sezione Santo Spirito* (The Santo Spiritual Branch, 1959), Doni developed the genre in increasingly ambitious works. He was eventually joined by others, including Mario Pomilio with *La compromissione* (The Compromise, 1965), Gino Montesanto with *La cupola* (The Dome, 1966), and Raffaele Crovi with *Il franco tiratore* (The Sharpshooter, 1967). The protagonists of other writers, though Christian Democrats, rarely have religious convictions as strong as those of Doni's central characters, who always live the conflict between the demands of politics, with the compromises imposed by everyday experience, and the imperatives of their moral and religious principles. Doni's novels always center on an anguished inner crisis, providing a richly structured story skillfully told in strikingly direct, highly effective language.

Doni was born Rodolfo Turco in 1919 in Pistoia, a Tuscan provincial capital, where he was raised and educated; the friendship of a young local priest influenced his early religious development. The financial difficulties of his family led him to take a business-oriented secondary-school diploma; although the desire to be a writer had already manifested itself in his early teens, the war later diverted any plans to earn a university degree. Given his lack of enthusiasm for the policies of Fascism and his aversion to a war on the side of the Germans, when the opportunity to choose sides finally came with the armistice on 8 September 1943, Doni crossed the battle zone to fight on what he regarded as the right side.

Immediately after World War II, Doni became involved in various activities of his political party, beginning as a representative of the Christian Democratic current within Italy's unified labor union at the local level and progressing to become the party secretary for the province of Pistoia. These were largely years of frustration: Tuscany was predominantly Communist; Doni was dissatisfied by the direction his own party was taking at the national level; and he encountered difficulties in dealing with the old Catholic guard, both lay and clergy, at the local level.

By 1950 Doni was ready to leave all of it behind. He married and moved to Florence, where he began a new career in banking, while continuing both his interest in politics—a lively sphere in that city—and his writing: in Florence he maintained direct contacts with other writers whom he asked to read and evaluate his work. When he began to pub-

lish, he decided to use the pseudonym Doni. Later, widely known by that name, he adopted it legally. By the time he retired in 1980, he had become the director of the Mediocredito Toscano, a bank set up to provide loans to small, developing industries. His three older children were establishing professional careers.

The works from *Società anonima* (The Giant Corporation, 1957) to *I numeri* (The Power of Numbers, 1969) belong to the formative phase of Doni's writing career, not in the sense that he was still learning how to write (for they clearly show that such an apprenticeship had already been completed) but because through them he explored and defined his characteristic themes and established his identity as a writer. He focused on the spheres familiar to him: the experience of the war; the world of politics; the workplace; the microcosm of the family and the difficult relationships between spouses, aging parents, and children. At first Doni's protagonists experience such conflicts singly in stories of limited scope; later, they become involved with several conflicts at once, as Doni explores increasingly complex characters and situations that will continue to appear in the works of his mature phase. Through these early narratives Doni develops the ability to render in forceful detail the world that envelops and conditions his protagonist, eventually wearing him out but not forcing a total surrender.

While the works of this period may be considered minor, they contain almost all the motifs that will later be found in his major works: the need to make a choice, to risk "crossing the front" in order to fight on the right side; the figure of thâ progressive young Catholic eager to participate in the reconstruction of the country and the establishment of a new political system and a new society in accordance with his religious convictions, who meets with many disappointments; the differences between the old and the new generations of "Catholic" politicians; the difficulty of family relationships. Above all, the typical protagonist of Doni's fiction emerges: a character whose religious convictions lead him not to abstract metaphysical speculation but to moral sensitivity to human relationships, whose idealism involves him in the inevitably unsatisfactory arena of political activity.

Doni's concept of the political novel is already well formulated in these early works. He presents the drama of individuals locked in political battles, not a political thesis; the interaction of individuals tackling concrete problems at a local level, not large-scale political intrigues. Doni does not create clichéd politicians, either all good or all bad, but ordinary, recognizable people, who frequently alternate between enthusiasm and frustration. His characters are human beings with whom the reader can empathize.

The two novels that follow this formative period, *Passaggio del fronte* (Crossing the Front, 1971) and *Le strade della città* (City Streets, 1973), bear a common subtitle, *diario di un cinquantenne* (The Diary of a Man of Fifty). Both deal with the present, yet one looks at the past, the other at the future. Having reached the age of fifty, Doni was prompted by an ethical impulse to take stock of his life and generation. He wanted to examine what had led his generation, where it was going, and what it had achieved for the generations to come. Having first explored the gray world of the office worker, the frustrating world of the labor organizer, and local party politics, he now turned to the political experience of an entire generation and nation.

Doni returned to some of his old material, put it in a wider perspective, and revised his narrative techniques in two novels of greater breadth than his earlier work. His earlier concerns are brought together in these two novels, which also focus on the experience of a disenchanted, new generation on whom the future depended despite their not having seen or understood the war and the reconstruction. Similarly, the narrative techniques developed in the course of the writer's apprenticeship are here joined in a synthesis that would remain characteristic of Doni's mature work: fusing the techniques of the diary and those of the novel, he could narrate present events, evoke those of the past, and provide a philosophical and moral meditation on the past and the present as well as the future.

The character of Andrea that had been evolving in the previous works, sometimes under other names, is clearly more autobiographical in the diary novels and narrates his story in the first person. The crossing of the front was for Doni's generation an event born of extraordinary courage, youthful hope, and anxious expectations. While others took cover to wait out the storm, Andrea risked his life to take part in the war to free Italy from Fascism. Yet, now middle-aged, he finds indifference and fatalistic discouragement among people. Andrea goes from hope and a will to contribute to disappointment, a movement that recurs in many of Doni's works, whether the protagonist is a politician or an industrial executive or the head of a family. But Andrea's convictions provide the moral imperative to try again, to get involved, even though at fifty he seems to feel that everything has gone counter to his ideals. He and his generation, as well as the discontented youth of the 1960s, find themselves at a new front line to cross. This is the message of the two

Self-portrait by Doni (Collection of Rodolfo Doni)

novels, the second of which especially trains a beam of light on the city of the future, pointing to new roads and the realization of new plans.

Doni's next novels, *Muro d'ombra* (A Wall of Darkness, 1974) and *Giorno segreto* (A Secret Day, 1976), are linked by a continuity of action as well as common themes and problems. *Muro d'ombra* begins with the protagonist, Marco, suffering a skiing accident. His subsequent hospitalization and operation bring back the memories and fears of a previous hospitalization and a similar operation following a war wound many years earlier. The narrative switches back and forth between the present and the past at almost every chapter, so that by the end of the novel the protagonist has fully explored his history from that wartime experience to the present. During his three months of quasi-immobility in a cast, he reviews his life thoroughly and calmly: the deterioration of his marriage and family life, the annoyances and responsibilities of a love affair that has produced an illegitimate child and has been dragging on for too long, and his exploitative management of a successful business. At the end, Marco's early resolve to put his life in order has become so strong that the overcoming of his physical infirmity marks the beginning of an intense new struggle.

In *Giorno segreto* Marco confronts incomparably more-painful troubles than he previously experienced in his effort to put into practice the religious

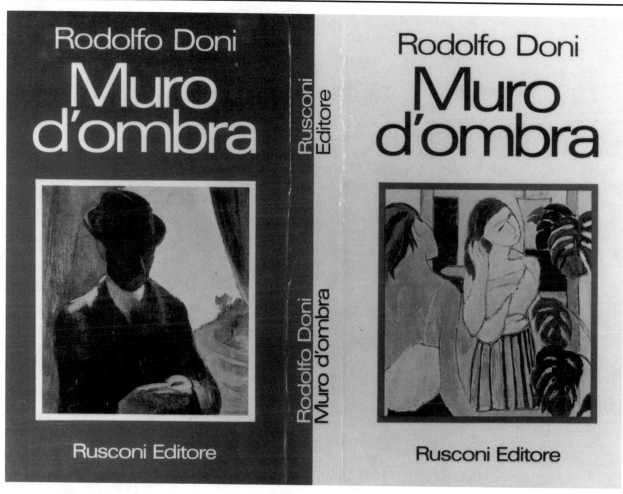

Dust jacket for Doni's 1974 novel, in which a skiing accident affords the protagonist the opportunity to reflect on his life

and moral convictions he has regained. Since his exploration and repudiation of the past have been completed, the narrative becomes more linear. Although the realization of his ethical vision is full of obstacles, the protagonist's unwavering resolve and the regained strength of his character allow him to move forward. But the results are not always positive. Some of the people he hoped to influence with his enthusiasm, those he most wanted to stand beside him, both within his family and among his business associates, prove to be rebellious and alienated. His new gospel of solidarity and responsibility is not understood in every quarter. The younger generation, in particular, is going through a phase of blind repudiation, and the father must acknowledge his mistakes and guilt even as he suffers at the rejection of his candor and concern. The religious and ethical dimension of the novels is as important to their artistic success as Doni's remarkable mastery of narrative. He is able to combine smoothly the sustained energy of the action with a continual filtering of experience through a strong moral sensibility.

Doni's *Se no, no* (Otherwise It's No Go, 1978) is a fascinating exploration of Italy's Byzantine politics of the 1970s and of the internal and external conflicts a conscientious Catholic politician inevitably experiences. The protagonist, Lucio, of the novel is one of a group of Catholic and Marxist intellectuals who have been conducting a politically constructive dialogue behind the scenes. The group plans to seek a seat in the senate in the June 1976 elections, and as the deadline for the submission of electoral slates approaches, the protagonist must choose between running as an independent on the Communist ticket or as a candidate for his own Christian Democratic Party.

Since an offer is supposed to be forthcoming from both parties in a couple of days, the protagonist must decide in a limited time which offer to accept. He endures two days of wrenching inner torment and passionate family disputes, two days in which the religious, intellectual, and social foundations of an entire life are tried. The protagonist holds firmly to his convictions. Despite the opposition of family and friends, he remains open to either offer in order to further the Catholic-Communist collaboration that has been in the planning stage for so long. For Lucio, party labels are irrevelant. However, he is informed at the end of his agonizing that, thanks to the conniving intervention of the party bosses, an offer will not be forthcoming from either side. All the novels of Doni's mature phase capture the experience and meaning of an entire lifetime, and *Se no, no* concentrates the life of the protagonist in the action of just a few days.

In *La doppia vita* (The Double Life, 1980), perhaps his best novel, Doni retrieved material from several previous novels and reworked it in a vast new canvas, re-creating the entire life of his protagonist, Andrea Di Lello, in an attempt to explore his inner consistency, despite the inevitable compromises his business and political activity have engendered, and to distill its meaning. Di Lello, a man of Doni's generation, has lived a life parallel to the author's in many respects: childhood in a provincial town, growing up under Fascism, military service, a return to faith, the crossing of the front, political involvement, marriage and family, and the avocation of writing. The story begins when Di Lello, finally about to enter a well-deserved and longed-for retirement, receives an anonymous letter that accuses him of having led a double life, challenging the integrity of a life supposedly dedicated to family and work.

Reexamining his life from early childhood on, Di Lello discovers a series of disjunctions that he and many of his generation experienced. However, the religious faith that guided his life and the writing he always pursued as a means of inner clarification render him unafraid to reveal his inner self. Strongly conscious of the unmarked borders between right and wrong in everyday reality, he is well prepared to order in a clear, coherent first-person narrative his memories, his complicated emotions, the historic events of his time, and his long struggle with a hostile social and political environment. His discoveries extend to the roots of the essential traits of his personality: his shyness, his feeling of rejection, his strong ethical bent, his sense of social responsibility, and the "doubleness," or inner conflict, with which he has always contended.

Open and friendly as a boy, Di Lello nevertheless felt somehow different from those around him. Family poverty impels him to early educational achievement, yet he has to beg for a job. A nonfascist in a fascist environment, his youthful religious beliefs lost, shy and depressed, he finds an outlet in writing. The war, a wound, and a hospital stay lead to a reawakening: a return to religious beliefs, to

moral and political commitment, beginning with the crossing of the front. But across the front and during the reconstruction, further inner turmoil and disappointment await him. This was to be the fate of his generation: their youth wasted in a Fascist war they did not believe in, they were redeemed in an antifascist resistance, worn down by a difficult period of political and economic reconstruction, and damned any way they turned. Di Lello meets each new phase of his life with a renewed sense of purpose and dedication, but each phase ends in disappointment. The last period of the protagonist's life, as a banker and as a father, after he leaves politics, is infinitely the most painful; even his reserves of hope and enthusiasm seem depleted.

The novel is unified and beautifully structured by the alert consciousness and sensibility of the narrator, who objectifies and analyzes facts and emotions in the private and public life of his eventful years, creating an organic interplay between past and present, memory and the struggles of the moment, youthful experience and maturity. *La doppia vita* is a summation and a definitive reorganization of various parts of previous narratives, and as such it represents the end of a cycle, in which most of Doni's personal experience has been mined and variously built upon. But its organization, structure, and narrative techniques reflect a craftsmanship so mature as to constitute the beginning of the high phase of Doni's creative career, which includes *Servo inutile, Legame profondo,* and *Medijugorje,* all of which draw on new narrative material.

Servo inutile (Useless Servant, 1982) centers on the crisis of an intellectual priest who falls in love with a woman and would like to marry her; the church he also loves and wants to serve compels him to make a choice. Enrico Cini is a priest in a suburban parish and a teacher in a high school in Rome. Largely uninvolved in either vocation, he is essentially a scholar, a student of early Christian literature. While his love relationship with Claudia—his brother's adopted daughter, who had been orphaned by an automobile accident—somewhat diminishes his aridity and aloofness, his profound sense of guilt prompts him to request permission to go as a missionary to Argentina, where he hopes to expiate his sin by serving the poor. His bishop instead assigns him to one of the poorest parishes in Rome, which has openly defied the diocesan Curia, particularly in regard to social ethics.

While Enrico discovers the essence of a priestly vocation through his work among desperately poor people, the Curia pressures him to choose between the priesthood and marriage. When the synod of bishops decides against any change in

Dust jacket for Doni's 1985 novel, in which a man makes a pilgrimage to a Croatian village in search of a stronger faith

try, the book is actually a long meditation on the critical state of contemporary Italy. The events, encounters, conversations, readings, and reflections the diarist records portray the social, political, and religious condition of a nation seriously adrift. To this frightened father modern life seems dedicated to materialism and ephemeral pleasures; everywhere he sees indifference to the intellectual life, to religious ideals, and to the needs of the spirit. He is worried that while those who call themselves Christians do not follow the dictates of their faith in their political activity, those who seem genuinely principled are not involved. As he tries to convey to his son the urgent need for the truly religious and the concerned to enter the realm of politics and inform it with their ideals, the father expresses a dark view as to how and why the forces of evil seem always to have the upper hand in dictating the direction of history.

In *Legame profondo* (Deep Bond) the narrator engaged in a struggle for the soul of the younger generation is the mother rather than the father. Angela Roio is the daughter of a domineering, violent, brutal father who, after destroying her mother, tries to subjugate her as well. Nevertheless, she succeeds in asserting her independence and completing her education thanks to the strength of her character and her religious beliefs. Later, the son she has raised with love and intelligence begins to show both a physical and emotional resemblance to his grandfather. He resents his mother's increasing concern and rebels against the authority of the family, the school, and his religious upbringing, particularly during his last years of high school, which coincide with the years of Italian student unrest. His conscientious mother responds by intensifying the study of her faith, by becoming involved both intellectually and practically in the pedagogical debate, and by joining in the common struggle against the anarchy of the moment. She never gives up on her son, although he leaves home and school and never returns to the affection of the family or its religious beliefs. In his later university years he lives alone, either indifferent to or rebellious against all that his mother cares about, while she is consumed by his rejection and her sense of responsibility for his destiny.

The narrative unfolds steadily in the form of a confession long after the event by a protagonist whose wounds have not been healed by time and whose voice still conveys the pain of an ongoing crisis, a troubled sense of final isolation. On reflection Angela can see that her mistakes often lay in the rigid coherence and fidelity of her convictions. Now she can appreciate the fact that the strength of her

the rule of priestly celibacy and his lover's depression becomes suicidal, Enrico decides he must leave the priesthood and marry her. This first-person narrative, with its dramatic handling of scenes and well-developed secondary characters, studies in depth the evolution of the man and the priest against the background of the pontificate of Paul VI. Enrico's crisis is a search for identity, for the meaning of his vocation, and ultimately for the essence of Christianity.

The theme of the complexity of love is central to Doni's next two novels as well. In *Memoria per un figlio* (Notes for My Son, 1983) a father, deeply concerned over the state of the world his beloved son will have to live in, records for him the thoughts he has been pondering during the troubled years of the late 1970s and early 1980s. He hopes by this means to explain, to advise, to communicate with a younger generation that has seemed quite unwilling to listen. Presented as a diary with dates for each en-own character was part of the "negative" inheritance from her father. But her abiding conviction is that maternal responsibility must include spiritual nurturing, that as a mother and teacher and citizen she must strive for the ideals of humanity and reason against the anarchic rebellion and violence of the times. As always in Doni's fiction, the private drama and the historic situation are richly interwoven and given a significance that transcends their particularity. The novel focuses on the loss of values, here the loss of religious faith, that triggers the perennial crisis of the generation gap. The present situation is made understandable and meaningful through repeated references to the past, and Doni, through connecting motifs and suggestive parallels, achieves an almost simultaneous presentation of various phases of the story.

In *Medijugorje* Doni similarly weaves together past and present so that events and figures of the past continually illumine the meaning of what is happening in the present. The protagonist, Alberto, is surrounded by an array of characters–his mother, his wife, and his political, intellectual, and ecclesiastical friends–who give rise to many of the questions that trouble him. Doni interconnects the events of Alberto's public life and inner struggle so that the private event takes on an emblematic dimension and epitomizes the experience of an entire generation, and he endows public events with the religious and existential significance inherent in the drama of the individual conscience. Alberto's deeply affecting spiritual experience in joining the hundreds of thousands of pilgrims who have travelled to Medijugorje–a village in Croatia where, beginning in 1981, six young people claimed to have silent communications with the Virgin Mary at 6:30 every evening–represents both an individual and a collective experience. The crisis of faith that motivates Alberto's trip reflects a general sense of spiritual malaise, a need for certitudes, for answers, experienced by many intellectuals.

Alberto's decision to go to Medijugorje is prompted by a desire to move from a problematic and troubled faith, the faith of the "discontented Catholic," to the tranquil certitude of his ailing mother and his wife. As a young man he lost his faith and searched for truth outside religion, in political activity and philosophical atheism, but never gained a sense of security. He returned to the practice and study of his faith, pursuing Christian studies and writing extensively on the necessity of the renewal of faith and the Christian spirit, not only as a road to the supernatural but also as a way of overcoming the social and political crisis of his time. Yet he remained a "discontented Catholic."

Though his faith is strengthened by the Medijugorje experience, Alberto does not find the reassuring truths he is seeking, and his faith remains troubled by doubts. He comes away convinced that the peaceful faith he longs for is given only to the simple people whom God loves, not to the "pharisees" like himself, but he realizes that faith, whether a gift or the fruit of an intense personal quest, need not be the same for everyone. His problematic faith is fitting for an intellectual like himself, in whom a faith preserved in tranquillity would "go to sleep and disintegrate" or revert to the deeper doubts and uncertainties that led him to Medijugorje. He understands that faith "must be spent and renewed continually, otherwise it vanishes." The narrator's language is beautifully fluent, spontaneous, and sincere, as are the emotions it attempts to convey.

The protagonist of *La città sul monte* (The City on a Hill, 1986), a novel incorporating recent historic events and characters, is Giorgio La Pira, the late mayor of Florence, whom Doni greatly admired. Once more Doni tells a story of a spiritual adventure, again centering on a Catholic intellectual who believes in a divine plan of justice and love for human history and works toward its realization in the arena of politics. Again, Doni's protagonist, often prey to doubts about himself and his mission, searches for certitude and is always deeply disappointed. The novel opens on a dejected La Pira contemplating the failure of his career and treats three salient episodes in descending order of success: his arduous fight to preserve the Pignone factory for the jobs of its workers; his peace mission to Vietnam, which achieved at best a partial success; and his unrealized project of making Florence the "city on the mount," a beacon to the world of the universal Christian values of unity, peace, and brotherly love.

Altare vuoto (A Bare Altar, 1989) takes up the story of Enrico Cini where it breaks off at the end of *Servo inutile,* when he decides to leave the priesthood, marry Claudia, and dedicate himself to actions of support and renewal, both in his personal relationships with his fellow men and in his work as a writer on ecclesiastical controversies. The novel covers a fifteen-year span in Cini's life that is full of tensions and setbacks after an initial period of satisfactory new activities and apparent success. Cini's family life and his work as a journalist and reformer have apparently lost all chance of regaining momentum. After the birth of a severely handicapped child and the deepening of the differences in the social, political, and religious interests of the couple, no exit seems possible from deadening habits and spiritual estrangement. Similarly, the various move-

Manuscript page for a work in progress (Collection of Rodolfo Doni)

ments for ecclesiastical reforms Cini was interested in reach such extremes of either triviality or outright heresy that they can no longer engage him. But, as is always the case for the Doni protagonist faced with the apparent conclusion of a phase of his life, Cini experiences a rebirth of energy, drawn from the profound moral and religious forces that nurture him, and the novel ends with a new point of departure, both in family relationships and in religious and political engagement.

I popolari (Missing the Popular Party, 1990) also picks up a character who had appeared in Doni's previous works: Giovanni Fedele, the representative of an older generation of sincere and selfless politicians, had appeared as the Honorable Fedele of *La provocazione* (The Provocation, 1967). He had also appeared as a type in *I numeri* and *Il senatore Mazzoni* (1981) as senator Mazzoni. Luigi, Fedele's son-in-law, is the discontented Catholic politician of Doni's generation. Under other names—Vasco, Marco, Andrea, as well as Luigi—he had appeared in various novels from *Sezione Santo Spirito* to *La doppia vita*. Luigi's background includes many of Doni's own experiences as well as those of his wife, Luisa. The development and the themes of the story, however, are quite new for Doni.

The novel follows two generations of Catholics who are disturbed by the unsatisfactory results of their party's political activity and caught in the frustrating and unforeseeable twists and turns of Italy's history and political evolution. It follows the old politician through more than half a century of engagement, struggle, defeat, fresh starts, and new disappointments. When he dies, Luigi, despite the frustrations that he and the new generation heretofore have been unwilling to bear, feels that he cannot abandon the fight that has been conducted with so many sacrifices and such a sense of dedication.

The title *I popolari* refers to the original Catholic party, called the Partito Popolare when it was organized in 1919 with the lifting of the papal prohibition against Italian Catholics taking part in political activity. Both Fedele and Luigi, as discontented Catholic politicians, share the progressive Christian ideals of the Partito Popolare that were subsequently compromised repeatedly by the new Christian Democratic Party after World War II. The older generation of politicians were willing to collaborate with the Christian Democratic Party in spite of the price they had to pay. Many in the younger generation, equally frustrated, were unwilling to work from within for the restoration of the party to its original ideals and have been hoping to found a separate progressive Catholic movement. Such a movement, however, has never materialized.

For the celebration of the five hundreth anniversary of the birth of Ignatius of Loyola, some influential Jesuits asked Doni to write a novel or a play about their founder. Doni's three-act play, titled *I duelli di Ignazio* (Ignatius' Duels), was published in 1991 along with two other plays written earlier: one on La Pira, called *I folli* (God's Fools) and the other on an unusual saint, Gemma Galgani of Lucca, a humble young housemaid, titled *La povera Gemma* (The Poor Gemma). While it was not difficult to find material for drama in the life of St. Ignatius or the controversial mayor of Florence, the life of Gemma Galgani had been so humble and uneventful as to compel the writer to abandon purely biographical material and rely on invention. The common theme of all three plays is suffering, accepted and indeed actively sought, as a price to be paid for the redemption of humanity following the example of Christ.

On 15 July 1990 Doni's youngest son, Lorenzo, still a college student in his early twenties, was killed in an automobile accident while traveling with four friends, from the same Florentine Catholic youth group, toward a center in France where young Catholics gather every summer for work and prayer. A week later, following many gatherings of families and friends to pray for the victims and express solidarity with those they left behind, Doni began to write a diary in the form of a conversation with his son, describing the initiatives undertaken to keep the memory of the dead alive and the inner growth that was taking place in the living. He kept the diary for three months and later let himself be persuaded to publish it as *Colloquio con Lorenzo* (A Dialogue with Lorenzo, 1992).

Human suffering endured within an intense yet subdued religious experience has been the subject of most of Doni's recent works. It seems clear that the tragic experience of his son's death has intensified his absorption with this theme. *Un filo di voce* (A Mere Whisper, 1993) is another "povera Gemma" story, whose ordinary protagonist, Anna, also has a religious experience that includes visions and stigmata. *Il Presidente e il Filosofo* (The President and the Philosopher, 1995) is about French president François Mitterand's grappling with metaphysical issues during the months in which he was awaiting death. *Premio Letterario* (Literary Prize, 1994) is a novel about the crossbreeding of finance, real estate speculation, and the arts in the waning years of the Italian economic boom. In *La vita aperta* (An Open Life, 1995) Doni rearranges the events and reworks the style of *La doppia vita*.

After four fertile decades, Rodolfo Doni's creativity is far from exhausted. More than any other contemporary novelist, he has explored the possibilities of the political and the religious novel. Perhaps because of his uniqueness, it has taken some time for his fiction to gain the recognition it deserves, but during the last two decades his work has been gathering increasing critical attention, a series of literary prizes, and a wide readership.

References:

Vincenzo Arnone, "Da *Servo inutile* ad *Altare vuoto*," *Il ragguaglio librario*, 56 (July–August 1989);

Alberto Bevilacqua, "Notabili sulla graticola," *Oggi*, 12 March 1969, p. 127;

Carlo Bo, "Le confessioni d'un cattolico," *Corriere della sera*, 14 March 1976;

Arnaldo Bocelli, "Bilancio senza fine," *Corriere della sera*, 9 March 1980;

Bocelli, "Rabbia dopo il diluvio," *La stampa*, 31 December 1971;

Ido Borlenghi, "Muro d'ombra di Rodolfo Doni," *L'approdo letterario*, 8 June 1974;

Ferdinando Castelli, "L'esame di coscienza di uno scrittore," *La civiltà cattolica*, 2 (1980): 250–261;

Cesare Cavalleri, "Il muro segreto di Rodolfo Doni," *Studi cattolici* (April–May 1976): 391–393;

Pasquale Maffeo, "Giovani popolari alla riscossa," *Avvenire*, 5 January 1991;

Giuliano Manacorda, "Fede cattolica e politica democristiana nei romanzi di Rodolfo Doni e Gino Montesanto," in *Il filone cattolico nella letteratura italiana del secondo dopoguerra*, edited by Florinda Iannace (Rome: Bulzoni, 1989), pp. 113–125;

Manacorda, *Vent'anni di pazienza. Saggi sulla letteratura italiana contemporeanea* (Florence: La Nuova Italia, 1972), pp. 363–368;

Gennaro Manna, "I misteri di Medjugorje," *La discussione*, 8 April 1985;

Claudio Marabini, "La città di Doni," *Il resto del Carlino*, 22 April 1973;

Umberto Mariani and Franco Zangrilli, eds., *Invito alla lettura di Rodolfo Doni. An Introduction to the Works of Rodolfo Doni*, 2 volumes (Florence: Vallecchi, 1989);

Walter Mauro, "Verso il futuro con speranza," *Messaggero veneto*, 21 March 1984;

Carmelo Mezzasalma, "Doni: *Legame profondo* in generazioni mute," *Città di vita*, 39 (July–August 1984): 331–342;

Mezzasalma, "*L'altare vuoto* di Rodolfo Doni," *Città di vita*, 44 (July–August 1989): 347–356;

Lorenzo Mondo, "*I numeri*, racconto lungo," *Meridiano* (March 1961): 192;

Geno Pampaloni, "Utopia e illusione: La città sul monte," *Il giornale*, 13 April 1986;

Giorgio Petrocchi, "Gli espliciti segni di una nuova ricerca religiosa," *Avvenire*, 24 June 1979;

Mario Pomilio, "Dall'autobiografia al romanzo d'epoca," *Il tempo*, 26 March 1980;

Pomilio, "Il colore storico di un dramma privato," *Il tempo*, 20 January 1984;

Michele Prisco, "Dopo la caduta diventa più forte," *Oggi*, 8 May 1974;

Prisco, "Servo inutile," *Oggi*, 22 February 1982;

Giorgio Pullini, "Doni" [*Fuori gioco*], *Comunità*, 16 (May 1963): 103–104;

Massimo Romano, "L'altare vuoto del servo inutile," *La stampa-Tuttolibri*, 8 September 1989;

Ines Scaramucci, "Rodolfo Doni, *Muro d'ombra*," *Il ragguaglio librario* (March 1984);

Alessandro Scurani, "*La città sul monte* di Rodolfo Doni," *Letture*, 41 (May 1984): 407–408;

Scurani, "Rodolfo Doni: il coraggio di testimoniare," *Letture*, 40 (June–July 1985): 483–508;

Mario Spinelli, "Un cattolico al bivio," *Il settimanale*, 17 May 1978;

Giancarlo Vigorelli, "L'italiano neoborghese di un romanzo di Doni," *Il giorno*, 3 April 1974;

Valerio Volpini, "Passaggio del fronte: romanzo di R. Doni," *Avvenire*, 2 January 1972;

Volpini, "Sezione Santo Spirito," *La fiera letteraria*, 21 May 1959;

Volpini, "La speranza e i tormenti di un padre," *Avvenire*, 7 April 1976;

Franco Zangrilli, *La voce e la storia. Ispirazione religiosa nell'opera di Rodolfo Doni* (Florence: Cultura Nuova, 1992).

Beppe Fenoglio

(1 March 1922 – 18 February 1963)

Mark Pietralunga
Florida State University

BOOKS: *I ventitrè giorni della città di Alba* (Turin: Einaudi, 1952);

La malora (Turin: Einaudi, 1954); translated by John Shepley as *Ruin* (Marlboro, Vt.: Marlboro Press, 1992);

Primavera di bellezza (Milan: Garzanti, 1959);

Un giorno di fuoco (Milan: Garzanti, 1963); enlarged as *Un giorno di fuoco e altri racconti* (Milan, Garzanti, 1965); —enlarged edition includes *Una questione privata*; translated by Maria Grazia Di Paolo as *A Private Matter* (New York: Peter Lang, 1988);

Il partigiano Johnny, edited by Lorenzo Mondo (Turin: Einaudi, 1968);

La paga del sabato (Turin: Einaudi, 1969);

Un Fenoglio alla prima guerra mondiale, edited by Gino Rizzo (Turin: Einaudi, 1973);

La voce nella tempesta, edited by Francesco De Nicola (Turin: Einaudi, 1974);

L'affare dell'anima e altri racconti (Turin: Einaudi, 1978);

Opere, edited by John Meddemmen, Maria Antonietta Grignani, Piera Tommasoni, Maria Corti, and Carla Maria San Filippo, 3 volumes (Turin: Einaudi, 1978);

Appunti partigiani 1944–1945, edited by Lorenzo Mondo (Turin: Einaudi, 1994).

Edition: *Romanzi e racconti,* edited by Dante Isella (Turin: Einaudi-Gallimard, 1992).

TRANSLATIONS: Samuel Taylor Coleridge, *La ballata del vecchio marinaio* (Turin: Einaudi, 1964);

Kenneth Grahame, *Il vento nei salici,* edited by John Meddemmen (Turin: Einaudi, 1982).

When Beppe Fenoglio died in 1963 at the age of forty, he had published only a collection of short stories, *I ventitrè giorni della città di Alba* (The Twenty-three Days of the City of Alba, 1952), and two novels, *La malora* (1954; translated as *Ruin,* 1992) and *Primavera di bellezza* (Springtime of Beauty, 1959). At the time of his death, he was known only

to a small circle of Italian readers. With the subsequent publication of other writings, he has become one of Italy's major postwar writers.

Isolated and reluctant to conform to the literary establishment, Fenoglio remained committed to linguistic experimentation, hoping to reinvigorate what he regarded as the sterile and rhetorical Italian language. He viewed his work as a translator as a means of experimenting with language and style, and his intense love for English literature had an enormous impact on his writings. A large share of Fenoglio's work is connected to his experiences in the antifascist Resistance and to life in his native region of Piedmont. The dominant features of his prose are a moral rigor and an epic representation of reality.

Fenoglio was always modestly laconic about the details of his life. His 9 February 1952 letter to Italo Calvino suggests his reserve:

> Circa i dati biografici è dettaglio che posso sbrigare in un baleno. Nato trent'anni fa ad Alba (1 marzo 1922), studente (Ginnasio-Liceo, indi Università, ma naturalmente non mi sono laureato), soldato nel Regio e poi partigiano; oggi, purtroppo, uno dei procuratori di una nota ditta enologica. Credo che sia tutto qui.

> (Regarding my biographical data, they are so brief that I can detail it in a flash. I was born thirty years ago in Alba [1 March 1922]—a student [Ginnasio-Liceo, then University, but naturally I didn't graduate], soldier in the King's forces and afterwards a partisan; today, unfortunately, I am one of the administrators of a well-known winery. I think that's about all.)

Alba is a large town lying in the southern part of Piedmont near the range of hills known as Le Langhe. Fenoglio was the first born of three children; his brother, Walter, was born in 1923 and his sister, Marisa, in 1933. Fenoglio's parents, Amilcare and Margherita Faccenda Fenoglio, owned a butcher shop in the center of town. Amilcare had experienced the harsh peasant life of the region and had moved to Alba from the town of Monforte.

Beppe Fenoglio in the Langhe region of Piedmont, 1961 (photograph by Aldo Agnelli)

Margherita Faccenda, also of peasant stock, came from Canale, a town on the plains crossed by the river Tanaro.

Fenoglio's parents contrasted both in character and background. Impulsive and temperamental, his mother was from a strict Catholic family; her husband, though, was extremely tolerant and a dreamer. In a passage from his diary, Fenoglio writes of his parents' strong influence upon him and of the visceral attraction he felt toward his father's side of the family:

> Io li sento tremendamente i vecchi Fenoglio, pendo per loro (chissà se un futuro Fenoglio mi sentirà come io sento loro). A formare questa mia predilezione ha contribuito anche il giudizio negativo che su di loro ho sempre sentito esprimere da mia madre. Lei è d'oltretanaro, d'una razza credente e mercantile, giudiziosissima e sempre insoddisfatta. Questi due sangui mi fanno dentro le vene una battaglia che non dico.

(I feel deeply a part of my Fenoglio ancestry. I am attracted to them–who knows if a future Fenoglio will feel for me what I feel for them. This attachment was formed in part by the negative opinion that my mother has always had of them. She comes from a region beyond the Tanaro, from a line of merchants who are re-

ligious, most judicious and always dissatisfied. These two blood lines cause a battle in my veins that I cannot describe.)

During the summers of his youth, Fenoglio would vacation with his father's family in the villages of the Langhe, either at San Benedetto Belbo or at Murazzano. These experiences would figure prominently in his formation as a writer, for on those occasions he came into contact with the harsh realities of peasant life. The severity and solitude of the environment touched a chord in his solitary and pensive nature. He developed an intense love for the hills of the Langhe, with their forests and torrents. He visited the region throughout his life and made it the setting for all his writings.

In school Fenoglio was an outstanding student; consequently, his parents decided to enroll him in the Ginnasio-Liceo Govone, rather than a vocational school. At the *ginnasio* (a secondary school marked by a concentration in the humanities) he excelled not only in his studies but also in athletics, particularly basketball and soccer. Despite his accomplishments, he remained shy and withdrawn, afflicted with a slight stutter. Inspired by his English instructor, Maria Lucia Marchiaro, Fenoglio developed a strong interest in English writers and in Anglo-Saxon culture, a civilization that doubtless appeared more open, more just, and more suitable to his temperament than the stifling provincial reality of Fascism.

Fenoglio, whose anti-Fascism was anchored in ethical and aesthetic considerations, found moral and intellectual support in two other instructors, Pietro Chiodi (philosophy) and Leonardo Cocito (Italian). Fenoglio recalled these men with affectionate esteem in his novel *Il partigiano Johnny* (Partisan Johnny, 1968). After receiving his diploma from the lyceum in June 1940, he enrolled in modern literature at the University of Turin the following September; however, after two years, his university studies were interrupted by military service. He attended courses at an officer's school in the nearby town of Ceva and subsequently was transferred to Rome. He was in Rome on 8 September 1943 when the armistice was declared. In *Primavera di bellezza*, Fenoglio records with lashing sarcasm the cataclysmic events of those days and traces his own adventurous return home by train.

After a period of concealment in January 1944, Fenoglio joined the Resistance movement against the German and Fascist forces that still controlled northern and central Italy. His first battle experience was in the ranks of a communist company in the upper hills of the Langhe. He remained briefly with this group and in the summer of 1944 enrolled in the partisan forces called *autonomi* (autonomous) or *azzurri* (blueshirts) under the command of the famed Resistance fighter Enrico Martini Mauri. With these detachments, Fenoglio engaged in combat against German soldiers and their Italian Fascist auxiliaries. He took part in the seizure and defense of his birthplace, an experience he narrated in his short story "I ventitrè giorni della città di Alba." In the final months of the war he worked as interpreter and liaison officer for the English mission located in the hills near the city of Asti.

After the war Fenoglio urgently needed employment and decided to forgo his university studies. Taking advantage of his skills in English, he found a job in the export division of a local winery, first as an interpreter and then as an administrator. Although he would later have the opportunity to leave for more fulfilling employment, he chose to remain at the winery because the routine work afforded him the time to write, his true vocation. The early stages of his literary career were long and arduous. In the November 1949 *Pesci rossi,* a bulletin of the Bompiani publishing house, he published his first short story, "Il trucco" (The Trick), using the pseudonym Giovanni Federico Biamonti. That same year he sent the publisher Einaudi a collection of short stories titled "Racconti della guerra civile" (Stories of the Civil War), which was met with silence.

The following year he submitted to Einaudi a novel titled *La paga del sabato* (Saturday's Pay), which was refused at the time but published posthumously in 1969. This second work focuses on the uneasiness that prevailed in the immediate postwar years and the difficulties that Ettore, a former partisan, experiences in finding employment. Many autobiographical elements are blended into *La paga del sabato,* especially the portrait of the protagonist's parents: the conciliatory, understanding father and the rigid, combative mother. Ettore's mother is her son's antagonist in bitter disputes over money, work, and smoking. Written at the height of Neorealism, the novel was described by Fenoglio in a 30 September 1981 letter to Calvino, who served as consultant for Einaudi, as "il frutto piuttosto difettoso, anche se magari interessante, di una mia cotta neoverista che ho ormai superato" (the rather faulty, perhaps interesting product of an infatuation with Neorealism that I have now overcome).

In *La paga del sabato* one finds many ingredients that identify a neorealist story. The subject matter is linked to the experience of the war and its influence on the postwar years. While the work depicts the everyday life of the lower classes within a provincial setting, Fenoglio clearly intends his regional world to suggest the larger history of a generation. Also indicative of the neorealist influence is Fenoglio's effort to realize spoken Italian in a written form. For Fenoglio, Neorealism meant remaining faithful to his Piedmontese roots while striving for universality.

Elio Vittorini, the consultant for Einaudi who refused *La paga del sabato,* recommended that he draw two short stories from it. Fenoglio followed Vittorini's advice in part, including the story "Ettore va al lavoro" (Ettore Goes to Work) in the collection of short stories titled *I ventitrè giorni della città di Alba*. After much hesitation and several revisions Einaudi published the book in 1952.

I ventitrè giorni della città di Alba is made up of twelve stories that draw from two rich narrative sources: the partisan war and the peasant life of the Langhe. Fenoglio's original title for the work, "Racconti barbari" (Barbarous Tales), suggests his harsh view of the world. The title story that introduces the volume centers on a remarkable episode of the Resistance, the twenty-three days during which the partisans held and defended the city of Alba, having seized it in a brutal fight from the Nazi and Fascist forces. Fenoglio's demystifying and ironic treatment of war distinguishes this work from many of the war chronicles or diaries of the period that indulge in the heroics rather than emphasize the death and violence.

Fenoglio's vision of the human condition is dominated by tragic violence. He makes no distinction between the executions, ambushes, and the punishment of traitors in the war stories and the suicides and destructive rains in the tales of peasant life. His antiheroic, unconventional, and bitterly realistic narrative of the Resistance initially evoked a sharp reaction, especially among leftist critics who accused Fenoglio of robbing the partisans of their ideological and political convictions. However, the originality of *I ventitrè giorni della città di Alba* lies in Fenoglio's refusal to conform to literary or ideological conventions.

Still unsure about his abilities as a novelist, Fenoglio proposed to Einaudi a short novel titled *La malora*. He resisted the publisher's attempt to change the title and later remarked on its aptness in a 1 July 1954 letter to Calvino: "Titolo sì deprimente ed anche puzzante un poco di verismo ottocentesco, ma che aveva il vantaggio grande di essere titolo riassuntivo e globale" (Yes, it was a depressing title which also smelled a bit of nineteenth-century verismo, but it had the advantage of being a synthetic and all-encompassing title). A masterpiece of the novella form, *La malora* tells the story of an impoverished and unfortunate family of the Langhe.

Fenoglio is extraordinarily faithful to authentic peasant speech. There is nothing superfluous in the narration, and the bareness of the language reflects the harsh life in the region. The opening lines spoken by Agostino, the young narrator, set the mood for the rest of the story:

> Pioveva su tutte le langhe, lassù a San Benedetto mio padre pigliava la sua prima acqua sottoterra.... Fortuna che il mio padrone m'aveva anticipato tre marenghi, altrimenti in tutta casa nostra non c'era di che pagare i preti e la cassa e il pranzo ai parenti.

> (It was raining all over the Langhe, and up in San Benedetto my father was getting wet underground for the first time.... It was a good thing my master had advanced me three napoleons, otherwise there was nothing in the whole house to pay for the priests and the coffin and the meal for the relatives.)

The novella is linguistically one of Fenoglio's most interesting works, for he effectively mixes languages (Italian and dialect) and styles (popular and literary).

Agostino is sold off as a "bond servant" by his poor peasant parents to the slightly less destitute Tobia, a sharecropper in a nearby village. Life in the Langhe, presented through Agostino's eyes, is a curse for everyone. In the midst of poverty and destitution, Agostino is offered a glimmer of hope when his master acquires another servant, Fede. The two fall in love and plan a life together. Their plans, however, are soon vanquished when Fede's parents arrange to marry her to someone else. Meanwhile, Agostino's seminarian brother, Emilio, is slowly dying of tuberculosis. The novel ends when the mother announces his imminent death and prays to a severe God who has violently struck her hopeless world once again:

> Non chiamarmi prima che abbia chiuso gli occhi a mio povero figlio Emilio. Poi dopo son contenta che mi chiami, se sei contento tu. E allora tieni conto di cosa ho fatto per amore e usami indulgenza per cosa ho fatto per forza. E tutti noi che saremo lassù teniamo la mano sulla testa d'Agostino, che è buono e s'è sacrificato per la famiglia e sarà solo al mondo.

> (Don't call me until I have closed the eyes of my poor son Emilio. After that you can call me, if you like, whenever you want. And then consider what I've done for love and be indulgent with me for what I've had to do. And all of us who'll be up there, we'll hold our hands over Agostino's head, because he's good and has sacrificed himself for the family and will be all alone in the world.)

In his comments on the volume's dust jacket, Vittorini expressed some reservations about *La malora*, perhaps as a result of Fengolio's reluctance to follow his editorial suggestions. He reproached the author for not treating "cose sperimentate personalmente" (things experienced personally) and for indulging in the details of provincial life, not unlike a realist writer of the late nineteenth century. Vittorini warned young writers (such as Fenoglio), armed with a modern style and a facile tongue, not to allow themselves to be taken by the vividness of the written page crammed with "afrodisiaci dialettali" (dialectal aphrodisiacs). These observations provoked a crisis of confidence in Fenoglio. He wrote in his diary in August 1954:

> La *Malora* è uscita il 9 di questo agosto. Non ho ancora letto una recensione, ma debbo constatare da per me che sono uno scrittore di quart'ordine. Non per questo cesserò di scrivere ma dovrò considerare le mie future fatiche non più dell'appagamento d'un vizio. Eppure la constatazione di non esser riuscito buono scrittore è elemento così disperante, che dovrebbe consentirmi, da solo, di scrivere un libro per cui possa ritenermi buono scrittore.

(*Malora* came out on the 9th of this August. I haven't read a single review yet, but I must realize on my own that I'm a fourth-rate writer. This won't stop me from writing, but I must regard my future efforts as nothing more than placating a bad habit. And yet the realization I have not made it as a writer is such a decisive and disheartening factor that it should enable me to write a book which will allow me to consider myself a good writer.)

La malora marks the end of Fenoglio's association with the publisher Einaudi.

Between 1954 and 1962 Fenoglio continued to write short stories, several of which appeared in literary journals. They deal primarily with life in the villages of the Langhe and the everyday experiences of his kinsfolk. Among the short stories written during this period, "Un giorno di fuoco" (A Day of Fire), the story of the bloody rebellion of a loner, Pietro Gallesio, clearly stands out as one of his best. The events are recounted in first person by a boy narrator (the young Fenoglio), who is staying with his relatives in the village of San Benedetto.

The boy recalls Gallesio's actions as "il più grande fatto prima della guerra d'Abissinia" (the most noteworthy occurrence before the Abyssinian war). Seeking to avenge himself of perceived wrongs done to him, Gallesio kills, in succession, his brother, his nephew, the parish priest, and a policeman sent to capture him; then he shoots himself with the only bullet left. The boy narrates the event, relying on what he hears from the men of San Benedetto, including his stepuncle, who had seen the shootout at the nearby village of Gorzegno. The young boy is receptive to the point of view of his stepuncle, who sympathizes with the murderer and sees the state as an enemy, indifferent to local problems.

Throughout the story a law of primitive, irrational violence seems to govern the actions of men. In the midst of the seemingly inexorable violence, the boy's aunt attempts to bring some hope of order to this hostile world, asking God for forgiveness and blaming the great ignorance of the people for the misfortunes that occur in the Langhe. Fenoglio's female characters appear to bear the only source of hope in this cruel existence.

Although he published few of his translations during his lifetime, Fenoglio remained an active translator until he died. In a letter to Calvino on 8 September 1951, he offered his services as translator to Einaudi: "Traduco tutto indifferentemente, ma ho una spiccata preferenza per il teatro e la poesia" (I translate everything indiscriminately, but I have a distinct preference for theater and poetry). Nevertheless, he considered his translations above all a literary exercise. The craft of translation was a funda-mental activity to which he devoted a great deal of his energies, especially when he felt he lacked creative inspiration.

In the December 1955 issue of the literary magazine *Itinerari,* Fenoglio published his translation of Samuel Taylor Coleridge's *The Rime of the Ancient Mariner* (1798), which was reprinted by Einaudi in 1964. In the preface to this edition, Claudio Gorlier speculates on the reasons that might have led Fenoglio to translate Coleridge. He emphasizes the inventiveness and balance of the poem's language and refers to its popularity, a break from a highly stylized and rhetorical language. Fenoglio doubtless was fascinated by the poem's mixture of the realistic and the supernatural and Coleridge's adoption of a popular language within a permanent and universal structure. More important than the rhyme, which Fenoglio abandons, is the poem's dramatic and narrative rhythm coupled with a fluent style. The decision to translate *The Rime of the Ancient Mariner* must have been a valuable literary exercise for Fenoglio.

Fenoglio never concealed his dissatisfaction with his writing. In an interview with Elio Filippo Accrocca in 1960, he spoke of his work and of a lack of confidence in his writing skills:

> Scrivo per una infinità di motivi. Per vocazione . . . anche per spirito agonistico, anche per restituirmi sensazioni passate . . . non certo per divertimento. Ci faccio una fatica nera. La più facile delle mie pagine esce spensierata da una decina di penosi rifacimenti.

> (I write for an infinite number of reasons. Out of a sense of vocation . . . also because of a competitive spirit, and to revive past sensations . . . certainly not for fun. The easiest of my pages emerges carefree after about ten painful rewritings.)

Fenoglio viewed writing as a discipline, with all the rigor and difficulties the term implies. "Io studio le parole" (I study words), he stated, when he revealed to his former professor of religion, Don Natale Bussi, that he had spent weeks in writing the first line of *La malora.*

Although he had switched publishing companies from Einaudi to Garzanti, Fenoglio continued to have strained relations with his editor. After two years of rewritings suggested by the editor Garzanti, *Primavera di bellezza* finally appeared in April 1959. The final version of the novel only vaguely resembled the initial draft. According to Fenoglio, he first wrote the novel in English and then produced two drafts. The novel is only a small part of the elaborate project he had planned for several years.

He had hoped to publish two volumes covering the five-year period from 1940 to 1945. Instead,

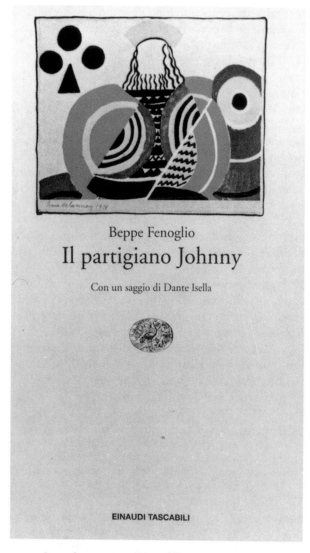

Beppe Fenoglio

Il partigiano Johnny

Con un saggio di Dante Isella

EINAUDI TASCABILI

Cover for a 1994 edition of Fenoglio's 1968 novel, which was assembled after his death from two incomplete versions

the published work details just nine months of the life of the protagonist, Johnny, from the day he is called to arms in January 1943 to his return from Rome in September, soon after the armistice. Through the use of flashbacks, Fenoglio includes in the final version descriptions of Johnny's high school years.

Primavera di bellezza introduces Fenoglio's alter ego, Johnny, a young anglophile with an inherent aversion for Fascist pomp. For much of the novel, Fenoglio traces his own traumatic experiences as a student at the officer's school in Piedmont and in Rome and his ensuing flight home after the sudden and turbulent events surrounding the armistice in September 1943. The final three chapters, which treat Johnny's experiences as a partisan, are far less autobiographically and historically accurate. In or-

der to affirm his faith in antifascist values, which had begun to fade by the 1950s, Fenoglio had his partisan hero die courageously. Many critics accused him of being too excessive in his search for a stylistic or linguistic expression. Eugenio Montale, Carlo Bo, and Giorgio Bàrberi Squarotti noted the incongruity between the novel's rich formalistic commitment and the lack of any clear thematic direction. In large part this preciosity of style is a result of the lengthy and laâorious gestation of the work.

In 1960 Fenoglio married Luciana Bombardi, whom he had met immediately after the war in a civil ceremony. Their daughter, Margherita, was born in 1961. Meanwhile he was beginning to receive recognition for his works. In 1960 he won the Prato literary prize for *Primavera di bellezza* and in 1962 the Alpi Apuane Prize for his short story "Ma il mio amore è Paco" (But My Love Is Paco), which appeared in the review *Paragone*. Despite the growing recognition, Fenoglio, a reserved man, continued to remain indifferent to the literary establishment. During this time, his health began to fail. He would spend long periods of time in his beloved high hills of the Langhe in the hope that the healthy air would cure him, but his condition only worsened. He was admitted to a private hospital in Bra and later to the Molinette hospital in Turin, where he died of lung cancer on 18 February 1963. Contemptuous of organized religion, he requested a civil burial.

A large part of Fenoglio's writings was left unfinished and was published posthumously. When he died, he was working on the novel *Una questione privata* (A Private Matter). Two months after his death, Garzanti published *Un giorno di fuoco,* which included a collection of short stories together with *Una questione privata*. In the preface to the 1964 edition of his first novel, *Il sentiero dei nidi di ragno* (The Path to the Nest of Spiders), Calvino examines the literary consequences of the Resistance movement with regard to the writers of his generation. He struggled to diagnose the *forma mentis* of Italian writers of the time, faced with the task of representing a country thoroughly devastated by both a civil and a world war. He pays tribute to Fenoglio, the most isolated and solitary member of his generation, whose novel *Una questione privata,* he asserts, represents the novel his generation had dreamed of writing. Thanks to Fenoglio, writes Calvino, a group of writers has acquired significance.

Una questione privata narrates the story of Milton, a university student from Alba, who has transferred from the king's army to the autonomous fighting forces of the partisans. It is not difficult to relate many aspects of this character to Fenoglio. Like his creator, Milton has a passion for Anglo-Saxon culture, which is reflected in the English uniform he insists on wearing, the poets he reads, the make of his military weapons, and his cigarettes. During military action near his hometown, Milton learns of a possible romantic relationship between Fulvia, with whom he is in love, and his friend and fellow partisan, Giorgio Clerici. Obsessed by thoughts of Fulvia's betrayal, Milton begins his personal quest for the truth in the midst of a raging civil war.

Among the other works published posthumously, *Il partigiano Johnny,* though incomplete, is considered one of the most original novels of twentieth-century Italian literature, distinguished by Fenoglio's exploration of language and his portrayal of the Resistance as an epic period. The manuscript was first edited and published by Lorenzo Mondo in 1968, who pieced together two incomplete versions found among the author's unpublished writings. Autobiographical in part, it is the story of the young anglophile, Johnny, the protagonist of *Primavera di bellezza.* Fenoglio narrates Johnny's war experiences beginning with his return home after the armistice on 8 September 1943 to the early months of 1945. During this period the protagonist flees from the Fascists' call-to-arms and joins the partisans. He remains alone in the Piedmontese mountains in the bitter winter of 1944, when the partisans are forced to disband and the Resistance becomes a dramatic struggle for survival, but finally rejoins the anti-Fascist troops in the spring of 1945. With this novel, Fenoglio succeeded once again in representing war as a universal human experience. He transformed the realities of the Resistance into a comprehensive symbol of the drama and cruelty of human existence. The richness of this text lies in its language, which demonstrates the influence of the English language on the author's lexical and syntactic choices.

Shortly after Fenoglio's death, his surviving manuscripts gave rise to a philological debate regarding the vexed question of compositional chronology. It was not until the publication of Fenoglio's *Opere* in 1978, however, that the controversy surrounding the chronology gained notoriety. The editors of this edition, directed by Maria Corti, chose to separate the two drafts of *Il partigiano Johnny* and include a third fragmented English version as the first phase of Fenoglio's partisan war epic. Following this arrangement of the texts, the editors advanced the theory that *Il partigiano Johnny* represents a narrative reservoir from which the author drew from the beginning of his career through to the end.

Although the complete works has come under sharp attacks by scholars, all acknowledge its documentary importance as testimony to the writer's tenacious spirit, his indefatigable work on language and style.

Distancing himself from Italian tradition—be it the postwar neorealist prose or the elegance of the pre–World War II *prosa d'arte*—Fenoglio turned to the Anglo-Saxon world for guidance. Once he was freed of what he saw as the stifling and rhetorical tradition of Italian letters, he sought to achieve a concise, lean, and rhythmic prose in consonance with his appreciation of English and American literature. Fenoglio's many drafts of his writings are a testimony to his labors in fashioning a distinctive style.

Interview:

Elio Filippo Accrocca, "Beppe Fenoglio" in *Ritratti su misura di scrittori italiani* (Venice: Sodalizio del Libro, 1960), pp. 180–181.

Bibliography:

Angelo Lacchini, "Beppe Fenoglio: notizia bibliografica," *Otto/Novecento,* 1 (January–February 1982): 275–281.

Biographies:

Davide Lajolo, *Fenoglio* (Milan: Rizzoli, 1978);

Franco Vaccaneo, *Beppe Fenoglio* (Cavallermaggiore: Gribaudo, 1990).

References:

Gian Luigi Beccaria, *La guerra e gli asfodeli. Romanzo e vocazione epica di Beppe Fenoglio* (Milan: Serra e Riva, 1984);

Roberto Bigazzi, *Fenoglio: personaggi e narratori* (Rome: Salerno, 1983);

Mariarosa Bricchi, *Due partigiani, due primavere* (Ravenna: Longo, 1988);

Italo Calvino, *Il sentiero dei nidi di ragno* (Turin: Einaudi, 1964), p. 9;

Pietro Chiodi, "Fenoglio, scrittore civile," *La cultura,* 3 (January 1965): 1–7;

Eugenio Corsini, "Ricerche sul Fondo Fenoglio," *Sigma,* 26 (June 1970): 3–17;

Maria Corti, *Beppe Fenoglio. Storia di un "continuum" narrativo* (Padua: Liviana, 1980);

Corti, "Realtà e progetto dello scrittore nel Fondo Fenoglio," *Strumenti critici,* 2 (1970): 38–59;

Corti, "Trittico per Fenoglio," in her *Metodi e fantasma,* second edition (Milan: Feltrinelli, 1977), pp. 15–39;

Francesco De Nicola, *Fenoglio partigiano e scrittore* (Rome: Argileto, 1976);

De Nicola, *Introduzione a Fenoglio* (Bari: Laterza, 1989);

Giuseppe Grassano, *La critica e Fenoglio* (Bologna: Cappelli, 1978);

Maria Grazia Di Paolo, *Beppe Fenoglio fra tema e simbolo* (Ravenna: Longo, 1988);

Maria Antonietta Grignani, *Beppe Fenoglio* (Florence: Le Monnier, 1981);

Grignani, "Virtualità del testo e ricerca della lingua da una stesura all'altra del *Partigiano Johnny*," *Strumenti critici,* 36–37 (October 1978): 275–331;

Giovanna Ioli, ed., *Beppe Fenoglio oggi,* (Milan: Mursia, 1991);

Gina Lagorio, *Fenoglio,* third edition (Florence: La Nuova Italia, 1982);

Walter Mauro, *Invito alla lettura di Fenoglio,* second edition (Milan: Mursia, 1983);

John Meddemmen, "L'inglese come forma interna dell'italiano di Fenoglio," *Strumenti critici,* 38 (1979): 89–115;

Mark Pietralunga, *Beppe Fenoglio and English Literature: A Study of the Writer as Translator* (Berkeley: University of California Press, 1987);

Michele Prandi, "Modificazioni oblique nel *Partigiano Johnny*," *Strumenti critici,* 56 (January 1988): 3–64;

Gino Rizzo, *Su Fenoglio tra filologia e critica* (Lecce: Milella, 1976);

Rizzo, ed., *Atti del Convegno dell'Incontro di Studio su Beppe Fenoglio* (Florence: Olschky, 1984);

Eduardo Saccone, *Fenoglio. I testi, l'opera* (Turin: Einaudi, 1988);

Elisabetta Soletti, *Beppe Fenoglio* (Milan: Mursia, 1987).

Carlo Emilio Gadda

(14 November 1893 – 21 May 1973)

Albert Sbragia
University of Washington

BOOKS: *La Madonna dei filosofi* (Florence: Solaria, 1931);

Il castello di Udine (Florence: Solaria, 1934);

Le meraviglie d'Italia (Florence: Parenti, 1939);

Gli anni (Florence: Parenti, 1943);

L'Adalgisa. Disegni milanesi (Florence: Le Monnier, 1944);

Il primo libro delle favole (Venice: Pozza, 1952);

Novelle dal ducato in fiamme (Florence: Vallecchi, 1953);

Giornale di guerra e di prigionia (Florence: Sansoni, 1955; enlarged edition, Turin: Einaudi, 1965);

Quer pasticciaccio brutto de via Merulana (Milan: Garzanti, 1957); translated by William Weaver as *That Awful Mess on Via Merulana* (New York: George Braziller, 1965; London: Secker & Warburg, 1966);

I viaggi la morte (Milan: Garzanti, 1958);

Verso la Certosa (Milan & Naples: Ricciardi, 1961);

I racconti: accoppiamenti giudiziosi, 1924–1958 (Milan: Garzanti, 1963);

La cognizione del dolore (Turin: Einaudi, 1963, enlarged edition, Turin: Einaudi, 1970); translated by Weaver as *Acquainted with Grief* (New York: George Braziller, 1969; London: Owen, 1969);

I Luigi di Francia (Milan: Garzanti, 1964);

Eros e Priapo—da furore a cenere (Milan: Garzanti, 1967);

Il guerriero, l'amazzone, lo spirito della poesia nel verso immortale del Foscolo. Conversazione a tre voci (Milan: Garzanti, 1967);

La meccanica (Milan: Garzanti, 1970);

Novella seconda (Milan: Garzanti, 1971);

Norme per la redazione di un testo radiofonico (Turin: ERI, 1973);

Meditazione milanese, edited by Gian Carlo Roscioni (Turin: Einaudi, 1974);

La verità sospetta—Tre traduzioni di Carlo Emilio Gadda, edited by Manuela Benuzzi Billeter (Milan: Bompiani, 1977);

Le bizze del capitano in congedo e altri racconti, edited by Dante Isella (Milan: Adelphi, 1981);

Carlo Emilio Gadda

Un radiodramma per modo di dire e scritti sullo spettacolo, edited by Claudio Vela (Milan: Il Saggiatore, 1982);

Il tempo e le opere: saggi, note e divagazioni, edited by Isella (Milan: Adelphi, 1982);

Il palazzo degli ori (Turin: Einaudi, 1983);

Racconto italiano di ignoto del Novecento (Cahier d'études), edited by Isella (Turin: Einaudi, 1983);

Gonnella buffone (Parma: Guanda, 1985);

Azoto e altri scritti di divulgazione scientifica (Milan: Scheiwiller, 1986);

I miti del somaro, edited by Alba Andreini (Milan: Scheiwiller, 1988);

Taccuino di Caporetto: diario di guerra e di prigionia (ottobre 1917–aprile 1918), edited by Sandra Bonsanti and Giorgio Bonsanti (Milan: Garzanti, 1991);

Il Tevere, edited by Isella (Lugano & Milan & New York: Annuario della Fondazione Schlesinger, 1991);

Poesie, edited by Maria Antonietta Terzoli (Turin: Einaudi, 1993).

Collections: *I sogni e la folgore* (Turin: Einaudi, 1955);

Opere, 5 volumes, edited by Dante Isella and others (Milan: Garzanti, 1988–1993).

Carlo Emilio Gadda is generally considered one of Italy's most important authors of this century. Gadda does not share the transparency of style one finds in Italo Svevo or Italo Calvino. His prose is characterized instead by a linguistic expressionism and a grotesque and baroque fantasy that have led Gianfranco Contini and other critics to see him as a contemporary practitioner of the Italian plurilingual, or macaronic, literary tradition.

Gadda worked for many years in Italy and abroad as an electrical engineer; he was seen for most of his career as a difficult and obscure author. Much of his work consists of short stories, novel fragments, and essays written in the 1920s, 1930s, and 1940s, originally published in elite literary journals such as the Florentine Solaria and *Letteratura* and appreciated by a small coterie of critics and literati. In 1957 the publication of his detective thriller *Quer pasticciaccio brutto de via Merulana,* (translated as *That Awful Mess on Via Merulana,* 1965) propelled the reclusive Gadda to instant national fame. "Sono diventato una specie di Lollobrigido, di Sofío Loren" (I've become a sort of Lollobrigido, of Sophia Loren), he wrote to friend Domenico Marchetti. In 1963 the seventy-year-old Gadda became a European cause célèbre when *La cognizione del dolore* (translated as *Acquainted with Grief,* 1969) was awarded the Formentor Prix International de Littérature and major European writers and critics such as Michel Butor and Hans Magnus Enzensberger commented on his work.

The success of *La cognizione del dolore,* originally written in 1938–1941, and of *Quer pasticciaccio brutto de via Merulana,* written in 1946, led to the exhumation of Gadda's unfinished manuscripts and correspondence, many of which were posthumously published. As had been the case four decades earlier with Svevo, Italy's first modernist writer, Gadda achieved recognition at the end of his life, decades after most of his works had been written. He is now regarded as a major figure in twentieth-century Italian letters, an author who is compared to James Joyce, Robert Musil, or Louis-Ferdinand Céline.

Gadda's plurilingualism is characterized by his use of archaic forms of literary Italian, scientific and technological terminology, frequent and bizarre neologisms, borrowings from foreign languages, and, most notably, regional dialects. In particular he incorporates the Milanese and Roman dialects, while also making significant forays into the Neapolitan and Venetian. The linguistic complexity is grounded in Gadda's vision of the *pasticcio,* the mixture, mess, or pastiche of life.

The link between Gadda's linguistic expressionism and the complex philosophical *groviglio* (knot) lurking behind his verbal pastiche was not fully understood until Gian Carlo Roscioni published his work on the author. In 1969 Roscioni produced a groundbreaking study, *La disarmonia prestabilita* (Preestablished Disharmony), on the speculative thought underpinning Gadda's prose and five years later edited Gadda's eccentric 1928 philosophical treatise, *Meditazione milanese* (Milanese Meditation, 1974). Gadda pursued a degree in philosophy with an emphasis on the thought of Gottfried Wilhelm Leibniz, Benedict de Spinoza, and Immanuel Kant in the mid 1920s. In the *Meditazione milanese* he elaborated his perception of reality and knowledge as open-ended multiplicity subject to continual flux and deformation. In keeping with his philosophy, Gadda's works typically seem unfinished, lacking clear resolutions and quite often lacking endings entirely.

Gadda's narrative work is a fusion of expressionism and personal neurosis. Perhaps no other Italian author has managed better than Gadda to cultivate the persona of the neurotic writer. His correspondence and writings are pervaded by the sense of his many ailments, including hypochondria, excitability, lethargy, depression, paranoia, and, above all, a debilitating hypersensitivity. Friends jokingly referred to Gadda's quirks, his fear of automobiles and electric razors, his misogyny and determination not to be collared into marriage, his homophobia, his hatred for the family villa, his troubles with landladies, and his need for mathematical precision. As Gadda grew older and more feeble, the eccentricities degenerated into frightful phobias. His letters gradually acquire by turns bitter, apologetic, and whimpering tones. His reclusiveness increased in the final years as he spent his days between his armchair and his bed. Possibly a manic-depressive, he broke into tears easily. His enormous unhappiness, Contini remarked, was punctuated by intervals of an equally enormous hilarity.

It has been said that Gadda is the author of a single work. Themes, images, character types, fixed ideas, obsessive metaphors, and linguistic tics recur with a frequency that would be intolerable in a writer of less afflatus and breadth. The Gaddian protagonist is haunted by the obsessive symptoms of an existential malaise, labeled in *La cognizione del dolore* as a "male invisibile" (invisible illness/evil). The hypersensitive Gonzalo Pirobutirro of that novel suffers from a tragic "delirio interpretativo" (interpretative delirium) brought on by the impossibility of imparting order to the chaos of reality.

Gadda was born on 14 November 1893 into a Milanese family that would shape the traumatic core for his most autobiographical works. His father, Francesco Ippolito, had married Adelaide (Adele) Lehr in a second marriage, and the couple had three children: Carlo Emilio, the oldest; a daughter, Clara; and a second son, Enrico. Gadda called his younger brother the better and dearer part of himself, and Enrico's death in an aviation accident during World War I was a devastating blow. Yet Gadda's love and near adoration of his brother were mixed, as is revealed in Gadda's fictional autobiography *La cognizione del dolore,* with strong feelings of jealousy and resentment. Gadda's father engaged in risky speculations in the Lombard silk industry, resulting in economic hardship for the family. He later complained that his father deprived his children of the basic necessities in order to construct the hateful family villa in the Brianza region north of Milan.

Gadda's family was of conservative stamp; he had been inculcated from childhood with strong patriotic and nationalist sentiments, and he was a convinced interventionist at the outset of Italy's entrance into the war in 1915. In the yearning felt by so many prowar European intellectuals to experience a Bergsonian élan, the young Gadda, who absorbed many of these sentiments through his avid reading of Gabriele D'Annunzio's poetry, saw the war as a last chance to overcome what he felt to be the "deviamento" (deviation) of his life and "sciupío di meravigliose facoltà" (waste of marvelous faculties). His participation in the fighting is a desperate attempt to avoid a bleak personal fate of indistinction and failure.

Gadda kept a private journal throughout the war, from his arrival in the Val Camonica on the Trentino front in August 1915, to his transfer to the main Isonzo front and capture at Caporetto on 25 October 1917, to the bitter experience of his imprisonment in Germany and return home to the horrific news of his brother's death. His final entry on 31

Portrait of Gadda by Ugo Capocchini, 1934

December 1919 reveals the profound abjection Gadda felt as the result of his shattered aspirations: "La mia vita è inutile, è quella di un autonoma sopravvissuto a sé stesso, che fa per inerzia alcune cose materiali, senza amore né fede" (My life is useless, it is that of an automaton that has outlived itself, who because of inertia does some material things, without love or faith).

Gadda's *Giornale di guerra e di prigionia* (War and Prison Journal, 1955) represents his first effort to reconstruct a "tragica vita" (tragic life), and it is a key document in understanding his emerging ethos. Gadda writes of the dual scourge of his youth, his extreme sensitivity "congenita e continua" (congenital and continual) and his "terrori infantili" (childhood terrors). He writes of his reverence for and resentment of his mother, her constant sacrifices and unyielding severity in raising her children. Gadda's "caro papà" (dear father) is remembered in the diary for having told him that he would never amount to anything in life.

Politically, Gadda's vision of the war as "necessaria e santa" (necessary and holy) was most consonant with the platform of the Italian Nationalist Association, of which he was a member until 1921 when he joined the Fascist Party. The Nationalist vision of the war as consecrating Italian national identity and pride is echoed throughout Gadda's diary,

First page of the manuscript for Giornale di guerra e di prigionia

but it is a vision that is repeatedly betrayed by the behavior of Gadda's countrymen. The war is a proving ground for Gadda's evolving thoughts on the importance of the common good over the individual self. A recurring motif in his often harsh criticism of the Italian war effort is the unbridled egoism of Italian soldiers and officers and their lack of self-sacrifice for the benefit of the nation. This egoism is denounced throughout Gadda's fiction, most clearly in Gonzalo Pirobutirro's desecration of the first person pronoun–"l'io, l'io! . . . Il più lurido di tutti i pronomi!" (I, I! . . . The foulest of all pronouns!).

In Gadda's war diary one also finds the first articulation of his obsession with order and disorder. Gadda continually associates order with rationality and sublimity, while disorder is the realm of the irrational. Gadda's militarism is born from his mania for order, and the military life is seen as the opportunity for the exertion of methodic discipline and rational order. In his diary Gadda denounces the nightmarish disorder of his fellow Italians, from the messy trenches of the soldiers to the cluttered desks of the officers.

Disorder, though, is not only a social aberration of "italianità" (Italianness) for Gadda: it is also a personal nemesis that conditions his behavior, saps his strength, and impedes his creativity. He dares not wash his hands in his basin or take a sip of grappa for fear of disturbing the alignment of his possessions. Dripping water in his tent enrages him and summer flies are "le più puttane troie scrofe merdose porche ladre e boje forme del creato" (the most slutty whoring sowlike shitty swinish thieving and damned forms of creation). The conflict between an obsessive will to order and its continual defeat at the hands of a prolific and destructive disorder will become a constant motif in Gadda's life and work.

After the war and urged on by the insistence of his mother, Gadda took his degree in engineering at the University of Milan in 1920 and worked in Lombardy and Sardinia. Adamantly opposed to the socialist agitation and factory occupations in Italy after the war, Gadda joined the Fascist Party in 1921. He was at the Central Station in Milan to witness the return of the Milanese participants in the march on Rome in October 1922 that brought Benito Mussolini to power. Gadda was hired by the Argentinean Compañía General de Fósforos and spent fourteen months in Argentina, from December 1922 to February 1924. Gadda initially envisioned the move as a way of escaping from what he felt to be the chaotic and debilitating environment of postwar Italy, but he continued his political involvement, joining the Buenos Aires Fascio all'Estero (Fascist Cell Abroad). Unhappy in Argentina, he returned to Milan in February 1924 and decided to use his savings to attempt a first novel, the *Racconto italiano di ignoto del novecento* (An Italian Tale by an Unknown Author of the Twentieth Century), which was eventually published in 1983. Although he sketched only a few fragments of the actual novel, his extensive compositional and critical notes provide a wealth of information concerning his emerging politics, poetics, and metaphysics.

Gadda's outline of *Racconto italiano* reveals an ambitious attempt to fuse a traditional nineteenth-century realist narrative with the conventions of tragic drama and lyricism. The complex story, of which Gadda wrote only a few incomplete episodes, is an odd pastiche of romance novel motifs and scenes of violent clashes between Fascists and Socialists. Gadda's sees the postwar Italian crisis as the result of a disintegrated ethos and political irresponsibility. The novel is to bear witness to the tragedy of individual achievement and greatness suffocated by an inadequate Italian environment: "Uno dei miei concetti . . . è l'insufficienza etnico-storico-economica dell'ambiente italiano allo sviluppo di certe anime e intelligenze che di troppo lo superano" (One of my long-standing concepts . . . is the ethnic, historical, and economic insufficiency of the Italian environment for the development of certain souls and intellects that stand too far above it).

The novel's protagonist, Grifonetto Lampugnani, launches into a particularly virulent diatribe against what he calls the "arcadia criminale" (criminal arcadia) of the socialists and the Catholic Popolari who for their own self-interest extol the lower classes as the only repository of all that is good. Grifonetto's sarcastic ire is representative of the disillusionment of many disgruntled middle-class veterans, who, like Gadda, reacted against the perceived defeatism and class agitation of the socialists, Bolsheviks, and Popolari. Grifonetto's profession of faith in the machine gun and his love of D'Annunzio's book of poetry *Laus vitae* (In Praise of Life) indicates an adherence to the course of violence. Gadda, however, did not participate in violence, though he initially shared Grifonetto's faith in fascism as "una reazione netta, pratica, umana contro il nodo-gordiano della balordaggine ideologica accumulata dal secolo 18^0 e 19^0" (a clear, practical, human reaction against the Gordian knot of ideological stupidity accumulated from the eighteenth and nineteenth centuries).

In 1924 Gadda also resumed a program in philosophy he had begun at the University of Milan in 1922 under the tutelage of Piero Martinetti. Although he passed all the required examinations, he never completed a projected thesis on Leibniz's *New Essays Concerning Human Understanding*. From that abandoned project Gadda composed the eccentric *Meditazione milanese*. Although this work is problematic in its attempt to present a rigorous and systematic philosophy, it is a fascinating speculative presentation of the obsessive crusade of Gadda's narrative: the dismantlement of the hackneyed notion of reality and the human psyche as self-contained "pacchi postali" (postal parcels) and its replacement with a vision of human and phenomenal reality as tangled, fissured webs of multiplicity.

Meditazione milanese is notable for Gadda's effort to link of his idea of analytic "metodo" (method) to an "accrescimento di ordine" (an increase of order). Method attains a greater order through critical selection and elimination. The system that has a method, Gadda declares, is "dotato di fagociti logici" (endowed with logical phagocytes), with "gatti che divorano la topaglia nell'organismo casa" (cats that devour the mice in the house-organism). The goal of rational method for Gadda is to impose order on reality. But when the system cannot be rid of mice, when the shelter can not be rid of flies, then method gives way to the terror of contamination, to the abjection of will, to the exorcism of invective. Faced with a world that no longer seems subject to order, reason, and method, Gadda often abandons himself in his fiction to a rhetorical exasperation with reality's disorder, not so much in a process of mimesis but, as Roscioni has pointed out, to remain in some way reality's *arbitro* (arbiter) or *artefice* (artificer).

During the middle to late 1920s Gadda made his first hesitant overtures to the Italian literary community and began to publish short narrative pieces and literary essays. In a letter of 6 March 1926, on the eve of his first publication in the Florentine literary journal *Solaria,* Gadda paints himself to friend and intercessor Bonaventura Tecchi as an extravagant oddity among the journal's rarified belletrists: "Come soggetto strano, come giraffa o canguro del vostro bel giardino: ecco quel che posso valere" (Like a strange character, like a giraffe or a kangaroo in your beautiful garden: that's what I can be). The self-effacing trepidation of his letters to Tecchi in this period are indicative of Gadda's mixed relationship with the elite Italian literary establishment of the 1920s, located in the splendid Liberty cafés of Florence and in the cultured Europeanism of *Solaria*. In 1926 engineer Gadda, at work on the planning and construction of synthetic ammonia plants for the Società Ammonia Casale in Italy and abroad, was still far from that world. Not until 1940 would Gadda definitively abandon his duties as an engineer and move to Florence.

Gadda's literary production from the late 1920s to the early 1940s is marked by his struggle between inspiration and form. Rich in stylistic experimentation, the period saw Gadda publish literary fragments and shelve longer unfinished projects, as he attempted to forge what he would later call a style that is not merely adequate but "necessary" to his vision of the tangled muddle of existence and his own psyche. In this time of literary apprenticeship Gadda engaged in three principal types of composition: literary and techical essays, literary narratives, and satire.

Gadda's essay writing is quite varied. He wrote essays combining his literary interests and technical expertise such as "Le belle lettere e i contributi espressivi delle techniche" (Belles-lettres and the Expressive Contributions of the Technical Fields) in the May 1929 *Solaria*. He described technical or semitechnical enterprises, ranging from the surgery room, to the geologists' mountainside, to the slaughterhouse or flea market. Many of these descriptions were gathered into *Le meraviglie d'Italia* (The Wonders of Italy, 1939), a collection in which Gadda seeks to hone the literary word by linking it with the precision of the technological word. He also contributed many technical essays to various periodicals and newspapers on matters such as metal alloys or the industrial uses of nitrogen and lignite. Some of Gadda's technical writings, Robert Dombroski points out, are not without a certain measured tone of support for the Fascist government's policies, such as the mining plan in the newly conquered Ethiopia, the massive projects of drainage and land reclamation, and the resettlement plan in Sicily. Many of these articles were written during and even after the veiled but scathing satire of Italian fascism in *La cognizione del dolore*. Only in the realm of technology, it seems, could Gadda remain somewhat consonant with a regime that in every other way had betrayed his hopes for a new pragmatic reality in Italy.

A large part of Gadda's narrative fiction during this early period is marked by what Alfredo Gargiulo, regarding Gadda's first book, *La Madonna dei filosofi* (1931), referred to as "una ironia oziosa o scherzo a vuoto, così da parere, nel complesso, un cincischiato e molto letterario esercizio di penna" (an indolent irony or empty joke, so as to appear, overall, a mangled and very literary exercise of the pen). This early characterization of Gadda as a *umorista* (humorist) immediately casts him into a Lombard lineage with, according to Gargiulo, the "letteratissimo spirito bizzarro" (most literary bizarre spirit) of Carlo Dossi (1849–1910). Contini emphasized Gadda's connection with Dossi and the late-nineteenth-century *Scapigliatura* authors, but Gadda largely dismissed the link, stressing that the humorous satire and expressionism of the *Scapigliati,* unlike his own, was artificial, unmotivated, and aristocratic. Much of Gadda's defense of his "baroque" and "bizarre" style from this period on would consist in defending its "motivation" as absolutely "necessary" to his understanding of human existence.

The third emergent strand in Gadda's literary apprenticeship is evidenced in his writings of sarcastic rage, born of an epistemological and ethical fury that was already present in his World War I diary. Gadda's most ambitious early attempt to develop this sort of discourse was in his novel *La meccanica* (Mechanics, 1970), sketched in 1928. It is especially apparent in his critique of Italian and socialist defeatism during World War I. *La meccanica,* though, is a highly uneven work; Gadda's literary rage would only reach fruition in the first of his two great novels, *La cognizione del dolore.*

La cognizione del dolore takes place in the fictitious South American nation of Maradagàl and chronicles the tragic relationship between the volatile Gonzalo Pirobutirro, the semi-autobiographical protagonist, and his mother, whom he terrorizes. Gadda wrote the novel, which began to appear in serial form in 1938, after his encounter with Freudian psychoanalysis in the early 1930s, the death of his mother in 1936, and his frenzied efforts to rid himself of the odious family villa in Longone al Segrino. For years Gadda had suffered from bouts of anger and remorse in his relationship with his mother. Gadda's understanding of Freudian psychology, rather than providing a curative analysis of the relationship, led to a narrative full of allusions to his troubled feelings for his mother.

Pirobutirro is largely a caricatured representation of what Gadda perceived to be his own neurotic traits. As his mother notes with reference to Molière, he is both a misanthropic recluse and a *malade imaginaire* (imaginary invalid). Pirobutirro explodes in uncontrollable fits of rage at his mother because of her friendship with the local peons, which he reads as one more instance of her denial of love to him and in keeping with his bitter remembrances of an overly strict upbringing of deprivation and punishment. Gadda's postwar anger at what he perceived to be the socialist and Catholic exaltation of the wretched at the expense of the nation is transformed into Pirobutirro's hatred of vulgar hordes who smell of urine and feces and continually invade the ancestral villa of the "ultimo hidalgo" (last hidalgo). He, in turn, is presented to the reader

Portrait of Gadda by Francesco Messina

through the gossip of the local inhabitants as an enemy of the people, possessed of the seven capital sins.

Gadda's troubled relationship with Italian Fascism is played out in the novel's climactic episode, the brutal, mysterious bludgeoning of the mother in her bed. In Gadda's notes for a final chapter that was never written, the killer is discovered to be the local night watchman who metes out punishment on the mother for the refusal of her son to subscribe to the protective services of the Nistitúo de Vigilancia para la Noche–a thinly veiled substitute for the local *fasci* of Mussolini's regime. But because of a resemblance between Pirobutirro and the guard, the mother thinks it is her son who tried to kill her and reels back in horror when he arrives at the scene. She dies and he remains with "il dolore eterno" (eternal grief).

Many critics have noted the tension between the carnivalesque and tragic discourses in *La cognizione del dolore.* Gadda uses both as narrative screens, or masks, to deal with his traumatic autobiographical material. Contini has called it an "arte maccaronica esercitata su una materia freudiana" (a macaronic art exercised on a Freudian material). While Pirobutirro's frenzied consumption of inordinately large sea delicacies casts his bilious gastric problems in a comic light, mother and son don the masks of the tragic stage through allusions to classical or Shakespearean plays, including *Coriolanus, King Lear, Julius Caesar,* and *Hamlet.*

Gadda's fascination with the idea of Hamlet's revenge restoring order to a disordered reality provides the focus for his protagonist's "interpretative delirium" vis-à-vis reality. Hamlet's mission of vengeance, Gadda argues in the 1952 theater review "Àmleto'al Teatro Valle" collected in *I viaggi la morte,* is similar to that of the matricidal Orestes, who avenges Clytemnestra's murder of his father, Agamemnon; however, Hamlet's revenge is necessarily self-destructive. The moral order of the world can only be restored at the cost of his life. Pirobutirro is not able to carry out his tragic mission to restore order in this heroic fashion. His neuroses get the best of him, diverting lucid ferocity into delirium and impotent rage. Pirobutirro's dilemma is evident in his central soliloquy in which the ontological "To be or not to be" is expressed in terms of whether one should acquiesce to the phenomenal world of false appearances—"Cogliere il bacio bugiardo della Parvenza" (To seize the lying kiss of Appearances)—or deny it and in so doing to deny one's own self: "O invece attuffarla nella rancura e nello spregio come in una pozza di scrementi, negare, negare . . . Ma l'andare nella rancura è sterile passo, negare vane immagini, le più volte, significa negare se medesimo" (Or instead to plunge them into rancor and into contempt as into a well of excrement, to deny, deny . . . But the progress of rancor is a sterile footstep; to deny vain images, most of the time, means denying oneself).

The characters of Pirobutirro and his mother are powerfully drawn in *La cognizione del dolore.* They seem more akin to the troubled and assaulted characters of Fyodor Dostoyevsky or Louis-Ferdinand Céline than to the protagonists of the Italian narrative tradition. Their tragic gestures—Pirobutirro's mother in the grip of her son's rage is described with the words Suetonius uses to capture Caesar's fear as he is murdered —and incurable angst are reminiscent of the mixture of ancient and modern archetypes of Eugene O'Neill's nearly contemporaneous *Mourning Becomes Electra* (1931).

Much more than mere sympathetic characters, Pirobutirro and his mother are dramatic icons who demand a cathartic release. Gadda's style, with its metaphorical allusiveness, word variants from the loftiest Italian tradition, and rhythmic repetition,

serves to enhance the distance between the reader and the characters, as in the opening scene of the second part of the novel in which the mother seeks refuge from the fury of a sudden autumn storm: "Il vento, che le aveva rapito il figlio verso smemoranti cipressi, ad ogni finestra pareva cercare anche lei, anche lei, nella casa. Dalla finestretta delle scale, una raffica, irrompendo, l'aveva ghermita per i capegli" (The wind, which had carried off her son toward the oblivion-making cypresses, at every window seemed to be seeking her, too, her, in the house. From the little window over the stairs, a gust, bursting in, had gripped her by the hair). With its forays into Milanese and Neapolitan dialects, its use of Spanish, and its high and low registers of diction, *La cognizione del dolore* is indicative of Gadda's increasing plurilingualism.

The sardonic yet nostalgic view of *L'Adalgisa. Disegni milanesi* (Adalgi. Milanese Sketches, 1944), which began to appear in journals in the early 1940s, constitute a somewhat different path in Gadda's linguistic gamesmanship. *L'Adalgisa* is a final, ironic tribute to the Milanese society of Gadda's formation, and in particular to the intertwined upper-middle-class clans of the Cavigioni, Trabattoni, Berlusconi, Gnecchi, Cavenaghi, and others. This closed world of Milanese society with its aged patriarchs, philological societies, young engineers, and name confusion constitutes a veritable regional tribe, one that finds its true expression only in its native dialect. Thus, the major linguistic innovation in *L'Adalgisa* is the prevalent use of Milanese dialect as the necessary form for the expression of Milanese thought.

In 1940 Gadda abandoned his engineering career and moved to Florence to pursue more seriously his career as a writer. In Florence, at that time the literary capital of Italy, he solidified his contacts with the literary world, most important his friendship with the poet Eugenio Montale, but not without a certain acrimony on his part toward the leftist-leaning elite of the city's café scene, especially after World War II. In Florence Gadda experienced the disarray of the war; his destitution and hunger revived his traumatic memories of being a prisoner of war in Germany during World War I. Gadda's meager savings were quickly consumed during the war and immediate postwar period. He was nearly penniless when he moved to Rome in 1950 and found work with the "Terzo programma" (Third Program) for the Italian state radio (RAI) until 1955.

From his wartime experiences is born the last great obsession in Gadda's writing: his continual desecration of the dictator Benito Mussolini. His attack on Il Duce (the Leader) reaches its apex in the satiric pamphlet *Eros e Priapo,* which he wrote in 1944 but was not published as a book until 1967. Gadda's reduction of the Fascist phenomenon to the unsublimated narcissism of Mussolini and his cohorts is cast in pseudo-Freudian terminology. Il Duce is a freak-show attraction, half ass, half man. Gadda creates imagery of the obscene dictator engaging in a bestial verbal fornication with the oceanic, female crowds below his balcony in Piazza Venezia, making a grotesque pantomime of the complex social, political, and historical phenomenon of Italian Fascism. Conceived as a satire on Mussolini's female followers, the pamphlet was originally titled "Le patriotesse" (The Female Patriots), and Gadda's psychopolitical analysis becomes a thin facade for the unleashing of his pent-up misogyny.

The distasteful elements of *Eros e Priapo,* which have occasioned comparisons to Céline's *Bagatelles pour un massacre* have rendered it the least appreciated of Gadda's mature works. Stylistically, though, *Eros e Priapo,* along with Gadda's *Il primo libro delle favole* (First Book of Fables, 1952), is the most notable work emerging from what has been called Gadda's Florentine stage. In its derision of the Fascist enterprise, the pamphlet employs an ancient Florentine dialect ripe with archaisms and the morphological peculiarities of the Tuscan tradition. This has led to the accusation that Gadda's work smacks of "bozzettismo" (fanciful sketches), which critics such as Guido Baldi see as the major fault of Gadda's writing. Yet it is in *Eros e Priapo* that Gadda most closely approaches the original Renaissance macaronic form, for not only does he exploit the plurilingual interference between high (official language) and low (dialect) codes, he also recuperates what Cesare Segre calls the diachronic layering of the original Renaissance macaronic works of Folengo or François Rabelais in his fusion of archaic and modern languages.

In the 1940s, a decade of intense linguistic experimentation, Gadda wrote his most popular and linguistically complex work, the detective thriller *Quer pasticciaccio brutto de via Merulana.* First published in serial form in 1946, the novel was expanded and edited for its 1957 book publication. Set in Rome in early 1927, it has a muddled plot that traces two crimes, a jewel heist and the brutal murder of Liliana Balducci, a sublime soul who excites a passionate compassion in detective Francesco Ingravallo. But whereas the traditional detective novel is cast as the triumph of analytical rationality over criminal evil, *Quer pasticciaccio* underscores the tangled interrelatedness of reality with its multiple causes and impossible closure. The "pasticciaccio," or awful mess, of the novel's title is indicative of Gadda's ad-

a novel by the author of THAT AWFUL MESS ON VIA MERULANA

Dust jacket for the American edition of the translation of Gadda's 1963 novel, in which the mother of the protagonist dies believing him to be her murderer

aptation of the literary notions of the pastiche (which is also rendered as *pasticcio* in Italian) and the macaronic to his existential vision of the often horrific messiness of reality. As if to underscore this ontological grounding, a wicked allusion to the poetics of macaronic pastiche appears when one might least expect it, in the description of the savagely severed neck of Liliana Balducci. As the horrified yet curious police agents gaze at the wound, the blackened blood is likened to a dark, frothy "pasticcio," or mess, and the severed arteries appear to the agents as red or pink "maccheroncini" (little pasta noodles). This is the concrete, physical reality of the pasticcio as mess for Gadda.

Gadda's macaronic use of language suggests both disordered messiness and man's confused attempt to understand reality. In their association of Liliana's wound with maccheroncini and later with a "sanguinaccio" (blood pudding), the agents grasp for a suitable analogy. Although Gadda was always wary of too simplistic an interpretation of the terms *macaronic* and *pastiche* as applied to his work, he also emphasized that, when used critically, the macaronic style "polverizza e dissolve" (pulverizes and dissolves) every abuse that reason and language commit through the words of fraud. Gadda's macaronic pastiche is self-consciously present in detective Ingravallo's opening observation that any notion of cause and effect must be replaced by that of a tangled skein of a multiple concurrence of causes and effects, and his articulation of these thoughts in plurilinguistic forms. Ingravallo's pastiche of juridical, philosophical, and popular codes and his macaronic mixture of both technical and everyday Italian with the dialects of Rome, Naples, and the Molise are tantamount to the declaration of a textual modus operandi in which the word is as complex and changeable as its referent.

Gadda in *Quer pasticciaccio brutto de via Merulana* is much more positive toward popular language and its attendant carnival-like backdrop than he was in *La cognizione del dolore*. In the earlier novel his presentation of popular discourse was vitiated by the neurotic hypersensitivity and class consciousness of Pirobutirro, but the sensibility expressed in his detective story permits a celebratory popular atmosphere. In the Roman novel Gadda is likewise removed from the negative associations of his native Milanese dialect.

Gadda's encounter with the Roman sonnets of Giuseppe Gioacchino Belli (1791–1863) when he was writing the original version of the novel in 1946 doubtless contributed to his presentation of popular speech. In a 1945 essay titled "Arte del Belli" (The Art of Belli), which was collected in *I viaggiomorte*, Gadda not only praises Belli's "dissolvimento della inanità nella maccheronea" (dissolution of inanity in the macaronic) but notes that this is achieved through the promotion of the plebeian spirit and its language to a "materia epica" (epic material). In *Quer pasticciaccio brutto de via Merulana* Gadda uses the popular dialect as the vehicle for much of his satire on Italian Fascism. He also emphasizes the stunning sexual beauty and vitality of the Roman underclasses, whereas popular Lombard speech in *La cognizione del dolore* was typically associated with filthy, withered serving women and peons.

While detective Ingravallo suffers from a jealousy not dissimilar to that of Pirobutirro, it is often described in humorous fashion. The detective maintains a sleepy mien under his heavy pitch of black hair, and his ponderous clumping often disturbs the rest of the tenant who occupies the room below his own. Even more lighthearted is the depiction of the Neapolitan inspector Fumi whose sonorous voice and moral passion add a warmth to this novel that is absent from *La cognizione del dolore*. Many of Gadda's neuroses are depicted in the comically timid, large-nosed suspect Filippo Angeloni, whose predilection for tasty morsels from the local delicatessens is the butt of much sardonic irony. Even Liliana Balducci becomes a subject of irony in the novel when her desperation at not being able to bear children from her husband is described with reference to serving maids with pregnant bellies as large as trunks and the comic use of Roman dialect.

Gadda employs a third-person indirect discourse in which the narration becomes imbued with the tonality of his characters' points of view, typically expressed in dialect. This is often used to comic effect as when the Neapolitan Fumi is described in the third-person voice with Neapolitan phrases and interjections that reflect his own speaking style. *Quer pasticciaccio brutto de via Merulana* is continually poking fun at itself, and the reader who has some knowledge of Italian dialects is frequently delighted by the surprising interplay. Unfortunately, most of this subtlety is lost in translations.

Quer pasticciaccio brutto de via Merulana is the masterpiece of Gadda's Roman phase and his last great narrative effort. After its publication Gadda became ever more reclusive as his fame continued to increase with the republication of his earlier works and his critical and popular exaltation in the late 1950s and early 1960s. His instant celebrity was connected to the widespread sense of restlessness with what was perceived by many authors as the exhausted neorealist legacy. Gadda himself had roundly criticized much of the neorealist school for what he viewed as its insipid social realism at the expense of any sort of Kantian "dimensione noumenica" (noumenal dimension).

Quer pasticciaccio brutto de via Merulana and *La cognizione del dolore* were seized by many as examples of a narrative in which form and expressiveness were one with the complexity and alienation of modern reality. There was a surge of novelists who dabbled in dialect, whom Alberto Arbasino called Gadda's "nipotini" (little nephews or grandchildren), including writers such as Giovanni Testori, Pier Paolo Pasolini, and Arbasino himself. The "neo-avant-garde" *Gruppo '63* declared at its 1965 convention that the new experimental novel must take Gadda's *Quer pasticciaccio brutto de via Merulana* as its starting point and improve on it. Group member Angelo Guglielmi's anthology of the same year, *Vent'anni di impazienza,* reiterated this position by casting Gadda as the founding inspiration for the new experimental writers. In a 1964 essay titled "Nuove questioni linguistiche" (New Linguistic Questions), Pasolini argued that Gadda was the only author who presented a successful model for the enrichment of the national language. Writing like Gadda's, he asserted, was needed to operate against the degradation of language caused the colorless bureaucratic and technological onslaught in the new industrialized Italy.

Gadda's funeral services were held in May 1973 at Santa Maria del Popolo among the paintings of his favorite artist, Michelangelo Caravaggio, another Lombard expatriate in Rome whose gritty realism Gadda had so admired that he dedicated to his "inarrivabile maestro" (unreachable master) his first attempt at a novel in 1924. Much of Gadda's philosophical work was published posthumously, thus adding speculative depth and coherence to his fame as an expressionist. The publishing house Garzanti has published (1988–1993) a meticulously edited and researched five-volume edition of his collected works.

Letters:

Piero Gadda Conti, *Le confessioni di Carlo Emilio Gadda* (Milan: Pan, 1974);

Giuliano Manacorda, ed., *Lettere a Solaria* (Rome: Riuniti, 1979);

Dante Isella, ed., *Carteggio dell'ing. Carlo Emilio Gadda con l' "Ammonia Casale S.A."* (Verona: Ammonia Casale, 1982);

Emma Sassi, ed., *Lettere agli amici milanesi* (Milan: Il Saggiatore, 1983);

Giuseppe Marcenaro, ed., *Lettere a una gentile signora* (Milan: Adelphi, 1983);

Marcello Carlino, ed., *A un amico fraterno. Lettere a Bonaventura Tecchi* (Milan: Garzanti, 1984);

Giulio Ungarelli, ed., *L'ingegnere fantasia: Lettere a Ugo Betti* (Milan: Rizzoli, 1984);

Gianfranco Colombo, ed., *Lettere alla sorella, 1920–1924* (Milan: Rosellina Archinto, 1987);

Gianfranco Contini, ed., *Lettere a Gianfranco Contini a cura del destinatario* (Milan: Garzanti, 1988).

Interviews:

Cesare Garboli, "Non sono un misantropo," *La fiera letteraria,* 10 August 1967, pp. 8–9;

Alberto Arbasino, "Carlo Emilio Gadda," in *Sessanta posizioni* (Milan: Feltrinelli, 1971), pp. 185–210;

"Carlo Emilio Gadda con le sue parole," *Studi cattolici,* 148 (June 1973): 365–369;

Dacia Maraini, "Carlo Emilio Gadda," in *E tu chi eri? Interviste sull'infanzia* (Milan: Bompiani, 1973), pp. 9–21.

Biography:

Giulio Cattaneo, *Il gran lombardo* (Milan: Garzanti, 1973).

References:

Alba Andreini, *Studi e testi gaddiani* (Palermo: Sellerio, 1988);

Guido Baldi, *Carlo Emilio Gadda* (Milan: Mursia, 1972);

Renato Barilli, "Gadda e la fine del naturalismo," in *La barriera del naturalismo. Studi sulla narrativa italiana contemporanea* (Milan: Mursia, 1964), pp. 105–128;

Manuela Bertone, *Il romanzo come sistema. Molteplicità e differenza in Carlo Emilio Gadda* (Rome: Riuniti, 1993);

Filippo Bettini and others, *L'alternativa letteraria del '900: Gadda* (Rome: Savelli, 1975);

Gian-Paolo Biasin, "The Pen, the Mother," in *Literary Diseases. Theme and Metaphor in the Italian Novel* (Austin: University of Texas Press, 1975), pp. 127–155;

Michel Butor, Juan Petit, Hans Magnus Enzensberger, Drago Ivnisevic, and Pier Paolo Pasolini, "Gadda Europeo," *L'Europa letteraria,* 4, nos. 20–21 (1963): 52–67;

Eleonora Cane, *Il discorso indiretto libero nella narrativa italiana del '900* (Rome: Silva, 1969);

JoAnn Cannon, "The Reader as Detective: Notes on Gadda's *Pasticciaccio,*" *Modern Language Studies,* 10, no. 3 (1980): 41–50;

Marcello Carlino and others, *Gadda: progettualità e scrittura* (Rome: Riuniti, 1987);

Luigi Cattanei, *Carlo Emilio Gadda: introduzione e guida allo studio dell'opera Gaddiana, storia e antologia della critica* (Florence: Le Monnier, 1975);

Giorgio Cavallini, *Lingua e dialetto in Gadda* (Messina: D'Anna, 1977);

Arnaldo Ceccaroni, ed., *Leggere Gadda: antologia della critica gaddiana* (Bologna: Zanichelli, 1978);

Pietro Citati, "Il male invisibile," *Il menabò,* 6 (1963): 12–41;

Gianfranco Contini, *Quarant'anni d'amicizia: scritti su Carlo Emilio Gadda (1934–1988)* (Turin: Einaudi, 1989);

Robert Dombroski, "Gadda: fascismo e psicanalisi," in *L'esistenza ubbidiente. Letterati italiani sotto il fascismo* (Naples: Guida, 1984);

Dombroski, "Overcoming Oedipus: Self and Society in *La cognizione del dolore,*" *Modern Language Notes,* 99 (January 1984): 125–143;

Gian Carlo Ferretti, *Ritratto di Gadda* (Bari: Laterza, 1987);

Enrico Flores, *Accensioni gaddiane. Strutture, lingua e società in C. E. Gadda* (Naples: Loffredo, 1973);

Alfredo Gargiulo, "Carlo Emilio Gadda," in *Letteratura italiana del Novecento* (Florence: Le Monnier, 1958), pp. 547–560;

Pietro Gelli, "Sul lessico di Gadda," *Paragone,* 230 (1969): 52–77;

Elio Gioanola, *L'uomo dei topazi. Saggio psicanalitico su C. E. Gadda* (Milan: Librex, 1977);

Dante Isella, *I lombardi in rivolta. Da Carlo Maria Maggi a Carlo Emilio Gadda* (Turin: Einaudi, 1984);

Guido Lucchini, *L'istinto della combinazione. L'origine del romanzo in C. E. Gadda* (Florence: La Nuova Italia, 1988);

Gregory Lucente, "System, Time, Writing, and Reading in Gadda's *La cognizione del dolore*: The Impossibility of Saying 'I,'" in *Beautiful Fables. Self-consciousness in Italian Narrative from Manzoni to Calvino* (Baltimore: Johns Hopkins University Press, 1986);

Paola Marinetto, "Mito e parodia in Gadda," in *Profili linguistici di prosatori contemporanei,* Quaderni del circolo filologico-linguistico padovano, no. 4 (Padua: Liviana, 1973), pp. 113–176;

Giuseppe Nava, "C. E. Gadda lettore di Manzoni," *Belfagor,* 20, no. 3 (1965): 339–352;

Giuseppe Papponetti, "Gadda e-o D'Annunzio. Fallimento e congedo del Superuomo," *Otto/Novecento,* 8 (January–February 1984): 23–42;

Pasolini, "Gadda," in his *Passione e ideologia* (Turin: Einaudi, 1985), pp. 274–283;

Giorgio Patrizi, ed., *La critica e Gadda* (Bologna: Cappelli, 1975);

Piero Pucci, "Il male oscuro," *Belfagor,* 23 (31 January 1968): 91–98;

Rinaldo Rinaldi, *La paralisi e lo spostamento: Lettura della "Cognizione del dolore"* (Livorno: Bastogi, 1977);

Gian Carlo Roscioni, *La disarmonia prestabilita. Studio su Gadda* (Turin: Einaudi, 1969);

Albert Sbragia, *Carlo Emilio Gadda, The Modern Macaronic* (Gainesville: University Press of Florida, 1996);

Cesare Segre, "La tradizione macaronica da Folengo a Gadda (e oltre)," in *Semiotica filologica* (Milan: Feltrinelli, 1979), pp. 169–183;

Darby Tench, "Quel Nome Storia: Naming and History in Gadda's *Pasticciaccio,*" *Stanford Italian Review,* 5, no. 2 (1985): 205–217;

Giulio Ungarelli, *Gadda al microfono: l'ingegnere e la Rai 1950–1955* (Turin: Nuova ERI, 1993).

Natalia Ginzburg

(14 July 1916 – 7 October 1991)

Giuseppe Faustini
Skidmore College

BOOKS: *La strada che va in città,* as Alessandra Tornimparte (Turin: Einaudi, 1942); enlarged as *La strada che va in città, e altri racconti* (Rome: Einaudi, 1945); translated by Frances Frenaye as *The Road to the City: Two Novelettes* (Garden City, N.Y.: Doubleday, 1949; London: Hogarth Press, 1952);

È stato così (Turin: Einaudi, 1947); translated by Frenaye as *The Dry Heart,* in *The Road to the City: Two Novelettes* (Garden City, N.Y.: Doubleday, 1949; London: Hogarth Press, 1952);

Tutti i nostri ieri (Turin: Einaudi, 1952); translated by Angus Davidson as *Dead Yesterdays* (London: Secker & Warburg, 1956) and as *A Light for Fools* (New York: Dutton, 1957); republished as *All Our Yesterdays* (Manchester: Carcanet, 1985; New York: Arcade, 1989);

Valentino (Turin: Einaudi, 1957)–includes *Sagittario;* translated by Avril Bardoni as *Two Novellas: Valentino and Sagittarius* (Manchester: Carcanet, 1987; New York: Seaver, 1988);

Le voci della sera (Turin: Einaudi, 1961); translated by D. M. Low as *Voices in the Evening* (London: Hogarth Press, 1963; New York: Dutton, 1963);

Le piccole virtù (Turin: Einaudi, 1962); translated by Dick Davis as *The Little Virtues* (Manchester: Carcanet, 1985; New York: Seaver, 1986);

Lessico famigliare (Turin: Einaudi, 1963); translated by Low as *Family Sayings* (London: Hogarth Press, 1967; New York: Dutton, 1967); revised translation (Manchester: Carcanet, 1984; New York: Seaver, 1986);

Cinque romanzi brevi (Turin: Einaudi, 1964);

Ti ho sposato per allegria e altre commedie (Turin: Einaudi, 1966);

Mai devi domandarmi (Milan: Mondadori, 1970; enlarged edition, Turin: Einaudi, 1989); translated by Isabel Quigly as *Never Must You Ask Me* (London: M. Joseph, 1973);

Caro Michele (Milan: Mondadori, 1973); translated by Sheila Cudahy as *No Way* (New York: Har-

Natalia Ginzburg

court Brace Jovanovich, 1974) and as *Dear Michael* (London: Peter Owen, 1975);

Paese di mare e altre commedie (Milan: Garzanti, 1973);

Vita immaginaria (Milan: Mondadori, 1974);

Famiglia (Turin: Einaudi, 1977); translated by Beryl Stockman as *Two Novellas. Family and Borghesia* (Manchester: Carcanet, 1988) and as *Family: Two Novellas* (New York: Seaver, 1988);

La famiglia Manzoni (Turin: Einaudi, 1983); translated by Marie Evans as *The Manzoni Family* (New York: Seaver, 1987);

La città e la casa (Turin: Einaudi, 1984); translated by Dick Davis as *The City and the House* (New York: Seaver, 1987);

Opere, raccolte e ordinate dall'autore, 2 volumes (Milan: Mondadori, 1986–1987);

L'intervista (Turin: Einaudi, 1989);

Teatro (Turin: Einaudi, 1990);
Serena Cruz o la vera giustizia (Turin: Einaudi, 1990).

PLAY PRODUCTION: *L'inserzione,* Brighton, Theatre Royal, 16 September 1968.

OTHER: Marcel Proust, *La strada di Swan,* 2 volumes, translated by Ginzburg (Turin: Einaudi, 1946);
Mario Soldati, *La carta del cielo: racconti,* edited by Ginzburg (Turin: Einaudi, 1980);
Carlo Cassola, *Paura e tristezza,* introduction by Ginzburg (Milan: Biblioteca Universale Rizzoli, 1981);
Antonio Delfini, *Diari, 1927–1961,* edited by Ginzburg and Giovanna Delfini (Turin: Einaudi, 1982);
Gustave Flaubert, *Madame Bovary,* translated by Ginzburg (Turin: Einaudi, 1983).

The larger share of Natalia Ginzburg's life was divided between Turin and Rome, the two cities that are associated with most of her works. Turin, where she spent her youth, became a valuable source of past memories; the eternal city of Rome, home for the rest of her life, served as a setting for many of her novels as well as her dramatic works. It is in Rome that her characters develop into emblematic figures of estrangement, troubled creatures alienated from self, family, and society. The most difficult years in Ginzburg's life were 1940 through 1943, the transitional years between the two cities when she accompanied her husband to a remote village in the southern region of Abruzzi. Many of her works carry the imprint of this painful experience.

Ginzburg was born in Palermo in an upper-middle-class family, the youngest of five children. Her father, Giuseppe Levi, a professor of anatomy at the university, was born into a Jewish family of bankers from Trieste; her mother, Lidia Tanzi, was from the northern region of Lombardy. Her maternal grandfather, a lawyer by profession, was a friend of Filippo Turati, the prominent socialist writer. Ginzburg's parents were Jewish and Catholic in name only since both were nonbelievers. At the age of three Ginzburg moved from Palermo to Turin when her father was appointed to the chair of anatomy at the university.

Fearing that Natalia would catch a disease in the public schools, which he distrusted, her father had her tutored at home for the duration of her primary education. Later he relented and allowed Ginzburg to attend the prestigious Liceo Alfieri, where she completed her secondary education. In 1935 she enrolled in the Faculty of Letters at the University of Turin but did not stay to complete her studies. She wrote poetry, imitating such writers as Giovanni Pascoli, Guido Gozzano, and Sergio Corazzini, and devoted considerable time to what she called "il mestiere di scrivere" (the craft of writing). She also read voraciously, including French and Russian authors, especially Marcel Proust and Anton Chekhov. She admired two women writers, the American poet Emily Dickinson and the English novelist Ivy Compton-Burnett.

Leone Ginzburg, who was to marry Natalia, was a frequent visitor to the Levi household. Professionally he was a specialist in East European literatures, and in 1933 he had been one of the founders of the Giulio Einaudi publishing house. Strongly anti-Fascist and active in underground activities, he was a leader in the opposition group Giustizia e Libertà (Freedom and Justice). He had been imprisoned from 1934 to 1936 for anti-Fascist activities and was closely monitored by the Fascist police. Leone and Natalia were married in 1938. Two years after his marriage, Leone Ginzburg was again arrested and this time sentenced to political confinement in Pizzoli, a small town about ten miles from the city of Aquila in Abruzzi. The Ginzburgs thus joined many others in suffering the consequences of the anti-Semitic laws passed in 1938, which prevented Italian Jews from publishing and teaching in public schools. Also affected by these restrictions were such well-known writers as Giorgio Bassani, Carlo Levi, Primo Levi, and Alberto Moravia. Other prominent Italian intellectuals and writers also forced into exile or confinement included Ignazio Silone, Antonio Gramsci, Giuseppe Antonio Borgese, and Gaetano Salvemini.

In 1940 Natalia, with her two children, Carlo and Andrea, followed her husband to Pizzoli (a third child, Alessandra, was born in that town), where they remained from 1940 to Armistice Day, 25 July 1943. In the three years Natalia lived with her husband in Abruzzi, she was forced to adapt to a life that strongly contrasted with her life in Turin and developed a strong sense of rural life. Her first novel, *La strada che va in città* (1942; translated as *The Road to the City,* 1949), was written in Pizzoli. It was accepted for publication by the writer Cesare Pavese, who worked as an editor at Einaudi, and was published under the pseudonym of Alessandra Tornimparte in order to circumvent the anti-Semitic laws. Ginzburg borrowed the name Alessandra from her daughter and took the last name Tornimparte from a town near Pizzoli that had a small railroad station.

La strada che va in città is narrated by sixteen-year-old Delia. Although she is in love with Nini, a distant relative who resides with her family, Delia nevertheless becomes enamored with and pregnant by Giulio, the doctor's son and a law student who, she believes, will be able to offer her all of the niceties of city life and take her away from her depressing life in the country. After Giulio seduces Delia, the two are quickly forced into marriage. During the wedding ceremony Delia realizes that she does not love her husband-to-be. Her feelings about her predicament become the focal point of the story that explores the dichotomy between the city and the countryside. For Delia, the city becomes a false promised land, for though her marriage to Giulio brings her a life in the city, with the nice house and clothes she always wanted, she still has feelings for Niní, who also moves to the city. Delia's story ends in desperation.

In the fall of 1941, when she wrote *La strada che va in città,* Ginzburg, feeling homesick for Turin, had a love/hate relationship with the Abruzzi village of Pizzoli. In *Opere* (Works, 1986–1987) she recalls, "Quel paese lo amavo e lo detestavo" (I both loved and loathed that town). The road connecting the village and the city became the central metaphor in her writing: "La strada che tagliava in mezzo il paese e correva, tra campi e colline, fino alla città di Aquila, era venuta anche lei dentro alla mia storia. . . . La città era insieme Aquila e Torino. Il paese era quello, amato e detestato, che abitavo ormai da più di un anno e che ormai conoscevo" (The road that intersected the village and ran amid the fields and hills, up to the city of Aquila, had also come into my story. . . . The city was at the same time Aquila and Turin. That village I loved and hated; there I lived for more than a year and by now I was familiar with it). In writing the novel, its title suggested by her husband, Ginzburg realized that part of her would always be present in all her stories.

After being released from confinement in Pizzoli and returning to Rome, Leone was arrested on 19 November 1943 for editing the anti-Fascist newspaper *L'Italia libera.* On 5 February 1944 he died from torture wounds inflicted by the gestapo in Regina Coeli prison. For a two-year period beginning in November 1943, Natalia and her three children lived in Rome, hiding in several temporary lodgings. In November 1945 she returned to Turin to work as editor and translator for the publisher Einaudi. Her Italian translation of Marcel Proust's *Du côté de chez Swann* (1913; translated as *Swann's Way,* 1922) was published in Turin in 1946 as *La strada di Swan.* During this period she came in contact with important postwar writers such as Cesare Pavese, Elio Vittorini, and Italo Calvino.

Ginzburg wrote her second novel, *È stato così* (1947; translated as *The Dry Heart,* 1949), in four months, from October 1946 to January 1947, about a year and a half after the war. It provided a means of escaping the unhappiness of the war years and the tragic death of her husband, to whom she dedicated the novel. Years later Ginzburg reminisced about the novel in *Opere:* "Questo racconto è intriso di fumo, di pioggia, e di nebbia" (This story is soaked in smoke, rain, and fog). It is a novel of long monologues that begins with a murder.

È stato così is told in the first person by the narrator, a teacher, who has fatally shot her unfaithful middle-aged husband, Alberto. She recounts her tragic love story while sitting on a park bench, unfolding its events in a series of flashbacks triggered by her repetition of the last sentence of the opening paragraph: "Gli ho sparato negli occhi" (I shot him in the eyes). She recalls all that led her to kill her husband: their first encounter, the birth of their sickly daughter who eventually died of meningitis, and their difficult and often separate marital lives. She has long lived an empty life of solitude, from the school where she teaches to the room in the *pensione* where she lives. At one point the narrator developed a friendship with another woman, but it did not replace the emptiness in her life from her failed marriage to the older Alberto, who often left home for extensive periods, sometimes to visit his mistress, Giovanna.

È stato così lacks the humor of Ginzburg's other novels. The bitter pessimism that infects the narrator's entire world can be better understood if the reader is mindful of the historical and personal circumstances of Ginzburg's life during the composition of the novel. *È stato così* can be read both as a murder story and as a story of a young woman's desperate search for happiness. When she realizes that she will never find happiness, she shoots her husband. The murder has more to do with her mental and emotional condition than her husband's infidelity. It is one of Ginzburg's most convincing and penetrating studies of a woman's psyche.

In the fall of 1949, at a convention of the Pen Club in Venice, Ginzburg met Gabriele Baldini, professor of Anglo-American literature, musicologist, and critic, whom she married the following year. In 1952 they moved to Rome when Baldini was appointed professor of English literature at Magistero, the teachers' college where Luigi Pirandello and Maria Montessori had taught in the early part of the century. Except for a two-year sojourn in London from 1959 to 1961, when her husband served as director of the Italian Cultural Institute, Ginzburg lived in Rome in the Campo Marzio section, near the Pantheon. Her second husband died in Rome in June 1969 from hepatitis.

Ginzburg took the title of her first full-length novel, *Tutti i nostri ieri,* from Shakespeare's *Macbeth,* act 5: "And all our yesterdays have lighted fools. The way to dusty death." Published in Italy in 1952, the novel was translated into English in 1956 as *Dead Yesterdays* in England and in 1957 as *A Light for Fools* in the United States. In 1985 it was republished under the most literal of the translated titles, *All Our Yesterdays.* The use of the possessive pronoun *our* for "i nostri" in the last title is appropriate, for Ginzburg's novel can be read as a chronicle of her generation, who grew up under Fascism. The title also seems in keeping with Dante's opening verse in the *Inferno*–"Nel mezzo del cammin di nostra vita" (In the midcourse of our life)–for the Florentine poet includes all of mankind as partners in his journey. T. S. Eliot remarked that this verse points to the "collective dimension" of the work. Thus, in Ginzburg's novel "i nostri" represents the collective story of a generation under Fascism and the plight it had to endure. In this light, *Tutti i nostri ieri* can be seen as the author's contribution to the literature of the Resistance against Fascism, which was popular in the immediate postwar.

The novel is set against the most difficult and disturbing years of recent Italian history: the final period of the Fascist regime and Italy's participation in World War II. Ginzburg describes the human toll of Fascism during the five years from 1939 to 1944, a period that coincides with her marriage to Leone Ginzburg, weaving fiction with the history of war-torn Italy. The unifying elements of the novel are the historical and political events: Italy's preparations to enter the war, the war years and the fall of Mussolini, the invasion of the Allies, and their forcing the Germans out of Italy. There are direct references to the plight of the Jews in Italy after the 1938 anti-Semitic laws and under German occupation. The atrocities, the ransacking, the ravaging, the destruction, and the killing are evidenced by the German soldiers' rape of the forester's wife.

Divided into two parts, *Tutti i nostri ieri* focuses on the stories of the young people of two neighboring families and their relationship with Cenzo Rena, who becomes the central, unifying character of the second part of the novel. Anna, whose sister Concettina is courted by several young men, is the center of a typical bourgeois family. Anna's father is a stubborn and argumentative old widower and committed anti-Fascist whose memoirs contain fierce attacks against the Fascists and the king of Italy. In some ways he resembles Ginzburg's own rather authoritarian father. The first part of the novel ends with the suicide of Anna's older brother Ippolito, who is disturbed by the evils of Fascism, the inception of the war, the fact that Italy had joined forces with the Nazis, and Anna's revelation that she is expecting a child by Emanuele Giuma, a neighbor. As a result she decides to marry Cenzo Rena, who is forty-eight years old and rather ugly.

In the second part of the novel the role of history is accentuated, and Rena takes on a pivotal role. In his empathy for the peasants, who are often at the mercy of, and exploited by, the ruling classes, Rena is similar to Antonio Gramsci, the Sardinian Marxist, who, like Leone Ginzburg, was interned and imprisoned and eventually died as a result of wounds suffered while in jail. Rena represents Gramsci's belief in the union of the intellectual and the peasants, which would result in the enlightenment of the peasants and the creation of a more egalitarian society. Rena's willing sacrifice of his own life for that of a peasant who is responsible for the accidental death of a German soldier attests to his sincerity and love of his countrymen. It is noteworthy that Ginzburg's characters are not plagued by the usual psychological problems of alienation and unfulfilled or betrayed love; rather, their unhappiness is the direct result of Italy's social and political problems. Moreover, characters such as Rena and Ippolito are not relegated to the role of spectators of life but deal with their own miseries; indeed, they often champion the lives of those suffering from war and Fascism, particularly the peasants.

Toward the end of *Tutti i nostri ieri,* when the Germans are occupying Rome, Emanuele is serving as editor of a secret newspaper, for which he is imprisoned twice by the Germans–circumstances that recall the activities of Ginzburg's husband. The novel ends with Anna, Emanuele, and Giustino thinking "a tutti quelli che erano morti, e alla lunga guerra e al dolore" (of all those who were dead, and of the long war and the sorrow). The ability to grieve seems a key factor in being able to survive the devastating experience of Fascism and the war. While permeated with suffering, the novel also offers a vision of humanity capable of redemption. *Tutti i nostri ieri* was awarded the Veillon Prize in 1952 and is considered Ginzburg's most important engagé novel.

Ginzburg wrote *Le voci della sera* (1961; translated as *Voices in the Evening,* 1963) in three weeks in the spring of 1961 when she was living in London. In the same vein as Ginzburg's first two short novels, *Le voci della sera* is the first-person story of Elsa, a small-town woman with high aspirations, and her strenuous relationship with the wealthy Tommasino. The story details the sad account of Tommasino's family, his father, his two brothers, and his sister, who is rejected by her paramour. The novel brings to light the father's initial hopes and gradual disenchantment with Fascism. In reviewing the work in the 21 September 1963 *Saturday Review* Thomas G. Bergin pointed to Ginzburg's concise style and her aversion to rhetoric. He characterized the book as an "honest and accurate depiction of small town life, chiefly for the sake of the protagonist, who arouses our interest and compassion."

In 1962 Ginzburg published *Le piccole virtù* (translated as *The Little Virtues*, 1985), a collection of essays that appeared from 1944 to 1962 in newspapers and other publications. The title, taken from the last essay of the collection, alludes to the necessary little virtues that must be imparted to children. In the essay "Ritratto d'un amico" (Portrait of a Friend) Ginzburg recalls her friendship with the writer Cesare Pavese, who committed suicide in 1950. Her essay "Elogio e compianto dell'Inghilterra" (Praise and Sorrow for England), written in London in 1961, offers a personal view of the English way of life seen from a strikingly different culture. Of the eleven articles, the most memorable and personal is the humorous essay "Lui e io" (He and I), in which Ginzburg contrasts her personality traits with those of her second husband. This is both an affectionate and critical assessment of her married life. Noteworthy as well is "Il mio mestiere" (My Vocation), written in 1949, in which Ginzburg comments on the art of writing as a skill and a craft perfected by continuous practice and the discriminate use of language.

In 1963 Ginzburg was awarded the prestigious Strega Prize for her unconventional memoir *Lessico famigliare* (1963; translated as *Family Sayings*, 1967). Although Ginzburg on more than one occasion asserted that *Lessico famigliare* is a true story, she did not call it an autobiography. In the preface she maintains that "benché tratto dalla realtà, penso che si debba leggerlo come se fosse un romanzo" (although the book is drawn from real life, I think it should be read as though it were a novel). She adds that the book is not about herself but is "la storia della mia famiglia" (the history of my family), in which she was the youngest child, with three brothers and a sister. Ginzburg as the first-person narrator recounts the story of the Levi family in Turin beginning in the 1920s. Her protagonists are not only the members of the Levi family and their friends but also the setting, the atmosphere, the intellectual and historical milieu, and even the family language—which brings to mind the Finzi-Continis' language in Giorgio Bassani's *Il giardino dei Finzi-Contini*

(1962; translated as *The Garden of the Finzi-Continis*, 1965).

In *Lessico famigliare* Ginzburg describes an explosive father who takes cold showers and eats a homemade yogurt, a jovial mother, and the raucous rivalries among siblings. Since the people and places are real, as are their hopes and fears, the book can be read as a sociological document detailing the life of an Italian family of Jewish extraction during the Fascist era and the postwar period. Ginzburg recreates the salient historical events of the time as well as her family memories.

In the twenty-five-year period beginning in 1964, Ginzburg wrote ten plays. Her first volume of plays, *Ti ho sposato per allegria e altre commedie* (I Married You for Fun and Other Plays, 1966), included *L'inserzione* (The Advertisement), which was awarded the international Marzotto Prize. It was staged in 1968 in London at the National Theatre under the direction of Sir Laurence Olivier, with Joan Plowright in the leading role. Her second collection of four plays was titled *Paese di mare e altre commedie* (A Town by the Sea and Other Plays, 1973). Her last two plays were *La poltrona* (The Armchair), which she wrote in 1985 and published in *Opere*, and *L'intervista* (The Interview, 1989).

Ginzburg's plays offer a microcosm of Italian society in transition. Her characters reflect the grief and anxiety that result from the disintegration of traditional social structures such as the institutions of marriage and family. She uses drama to examine the changing roles of marital and familial relationships and the effects of the political and social reforms that took place primarily in the 1960s and 1970s. However, Ginzburg's primary interest, in her plays as in her novels, is the human condition, what the Nobel poet Eugenio Montale aptly called "il male di vivere" (the evils of living).

As a playwright Ginzburg spares no one. She criticizes political leaders who have failed in their efforts to create a better society; she attacks and indicts the ruling middle class as well as the dissatisfied working class. And she attempts to liberate female characters who are often controlled by their male partners. The female characters—notably Giuliana in *Ti ho sposato per allegria*, Barbara and Flaminia in *Fragola e panna* (Strawberries and Cream), and Elena and Teresa in *L'inserzione*—struggle within a male-dominated world as they seek to assert themselves within the changing roles of wife and mother. These women try to adjust to marriage and divorce as they attempt to make sense of their chaotic emotions resulting from their inability to communicate.

The first page of the manuscript for Lessico famigliare *(Natalia Ginzburg Collection)*

One of the strongest aspects of Ginzburg's plays is the characters' lively, contemporary speech, which makes them appear real on the stage. Through Ginzburg's skillful use of language her characters assume realistic and individual identities free from social and psychological stereotypes. Although her plays mirror the novels and especially the essays written during the same period, it is in the plays that Ginzburg is able to express her preoccupation with women's dependence on men as fathers, husbands, or lovers. She shows deep concerns about the disintegration of family life and about what she regards as parasitic male behavior. Ginzburg does not free anyone from moral responsibilities: men and women are judged according to the same values. Compared to her novels, Ginzburg's plays have received marginal attention. While most of her novels and essays are readily available in English, only *L'inserzione* has been translated.

Ginzburg frequently contributed to the cultural section of Italy's major newspapers. In 1969 she became a regular contributor to Turin's *La Stampa* and Milan's *Il Corriere della sera*. Ginzburg collected many of her short articles in *Mai devi domandarmi* (1970; translated as *Never Must You Ask Me*, 1973) and in *Vita immaginaria* (Imaginary Life, 1974), though much of her periodical writing remains uncollected. The first volume consisted originally of thirty-one articles ("Luna pallidassi" was added to the 1989 edition). The range of her subjects can be indicated by a few of her titles: "Childhood," "Old Age," "Literary Criticism," "Cinema," "My Psycho-analysis," and "On Believing and Not Believing in God." She discusses one of her friends, the prolific writer Alberto Moravia, films by Federico Fellini and Ingmar Bergman, and the problems and politics of the city of Rome.

Most of these writings were published in a two-year period, from December 1969 to October 1970, in *La Stampa* of Turin. In the preface of the 1989 edition of *Mai devi domandarmi*, Ginzburg confesses that since she was not successful in keeping a diary, the contents "sono forse qualcosa come un diario, nel senso che vi annoto via quello che mi capitava di ricordare o pensare" (are perhaps something like a diary to the extent that I made a note of what I happened to remember or think). Taken together, the two volumes offer an instructive and perceptive account of Italian society in the early 1970s.

In 1973 Ginzburg published a semiepistolary novel, *Caro Michele* (translated as *No Way*, 1974, and *Dear Michael*, 1975), which was subsequently made into a film by Mario Monicelli in 1976. In order to escape arrest as a political activist, Michele is forced to leave his middle-class family. He travels through-

out England and, after many escapades, marries an alcoholic American physicist. Traveling erratically from city to city, he eventually meets a violent death at a political demonstration in Bruges, where he is stabbed by a neofascist. *Caro Michele* consists of thirty-six letters addressed to Michele by his mother, Adriana, his sister Angelica, and his former girlfriend Mara, whose son could have been fathered by Michele. The twenty-one-year-old Michele answers a few of these missives in a terse and truncated manner, and though the letters are about Michele, his character remains elusive.

Caro Michele is a social, existential, and psychological novel affording a squalid vision of a frayed Italian society. Its crisis is suggested by a self-absorbed, introspective, and ultimately selfish mother; a vain and egocentric father; an unstable teenage mother; an ambivalent homosexual character; a separated couple whose unconventional marital arrangement is treated as perfectly normal in the novel; and the misguided and disoriented Michele. Michele's family symbolizes Italy's sociopolitical instability and the uncertainties of the early 1970s.

In 1977 Ginzburg resumed her editorial work with Einaudi and published *Famiglia* (translated as *Two Novellas. Family and Borghesia* and *Family: Two Novellas*, 1988), a volume that contained two novellas, the title story and *Borghesia* (Bourgeoisie). The latter had appeared in installments in the Milanese daily *Il Corriere della sera* during the summer of 1977. These works underscore Ginzburg's primary concerns. In *Famiglia* she treats the breakup of the family unit, and in *Borghesia* she examines the failures of the ruling class. Ginzburg's other evident themes are divorce and separation, the relationships between parents and children, suicide, love, and the inability to communicate and maintain solid relationships.

The year 1983 was eventful for Ginzburg. After extensive research into the life of Alessandro Manzoni, Italy's most important nineteenth-century writer, Ginzburg published *La famiglia Manzoni* (translated as *The Manzoni Family*, 1987), a work whose social, historical, and literary value proved to be controversial in Italian literary circles. More than a social, cultural, and historical reconstruction of the celebrated life of Alessandro Manzoni, Ginzburg weaves a psychological portrait not only of the novelist but also of his mother, Giulia Beccaria; his first wife, Enrichetta; and his second wife, Teresa. Ginzburg describes the sociopolitical and cultural background of Milan and Paris as she tells the story of the Manzoni family, spanning almost 150 years from the French prerevolutionary year of 1789 to

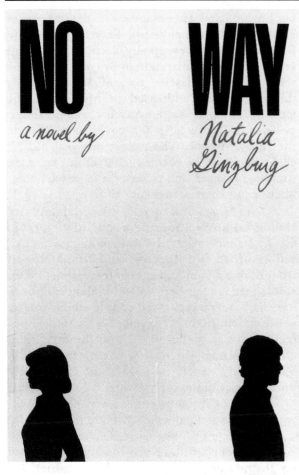

Dust jacket for the American edition of the translation of Ginzburg's 1973 novel, in which frayed relationships are indicative of deep conflicts within Italy in the 1970s

the Italian post-Risorgimento. She also published her long-awaited translation of Gustave Flaubert's *Madame Bovary* (1857). The same year she was elected deputy to the Italian Parliament among the independent Left.

La città e la casa (1984; translated as *The City and the House,* 1987), another epistolary novel, can be seen as a sequel to *Caro Michele,* though it explores the lives of new characters. It begins with an affair between Giuseppe, a widower, and Lucrezia, a married woman with five children. When Lucrezia has a second affair, with Ignazio Fegiz, her husband, Piero, leaves her. Giuseppe goes to America, and after his brother's death he marries his sister-in-law. He has a strained relationship with his son Alberico, a homosexual whom he ignored as a child and now rejects as an adult. Not one of Ginzburg's characters is able to sustain a relationship. They are estranged and alienated from self, family, and society, much like the characters in *Caro Michele.*

The city in the title of *La città e la casa* is Rome, and the house, called Le Margherite, is home to

Piero and Lucrezia until their marriage breaks up. Before being sold and turned into the hotel Panorama, the house served as a meeting place for many of the characters. The transformation of a warm home into a cold, impersonal, commercial establishment symbolizes the breakdown of the traditional family, one of Ginzburg's recurrent themes. Ginzburg maintains the humor of earlier novels but mixes in a larger dose of pessimism. This is especially true in her treatment of the children, a subject dear to the novelist.

In February 1990 Ginzburg published her last complete work, the lengthy essay *Serena Cruz o la vera giustizia* (Serena Cruz or True Justice). It is about the life of an adopted four-year-old Filipino girl, Serena Cruz, and her adoptive parents' battle with Italy's archaic adoption laws. Ginzburg was touched by the much debated plight of Serena Cruz and her Italian adoptive parents' rights as they battled the court system that impeded the legal adoption process. Ginzburg died of cancer in Rome on 7 October 1991.

One finds little action in Ginzburg's short stories, novels, and plays. Her fiction has thin, and at times almost nonexistent, plots. Yet she has an uncanny ability to capture the environment that surrounds her characters. Her style is subdued, antirhetorical, direct, and often ironic. As William H. Honan noted in his 9 October 1991 appreciation of Ginzburg in *The New York Times,* "The subtlety and economy of Miss Ginzburg's style has prompted critics to liken her to Chekhov." In *A Guide to Contemporary Italian Literature* (1962) Sergio Pacifici, one of the first Americans to write on Ginzburg's fiction, alludes to "the impact of Gertrude Stein's stylistic device of repeating and elaborating the same sentence."

In a 1993 interview in *Italian Journal* the novelist Francesca Sanvitale was asked which writers have influenced her. She mentioned Stendhal, Leo Tolstoy, Katherine Mansfield, and Dickinson, and then she added:

> Finally, there is Natalia Ginzburg, who should never be forgotten by Italian women writers. For the first time in our country, Natalia represents the painful but steadfast involvement of a woman who tackles the concerns of a society on the boil, in flux since the time of Fascism (when Natalia was an adolescent), a society going through war and resistance, well-being and an economic boom, terrorism and massacres.

In Mary Gordon's 25 March 1990 *New York Times* article "Surviving History," Natalia Ginzburg best summarizes her writing career: "I was formed by the war because that was what happened to me. I think of a writer as a river: you reflect what passes before you. The trees pass, and the houses, you reflect what is there." Throughout her life Natalia Ginzburg remained religiously committed to her writing. Her fiction always focused on the human condition, on the joys and, more often, the pains of living. Her characters constantly struggle to survive and master *l'arte del vivere* (the art of living).

References:

Gian-Paolo Biasin, "A Family Portrait," *Italian Quarterly,* 7 (1963): 82–83;

Alan Bullock, *Natalia Ginzburg* (New York: Berg, 1991);

Elena Clementelli, *Invito alla lettura di Natalia Ginzburg* (Milan: Mursia, 1977);

Piero De Tommaso, "Elegia e ironia in Natalia Ginzburg," *Belfagor,* 17 (31 January 1962): 101–104;

De Tommaso, "Natalia Ginzburg," in *I contemporanei* (Milan: Marzorati, 1969), pp. 817–833;

De Tommaso, "Una scrittrice geniale," *Belfagor,* 18 (May 1963): 335–340;

Mary Gordon, "Surviving History," *New York Times,* 25 March 1990, pp. 44–46, 62;

Maria Antonietta Grignani, ed., *Natalia Ginzburg: la narratrice e i suoi testi* (Rome: La Nuova Italia Scientifica, 1986);

Donald Heiney, "The Fabric of Voices," *Iowa Review* (Fall 1970): 87–93;

H. S. Hughes, *Prisoners of Hope: The Silver Age of the Italian Jews* (Cambridge, Mass.: Harvard University Press, 1983);

Olga Lombardi, "Natalia Ginzburg," in *I contemporanei,* volume 7, edited by Gianni Grana (Milan: Marzorati, 1979), pp. 7606–7627;

Anne-Marie O'Healy, "Natalia Ginzburg and the Family," *Canadian Journal of Italian Studies,* 9 (1986): 21–36;

Gino Pampaloni, "Natalia Ginzburg," in *Storia della letteratura italiana,* volume 9, edited by E. Cecchi and N. Sapegno (Milan: Garzanti, 1969);

Luciana Picchione Marchionne, *Natalia Ginzburg* (Florence: La Nuova Italia, 1976);

Rosetta Piclardi, "Forms and Figures in the Novels of Natalia Ginzburg," *World Literature Today,* 53 (1979): 585–589;

Salmagundi, special issue on Ginzburg, 96 (Fall 1992): 54–167;

C. Soave Bowe, "The Narrative Strategy of Natalia Ginzburg," *Modern Language Review,* 68 (1973): 788–795;

Giacinto Spagnoletti, "Natalia Ginzburg," *Belfagor,* 39 (31 January 1984): 41–53;

Jen Weinstein, "Il maschio assente nell'opera narrativa e teatrale di Natalia Ginzburg," in *Donna: Women in Italian Culture,* edited by Ada Testaferri (Toronto: Dove House, 1989), pp. 89-98.

Tommaso Landolfi
(9 August 1908 – 8 July 1979)

Charles Fantazzi
University of Windsor

BOOKS: *Dialogo dei massimi sistemi* (Florence: Parenti, 1937);

Il mar delle blatte e altre storie (Rome: Edizioni della Cometa, 1939);

La pietra lunare (Florence: Vallecchi, 1939);

La spada (Florence: Vallecchi, 1942);

Il principe infelice. Romanzo per bambini (Florence: Vallecchi, 1943);

Le due zittelle (Milan: Bompiani, 1946);

Racconto d'autunno (Florence: Vallecchi, 1947); selections translated by Raymond Rosenthal and others as *Gogol's Wife and Other Stories* (Norfolk, Conn.: New Directions, 1963);

Cancroregina (Florence: Vallecchi, 1950); translated by Rosenthal as *Cancerqueen and Other Stories* (New York: Dial, 1971);

La biere du pecheur (Florence: Vallecchi, 1953);

La raganella d'oro (Florence: Vallecchi, 1954);

Ombre (Florence: Vallecchi, 1954);

Mezzacoda (Venice: Sodalizio del Libro, 1958);

Ottavio di Saint-Vincent (Florence: Vallecchi, 1958);

Landolfo VI di Benevento (Florence: Vallecchi, 1959);

Se non la realtà (Florence: Vallecchi, 1960);

In società (Florence: Vallecchi, 1962);

Rien va (Florence: Vallecchi, 1963);

Scene dalla vita di Cagliostro (Florence: Vallecchi, 1963);

Tre racconti (Florence: Vallecchi, 1964);

Un amore del nostro tempo (Florence: Vallecchi, 1965);

Racconti impossibili (Florence: Vallecchi, 1966);

Des mois (Florence: Vallecchi, 1967);

Un paniere di chiocciole (Florence: Vallecchi, 1968);

Faust '67 (Florence: Vallecchi, 1969);

Breve canzoniere (Florence: Vallecchi, 1971);

Gogol a Roma. Articoli letterari (Florence: Vallecchi, 1971);

Viola di morte (Florence: Vallecchi, 1972);

Le labrene (Milan: Rizzoli, 1974);

A caso (Milan: Rizzoli, 1975);

Il tradimento (Milan: Rizzoli, 1977);

Del meno (Milan: Rizzoli, 1978);

Il gioco della torre (Milan: Rizzoli, 1987).

Tommaso Landolfi

Collections: *Opere I. 1937–1959* (Milan: Rizzoli, 1991);

Opere II. 1960–1971 (Milan: Rizzoli, 1992).

TRANSLATIONS: Nikolay Gogol, *Racconti di Pietroburgo* (Milan: Rizzoli, 1941);

Prosper Mérimée, *I falsi Demetrii* (Turin: Einaudi, 1944);

Narratori russi (Milan: Bompiani, 1948);

Alessandro Pushkin, *Poemi e liriche* (Florence: Vallecchi, 1960);

Pushkin, *Teatro e favole* (Florence: Vallecchi, 1961);

Novalis, *Enrico di Oftlerdingen* (Florence: Vallecchi, 1962);

Mikhail Lermontov, *Liriche e poemi* (Turin: Einaudi, 1963);

Fëdor Tjutcev, *Poesie* (Turin: Einaudi, 1964).

Those who knew Tommaso Landolfi from his student days in Florence and might be considered his closest friends, such as the literary critic Carlo Bo, confess to their inability ever to get to know him. He always shrouded himself in mystery, even as to his origins, and cultivated the image of the dandy and the disdainful recluse. Landolfi struck a romantic pose in his fiction as well as in his life. In some autobiographical essays he wrote in the 1960s he does vouchsafe some of the formative influences in his literary career. In a short piece titled "Morte di un amico" (Death of a Friend), which was included in *Un paniere di chiocciole* (1968), Landolfi recounts how his friend, Renato Poggioli, had introduced him to the secrets of the Cyrillic alphabet, which led him to major in Russian at the University of Florence and later to translate brilliantly many of the great Russian classics into Italian. Fyodor Dostoyevsky's remark about all subsequent Russian literature emerging from the overcoat of Nikolay Gogol holds true also of Landolfi. His prose is in the mold of the great Russian novelists and short-story writers, and his characters resemble theirs—wan, surly, sometimes deformed individuals who wander about the world but cannot be ignored. They seem to be mere puppets, speaking their lines only to reveal their impotence and sterility.

Landolfi probably learned from the Russians, from Gogol and Anton Chekhov in particular, to tell his stories with the awareness that they are susceptible to multiple interpretations, that they do not end on the page but in the mind. Often his stories are only half finished, mere sketches, especially in his later works, when he actually suspends the narrative in the middle of the story, as if it were of no use to continue.

Landolfi's tone is cold, cerebral, and detached, to such an extent that at times he seems to be transcribing a foreign, bodiless voice. He often begins a story in a disarmingly simple, banal setting that subsequently suddenly verges toward the mysterious and the occult. His characters are drawn toward the taboo in search of new dimensions of reality but then withdraw in terror. Even in his diaristic writings, behind the voice there is a countervoice that is not directed to the reader. The poet Eugenio Montale put it well in a review in the 20 June 1963 *Corriere della sera*: "Quando scriveva in proprio non faceva altro che tradursi, tenendo nascosto in sè l'originale" (When he wrote in his own voice he did nothing other than translate himself, keeping the original hidden in himself).

In contrast to the eccentric, surrealistic content of the stories his prose style is of a limpid purity, showing an exceptional mastery of the rich resources of the Italian language. Landolfi prefers the rare word, the precious construction, the unusual meaning, and he admits his virtuosity sometimes seems to be an end in itself: "falsamente classicheggiante, falsamente nervosa, falsamente sostenuta, falsamente abbandonata" (falsely classicizing, falsely nervous, falsely sustained, falsely abandoned). Yet with all of his formal precision he is careless about final results and often seems to abandon the work to its destiny, acting as a writer much like the passionate gambler that he was in real life. Indeed his feverish devotion to the god of chance is the leitmotiv that runs through all his works. Through the almost ceremonial urbanity of his style he lures his readers into the strange world of his fiction and makes them his accomplices in macabre adventures.

Tommaso Landolfi was born on 9 August 1908 in the town of Pico. Since 1926 Pico has been part of the province of Frosinone and the capital of Ciociaria, but when he was born it was under the jurisdiction of Caserta. In language and traditions Pico has remained in the Neapolitan rather than the Roman sphere, as Landolfi always maintained. In *Se non la realtà* (1960) he writes: "Di qua Longobardi, Normanni, Angioini, di là papi e loro accoliti; di qua una lingua di tipo napoletano-abruzzese, di là una specie di romanesco suburbano." (On this side, Lombards, Normans, Angevins, over there popes and their followers; here a Neapolitan-Abruzzese type of language, there a kind of suburban Roman dialect).

Landolfi's father, Pasquale, scion of an ancient Lombard family of the region with ties to the Bourbon dynasty, was a lawyer, though he probably never actively practiced. He acted as mayor of the town for several terms of office, as his father had done before him. Pasquale was partial heir to a manor house and a ruined medieval castle that dominates the town. In 1907 he married his cousin, Maria Gemma Nigro, always known as Ida, from the region of Basilicata. They spent their honeymoon in Paris, where, as Landolfi liked to recall, little "Tommasino" was conceived.

At the tender age of a year and a half, Tommaso lost his mother, who died pregnant with her second son. The little boy was brought before his dead mother so that her features would be imprinted in his memory, as Landolfi recounts at the beginning of his autobiographical *Prefigurazioni: Prato,* which was included in *Ombre* (Shadows, 1954). Father and son passed the following years either in Pico at the home of Landolfi's maternal grandmother or ever more frequently in hotels and rented rooms in Rome. Landolfi developed a lifelong friendship with his cousin Fosforina who probably taught him how to read and write and encouraged his early ambitions to be a writer.

Another traumatic experience in the life of young Landolfi was his stay at the Collegio Cicognini in Prato (where writer Gabriele D'Annunzio had also been a student). Landolfi describes the painful moment when his father accompanied him down the long corridor of the school to the front door and then took leave of him, as both wept tears of inconsolable desperation. Sensitive child that he was, Landolfi found it hard to adapt and was treated with great scorn by his schoolmates. Here began his flight from ordinary associations and his acquisition of a sense of guilt that never left him. Scholastically he did not fare well at this famous institution, save for his proficiency in Italian, Spanish, and French; for Latin he had no great love. He spent summers, as he would throughout his life, partly in Pico and partly at seaside resorts such as Formia and Gaeta. It took much persuasion on the part of his father and severe reprimands from his superiors to get him through the classical lyceum. In the end, however, he passed with high marks, but his scholastic record did not at all reflect the knowledge of foreign languages that he had acquired and his voracious reading habits. In these adolescent years he dabbled in such languages as Arabic, Polish, Hungarian, Japanese, and Swedish.

After sporadic attendance at the University of Rome, Landolfi moved to Florence to continue his university studies. The Florentine years would prove decisive for the young writer, especially for the friendships he established with such future luminaries as Bo; Poggioli, who encouraged him in his study of Russian; and Leone Traverso, who would become a famous Germanist at the University of Urbino. His passion for gambling—"la volontà di potenza" (the will to power), as he called it in one of his autobiographical essays—was born in the gambling dens of Florentine bars. Landolfi's creative spirit came spontaneously to life during his summers in Pico. The fruit of the summer of 1929 was his first published short story, "Maria Giuseppa." It appeared in the Florentine student journal *Vigilie letterarie,* which he edited with Poggioli. Later he included the story in his first collection. In 1932 he finished his thesis on the Russian writer Anna Achmatova, which he defended brilliantly before experts from various universities.

During the years 1934 and 1935 Landolfi lived mostly in Rome with his father and made periodic visits abroad to Berlin, Cologne, Paris, and London. He actively collaborated with various periodicals, all published in Rome, on the subject of modern Russian letters—Ivan Bunin, Aleksandr Lebedenko, Boris Pasternak, Yefgeny Petrov, and others. He published his doctoral thesis in four installments in the review *Europa Orientale,* edited by Ettore Lo Gatto.

Landolfi's first collection of stories, *Dialogo dei massimi sistemi* (Dialogues of the Greatest Systems, 1937), contains in essence all of his themes and narrative techniques. Maria Giuseppa, the title character of his first published story, was the name of a servant who lived in his ancestral home, as he recalls in an autobiographical account included in *Ombre.* The narrator and male protagonist of the tale, Giacomo, is the master of the household. He is described in the essay as "un tal disutilaccio o psicopatico" (a useless good-for-nothing or psychopath), who treats his servant as his slave and brutalizes her. The climax of the story is his sadistic rape of the old woman, whom he discovers at the window throwing oleander branches upon a passing religious procession. It is both an act of sudden passion and unexplained violence, an *acte gratuit* in the Gidean sense. The narrator thinks nothing of his vile action and tells his imaginary audience to refrain from giving him contemptuous looks. Maria Giuseppa is a symbol of the house, whose mysteries always eluded him and nourished his perennial nostalgias for a better life. But a perverse and malignant instinct drives him to commit violence against the woman and to send her away, perhaps so that he may remain alone in the house. From that moment no one else may enter the house. Like his character, Landolfi would remain largely inaccessible to the world at large.

Another story in the same collection is titled "La morte del re di Francia" (The Death of the King of France), an Italian expression used to signify a long and tedious piece of music. The narrator is an old, flaccid captain, who opens the story with remembrances of his past glories, phrased in seamen's jargon, which allows Landolfi a show of stylistic bravura. He lives with a thirteen-year-old adopted daughter, Rosalba, whom he has raised as an innocent, free of all sexual taboos, so that she is used to taking her daily bath in his presence. His object in providing this uninhibited education is to behold the growth and flowering of the female body. One evening, however, the girl attracts the attention of a young man invited to the house, and his amorous conversation awakens Rosalba's dormant femininity. That night she is unable to sleep.

Landolfi indulges in another display of linguistic virtuosity to describe the young girl's erotic dreams, filled with various species of animals. This empathy of Landolfi for the animal kingdom, especially his predilection for insects and creatures equipped with suckers, is evident in all his narratives and recalls the hallucinatory prose of Le Comte de Lautréamont. As she writhes with pleasure in her erotic fantasy, the captain lies in sleepless terror imagining the horrid presence of a spider, which is an obsessive fear with him. The tale ends with his desperate flight through a grotesque garden filled with dark birch trees, gnarled gnomes, and sylphs. Landolfi is not interested in telling the reader how all of this ends up. He lets the psychological possibilities resonate in the mind of the reader, content with his artful verbal contrivances that lend a kind of scientific realism to the strange narration.

Semidarkness envelops the intense drama of "Mani" (Hands), a short, terrifying vignette depicting the uneven struggle to the death between a mouse and a dog. The hands of the title are actually the front feet of the mouse, which take on the aspect of flabby human hands when the animal throws itself on its back in fighting position. They appear even more human when in the convulsions of death the tiny creature holds them out parallel to the ground. Landolfi's morbid description adds to the pathos and horror of the scene: "Si trascinava dietro una specie di lungo cordone, di una lucentezza opaca, che a volte gli si avvolgeva intorno al corpo, a volte strisciava, lungo disteso, nella polvere del cortile, sicché finì presto col perdere anche quel po' di splendore" (It dragged behind it a kind of long string that had a dull sheen about it, which at times wrapped itself around its body and at other times slithered, fully extended, in the dust of the courtyard so that it quickly lost whatever luster it had). The umbilical-cord-like string is part of the mouse's intestines. When the dog finally finishes off the agonizing mouse, the extraordinary thing is that there is not a drop of blood anywhere. Somehow this bloodless extinction is the most horrific part of the tale, suggesting the hopelessness of the struggle for life that Landolfi will later identify as the syndrome of insufficiency. The story ends in a surrealistic mock funeral for the mouse, a mixture of black humor, revulsion, and pity.

In the English-titled "Night Must Fall" the narrator, after a night of carousing, is haunted by the solitary, prolonged, unchanging note of the horned owl; to him it symbolizes the perfect concentration of restless energies that contrasts with his own futile striving, likened to the diffused, meandering melody of a nightingale. During these nocturnal meditations Landolfi evinces a Virgilian sense of participation in the intimate secrets of nature. He imagines the depression of the lark, tricked by the clarity of the moon into singing its dawn song only to cease suddenly and abjectly when the light fails to grow.

Fascination with language for its own sake is at the heart of the title story, "Dialogo dei massimi sistem." The narrator advances the novel thesis that it is best for a writer to use a language that he only partially knows in preference to one with which he is wholly familiar. In this way he is forced to paraphrase, to be inventive, to substitute images for words. To illustrate his argument he tells of his acquaintance with a man who wished to teach him Persian, which he did orally without the aid of any written text. Ultimately the pupil discovers that what was taught him was not Persian at all but a fictitious language. The rest of the dialogue is a rather sophistic disquisition on the independence of language from any set rules of grammar, syntax, or lexicon. The narrator argues that even indecipherable inscriptions in unknown languages have their own intelligibility.

Back in Florence in 1937 Landolfi began a long association as a freelance writer with the review *Letteratura,* founded by Alessandro Bonsanti, and became part of the famous literary circle that met at the Caffé delle Giubbe Rosse. His stories, reviews, and translations appeared in various literary journals both of Florence and Rome, including the *Campo di Marte,* newly founded by Alfonso Gatto and Vasco Pratolini. His first translation from Russian, *Racconti di Pietroburgo* (Tales of St. Petersburg) by Gogol, was commissioned by Rizzoli and finished at this time but was not published until 1941. In addition to his skillful translations from Russian Landolfi was also an excellent translator of German, as can be seen in his idiomatic versions of seven Grimm fairy tales in an anthology of German literature, *Germanica,* edited by his friend Traverso for Vallecchi in 1942.

Landolfi's first novel, *La pietra lunare* (The Moonstone, 1939), is a clear harbinger and one of the best examples of his penchant for the fantastic. Modeling his narrative on his own experience, Landolfi depicts a young student, Giovancarlo, returning to the quiet of his country home from his studies in the city. In a nocturnal walk in the garden of the

Piccola Biblioteca 358

Tommaso Landolfi

LA PIETRA LUNARE

ADELPHI

Cover for a 1995 edition of Landolfi's first novel, in which a young student is caught up in the powerful myths of the country people

villa Giovancarlo suddenly becomes conscious that he is being watched, a feeling endemic to many of Landolfi's characters. "Dal fondo dell'oscurità resa più cupa da un taglio alto di luce sul muro di cinta, due occhi neri, dilatati e selvaggi, lo guardavano fissamente" (From the depths of the darkness rendered more obscure by a high sliver of light on the boundary wall, two black eyes, wide open and savage, were fixed on him). The female figure, who has goatlike bifurcate feet, wears a white, décolleté dress. Strangely, this incongruous joining of animal and human forms does not seem monstrous, as is often the case in Landolfi's work: "Queste zampe, a guardarci bene, parevano la logica continuazione di quelle cosce affusolate" (These hooves, if one were to look closely, seemed to be the logical continuation of those tapering thighs). The villagers, he soon

discovers, accept Gurù, as she is called, as they do anyone else. Animals, too, are friendly with her, although they seem to be submissive in her presence.

Giancarlo, as is typical of a Landolfi character, is both attracted and repelled by this grotesque creature, and his love is reciprocated. On another night he follows her to a moonstone on a remote hillside, where in the light of the full moon before his terrified gaze she metamorphoses into a goat and copulates with a mate of her own species. This is only the beginning of many eerie discoveries in this archaic world, culminating in the apparition of the Three Mothers, figures of death like the Graeae of Greek mythology. Horrid in their immobility, their eyes are silvery like hemp, staring at the moon. The story ends with the young student returning to his studies in the city. Landolfi sees in the mysterious, atavistic beliefs of the country people a strange power. They are more real than the world of conventional reality.

An even more bizarre tale, written at about the same time, is the long title story of *Il Mar delle blatte e altre storie* (The Sea of Cockroaches and Other Stories, 1939). The reader is catapulted without warning from the narration of a banal, everyday occurrence into the uncanny dream world of surrealism. On a spring afternoon Coracaglina, a colorless lawyer, is walking with unusual alacrity down the street when his son, a fainéant, emerges from the barbershop and runs up to him. He shows his father a deep cut in his forearm, from which he calmly extracts a length of string, a piece of macaroni, a hobnail, some hunting pellets, a grain of rice, a blowfly, and a worm. They are all seemingly innocent objects, perhaps souvenirs of a carefree childhood, but they assume a grotesque character in their collocation here. The scene is reminiscent of a famous sequence in Luis Buñuel and Salvador Dalí's film *Un Chien andalou* (1928), in which ants swarm out of a wound in the hand of the protagonist.

In the adventure that follows, the objects become personified as the members of a desperate crew that will sail for destinations unknown under the young Coracaglina, who is transformed into the personage of Alto Variago. The voyage, especially in its black humor, might be compared to Jonathan Swift's *Gulliver's Travels* (1726) or to the dream world of Dutch painter Hieronymus Bosch. The ship sails past a lonely, uninhabited city that resembles a vast amphitheater facing the sea, with gigantic buildings, frightening in their appearance, pierced by black streets and bottomless abysses. After this last bulwark of what used to be a human habitation the ship enters upon a sea of inert roaches that extends to the limits of the horizon. Aboard ship, in contrast to the hideous lethargy of the sea, a female passenger, Lucrezia, is the object of the erotic contention between the former worm and Captain Variago. In this Boschian nightmare her breasts weep milk that is consumed by two serpents, and it is the blue, diaphanous worm who wins the sexual duel. In the ironic ending the two lovers escape through the sea of enraged roaches and reach their desired paradise. The reader, however, is so disoriented and disgusted by the repulsive manifestations of repressed sexual desires that he can give little credence to this happy ending. If this is a metaphor of life, it is a pitiless, desecrating *mal de vivre,* and the idyllic epilogue is but a facile irony.

Landolfi's next collection of stories, *La spada* (The Sword, 1942), contains both stories of pure fantasy that have a semblance of a catharsis at the end and those that are dominated by the specter of fear. One of the most memorable stories, only a few pages in length, is titled simply "La paura" (Fear). The emotion generated in the brief episode is not a physical fear but a general feeling of malaise and helplessness inspired in the onlookers of an act of wanton cruelty. A woman, impatiently awaiting the return of her teenage daughter in the middle of the night, sees a toad in the middle of the street, chases it into a corner and pours embers and hot ashes on it, as if venting her frustrated feelings upon the abject creature. Passersby scream at her and call her a witch, but the hysterical woman continues her sadistic ritual. In the last line of the gruesome tale the toad leaps back in the direction of its tormentor. "Il babbo di Kafka" (Kafka's Daddy) is a weird little apologue, in which the father of Franz Kafka appears as a huge spider with a human head. Like the face of Kafka's father in a fit of anger, the head's eyes are distorted and its upper lip is arched to one side. Kafka finally kills this evil personification of his childhood anguish.

On 23 June 1942 Landolfi was imprisoned for a month in Florence for his antifascist conversations overheard in the Café della Giubbe Rosse. Greater troubles awaited him in Pico, where his home was commandeered first by the Germans and then by the Allies from the fall of 1943 until May of 1944. A bombardment of the region resulted in the destruction of an entire wing of the Landolfi palazzo, which in its ruined state became the asylum for many refugee families. Valuable furnishings and precious books were lost in these occupations, leaving an indelible mark on Landolfi. What he felt most poignantly was the profanation of the sacred memories of this antique family sanctuary.

Landolfi spent the years from 1945 to 1950 mostly in Florence, where he continued at the Giubbe Rosse to meet his friends, among them the writers Mario Luzi, Carlo Emilio Gadda, Montale, Carlo Betocchi, and Piero Bigongiari and the painter Ottone Rosai. Some of his most commercially successful works were published, including the novellas *Le due zittelle* and *Racconto d'autunno*. He had a stroke of luck in his gambling and from his winnings bought a whole new wardrobe and a motorcycle, astounding all his friends with his sportsman's verve and ability. There were many side trips to the casinos of Venice and San Remo and even an unexpected appearance at the P.E.N. Congress held in Venice in 1949; he usually sedulously avoided all public appearances of this kind.

Le due zittelle (The Two Old Maids, 1946)—Landolfi arbitrarily insisted on the anomalous Italian spelling for *maid*—is supposedly based on an actual news item. The two old maids live together with a monkey, Tombo, left to them by their dead brother. In a sense Tombo, the chief object of their affections, functions as the man of the house. One night the monkey sneaks off to a nearby convent, where he dons the priest's garments and celebrates mass after his fashion, eating the host and urinating on the altar. This incident allows Landolfi to stage a discussion between two priests, one obscurantist and intolerant, the other progressive. It leads to some rather facile casuistry, raising the questions of whether an animal can be charged with profanation and the meaningfulness of human morality. The younger priest maintains that morality does not consist in the ability to choose between good and evil; instead, he holds that man is defenseless before both moral choices. Tombo is a surrogate for secret instincts averse to religious prohibitions and ecclesiastical censures (friends sometimes called the author Tom, so perhaps the monkey is Landolfi's alter ego). The two maids are not so liberal as the theological disputants. They torture and kill the monkey with a huge hat pin in a symbolic example of human injustice and cruelty. For Landolfi, they seem to be the real culprits, having never loved nor been loved.

In *Racconto d'autunno* (Autumn Story, 1947) Landolfi reverts to the more mysterious and sinister side of his genius. The scene is a forbidding house that recalls Edgar Allan Poe's house of Usher in his famous short story. In Landolfi's fiction houses are usually emblematic of the attempt to escape from external chaos into warmth and security. From the outside they promise refuge and protection, but once inside them their visitors find arcane secrets and a world of phantasmagoria. To escape the enemy, a soldier enters the house, first getting past two watchdogs whose violent behavior suggests some foreboding secret contained within. He then encounters the hairy, unkempt old man who is the master.

An invisible presence hangs over the house, and one night the soldier comes upon a young girl, who has obviously been brought up in ignorance and squalor, incapable of uttering a single word. The soldier sees at once that she is the perfect image of a woman in a portrait that the old man holds in great veneration. He eventually learns that the house had been the scene of sadomasochistic orgies first between husband and wife and then between father and daughter. The soldier had wandered through the labyrinthine passages of the house hoping to find salvation for himself, but he finds the girl who looks to him for salvation. One door leads to another in this gothic darkness, where one seeks oneself but ends by becoming a prisoner.

Many critics speak of Landolfi as experiencing an artistic crisis in mid career at the beginning of the 1950s. Critics have suggested that Landolfi lost faith in the possibility of representing man's existential quandaries through literature and cite the collection *Cancroregina* (1950, translated as Cancerqueen and Other Stories, 1971) as evidence of Landolfi's loss of faith. The title story seems a rather halfhearted attempt at writing science fiction, for the allegory dominates the narrative development and invention and artifice are cultivated for their own sake. The story is strictly not science fiction at all but more in the style of Jules Verne. The spaceship, called the *Cancroregina* by its mad designer, Filano, is anything but a model of technical perfection. Like Verne's machines, the ship can take on human qualities and seems an unlikely vehicle for conquering space.

In the voyage of the *Cancroregina* the narrator accompanies the ship's designer, a madman who has escaped from an insane asylum. As the trip proceeds the designer becomes more and more incoherent, mumbling in an incomprehensible babble. Finally he demands that the narrator be jettisoned in order to ensure a freer flight. A struggle ensues and the madman is thrown into the void, where his corpse flattens out against his creation, becoming part of it. Landolfi expresses the supreme alienation of his narrator, imprisoned in the machine, condemned neither to live or die but exist in an interstellar twilight zone: "E pensare che tutto quanto occorre a menarmi in salvo è qui, qui dentro e a portata di mano; ma è come se non ci fosse, non so trarne profitto" (And to think that all that is necessary to lead me to safety is here, in here and within my reach; but it is as if it were not there, I do not know how to make use of it).

By 1951 Landolfi had abandoned Florence, as did many of his fellow writers, and began to spend more time in his native Pico. For the next twenty years he contributed hundreds of literary articles and reviews—*elzevirs* as the Italians call them—to *Il Mondo*. He also dedicated himself to his diaristic writings and took up the study of the piano.

With the publication of *La biere du pecheur* (1953) Landolfi turned from fantasy to a type of autobiographical confession by recording a man's febrile infatuation with Dame Fortune. The deliberate ambiguity of the French words of the title, presented without accentuation, yields either "The Beer of the Fisherman" or "The Bier of the Sinner." Landolfi writes in a deliberately plain style, renouncing rhetorical frills for a more meditative discourse. He describes his condition dispassionately: "Sempre io mi son voltolato e rivoltolato nella vita come un ammalato smanioso nel suo letto; anche mi somiglio a quelle farfalle notturne sorprese dalla luce o dall'agonia che rimangono a sbattere disperatamente le ali sui nostri pavimenti" (I have always tossed and retossed in life like a restless sick man in his bed; I resemble, too, those nocturnal moths surprised by the light or by the pangs of death, that continue to beat their wings desperately on our floors).

The rhythm of the book is the disjointed, unpredictable rhythm of chance. The protagonist wanders from place to place, usually in the company of one of his many female companions in Florence; then suddenly he is off to San Remo; then he is back again in Florence, physically exhausted and morally defeated. In his moments of greatest despair he returns to the country house, "la gran casa vuota e cadente" (the big, empty, and decrepit house), where he can rediscover his fantasies, find refuge from the pretense of social relationships, and reconnect with his ancestors and his own people. In the pages of these diaristic jottings Landolfi diagnoses his predicament as "uno stato d'insufficienza" (a state of insufficiency) for the first time: "Tutto si potrà trovare nelle mie passate opere e in me fuorché . . . la vita" (One will find everything in my previous works and in me except . . . life).

In the collection *Ombre* Landolfi continues in his more personal vein, writing short stories, essays, moral exhortations, and divertissements in prose and in verse. The most famous piece is "La moglie di Gogol" (Gogol's Wife), obviously inspired by German writer E. T. A. Hoffmann's terrifying story "The Sandman." In Landolfi's tale the wife is a rubber doll named Caracas, a grotesque fetish, whose appearance can be changed at will from voluptuous curves to anorexic emaciation. Little by little the doll begins to take on more human qualities and a personality of her own, which prompts its owner to destroy it. The scene in which Nikolay Vasilyevich, as the narrator familiarly calls Gogol, inflates the doll until it bursts is a mixture of the ludicrous and the horrifying, as is so often the case in Landolfi's work. The final turn is Nikolai's furtive consigning to the flames a rubber doll, which can be nothing other than the child of Gogol's wife.

In November of 1956 the forty-eight-year-old Landolfi married Marisa, a woman much younger than himself, and took up residence in his ancestral home, restored once more to its original splendor. He continued, though, to make frequent trips to the gaming rooms of San Remo. After the birth of his two children Landolfi spent more and more time living alone in a small apartment in Arma di Taggia on the Riviera di Ponente, while his family moved to nearby San Remo. Stories and translations from the Russian classics still flowed from his pen.

Landolfi's obsession with gambling informs his novel *Ottavio di Saint-Vincent* (Octavio from Saint-Vincent, 1958), in which an incurable card-player reduced to poverty wins the affections of a Russian duchess, a descendant of the czars who desires to elevate someone of lowly station to her own class. Somewhat like Luigi Pirandello's nameless madman in *Enrico IV* (Henry IV, 1922), the gambler identifies with his new role as duke, conniving with those who are aware of the comedy and lying to those who know nothing. The fairy-tale ending is denied, however, for Ottavio is bored by royal life and returns to his shiftless but free existence in the streets of Paris, to the state of nothingness, the natural condition, according to Landolfi, of all existence.

Beginning in the late 1950s Landolfi began to write drama. He meditated and finally produced a play, *Landolfo VI di Benevento* (1959), on one of his remote ancestors, Landolfo VI, the last Lombard prince of Benevento, who fell under the dominion of Robert Guiscard, king of the Normans. It is a play of death and dissolution, showing the indifference of the world to the death of the individual. In polemical disputes with Cardinal Hildebrand, the future Pope Gregory VII, and Desiderio, abbot of Montecassino, also destined to become Pope, Landolfo fiercely denies the Christian view of death as the beginning of a new life with God. The sentiments expressed by the despairing king are reminiscent of the teachings of the Roman philosopher, Seneca:

> E come infatti
> Potrebbe mai la morte essermi lieta?

Dust jacket for the American volume that includes translations of some of the stories in Landolfi's 1947 collection, which shows a Gothic influence

> La morte è perfezione della vita.

> (And how indeed
> Could death ever bring me happiness?
> Death is the perfection of life.)

The style of the hendecasyllables is fustian, as Landolfi himself admits in his diaries: "Sempre più sfumata in una vaga verbosità, in una eloquenza ed oratoria quasi fine a se stessa" (More and more indistinct in a vague verbosity, in an eloquence and oratory that is almost an end in itself).

In May 1961 another of Landolfi's theatrical experiments, *Scene dalla vita di Cagliostro* (Scenes from Cagliostro's Life, 1963), was presented on Italian television by a group of some of the best actors in Italy, including Angela Cavo and Giorgio Albertazzi. It tells of the rise and fall of Count Alessandro di Cagliostro, a famous figure in Italian history, who is usually branded as an imposter but to whom magical and miraculous or occult powers were attributed. Denounced to the authorities by his wife, he died of famine in the fortress of San Leo. Landolfi has him utter these anguished words at the end of the play: "Volli illudermi che le cose non fossero quello che sono, che da ogni cosa si potesse cavare una riposta virtù che . . . la riscattasse: dalla noia, dal tedio, e da se medesima. Ah, voi beati che potete vivere senza affanno in un mondo di parvenze immutabili!" (I wanted to delude myself into thinking that things are not as they are, that from everything some hidden virtue might be extracted that . . . would redeem it: from boredom, tedium, and itself. Ah, you lucky ones who can live without anxiety in a world of unchangeable appearances!).

The 1960s were generally fallow years in Landolfi's literary career. Only a volume of his travels through Italy, originally published in *Il Mondo,* and an anthology of most of his stories, titled *Raconti,* was published in 1961. He returned to the themes of many of his earlier stories in several new collections, but the tales lack inspiration and are written in a precious, artificial style. One collection is justly titled *Racconti impossibili* (Impossible Tales, 1966), for the stories are indeed proof that he could neither come to terms with contemporary reality nor fruitfully return to a past that was patently anachronistic. He obtained better results in the continuation of his diaries, *Rien va* (Nothing Goes, 1963) and *Des mois* (Months, 1967), a monthly diary recording intimate reflections on such favorite subjects as man's condition, work, democracy, gambling, and family affections.

The title *Rien va* is an abbreviation of the croupier's call in the casino, "rien va plus" (no more bets). For Landolfi the call was a peremptory warning of the approaching end of the game of life. He confesses that he writes these diaries for "necessità igienica" (reasons of health)—health of the body, not the soul. They permit him to go on living. He evinces great affection in these pages for his small children—his daughter, whom he calls Minor, and his two-year-old son, to whom he gives the name Minimus—although at times he manifests a certain morbidity even in their regard. The notebooks slip from one subject to another, meditations on such subjects as smoking in the dark, being in love with a voice, and the contaminating effects of photography on the ideal images of nature and love. He also writes of the fragility of the city of Venice, threatened by the smokestacks of the terra firma, and one day in the not-too-distant future doomed to surrender itself once again to the lagoon. One of the versified divagations interspersed in the writing echoes a Horatian remark on the indiscriminate zeal of writers of his day: "Non so che dir, però scrivo lo stesso" (I do not know what to write, but I write all the same).

Un paniere di chiocciole (A Basketful of Snails, 1968) is a collection drawn from Landolfi's columns for the literary pages of the Milanese newspaper *Il corriere della sera.* The title piece concerns a man obsessed with what he imagines to be the sound of a basket of snails that prevents him from sleeping at night. None of his neighbors hears it and they wonder at his complaints. One night he finally concludes that, as with Jean-Jacques Rousseau, who claimed to hear the roar of the waves constantly in his ears, the sound must exist within himself. He smiles to himself remembering that the word *chiocciola* also refers to an organ of the inner ear (cochlea). "Perhaps," he reasons in the end, "we are all nothing but a basket of snails," to which one might add "that emit faint sounds when shaken."

The leitmotiv of many of these musings seems to be the tenuousness of human existence, as, for example, in the brief tale of an astronaut who has captured a nebulous particle during his flight in space and is gradually absorbed into its extraterrestrial state of being. Among the other parodic divertissements of the collection is the story of a harmless old bachelor who has the sensation, as he lies in bed at night, of being the recipient of a bodiless kiss. The kiss becomes more and more insistent until it consumes him utterly. Landolfi writes one story apparently to illustrate the impossibility of finding true happiness in life. It is the tale of the perfect wife, who is so compliant to the wishes of her husband that she actually becomes him and consequently hateful to him. Landolfi directly addresses the reader with his moral: "La gente, quando non è noi, è odiabile perché non è noi; quando è noi, è odiabile perché è noi. E chiedo ora: a che gioco si gioca?" (People, when they are not us, are hateful because they are not us; when they are us, they are hateful because they are us. And I ask you now: what game are we playing?).

Landolfi's third play, *Faust '67,* an adaptation of Pirandello's *Sei personaggi in cerca d'autore* (Six Characters in Search of an Author, 1921), was published in 1969. In his preface Landolfi calls the play an empty canvas or "commedia da fare" (a comedy in the making), exhorting the reader to fill in the action with his own personal experiences. The protagonist, Signor Nessuno—No Man in the place of Everyman—is not, as in Pirandello's play, simply looking for a part to play but a part in which he can recognize himself. He refuses three roles that are offered him—those of the arrogant dictator, the successful gambler, and the famous writer—choosing instead to play a middle-aged intellectual falling in love with a washerwoman, who corresponds to Marguerite in *Faust.* Unlike Pirandello's play there is no solution, no catharsis that evolves out of the staging of the play. The only liberation for No Man comes from an outside force, a specious deus ex machina. Thunder and lightning flood the stage as a voice cries out "Nessuno si salverà, perché non accettò mai di essere qualcuno!" (No one will be saved, because he never wanted to be someone!). As in his *Racconti impossibili* Landolfi reached the point of no return in his negativity.

Landolfi's constitution was weakened by winters passed in his poorly heated palazzo and his addiction to smoking. His health began to falter in the winter of 1971, when he suffered a heart attack. In 1973 he was stricken with cancer and remained for a month in a clinic in Rome. In his last years he turned more to poetry, publishing two volumes of poetry, *Viola di morte* (Viola of Death, 1972) and *Il tradimento* (The Betrayal, 1977), which won the Viareggio Prize. Landolfi's stately style—a style called *aulico,* or "courtly"—is incongruous in the context of modern Italian poetry. It is redolent of the late romantic, nocturnal poetry of D'Annunzio, especially in its diction, while being closer in sentiment to Leopardian pessimism.

Landolfi is obviously considering his own death and fate in some of his poems, as in "Epitafio" (Epitaph), an eloquent expression of his separateness:

> nacque,
> fu sempre solo
> tra tanta gente;
> in molte parole
> tacque;
> indi morì, s'accomiatò dal sole.

> (he was born,
> he was always alone
> among so many people;
> in many words
> he was silent;
> then he died, he took leave of the sun.)

But death and the idea of nothingness had always been an overriding theme in Landolfi's writing. In the diaristic *Rien va* Landolfi wrote of his fear that nothingness itself may not exist:

> L'esistenza è una condanna senza appello e senza riscatto; niente vi è da fare contro di essa; ed è forse la nostra speranza soltanto, il nostro bisogno di riprender fiato come dall'acuto dolore di una ferita, che ha immaginato uno stato altro dall'essere, un nulla. Forse, mio Dio, tutto esiste, è esistito, esisterà in eterno. Non c'è niente da fare contro la vita, fuorché vivere, press' a poco come in un posto chiuso, dove si sia soffocati dal fumo del tabacco, non c'è meglio che fumare.

Dust jacket for the American edition of the translation of Landolfi's 1950 book, whose title refers to the name of a spaceship designed by a madman

> (Existence is a condemnation without appeal and without redemption; there's nothing to be done to oppose it. And perhaps it is only hope, our need to catch our breath, as if from the sharp pain of a wound, that conceived of a state outside of existence, a nothingness. My God, perhaps everything exists, has existed, and will exist in eternity. There is nothing we can do against life but live it, just as there is nothing to do in a closed, suffocating smoke-filled room but go on smoking.)

In 1974 Landolfi returned to storytelling with a collection, *Le labrene* (The Labrenas), that seems almost to parody his own themes and obsessions. In the title story "Le labrene" Landolfi invents a fictitious specimen of lizard, similar to the gecko, to which he gives a facetious zoological classification, *Platidattilo muraiolo.* The narrator is terrified by this innocuous creature and sees it everywhere. When one day it actually lands on his face, he loses all vital signs, but remains fully conscious. He is thought to be dead, but as the coffin is about to be consigned to

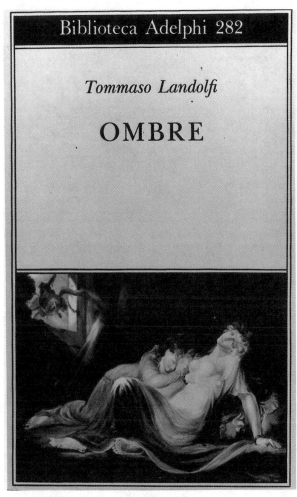

Cover for a 1994 edition of Landolfi's 1954 book, which includes stories as well as essays and verse

chapel in Pico, with his parents, grandparents, and the relatives of his beloved cousin, Fosforina.

Critics have always been unanimous in recognizing the genius and pure intelligence of the idiosyncratic Landolfi but awaited in vain his one definitive work. Perhaps Landolfi aspired to be another Anton Chekhov, who, he says in one of his literary articles, wished to write a novel, but never succeeded in doing so:

> Uno ne andava scrivendo, sebbene a minuzzoli, tra i maggiori di tutte le letterature; aperti sul mondo come i mille occhi di un insetto, i quali ne formano poi uno solo. Ed è tra le pagine di questo sparso romanzo che bisognerà con amore, con pazienza persino, cercare il suo vero volto.

> (He was in the process of writing one, even if it consisted of tiny pieces, among the greatest of all literatures; open upon the world like the thousand eyes of an insect, which in the end form one single eye. And it is among the pages of this scattered novel that with love and even with patience it will be necessary to seek out his true countenance.)

Landolfi succeeded to the end in not revealing his true countenance, remaining a "mantrugiatore di libri o topo di bisca" (devourer of books or gambling-den rat), as he described himself. It is difficult to determine how much of his confessions, implicit or explicit, are part of the gambler's bluff, but in his poetics of despair and fin de siècle diabolism he is a figure to be reckoned with in the annals of twentieth-century Italian letters.

the earth he manages to emit an audible sound and is rescued from his premature death, not, however, before having heard his wife plighting her love to his cousin. The rest of the contrived tale is almost farcical. The burial alive could be a subtle pastiche and ironic homage to Edgar Allan Poe, as Italo Calvino remarked, but there is not even a shadow of the intensity of Poe's work. At the end the protagonist seems to be in a padded cell as the instigator of his fears stares at him "coi tondi, sporgenti, lucenti occhi" (with its round, bulging, glittering eyes). This image of death, however, is not frightening. Landolfi seems to be playing his last cards.

Landolfi published one more collection, *A caso* (At Random, 1975), which was centered upon the vagaries of his god, chance. Already the recipient of many prestigious literary prizes, Landolfi was awarded the Premio Strega in 1975 for the entirety of his works. On 8 July 1979 Landolfi died in a hospital outside Rome. He was buried in the family

References:

Renato Aymone, "Tommaso Landolfi," *Otto/Novecento,* 3 (1979): 169–197;

Aymone, *Tommaso Landolfi: Analisi e letture* (Salerno: Palladio Editrice, 1978);

Giorgio Barberi-Squarotti, "Tommaso Landolfi," in his *La narrativa italiana del dopoguerra* (Bologna: Cappelli, 1965);

Giorgio Bernabò Secchi, *Invito alla lettura di Landolfi* (Milan: Mursia, 1978);

Carlo Bo, "Nota introduttiva a *Racconto d'autunno*" (Milan: Rizzoli, 1975);

Arnaldo Bocelli, *Letteratura del Novecento* (Rome & Caltanissetta: Sciascia, 1975), pp. 404–409;

Italo Calvino, "L'esattezza e il caso," in *Le più belle pagine di Tommaso Landolfi scelte da I. Calvino* (Milan: Rizzoli, 1983); translated by Katherine Jason as *Words in Commotion* (New York: Viking, 1986);

Lanfranco Caretti, *Sul Novecento* (Pisa: Nistri-Lischi, 1976), pp. 198–203;

Silvana Castelli, "Saggio su Landolfi," *Nuovi argomenti*, 40–42 (1974): 129–153;

Gianfranco Contini, "Tommaso Landolfi," in *Letteratura dell'Italia unita* (Florence: Sansoni, 1968), pp. 931–934;

Giacomo Debenedetti, "Il *Rouge et noir* di Landolfi," in *Intermezzo* (Milan: Mondadori, 1963), pp. 215–238;

Debenedetti, "La roulette di Landolfi," in *Novecento. I contemporanei,* volume 6 (Milan: Marzorati, 1979), pp. 5624–5630;

Diego Dejaco, "Un punto di svolta nella narrativa landolfiana," *Strumenti critici,* 4 (1989): 395–414;

Enrico Falqui, *Novecento letterario* (Florence: Vallecchi, 1970), pp. 809–828;

Luigi Fontanella, *Il surrealismo italiano* (Rome: Bulzoni, 1983), pp. 189–218;

Claudio Gorlier, "Considerazioni su Landolfi," *Aut-Aut,* 19 (1954): 49–53;

Stefano Guidi, "Prodigalità landolfiana," *Il Ponte,* 44 (1988): 178–186;

Idolina Landolfi, ed., *Le lunazioni del cuore. Saggi su Tommaso Landolfi* (Florence: Nuova Italia, 1996);

Giorgio Luti, "Tommaso Landolfi," in *Novecento. I contemporanei,* pp. 5595–5624;

Oreste Macrí, *Tommaso Landolfi: Narratore poeta critico artefice della lingua* (Florence: Le Lettere, 1990);

Claudio Marabini, "Tommaso Landolfi," in *Gli anni Sessanta. Narrativa e storia* (Milan: Rizzoli, 1969), pp. 197–218;

Giuseppe Montesano, "Rassegna di studi critici su Tommaso Landolfi (1937–1978)," *Critica letteraria,* 10 (1982): 593–599;

Geno Pampaloni, *Storia della letteratura italiana. Il Novecento,* volume 9 (Milan: Garzanti, 1969), pp. 795–806;

Giancarlo Pandini, *Tommaso Landolfi* (Florence: La Nuova Italia, 1975);

Walter Pedullà, *La letteratura del benessere* (Rome: Bulzoni, 1973), pp. 342–353;

Alberto Pezzotta, "Tommaso Landolfi," *Belfagor,* 48 (1993): 543–558;

Giorgio Pullini, "Landolfi e il suo Enigma," *Lettere italiane,* 32 (1980): 356–363;

Edoardo Sanguineti, *Letteratura italiana. I contemporanei,* volume 2 (Milan: Marzorati, 1963), pp. 5595–5624;

Tarcisio Tarquini, ed., *Landolfi, libro per libro* (Alatri: Hetea, 1988).

Primo Levi

(31 July 1919 – 11 April 1987)

Ilona Klein
Brigham Young University

BOOKS: *Se questo è un uomo* (Turin: De Silva, 1947); translated by Stuart Woolf as *If This Is a Man* (New York: Orion, 1959; London: Orion, 1960); published as *Survival in Auschwitz* (New York: Collier, 1961);

La tregua (Turin: Einaudi, 1963); translated by Woolf as *The Reawakening* (Boston: Little, Brown, 1965) and *The Truce* (London: Bodley Head, 1965);

Storie naturali, as Damiano Malabaila (Turin: Einaudi, 1966); selected stories translated by Raymond Rosenthal in *The Sixth Day and Other Tales* (New York: Summit Books, 1990; London: M. Joseph, 1990);

Vizio di forma (Turin: Einaudi, 1971); selected essays translated by Rosenthal in *The Sixth Day and Other Tales*;

Il sistema periodico (Turin: Einaudi, 1975); translated by Rosenthal as *The Periodic Table* (New York: Schocken Books, 1984);

L'osteria di Brema (Milan: Scheiwiller, 1975);

La chiave a stella (Turin: Einaudi, 1978); translated by William Weaver as *The Monkey's Wrench* (New York: Summit Books, 1986);

La ricerca delle radici (Turin: Einaudi, 1981);

Lilìt e altri racconti (Turin: Einaudi, 1981); selected stories translated by Ruth Feldman as *Moments of Reprieve* (New York: Summit Books, 1986; London: M. Joseph, 1986);

Se non ora, quando? (Turin: Einaudi, 1982); translated by Weaver as *If Not Now, When?* (New York: Summit Books, 1985);

Dialogo, by Levi and Tullio Regge (Milan: Edizioni di Comunità, 1984); translated by Rosenthal (Princeton: Princeton University Press, 1989; London: I. B. Tauris, 1989);

Ad ora incerta (Milan: Garzanti, 1984);

L'altrui mestiere (Turin: Einaudi, 1985); translated by Rosenthal as *Other People's Trades* (New York: Summit Books, 1989);

I sommersi e i salvati (Turin: Einaudi, 1986); translated by Rosenthal as *The Drowned and the Saved* (New York: Summit Books, 1988);

Primo Levi (photograph © Jerry Bauer)

Racconti e saggi (Turin: La Stampa, 1986); essays and selected stories translated by Rosenthal as *The Mirror Maker* (New York: Schocken Books, 1989);

Autoritratto di Primo Levi, edited by Ferdinando Camon (Padua: Nord-Est, 1987); translated by John Shepley as *Conversations with Primo Levi* (Marlboro, Vt.: Marlboro Press, 1989).

Collections and Editions: *Opere,* 3 volumes (Turin: Einaudi, 1987–1990);

Collected Poems, translated by Ruth Feldman and Brian Swann (London & Boston: Faber & Faber, 1988).

OTHER: Simon Wiesenthal, *The Sunflower,* response by Levi (New York: Schocken Books, 1976), pp. 161–162;

Hermann Langbein, *Uomini ad Auschwitz,* introduction by Levi (Milan: Mursia, 1984);

Rudolf Höss, *Comandante ad Auschwitz,* preface by Levi (Turin: Einaudi, 1985);

Anna Bravo and others, *La vita offesa,* preface by Levi (Milano: Franco Angeli, 1986);

"The Memory of Offence," in *Bitburg in Moral and Political Perspective,* edited by Geoffrey H. Hartman (Bloomington: Indiana University Press, 1986), pp. 130–137.

SELECTED PERIODICAL PUBLICATION – UNCOLLECTED: "Beyond Survival," *Prooftexts,* 4 (1984): 9–21.

Chemistry and literature, viewed by most people as widely different subjects, come together in the works of Primo Levi, an Italian Jew who was both a professional chemist and a professional writer. Levi said that he wanted to fill the gap between the imaginative world of literature and the analytical world of science. Believing such a gap absurd, he was never daunted by the purported incompatibility between the two fields of knowledge. Levi's literary work is also marked by his experience in Auschwitz's concentration camp, where he was interned from February 1944 to January 1945. Through his characteristically clear and precise prose, he dealt with political and social issues as a survivor of the Nazi regime.

Levi was born in Turin in an elegant apartment building at 75 Corso Re Umberto. He lived there all his life, and in the same house he died tragically in 1987. His ancestors were Jews of ancient Spanish descent who found their way to Piedmont after their expulsion from Spain in 1492. Levi's paternal grandfather was a local civil engineer; his maternal grandfather was a businessman in fabrics. Born in a well-to-do family, Levi's father, Cesare, was a bookworm who did not enjoy weekend outings, lived extensively abroad in Hungary, Belgium, and France, spoke several foreign languages well, and was a well-known electrical engineer.

Levi received a classical education at Turin's Ginnasio-Liceo D'Azeglio, where the writer Cesare Pavese was one of his teachers for a few months. Later he enrolled at the University of Turin, where, despite the racial laws against Italian Jews promulgated in 1938, he received a degree in chemistry in 1941. His degree indicated not only that Levi had graduated "maxima cum laude" but also that he belonged to the "razza ebraica" (Jewish race).

In 1943, appalled by the German invasion of northern Italy, he joined a group of inexperienced partisans in the region of Valle d'Aosta who were fighting against Fascism. In December of that year he was arrested and sent to Carpi-Fossoli, an internment camp near Modena. During the interrogation, Levi identified himself as a "cittadino italiano di razza ebraica" (Italian citizen of the Jewish race). As a result he was deported to the Buna-Monowitz camp at Auschwitz, where he worked as a slave laborer. He was able to survive the horrors of the systematic extermination of European Jews, which ultimately accounted for an estimated six million lives. When the camp was liberated by Russian troops in January 1945, Levi's incredible journey back to Turin took him through the countryside of Eastern Europe and Belorussia. In October 1945 he rejoined his family in Turin. Two years later, he married Lucia Morpurgo; they had a daughter, Lisa Lorenza, born in 1948, and a son, Renzo, in 1957.

After the war Levi worked as a chemist in a small factory near Turin while also pursuing his writing, publishing four books between 1947 and 1971. In 1975 he retired from his successful factory career and began to work full-time as a writer. During the last years of his life, Levi was subject to frequent bouts of depression, due in part to his frustration with the theories on the Holocaust advanced by historical revisionists during the late 1970s and early 1980s. He also suffered from the feeling that he may have failed to communicate adequately his war experience to posterity. Furthermore, he was aging and his body was no longer healthy. A few months before his death, he had been operated on for prostate cancer. Levi died in the morning of 11 April 1987, apparently by his own hand.

Se questo è un uomo (1947; translated as *If This Is a Man,* 1959) is Levi's first, and probably his best-known, book. In the preface to the work Levi writes: "Per mia fortuna sono stato deportato ad Auschwitz solo nel 1944" (It was my good fortune to be deported to Auschwitz only in 1944). Since the need for slave workers was so critical for the German economy during 1944, the concentration camp prisoners of that year had a slightly better chance of survival than inmates had had in earlier years. Reading Levi's memories, one is puzzled by his use of the word *fortune* in the account of the horrible eleven months he spent in the Nazi death camp. Indeed, Levi's experiences seem completely opposite of any semblance of "good fortune," though he was certainly lucky to survive. Levi's style is surprisingly calm even when he narrates the most harrowing moments of his life. Yet it is obvious that he was obsessed by the need to remember every detail of his detention and to recall his comrades killed in Auschwitz.

Levi wrote the book as an autobiographical and testimonial work: hence it is impossible to call it a novel. Moreover, the author is quick to add in the preface that "nessuno dei fatti è inventato" (none of the facts are invented). Levi remarks in the preface to *Se questo è un uomo* that he was motivated to write the book by the "bisogno di raccontare agli 'altri' " (the need to tell to the "rest") about the genocide he witnessed. He also points out that he did so "a scopo di liberazione interiore. Di qui il suo carattere frammentario: i capitoli sono stati scritti non in successione logica, ma per ordine di urgenza" (in order to achieve an inner freedom. Hence its fragmentary character: the chapters were written not in logical succession, but in order of urgency).

In 1947 Levi submitted his manuscript to Einaudi; when it was rejected, he had it published at his own expense by De Silva. A decade later Einaudi, sensing that Italian readers were ready for the book, published *Se questo è un uomo*. Clearly a standout among similar accounts of concentration camp life, *Se questo è un uomo* met with immediate success, gained wide acceptance, and is still required reading in most public schools in Italy. Levi recounts his experiences in a quasi-journalistic fashion, without hyperbole, and what he had to endure is impressed indelibly on the reader's mind. He writes about his ordeal as a slave worker in Buna, the Nazi rubber factory that never produced a single pound of rubber. He recalls his friendship with Lorenzo, a civilian worker who at great personal risk brought extra food to Levi and whom Levi credits for his survival. Other memorable figures are Alberto, who died during the evacuation of the camp, and Jean, nicknamed Pikolo, a twenty-four-year-old French student to whom Levi tried to teach some Italian using the episode of Ulysses from Dante's *Divine Comedy*.

Throughout *Se questo è un uomo* Levi shifts verb tenses from the present to the past tense to emphasize the difficulty of focusing on memories that slip away and then reappear stronger than before only to fade away again. Part of Levi's early success as an author is due to his literary style, characterized by short, strong sentences that contain no superfluous information. His prose is descriptive and to the point. He understands his limited perspective, explaining that war memories at times are misunderstood because the prisoners themselves did not clearly understand how the camps were organized and what was expected of them. Indeed, not understanding German turned into a tragedy for many prisoners who, unable to follow orders, were executed. Levi nevertheless attempts to understand the killing machine of Auschwitz.

Levi is unambiguous in his conviction that outside Polish and German civilians must have been aware of (but did not further inquire about) the concentration camps. In the chapter titled "I fatti dell'estate" (The Events of the Summer) he speculates that, given the miserable conditions of Auschwitz prisoners, civilians must have assumed that slave workers had committed unthinkable sins for which they were being punished. Several undercover smuggling operations involving small items existed between interned prisoners and outside civilians: the author describes these in great detail in the chapter titled "Al di qua del bene e del male" (This Side of Good and Evil).

Levi remains firm in his intent to write as a witness to history and not to become a judge who delivers a verdict. He leaves the verdict to his readers and to the coming generations of readers. *Se questo è un uomo* is a remarkable book by virtue of the courage it displays in treating a compelling experience and for the compassion it shows toward the suffering of other human beings. Levi writes about men who became "vermi vuoti d'anima" (vermin without soul) as a consequence of the Nazis' systematic dehumanization of prisoners. Eventually, senseless violence was met by indifference: "Non era rassegnazione cosciente, ma il torpore opaco delle bestie domate con le percosse, a cui non dolgono più le percosse" (It was not a conscious resignation, but the opaque torpor of beasts broken in by blows, whom the blows no longer hurt). In Auschwitz, these weak men were called "Muselmänner": they had become completely indifferent to everything, including their own lives. They were the walking dead.

Levi's survival can largely be attributed to favorable circumstances and timing. One morning, the announcement came that a specialized group of workers was sought for the magnesium chloride warehouse. Levi and his friend, Alberto, who was a third-year chemistry student before the deportation, were assigned to Kommando 98 (Squad 98). Levi partially credits his survival to his being selected for this work. Some of his work was performed inside, in the laboratory in Buna, and he was no longer exposed to inclement weather. In the beginning of January 1945, Levi fell sick with scarlet fever just as the Russian troups were advancing to liberate Auschwitz. His illness did not allow him to join the column of tens of thousands of prisoners whom the Nazis forced to march in a vain effort to hide the evidence of the horrors of the camp. The exhausting march in subfreezing winter temperatures killed almost all prisoners who were forced to go.

La tregua (1963; translated as *The Reawakening* and *The Truce,* both 1965) continues Levi's story begun in *Se questo è un uomo*. He re-creates his long odyssey, filled with adventures, from Auschwitz to Turin, which took about ten months. Levi experienced firsthand the devastation and confusion that reigned everywhere in Europe as he traveled through Poland, Ukraine, Belorussia, Romania, Hungary, and Austria. Since Levi wrote the book fifteen years after the experiences he relates, he is less obsessed than in his first book with recounting his experiences from memory; he is more interested in creating a literary work than a journalistic narrative. He remarked in the preface that this book forced him to think about sentence structure, to understand the texture of narration, and to become cognizant of different ways in which literature is created.

Levi knew that what he experienced during the first months of freedom were unique to him, and it is this uniqueness that he tries to convey to the reader. In his characteristic detached style, Levi offers abundant picaresque details without becoming too personally involved in the narration, thus allowing his readers to enjoy the description of his adventurous return and draw their own conclusions. Rather than harrowing scenes, Levi relates both sad and funny tales as he writes about foreign lands and cultures. He observes, for example, how the entertaining Cesare, a former inmate from Rome, became an entrepreneur on the black market in Katowice and procured food for himself and for Levi.

Levi wrote his third book, *Storie naturali* (1966; selected stories translated in *The Sixth Day and Other Tales,* 1990), under the pseudonym Damiano Malabaila because, as Levi himself stated, he did not wish to be associated with "entertaining" literature after two works that dealt with the Holocaust and its aftermath. At first Levi maintained that his pseudonym did not carry a specific meaning, but in the 12 October 1966 *Il Giorno* he observed that Malabaila could be read as a deformation of the Italian *mala balia* (evil nurse), for Nature had turned sour on humanity and could no longer be regarded as a nurturing, protective mother after the tragic occurrence of World War II.

While some stories are tragic in concept, many others are truly entertaining and brilliantly witty. Levi moves stylistically from a tight and somber prose in some stories to fast and engagingly funny writing in others. His most powerful stories, though, depict the universal wickedness of human nature and the pseudomedical experimentation that the Nazis carried out in concentration camps. Levi is particularly sensitive to the ethical questions arising from the traditional schism between the scientific and the humanistic worlds. What stays with the reader of *Storie naturali* is Levi's exhortation to ponder the developments of technology and scientific experimentation in society. He urges readers to re-

main informed about biogenetic experimentations and their potentially adverse consequences.

The short stories of *Vizio di forma* (Procedural Error, 1971; selected essays translated in *The Sixth Day and Other Tales*) continue to bind Levi the scientist with Levi the writer, both of whom search for truth. The title of the collection is taken from the science-fiction story "Procacciatori d'affiar" (The Hard-Sellers), which tells of the efforts of an extraterrestrial civilization to find a way to fight and to conquer human misery and hunger on the planet Earth. Even though mankind is given free will, "qualcuno da qualche parte ha sbagliato, ed i piani terrestri presentano una faglia, un vizio di forma" (someone somewhere has made a mistake, and the terrestrial plans present a fault, a procedural error). Themes treated in the collection include death, natural and by one's own hand; otherness, or being "different" or an "outsider," viewed as a positive quality no matter the circumstances; innate biological versus socially ingrained behaviors; the role of a writer and his or her responsibilities; and how humanity is judged by its collective actions and their consequences. The tone of the collection varies from pessimism to a somewhat lighter, entertaining accent.

In *Vizio di forma*, as in *Se questo è un uomo* and *La tregua*, Levi provides one of his poems for an epigraph. As is the case for most of Levi's poetry, his verse reveals a more pessimistic view than he allows in his prose:

Eran cento uomini in arme.
Quando il sole sorse nel cielo,
Tutti fecero un passo avanti.
. . . .
Quando suonarono le campane,
Tutti mossero un passo avanti.
. . . .
quando fiorì in cielo la prima stella,
Tutti insieme, fecero un passo avanti.
"Indietro, via di qui, fantasmi immondi:
Ritornate alla vostra vecchia notte":
Ma nessuno rispose, e invece,
Tutti in cerchio, fecero un passo avanti.

(There were one hundred men in arms.
And when the sun rose in the sky,
They all took a step forward.
. . . .
But when the bells tolled,
They all moved a step forward.
. . . .
But when the first star flowered in the sky,
Then all of them together took a step forward.
"Get back, get out of here, filthy ghosts,
Return to your old night":
But no one replied, and instead

Dust jacket for the American edition of the translation of Levi's 1978 novel, which depicts a skilled worker's love of his craft

All in a circle took a step forward.)

The poem suggests humanity's inadequacy in understanding and dealing with life's great questions by showing its ignorant and presumptuous response to grand philosophical, ethical, and scientific dilemmas.

When *Il sistema periodico* (1975; translated as *The Periodic Table,* 1984) was published, it became an immediate success, reaching a third reprint within a few months. The book takes its name from the periodic table of elements fashioned by the Russian chemist Dmitry Mendeleyev; each title of the twenty-one chapters carries the name of one of the chemical elements, around which Levi creates a story.

Levi recounts among other things the origins of his family, his love for chemistry, his arrest and deportation, and his lifelong friendships. In the first chapter, "Argon," he draws the story of his ancestors by establishing analogies with the chemical properties of argon, an inert gas. Argon is rare – as rare, Levi writes, as the first group of Jews who moved to Piedmont after the Spanish Diaspora to create a new community. From "Argon" to the last chapter, titled for vital element "Carbon," the only element that delineates inorganic material into organic matter, Levi leads his reader through a labyrinth of enticing short stories written in a style marked by precision and clarity. The author's autobiographical moments set in fictional frame include "Nitrogen," with its description of the chemical transformation of excrements into cosmetics; "Gold," in which Levi recounts his arrest as a partisan by the Fascist militia and subsequent interrogation; "Zinc," which recounts the author's discovery of his Jewishness as a "small, amusing anomaly" when he was still an adolescent; "Potassium," which describes Levi's love for chemistry; and "Iron" and "Cerium," where he tells touching stories of deep friendships. Fully cognizant that most of his readers are not chemists, Levi is able, through extended metaphors and examples, to make his passion for the periodic table come alive.

Dust jacket for the American edition of the translation of Levi's 1982 novel, in which a Jewish watchmaker becomes a member of the Resistance during World War II

After retiring in 1975 from his position of director with the chemical firm Siva, Levi was able to devote himself full-time to writing. One of the first books he wrote after his retirement bears the title *La chiave a stella* (1978; translated as *The Monkey's Wrench,* 1986), a novel quite unlike any of his previous works. He portrays a specialist in cranes and giant derricks, Tino Faussone, a hardworking man who takes great pride in his labor and who is enamored by the precision it requires. In *La chiave a stella*, Levi gives voice to a skilled blue-collar worker who is in demand around the world and who enjoys many adventures. Levi writes that "l'amare il proprio lavoro (che purtroppo è privilegio di pochi) costituisce la migliore approssimazione concreta alla felicità sulla terra: ma questa è una verità che non molti conoscono" (loving one's work [unfortunately, the privilege of a few] represents the best, most concrete approximation of happiness on earth. But this is a truth unknown to many).

The unnamed narrator of the novel, a paint chemist from Turin on assignment to the Soviet Union, gets to know Faussone slowly. The way in which Levi writes the first chapters mirrors the way people meet each other in life: superficially at first, through small talk; gradually learning more as bits and pieces of meaningful information come together, until the knowledge of a character becomes complete. The use of regional slang for the Piedmontese Faussone and his dexterity in describing tools of manual trade are admirable. Faussone's enthusiasm for his work and his adventures while on job assignments in Africa and in the Soviet Union indicate the profound sense of freedom and accomplishment that his job affords him.

Se non ora, quando? (1982; translated as *If Not Now, When?,* 1985) received both the Premio Viareggio and the Premio Campiello. The novel explores what might have been Levi's experience as a partisan had he not been arrested after only three months of activity. The title comes from Rabbi Hillel's commentary in *Talmud, The Maxims of the Fathers:* "If I am not for myself, who will be for me? And even if I think of myself, what am I? If not now,

*Dust jacket for the American edition of the translation of Levi's
1986 book of essays, in which he explores the horror of
the Holocaust*

when?" The passage of time, gaining control of time, and mending the past are the major themes of the work. The protagonist, Mendel, is a watchmaker turned partisan. Levi employs a quick narrative pace, like a clock ticking too fast, to describe the frenetic actions of a group of partisans, including their combat techniques and sabotage missions.

Se non ora, quando? also explores the world of Ashkenazi Judaism in Eastern Europe, a language and a culture to some extent unknown to Levi, an integrated Italian Jew who did not speak Yiddish. During World War II most Italian Jews were viewed with suspicion by eastern Jews because, as they would say in Yiddish, "Redest keyn jiddisch, bist nit keyn jid" (If you do not speak Yiddish, you are not a Jew). Although Levi was an agnostic and his work has been valued and respected by critics for its humanism, a strong religious theme permeates this novel, in which he celebrates Judaism.

The novel stresses the individual's obligations toward society. While carefully weighing coexistent

political and moral duties, Levi pays tribute to the thousands of Jews and Gentiles who fought against the genocidal Nazi effort. The novel covers a time span of twenty-five months, from July 1943 to Tuesday, 7 August 1945, the day after the United States dropped an atomic bomb on Hiroshima. The novel ends on a tragic note, with the news of the bombing dampening the joy of White Rokhele, one of the protagonists of the novel, upon the birth of her son. Even a newborn's presence is unable to disperse the novel's omnipresent sense of death.

Levi also ends the essay collection *L'altrui mestiere* (1985; translated as *Other People's Trades,* 1989) by considering the effect of the bomb. In the last essay, "Eclissi dei profeti" (Eclipse of the Prophets), he explores the malaise of post–World War II humanity and encourages wisdom in making collective and individual decisions that will shape the future. Although the volume does not close on an optimistic note, most of the essays are not pessimistic. They record the thoughts of a chemist-turned-writer on diverse topics such as zoology (his great love and respect for animals is evident on almost every page), astronomy, linguistics, computers, world literature, submarines, sidewalks, plants, education, and translating and being translated, to mention just a few. Levi asserts that his essays "sono il frutto di questo mio più che decennale vagabondaggio di dilettante curioso. Sono 'invasioni di campo', incursioni nei mestieri altrui, bracconaggi in distretti di caccia riservata; scorribande negli sterminati territori . . . che non ho mai studiato sistematicamente" (are the fruit of my roaming about as a curious dilettante for more than a decade. They are "invasions of field," incursions into other people's trades, poaching in private hunting preserves, forays into the boundless territories . . . which I have never studied systematically).

In this book, more than in any of his other works, Levi purposefully sets out to build a bridge across the cultures of science and literature: "Mi auguro che questi miei scritti, entro i loro modesti limiti d'impegno e di mole, facciano vedere che fra le due 'culture' non c'è incompatibilità" (I hope that these essays, within their modest limits of commitment and scope, will make clear that between "the two cultures" there is no incompatibility). An important essay in light of Levi's own death is "Dello scrivere oscuro" (On Obscure Writing), in which he writes with great compassion about Paul Celan's reasons for being an obscure poet and sheds light on some clues to Celan's suicide. Levi intuitively connects the cathartic value of writing with the need to communicate with others, and he explains why, contrary to Celan, in his own prose he strives to make every sentence as clear to the reader as possible. When a writer's work turns obscure, Levi writes, it is because obscurity mirrors the darkness and hopelessness of a person's view of life. The gloom is like the last, unintelligible sound from the mouth of a moribund man.

I sommersi e i salvati (1986; translated as *The Drowned and the Saved,* 1988) is the last book Levi published in his lifetime. In it he relives, forty years later, his harrowing experience in Auschwitz and its aftermath. The calm and rationality with which he approaches the analysis of the deportation and death of millions of people makes this volume a milestone in the documentation about concentration camps. However, by Levi's own admission, he felt compelled to write *I sommersi e i salvati* in a manner similar to the way in which Samuel Taylor Coleridge's Ancient Mariner felt coerced to stop the wedding guests and tell his tale. Likewise, Levi succumbed to the impulse of rationalizing in words the horrible truth of Auschwitz. Perhaps these essays represent the survivor's way of coping with the haunting ghosts from his past. In each essay the reader comes to appreciate and to understand the way in which memory operates.

Levi explores the feeling of guilt and/or shame that concentration camp survivors experience vis-à-vis the prisoners who died. He also writes about the importance of Yiddish as a common language for the Jewish prisoners deported to Auschwitz from different nations and cultures throughout eastern Europe. He treats the fate of Italian Jews with great compassion, for though they generally fared a bit better than their European brothers and sisters, only 5 percent of those deported made it back to Italy. When Levi takes upon himself the task of recounting the unspeakable, his scientific training enables him to choose precise words and details. The characteristic *impotentia judicandi* (powerlessness to judge) that permeates Levi's work is strongly present in *I sommersi e i salvati,* especially when he deals with Jewish prisoners who collaborated with Nazi officials, the so called privileged prisoners.

In addition to his prose, Levi wrote two volumes of poetry, *L'osteria di Brema* (Brema's Inn, 1975) and *Ad ora incerta* (At an Uncertain Hour, 1984), that are essential to understanding his work. In his poetry Levi shows aspects of his personality and intellectual makeup that are not found in his prose works. His poetry is consistently pessimistic, permeated by helplessness, anger, and nightmares. All of his poems are dated, so that the reader may analyze them both synchronically and diachronically. Spanning a period from 1943 ("Crescenzago") to January 1987 ("Almanacco"), the lyrics offer a clear picture of emotional states that Levi never allows to transpire in his neatly controlled prose.

"Shemà," which serves as the epigraph of *Se questo è un uomo,* is perhaps Levi's best-known poem. Written shortly after his return to Turin in 1946, it echoes Deut. 6:4–9. Levi, however, twists the important Jewish prayer: rather than reminding Jews to love the Lord, he urges posterity to remember the Holocaust, never to forget, lest "vi si sfaccia la case, / la malattia vi impedisca, / i vostri nati torcano il viso da voi" (your house crumble, / disease render you powerless, / your offspring avert their faces from you). He questions the purpose of human existence, betraying a hopelessness that is not detectable in his prose. Although a few of the poems appear to be humorous or amusing, such as "Vecchia talpa" (Old Mole), "Il primo atlante" (The First Atlas) and "Avigliana" (Avigliana), they are not meant to be entertaining. Most of them lack the sense of calm observation and serene balance that mark his prose. Levi is anguished by the unrelenting passing of time, by an obsessive need to communicate and exorcise the ghosts from his past. He portrays humanity as self-destructive, presumptuous, and irresponsible toward nature.

Levi was already well known in Italy but was just beginning to be discovered in the United States in the early 1980s. The literary world was left aghast at the news of his sudden death in April 1987. With Levi died a strong voice willing to bear witness to events that younger generations did not experience and had difficulty imagining; with him also died the hope of many who had survived the Holocaust and found him a source of fortitude and resolution. Rather than searching for general solutions to grand questions, Levi focused on specifics and small truths. His wisdom lay in the intellectual rigor that permeates his reasoning and in his capacity to describe in detail every memory, observation, and inquiry and to draw conclusions from his experiences. To Italians Levi represents a man whose interests ranged from chemistry to Dante, from psychology to economy, from politics to physics. He was, indeed, one of the few true humanists of his time.

Interviews:

Claudio Toscani, "Primo Levi," in his *La voce e il testo* (Milan: Istituto Propaganda Libraria, 1985), pp. 119–132;

Risa Sodi, "An Interview with Primo Levi," *Partisan Review,* 54 (Summer 1987): 355–366;

Sodi, "Primo Levi: A Last Talk," *Present Tense,* 15 (1988): 40–45.

References:

Giancarlo Borri, *Le divine impurità. Primo Levi tra scienza e letteratura* (Rimini: Luisè, 1992);

JoAnn Cannon, "Canon-Formation and Reception in Contemporary Italy: The Case of Primo Levi," *Italica,* 69 (1992): 30–44;

Alberto Cavaglion, "Argon e la cultura ebraica piemontese," *Belfagor,* 5 (1988): 541–562;

Cavaglion, ed., *Primo Levi: il presente del passato* (Milan: Angeli, 1991);

Mirna Cicioni, "Bridges of Knowledge: Re-reading Primo Levi," *Spunti e ricerche,* 3 (1987): 59–94;

Cicioni, *Primo Levi: Bridges of Knowledge* (Oxford & Washington, D.C.: Berg, 1995);

Vania De Luca, *Tra Giobbe e i buchi neri* (Naples: Istituto Geografico Editoriale Italiano, 1991);

Massimo Dini and Stefano Jesurum, *Primo Levi: le opere e i giorni* (Milan: Rizzoli, 1992);

Pietro Frassica, ed., *Primo Levi as Witness: Proceedings of a Symposium Held at Princeton University* (Fiesole: Casalini Libri, 1990);

Sander L. Gilman, "Primo Levi: The Special Language of the Camps and After," *Midstream,* 35 (October 1989): 22–30;

Giuseppe Grassano, *Primo Levi* (Florence: La Nuova Italia, 1981);

Lynn M. Gunzberg, "Down among the Dead Men: Levi and Dante in Hell," *Modern Language Studies,* 16 (1986): 10–28;

Ilona Klein, "Primo Levi: The Drowned, the Saved, and the 'Grey Zone,'" *Simon Wiesenthal Center Annual,* 7 (1990): 77–89;

Rita Levi-Montalcini, "Epilogue: Primo Levi's Message," in her *In Praise of Imperfection. My Life and Work* (New York: Basic Books, 1988), pp. 212–214;

Guido Lopez, *Se non lui, chi* (Rome: Centro di cultura ebraica della Comunità israelitica di Roma, 1987);

John Murawski, "In Order to Tell: Primo Levi and the Subversion of Literary Language," *Prose Studies,* 14 (1991): 81–96;

Cynthia Ozick, "Primo Levi's Suicide Note," in her *Metaphor and Memory. Essays* (New York: Knopf, 1989), pp. 34–48;

Nicholas Patruno, "Primo Levi: Science and Conscience," *Italian Culture,* 10 (1992): 159–166;

Patruno, *Understanding Primo Levi* (Columbia: University of South Carolina Press, 1995);

Gabriella Poli and Giorgio Calcagno, *Echi di una voce perduta: incontri, interviste e conversazioni con Primo Levi* (Milan: Mursia, 1992);

Primo Levi, directed by Henry Colomer, Archipel 33 – la Sept Arte, 1995, videocassette;

Anthony Rudolf, *At an Uncertain Hour: Primo Levi's War Against Oblivion* (London: Menard, 1990);

Giuseppina Santagostino, "Dalle metafore vive alla poetica di Primo Levi," *Letteratura italiana contemporanea,* 35 (1992): 237–253;

Santagostino, "Destituzione e ossessione biologica nell'immaginario di Primo Levi," *Letteratura italiana contemporanea,* 32 (1991): 127–145;

Lawrence R. Schehr, "Primo Levi's Strenuous Clarity," *Italica,* 66 (1989): 429–443;

Risa B. Sodi, *A Dante of Our Time: Primo Levi and Auschwitz* (New York & Bern: Peter Lang, 1990);

The Suicide of a Camp Survivor: The Case of Primo Levi (Princeton, N.J.: Films for the Humanities and Sciences, 1994), videocassette;

Susan Tarrow, ed., *Reason and Light: Essays on Primo Levi* (Cornell, N.Y.: Center for International Studies, Cornell University, 1990);

Claudio Toscani, *Come leggere "Se questo è un uomo" di Primo Levi* (Milan: Mursia, 1990);

Giuseppe Varchetta, *Ascoltando Primo Levi: organizzazione, narrazione, etica* (Milan: Guerini, 1991);

Fiora Vincenti, *Invito alla lettura di Primo Levi* (Milan: Mursia, 1973);

Wallis Wilde-Menozzi, "A Piece You've Touched is a Piece Moved: On Primo Levi," *Tel Aviv Review,* 2 (Winter 1989–1990): 149–165.

Gianna Manzini
(24 March 1896 – 31 August 1974)

Giovanna Miceli-Jeffries
University of Wisconsin–Madison

BOOKS: *Tempo innamorato* (Milan: Corbaccio, 1928);

Incontro col falco (Milan: Corbaccio, 1929);

Boscovivo (Milan: Treves, 1932);

Un filo di brezza (Milan: Panorama, 1936);

Rive remote (Milan: Mondadori, 1940);

Venti racconti (Milan: Mondadori, 1941);

Forte come un leone (Rome: Documento, 1944);

Carta d'identità (Rome: Nuove Edizioni Italiane, 1945);

Lettera all'editore (Florence: Sansoni, 1945);

Ho visto il tuo cuore (Milan: Mondadori, 1950);

Il valtzer del diavolo (Milan: Mondadori, 1953);

Animali sacri e profani (Rome: Casini, 1953);

Foglietti (Milan: Scheiwiller, 1954);

La sparviera (Milan: Mondadori, 1956);

Cara prigione (Milan: Mondadori, 1958);

Ritratti e pretesti (Milan: Il Saggiatore, 1960);

Arca di Noè (Milan: Mondadori, 1960);

Un'altra cosa (Milan: Mondadori, 1961);

Il cielo addosso (Milan: Mondadori, 1963);

Album di ritratti (Milan: Mondadori, 1964);

Allegro con disperazione (Milan: Mondadori, 1965);

Ritratto in piedi (Milan: Mondadori, 1971);

Sulla soglia (Milan: Mondadori, 1973).

Gianna Manzini

The work of Gianna Manzini is central to understanding twentieth-century Italian literature. Her novels and short stories, spanning from 1928 to 1973, have established her as an influential and original writer whose art combines the most salient expressions of Italian prose. Receptive to experimentation, she played an important role in both the theory and practice of the novel.

Manzini's narratives are characterized by her loyalty to the *prosa d'arte* (artistic prose), with its intensely lyric fragmentism and linguistic refinement, and to the *rècit,* the story itself and its structural organization. The two tendencies, present in many Italian writers between the two world wars, inform Manzini's writings with a strong lyric quality and self-reflectivity. To the younger generation of writers who matured in the postwar years, Manzini rep-

resented a writer with a modern conception of the novel and far-reaching linguistic ability.

Although Manzini's novels and stories show a mastery of style and profound perception of life, especially of its poetic and mysterious aspects, she never achieved the popularity of women writers such as Elsa Morante or Natalia Ginzburg. According to some critics, her tendency to deal with intimate aspects of life, with the complexity of human emotions, coupled with a refined and lyrical prose make her art too difficult for the general public. None of Manzini's works has been translated into English. Her prose would certainly prove a challenge to a translator.

Born in Pistoia, Tuscany, in 1896, Manzini was the only child of an ill-fated marriage. Her mother, who came from a middle-class, politically conservative family, separated early from her husband, the anarchist Giuseppe Manzini, who later died in Fascist confinement. Manzini's deep admiration for her father's unshakable integrity left its mark on her emotional development and artistic commitment. She graduated with a degree in Italian literature at the University of Florence, where she was a student and admirer of Giuseppe De Robertis, the second editor of the journal *La Voce.*

In Florence, during the 1920s and early 1930s, Manzini absorbed the lessons of the influential literary journals *La Ronda,* which stressed the preservation of the language and style of the literary tradition that included Petrarch, Giacomo Leopardi, and Alessandro Manzoni, and *La Voce,* which emphasized a concept of literature–stemming from Benedetto Croce's aesthetic ideas–concerned only with the spiritual world. In 1929 Manzini started contributing to the journal *Solaria.* The exposure to the dynamic, European-minded writers associated with the journal proved important to her artistic maturation.

Solaria integrated the programmatic ideas of *La Ronda* and *La Voce* but also voiced a healthy criticism of the stylistic abuses and thematic abstractions identified with the other two journals. *Solaria* became an open forum for young Italian writers such as Elio Vittorini, Emilio Cecchi, and Eugenio Montale, as well as for European and American authors such as Marcel Proust, Virginia Woolf, William Faulkner, Katherine Mansfield, and James Joyce. This opening to experimentation with different narrative styles brought about a renewed interest in the forms and structure of the novel, which the long practice of the *frammento* (fragment) had minimized and brought to a crisis.

Manzini's narrative style has often been compared to that of Woolf to the point that she has been called the Italian Virginia Woolf. To be sure, in the early 1930s Woolf had a profound influence on Manzini's literary development. In the essay "La lezione della Woolf" (Virginia Woolf's Lesson), which is collected in *Album di ritratti* (1964), Manzini writes:

> In me, il coraggio di non rinunciare si chiama precisamente Virginia Woolf. La leggevo e imparavo a raccogliermi l'anima a tenerla in fronte come la lampada dei minatori. . . . Nient'altro che una particolare attenzione, in virtù della quale le cose escono da un'ombra che le preserva, un'ombra fermentante, faticosa, bruta, l'ombra dell'attimo che precede la nascita, per entrare in un cerchio di chiarità.

> (For me, the courage to endure has a name: Virginia Woolf. In reading her, I learned to collect my soul and to keep it in front of me as mine workers do with their lamp. . . . It was a particular attention, through which things come out from a shadow that preserves them–a fermenting shadow, harsh, crude, the shadow of the moment that precedes birth–to enter into a circle of clarity.)

What Manzini calls the lesson of Virginia Woolf's art is in effect a confirmation of her narrative approach that centers on a penetrating observation of reality–individuals, animals, plants, and objects. Her process generates a narrative voice intensely involved in discovering and scrutinizing reality. Manzini's language creates a web of evocative and symbolic meaning through which one comes to appreciate her passionate, indomitable interest in *la parola* (the word), her search for a visual language and a resonant lexicon. She always aims to uncover the connections, analogies, and recognitions underneath the word or sign.

In Manzini's narratives there is always a mystery to unveil in the characters' lives, especially in their love experiences. Love, in all its manifestations, is by far her most recurrent and powerful theme. Love appears not simply as the main thread that ties a story together but as a source of constant tension. In Manzini's fiction love is like a lens that magnifies common sensations or a catalyst that changes sentimental experiences into intellectual quests. To further her larger theme of love, Manzini in several of her works uses physical illness to bring about in a character an experience of rare lucidity and spiritual exaltation. She represents illness as allowing a deeper apprehension of the fragility of the body, thus freeing the spirit of its power.

Autobiographical elements appear directly and indirectly in all of Manzini's works. Whether she writes in the third or first person, Manzini's narratives allow her to plumb a deeper understanding of her personal identity as woman, daughter, lover, and artist. It is certainly not an accident that authors, publishers, and friends in talking about Manzini the artist never fail to mention the refinement and elegance of her personality. A woman of impeccable taste and fascinating conversation, she liked to discuss narrative issues and contemporary world literature. She was especially fond of Japanese literature and was not at all surprised when the first request to translate her novel *Ritratto in piedi* (A Standing Portrait, 1971) came from Japan.

Under the pseudonyms of "Vanessa" and "Pamela," Manzini beginning in 1935 served for many years as the fashion editor of the literary journal *La fiera letteraria* as well as the fashion columnist for other Italian magazines and newspapers, such as *Il giornale d'Italia, Oggi,* and *Tempo.* Manzini's interest in fashion was more than a personal habit; she cultivated an understanding of the subject, which she integrated in her writing. There is an osmotic relationship between the visual and graphic codification of the fashion editorial page and the literary refinement of her prose, stemming from an educated, discriminating sense of language and rhythm.

Clothing, textures, colors, and shapes occupy a significant space in Manzini's fiction. Clothes and colors, especially with women characters, often offer visual clues to characters' identities. Manzini's interest in fashion is also clear in her autobiographical novel *Ritratto in piedi.* Here she reveals that she was educated early in life to the importance of clothes by her mother, who not only dressed well herself but gave extraordinary attention to her young daughter's clothing. However, as the adult author-narrator recognizes the "bewitching" hold that clothes had on both her mother and herself, she is at the same time pointing to the effects of the conditioning and social genderization of women, exemplified by her mother's unhappy life.

There is no doubt that the idea of femininity Manzini evokes through her work affects attentive readers and critics alike. Gianfranco Contini points to the "rare" refinement of Manzini's prose and finds in her lyrical analogies "uno stile eminentemente femminile" (an eminently feminine style). Similarly, Giansiro Ferrata, in his preface to the 1973 edition of *Tempo innamorato* (Time in Love, 1928), praises "l'intensa ricchezza del punto di vista femminile" (the intense richness of the feminine viewpoint) as a mark of distinction and originality in Manzini's writings. In ascribing to her art a gendered difference and regarding such a difference as a mark of uniqueness and artistic quality, the critics uniformly limit Manzini's refined narrative style and emotional qualities to gendered attributes.

Manzini's literary career can be divided into three phases, the first beginning with the publication of her first novel. *Tempo innamorato* is the result of Manzini's apprenticeship in Florence. After her graduation from the university and a brief teaching experience, she concentrated all her attention on writing while actively participating in the intellectual Florentine circles of young artists. Her book received immediate attention by reviewers, who praised the novelty and inventiveness of its narrative structure and the rare blend of sensitivity and intelligence shown in the representation of the characters' complicated relations.

The story revolves around four characters, two couples whose destinies intersect. Rita, a beautiful woman determined to live life fully, is responsible for the change of directions in the lives of the other characters. After she becomes a widow—her husband commits suicide—she attracts to herself and starts to live with Ugo, Clementina's husband. As Rita personifies the exuberance and joy of living, Clementina is at the opposite end of the spectrum. Rita emanates "light" and "splendor" while Clementina is marked by "opacity." A rather unattractive and self-giving person, Clementina accepts her husband's infidelity as inevitable and lives vicariously in the shadow of the two lovers.

The novel displays an unusual narrative style through the presence of an indefinable narrating voice. This unnamed, always-present narrator acts as a medium or a filter operating in and out of the lives of the characters, witnessing, assuming, hypothesizing, sympathizing, and apostrophizing as in a confessional novel. Manzini breaks the traditional linear plot in favor of a layered composition in which the narrator controls the flow of the narrative: "È bella la lettera nella quale Clementina mi fa questo racconto; ma io non posso riferirla uguale. Trascriverò soltanto quello che a me e a te, lettore, piace, purtroppo, di più" (Lovely is the letter where Clementina tells me this story; but I cannot retell it as it is. I will only transcribe those parts that you, the reader, and I admittedly like most).

Even in her first novel Manzini shows technical and linguistic sophistication as she strives to create a prose more attuned to an interior rhythm than to an exterior logical organization of the facts. Her stylistic tools include syntactic displacement, isolation through punctuation, inversions, interruptions, and suspensions. Manzini's use of synesthesia, oxymoron, analogy, and metaphor gives her prose a distinctive lyrical flow and a sense of complete correspondence between characters and their environment, as in the description of Clementina's living room:

Le somigliava veramente il salotto disadorno, e pareva educata dalla sua malinconia l'iridescenze distratta ed insocievole di due vasi di Murano sulla credenza, e sapevano del suo monologo le sedie con lo schienale al muro, e c'era lei, tutta lei, in quel respiro di cose riposte, protette dall'ombra. M'accoglieva, *l'assente,* con una pacatezza di pantofola.

(It really looked like her the unadorned living room; and the distracted, and asocial iridescence of two Murano vases on the top of the china closet seemed nurtured by her melancholy, and the chairs against the wall knew of her monologue, and there she was, all of her, in that breath of things put away, protected by the shadow. *The absentee* was welcoming me, with the quietness of a slipper.)

Manzini's early work suggests some of the stylistic refinement of the prose and poetry of the first decades of this century: Gabriele D'Annunzio's decadence, vitalism, and linguistic exaltation as well as the prosaic melancholy of the *crepuscolari* (twilight) writers. Manzini artfully exploits the possibilities of her prose, searching for linguistic shades much like the visual fragmentism and descriptive impressionism practiced by Tuscan writers and poets of her time, such as Federigo Tozzi, Cecchi, and Ardengo Soffici. But alongside her practice of the prosa d'arte, Manzini shows a deep interest in the structural aspects of the novel, searching from her first novel for narrative modes that allow a free flowing of points of view and emotions between characters and author.

In 1929, a year after the publication of *Tempo innamorato,* Manzini married the Florentine journalist Bruno Fallaci, but the marriage did not last long. That same year the writer published her first collection of stories, *Incontro col falco* (Encounter with the Hawk). For more than a decade Manzini would write stories rich in detailed observation, shifting her attention from human beings to the representation of the animal world. Her failed marriage, a reminder of the unhappy marital experience of her parents, was probably responsible in no small measure for Manzini's hesitation to represent human relations. Her several collections of stories during the 1930s and early 1940s indicate that it was a period of gathering narrative materials, of testing new possibilities to interpret reality, especially the vegetable and animal worlds. Her innovative writing style became more assured and bold as Manzini brought her self-reflectiveness about her work into her narration. As in *Tempo innamorato,* the narrating voices in her stories blur the line between subjective and objective reality.

Manzini had a lifelong interest in and love for animals. In 1932 she published *Boscovivo* (Woods Alive), a collection of sixteen stories, five of which have animals as protagonists. In the preface to the collection *Animali sacri e profani* (Sacred and Profane Animals, 1953), which included some of her early stories, she talks about the recurrence of certain themes in her fiction and how sometimes an author needs to abandon such interests either temporarily or permanently. She confesses, though, that she cannot stay away from her interest in animals: "Questo lo salvo e lo salverò finchè campo. È un regno. Non si può passarsela d'un regno" (This I shall save it as

long as I live. It is a Kingdom. And one cannot renounce to a Kingdom).

Manzini's interpretation and exploration of the poetry that she saw in animals place her among the best writers about the animal world in the twentieth century. Animals combine innocence and mystery, an inscrutable world that Manzini yearned to penetrate. In the story "Allo zoo di Roma" (At Rome's Zoo) Manzini reflects:

Ma ogni animale è una forma e un significato splendidamente raggiunto. Ed io penso che i loro visi siano così ben modellati dal di dentro a causa delle parole cui hanno inutilmente anelato: tanti segreti mentenuti, tanti ragionamenti mai articolati. È nell'intensità della loro espressione che oguno di noi trova uno speciale silenzio, uno speciale spazio: quello che rese sacro il gatto, o la tigre, o il serpente, o il pavone.

(But every animal is a splendidly accomplished form and meaning. And I believe that their faces are so well fashioned from the inside because of the words they have yearned for in vain: so many secrets kept, so much reasoning never articulated. It is in the intensity of their expression that each of us finds a special silence, a special space: that quality which made the cat, the tiger, or the serpent, or the peacock sacred animals.)

In 1933 Manzini moved to Rome, and though she made her home and lived the rest of her life in that city, she would always miss her beloved Tuscany, especially the gentle lines of the Tuscan countryside. In Rome she began a lifelong artistic and sentimental relationship with the critic Enrico Falqui, grounded in their common passion for literature. Falqui had already published two anthologies, *Scrittori nuovi* (New Writers, 1930) and *La palla al balzo* (The Jumping Ball, 1932), that proved him to be a timely and acute reader of contemporary Italian literature. Manzini experienced a renewed vigor and enthusiasm for her work as she intensified her search for new narrative forms.

In 1945 Manzini became the editor of the international journal *Prosa,* a companion journal to *Poesia,* which was directed by Falqui. *Prosa* became an open forum for many European and American writers. The experience of war had changed the social, historical, and economic landscape of the world, especially of Europe, and artists and intellectuals were facing a new set of questions regarding the validity and role of literature. In a 1946 issue of *Prosa,* Manzini organized a debate titled "La struttura e la forma stessa del romanzo sono in continua evoluzione" (The Structure and Form of the Novel in Continuous Evolution), which included articles by André Malraux, Marcel Arland, Paul Valéry, and Leon Bopp, among others.

Also in the year 1945 Manzini published her second novel, *Lettera all'editore* (Letter to the Publisher). The book was well received and immediately gave rise to considerable critical acclaim and debates about its audacious structure as a work in progress. The novel is structured around two narratives: one is a story about a couple's tormented relationship that the author is writing; the other is a series of letters she sends to her publisher addressing the artistic and personal crisis she is facing in the process of writing her novel.

In her letters the author views her novel as an objective fact, but she also talks about her developing story from within the work. She discusses her vision of and theories about the novel as well as her emotional involvement and interaction with her characters: "Accompagnare i miei personaggi non so più: li esorto, li trattengo: da che la mia vita, riflettendo il loro destino, me li traveste da oracoli" (I cannot escort my characters any longer: I exhort them, I hold them back: since my life which I see reflected in their destiny disguises them as oracles). Her idea of the novel has changed, she confesses to her publisher, and she can no longer see it as a closed form:

È anche l'idea del romanzo che si è modificata in me. Sono giunta perfino a rinunciare ad argomenti salienti. Se ripenso al lavoro che anni fa avevo vivacemente affrontato, al movimento uniforme con cui si svolgeva, al mio proposito di far convergere l'interesse essenziale nella soluzione della storia, non riesco a ravvisarmi in quello che io fui.

(It is also the idea of the novel that has undergone a change in me. I have even reached the point of doing away with salient themes. If I think back at the work that years ago I embraced with enthusiasm, at its uniform development, at my intention to converge the essential interest of the story with its resolution, I cannot recognize myself in what I was.)

As the planes of fiction, autobiography, and self-consciousness intersect, the message of *Lettera all'editore* is that the novel, as a fictive construction and an attempt to represent reality, far from being a codified form, is always, at least potentially, in the making. Manzini's voice is that of the lyrical, introspective narrator who overtly claims a space and a relationship within the representation; her articulate presence legitimizes her involvement in the work. As a manifesto of Manzini's poetics, this novel assembles all the thematic and stylistic elements of her previous works in a context where they can be seen at work in the developing story while simultaneously being questioned by the narrator-

Caricature of Manzini by Mario Vellani Marchi (Bagutta Collection)

author. The story of the couple's relationship, as originally conceived and abandoned by the author, is carried on through the device of the letters sent to the publisher—and regularly interrupted by the writer's hesitations, crises, and moments of illumination. Though a possible tragic conclusion is hinted, the story never reaches an end, further suggesting the open-endedness of the novel.

The impact of *Lettera all'editore* on Manzini's career and on the development of the Italian novel is comparable to that of Luigi Pirandello's *Sei personaggi in cerca d'autore* (Six Characters in Search of an Author, 1921). Critics of the time, undecided whether to consider the book, as Cecchi remarked, "una vera e propria opera d'arte o un superbo esercizio di stile e di volontà" (a legitimate work of art or a superb exercise in style and will), immediately recognized it as the culmination of a major phase of Manzini's art and a turning point in the conceptualization of the novel. Cecchi suggested that "il romanzo della Manzini dovrà essere attentamente studiato, da quanti sul serio s'interessano ai problemi della letteratura contemporanea" (Manzini's novel must be closely studied by those who are seriously interested in the problematics of contemporary literature).

Whereas in *Lettera all'editore* Manzini makes her poetics the structuring theme, her next novel, *La sparviera* (The Sparrow Hawk, 1956), presents a less exotic design. The novel earned Manzini the Premio Viareggio, which she shared with Carlo Levi. In the decade between the two novels, Manzini had published collections of short stories and novellas in which her attention had progressively shifted toward a symbolic and allusive interpretation of reality. In *La sparviera* she intensifies the characters' process of self-exploration by introducing epiphanic moments. She also gives her narration a more cohesive and consistent structure in order to balance, as she points out in *Forte come un leone* (Strong as a Lion, 1944), the lyric fragment—the privileged, purely descriptive moment of the prosa d'arte—with "un senso di superiore geometria e architettura" (a sense of superior geometry and architecture).

Manzini constructs her novel entirely around an elusive and mysterious illness in the protagonist's life: a persistent cough, contracted when he was a young boy, to which he gives a name, "la sparviera" (the sparrow hawk). Born out of a nightmare in a child's mind, the illness, through the perception of the child and later the grown man, gradually acquires both physical and metaphysical connotations. When the young protagonist meets a little girl who is eager to understand and interpret the meaning of his illness, a lifelong dialogue starts between the two. Through their private talks the two discover and define various qualities of the ineffable sparviera. In the process they recognize, as they become adults, their passionate love for each other and an awareness of being endowed with a heightened perception of reality.

Each chapter of the novel represents an epoch of the protagonist's life. Through a masterful use of linguistic allusiveness and displacement of scenes and dialogues, Manzini maintains throughout the narration a continuous atmosphere of suspense and mystery as well as a sense of timelessness. The extent of the symbolic interplay between the protagonist and his illness, as a process of self-creation, is finally revealed by the man before his death as he is afflicted by a last attack of his sparviera: "Questa malattia, non parlo della polmonite, tutta la mia malattia, è stata una specie di costruzione, che poi mi ha imprigionato. . . . Sì, obbrobriosa, eppure condizione per mettere una certa luminosa frenesia al centro di ogni azione; il prezzo d'una vita immaginativa" (This sickness, I am not talking about the pneumonia, all my sickness, has been a sort of construction, that eventually has imprisoned me. . . . I felt it as something shameful, dreadful and yet a condition for putting a certain luminous frenzy at the center of each action: the price of an imaginative life).

Manzini's treatment of illness in the novel stems from her personal experience with a lung ailment that affected her health for years, from around the time of her father's death in 1925 until her death. Her condition of "non salute" (non-health), as she puts it in the autobiographical piece "Diciamo 'mestiere'" (Trade) that was collected in *Album di ritratti,* elicited in the writer a meditation on illness that points to the sensorial and intellectual ramifications found in D'Annunzio, Thomas Mann, and Proust.

In the works that follow *La sparviera,* Manzini favors always deeper introspective analyses of characters and brings her language to higher levels of abstraction and analogy. At the time, however, as an effort to clear literature from Fascist mystification and propaganda, the ascendant poetics of Neorealism in cinema and narrative advocated a committed representation of social reality in its immediacy. Manzini did not respond to the militant program of the neorealists, for she believed strongly in the interpretative function of literature. In an interview with Carlo Bo, in his *Inchiesta sul Neorealismo* (Inquiry about Neorealism), Manzini declared that the writer's function is to interpret reality in a way that, once written, it becomes clearer, more transparent, "più viva" (more alive) than its confused state in accidental events. The clarity Manzini talks about is not the neorealistic nudity of a social document; it is, rather, the result of "un'attenzione docile e ardente" (a lively and patient attention) that enables the writer to look beyond mere happenings to unveil the absolute essence of reality.

In Manzini's view, the novel cannot be the vehicle of a political or social ideology; its aim is to express the inner world, the possibility of a deeper connection with reality. Even in her 1971 novel, *Ritratto in piedi,* where she had the perfect opportunity to write a historical novel dominated by the figure of her father—an anarchist and victim of Fascism—she did not allow history to become her focus. History, especially Italy's Fascism, is always filtered through the characters' personal experience—in this case Manzini and her father—and so is humanized and understood through the private dimension.

Perhaps no other work by Manzini expresses more completely her passionate, almost missionary view of literature than *Ritratto in piedi,* which won the Premio Campiello, one of Italy's most prestigious literary prizes. Most critics consider it Manzini's most accomplished and ambitious work as well as one of the most interesting Italian post–World War II novels. Drawing on her memory Manzini with consummate technical skill combines autobiography with her penchants for symbolically representing reality and self-reflectively commenting on her process of writing. The result is a further demonstration of the flexibility of the novel in Manzini's hands.

A project that haunted her for years, *Ritratto in piedi* is Manzini's tribute to the memory of her father. Giuseppe Manzini was born to wealth—in the preface she asserts that her father's family lineage could be traced back to the fifteenth century—but he divested himself of his possessions to become totally committed to his faith in an anarchic society, free of inequalities, injustices, and privileges. Rejected by his wife's family as irresponsible, he lived alone in a rented room repairing and selling watches, separated from the wife and daughter he dearly loved. After being chased by the fascist Blackshirts, he died of a heart attack in political confinement.

There is an ongoing tension between the memories of the daughter-author-narrator and their actualization in the narration of the novel, where the memories are questioned and acquire refractions, connections, and a deeper emotional and intellectual impact. This effect is accomplished through frequent shifts to dialogues between the narrator and her father. In these dialogues Manzini continually apostrophizes her father, asking for his participation and guidance, as the past is revised and corrected:

> Ha le spalle larghe, il babbo. È sempre stato dritto. Tiene, al solito, la testa alta. Un atteggiamento non di alterigia; ma di sfida, sì. Lealtà e chiarezza dichiarate esponendo la fronte spaziosa. . . . "Vedi, nemmeno la morte mi ha scoraggiato. Nemmeno la morte può qualcosa, contro ciò che abbiamo in noi d'immortale, idea e sentimento. Non la senti, Giannina, la grandezza d'essere obbligati a esistere, a essere se stessi eternamente, legati, legati da qualcosa che sfugge all'amore e all'odio."

> (Dad has wide shoulders. He is always erect. As usual, he keeps his head high. His demeanor is not haughty but challenging. Loyalty and clarity appear on his spacious forehead. . . . "See, not even death has discouraged me. Not even death can do anything against what we have in us which is immortal—ideas and sentiments. Don't you hear, Giannina, the greatness of having to exist, of being eternally ourselves, bound, bound by something that eludes love and hate.")

Manzini was determined to re-create in her language her father's life and words as action. She wrote to present both the objective "full size" portrait of her father and to free her memory from the remorse of not having been close to him during the last years of his life. The novel allows father and

Cover for a 1995 edition of Manzini's 1971 novel, in which the narrator speaks directly to her dead father

daughter to find understanding and love, as is clear in the last imaginary dialogue between the two:

> Vedi, finiamo sempre col parlare della stessa cosa; volevo dire: della nostra idea: e che è viva lo dimostra il fatto che continua a nutrirci. In ogni apparizione un emblema. Tutto diventa allusione, o conferma, o promessa. Le cose, a volte, sono un velo: anche le parole, anche le persone. Di certe trasparenze, io e te siamo assai esperti, vero?

> (You see, we always end up talking about the same thing; I meant to say our idea: and that it is alive is demonstrated by the fact that it keeps nurturing us. In every apparition, an emblem. Everything becomes allusion, confirmation, or promise. Things, at times, are a veil: even words, even people. You and I are expert of these transparencies, aren't we?)

Manzini experienced the success of *Ritratto in piedi* in the last years of her life, when her chronic asthmatic and lung condition had worsened considerably. She kept a strong facade and was determined to give a symbolic closure to her prolific writing career with the publication in 1973, a year before she died, of her last work, *Sulla soglia* (On the Threshold). The book's four stories are centered around the theme of death; they are explorations and meditations to find in death another possible meaning of life. In this last work Manzini takes to another level the thematic and linguistic experimentation that so characterizes her work, setting the last challenge for her art to represent a hyperreality along the blurry line of life and death. "Che cos'è l'arte, per me, se non uno strumento per cercare vita dietro la vita?" (What also is art to me if not an instrument to search for life behind life?), says the protagonist of "Autoritratto involontario" (An Involuntary Self-Portrait), the first story in the book.

The title story, the last in the collection, is a long novella about Manzini's imagined encounter with her dead mother in an emblematic situation bordering life and death, the threshold. The dialogue takes place in the wagon of a one-way train where the author-narrator meets her mother and five other passengers: an old man, a musician, an actor, a dignified horse breeder, and a little girl. The writer uses these emblematic characters as a window of observation on her mother's character. The mother's subtle reactions reveal her to be a beautiful, sensitive woman. Although she was separated from her idealistic husband, she continued to love him and always remained faithful. As in the previous novel, daughter and parent recall the past and bring it into the present in order to relive and confront it.

The mother's fundamental ambiguity is posited as a contrast to the father's integrity and fully lived life. But this bias—what Anna Nozzoli calls Manzini's "adoption of a decisively male optics"—does not result in a lessening of interest in the mother or invalidate her. While the father figure acquires a heroic solemnity, the mother's personality becomes more convincing and human as she oscillates between love and admiration for her husband and fear and insecurity about life.

In this autobiographical novella Manzini wants to rediscover her mother, to free her from the author's confused and conflicted memory of her as well as from the literary persona she had established for her in other works. She insists to another passenger on the train that words are not irrevocable, that they can resurrect as well as cause death:

Ma l'arte dello scrittore consiste proprio, a volte, nel vincere e nello sfruttare quello che lei chiama implaca-

bilità. Può bastare un effetto di opposizione a farle risplendere, le parole, come un gioiello mosso in un raggio di sole; a cavarne una specie di fruttuoso sbaraglio.

(But a writer's art sometimes consists precisely in winning, or in taking advantage of what you call implacability. A movement of opposition is sufficient to make words shine, like a jewel moving in the sun; to extract from words a sort of fruitful risk.)

As with her father in *Ritratto in piedi,* Manzini discovers the genetic and spiritual link with her mother in her own writing: "Come me, amavi le cose che ti aiutavano a esprimerti; a somigliare una tua immagine di te. Quelle cose erano ciò che per me sono le parole" (Like me, you loved the things that helped you to express yourself; to look like an image of yourself. Those things were for you what words are for me).

By devoting her last two books to the memory of her parents and re-creating their lives, Manzini summed up her life as daughter and writer, reiterating her effort to integrate life and art. In *Lettera all'editore* Manzini had formalized the autobiographical characteristic of her writing as the guideline of her poetics: "Il vero Romanzo per me consiste nei punti di concomitanza dell'intreccio con alcuni episodi della mia vita" (For me, the true Novel lies in the meeting point between the plot and some episodes of my life). Writing about her last visits with Manzini in Marco Forti's *Gianna Manzini tra letteratura e vita* (1985), Mimma Mondadori remembered the refinement she displayed even in her illness: "Poteva avere le cannucce dell'ossigeno nelle narici e le bombole di ossigeno a fianco, era sempre stupendamente vestita, con i suoi gioielli indosso e truccata. Una donna spinta da una forza straordinaria, una donna che veramente ha lottato tutta la vita per vivere" (She could have had the oxygen tubes in her nose and the oxygen tank next to her, but she was always stupendously dressed, wearing her jewels and makeup. A woman driven by an extraordinary inner strength, a woman who truly fought all her life to live). Manzini died in Rome on 31 August 1974, surviving only by a few months her beloved companion, Enrico Falqui.

References:

Emilio Cecchi, "Gianna Manzini," in *Storia della letteratura italiana: il Novecento,* volume 9, edited by Cecchi and Natalino Sapegno (Milan: Garzanti, 1969), pp. 683–687;

Cecchi, *Letteratura italiana del Novecento,* volume 2 (Milan: Mondadori, 1972), pp. 919–928;

Gianfranco Contini, "Gianna Manzini," in his *La letteratura italiana Otto-Novecento* (Florence: Sansoni, 1974), pp. 361–362;

Lia Fava-Guzzetta, *Gianna Manzini* (Florence: La Nuova Italia, 1974);

La fiera letteraria, special issue on Manzini, 19 (6 May 1956);

Marco Forti, "Gianna Manzini," in *Prosatori e narratori del Novecento italiano,* edited by Forti (Milan: Mursia, 1984), pp. 111–121;

Forti, ed., *Gianna Manzini tra letteratura e vita* (Milan: Mondadori, 1985);

Giovanna Miceli-Jeffries, "Gianna Manzini's Poetics of Verbal Visualization," in *Contemporary Women Writers in Italy,* edited by Santo Aricò (Boston: University of Massachusetts Press, 1990), pp. 90–106;

Anna Nozzoli, "Gianna Manzini: metafora e realtà del personaggio femminile," in her *Tabù e coscienza: La condizione femminile nella letteratura italiana del Novecento* (Florence: La Nuova Italia, 1978), pp. 65–84;

Enzo Panareo, *Gianna Manzini* (Milan: Mursia, 1977);

Maria Assunta Parsani and Neria De Giovanni, *Femminile a confronto: Tre realtà della narrativa italiano contemporena: Alba De Céspedes, Fausta Cialente, Gianna Manzini* (Manduria: Lacaita, 1984);

Ornella Sobrero, "Gianna Manzini," in *Novecento. I contemporanei,* volume 6 (Milan: Marzorati, 1979), pp. 5469–5495;

Ferruccio Ulivi, "G. Manzini fra prosa e racconto," in *Novecento. I contemporanei,* volume 6, pp. 5495–5501;

Ulivi, "Narrativa emozionale di G. Manzini," in *Novecento. I contemporanei,* volume 8, pp. 7515–7526;

Ulivi, "'La prosa d'arte' nel Novecento," in *Novecento. I contemporanei,* volume 5, pp. 3922–3938.

Lucio Mastronardi
(28 June 1930 – 29 April 1979)

Augustus Pallotta
Syracuse University

BOOKS: *Il calzolaio di Vigevano* (Turin: Einaudi, 1962);

Il maestro di Vigevano (Turin: Einaudi, 1962);

Il meridionale di Vigevano (Turin: Einaudi, 1964);

A casa tua ridono (Milan: Rizzoli, 1971);

L'assicuratore (Milan: Rizzoli, 1975);

Quattro racconti (Pavia: Aurora Edizioni, 1981).

Collection: *Gente di Vigevano* (Milan: Nuova Accademia, 1977).

OTHER: *Racconti,* in *Per Mastronardi,* edited by Maria Antonietta Grignani (Florence: La Nuova Italia, 1983).

Lucio Mastronardi's work is tied to a significant, albeit short-lived, effort in postwar Italian fiction that relied on linguistic experimentation to underscore new social realities, including rapid industrialization, materialism, internal immigration, and the problem of a large underclass found mostly in southern Italy. Unlike other avant-garde writers whose experimentations with language were motivated by a desire for formal innovation, Mastronardi was moved, as Gianfranco Contini points out, by his angst about social conditions and his deeply felt need for social change.

The forces that guided Mastronardi's direction as a writer can be identified with Antonio Gramsci, the influential Marxist intellectual who was arrested by the Fascists and died in prison in 1937, and Carlo Emilio Gadda, whose work combines standard Italian and the dialects of various Italian regions. Gramsci saw language as a sociopolitical tool that committed Marxist writers should use to broaden self-consciousness within the proletarian class. Gadda's linguistic experimentation in his detective novel, *Quer pasticciaccio brutto de Via Merulana* (1957; translated as *That Awful Mess in Via Merulana,* 1965), laid bare, in Pier Paolo Pasolini's words, "l'urto violentissimo tra una realtà oggettiva . . . e una realtà soggettiva incompatibili ideologicamente e stilisticamente" (the violent clash between objective and subjective reality that proved ideologically

Lucio Mastronardi

and stylistically incompatible). In his own *Ragazzi di vita* (1955; translated as *The Ragazzi,* 1968) Pasolini had made generous use of the Roman dialect to identify the proletarian condition of his youthful protagonists. For Mastronardi as well as for Gadda, the clash between subjectivity and objectivity becomes a metaphor for the tension present in society.

Mastronardi was born in 1930 in Vigevano, a provincial town some thirty miles southwest of Milan known for its thriving shoe industry. His father, a man of progressive ideas, was a teacher from the southern region of Abruzzi. He settled in Vigevano and married a local schoolteacher. Their financial resources being quite modest, they lived in a tenement house inhabited by artisans and factory workers. Mastronardi followed in his parents' footsteps and became a teacher. To gain experience and to improve his chances of finding employment, he taught inmates in the local prison. He also taught evening classes in nearby villages before he was assigned to an elementary school in Vigevano.

In time Mastronardi grew disenchanted with teaching. He included in his best novel, *Il maestro di Vigevano* (The Schoolteacher of Vigevano, 1962), a scathing, satiric account of his experiences in the classroom. In a letter to Elio Vittorini in 1955 he writes that he became interested in literature at the age of fifteen. Among his favorite authors he cites Giovanni Verga, Luigi Pirandello, Ernest Hemingway, and John Steinbeck. He began to write in his early twenties and at the age of twenty-five he published four short stories in the town's weekly newspaper, *Il corriere di Vigevano*. What stands out in these youthful efforts is a simple, low-key narrative coupled with the presence of humble people much like his neighbors. Significantly, the stories are free of linguistic experimentation, which proved to be the most important element in Mastronardi's first novel. (In 1983 these stories, along with ten stories later published in *L'Unità,* were included in a collection of essays on the author, *Per Mastronardi,* edited by Maria Antonietta Grignani.)

Il calzolaio di Vigevano (The Shoemaker of Vigevano, 1962) originally was published in 1959 in *Il menabò di letteratura,* a socially engaged review published by Vittorini. An established writer and a Marxist, Vittorini was interested in exploring the impact of rapid industrialization on Italian society and the forms literature could assume to address this problem. Language, he felt, afforded fiction the potential to mirror the profound changes in social behavior that would inevitably arise from the industrial development of the postwar era. In the fourth issue of *Il menabò* he wrote:

> La narrativa che concentra sul piano del linguaggio tutt' intero il peso delle proprie responsabilità verso le cose risulta a sua volta, oggi, più vicina ad assumere un significato storicamente attivo di ogni narrativa che abbordi le cose nella generalità.

> (The narrative that places on language the full weight of its responsibilities toward different matters today proves to be closer to assuming historically active mean-

ing than any other narrative that approaches matters in a broader sense.)

Mastronardi's novel mirrors these concerns, and Vittorini accepted it with little hesitation. Indeed, in the introductory remarks to the first issue of *Il menabò,* which included Mastronardi's novel, Vittorini singled out the salient theme of the work, "la 'decadenza' dell'individuo come soggetto di autodeterminazione ideologica e insomma come eroe" (the decline of the individual as a subject of self-determination and, essentially, his decline as a hero).

Il calzolaio di Vigevano was published in book form by Einaudi in 1962. As the title indicates, the novel is set in Vigevano. Much like the city of Ferrara in Giorgio Bassani's work, Vigevano is the focal point for all of Mastronardi's writing. Through the reiterated and manifold views of its physical setting and the often satiric parade of its fictional characters, Vigevano comes to represent the soul of Mastronardi's work. However, whereas Bassani's kinship to Ferrara unfolds in emotionally ambivalent terms firmly anchored to the city's Jewish community, Mastronardi's uneasy relationship to Vigevano is marked by constant alienation. Both writers, though, confront questions that are deeply human and of substantial sociological interest.

Rinaldo Rinaldi, the author of a long essay on Mastronardi, has called *Il calzolaio di Vigevano* "un racconto che non racconta nulla" (a tale that does not tell anything). In some ways this is not an exaggeration, for Mastronardi's characters as a rule are engaged in physical labor and react to machines more often than they interact with others; his story is one of personal identity, rather than an interactive or communal story, as is the case with the traditional novel. *Il calzolaio di Vigevano* revolves around the largely uneventful life of a married couple, Mario and Luisa, who share with hundreds of others in Vigevano their work as part of the shoe industry and their inordinate desire to get ahead in life. They want to open a small shoe factory and one day become rich enough to build a villa on the outskirts of the town.

The action is set during World War II: Italy is under Fascist rule and at war with Greece and Albania. The military demand for shoes is considerable, and business is booming in Vigevano. Mario and Luisa have become successful entrepreneurs when they decide to join Pelagatta, the owner of a much larger firm. Before Mario has had a taste of success, he is drafted and sent to the front in Albania. During his absence, Luisa betrays Mario with Netto, a trusted family friend. Pelagatta severs his business

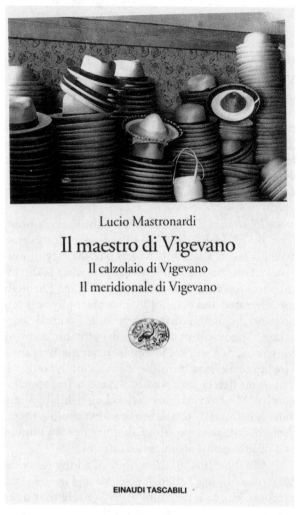

Lucio Mastronardi

Il maestro di Vigevano

Il calzolaio di Vigevano
Il meridionale di Vigevano

EINAUDI TASCABILI

*Cover for a 1994 edition of Mastronardi's second novel, in
which a teacher writes a satirical essay on the language and
practices of Italian schools*

ties with Luisa and starts a successful but short-lived
partnership with Netto. At the end of the war Mario
returns to Vigevano and forgives his wife, and the
two, having lost their financial assets, start anew
with a small shoe shop, dreaming of repeating their
earlier success.

The novel exemplifies what will become the
hallmark of Mastronardi's treatment of characters.
Sketched rather than fully painted, Mario and Luisa
bring to mind Dante's diaphanous characters: they
define themselves through speech, leaving readers
with a disquieting sense of incompleteness. As
Rinaldi points out, money is the true protagonist of
the novel: "Uomini e merci diventano semplice-
mente dei mezzi per raggiungere il fine ultimo, il denaro" (People and merchandise become simply a
means of reaching the ultimate objective, money).
The novel is structured much like a play, with long
streams of dialogue, but unlike a play, verbal interaction dwells on external, physical matters, hardly
ever on feelings, emotions, or ideas. Introspection is
systematically avoided.

The other distinctive feature of *Il calzolaio di Vigevano* is the use of the dialect spoken in the town.
The characters express themselves in exactly the
same way that the people speak to each other in the
street, giving the novel a strong regional flavor. Indeed, the prevalence of dialect makes the work difficult to understand for readers who are not from
Lombardy.

Il maestro di Vigevano, Mastronardi's most successful novel, is a much more ambitious effort than
his first work. Its success lies in a broader view of society, coupled with the author's more sophisticated
understanding of the introspective and intellectual
uses of fiction than is evident in *Il calzolaio di Vigevano*. Mastronardi avails himself of a far richer narrative technique that includes parody, satire, the
surreal, and the grotesque in conveying a complex
and troublesome view of Italian society that goes beyond the town of Vigevano. The central character
and narrator of the story is a schoolteacher approaching middle age, Antonio Mombelli. Disenchanted with his professional and family life, he
leads a sterile, aimless life that includes absurd
erotic fixations and surrealistic daydreams. His
wife, Ada, is venal and materialistic, a woman
whose main interest in life is to climb the social ladder. When their son dies, the marriage, which suffered from strains, suspicions, and mutual ill feelings, comes to an end.

The book is divided not into chapters but into
three diary-like parts, which the narrator uses skillfully to depict Mombelli's daily routine and the
dreary social atmosphere of his hometown, with its
monotonous life and puppetlike parade of familiar
faces. Much of Mastronardi's caustic irony is directed at the appearance-conscious decorum of the
middle class, which is symbolically likened to tar
smears ("catrame"), underscoring both its ugliness
and its permanence. Part of Mombelli's predicament
is the difficulty he experiences shedding the pseudo-
dignity of his upbringing and his perceived need to
defuse the tension with his status-conscious wife.
His struggles leave him spiritually weary. "Mi ac-
corgo," remarks the narrator at one point, "che la
mia vita è tutto un seguito di ore bruciate, di tempo
perduto. Ma che devo fare, mi domando" (I realize
that my life is a chain of wasted hours, of wasted
time. But, what can I do? I ask myself).

Mombelli needs a spiritual refuge, and he finds
it in the countryside, in a secluded spot of the Ticino
valley not far from Vigevano. Left to his thoughts,

Mombelli's ill-concealed fear and insecurity is manifest. He sees himself as a stranger or misfit in a community that judges individual worth by the ability to compete and succeed:

> E mi penso che sono come un naufrago attaccato nel mare della vita a uno scoglio e rimango attaccato mentre attorno a me tutt' un'umanità nuota, cerca di raggiungere scogli più comodi. . . . Ed io rimango aggrappato allo scoglio, fermo. Ho paura di annegare in questo mare-vita dove ogni giorno tanti ne annegano e tanti ne nascono. La parola paura mi suona male. Dico: non è paura; è prudenza. Questa mi suona meglio, è accettabile.

> (And I think of myself as a shipwrecked person in the sea of life holding on to a reef; I hold on while countless other people try to reach more secure reefs. . . . And I remain motionless, clinging to my reef. I am afraid of drowning in this sea life where every day as many drown as are born. I don't like the word fear. I say: it is not fear; it is prudence. That word sounds better; it is acceptable.)

The depth of Mombelli's existential anguish is intensified by his words' affinity with the image of the lost, shipwrecked individual found in "L'infinito" (1819), a famous poem by Giacomo Leopardi, the early-nineteenth-century writer who gave perhaps the most incisive expression to the perception of life as constant suffering.

Implicit in Mombelli's insight is the recognition of his own unwillingness—born of deep insecurity and the fear of failing—to enter the race for success and material rewards, to swim with competitors. The hallmarks of capitalism—competition, materialism, the obsession with money and wealth—are present and forcefully contested in all of Mastronardi's works. This ever-present drive is voiced by a character in *Il calzolaio di Vigevano:* "Gira la manopola, e la musica è sempre la stessa: danè fanno danè" (Turn the dial and the music is always the same: money makes money). The money-making activity carried out with alacrity by the shoe merchants in *Il calzolaio di Vigevano* is toned down in Mastronardi's second novel, but the entrepreneurial fever affecting the townspeople does not spare Mombelli. He decides to quit teaching and join his wife and brother-in-law in a shoemaking partnership at their home. Yet Mastronardi's thrust is at once ironic and despairing, for what Mombelli perceives as the dehumanizing force of capitalism leads to the discovery that his newly won identity and his success as an entrepreneur make him feel no less useless than he had felt as a schoolteacher.

While the linguistic experimentation of *Il calzolaio di Vigevano* takes the form of literal imitation of dialect speakers, the dialect of the town is nearly absent in *Il maestro di Vigevano,* replaced by an acceptably literate Italian, which is also mimetic in that it reflects the language used by schoolteachers. The narrative shifts to a different linguistic register upon Mombelli's decision to quit shoemaking and return to teaching. To do so, he has to retake a competitive examination that requires an essay on the Italian language taught in public schools. This occasion allows Mastronardi to create a self-reflecting instrument of parody and thus ridicule the ossified bureaucratic apparatus of the Italian school system, its cynical and often clownish faculty, and its backward pedagogical tenets.

Mombelli feels obliged to reenter the "circus" because at his age he could not find any other employment. Moreover, he remains steadfast in his conviction that not only his occupation but also life itself can only be understood as an expression of the absurd. Indeed, toying with the idea of the absurd, the narrator introduces the ludic function of language as an effective tool of social satire. In this vein, writing becomes "una frase fatta che ci rimbalziamo dall'uno all'altro collega, come i giocatori di calcio si rimbalzano il pallone" (a ready-made phrase that one instructor passes to another like soccer players passing a ball). In other instances Mombelli's surreal imagination leads him to envision an Orwellian world dominated by the triumph of numbers over words: "Le parole non possono! Bisogna abolire le parole! Noi ci dobbiamo intendere coi numeri. I numeri sostituiranno le parole" (Words cannot do it! We must do away with words! We must communicate with numbers. Numbers will replace words).

From 1962 to 1966 Mastronardi continued to write short stories, ten in all, which he submitted to a single publication: *L'Unità,* the official organ of the Italian Communist Party (renamed the Democratic Party of the Left in 1992). Like many idealistic youths of his generation, Mastronardi looked to a Marxist party as the only viable political structure capable of creating an egalitarian society. He marched with factory workers at demonstrations and was with them at the picket line when they went on strike. But like most writers, Mastronardi soon became disenchanted with the Communist Party: as early as January 1956, in a letter to Vittorini that was published in the first issue of *Il menabò* in 1959, he calls himself a former communist, though he remained sympathetic to Marxist thought.

In these *L'Unità* stories Mastronardi brushes Marxist dialectics aside in favor of a faithful representation of different social groups, such as struggling entrepreneurs, successful businessmen, and schoolteachers, as well as factory workers. The stories are not held together by the force of leftist ideology but by Mastronardi's deep sense of humanity and resourceful comedy. There are characters such as the former domestic worker Girini, who has gone from rags to riches and boasts about the seven luxury automobiles (one for every day of the week) parked in the garage of his villa and the two chamber pots of pure gold (one for him, one for his wife). As to the dowry promised to his daughter, he says to interested parties: "Ricordatevi che mia figlia vale un milione al pelo. Ed è molto pelosa!" (Remember that my daughter is worth one million liras for every hair on her body. And she is very hairy!).

Mastronardi notes a pragmatic accommodation between Marxism and Italian culture even among schoolteachers. In the story "Io, un ribelle" (I Am a Rebel) one character explains his peculiar views of Marxism:

> Una volta dissi a un maestro laico socialdemocratico:–Tu sei un marxista!–Quello diventò bianco, disse:–Io sono anche marxista–e sottolineava l'anche–pero sono cattolico. Io, prima di iscrivermi alla sezione socialdemocratica di Vigevano, ho dichiarato che io credo. Perchè io sono credente. Ho chiesto al caposezione del partito: rispettate voi il mio credo? Il caposezione mi ha risposto: certo. Perchè anch'io credo come te, compagno, nella nostra religione. Allora io mi sono iscritto. Io dal marxismo accetto solo qualche idea, per quel che mi riguarda l'economia, perchè io sono cattolico, e cattolico praticante.

> (Once I said to a sociodemocratic teacher:–You are a Marxist!–He turned pale and said:–I am also a Marxist–placing the stress on also–but I am Catholic. Before joining the local branch of the party in Vigevano, I asked the party official: Do you respect my religious beliefs? He answered: Certainly. Because I too believe in our religion, comrade. Then I joined the party. From Marxism I draw and accept a few ideas that pertain to economics; other than that, I am Catholic, a practicing Catholic.)

"Racconto stracciato" (The Discarded Story) is the only story–actually more a sketch of a story–in which Mastronardi refuses the role of fiction writer and takes a strong position as a committed intellectual. Published in *L'Unità* on 4 March 1965, the story begins with this line: "Volevo pubblicare un racconto tratto dalla realtà" (I wanted to publish a short story drawn from real life) and goes on to say that the story deals with the death of a young factory worker from the effects of benzene, officially the thirteenth such death in Vigevano. The occurrence, says Mastronardi, was totally ignored, public attention being focused on the annual shoe fair that brought riches to the city and handsome profits to the local factory owners. The writer's moral outrage is conveyed through a poignant antithesis: "Mentre quell'operaio agonizzava in una stanza della clinica, nei saloni della Mostra si contrattavano affari per miliardi" (While the worker was dying in a hospital room, in the halls of the Fair they were making business deals worth billions of liras). By refusing to publish the fleshed-out short story that he says he wrote and then discarded, Mastronardi as an act of protest withheld his creative work in the same way that a factory worker withholds his labor through a strike.

Mastronardi's portrait of the petite bourgeoisie in Vigevano became a trilogy with his novel *Il meridionale di Vigevano* (The Southerner of Vigevano, 1964). The title refers to the narrator and main character of the story, Camillo, a government revenue officer transferred from his native Sicily to Vigevano. The novel explores an important sociological issue, for the early 1960s saw the phenomenon of immigration by southerners to Vigevano and many other cities in northern Italy.

Italy suffered from a lack of cultural cohesiveness fostered by centuries of regional separatism. Southern immigrants were generally viewed by northern Italians as foreigners, which, in a narrow sense, they were. The immigrants spoke a different language, had less education, and were brought up with different values. When they immigrated to the North, they were at best looked upon with suspicion; more often than not, they were treated as intruders and regarded as untrustworthy. What northerners and southerners had in common–Catholicism, a sense of tradition, a deep attachment to the family–were not distinctively Italian traits; they could as easily be found among other national groups, such the Irish, the Poles, or the Spaniards.

The perception of southern Italians as foreigners is reflected in the remarks that a woman born in Vigevano addresses to Camillo:

> Al vaga: noi Vigevano la ioma fai per noialtri: le strade tranquille; le casette col giardino; la Piazza, le lee. Adesso insomma siete venuti a invaderci voialtri.

> (Look here: we built Vigevano for ourselves: quiet streets, attractive homes with front yards, the main square, the avenues. And now you people have come and invaded us.)

Nothing in this passage underscores more clearly the tension and the sociocultural differences between two classes of Italians than the polar expressions *noialtri* (ourselves) and *voialtri* (you people).

Mastronardi (center) with Alberto Moravia (left) and Giulio Einaudi (right)

But southern Italians, who for more than a century had immigrated to foreign countries, adjusted quite well in Vigevano, proving themselves as enterprising and successful in commerce as the natives. In the January 1956 letter to Vittorini Mastronardi observed:

> Conosco parecchia gente che lavorano tutti in famiglia, chi al banchetto, chi alla macchina, e un tre quattro dozzine di paia in un giorno le fanno. E sa chi sono i veri lavoratori? I meridionali. Tutti, arrivati qui, pensano alle scarpe, soltanto alle scarpe.

> (I know many people who work together, all of them, as a family: some at the bench, others with machines, and they can make three or four dozen pairs of shoes in one day. And do you know who the real workers are? The southerners. Every one of them, as soon as they get here, they think of one thing, and one thing only: making shoes.)

Even so, the narrator feels like a stranger in his adopted town and has occasion to experience discrimination at work and in his search for an apartment. As far as Camillo is concerned, and regardless of how successful he will be, he will never be accepted as an equal by northern Italians; he, and perhaps his children, will always be southerners first.

Il meridionale di Vigevano has little in common with *Il maestro di Vigevano,* and in some ways it seems a step backward for Mastronardi to *Il calzolaio di Vigevano.* The plotline is quite tenuous and entails inconsequential experiences by Camillo, who falls in love with Olga, a native of Vigevano. At the end the reader does not know whether they will get married. In *Il meriodionale di Vigevano,* as in his first novel, Mastronardi relies heavily on dialogue, sometimes juxtaposing local dialect and standard Italian in the same sentence, thereby confusing and disorienting the reader. He possesses an uncanny ability to elicit comic responses from lexical constructs, but his ability for linguistic manipulation can only be appreciated in the original form by those who understand the dialect.

Il meridionale di Vigevano is notable for Mastronardi's representation of Vigevano's industrial heart. The feverish activity of shoe manufacturing mushroomed everywhere in Vigevano after the war, housed in large and small factories and in garages, kitchens, and living rooms of private homes. These were the boom years of the Italian economy, the years of increased productivity and rising demand for material goods that laid the foundation for the consumer society of the following decades. Ostensibly the novel shows the material rewards of entrepreneurship. When the narrator is shown the outskirts of Vigevano, his girlfriend's brother points with pride to the fruits of successful capitalism:

> Questa fabbric l'è del detto Ortolino. Conoscete il Detto? Quello che l'ha fai quella tarmenta villa, con la

piscina in ceramica, e al podanò fare il bagno in bella biotto che ci vedono dentro il giardino, dai condomini che ci hanno costruito intorno? Questa fabbrica è del Potti. Ha piantato fabbriche sino in Sud Africa. Il Potti! Quello che l'è andài a piantare una fabbrica anche in Persia, per gli arabi, e l'è turnà a Vigevano, con un bordello di danè.

(This factory belongs to Ortolino. Do you know him? The guy who built himself that gorgeous villa with a swimming pool covered with ceramic tiles; they can no longer swim naked there because the tenants in the condominiums built around the villa can look inside the pool. This factory belongs to Potti. He has built factories even in South Africa. Potti! That's the guy that built a factory in Iran, for the Arabs, and came back to Vigevano loaded with dough.)

Businessmen like Ortolino and Potti, Mastronardi points out, are more than role models worthy of imitation; in a setting such as Vigevano they hold the same fascination for young entrepreneurs as Hollywood stars have for teenagers in America.

But Mastronardi's novel is veined with caustic irony and a compelling, dark humor that casts a shadow on the perceived merits of capitalism. Many of his characters, consumed by an obsessive drive to make money, turn into one-dimensional, neurotic caricatures of themselves. Reduced to its essence, Mastronardi's basic theme is that the relentless pursuit of material wealth can—and quite often does—become a spiritual disease that ultimately subjugates and dehumanizes people.

A casa tua ridono (At Home They Laugh at You, 1971) marks the last, difficult stage of Mastronardi's career, in which he attempted to transcend linguistic experimentation while remaining within the socio-economic milieu of Vigevano—the only setting he seems interested in or capable of portraying. The results are largely negative. The surreality that played an importatnt role in *Il maestro di Vigevano* here becomes the dominant narrative mode, affecting both setting and action in ways that clearly separate this book from Mastronardi's previous work. The novel's internal disharmony is embodied in the central figure, Pietro. In the first part of the work he is drawn as an insecure and confused young man struggling to find a modicum of self-esteem and live an ordinary life. Yet in the latter part Pietro seems a different person. He is married to Angela and running his father-in-law's shoe factory. He neglects his wife and only son to devote all his energies to the management of the company, discovering in the end that his workers are unhappy with their jobs and dislike him.

What remains constant in this work is the sense of solitude and existential grief that Pietro has experienced since his adolescence. As a child Pietro shunned sympathy, considering it "la parte esterna del disprezzo" (the outer part of contempt). On the other hand, as an adult he indulges in self-pity: "Ogni giornata di lavoro mi sfibra. Torno a casa sfibrato. Non ho amico, non ho nessuno. . . . mi si tiene alla larga come il disonesto e come l'appestato" (Every working day exhausts me. I go home exhausted. I have no friends, I have no one. . . . People avoid me like a dishonest person or a plague victim). Solitude is filled with unhappy childhood memories; the anxieties of the present are exorcised through escapist, delusional flights of fancy that betray a threatening, darker side of Pietro's psyche. Ultimately the merit of the book lies in its existential theme, which is depicted through the arresting image of a blind horse pulling the merry-go-round at a fair. The horse—Pietro's symbolic correlative—goes around in circles but believes it is traveling on a straight path leading somewhere.

Structurally Mastronardi juxtaposes different narrative strands and changes viewpoints unexpectedly. Blocks of narrative that appear early in the book are reintroduced in its latter part and are reelaborated with a different perspective. His writing often takes a staccato rhythm, as in this portrait of a young woman: "Il corpo grasso nelle rughe carnose. La pancia rotonda, Molle. Il seno pendente. La gamba muscolosa" (Fat body with flashy wrinkles. Round stomach. Soft. Drooping breasts. Muscular legs). The writer directs the reader's attention to each unappealing part of Marta's body, and, much like a Picasso painting, the whole suggests a nonorganic, disjointed vision of the individual and her spiritual condition.

L'assicuratore (The Insurance Salesman, 1975) is a collection of twelve short stories in which the reader will find a familiar setting, Vigevano, and familiar characters: schoolteachers, factory workers, and small entrepreneurs involved in some way in the shoe industry. "L'assicuratore," the story that lends the title to the collection, deals with the bitter and degrading experiences borne by a salesman whose desire to succeed is vitiated by his unsuitable personality and by repeated bungled efforts in selling insurance. In "Dalla santa" (At the Psychic), the most innovative story in the collection, Mastronardi fuses humor, superstition, and a sense of empathy for both the ignorance and the needs of lower-class women; the result is a convincing sketch of proletarian life in an urban setting.

In a moment of extreme depression, the main character of *A casa tu ridono* tries to take his life in the deep waters of the river Ticino. Years after writing that scene, Mastronardi apparently played it out himself. On 29 April 1979 his body was found in the Ticino. Five days earlier he had disappeared from home, and all search efforts had proven fruitless. Mastronardi had suffered from severe chronic depression most of his life. At the age of twenty-six, writing to Vittorini, he had lamented the fact that his frequent periods of depression robbed him of the two activities he cherished most in life: reading and writing.

Mastronardi was among the first postwar Italian writers to deal with the social consequences of the industrialization that transformed Italian life and culture. A narrative project akin in spirit with the socially conscious novel of the nineteenth century, Mastronardi's Vigevano trilogy points ultimately to the dehumanization caused by materialism when the quest for individual success and the acquisition of wealth become the cornerstone of social ethos. In this sense the trilogy is provincial only on the surface. Mastronardi's Vigevano comes to represent a large part of Italian society.

References:

Alberto Asor Rosa, "Uno scrittore ai margini del capitalismo: Mastronardi," *Quaderni piacentini,* 14 (January–February 1964): 36–40;

Gualtiezo Amici, *Il realismo nella narrativa da Verga a Mastronardi* (Bologna: Ponte Nuovo, 1963);

Gianfranco Contini, *Letteratura dell'Italia unita, 1861–1968* (Florence: Sansoni, 1968), pp. 1033–1035;

Marco Forti, "Tecnologi arrabbiati e favolisti," *Aut-aut,* 76 (July 1963): 36–74;

Forti, "Termi industriali della narrativa italiana," *Il menabò,* 4 (1961): 213–239;

Maria Antonietta Grignani, ed., *Per Mastronardi* (Florence: La Nuova Italia, 1983);

Michele Leone, "*Il maestro di Vigevano:* l'industria tra benessere e perdizione," in his *L'industria nella letteratura italiana contemporanea* (Saratoga, Cal.: Anma Libri, 1976), pp. 97–106;

Giuliano Manacorda, *Vent'anni di pazienza. Saggi sulla letterature italiana contemporanea* (Florence: La Nuova Italia, 1972), pp. 387–392;

Giorgio Pullini, *Volti e risvolti del romanzo italiano contemporaneo* (Milan: Mursia, 1974), pp. 219–222;

Rinaldo Rinaldi, *Il romanzo come deformazione. Autonomia ed eredità gaddiana in Mastronardi, Bianciardi, Testori, Arbasino* (Milan: Mursia, 1985);

Antonietta Sardi, "Scarpari, donne, meridionali in Mastronardi," *Letture,* 8–9 (1970): 559–563.

Elsa Morante

(18 August 1912 – 25 November 1985)

Rocco Capozzi
University of Toronto

BOOKS: *Le bellissime avventure di Caterì dalla treccio-lina* (Turin: Einaudi, 1941); revised and enlarged as *Le straordinarie avventure di Caterina* (Turin: Einaudi, 1959);

Il gioco segreto (Milan: Garzanti, 1941);

Menzogna e sortilegio (Turin: Einaudi, 1948); translated by Adrienne Foulke as *The House of Liars* (New York: Harcourt, Brace, 1950);

L'isola di Arturo (Turin: Einaudi, 1957); translated by Isabel Quigly as *Arturo's Island* (London: Collins, 1959; New York: Knopf, 1959);

Alibi (Milan: Longanesi, 1958);

Lo scialle andaluso (Turin: Einaudi, 1963);

Il mondo salvato dai ragazzini e altri poemi (Turin: Einaudi, 1968);

La storia: romanzo (Turin: Einaudi, 1974); translated by William Weaver as *History. A Novel* (New York: Knopf, 1977; London: Allen Lane, 1978);

Aracoeli (Turin: Einaudi, 1982); translated by Weaver as *Aracoeli* (New York: Random House, 1984);

Pro o contro la bomba atomica e altri scritti, edited by Cesare Garboli (Milan: Adelphi, 1987);

"Piccolo manifesto" e altri scritti (Milan: Linea d'ombra, 1988);

Diario 1938, edited by Alba Andreini (Turin: Einaudi, 1989).

Collection: *Elsa Morante. Opere,* 2 volumes, edited by Carlo Cecchi and Cesare Garboli (Milan: Mondadori, 1988–1990).

Elsa Morante

Elsa Morante was not a prolific writer. Beyond her two children's books and her many articles and stories that appeared in newspapers and periodicals in the early stage of her career, her work consists of four novels, two volumes of short stories, and one book of verse. However, few contemporary writers in Italy enjoyed as much success as did Morante. Ever since the Marxist critic György Lukács praised her first novel, *Menzogna e sortilegio* (1948; translated as *The House of Liars,* 1950), and called her one of the best European novelists, Morante saw her popularity rise with each subsequent book. Her death stimu-

lated reprints of her works, literary conventions in her honor, and renewed critical interest. There is general consensus today that Morante is a major writer.

Morante's deep love for literature can be traced to her early teens when she began to write poems and stories for friends and relatives. Her children's story *Le bellissime avventure di Caterì dalla trecciolina* (The Most Beautiful Adventures of Caterì with a Pigtail) was written when she was fourteen, though it was not published until 1941. As she progressed as a writer Morante drew inspiration from

188

ancient Greek writers and philosophers, as well as from Stendhal and Fyodor Dostoyevsky. For Morante writing became not only an art but a personal imperative. One of her first poems affords an excellent self-portrait, for she describes herself as a modern Sheherazade who tells stories for herself and for others in the middle of the night.

On the rare occasions that she agreed to be interviewed, Morante refused to talk about herself, insisting that her "complete self" could be found in her work. She was a private person, and only after her death has much been learned about her life, with many aspects remaining shrouded in an aura of secrecy, lies, and incredible stories. It is exactly the way she wanted her private life to appear: full of magic and intriguing rumors. Morante preferred that her faithful readers create an image of her based on the characters and the narrative voices they found in her books.

Elsa Morante was born in Rome on 18 August 1912. Her mother, Irma Poggibonsi, was from Modena, in northern Italy. Her legal father, Augusto Morante, was an instructor in a school for problem children. When Irma discovered that her husband could not father children, she agreed that Augusto's friend Francesco Lo Monaco, a Sicilian police officer, could be the surrogate father. Elsa and her four brothers and sisters were all fathered by Lo Monaco. This was one of the family secrets that Elsa discovered before she moved out of her house at the age of sixteen. She began to reveal this and other secrets in her first novel, but she never discussed them with anyone. It was not until a year after her death, when her brother Marcello published a brief family biography, *Maledetta benedetta* (Cursed and Blessed, 1986), that readers learned her real age and other private information.

In 1936 Morante met Alberto Moravia; after a long relationship, they were married in 1941. Following their marriage they spent nearly two years on the island of Capri, both engaged in literary projects. During the last nine months of World War II they were forced to take refuge in the hills of Ciociaria, south of Rome—an experience that is reflected in one of Moravia's most neorealistic novels, *La ciociara* (1957; translated as *Two Women,* 1958). This same experience reappears in part in Morante's *La storia* (1974; translated as *History. A Novel,* 1977). Morante accompanied Moravia on many of his trips around the world. However, theirs was a difficult marriage, which began to deteriorate in the early 1950s. In 1961 she traveled with Moravia for the last time, on a trip to India, in the company of Pier Paolo Pasolini. Morante and Moravia decided to separate in 1962 but were never divorced. She had brief relationships, first with director Luchino Vis-

conti and then with a young American painter named Bill Morrow. Her closest friends were the poets Sandro Penna, Umberto Saba, and Pasolini.

In the 1960s Morante became a virtual recluse; she avoided interviews, literary gatherings, and even friends. Her isolation was no doubt prompted by factors such as her separation from Moravia; the suicide of her lover, Morrow; and her disillusionment with Italian political realities. Morante also may have felt that she had to prove to skeptics that her success did not come from her close association with Moravia, who was a more popular author at the time. She was not a fast writer, and her works took years before they were published. During the long composition of *La storia* she also collected some of her favorite short stories in *Lo scialle andaluso* (The Andalusian Shawl, 1963) and began writing what was her most experimental work, *Il mondo salvato dai ragazzini e altri poemi* (The World Saved by the Little Children, 1968). Some critics see this text as the beginning of a new development in her fiction in which she stakes out an ideological position that has its roots in anarchy and in a rejection of all forms of power. In the next fourteen years Morante published the much revised *La storia* and *Aracoeli* (1982; translated as *Aracoeli,* 1984), which betrays a gloomy, nihilistic view of human existence.

The last five years of Morante's life were painful, for she was confined to a wheelchair and spent a great deal of time in hospitals. Her physical condition deteriorated rapidly after she broke her hip in 1980; she had surgery but continued to suffer pain. In 1983, following an attempted suicide, she had a brain operation. She died of cardiac arrest in a Roman clinic on 25 November 1985. Tragically, Morante experienced in life what her characters feared in her fiction, for her major characters all share deep fears of aging, of losing their rational faculties, of being alone and becoming helpless.

It is clear that Morante, who refused to speak about her private life, used her work to bring to life her family, childhood, and early youth. Her novels show a strong autobiographical strain and through their narrative voices explore, at times obsessively, different aspects of unrequited love. Morante's works reinforce time and again the conviction that love is the most important need in life.

Morante's early stories, some of which were included in *Il gioco segreto* (The Secret Game, 1941) and *Lo scialle andaluso,* were published in periodicals between 1930 and 1941. They received little attention at the time and were long neglected by critics. For example, the significance of the story "Qualcuno bussa alla porta" (Someone Is Knocking at the Door), which was published in installments in the

Morante in Capri (photograph by D'Elia)

parenthetical statements. Stories such as "Il ladro dei lumi" (The Candle Thief), which was written in 1935, show that Morante's earliest elaboration of fables, oneiric descriptions, and other allusive elements preceded and so are not mere imitations of Massimo Bontempelli's magical realism. They illustrate her fundamental belief that literature can bring to the foreground those life experiences that from early childhood remain impressed in the mind and the subconscious of individuals. The early stories contain her first treatment of desires, fears, anxieties, passions, secrets, and obsessions that were fully developed in the course of her narrative career.

Morante uses the term *alibi* to allude to the literary personae present in her works. She uses the same word in her well-known reply to "Nove domande sul romanzo" (Nine Questions on the Future of the Novel), which were posed by the editor of *Nuovi Argomenti* in 1959. Her response was included with other essays in the posthumous *Pro o contro la bomba atomica e altri scritti* (For or Against the Atomic Bomb, 1987). She stated that modern novelists no longer invoke the muses for inspiration but resort to a "narrating-I" that serves as an "alibi" to represent realities pertinent to their own selves and to others. Critics often quote this essay to indicate Morante's position on art and on the role of writers in portraying "incorruptible poetic truths," yet they largely ignore how she employs the expressions *alibi* and the *narrating/ reciting-I*—words that suggest her almost autobiographical identification with her narrators. In her poems, specifically in "Alibi," Morante speaks forthrightly about her characters as alibis and how, like a phoenix, she returns in each work to narrate like a modern Sheherazade.

In most instances it is through male alibis, especially young boys, that Morante has represented both the effects of excessive love and the anxieties of feeling neglected or rejected. Children and adolescents play an important role in Morante's work because she sees them as the custodians of fables, myths, idols, and heroes. They are also vulnerable to love, confused about death, always craving attention, and blessed with the necessary fantasy needed to communicate with nature.

Menzogna e sortilegio, winner of the 1948 Viareggio literary prize, is in many ways the source from which Morante draws characters, situations, themes, and narrative techniques for her subsequent fictions. This long novel, written in the tradition of eighteenth- and nineteenth-century "well-made" realistic novels, deals with the tragic results of lies told by practically every major character. As Elisa indicates in the reconstruction of her family's long history of telling lies, the characters are ad-

journal *I diritti della scuola* from 25 September 1935 to 15 August 1936, was not appreciated until the late 1980s. It is an elaborate and dramatic love story whose characters and themes prefigure Morante's mature work. The earliest prototypes of Morante's parents, lovers, and children can be found in the characters of Michele Waug, the tall, handsome gentleman who leaves the woman he has infatuated; Mirtilla, the young woman who falls madly in love with Michele and who abandons her child to pursue him; and Lucia, the young girl who grows up respecting but not loving her adopted father. The main themes found in Morante's youthful work—evident also in the story "La nonna" (The Grandmother) —are centered around possessive and blind love; concern for physical attractiveness; narcissism; difficult relationships between parents and children; feelings of betrayal or abandonment; and tragic consequences of morbid and unrequited love.

In many of the stories of *Il gioco segreto* and *Lo sciale andaluso* the implied author intrudes in the narration through a variety of authorial interjections and

dicted to false secrets, fantasies, dreams, and invented stories. Elisa, as well as her grandparents, Teodoro and Cesira; her parents, Anna and Francesco; her relatives; and her close friend Rosaria, the woman who will care for Elisa after Anna's death, are all victims of lies motivated by the strong need to love and feel loved.

As in the case with these and other Morante characters, possessive, blind love at times becomes the principal cause of their suffering, their mental disorder, and eventually their death. *Menzogna e sortilegio* abounds with examples of unrequited love. The best representative of rejected lovers is no doubt Anna, who loves but is not loved by her beautiful and narcissistic cousin Edoardo. Anna's blinding passion for her idol will make her neglect both her husband and her daughter. Moreover, this same passion will be responsible for her slow disintegration and her death. To some degree, Anna's fate is experienced by other lovers: by Rosaria, the generous and protective prostitute who adores Francesco; by Francesco, who loves his wife, Anna; by Concetta, who idolizes her son Edoardo; and by Elisa, who worships her mother, Anna.

The network of love experiences that unfolds in *Menzogna e sortilegio* is brilliantly portrayed through dialogues, monologues, dreams, memories, and letters. Morante demonstrates her art as a great storyteller as she focuses with equal skill on the psychology of her characters and on the bourgeois setting. The story follows two generations of two families, first in southern Italy and then in Rome, from the late part of the nineteenth century to the beginning of the twentieth century.

The presence of the narrator-protagonist Elisa, the link for all the digressions and all the minor characters, is felt throughout the novel, including the first part where an omniscient narrator reconstructs the background of the characters and the events in the story. Elisa is Morante's first major alibi, the first fully developed prototype of the author's dramatis personae, a role filled by the narrator-protagonists Arturo and Emanuele in later novels. Elisa has been raised with little parental attention, loves books, and has undergone a traumatic experience during her childhood. Most important, she, like her creator, has the ability to articulate the psychological afflictions she experienced while growing up. Nonetheless, Elisa and any other of Morante's so-called alibis should not be taken merely as autobiographical portraits; they are excellent depictions of characters whose psychological makeup and life experiences correspond to the experiences of men and women who have undergone the pains and disillusionments of loving and not feeling loved.

Menzogna e sortilegio contains the salient stylistic and narrative techniques evident in Morante's later works: the fusion of a subjective first-person narration with an omniscient third-person point of view; the use of memory, flashbacks, dreams, digressions, authorial intrusions, parenthetical statements, and dialogues with the reader; and the juxtaposition of psychological and sociohistorical realism. Contemporary readers and literary critics neglected Morante's first novel because she was not well known. This was not the case for her second novel, *L'isola di Arturo* (1957; translated as *Arturo's Island,* 1959), which won the 1957 Strega Prize and proved to be an immediate success. Critics offered high praise for the work, lauding Morante's extraordinary talent as a novelist.

L'isola di Arturo is the story of Arturo Gerace, a boy who grows up in the idyllic setting of the island of Procida. His mother dies giving birth to him, and thus the little boy with dark hair, who had been fed on goat's milk by the handyman Silvestro, grows up mostly alone and free to roam around the island. Arturo has no formal schooling and yet, like many of Morante's narrator-protagonists, has developed a great passion for books, especially adventure stories. His father, Wilhelm Gerace, is half German and half Italian, with blue eyes and blond hair. He spends little time on the island, but Arturo sees him as a hero who travels to exotic places in search of great adventures. The story, the reader discovers, is narrated with hindsight by a disillusioned man who recognizes that he has lost forever his private Eden in his early teens.

Arturo's problems begin when he is about fourteen and Nunziatella, a sixteen-year-old Neapolitan girl, is introduced to him as his new mother. She is brought into the Gerace home, the notorious "Casa dei Guaglioni," a run-down former monastery where no woman had been allowed to enter by the former owner Romeo l'Amalfitano. It is shortly after the arrival of Nunziatella that the protagonist discovers love and sex as well as some bitter truths about himself and his father as an Oedipal drama unfolds.

Arturo at first hates his stepmother and is jealous of her baby, his half brother, because he receives so much attention. His hate for Nunziatella turns into love not because she is beautiful but because she is a mother who kisses, caresses, and loves her newborn child. Arturo, on the other hand, had never received kisses and caresses from his mother. The idea of winning Nunziatella's maternal affection soon turns into an obsession for Arturo, as he dreams and fantasizes about her kisses. After faking a suicide attempt, Arturo forcefully steals a kiss from Nunziatella. From this moment his life changes drastically. Arturo can no longer face Nunziatella, and worse yet, he soon discovers that his idolized father

Dust jacket for the American edition of the translation of Morante's first novel, which examines the consequences of lies told for the sake of love (courtesy of the Lilly Library, Indiana University)

is not a hero. Far from being an adventurous man, Wilhelm proves to be a wretched individual who abandons his family for an escaped convict, Tonino Stella. Arturo discovers the truth about his father when Stella rejects Wilhelm's homosexual attraction by openly ridiculing him, calling him a "parody." Wilhelm, readers learn, suffers the same pains of rejection he had inflicted upon his old friend Romeo. Between his fourteenth and sixteenth birthdays, Arturo's once enjoyable and innocent life becomes a prison from which he must run away. As World War II breaks out, Arturo leaves the island with the bitter realization that "outside of limbo there is no Elysium."

L'isola di Arturo has an underlying theme of misogyny, first introduced by Romeo and then more acrimoniously expressed by Wilhelm, who suffered from a possessive motherly love in his childhood and from an equally tyrannical affection by Romeo in later years. Arturo's misogyny results from Wilhelm's many lectures on the dangers of mothers. Morante deals in greater detail with the theme of misogyny and with a son's love/hate relationship with his mother in her last novel, *Aracoeli*.

The love/hate relationship between mother and son is clearly at the center of one of Morante's best-known short stories, "Lo scialle andaluso,"

written in 1951 when she was working on *L'isola di Arturo;* it became the title story of her 1963 story collection. The story is a drama of jealousy and possessive love between a young boy, Andrea, and his mother, Giuditta (her name is symbolic of her betrayal), who leaves her two children to become a dancer. To lessen the pain of the separation, Andrea enters a seminary. A few years later, when Giuditta's company plays in the town where Andrea is studying, the young man is unable to resist the temptation of seeing his mother perform. He finds that she is neither a star nor a good dancer, and the audience openly ridicules her. After the performance Giuditta and Andrea meet and vow to be together once again. On the way home the mother puts her "Andalusian shawl" over Andrea's shoulders to keep him warm. The happy reunion does not last long because Andrea soon realizes that Giuditta has returned not because she loves him but because she is getting old, lacks talent, and is no longer needed by her employer. Andrea must live with the bitter realization that his mother has again acted out of selfishness and not out of love.

The sixteen poems of *Alibi* (1958) were written between 1941 and 1957. In a brief preface Morante explains that they are an "echo" and a "chorus" of her prose; in fact, some verses were written specifically for her first two novels. She also remarks that to some extent writing poetry was a hobby and a form of divertissement for her, because she enjoyed the musical quality of her verses. Perhaps because of such deprecations, Morante's poetry has received little critical attention. Yet *Alibi* is an important book that should not be taken lightly. In these poems one hears the voice of Sheherazade, who desires that her stories should bring pleasure to others and hope to herself. *Alibi* is about fables, allegory, Hamlet, childhood friends, and love. It is also about Morante the novelist, addressing in the title poem (written in 1955) all of her "alibis" who chose to hide their real names but not their identities.

Il mondo salvato dai ragazzini was published during the so-called revolution of 1968–a year of widespread and often violent protests led by factory workers, students, and women. This may explain why some critics assumed that it was Morante's contribution to the politicized works that at the time appeared under the label of the *Neoavanguardia* (new avant- garde). With the exception of Pasolini and a few other sagacious reviewers, critics showed little appreciation for this unusual lyrical collection. Leafing through the text, one notices verses, drawings, musical notes, and pages on which the writing appears vertically rather than horizontally. Was this Morante's example of the experimental works in vogue in the 1960s? Certainly not, because Morante was not a follower of trends. She detested the new avant-garde Italian, the French *nouveau roman* (new novel), and all formalistic literature whose overall intentions seemed to begin and end with wordplay.

After the republication of *Il mondo salvato dai ragazzini* in 1971 and especially the appearance of *La storia* in 1974, critics began to examine more closely *Alibi* and noted that its third part in particular could be considered a preamble to the novel. Several poems are said to indicate Morante's embrace of anarchy as a means of distancing herself from the scandalous behavior of those who seek power. The verses cited in support of this point include the "popular songs" of the "F.P." or "Felici Pochi" (Happy Few), and "I.M." or "Infelici Molti" (Unhappy Many) sections; the opening poem "Addio," a farewell written in memory of the artist Bill Morrow; the tragic "La serata a Colono" (An Evening at Colono), a parody of Oedipus and Antigone; and the song describing the trials of "Pazziarello," a carefree boy who is destroyed by the establishment because he is seen as a threat to law and order.

Morante's favored characters are the *ragazzini* (children) and those such as Pazziarello, who choose to live outside social institutions. However, it is in

the voices of Antigone (who in some ways recalls Nunziatella) and of Oedipus that one most clearly hears the familiar voices of Morante's alibis. The refrain "It's all a joke," which appears at the end of each song of the *Il mondo salvato dai ragazzini,* is echoed in *La storia* when Useppe hears the birds chirping away "It's a joke, it's a joke."

The composition of *La storia: romanzo* kept Morante busy for more than ten years. On several occasions she announced that she was working on a novel to be called "Senza il conforto della religione" (Without the Comfort of Religion). When *La Storia* finally came out, the novel immediately became the center of a heated literary debate that in the long run strengthened Morante's role as one of Italy's most important writers.

La storia was attacked principally by marxist critics who alleged it was superficial and who disliked its unprecedented success as a best-seller. But most readers were able to see beyond the novel's minor structural weaknesses, linked primarily to the use of an omniscient narrator, and appreciate Morante's powerful denunciation of needless suffering and destruction. *La storia* depicts the misfortunes and the deaths of poor people whose presence is hardly felt in the scandalous "history" that, as noted in the subtitle, "has been going on for 2000 years." Its core deals with a series of tragedies that falls upon the Raimundo family–Ida, Useppe, and Nino–and minor characters, including persecuted Jews, dispersed families, and antifascist soldiers, all of whom are drawn together by war in and around Rome, mainly between 1941 and 1947.

Ida Raimundo, whose mother was Jewish, is a schoolteacher who in the opening pages of the novel is raped by a German soldier as she returns home to her child, Nino. Ida gives birth prematurely to Useppe, a little boy who does not develop normally and dies before the age of seven. Useppe has some learning disabilities but he is unique in many ways, especially in his unusual gift to communicate with birds, cats, and particularly with his dogs, Blitz and Bella. Like all of Morante's children, he believes in fables, myths and idols; he is the embodiment of goodness and innocence. He is completely free and appears unaware of the brutalities inflicted by history on humanity. Moreover, he is the only one who keeps his innocence whether he witnesses physical acts of love, human atrocities, or violent deaths.

The omniscient narrator of *La storia* wishes to say everything but at times either does not remember or claims not to have sufficient information about certain events or characters. There are instances when one may question Morante's decision to employ this seemingly unreliable narrator who for the most part knows everything about every-

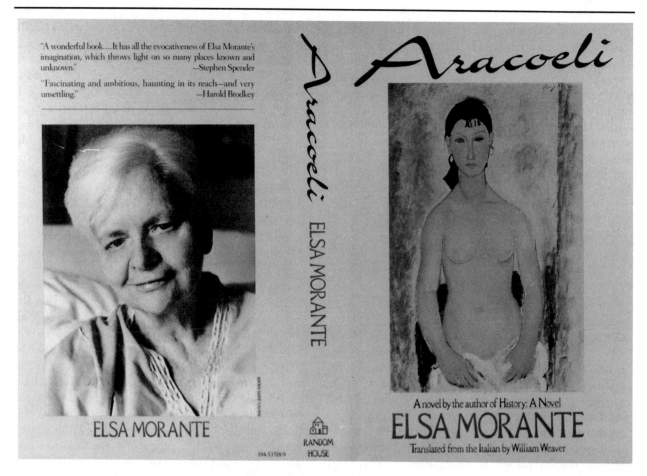

Dust jacket for the American edition of the translation of Morante's 1982 novel, in which the protagonist's search for his mother's roots in Spain are sparked by his "excessive hunger for love"

body, including their thoughts and dreams. Nonetheless, the language, style, events, and most of the characters of the novel have been carefully orchestrated to underline the message that history is synonymous with war, suffering, death, power, and, most of all, the destruction of innocence in children. The title of the novel must be understood as encompassing Morante's intent to juxtapose the fictional story of Ida, Nino, and Useppe, with the historical chronicles documenting some of the major events from 1900 to 1967 that appear at the beginning of each chapter in smaller print.

The pessimism that dominates *La storia* is not linked merely to the obvious evils and atrocities of war; it is instead rooted in Morante's views of a society that appears to have lost all respect for humanity. And if Davide Segre, a disillusioned bourgeois Jewish student, appears to preach rather than to speak to those who are willing to listen to him, it is primarily because he embodies many of Morante's own anarchist views. Segre's speeches seem to echo as well the writings of Simone Weil, which must have made a strong impression on Morante from the 1960s on-

ward. Morante's pessimism regarding contemporary society, already present in *Il mondo salvato dai ragazzini,* is underscored even more in this work.

A statement on the back cover of *La storia* claimed that the novel was written in a language accessible to all as it intended to speak to all. More than a strategy for selling novels, this assertion reflected Morante's wish to write a novel about and for the masses at a time when many writers were more interested in impressing critics with experimental and formalistic techniques than in writing fiction that would be enjoyed by the general public. *La storia* in any case is clearly more than Morante's reaction to elitist literature; it is a human drama that can be understood universally, written with the same passion that she showed in writing her previous works.

Morante's bitterness toward what the world was becoming and also toward herself as an aging invalid is transparent in every page of the last work published in her lifetime, *Aracoeli,* which she completed just three years before her death. From the opening pages, one recognizes various themes that date back to Morante's first short stories. However, it soon becomes clear that the narrator, Manuele, has lost all hope in the future. As Morante's last alibi, Manuele is given the unpleasant task of shattering all the illusions that his predecessors had about love, innocence, and happiness. As in *Menzogna e sortilegio* and in *L'isola di Arturo,* every major character is a victim of unrequited love. Aracoeli idolizes her brother Manuelito and for many years has loved blindly her husband, Eugenio, who cannot live with her. Manuele loves his mother, Aracoeli; with her, he idolizes the myth of his uncle Manuelito; and he also desires his homosexual friends. The only character who does not feel betrayed is Ramona, Manuele's aunt, who idolizes Mussolini.

Aracoeli deals with the tragic drama of Manuele, a man who at the age of forty-three, feeling unattractive, alone, and hopeless, embarks on a journey from Milan to El Almendral, in Andalusia, in search of his mother's roots. Manuele's allegorical journey is an attempt to find anything that may draw him close again to his former idolized love, Aracoeli, who has been dead for years. The trip from Italy to Spain lasts only five days, but as Manuele travels on planes and buses he takes a much longer inner journey. Thanks to his unusual ability to remember practically everything that he wishes to recall, including the happy days when he was feeding on his mother's breast, Manuele reconstructs through his "apocryphal memories" much of his childhood and adolescent years. His flashbacks are long digressions that take him back through his entire life so that he can rewitness the metamorphoses in his parents and in himself.

Manuele's memories do not provide any relief or any form of escape; instead, they aggravate even more his pains as each recollection intensifies his trauma of feeling abandoned like an "unloved puppy." Manuele's desperate desire to return to the womb follows his realization that he has no chance of ever changing his hopeless condition as an unloved misfit. And thus as Manuele recounts his life, he can only denounce his mother, his father, his relatives, friends, prostitutes, and anyone else he can blame as the cause for his anguishing solitude, his neuroses, his homosexuality, and his misanthropy.

Manuele's "excessive hunger for love" does not seem to exceed that of any of Morante's previous alibis. What exactly, then, has driven him to such a miserable state? The answer must be found in Manuele's analysis of events as he reconstructs why he has come to desire death. Never before had Morante's characters become so self-destructive in the process of destroying the few happy memories of childhood. Manuele surpasses even Elisa in admitting that the events being narrated (the apocryphal memories)

may not have happened exactly in the manner that they are presented to the readers. More than any other previous novel, *Aracoeli* contains the intrusions of a narrative voice that through innumerable parenthetical statements seeks to guide and possibly convince the reader of the message being delivered.

In Manuele the reader recognizes the implied narrator of previous novels, aged and embittered by solitude and suffering. If Manuele were to look back on his predecessors, he would surely do so with the uneasy feeling that they were victims of deceptions and lies. During his journey Manuele desecrates all myths about happiness as he attacks religion, society, and his parents in a way that makes the reader wonder whether his strong denials are not actually the manifestations of his need to believe in God, his fellowman and, most important, his mother's love. The novel closes with Manuele's confession that some individuals are more "inclined to weep for love than for death." These final words, precisely because they come from Morante's last alibi, seem to invite her faithful readers to journey back through her canon in search of clues that may help to unveil the painful personal truths of an artist who used fascinating alibis to both hide and at the same time reveal her most private self.

The writer and critic Carlo Sgorlon offers a fitting summary of Morante's unique art when he states that Italy has had many excellent poets but very few great novelists, and that Morante is one of the few true narrators that Italy has produced in ages. Lukács, though, was the first to proclaim Morante a writer of stature, the equal of Thomas Mann. After the publication of *L'isola di Arturo,* critics began to study her work seriously, searching for possible literary influences of great writers such as Gustave Flaubert, Jane Austen, Charles Dickens, Stendhal, Dostoyevski, and Alessandro Manzoni. Moravia's name has been mentioned in regard to similarities between his *Agostino* (1944) and Morante's *L'isola di Arturo.* Surprisingly, there are no studies that examine in detail the similarities and differences between Moravia's *La ciociara* and Morante's *La storia,* even though the novelists' shared experiences of the war shaped both works.

The few existing monographic studies on Morante were published either before or immediately after *La storia,* and thus they do not provide a comprehensive picture of her work. In many cases far too much emphasis has been given to the marxist polemics surrounding *La storia,* which critics agree is not her best work. Giacomo Debenedetti and Michel David were among the first critics to focus on the psychoanalytical elements, both Freudian and Jungian, in Morante's work. In his illuminating brief essay on *L'isola di Arturo* Debenedetti laid the ground for some interesting interpretations of Morante's mythical allusions that other scholars have used extensively in their own works. Donatella Ravanello's study is notable for the remarkable insight on Morante's treatment of insanity from *Menzogna e sortilegio* to *La storia*.

Since 1985 there have been several literary symposia in honor of Elsa Morante; some of them have seen the proceedings published in book form, such as *Per Elisa* (For Elisa, 1990), which is devoted entirely to *Menzogna e sortilegio*. In the late 1980s there appeared several essays that examined *Aracoeli*. Cesare Garboli and Carlo Cecchi coedited the two volumes of Morante's *opera omnia* and in their detailed introduction have corrected some of the misconceptions about Morante's life (such as her actual date of birth and who her birth father was) and have included an outline of the most significant criticism published on the author.

It was only after Morante's death that some critics have suggested Simone Weil's probable influence on Morante's life and works. This is an important area of inquiry and should prove fruitful in the examination of the literary sources of Morante's pessimism. But regardless of the hypotheses on what Harold Bloom calls the "anxiety of influences," the essential elements of narrative art in Elsa Morante's work—style, language, characters, narrative voices, and recurring leitmotivs—are unmistakably those of one of the best contemporary Italian novelists.

References:

Michael Caesar, "Elsa Morante," in *Writers and Society in Contemporary Italy,* edited by Caesar and Peter Hainsworth (Warwickshire: Berg, 1986), pp. 211–213;

Rocco Capozzi, "Elsa Morante's *Aracoeli:* The End of a Journey," in *Donna,* edited by Ada Testaferri (Toronto: University of Toronto Italian Studies, 1989), pp. 47–58;

Capozzi, "'Sheharazade' and Other 'Alibis': Elsa Morante's Victims of Love," *Rivista di studi italiani,* 1–2 (1987–1988): 51–71; revised in *Contemporary Women Writers in Italy,* edited by Santo L. Aricò (Amherst: University of Massachusetts Press, 1990), pp. 11–26;

Carlo Cecci and Cesare Garboli, eds., *Elsa Morante. Opere,* 2 volumes (Milan: Mondadori, 1988–1990), pp. 10–90, 1635–1681;

Concetti D'Angeli and Giacomo Magrini, eds., *Vent'anni dopo* La storia. *Omaggio a E Morante* (Pisa: Studi Novecenteschi, 1994);

Michel David, "Elsa Morante," *Le monde* (13 April 1968);

Giacomo Debenedetti, "L'isola di Arturo," in his *Saggi (1922–1966)* (Milan: Mondadori, 1982), pp. 379–396;

Franco Ferrucci, "Elsa Morante's Limbo Without Elysium," *Italian Quarterly,* 27–28 (1963): 28–52;

La fiera letteraria, special issue on *La storia,* 40 (6 October 1974);

Valeria Finucci, "The Textualization of a Female I. Elsa Morante's *Menzogna e sortilegio,*" *Italica,* 4 (1988): 308–323;

Luisa Guy, "Illusion and Literature in Morante's *L'isola di Arturo,*" *Italica* (1988): 144–153;

Gregory Lucente, "Everyday Life in Morante's *La storia,*" in his *Beautiful Fables* (Baltimore: Johns Hopkins University Press, 1986), pp. 248–265;

E. Allen McCormick, "Utopia and Point of View: Narrative Method in Morante's *L'isola di Arturo,*" *Symposium,* 14–15 (1960–1961): 114–129;

Marcello Morante, *Maledetta benedetta* (Milan: Garzanti, 1986);

Per Elisa (Pisa: Nistri-Lischi, 1990);

Angelo Pupino, *Struttura e stile della narrativa di Elsa Morante* (Ravenna: Longo, 1968);

Eugenio Ragni, "Elsa Morante" in *Il Novecento* (Rome: Lucarini, 1980), pp. 767–781;

Donatella Ravanello, *Scrittura e follia nei romanzi di Elsa Morante* (Venice: Marsilio, 1980);

Giovanna Rosa, *Cattedradi di carta* (Milan: Saggiatore, 1955);

Schifano, "Parla Elsa Morante. Barbara e divina," *L'Espresso* (2 December 1984): 122–133;

Schifano, ed., *Cahiers Elsa Morante* (Naples: ESI, 1993);

Jean-Noel Schifano and Tjuma Notarbartolo, eds., *Cahiers Elsa Morante* (Rome: ESI, 1993);

Carlo Sgorlon, *Invito alla lettura di Morante* (Milan: Mursia, 1972);

Luigina Stefani, "Elsa Morante," *Belfagor,* 26 (1971): 290–308;

Gianni Venturi, *Morante* (Florence: La Nuova Italia, 1977);

Sharon Wood, "The Bewitched Mirror: Imagination and Narration in Elsa Morante," *Modern Language Review* (April 1991): 310–321.

Alberto Moravia
(28 November 1907 – 26 September 1990)

Louis Kibler
Wayne State University

BOOKS: *Gli indifferenti* (Milan: Alpes, 1929); translated by Aida Mastrangelo as *The Indifferent Ones* (New York: Dutton, 1932); translated by Angus Davidson as *The Time of Indifference* (New York: Farrar, Straus & Young, 1953; London: Secker & Warburg, 1953);

La bella vita (Lanciano: Carabba, 1935);

Le ambizioni sbagliate (Milan: Mondadori, 1935); translated by Arthur Livingston as *The Wheel of Fortune* (New York: Viking, 1937; London: Cassell, 1938); republished as *Mistaken Ambitions* (New York: Farrar, Straus & Young, 1955);

L'imbroglio: Cinque romanzi brevi (Milan: Bompiani, 1937);

I sogni del pigro: Racconti, miti e allegorie (Milan: Bompiani, 1940);

La mascherata (Milan: Bompiani, 1941); translated by Davidson as *The Fancy Dress Party* (London: Secker & Warburg, 1947; New York: Farrar, Straus & Young, 1952);

L'amante infelice (Florence: Bompiani, 1943);

La speranza: ossia, cristianesimo e comunismo (Rome: Documento, 1944);

La cetonia (Rome: Documento, 1944);

Agostino (Rome: Documento, 1944); translated by Beryl de Zoete as *Agostino* (London: Secker & Warburg, 1947);

L'epidemia: Racconti (Rome: Documento, 1944);

Due cortigiane e Serata di don Giovanni (Rome: L'Acquario, 1945);

La romana (Milan: Bompiani, 1947); translated by Lydia Holland as *The Woman of Rome* (New York: Farrar, Straus, 1949; London: Secker & Warburg, 1949);

La disubbidienza (Milan: Bompiani, 1948); translated by Davidson as *Disobedience* (London: Secker & Warburg, 1950);

L'amore coniugale e altri racconti (Milan: Bompiani, 1949); translated by Davidson as *Conjugal Love* (New York: Farrar, Straus & Young, 1951; London: Secker & Warburg, 1951);

Alberto Moravia at the University of California, Los Angeles, in 1981

Il conformista (Milan: Bompiani, 1951); translated by Davidson as *The Conformist* (New York: Farrar, Straus & Young, 1951; London: Secker & Warburg, 1952);

I racconti (Milan: Bompiani, 1952); selected stories translated by Bernard Wall, Baptista Gilliat Smith, and Frances Frenaye as *Bitter Honeymoon, and Other Stories* (London: Secker & Warburg, 1954; New York: Farrar, Straus & Cudahy, 1956); selected stories translated by Davidson as *The Wayward Wife, and Other Stories* (New York: Farrar, Straus & Cudahy, 1960; London: Secker & Warburg, 1960);

Racconti romani (Milan: Bompiani, 1954); selected stories translated by Davidson as *Roman Tales* (London: Secker & Warburg, 1956; New York: Farrar, Straus and Cudahy, 1957);

Il disprezzo (Milan: Bompiani, 1954); translated by Davidson as *A Ghost at Noon* (New York: Farrar, Straus & Young, 1955; London: Secker & Warburg, 1955);

La ciociara (Milan: Bompiani, 1957); translated by Davidson as *Two Women* (New York: Farrar, Straus and Cudahy, 1958; London: Secker & Warburg, 1958);

Teatro: La mascherata. Beatrice Cenci (Milan: Bompiani, 1958); second play translated by Davidson as *Beatrice Cenci* (London: Secker & Warburg, 1965; New York: Farrar, Straus & Giroux, 1966);

Un mese in U.R.S.S. (Milan: Bompiani, 1958);

Nuovi racconti romani (Milan: Bompiani, 1959); selected stories translated by Davidson as *More Roman Tales* (London: Secker & Warburg, 1963; New York: Farrar, Straus, 1964);

La noia (Milan: Bompiani, 1960); translated by Davidson as *The Empty Canvas* (New York: Farrar, Straus & Cudahy, 1961; London: Secker & Warburg, 1961);

Un'idea dell'India (Milan: Bompiani, 1962);

L'automa (Milan: Bompiani, 1963); translated by Davidson as *The Fetish: A Volume of Stories* (London: Secker & Warburg, 1964); republished as *The Fetish, and Other Stories* (New York: Farrar, Straus & Giroux, 1965);

L'uomo come fine e altri saggi (Milan: Bompiani, 1964); translated by Wall as *Man as an End: A Defense of Humanism: Literary, Social, and Political Essays* (London: Secker & Warburg, 1965; New York: Farrar, Straus & Giroux, 1966);

L'attenzione (Milan: Bompiani, 1965); translated by Davidson as *The Lie* (New York: Farrar, Straus & Giroux, 1966; London: Secker & Warburg, 1966);

Il mondo è quello che è. L'intervista (Milan: Bompiani, 1966); *Il mondo è quello che è* translated by A. Coppotelli as *The World's the World, Salmagundi,* 14 (Fall 1970): 39–104;

La rivoluzione culturale in Cina: ovvero, il convitato di pietra (Milan: Bompiani, 1967); translated by Ronald Strom as *The Red Book and the Great Wall: An Impression of Mao's China* (New York: Farrar, Straus & Giroux, 1968; London: Secker & Warburg, 1968);

Una cosa è una cosa (Milan: Bompiani, 1967); selected stories translated by Davidson as *Command and I Will Obey You* (New York: Farrar, Straus & Giroux, 1969; London: Secker & Warburg, 1969);

Il dio Kurt: Tragedia in un prologo e due atti (Milan: Bompiani, 1968);

La vita è gioco (Milan: Bompiani, 1969);

Il paradiso (Milan: Bompiani, 1970); translated by Davidson as *Paradise and Other Stories* (London:

Secker & Warburg, 1971); republished as *Bought and Sold* (New York: Farrar, Straus & Giroux, 1973);

Io e lui (Milan: Bompiani, 1971); translated by Davidson as *Two: A Phallic Novel* (New York: Farrar, Straus & Giroux, 1972); republished as *The Two of Us: A Novel* (London: Secker & Warburg, 1972);

A quale tribù appartieni? (Milan: Bompiani, 1972); translated by Davidson as *Which Tribe Do You Belong To?* (New York: Farrar, Straus & Giroux, 1974; London: Secker & Warburg, 1974);

Un'altra vita (Milan: Bompiani, 1973); translated by Davidson as *Lady Godiva, and Other Stories* (London: Secker & Warburg, 1975); republished as *Mother Love* (St. Albans, U.K.: Panther, 1976);

Al cinema: Centoquarantotto film d'autore (Milan: Bompiani, 1975);

Boh (Milan: Bompiani, 1976); translated by Davidson as *The Voice of the Sea, and Other Stories* (London: Secker & Warburg, 1978);

Tre storie della preistoria (Milan: Emme, 1977);

Quando Ba Lena era tanto piccola (Teramo: Lisciani Zampetti, 1978);

La vita interiore (Milan: Bompiani, 1978); translated by Davidson as *Time of Desecration* (New York: Farrar, Straus & Giroux, 1980; London: Secker & Warburg, 1980);

Un miliardo di anni fa (Turin: Stampatori, 1979);

Cosma e i briganti (Palermo: Sellerio, 1980):

Impegno controvoglia: Saggi, articoli, interviste: Trentacinque anni di scritti politici, edited by Renzo Paris (Milan: Bompiani, 1980);

Lettere dal Sahara (Milan: Bompiani, 1981);

Come Cama Leonte diventò verde lilla blu (Teramo: Lisciani e Zampetti, 1981);

Storie della preistoria (Milan: Bompiani, 1982);

1934 (Milan: Bompiani, 1982); translated by William Weaver as *1934* (New York: Farrar, Straus & Giroux, 1983; London: Secker & Warburg, 1983);

La cosa e altri racconti (Milan: Bompiani, 1983); translated by Tim Parks as *Erotic Tales* (London: Secker & Warburg, 1985; New York: Farrar, Straus & Giroux, 1986);

L'uomo che guarda (Milan: Bompiani, 1985); translated by Parks as *The Voyeur* (London: Secker & Warburg, 1986; New York: Farrar, Straus & Giroux, 1987);

L'angelo dell'informazione e altri testi teatrali (Milan: Bompiani, 1986)—includes *Omaggio a James Joyce: ovvero, Il colpo di stato, La cintura,* and *Voltati parlami;*

L'inverno nucleare, edited by Renzo Paris (Milan: Bompiani, 1986);

Passeggiate africane (Milan: Bompiani, 1987);

Il viaggio a Roma (Milan: 1988); translated by Parks as *Journey to Rome: A Novel* (London: Secker & Warburg, 1990);

Il vassoio davanti alla porta (Milan: Bompiani, 1989);

La villa del venerdì e altri racconti (Milan: Bompiani, 1990);

Diario europeo: Pensieri, persone, fatti, libri, 1984–1990 (Milan: Bompiani, 1993);

La donna leopardo (Milan: Bompiani, 1991);

Romildo, edited by Enzo Siciliano (Milan: Bompiani, 1993);

Viaggi: Articoli 1930–1990, edited by Sicilano (Milan: Bompiani, 1994).

Editions and Collections: *Romanzi brevi: La mascherata. Agostino. La disubbidienza. L'amore coniugale* (Milan: Bompiani, 1953);

Opere complete di Alberto Moravia, 17 volumes (Milan: Bompiani, 1952–1967);

Racconti surrealisti e satirici: L'epidemia. I sogni del pigro (Milan: Bompiani, 1956);

Tutti i racconti romani (Milan: Bompiani, 1971);

Teatro (Milan: Bompiani, 1976)—includes *La mascherata, Beatrice Cenci, Il mondo è gioco,* and *Il dio Kurt;*

Opere: 1927–1947, edited by Geno Pampaloni (Milan: Bompiani, 1986);

Opere: 1948–1968, edited by Enzo Siciliano (Milano: Bompiani, 1989).

Editions in English: *Two Adolescents: The Stories of Agostino and Luca* (New York: Farrar, Straus, 1950; London: Secker & Warburg, 1952)—includes *Agostino* and *La disubbidienza;*

Five Novels: Mistaken Ambitions. Agostino. Luca. Conjugal Love. A Ghost at Noon (New York: Farrar, Straus & Young, 1955; London: Secker & Warburg, 1955);

Three Novels: The Conformist, The Fancy Dress Party, A Ghost at Noon (New York: New American Library, 1961).

PLAY PRODUCTIONS: *Gli indifferenti,* adapted by Moravia and Luigi Squazini, Rome, 1948;

La mascherata, Milan, Piccolo Teatro della Città di Milano, 14 April 1954;

Beatrice Cenci, Sao Paulo, Brazil, Teatro Santana, summer 1955;

Il provino, and *Non approfondire,* Milan, 22 November 1955;

Il mondo è quello che è, Venice, Teatro Stabile di Torino, 8 October 1966;

L'intervista, Rome, Teatro del Procospino, 20 October 1966;

Il dio Kurt, L'Aquila, Teatro Comunale, 27 January 1969;

La vita è gioco; Rome, Teatro Valle, 1 October 1970;

Le donne di Moravia, adapted from *Il paradiso,* Compagnia del Teatro dei Commedianti, 1970–1971;

Omaggio a James Joyce ovvero il colpo di stato, Venice, Teatro di Cal Foscari, 1970–1971.

MOTION PICTURES: *Senza cielo,* screenplay by Moravia, Ugo Betti, Sandro De Feo, Ercole Patti, Viccenzo Talarico, Piero Tellini, Cesare Zavattini, and Alfredo Guarini, Artisti Associati/Continentalcine, 1940;

Un colpo di pistola, screenplay by Moravia, Mario Bonfartini, Corrado Pavolini, and Mario Soldati, Lux, 1942;

Ossessione, screenplay by Moravia, Pietro Ingrao, Mario Alicata, Antonio Pietrangeli, Giuseppe de Santis, Gianni Puccini, and Luchino Visconti, ICI, 1942;

Perdizione, screenplay by Moravia and others, Scalera, 1942;

Tragica notte (La trappola), screenplay by Moravia, Mario Bonfantini, and Emilio Cecchi, Scalera, 1942;

Zaza, screenplay by Moravia, Lux, 1942;

La freccia nel fianco, screenplay by Moravia, Ennio Flaiano, and Cesare Zavattini, Ponti/Ata, 1945;

Monastero di Santa Chiara, screenplay by Moravia and Fulvio Palmieri, Avis Film, 1948;

Il cielo sulla palude, screenplay by Moravia, Lux, 1949;

Documento mensile, one episode of documentary written and directed by Moravia, 1951;

Ultimo incontro, screenplay by Moravia, Edoardo Anton, Antonio Pietrangeli, and Gian Paolo Callegari, Lux, 1951;

La donna del fiume, screenplay by Moravia, Ennio Flaiano, Giorgio Bassani, Pier Paolo Pasolini, and Florestano Vancini; Excelsa/Carlo Ponti, 1954;

La romana, screenplay of his novel by Moravia, Luigi Zampa, Giorgio Bassani, and Ennio Flaiano, Ponti/De Laurentils/Excelsa, 1954;

Sensualità, screenplay by Moravia and Ennio De Concini, Ponti/De Laurentiis/Paramount, 1954;

Stazione Termini screenplay by Moravia, Cesare Zavallini, Truman Capote, and others, directed by Vittorio De Sica, Columbia, 1954;

Villa Borghese, screenplay by Moravia, Sergio Amidei, Liana Ferri, Ennio Flaino, and Rodolfo Sonego, Astoria Film, 1954;

Racconti romani, screenplay, based on Moravia's sto-
  ries by Moravia, Sergio Amidei, Francesco
  Rosi, and Furio Scarpelli, Ics, 1955;
Racconti d'estate, screenplay by Moravia, Alberto
  Sordi, Sergio Amidei, Ennio Flaiano, Edoardo
  Anton, Rodolfo Sonego, and René Barjavel,
  Maxima/Montflour/Gallus, 1958;
On the Beach, dialogue for the Italian version (*L'ul-
  tima spiaggia*) by Moravia, United Artists,
  1959;
I delfini, screenplay by Moravia, Francesco Maselli,
  Ennio De Concini, and Aggeo Savioli,
  Lux/Vides, 1960;
La giornata balorda, screenplay based on Moravia's
  stories by Moravia, Pasolini, and Marco Vis-
  conti, Intercontinental/Euro Film Interna-
  tional/Euro Film International/Transcontinen-
  tal, 1960;
Una domenica d'estate, screenplay by Moravia, Sergio
  Amidei, and Ugo Pirro, Cineproduzioni Emo
  Bistolfi/Leo Film, 1961;
Agostino (*La perdita dell'innocenza*), screenplay based
  on Moravia's novel by Moravia, Mauro Bo-
  lognini, and Goffredo Parise, Dino De Lauren-
  tiis/Baltea, 1962;
Le ore nude, screenplay, based on Moravia's story
  ("Appuntamento al mare"), by Moravia Antonio
  Guerro, and Marco Vicario, Atlantica, 1964;
L'occhio selvaggio, screenplay by Moravia, Paolo Ca-
  vara, and Tonino Guerra, directed by Paolo
  Cavara, Cavara/American International Pic-
  tures, 1967.

UNCOLLECTED PERIODICAL PUBLICATION:
  "About My Novels," *Twentieth-Century,* 164 (1958):
  530.

Alberto Moravia is a dominant figure in Italian
literary and cultural life in the twentieth century.
His first novel appeared in 1929, and for the next
sixty years he published profusely: novels, short
stories, essays, plays, film scripts, travel pieces,
movie reviews, and tales for children. The first Italian writer to achieve international renown after
World War II, he had become a public figure in Italy by the 1970s: political parties vied for his support and even his candidacy in elections; articles on
his personal life and literary career appeared regularly in mass-market magazines; and the press and
television sought him for interviews.

Moravia's appeal to three generations of Italian readers was undeniable: sales of his works
eventually made him wealthy—an uncommon phenomenon in Italy where few writers can support
themselves solely by their art. Critical reception of

his work has been less consistent. For some critics
his style lacks luster and his realism is as unimaginative as his themes are repetitive. Others have
supported him ardently, emphasizing his formidable skill as a storyteller and his sustained commitment to humanist ideals. Even his detractors usually agree that his fiction reflects the profound
changes that revolutionized Italian civilization in
the twentieth century: the experience of fascism,
the devastation of World War II, the postwar difficulties that were only partially resolved by the economic miracle of the 1960s, the student revolution,
the feminist movement, and the general malaise
and disarray of the 1980s.

Alberto Pincherle Moravia was born in Rome
on 28 November 1907. He inherited the double
name from his father's Venetian forbears, although
the family was commonly known as Pincherle.
However, only the author's first article, which appeared in a newspaper, carried the signature of Alberto Pincherle; thereafter, he used the pen name
Alberto Moravia in order to avoid confusion with a
professor of religion at the University of Rome who
had the same name. (Some scholars have errone-
ously attributed Professor Pincherle's 1920 volume
of poems, *Diciotto liriche,* to Moravia).

Moravia's father, Carlo, was a well-to-do architect and amateur painter who married Teresa
Iginia De Marsanich, a young woman from an impoverished though reputedly noble family of Ancona. The two could hardly have been more different: Carlo—blond, Jewish, and twenty years older
than his bride—was solitary, conservative, and a
creature of habit. His brunette wife was socially ori-
ented, forward-looking, and Catholic. A strong-
willed and active woman, she overshadowed her
quiet, retiring husband and appears to have dominated family life. The couple had four children:
Adriana, Alberto, Elena, and Gastone. Gastone was
killed in battle in World War II. It is perhaps significant that, although mothers figure prominently as
characters in many of Moravia's novels, fathers appear only in two novels written during the last decade of the author's life.

Teresa Pincherle hoped that her older son
would enter the diplomatic service, and to that end
she employed a succession of foreign governesses to
instruct her children. Languages were emphasized:
young Alberto learned French before he could
speak Italian and acquired a good knowledge of
English. Storytelling appears to have been almost instinctive in Moravia; as a youngster he asked for
and received a puppet theater and produced shows
to amuse his sisters and brother. He composed and
recited stories to himself, and, as he learned to

write, committed them to paper. Carlo Pincherle's library was rich in the dramatic literature of William Shakespeare, Molière, and Carlo Goldoni; Moravia also read classic comic writers such as Petronius, Lucius Apuleius, Giovanni Boccaccio, Ludovico Ariosto, Miguel de Cervantes, and François Rabelais. Giacomo Leopardi and Arthur Rimbaud were his preferred poets. Although Moravia attributed his penchant for narration to Alessandro Manzoni, he also read Daniel Defoe, Honoré de Balzac, Stendhal, Marcel Proust, and James Joyce. His acknowledged master, though, was Fyodor Dostoyevsky, whose obscure passions and somber atmospheres are sometimes echoed in Moravia's works.

Moravia's formal education was scanty and even deficient, especially in mathematics and science, for he fell ill at the age of eight with tuberculosis of the bone. His absences from school grew increasingly frequent and by the time he was twelve, he was bedridden. The treatment he received in Rome was of little benefit: his health deteriorated, and the prescribed casts for his legs were painful. Only the intervention of his father's sister, Amelia Rosselli, led to Alberto's recovery: she insisted that her nephew be taken to the Codivilla Sanitarium in Cortina d'Ampezzo. Moravia arrived there in March 1924, and the clinic's modern procedures effected over time a recovery.

Upon his release from the Codivilla in October 1925, Moravia began writing with the intention of publishing his work. His first story, "La cortigiana stanca" (1927; translated as "Tired Courtesan," 1954), appeared in *Novecento*, a review edited by Massimo Bontempelli, Corrado Alvaro, and Curzio Malaparte and was later collected in *I racconti*. Bontempelli encouraged and even challenged the young authors associated with the journal to write a novel in a modern vein that would reflect the character of the times and the somewhat avant-garde nature of *Novecento*. Only Moravia completed the task, but when he submitted the manuscript to the publisher of *Novecento*, it was rejected, according to Alain Elkann in his *Vita di Moravia* (1990), as "una nebbia di parole" (a fog of words).

Moravia then took his work to the Alpes publishing house in Milan, which agreed to print it in return for a subsidy of 5,000 lire. Moravia's father lent him the money and *Gli indifferenti* (translated as *The Indifferent Ones*, 1932) appeared in 1929. The novel was an instant, though not unmitigated, success, provoking a violent debate among Italian readers. Several critics, among them Giuseppe Antonio Borgese, praised its unadorned realism and straightforward style; many readers, however,

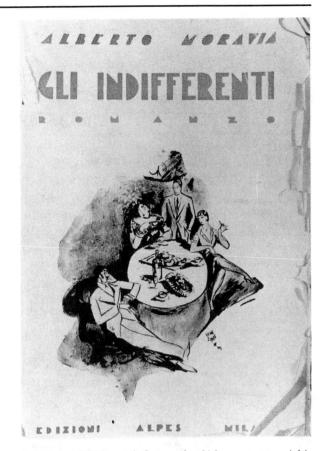

Dust jacket for Moravia's first novel, which was controversial in part because of its frank descriptions of sex

chastised the work for its explicit descriptions of sexuality and for an unsavory portrayal of Rome's upper middle class. As depicted in the novel the bourgeoisie seems to be motivated by greed, lies, and sexual appetite, a view that was contrary to the idealized picture of Italian life promulgated by Fascist propaganda.

Moravia was surprised at the clamor aroused by his first novel. In "Ricordo de *Gli indifferenti*" (translated as "Recalling *Time of Indifference*"), a 1945 essay collected in *L'uomo come fine e altri saggi* (1964; translated as *Man as an End: A Defense of Humanism: Literary, Social, and Political Essays*, 1965), he recalled his dispassionate, experimental approach to the work:

Mi ero messo in mente di scrivere un romanzo che avesse al tempo stesso le qualità di un'opera narrativa e quelle di un dramma. Un romanzo con pochi personaggi, con pochissimi luoghi, con un'azione svolta in poco tempo. Un romanzo in cui non ci fossero che il dialogo e gli sfondi e nel quale tutti i commenti, le analisi e gli interventi dell'autore fossero accuratamente aboliti in una perfetta oggettività.

(I had decided to write a novel that possessed the qualities of both fiction and drama. It was to be a novel with

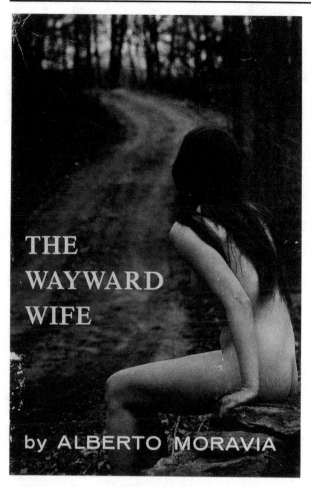

Dust jacket for the American edition of some of the stories from Moravia's 1952 collection, which won the Strega Prize

few characters, very few scenes, and with action restricted to a short period of time; a novel in which there would be only dialogue and descriptive narration and in which all the comments, analyses, and interventions of the author would be scrupulously omitted in order to achieve a perfect objectivity.)

The resulting novel was indeed theatrical: most of the settings are interior scenes; the action occurs in little more than two days; and there are only five characters.

The widow Mariagrazia Ardengo and her former rival, Lisa, are middle-aged women who dream of renewing or initiating love affairs and rising to new heights of power and wealth (Mariagrazia) or sentimental rapture (Lisa). Mariagrazia's children, twenty-four-year-old Carla and her younger brother, Michele, are tired of the numbing routine in the Ardengo villa and imagine a meaningful "new life" of ideal love, firm relationships, and careers. The focal character is the sinister Leo Merumeci, who years earlier had jilted Lisa in order to become Mariagrazia's lover and financial advi-

sor. Perversely, he intends to desecrate both of these roles by seducing Carla and foreclosing the mortgage on the villa.

Unlike the other characters in the novel, Leo has his feet planted firmly on the ground; he wastes no time daydreaming and conducts his life according to an almost Machiavellian discipline. In comparison to the cynical Leo, the other characters seem immature and unrealistic, suspended between what is and what may be. Their common failing is self-delusion: Lisa fancies that Michele will love her; Mariagrazia is confident that she can recapture Leo's affection; Carla believes that sleeping with Leo will put a definitive end to her old life and lead to the new life; Michele imagines that he can find within himself a reason to act authentically and so dispel the indifference that overwhelms him. Only Leo achieves his goal: the others relapse into a routine that has been rendered even more loathsome by the moral defeats experienced by Michele and Carla.

Gli indifferenti sets not only the despairing tone for much of Moravia's later fiction but also introduces the prototypes of many of the characters who will appear throughout his work: Michele, the young intellectual alienated from reality; Carla, who senses that there is something wrong with her life and the world in which it unfolds, but who has neither the intellectual capacity nor the moral stamina to come to grips with her problem; and Mariagrazia and Lisa, almost classic examples of self-deluding persons whose perceptions of the world have nothing to do with reality. *Gli indifferenti* also states the themes and problems that Moravia would treat in his fiction until the late 1960s, all arising from the individual's view of the self in the world and in relationship with other people. The question of how one can achieve a fulfilling life, of how one can reconcile ideals and dreams with the limitations imposed by existence, has motivated most of Moravia's work as well as much of the literature of the twentieth century.

Although many critics have maintained that *Gli indifferenti* is an indictment of Italian society under Fascism, Moravia always insisted that he wrote the novel without any political intentions. Indeed, it is difficult to connect the decadent family portrayed in the novel with the Fascist regime. Politics are never mentioned, nor is there even an allusion to the Fascist government. In its essence *Gli indifferenti* attacks not a political entity but bourgeois capitalist society. Such criticism goes beyond *Gli indifferenti* and is one of the constants in Moravia's career, present in the novels and stories he wrote even thirty and forty years after the fall of the Fascists. Carla and Michele became young adults under Fascist rule but are not unique to Italy: their peers are scattered throughout the Western world, members of the Lost Generation and the generation between the wars. The affliction of Michele and Carla has its roots not in Italian Fascism but in an international malaise.

The new realism of *Gli indifferenti*—its sparse style so uncharacteristic of traditional literary Italian as well as its treatment of existential anguish, which would later become common in the Continental novel—has led critics to regard *Gli indifferenti* as the first European novel to come out of what had been a decidedly regional Italian literature. As had been the case with Luigi Pirandello and Italo Svevo, the French were among the first to recognize the originality of Moravia's work and its existentialist themes. When Moravia traveled to France after World War II, Jean Paulhan asked him if he had come to visit his disciples, Jean-Paul Sartre and Albert Camus. Dominique Fernandez, pointing to the moral justification of action as the central theme of *Gli indifferenti,* called it the first European existentialist novel.

Shortly after the publication of *Gli indifferenti*, Moravia began a series of trips that continued almost uninterrupted during the 1930s, visiting Europe, North America, and Asia. In addition to the usual pleasures and benefits of travel, Moravia's sojourns abroad gave him the opportunity to escape the growing political repression in Italy. *Gli indifferenti* had not pleased the Fascists, who eventually prohibited its reprinting. Although Moravia did not engage in either overt or clandestine activities against the regime, he openly associated with antifascists. From at least 1931 onward he was under surveillance by the police.

Although Moravia's father provided the funds for his son's travels, the young author was also a special correspondent first for *La stampa* and then for *La gazzetta del popolo,* newspapers published in Turin. During the first half of the 1930s he reported on his European travels in a series of articles; he published little, though he did translate some stories by Ernest Hemingway, Ring Lardner, Theodore Dreiser, and James Cain. Eleven of his own stories were collected under the title *La bella vita* (The Good Life) in 1935. Included among them was one of Moravia's masterpieces, "Inverno di malato" (translated as "A Sick Boy's Winter," 1954), in which the protagonist, seventeen-year-old Girolamo, struggles to make sense of the world of adults. His perplexity when confronted with sexuality and class differences as well as his profound yet undeserved sense

of guilt lay a pattern for many of Moravia's later adolescent characters.

Moravia spent more than five years writing his second novel, *Le ambizioni sbagliate* (1935; translated as *Wheel of Fortune,* 1937). He clearly shows his debt to Dostoyevsky in this long novel of greed, passion, and murder. Unfortunately, the plot is extraordinarily complicated and melodramatic, and its characters are neither believable nor convincing: their motivations are vague, their actions are often inconsistent with their personalities, and even the idealistic hero comes off as hypocritical. Moravia agreed with his critics that the novel was a thorough failure.

In late 1935, following the publication of his novel, Moravia made his first trip to the United States with the help of a grant arranged by Giuseppe Prezzolini, then a professor of Italian at Columbia University. Except for a short visit to Mexico he remained principally in New York City during his six-month stay. Although he gave a few lectures at various colleges, he apparently wrote nothing during this period, nor did he publish any articles on his experiences in America. Most of his time was spent observing American life and the workings of capitalism. Despite his admiration for the modern and industrialized nation, he disapproved of its materialism and the chasm that separated the poor from the wealthy classes. Class differences, his unhappy experience under Fascism, and his reading of Karl Marx's *Das Kapital* (1867–1894) inclined Moravia increasingly toward Marxist ideology.

Toward the end of the 1930s Moravia made two more voyages abroad, the first to China in 1937 and the other a year later to Greece. Again, the trips were welcome respites from life in Italy and his increasing difficulties with its government. His perceived antifascism was the probable cause for his losing his position with *La gazzetta del popolo*; his political views coupled with the critical and commercial failure of *Le ambizioni sbagliate* also rendered uncertain the publication of his second volume of short stories. Valentino Bompiani finally agreed to publish them in 1937 under the title of *L'imbroglio* (The Imbroglio). Except for some works published in Rome during the war years, all of Moravia's books were produced by Bompiani.

On 18 October 1934 Moravia published in *La gazzetta del popolo* a short story, "Tiberio a Capri" (Tiberius at Capri), that marked a notable change from his previous fiction: for the first time the setting was not a bourgeois milieu in contemporary Italy. Encouraged if not impelled by the growing restraints on artistic expression in Italy, Moravia turned increasingly to satire, allegory, and surrealism in his short fiction. Many such stories were col-

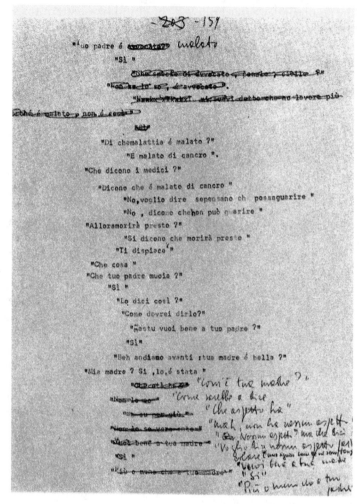

Page from the revised typescript for La noia *(Alberto Moravia Collection)*

lected in *I sogni del pigro* (Lazy Man's Dreams, 1940) and *L'epidemia* (The Epidemic, 1944) and later published in one volume, *Racconti surrealisti e satirici* (Surrealist and Satiric Stories, 1956). The majority of these stories criticize in a veiled way Fascism, society, or human weaknesses. They reveal a bountiful imagination that is sometimes difficult to discern in Moravia's realistic fiction. The stories also show his qualities as a moralist, a role that has been recognized by several critics.

Moravia again encountered difficulties when he tried to publish *La mascherata* (1941; translated as *The Fancy Dress Party,* 1947), a novel set in an imaginary Latin American country ruled by the dictator Tereso. Although the Fascist censors were aware that such a tale might conceal a satire, they eventually allowed its publication. To a contemporary reader, the farcical elements of the novel seem more notable than its satire. The scenario recalls traditional classic comedy, replete with mistaken identi-

ties, masked characters, servants who instigate and control the action, and several cleverly arranged scenes. The theatrical character of the novel led Moravia to adapt it for the stage, and it was produced by the Piccolo Teatro di Milano in 1954.

Moravia maintained that he intended *La mascherata* as a satire of Benito Mussolini and his regime. Certainly the fictitious Latin American dictatorship, with its oppression, police spies, and self-centered functionaries, calls to mind Italy in the 1930s. Tereso, however, resembles Il Duce only in his bald, protruding forehead and in his swagger. The Latin American ruler has simple tastes, is modest to the point of being almost antisocial, and considers himself an "ordinary man." He is also shy and awkward around women. Moreover, Tereso's plans for his nation contrast significantly with those envisioned by Mussolini. The government of the beloved Tereso becomes increasingly kind and paternal; to further his goal of a benign political structure, Tereso is about to rid himself of Cinco, the odious chief of police and the real villain of the novel.

If Tereso was modeled on Mussolini, then one can only conclude that Moravia regarded Il Duce as not too bad a fellow, a victim of circumstances and bad advisers. The Italian government's decision to seize the novel soon after its publication was probably occasioned more by Moravia's antifascist reputation than by any harm that *La mascherata* caused the regime. In addition, Moravia may have suffered for the more rigid enforcement of the laws of 1938 against Italian Jews. Although his mother had officially changed the family name to Piccinini, her own mother's maiden name, and though she produced baptismal certificates for all her children, the "taint" of Jewishness lingered nonetheless. Whatever the reasons, Moravia was forbidden to publish under his own name; until the collapse of Fascism he signed his articles with the transparent pen name of "Pseudo."

In 1941 Moravia married Elsa Morante, a writer whom he had met in 1936. The couple was living in Rome when the Fascist Grand Council deposed Mussolini on 25 July 1943 and turned political control over to Marshal Pietro Badoglio. From July until the announcement on 8 September of the armistice between Italy and the Allies, Rome enjoyed a brief period of liberty during which Moravia published two antifascist articles in the newspaper *Il popolo di roma*. Shortly after the Nazi forces seized control of the city, however, a Hungarian journalist told Moravia that his name was on a list of persons to be arrested. Hoping to cross the Allied lines north of Naples, Moravia and Morante boarded a southbound train; it traveled no farther than the small town of Fondi, halfway between the two major cities. Unable to continue south, the couple took refuge in the mountains, where they passed the winter of 1943–1944 living in a peasant's hut and often foraging for food. It was Moravia's first sustained direct contact with the lower classes, and it influenced not only his personal life but also the development of his career.

Moravia's two volumes of stories, *L'amante infelice* "The Unfortunate Lover," 1943) and *Due cortigiane* (Two Courtesans, 1945), were eclipsed by his short novel of 1944, *Agostino* (translated as *Agostino*, 1947), for which he received his first literary prize, the Corriere Lombardo. The Agostino of the title is similar to the protagonist of "Inverno di malato." The thirteen-year-old Agostino, like Girolamo, belongs to the middle class and is completely unaware of sexuality and class differences. During a vacation at the sea with his mother, Agostino meets a group of young boys from the lower classes. Their cruelty

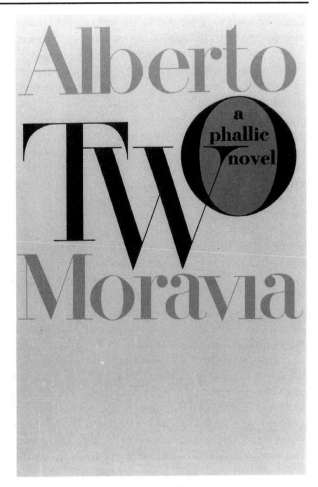

Dust jacket for the American edition of the translation of Moravia's 1971 novel, in which an ineffectual intellectual is ruled by his sexual desires

and vulgarity are for Agostino a new experience that he can neither understand nor accept. Even more perplexing is the question of sex. He is bewildered by the language of the boys, the homosexuality of an adult beach attendant, and by the sexual attraction that he feels for his mother. Not accepted by the lower-class boys yet unable to return uncritically to his bourgeois life and still mystified by sex, Agostino is stranded in the limbo of adolescence, no longer a boy but not yet a man.

Agostino is perhaps Moravia's most artistic novel. Despite the somewhat raw themes of homosexuality and Oedipal love (Moravia had discovered Sigmund Freud in the 1930s), the simple literary style and subtle imagery of the work imparts a natural and sympathetic tone that emphasizes Moravia's sensitivity, perception, and understanding of the complexities of adolescence. This same understanding is evident in *La disubbidienza* (1948; translated as *Disobedience*, 1950), often regarded as a sequel to *Agostino*, in which fifteen-year-old Luca also finds himself at a pivotal point in his life. Disillusioned by the hypocrisy of his parents, he becomes "disobedient" and rejects the bourgeois values of his social class. Adrift in uncertainty, his health deteriorates until he is reconciled with the world through the physical affection of a nurse.

La disubbidienza is a less satisfactory novel than *Agostino*. Overburdened by symbols and dreams, the novel at times resembles a Freudian casebook study and lacks the natural grace of the earlier novel of adolescence. Both, however, place sexuality at the center of human experience and suggest that it is an important means—perhaps the only one—of establishing a relationship with others and with the world. The primacy of sexuality would remain a constant element in Moravia's work.

While *Agostino* has the distinction of being Moravia's first sustained treatment of the proletariat, his sympathy with the lower classes was evident indirectly in *Gli indifferenti*: the ridiculous Mariagrazia despised them and thus unwittingly gave them value in the eyes of the reader. During his travels in England in the early 1930s, Moravia often mingled with the poor, writing more favorably of their values than of those of the British aristocracy. He began to understand and appreciate the Italian poor more deeply when he came to live among them in the winter of 1943–1944. In time his admiration transformed itself into what he termed "il mito del popolo" (the myth of the lower classes)—the idea that the masses were more in touch with reality than was the bourgeoisie.

Before World War II Moravia's protagonists were mostly middle-class men, often intellectual and usually alienated, leading lives of unrelenting boredom caused by an absence of values. Moravia discovered that the common people—peasants, domestic workers, small shopkeepers, skilled and unskilled laborers—did not suffer such problems. They were at home in their world, and life was closely connected to a reality that they did not doubt. Their lives were composed of actions undertaken freely and with the conviction that they were justified and justifiable. Alienation was unknown to them. Practical and material concerns aside, they were content with taking and enjoying life as it came. In Moravian terms they were authentic individuals.

The appearance in 1947 of *La romana* (translated as *The Woman of Rome*, 1949) marked a major change in Moravia's career. The work was a critical and commercial success in Europe, and it brought him to the attention of readers and critics in the United States. (The English translations of *Gli indifferenti* and *Ambizioni sbagliate* had passed almost unnoticed.) In *La romana* Moravia chose to write in the first person instead of the omniscient third person that had characterized his previous works. He also created a female protagonist, Adriana, who is from the lower classes of Rome.

Adriana's initial aim in life is to marry her working-class lover, Mino, and raise a family. Disillusioned when she discovers that he is already married, the young woman drifts into prostitution. She encounters men from all strata of Italian society, including self-centered, bourgeois gentlemen; powerful, sadomasochistic Fascists; brutish criminals; and feeble intellectuals such as Mino. Adriana's values contrast with theirs. They represent the forces of death and chaos; she is a life force firmly rooted in nature. Her sense of reality and of herself is clear and instinctive: life is concrete, real, here and now. Difficult as it may be, she accepts life freely and affirms it:

> Io mi sono sovente domandata perché la tristezza e la rabbia abitino così spesso l'animo di coloro che vogliono vivere secondo certi precetti o uniformarsi a certi ideali e perché invece coloro che accettano la propria vita . . . sono così spesso gai e spensierati. Del resto, in questi casi, ciascuno obbedisce non a precetti ma al proprio temperamento. . . . Il mio, come ho già detto, era di essere, a tutti i costi, lieta, dolce e tranquilla; e io l'accettavo.

> (I have often wondered why sadness and anger are so frequently found in those who try to live according to certain precepts or ideals and why those who accept their own life . . . are usually happy and carefree. But in these cases each obeys not a precept but his or her own temperament. . . . Mine was to be, at any cost, happy, sweet, and calm; and I accepted it.)

Adriana is Eros incarnate and, like nature, she guarantees the continuity of life: she bears a child in her womb as she ends her story.

The milieu of Rome's workers and small shopkeepers reappears in a series of short stories that Moravia began writing for Milan's *Corriere della sera* in late 1948 and continued to publish regularly for the next ten years. Narrated from the first-person point of view of a male protagonist, each story recounts with humor or pathos the difficulties of love, work, and life in a society plagued by poverty and unemployment. Popular with readers and praised by critics, the tales were collected in two volumes: *Racconti romani* (1954; translated as *Roman Tales*, 1956) and *Nuovi racconti romani* (1959; translated as *More Roman Tales*, 1963).

Moravia depicts the world of the lower classes and the petty bourgeoisie for the last time in *La ciociara* (1957; translated as *Two Women*, 1958), a novel some regard as Moravia's best. A country girl by

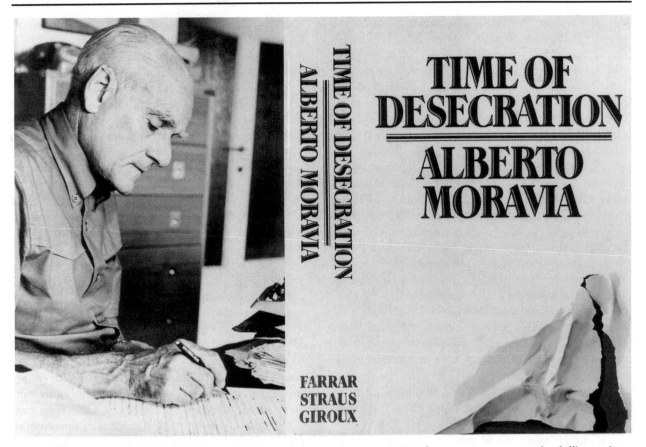

Dust jacket for the American edition of the translation of Moravia's 1978 novel, which focuses on a young woman's rebellion against bourgeois values

birth, Cesira runs a small grocery after the death of her husband, who brought her to Rome. She is fundamentally moral and honest, but it is 1943, a desperate time. With foodstuffs procured from her relatives, Cesira earns considerable sums on the black market. Her sole aim is to assure the security of her timid and religious eighteen-year-old daughter, Rosetta.

Eventually, Cesira can no longer obtain merchandise, and when it appears that Rome will be bombed, she decides to return with Rosetta to her parents' home in Fondi. They find on their arrival that their family has already fled the town. Forced to spend the winter in a small village in the mountains, they meet Michele, an antifascist intellectual who tries to rouse the villagers from their apolitical lethargy and selfishness. After the Allies break through the Gustav Line in the spring, Cesira and Rosetta set out for Rome. On the way, both are raped. Rosetta becomes cynical and promiscuous, while the despondent Cesira contemplates suicide and reaches a moral nadir when she steals money from Rosetta's murdered lover. Michele's teachings, however, eventually have their effect, and the novel ends in an affirmation of hope.

While enjoying considerable success with his *racconti romani* and populist novels during the late 1940s and into the 1950s, Moravia also continued to write works centered on the bourgeoisie. In 1951 he published *Il conformista* (translated as *The Conformist,* 1951), a novel loosely based on the 1937 assassination in France of Moravia's cousins, Carlo and Nello Rosselli, who were among the earliest and best-known antifascists: Carlo was the leader and theorist of the Giustizia e libertà (Justice and Liberty) movement.

The novel focuses on Marcello Clerici, who reacts to his self-perceived abnormality by conforming to the social and political standards of the era. He marries a middle-class woman, and he not only joins the Fascist Party but also collaborates with its secret police. A monster of egoism and self-delusion, Marcello is perhaps Moravia's most despicable creation. As a fictional character he is wooden and only barely believable. While director Bernardo Bertolucci based an excellent film on the work (1970), the novel offers only a facile and unconvincing case study of a psychotic. The plot becomes strained as Moravia pushes his message that Fascism was a pathological aberration of middle-class values.

Two other novels of this period, *L'amore coniugale* (1949; translated as *Conjugal Love,* 1951) and *Il disprezzo* (1954; translated as *A Ghost at Noon,* 1955), treat marital crises. In *L'amore coniugale* Moravia fashioned a situation to which he would return in the 1960s: the artist, stymied by interrelated creative and personal problems, who to recapture his creativity must analyze himself and investigate the world about him.

The domestic conflict of *Il disprezzo* is set against the world of filmmaking, which Moravia was well qualified to depict. From 1936 to 1960 he collaborated on film scripts for a variety of directors, among them Mario Soldati, Luchino Visconti, Renato Castellani, Alberto Lattuada, and Luigi Zampa. In addition, more than twenty of his novels and stories were adapted for the screen, including Zampa's *La romana* (1955), Vittorio De Sica's *La ciociara* (1960), Damiano Damiani's *La noia* (1963), Francesco Maselli's *Gli indifferenti* (1964), and Jean-Luc Godard's *Il disprezzo* (1965). Moravia began reviewing films for *L'Europeo* in 1944 and later became film critic for *L'Espresso,* an activity that he continued almost until his death. A selection of his reviews is collected in *Al cinema: Centoquarantotto film d'autore* (At the Movies: 148 Films, 1975).

The 1950s were a particularly productive decade in Moravia's career. His collected stories, *I racconti* (The Stories, 1952), earned him the Strega Prize in 1952. The following year Moravia and his longtime friend Alberto Carocci, a former editor of the highly respected journal *Solaria,* founded *Nuovi argomenti* (New Topics), a cultural review that would prove to be especially receptive to young writers. He also continued his travels abroad and began publishing books about his journeys.

Un mese in U.R.S.S. (A Month in the U.S.S.R.), the first of Moravia's many travel books, was published in 1958. In 1962 he published *Un'idea dell'India* (An Idea of India), which he followed five years later with *La rivoluzione culturale in Cina* (1967; translated as *The Red Book and the Great Wall,* 1968). The three volumes chronicling Moravia's travels in Africa are especially highly regarded in the field of travel literature: *A quale tribù appartieni?* (1972; translated as *Which Tribe Do You Belong To?,* 1974), *Lettere dal Sahara* (Letters from the Sahara, 1981), and *Passeggiate africane* (Walks in Africa, 1987). Unlike many other European visitors to other continents, Moravia avoided comparing exotic lands to Europe and sought instead to distinguish what was unique in each culture—and what might be adopted to improve the lot of humanity in Europe and elsewhere.

Moravia's interest in improving humanity permeates much of his nonfiction. An early essay, *La speranza: ossia, Cristianesimo e comunismo* (Hope: or, Christianity and Communism), appeared in 1944. After seeing the abuses of human rights under Fascism, Moravia along with many Italian intellectuals of his time took a utopian view of communism and regarded Marxism as the hope of the world. Christianity, he asserted, had lost its impetus as an active force for good and justice Moravia scarcely touched upon the economic or political features of Marxism; instead, he dealt principally with its humanistic aspects. Although Moravia later became disenchanted with communism as it was practiced in the Soviet Union, he never abandoned his idealistic view of Marxism, nor did he waver in his dedication to humanistic principles.

Moravia detailed his humanism in a major essay titled "L'uomo come fine." Written about 1946, the long essay was not published until 1954, when it appeared in *Nuovi argomenti;* it was later collected in *L'uomo come fine e altri saggi.* The modern world, Moravia maintains, has betrayed the Renaissance ideal of the improvement of the human being as an end, the only aim of human activity. Since all current political systems and institutions regard the individual as a means and not as an end, the world has become a nightmare: "Evaporato il cristianesimo, non essendo più l'uomo il fine ma il mezzo, il mondo moderno rassomiglia ad un incubo perfettamente organizzato ed efficiente" (With Christianity dead and man no longer being an end but a means, the modern world resembles a perfectly organized and efficient nightmare).

Moravia argues that the root of the modern condition is the indiscriminate application of reason in the lives of human beings, which always results in violence and in the use of human beings as instruments to achieve an end. But it is reason, not the human being, that should be the instrument: "La ragione non può servirci che a ragionare ossia a distinguere, conoscere e apprezzare secondo il loro giusto valore i mezzi e il fine. . . . La ragione, se è ragionevole, può dirci, come infatti talvolta ci dice, che il solo fine giusto e possibile è l'uomo." (Reason is useful only for reasoning, that is, for distinguishing, knowing, and evaluating accurately the means and the end. . . . Reason, if it is reasonable, will tell us, as indeed it sometimes does, that the only just and possible end is man himself.)

Although the 1950s witnessed significant critical and popular success for Moravia, they also were the years of crises in his personal life. His marital bond with Elsa Morante had never been strong: theirs was a tempestuous marriage, fraught with quarrels, professional jealousies, and infidelity. The marriage was in reality finished by the mid 1950s, though they continued to live in the same apartment until 1963. As Moravia later remarked to Enzo Siciliano:

> A cinquant'anni attraversai una crisi psicologica orrenda.... Ero arrivato a una svolta: forse non mi piaceva più vivere; e ho avuto il coraggio di spezzare tante cose che allora mi erano molto care e che avevano per me un grande significato. Ma non potevo fare altro.... Quel distacco, quella rottura hanno prodotto una forma di rinnovamento, credo.

> (At the age of fifty, I went through a severe psychological crisis.... I had arrived at a turning point: perhaps I did not like life any longer, and I had the courage to shatter many things which at that time were very dear and meaningful to me. But there was nothing else I could do.... That severance, that rupture produced, I believe, a kind of rebirth.)

Following the end of his marriage Moravia began living with novelist and playwright Dacia Maraini, whom he had met about 1954 and with whom he shared his life from 1962 until 1978.

Moravia renewed his art as well as his life. Although he still clung to the notion that the lower socioeconomic classes have stronger ties to reality than does the bourgeoisie, he ceased basing his fiction on the "myth of people." He came to the conclusion that the relationship between the individual and reality was fundamentally different for the two classes. The proletariat was bonded to reality by the necessity of securing food and shelter: alienation simply did not occupy their minds, nor did it pose a problem for them. Freed from such constraints, the bourgeoisie experienced alienation as *noia* (boredom, existential malaise), or a lack of meaning in their lives. For many of them intellectual myopia precluded their seeing beyond personal or professional interests, and they consequently did not confront, analyze, or resolve the problem. Moravia believed that this was the task of the intellectual, the only positive element that he recognized in the middle class. Moravia's fiction after 1958 dealt exclusively with a bourgeois milieu, and the protagonists of all his novels were intellectuals.

Moravia also modified his concept of the novel. Movies and television, he maintained, had supplanted the traditional narrative function of the novel. Film was more effective in detailing physical surroundings, depicting actions, and in telling a story. The new appropriate role of fiction, according to Moravia, was to treat what the camera could not capture, such as ideas and analytic investigations. In "Note sul romanzo" (translated as "Notes on the Novel"), an important 1956 essay included in

L'uomo come fine e altri saggi, Moravia envisioned a *romanzo-saggio,* an "essay-novel," in which the author's perceptions and convictions would give "senso e ordine ad una realtà altrimenti insensata e caotica" (meaning and order to an otherwise meaningless and chaotic reality).

Moravia's concept of reality also became more complex during this third phase of his career. In his earlier works Moravia used the term *reality* vaguely, to refer to objects and factual events, to that which was always outside his fictional characters. He had come to understand that reality and language are not absolute and objective, but relative and subjective: "Non ci saranno più una sola realtà e un solo linguaggio ma tante realtà e tanti linguaggi quanti sono i romanzieri" (There is no longer a single reality and a single language, but as many realities and languages as there are novelists).

The exclusive use of narration in the first person lay at the root of Moravia's new direction. He contended that the omniscient point of view was based on a belief in an objective and knowable reality; first-person narration implied multiple subjective and relative realities. Moreover, the first person was necessary for the essay-novel. In 1959 he wrote in "Risposta a nove domande sul romanzo" (translated as "Answers to Nine Questions on the Novel,"), another essay collected in *L'uomo come fine e altri saggi,* that "la terza persona non consente che la rappresentazione immediata, drammatica dell'oggetto; la prima persona permette di analizzarlo, di scomporlo e, in certi casi, addirittura di farne a meno" (third-person narration permits only the immediate and dramatic representation of the object; the first person allows it to be analyzed, deconstructed and, sometimes, done away with).

The short stories that Moravia wrote from 1958 to 1970 reflected his new approach to fiction as well as his criticism of the consumerism that accompanied Italy's economic boom. The stories collected in *L'automa* (1962; translated as *The Fetish,* 1964), *Una cosa è una cosa* (1967; translated as *Command and I Will Obey You,* 1969), *Il paradiso* (1970; translated as *Paradise,* 1971), *Un'altra vita* (1973; translated as *Lady Godiva,* 1975), and *Boh* (1976; translated as *The Voice of the Sea,* 1978) feature bourgeois protagonist-narrators, the mindless robots of a society that has transformed individuals into a means of production. Confusing dreams with reality, they lose their memories, their sense of time and, eventually, even their identities.

Moravia's investigation of language and reality is especially notable in some of these works. Is reality physical, he asks, or is it linguistic? Do words represent reality or do they create it? Moravia had touched upon such questions as early as 1947 through Mino, the intellectual of *La romana,* but his later reading of Ludwig Wittgenstein's *Tractatus Logico-Philosophicus* (1922) elevated the matter to a central position in his stories of the 1960s. Wittgenstein concluded that it is often not possible to say what a thing is; one can only state tautologically that it is what it is. In some cases, language fails completely, and the subject must be passed over in silence.

Moravia incorporated Wittgensteinian ideas into his novel *La noia* (1960; translated as *The Empty Canvas,* 1961), which received the prestigious Viareggio Prize. The critic Edoardo Sanguineti noted that *La noia* completes a thematic trajectory begun with *Gli indifferenti,* both of which ask the same questions: What is reality and how can one establish a rapport with it? One might say that this was the problem that Moravia investigated during the first forty years of his career. In 1958 he reviewed his previous efforts in "About My Novels": "All my books have been worked out in more or less the same way; that is to say, their point of departure has been an effective and objective reality–a reality that I have sought to define and explain and reveal to myself, either to sing its praises or to use it as an instrument of knowledge." In *La noia,* though, Moravia was no longer simply trying to present objective reality. There is increased emphasis not only on subjective reality but even a strong suggestion of a transcendent reality bordering on mysticism, a quality that was absent from his previous novels.

As the novel opens, the protagonist-narrator Dino, an artist, is undergoing a crisis. He is beset by noia, which he defines as "una specie di insufficienza o inadeguatezza o scarsità della realtà . . . una malattia degli oggetti" (a kind of insufficiency or inadequacy or scarcity of reality . . . a sickness of objects). Dino puts a metaphorical end to this noia by slashing his canvas, an act that is not so much a confession of his inability to paint as it is a revolt against his entire life. He is obsessed by the memory of a recently deceased fellow artist, Balestrieri, whose works are those of a man whose world was concrete and coherent, free of flaws and contamination. With the hope of discovering the secret of Balestrieri's rapport with reality, Dino initiates a liaison with Cecilia, the old man's last and favorite mistress-model. Almost immediately, however, his interest shifts from Balestrieri to Cecilia. Why does she behave as she does? What does she think about? Who is Cecilia?

Dino concludes that he will solve the riddle of Cecilia–and of reality–only if he can possess her to the degree that she will no longer be able to exercise the obsessive hold that she has on him. The substance of *La noia* is Dino's slow and sometimes tedious attempt to destroy Cecilia's mysterious autonomy and to reduce her to an object of insignificance. He tries in many ways to bring Cecilia under his control: seduction, money, even a marriage proposal. Nothing works. He is about to strangle her when he realizes that death would assure her a definitive autonomy. Desperate, Dino attempts suicide by crashing his car into a tree.

When Dino regains consciousness in a clinic, he dispels his noia by contemplating a Lebanese cedar: "Non pensavo a niente, mi domandavo soltanto quando e in che modo avevo riconosciuto la realtà dell'albero, ossia ne avevo riconosciuta l'esistenza come di un oggetto che era diverso da me, non aveva rapporti con me e tuttavia c'era e non poteva essere ignorato." (I thought about nothing, I wondered only when and how I had come to recognize the reality of the tree; that is, I had recognized its existence as an object which was different from me, which had no relation to me, and yet was there and could not be ignored.) In a similar fashion he establishes a rapport with Cecilia:

> Noi eravamo due e lei non aveva niente a che fare con me e io non avevo niente a che fare con lei, e lei era fuori di me, come io ero fuori di lei. E, insomma, io non volevo più possederla bensì guardarla vivere, così com'era, cioè contemplarla, allo stesso modo che contemplavo l'albero attraverso i vetri della finestra. . . . In realtà, come mi accorsi improvvisamente, con un senso quasi di meraviglia, io avevo definitivamente rinunciato a Cecilia; e, strano a dirsi, proprio a partire da questa rinunzia, Cecilia aveva cominciato ad esistere per me.

> (We were two, and she had nothing to do with me and I had nothing to do with her, and she was outside me as I was outside her. In short, I no longer wanted to possess her but to watch her live, just as she was, to contemplate her in the same way that I was contemplating the tree through the window pane.... Actually, as I suddenly realized to my wonder, I had once and for all renounced Cecilia; and, strangely, from the moment of that renunciation, Cecilia had begun to exist for me.)

Dino discovers that a rapport with others and with reality is established not through possession or analysis but by recognizing and accepting the autonomy of others' existence. His conclusion recalls that of Silvio in *L'amore coniugale,* who noted that the essential "mistero di tutte le cose, dalle grandi alle piccole, [è che] tutto si può spiegare salvo la loro esistenza" (mystery of all things big and small [is that] everything can be explained except their existence). Given this ineluctable fact, the only authentic rapport with reality must reside in disinterested con-

Dust jacket for the American edition of the translation of Moravia's 1982 novel, in which a scholar hopes to overcome his despair through a love affair

templation, an attitude that is at the same time mystic and aesthetic.

L'attenzione (1965; translated as *The Lie,* 1966) explores in a new way a situation similar to that of *La noia*. Like Dino, Francesco Merighi is an artist who seeks to establish a rapport with reality, represented again by a woman, his wife, Cora, and with his work, in his case as a novelist. Merighi returns to Italy and to his estranged wife after nearly a decade of travels abroad, bringing with him the manuscript of an idealistic novel based on their courtship. The novel, though, does not ring true; it is "inauthentic." The traditional past tense and third-person narration in which the novel is written are belied by the present reality of his unfortunate marriage. Beyond this superficial falseness of the novel, however, Francesco perceives that its inauthenticity resides in the events themselves, and he concludes that the dramatic novel, the novel of action, is by its nature inauthentic. Consequently, he decides to investigate whether a nondramatic novel, one in which nothing happens, will prove to be authentic. The opposite of the dramatic is the quotidian, the routine and trivial happenings of each day, and he determines to re-

cord them carefully and objectively in a diary, which he will then use as notes for rewriting his novel.

But not only do the events Francesco observes—including his semi-incestuous relationship with his stepdaughter, Baba—prove to be far from commonplace but he also discovers that objectivity is not possible: he must choose which events to set down and selectivity is implicitly subjective. He finally resolves to embellish reality with his own invention and imagination. The resulting chronicle thus details not "authentic" daily life, but daily life as it is perceived, filtered, and changed by the consciousness and imagination of the observer. The diary becomes an admixture of actuality and lies. The question of the veracity of Francesco's diary directs the reader's attention from the novel's apparent subject—Merighi's relations with his family and his attempts to write a novel—to its real subject: the "instrument," the novel itself. Both structurally and thematically, the central drama of *L'attenzione* is the internal drama of the creative process and of the realization of the work of art. The fruit of much thought, *L'attenzione* is Moravia's most intelligent and coherent work. It is also his most personal novel in that it summarizes and solves many of the problems that he as a novelist confronted, and it embodies many of the literary ideas that he had expounded during the ten years preceding its publication.

After the publication of *L'attenzione,* Moravia turned for a while to the theater. He stated on several occasions that he would have preferred writing plays to novels, but the sparse audiences and low box-office receipts of the Italian theater discouraged him. Nevertheless, in 1954 he had adapted *La mascherata* for the stage and in 1958 a historical tragedy, *Beatrice Cenci* (translated as *Beatrice Cenci,* 1965), considered by many his finest play, was relatively successful. These plays were published in one volume as *Teatro* (1958). Eight years passed before Moravia, Dacia Maraini, and Enzo Siciliano created in 1966 the Compagnia del Porcospino theater group in Rome. Although the company staged Moravia's one-act *L'intervista* (The Interview), which was published with a second play in the volume *Il mondo è quello che è. L'intervista* (1966), as well as plays by Pier Paolo Pasolini, Carlo Emilio Gadda, and Siciliano, the enterprise was not successful. Moravia himself did not give it full support, for what he regarded as his principal plays were performed by better known and more established companies. *Il mondo è quello che è* (translated as *The World's the World,* 1970), a rather tedious dialectic between the ideas of Marx and Wittgenstein, was staged in Venice. More successful was *Il dio Kurt* (Kurt the God, 1968), which was set in a Nazi concentration camp where the inmates present Sophocles' *Oedipus Rex. Il dio Kurt* was the high point of Moravia's playwriting career: subsequent works such as *La vita è gioco* (Life is a Game, 1969) and the plays now collected in *L'angelo dell'informazione e altri testi teatrali* (The Angel of Information and Other Dramatic Works, 1986) did not enhance his reputation as a playwright. In general Moravia's intellectualizing and socially relevant content overwhelmed the dramatic force of his plays.

The late 1960s were a time of change in Italy. The 1968 student protests swept away much that had been traditionally regarded as sacrosanct in the life and culture of Europe: authority was discredited; class distinctions faded; women discovered a new consciousness of self; and sexual expression became freer and more public. Ever sensitive to matters of culture, Moravia's attention turned increasingly toward social and political questions. The many essays that he wrote during the late 1960s and throughout the 1970s were collected in *Impegno controvoglia* (Involved in Spite of Myself, 1980). In his fiction Moravia evaluated and gave literary form to this new and often confused world.

Sexuality is present in almost all of Moravia's fiction, so much so that many accused him of writing pornography and the Catholic Church placed his complete works on its Index of Prohibited Books in 1952. Moravia denied vigorously that the sex of his fiction was gratuitous or that he exploited sex to increase sales. He regarded sexuality as a fundamental drive that conditions lives and behavior. Furthermore, he maintained, sex was a principal means of establishing a relation with others and with reality. The new permissiveness in Italian society gave to Moravia greater freedom of expression, and he profited by exploring not only the phenomenon of sexuality but also by using sexuality as a device to demonstrate attitudes toward life.

Moravia's only comic novel, *Io e lui* (translated as *Two: A Phallic Novel,* 1972), was published in 1971. The work's protagonist, Rico, is clearly a parody of the typical Moravian hero. He is a screenwriter who, like Silvio in *L'amore coniugale,* has temporarily separated from his wife in order to sublimate his sexual drive into creative potency. His preoccupation with reason, with abstract concepts, and with the analysis of his own consciousness recalls the concerns of Francesco Merighi of *L'attenzione* and Dino of *La noia.* His abstract vagaries are held in check by his conversations with the antagonist of the novel, Rico's own elephantine sexual member designated by the name Federicus Rex. The latter combats Rico's impotent intellectualism with his insistence on the primary importance of instinct, sexuality, and the physical. It is scarcely a fair contest, for Rico, like so many of Moravia's intellectuals, is weak and ineffective. Federicus Rex is victorious, and Rico at the end of the novel returns to the waiting arms of his wife.

Although disappointing as a novel and only mildly humorous, *Io e lui* is a transitional work in Moravia's development. Rico's renunciation of intellectual pretensions and his return to concrete realities are clear repudiations of the philosophical tendencies of *La noia* and *L'attenzione.* At the same time, Moravia's emphasis on sexuality and social commitment suggests the course of his writing for the final two decades of his career. *Io e lui* was Moravia's first novel since *La mascherata* to deal with contemporary political and social questions. Despite his longstanding support of the Left, he disparages the *contestatori* (protestors). They are presented as the immature and pampered brats of an alienated bourgeoisie. Robotlike, they chant slogans and blindly obey leaders whose exploitative methods are no different from those of the middle class.

Dust jacket for the American edition of the translation of Moravia's 1985 novel, in which a professor discovers that his wife is having an affair with his father

La vita interiore (1978; translated as *Time of Desecration,* 1980) is representative of Moravia's concerns during the 1970s. The protagonist, Desideria, is reared by her foster mother in a wealthy, middle-class environment. When she reaches her teens, she begins hearing a disembodied Voice that apparently represents the consciousness of youth, for it will disappear when Desideria loses her virginity. Under the direction of the Voice, Desideria elaborates, in a fashion reminiscent of Arthur Rimbaud, a plan of transgression and desecration: she will systematically profane all the sanctioned precepts of bourgeois society—property, language, culture, religion, money, love, and even life itself. The Voice also orders Desideria to seek an opportunity to join a group of *contestatori*. The quest is fulfilled when she meets a revolutionary organizer; she yields to him only to discover, like Carla in *Gli indifferenti,* that the new life he promises is scarcely distinguishable from the bourgeois life she has so despised. The Voice disappears, and Desideria's story ends.

In the midst of his involvement with social and political issues, Moravia in 1977 began writing a series of imaginative and witty fables for children. Bearing clever names, the characters in these tales are usually the primeval ancestors of animals familiar to everyone, such as Pin Guinone (big penguin), An Guilla (eel), and O Ran Gu Tang. Twenty-four of the stories were collected in *Storie della preistoria* (Prehistoric Stories, 1982).

Moravia surprised many with his second marriage in 1986. Despite a separation of more than two decades, Moravia and Morante had never legally divorced. Less than a year after Morante's death in 1985, Moravia married the Spanish-born Carmen Llera, with whom he had been living for about five years and who was younger than he by nearly half a century. Like his previous wives (Moravia often referred to Dacia Maraini as his wife), Llera is also a writer.

Although advanced in years, Moravia continued to be remarkably active during the 1980s. His first novel of that decade was *1934* (1982; translated as *1934,* 1983). Lucio, a scholar of German literature, goes to Capri to work on a translation of one of Heinrich von Kleist's stories and to come to terms with his chronic state of despair. He seeks to "stabilize" his hopelessness and reduce it to a normal condition of life. On the boat to the island he falls in love with Beate, a young German actress. The pair have much in common: like Lucio, Beate has asked herself whether one can live without hope and not desire death. Her response is negative, and, in emulation of the double suicide of Kleist and his mistress, she is apparently seeking a partner with whom to die.

Beate stays only briefly on Capri, but she tells Lucio of the expected arrival of her twin sister, Trude, and her mother, Paula. Lucio is astounded at the physical resemblance between the sisters. In contrast to the timid, liberal-thinking, sensitive, intellectual Beate, however, Trude is aggressive, vulgar, and a zealous Nazi. Lucio rejects her offer to play the role of Beate in a lovemaking game and decides to follow Beate to Germany. It would be useless, Paula confesses, because everything has been an elaborate joke: Beate and Trude are in reality the same person and Paula is her lesbian lover. Neither resentful nor angry, Lucio maintains that the problem of his despair is solved:

> Io mi accorgevo di essere innamorato non tanto dell'immaginaria Beate o dell'immaginante Trude; ma di una donna che era insieme Beate e Trude, cioè, al tempo stesso, l'inventata e l'inventrice. Questa donna aveva tutto quello che potevo desiderare. . . . Così il cerchio si chiudeva a mio favore; Trude e Beate fuse in una sola persona, mi avrebbero permesso di mettere in atto il mio progetto di stabilizzazione del disperare come condizione normale dell'esistenza umana.

> (I realized I was in love not so much with the imaginary Beate or with the imaginative Trude, but with a woman who was at the same time both Beate and Trude, the invented one and the inventor. This woman was all I could desire. . . . Thus, the joke came full circle and closed to my advantage; Trude and Beate fused in a single person would permit me to realize my project of stabilizing despair as a normal condition of human existence.)

Lucio's hopes soon perish, however. In the wake of a Nazi purge Trude and Paula carry out the Kleistian suicide pact.

Moravia's best novel since *L'attenzione, 1934,* despite its reliance on unlikely coincidences, is imaginative and well told. Although Lucio is the typical Moravian intellectual—naive, passive, almost comic—Beate, Trude, and many of the lesser characters enrich the novel. Particularly successful is the evocation of the ambiguous atmosphere that engulfed Europe in the 1930s. The rampant deceit and treachery, the masquerade that deforms values, and the substitution of propaganda for common sense recalls *La mascherata* and *Il conformista.* Though set in the past, the world of *1934* presages the late twentieth century. Lucio, for example, says: "Certo, non mi piaceva di vivere sotto il fascismo; ma non avrei voluto davvero vivere in alcun tempo del futuro perché ero sicuro . . . assolutamente sicuro, che la speranza di un mondo migliore non poteva che essere inganno o illusione." (I did not like living under fascism; but I really would not have wanted to live in any future time because I was sure . . . that the hope of a better world could only be a deception or an illusion.) Contemporary culture, Moravia indicates, harbors the same deceit and hypocrisy that he found so unbearable under Fascism, and political and economic injustice is as prevalent as it was in the past. Worst of all, stabilized despair as the normal human condition has been perpetuated by the threat of nuclear disaster, a problem that preoccupied Moravia more than did all others during the 1980s.

Such was Moravia's concern with the nuclear threat that in contradiction to his earlier refusals to engage directly in politics (in 1983 he had declined to run for the Italian Senate on the grounds that literature and politics should not be mixed), he ran in 1984 for the European Parliament as an independent on the Communist ticket. He accepted the candidacy only on the condition that he could devote all of his energies to the single issue of nuclear disarmament. After his election he recorded his experience as a political activist in *Diario europeo: Pensieri, persone, fatti, libri, 1984–1990* (European Diary: Thoughts, People, Deeds, Books, 1993). His essays on the subject of the nuclear threat were collected in *L'inverno nucleare* (The Nuclear Winter, 1986). The theme of nuclear disaster is present also in some of the stories collected in *La cosa e altri racconti* (1983; translated as *Erotic Tales,* 1985); it is central to the play *L'angelo dell'informazione*; and it underlies the structure of the novel, *L'uomo che guarda* (1985; translated as *The Voyeur,* 1986).

The voyeur of *L'uomo che guarda* is Edoardo, a professor of French literature who, in addition to an Oedipal complex and his proclivity for voyeurism, is obsessed by thoughts of a nuclear holocaust. He begins every day by thinking about the end of the world; each afternoon he watches clouds float over Saint Peter's Cathedral. On rare occasions, a mushroom-shaped cloud will hover overhead, and Edoardo imagines that an atomic explosion is destroying the basilica. As in *L'attenzione,* one of the problems of the novel centers on the question of incest. In Moravia, the question is never that of sexual intercourse between blood relatives but between persons related through marriage or through other long-standing sexual alliances, as is the case in *Gli indifferenti*: Leo's seduction of Carla, the daughter of his mistress, is tantamount to the seduction of one's stepdaughter.

In *L'uomo che guarda* Edoardo's adored wife, Silvia, has gone to live with an aunt. The impoverished professor believes that she is dissatisfied because they do not have their own home and must live in two rooms of his father's apartment. He moves to a new house and Silvia returns to him, but she confesses that the real issue is not their living quarters but her affair with another man. Insisting that she is not in love with her illicit mate and that they have ended the affair, she nevertheless admits to a continuing attraction toward him. Although he never reveals his knowledge, Edoardo discovers that his rival is his father. The couple then find that they cannot continue to maintain their own apartment and must return to live with the father. Edoardo finds himself in a state of perpetual uncertainty much like Lucio's stabilized despair: he will never know when Silvia may backslide, just as he never knows when a mushroom cloud will appear above Saint Peter's. The disaster may never occur, but living with the possibility is an unending nightmare.

L'uomo che guarda was the first of Moravia's novels in which a father had a significant role, although mothers had been common in his work from *Gli indifferenti* to *La vita interiore*. In *Il viaggio a Roma* (1988; translated as *Journey to Rome,* 1990) twenty-year-old Mario De Sio, who has been living with a relative in Paris since he was five, is invited by his father to return to Rome for a visit. He finds himself in a web of questionable relationships with his father as well as his father's girlfriend, an expatriate Frenchwoman, and her adolescent daughter. The memory of the narrator's long-dead mother also figures prominently in the novel, as does Guillaume Apollinaire, Mario's mentor, a self-styled poet who has never written a poem. Although it purports to be a burlesque, the novel never succeeds in achieving an identity—it is neither parody nor drama. Moravia's repetitive and frequently unconvincing exhibitions of voyeurism, sadomasochism, and Oedipal complexes—present also in his last collections of stories, *La cosa* and *La villa del venerdì* (The Friday Villa, 1990)—unfortunately taint with monotony much of the fiction written during the last decade of his life.

Moravia's final novel is unique because it is the only one by the indefatigable traveler that is set outside Italy. *La donna leopardo* (The Leopard

Moravia with his wife, Carmen Llera (photograph by M. Radogna)

Woman, 1991) takes place in Africa. Lacking the voyeurism, Oedipal complexes, incest, and adolescent girls, the novel is more restrained than most of his work of the 1980s. But it is also less original: the theme of marital infidelity and the circumstance of the young writer who facilitates an affair between his wife and his boss was treated earlier and more successfully in *Il disprezzo.*

Moravia died of a cerebral hemorrhage in his Rome apartment on the morning of 26 September 1990. He had just finished showering and was preparing to set to work as he had done almost every morning for the past fifty years. His body was taken to Rome's city hall, the Capitoline, where it lay in state, an honor rarely bestowed on Italian artists. Except for a few small bequests to friends and family, his considerable estate was bequeathed jointly to Carmen Llera and Dacia Maraini. They used part of the inheritance to establish the Fondazione Alberto Moravia in Rome, which houses an archive dedicated to the life and works of the novelist.

Throughout most of the twentieth century Alberto Moravia was a leading figure in Italian letters and his place in literary history is secure. The unequivocal realism and the lean style of his early works dispelled some of the literary traditions that had restrained and even inhibited the Italian novel, opening the way for more innovative stylists such as Elio Vittorini, Cesare Pavese, and Italo Calvino. With little formal education but possessing a broad background in world literature, Moravia extended Italian fiction beyond provincial bounds and the time lock that gripped it. While such modern writers as Luigi Pirandello and Italo Svevo were original artists, they still presented a fictional world that is unmistakably pre–World War I, a world closer to the nineteenth than to the twentieth century. Moravia's characters–even his earliest–definitely belong to the twentieth century. Moravia, though, was not a technical innovator: in only one work, *L'attenzione,* did he consciously apply a new theory of narrative, although he talked often about the crisis of the novel. Perhaps his attitude toward the matter was best expressed in his belief that there was no crisis in the novel, just a crisis of the novelist. With such self-assurance, he was content to follow in almost all cases the narrative techniques codified by the nineteenth-century realists or, later, to adopt and adapt means already established by others.

Many critics reproached Moravia for his conservative stance. They maintained that he brought nothing new to the novel, that he repeated the themes of his early work, that his works were overburdened by detail and explanations. Although there is a basis for each of these criticisms, there is also much of worth in Moravia's fiction. Novels such as *Gli indifferenti, Agostino,* and *La ciociara* are distinguished works of art that occupy unique places in Italian literature. As a chronicler of twentieth-century Italy, Moravia has no peer. He was attuned to the times in which he lived and to the spirit of his culture. His novels reflect and at times define the problems and concerns of his contemporaries. Like the Balzac of the *Comédie Humaine,* Moravia viewed his century with the eye not only of the social historian but with that of the moralist. Independent in his thought and eschewing literary and political fashions, he scrutinized the fabric of Italian life and held up to the light of reason and public discussion those parts that were threadbare or timeworn. That he maintained the regard not only of the reading public but also of succeeding generations of young writers and intellectuals is evidence of the vitality and relevance of his ideas and of his artistic creations.

Letters:

Alberto Moravia and Giuseppe Prezzolini, *Lettere* (Milan: Rusconi, 1982).

Interviews:

Jean Duflot, *Entretiens avec Alberto Moravia* (Paris: Pierre Belfond, 1970);

Enzo Siciliano, *Moravia* (Milan: Longanesi, 1971); enlarged as *Alberto Moravia: Vita, parole e idee di un romanziere* (Milan: Bompiani, 1982);

Carla Ravaioli, *La mutazione femminile: Conversazioni con Alberto Moravia sulla donna* (Milan: Bompiani, 1975);

Sergio Saviane, *Moravia desnudo* (Milan: SugarCo, 1976);

Nello Ajello, ed., *Intervista sullo scrittore scomodo* (Rome & Bari: Laterza, 1978);

Le roi est nu: Conversations en français avec Vania Luksic (Paris: Stock, 1979);

Dacia Maraini, *Il bambino Alberto* (Milan: Bompiani, 1986);

Io e il mio tempo: conversazioni critiche con Ferdinando Camon (Padova: Nord-Est, 1988);

Alain Elkann, *Vita di Moravia* (Milan: Bompiani, 1990);

Brigitte Chardin, *Sollers, Moravia* (Paris: Editions Ramsay / de Cortanze, 1991);

Moravia: Dialoghi confidenziali con Dina d'Isa (Rome: Newton Compton, 1991).

Bibliography:

Ferdinando Alfonsi and Sandra Alfonsi, *An Annotated Bibliography of Moravia's Criticism in Italy and in the English Speaking World, 1929–1975* (New York: Garland, 1976).

References:

Ferdinando Alfonsi, *Alberto Moravia in America: Un quarantennio di critica (1929–1969)* (Catanzaro: Carello, 1984);

Alfonsi, *Alberto Moravia in Italia: Un Quarantennio di critica (1929–1969)* (Catanzaro: Carello, 1986);

Bruna Baldini Mezzalana, *Alberto Moravia e l'alienazione* (Milan: Ceschina, 1971);

Cristina Benussi, ed., *Il punto su Moravia* (Rome, Bari: Laterza, 1987);

Rocco Capozzi and Mario B. Mignone, eds., *Homage to Moravia* (Stony Brook, N.Y.: Forum Italicum, 1993);

Rocco Carbone, *Alberto Moravia e gli indifferenti* (Turin: Loescher, 1992);

Nicola F. Cimmino, *Lettura di Moravia* (Rome: Volpe, 1966);

Jane E. Cottrell, *Alberto Moravia* (New York: Ungar, 1974);

Lilia Crocenzi, *La donna nella narrativa di Alberto Moravia* (Cremona: Mangiarotti, 1964);

Giuliano Dego, *Moravia* (Edinburgh & London: Oliver and Boyd; New York: Barnes & Noble, 1967);

Eurialo De Michelis, *Introduzione a Moravia* (Florence: Nuova Italia, 1954);

Oreste del Buono, *Moravia* (Milan: Feltrinelli, 1962);

Roberto Esposito, *Il sistema dell'indifferenza: Moravia e il fascismo* (Bari: Dedalo, 1978);

Dominique Fernandez, "Essai sur Alberto Moravia," in his *Le Roman italien et la crise de la conscience moderne* (Paris: Grasset, 1958), pp. 9–138;

Luca Gervasutti, *I fantasmi di Moravia: Gli intellettuali tra romanzo e realtà* (Tricesimo, Aviani, 1993);

Enrico Groppali, *L'ossessione e il fantasma: il teatro di Pasolini e Moravia* (Venice: Marsilio, 1979);

Donald Heiney, "Alberto Moravia," in his *Three Italian Novelists: Moravia, Pavese, Vittorini* (Ann Arbor: University of Michigan Press, 1968), pp. 1–82;

Janice M. Kozma, *The Architecture of Imagery in Alberto Moravia's Fiction* (Chapel Hill: University of North Carolina Press, 1993);

Alberto Limentani, *Alberto Moravia tra esistenza e realtà* (Venice: Pozza, 1962);

Fulvio Longobardi, *Alberto Moravia* (Florence: Nuova Italia, 1969);

Longobardi, *Alberto Moravia: Il narratore e i suoi testi. Saggi* (Rome: Nuova Italia Scientifica, 1987);

Marinella Mascia Galateria, *Come leggere "Gli indifferenti" di Moravia* (Milan: Mursia, 1975);

Sergio Pacifici, "Alberto Moravia: Sex, Money and Love in the Novel," in his *The Modern Italian Novel from Pea to Moravia* (Carbondale: Southern Illinois University Press, 1979), pp. 200–239;

Giancarlo Pandini, *Invito alla lettura di Moravia* (Milan: Mursia, 1973);

Renzo Paris, *Alberto Moravia,* preface by Enzo Siciliano (Florence: Nuova Italia, 1991);

Paris, *Moravia: Una vita controvoglia* (Florence: Giunti, 1996);

Per Moravia: Press-book della sua morte (Rome: Salerno, 1990);

Thomas E. Peterson, *Alberto Moravia* (New York: Twayne, 1996; London: Prentice Hall International, 1996);

Memi Piccinonno, *Discorrendo di Alberto Moravia* (Lecce: Edizione del Grifo, 1992);

Luciano Rebay, *Alberto Moravia* (New York: Columbia University Press, 1970);

Joan Ross and Donald Freed, *The Existentialism of Alberto Moravia* (Carbondale: Southern Illinois University Press, 1972);

Edoardo Sanguineti, *Alberto Moravia* (Milan: Mursia, 1962);

Lucia Strappini, *Le cose e le figure negli "Indifferenti" di Moravia* (Rome: Bulzoni, 1979);

Roberto Tessari, *Alberto Moravia: Introduzione e guida allo studio dell'opera moraviana: Storia e antologia della critica* (Florence: Le Monnier, 1977);

Carmen Vitter, *L'interpretazione psicanalitica dell'opera di Alberto Moravia attraverso quarant'anni di critica* (Rome: Pastena, 1973);

Sharon Wood, *Woman as Object: Language and Gender in the Work of Alberto Moravia* (London: Pluto, 1990; Savage, Md.: Barnes & Noble, 1990).

Guido Morselli
(15 August 1912 – 31 July 1973)

Charles Fantazzi
University of Windsor

BOOKS: *Proust o del sentimento* (Milan: Garzanti, 1943);

Realismo e fantasia (Milan: Bocca, 1947);

Roma senza papa (Milan: Adelphi, 1974);

Contro-passato prossimo: Un'ipotesi retrospettiva (Milan: Adelphi, 1975); translated by Hugh Shankland as *Past Conditional: A Retrospective Hypothesis* (London: Chatto & Windus, 1989);

Divertimento 1889 (Milan: Adelphi, 1975); translated by Shankland (London & New York: Dutton, 1986);

Il comunista (Milan: Adelphi, 1976);

Dissipatio H.G. (Milan: Adelphi, 1977);

Fede e critica (Milan: Adelphi, 1977);

Un dramma borghese (Milan: Adelphi, 1978);

Incontro col comunista (Milan: Adelphi, 1980);

Diario, edited by Valentina Fortichiari (Milan: Adelphi, 1988);

La felicità non è un lusso, edited by Fortichiari (Milan: Adelphi, 1994).

Guido Morselli

The *caso* (case) of Guido Morselli bears some resemblance to the famous "il caso Svevo," for, like Italo Svevo, through most of his career Morselli was unknown in his lifetime and his reputation as a writer has been a matter of posthumous debate. During their lives both writers had little contact with the Italian literary establishment and lived on the fringes of the Italian cultural scene. Svevo lived in Trieste, a city of the Hapsburg Empire, while Morselli was a lover of old Austria, obsessed by love/hate feelings for neighboring Switzerland. In their cultural affinities both might be regarded as belonging more to *Mitteleuropa* (Central Europe) than to Italy.

Morselli's introspective, antirhetorical style and his secluded, solitary life placed him outside the mainstream of Italian writing and contributed to his lack of success with publishers, who rejected one manuscript after another during his lifetime. He suffered greatly from these refusals, as Maria Bruna Bassi, heir of his unpublished writings, testifies. She remembers Morselli saying in a moment of exasperation: "Se mi permettessero di pubblicare, ogni giorno potrei trattare un argomento diverso" (If they would let me publish, I could treat a different subject every day).

Guido Morselli was born in Bologna on 15 August 1912, the last of four children of a well-to-do family. His parents, Giovanni Morselli and Olga Vincenzi, were from Modena. In his infancy the family moved to Milan, where his father was a manager in the Carlo Erba firm, one of the largest pharmaceutical companies in Italy. His mother died when he was twelve, and the loss would have far-reaching effects on his already introverted character. He attended a school run by the Jesuits, an order that he held in little esteem, and then pursued the *liceo classico* curriculum at one of the better secondary schools in Milan. In 1935 he received a law degree from the University of Milan, but instead of setting up a legal practice, as his father wished, he spent the next few years traveling extensively in England and Scandinavia, where he perfected his knowledge of the major European languages.

During World War II, when his military unit was disbanded, Morselli spent three difficult years in Calabria, unable to get in touch with his family and the woman he loved. Nevertheless, he was able to write diaries and notes that would later be useful in his work. On his return to Varese, where the family had moved, he gave himself to the task of writing, contributing to various newspapers of the region, including *Il tempo* of Milan, *La prealpina* of Varese, and *Il corriere del Ticino*. The only books he published during his lifetime, one on the French writer Marcel Proust and the other a philosophical dialogue, appeared in the 1940s.

In 1958 Morselli went to live permanently in a small villa that he had built at Sasso di Gavirate, on an isolated slope near Lake Maggiore. At Santa Trínita, as he called it, he worked assiduously on his novels, articles, and essays. Practically a recluse save for his occasional amours, he led a simple outdoor life, tending his small farm and ranging over the mountainside on his horse, Zeffirino. Little by little, however, his mountain retreat was invaded by land developers and motocross enthusiasts. All his efforts to stem the tide were in vain, and in 1973 he returned to Varese, where he chose to live in a tiny apartment near the guardian's house at his family villa. He committed suicide on 31 July 1973, after he returned from a brief vacation in the mountains. In his mail he had found two returned manuscripts of his latest novel, *Dissipatio H. G.* (The Dissolution of the Human Race, 1977). Immediately after his death, the task of getting his work published was undertaken by his friends, chiefly the well-known critic Dante Isella, who persuaded Luciano Foà, director of the Adelphi publishing house of Milan, to bring out Morselli's works posthumously.

His first work was published in 1943 by Garzanti in Milan while Morselli was in far-off Calabria at the beginning of his three-year enforced isolation. As he noted in his diary on 21 November 1943, he saw it as a strange sign of his destiny that his first work should be published far away from where he was and that he should have no news of it. The book was titled *Proust o del sentimento* (Proust or Concerning Sentiment), a perceptive essay on a writer who had suffered from long neglect in Italy. It bore a laudatory preface by Antonio Banfi, professor of philosophy at the University of Milan, who had been his teacher. More than a simple introduction to Proust, as Morselli modestly claims, it is a penetrating, lucid analysis of the Proustian *temps perdu,* the evocation of the past that comes from a profound intimacy with oneself and a receptivity to external things. The affinity of Morselli's own creative canons with those that he describes is revealed in a passage from his diary from 26 November 1943: "Chi sa ascoltarsi, vive più vite" (He who knows how to listen to himself leads many lives).

Morselli's interest in involuntary memories of lost sensations indissolubly linked with places and objects reappears in a more philosophical key in *Realismo e fantasia* (Realism and Imagination, 1947), begun during his exile in Calabria and finished on his return to Varese. The book is in the form of nine Socratic dialogues with a friend named Sereno, who is obviously Morselli's alter ego for that part of himself that tries to see the world as it really is. Morselli considered his musings to be merely those of a dilettante, a philosopher to his mind being any individual endowed with good sense. He broaches a multitude of subjects—the concept of knowledge, art and aesthetics, religion, being and nonbeing—and gives evidence of his extensive readings, quoting with familiarity writers as diverse as Saint Augustine, Michel de Montaigne, Giacomo Leopardi, Miguel de Unamuno y Jugo, Meister Eckehart, and Aldous Huxley. His goal was not to offer solutions to transcendental inquiries but to capture philosophical thought in its nascent state. This second book was the last Morselli would see published, though he continued to write and seek publication for more than twenty-five years.

Morselli continued his philosophical discussions in a treatise titled *Fede e critica* (Faith and Criticism, 1977), which he wrote in the mid 1950s. Once again Morselli disclaims any special qualifications for treating such topics, simply allowing himself the freedom of engaging in religious speculative thought as he would in any other intellectual activity. These are extemporaneous jottings, not the distilled wisdom of a rational system of philosophy. They draw on ancient writers, such as Epictetus and Saint Augustine, as well as contemporary thinkers

Père Antonin Gilbert Sertillanges and Fulton J. Sheen, whom Morselli's diaries reveal he was then reading.

The center of Morselli's obsessive anxieties is the problem of evil. He uses as his exemplary text the Book of Job, to which he gives a personal interpretation, although it is somewhat indebted to Saint Augustine. He sees Job as a rebel against God who cries out in anguish to his Creator: "Why me?" In his ultimate surrender Job acknowledges a divine power that has put him to the test and granted him clemency in the end. However, God gives no explanation for his conduct or for the existence of evil in the world. In an inserted intermezzo, Morselli recounts an Irish legend, according to which God left his throne to see the beauty of his creation and the devil took his place. This was when evil was introduced into the world, the diabolical usurper leaving enough good for humans not to renounce the world altogether and too much evil for them to be able to live decently.

Morselli never resolved his religious doubts, choosing to live in a state of suspended judgment. For him blasphemy is prayer and doubt is the essence of faith. He preferred the obscure disquietude of the mystics to arid rational theology, since their struggle embraces both God and evil. Morselli often returned to these quandaries in his diaries and unpublished papers, including an unfinished treatise on what he saw as the crisis of theology, mass atheism versus the atheism of the learned, and an abortive attempt to engage in a doctrinal dialogue with the theologians of his day.

Morselli's first attempt at writing a novel is mentioned in his diary as early as 1944, where he alludes to his unfinished "Uomini e amori" (Men and Love Affairs). By 1949 his reading of the Swiss writer Henri-Frédéric Amiel's *Fragments d'un journal intime* (Fragments of an Intimate Diary) had inspired him to write *Incontro col comunista* (Encounter with a Communist, 1980), a novel in the form of a diary. Two opposing worlds come together in the encounter of the rich Ilaria, widow of an architect but of humble origin, and the younger metalworker Gildo. The meeting comes about fortuitously through the intermediacy of her son, who was Gildo's comrade on the Libyan front in World War II. He asks his mother to visit Gildo in the hospital, where he is recovering from wounds received in battle. Gildo is a closed, difficult character, resistant at first to Ilaria's solicitude, but eventually the two are united, mostly on his terms.

Ilaria leaves her hotel and goes to live with him in a poor tenement on the outskirts of Milan. She comes to share his political views and discovers for the first time the joys of sensual love that had been denied to her in her bourgeois marriage. In his membership in the party as well as in his relations with Ilaria, Gildo seeks his own advantage and self-aggrandizement. Ilaria, in turn, relishes her new experiences and records them minutely in her diary. The affair comes to an abrupt end one day when she sees Gildo in the arms of the concierge, Armida. She attempts a smile as she makes a last incisive entry in her diary: "Non sorridere significa non vivere" (Not to smile is not to live). In this exordium Morselli gives evidence of his careful adaptation of language and sentiment to character. With its detached irony and lack of a hero, *Incontro col comunista* would surely have aroused critical attention in the Italy of the early 1950s had it been published.

Morselli returned to the theme of communism with an honest, searing analysis of the Italian Communist Party in *Il comunista* (The Communist, 1976). Unlike its predecessor *Incontro col comunista, Il comunista* is a novel of political dissension, though the focus is more psychological than ideological. Written in 1964, it is set in the year 1958 in the full fervor of de-Stalinization. The protagonist, Walter Ferranini, has gone from active participation in an agricultural cooperative in Reggio Emilia to a parliamentary seat in Rome. This role is ill suited to him; rather than engage in party politics, he spends his time scrupulously reading the works of Karl Marx and Friedrich Engels and studying Russian. He finds himself at odds with the party and is termed a deviationist, to the point of being brought before a committee and receiving a paternal reprimand.

The investigation into Ferranini's life was occasioned by an article he wrote titled "Il lavoro, il mondo fisico, l'alienazione" (Work, the Physical World and Alienation), which had been accepted by Alberto Moravia for the review *Nuovi argomenti* (Morselli regularly peoples his novels with actual historic figures). In the article Ferranini takes issue with the Marxist doctrine of work as part of an economic law, maintaining instead that work is a biological fatality, an unceasing Darwinian struggle against the forces of nature. Contemporaneously with the writing of this novel, Morselli wrote an article on the same subject, leaving it among his unpublished papers. He was much influenced at this time by Hanna Arendt's *The Human Condition,* which appeared in Italian translation in 1964.

When *Il comunista* was published in 1976, it drew sharp reaction from Communist commentators, but even party hard-liners conceded that Morselli had correctly diagnosed the torpor of the party in the late 1950s and foreseen the coming crises of 1966 and 1968. Writing without ulterior motives and holding to a clear-eyed neutrality, he recognizes a hierarchy within the Communist Party not dissimilar from that of the Catholic Church. He shows a much greater mastery of the historical milieu and doctrinal disputes in this novel than he did in the preceding one. Not only does he display a thorough knowledge of the classic texts of communism but he also draws inspiration from the contemporary ideological debates carried on in the pages of *L'Unità*, the official party organ, which he recorded sedulously in the pages of his diary. His careful research enabled him to create a persuasive, realistic narrative.

Written in 1962, *Un dramma borghese* (A Bourgeois Drama, 1978), a psychological drama played out in the aseptic neutrality of a Swiss rest home on the shores of Lake Lugano, is aptly named. Protagonists are a fifty-year-old father and his eighteen-year-old daughter, who have been estranged for many years and now find themselves convalescing together, he from an attack of rheumatism and she from an appendicitis operation. A heavy, languid atmosphere, almost redolent of putrefaction, pervades the scene. The humid autumnal wind and the physical confinement awaken feelings of sexual passion in the daughter, which are repudiated by the father. Morselli thought of wind as having a debilitating effect on the soul as well as the body, bringing out suppressed feelings. (He uses the wind in *Dissipatio H. G.* to signal the end of humanity.) The threat of incest is ultimately averted by the arrival of another woman, a friend of the daughter.

In many ways this experimental novel might be considered a *roman à thèse* (novel with a thesis), illustrating the ideas of Stendhal's *De l'amour* (1822), a favorite text of Morselli's at the time. A thinly veiled portrait of himself and his own obsessive, neurotic fears, it is also a kind of dialectic dramatization of the victory of egoism over altruism and rational behavior over emotion. The theme of suicide runs through the book both in the minor characters and in the attempted suicide of the daughter at the end, the circumstances of which are left rather vague. Morselli is obviously not comfortable exploring the female psyche, and in his analysis of the illicit passion he makes patently ironic use of Freudian ideas. Evident in the writing is a Proustian delight in the description of clothing and material objects, including a Browning pistol, which would appear again in his last apocalyptic novel and be the instrument of Morselli's suicide.

Morselli's first work to be published after his death, *Roma senza papa* (Rome without a Pope, 1974) was written in 1967. Subtitled *Cronache romane di fine secolo ventesimo* (Roman Chronicles at the End of the Twentieth Century), the novel is a pungent satire of the decadence of papal Rome projected into the year 1997. The chronicler is a Swiss priest, Don Walter, who has come to Rome for a papal audience. He encounters a sleepy, provincial capital, bereft of all its grandeur, a crossroads for the hordes of mass tourism. Don Walter is an impartial observer, a theologian of the old school who has written a tract on hyperdulia, the worship of the Virgin Mary. He is married but more out of conformity with prevailing ecclesiastical customs than through conviction. He spends the hot summer awaiting his longed-for audience with the mysterious new pope, John XXIV, an Irish Benedictine, who has transferred the papal residence to a motel complex in Zagarolo, a rustic town about thirty kilometers away.

In the diaristic accounts that the Swiss priest sends back to the newspaper of his native town, Morselli gives expression to his own misgivings about the church of Rome. The Vatican secretary of state has forged a concordat with the Soviet government called the "White Bomb," and the two forces are allied in their opposition to secularized schools and divorce while espousing birth control, euthanasia, and the use of drugs to induce mystical experience. The new church is more inclined to channel social movements than to ignore or combat them, as Morselli cynically observes. Drastically reversing its attitude to Sigmund Freud, the Viennese Antichrist, the church has established the Institute for the Promotion of Catholic Psychoanalysis (IPPAC). The Jesuits, as militant a wing of the church as ever, have organized a collectivist regime south of Naples on the model of the revolutionary communities of South America.

In the place of theological disputations, Morselli imagines two electronic brains discussing the problem of evil and Don Walter's thesis of hyperdulia; thus, he indulges in self-irony, ridiculing his own serious attempts to grapple with the problem of evil and other more abstruse theological questions in the pages of his diary and his early essays, *Fede e critica*. Another debate swirling in Morselli's future church concerns a new social doctrine, called "socialidarity." The term is Morselli's coinage, meant to satirize both leftists and Catholics in their efforts to placate the insurrectionists of the Third World. Morselli also foresees computerized confessionals that expedite the work of shriving the transitory penitents. In the absence of a resident pope, there is a film projection of the retinue of the former pope, Paul VI, whom Morselli ridicules as the first of the globe-trotting pontiffs.

Unlike his predecessor the new pope called the missionary of antirhetoric by the London *Times*, is

Cover for a 1987 edition of Morselli's 1975 novel, in which a major's military strategem results in the triumph of the Austrian Empire in World War I

not an exponent of the latest theories of *homo vagans,* kangaroo-man, equipped with his marsupium, the suitcase. He is content to remain in his humble backwater, cultivating serpents with a female Indian theosophist. Morselli keeps his readers in suspense throughout the novel regarding a potential meeting between the Pope and Jacqueline Kennedy, which, when it finally does take place, turns out to be the most banal of occurrences, recalling meetings in Samuel Beckett's *En attendant Godot* (1952; translated as *Waiting for Godot,* 1955).

The Pope's message is both obvious and cryptic: "Dio non è prete. E nemmeno frate" (God is not a priest. And not even a friar). As in his religious essays Morselli seems to be saying in this mock oracular utterance that religion belongs to the common man and not to age-old institutions. The novel ends in a Fellini-like vignette of unchanged papal Rome as a female tourist removes her shoes and dances over the cobblestones of Saint Peter's Square. As in the Horatian dic-

tum "ridendo dicere verum" (To tell the truth with a smile), Morselli in his clever burlesque makes many telling criticisms of the Catholic Church.

The protagonist of *Contro-passato prossimo* (1975; translated as *Past Conditional,* 1989) is Maj. Walter von Allmen, who at the beginning of the novel is traveling on a train and writing down impressions of his visit to a small church in the western part of Tyrol. (Morselli had a predilection for the name Walter, which perhaps symbolized for him a union of Germanic and Latin.) He is struck by the contrast between the creamy Austrian baroque architecture and the rugged ramparts of the surrounding mountains. From these idle imaginings an intuition emerges that later rescues the crumbling Austrian empire. He conceives of a brilliant military tactic of building on an old mine shaft and tunneling through the mountains, thus enabling the Austrians to overrun northern Italy in a lightning operation. In December 1915 the plan, given the code name E.E. for Edelweiss Expedition, is put into effect. In Morselli's imagined counterhistory an obscure major thus puts an end to the stalemate of the "mole war" that resulted in trenches stretching from the Dardanelles to the Baltic Sea. Young Erwin Rommel executes the nocturnal raid, and the central powers go on to conquer the Triple Alliance.

As opposed to actual events, a German victory is a much more logical outcome, Morselli argues in an imaginary conversation with the publisher, included as a kind of intermezzo. The author maintains that "in November 1918 there were too many victors: France, England, and most of all the outsider America. There could have been—considering its initial overall superiority—one sole victor: a country strong enough and central enough, and European, to bring about Europe's rapid evolution towards unity." With the end of the war, the work of reconstruction begins, a gradual evolution of socialism engineered by the new head of the Reich, Walter Rathenau, with the cooperation of Lenin, who is destined to bring socialism to America.

Many influences are evident in this historical fantasy, among them Robert Musil's *Der Mann ohne Eigenschaften* (1930–1932; translated as *Man without Qualities,* 1953–1960) and its rejection of official history, Bertrand Russell, and the historical personage Rathenau himself. As Morselli argues in the intermezzo that the historical law of irreversibility does not preclude criticism or a spirited foray against the sacred determinism of history. He is more interested in the history of what should or might have happened than in the history of actual events. *Contro-passato prossimo* is a mixed genre of history and invention (the *realismo* and *fantasia* of an earlier essay), Morselli's genial version of a counterreality that is still within the bounds of realism. It is not surprising that the novel did not find favor with traditional publishers.

Morselli's next excursion into the past, *Divertimento 1889* (1975; translated with the same title, 1986), has as its protagonist the ill-starred Umberto I, the second king of Italy. The opening image–a sea of gray, pink, and white parasols that look like a speckled, slow-moving river–sets the tone for this richly visual evocation of the Belle Epoque. Tired of his endless journeys up and down the length of the dusty and disjointed peninsula, the king decides to escape beyond the Alps incognito. Using a hunting expedition as a pretext, the king plans a secret sale of Savoy properties near Monferrato to a German noblewoman related to the Krupp family.

Morselli first gives readers a glimpse of the king's routine existence through a reception sponsored by the queen at the Gymnastic Society of Monza (where the historic Umberto was later assassinated by a silk worker, an event presaged here when a giant cedar is struck by lightning) and his visit to his mistress, the Countess Litta, intent on her mundane travels. Amorous adventures await him in the Alps in a tiny village of the canton of Uri with the extravagant Frau von Klotz, the millionairess of the financial affair, and also with the young fiancée of an accompanying navy official. It all comes to a swift end, however, when Kaiser Wilhelm II and a prying English journalist become aware of the king's presence in Switzerland.

In this divertissement Morselli re-creates a world that is about to give way to the modern era. The contrasting periods are symbolized by the Saint Gothard diligence with its postillions and spirited horses and the new steaming locomotive that will replace it. Morselli thought of the work as pure escapist literature, a sort of literary operetta in the style of Fromental Halévy without the champagne music of Jacques Offenbach. In an afterword to his intended female public he makes no apology for this re-creation of a vanished world, complete with its own particular language, which he skillfully imitates: "In conclusione, cara lettrice, prendi per buono il titolo che il raccontino si è dato. Uno almeno, io che l'ho scritto, ci si è divertito" (Lastly, Madame Reader, take this little tale in the spirit of its title. One person at least, I who wrote it, found pleasure in it).

Dissipatio H. G., a title supposedly taken from a Latin translation of the Neoplatonic philosopher Iamblichus, is Morselli's somber adieu to his reading public and clearly presages his own suicide a few months later. The first-person narrator is strongly autobiographical, betraying many of Morselli's fa-

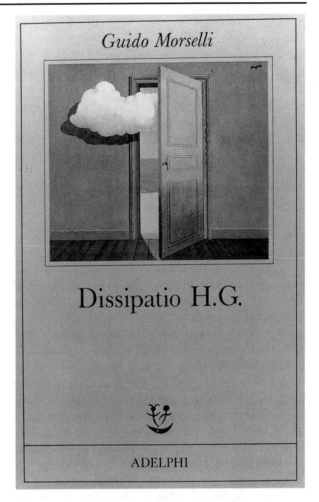

Cover for a 1994 edition of Morselli's 1977 novel, an apocalyptic story of nuclear devastation

vorite recriminations against the ugliness of modern urban civilization. The sole survivor of a universal cataclysm, he emerges from a subterranean lake at the bottom of a cavern, where, ironically, he had gone to drown himself. He had wanted to be alone, to flee from his fellowman but his body will not submit to death; now he finds himself the one thinking being in a deserted creation. Humanity has disappeared into thin air, leaving behind merely the outline of human forms, like the imprints left by Pompeian corpses in volcanic ash.

Other forms of animal and plant life continue to exist, however, and all the man-made machines of a modern metropolis keep on functioning in an eerie vacuum: traffic lights are still blinking; recorded announcements of flights drone out their unheeded messages at airports. The last "ex-man" conjectures that perhaps in the manner of a Dantean *contrappaseo* (counterbalance) the excesses of materialism have produced incorporeality; a world that was all body has become disembodied with the elimination of the infernal two-legged creature, man. In the usual eschatological theories it is assumed that the end of the human race would involve the end of all creation. But, Morselli suggests, the world may end peacefully without man.

Wandering through this uninhabited world, the lonely protagonist tries to communicate with the dead, piecing together fragments of memories and searching for survivors, especially a dear friend, the psychiatrist Dr. Karpinsky. At times he wonders whether he himself is dead or if perhaps as sole survivor he is really a condemned man rather than a privileged member of the species. But along with the bleakness, there is also a certain serenity. Little by little the natural world gains new confidence, and the creatures of the night sing more freely. At the end, a thin cover of earth invades the streets of Chrysopolis (Zurich, the city of gold, marketplace of marketplaces). Instead of the anonymous urban grass, chicory and crowfoot sprout up. The last man sits, "waiting for Karpinsky" with a pack of Gauloises, his favorite cigarettes, in his pocket.

On this quiet, unrhetorical note Morselli ended his literary career. He had always been averse to the excesses of rhetoric and bombast, which he regarded as the chief bane of Italian writing, and was the fierce enemy of all forms of exaggerated romanticism and idealism. His own style was terse and succinct, yet limpid and persuasive, especially in the apocalyptic pages of his last novel. He was a man of wide culture and vast reading, a writer of inexhaustible intellectual curiosity, possessed of a rare talent to evoke social or historical settings in appropriate contemporary language. Whatever his subject, he punctiliously documented its historical and cultural milieu. In passages of his diary that are first drafts of his novels he seems to be speaking through his characters, but he also always maintained a distance from his creations. As he said in one of his novels: "L'arte stilizza la realtà, non la riproduce, vuole l'unità o la concentrazione, mentre la vita per sua natura è molteplice e dispersiva" (Art stylizes reality, it does not reproduce it; it wants unity or concentration, while life by its very nature is many-sided and dispersive).

Immediately after his death Morselli was hailed as "the Gattopardo of the North," since he suffered the same fate as Giuseppe Tomasi di Lampedusa, author of *Il Gattopardo* (1958), who also acheived recognition only after his death. While there were some dissenting voices, the majority of critics lamented the tragic neglect of Morselli by the publishing industry. As his novels have appeared one by one, they have received the usual critical notice in newspapers and literary reviews. Two congresses have been held in his memory, one at Cortina d'Ampezzo on 24 August 1978 and another in Gavirate (Varese) on 22 and 23 October 1983. But though his reputation is growing and his work has attracted some critical attention, Morselli's stature as a novelist is still uncertain since he has not yet been accorded full recognition by the Italian literary establishment.

References:

Sebastiano Bastianetti, "Guido Morselli, scrittore vivo," *Letture,* 35 (December 1980): 803–832;

Angelo Piero Cappello, "La metafora negata. 'Il capitolo breve sul suicidio di Guido Morselli,'" *Otto/Novecento,* 27, no. 1 (1993): 129–141;

Vittorio Coletti, "Guido Morselli," *Otto/Novecento,* 2, no. 5 (1978): 89–115;

Simona Costa, *Guido Morselli* (Florence: Nuova Italia, 1981);

Valentina Fortichiari, *Invito alla lettura di Morselli* (Milan: Mursia, 1984);

Carlo Mariani, "Guido Morselli," *Studi novecentesdi,* 18 (June 1991): 7–48.

Papers:

The manuscript collection of the University of Pavia holds all of Morselli's papers, including the completed novel "Uomini e amori" and the sketch of another novel, "Uonna." The Fondo Morselli in the Biblioteca Civica of Varese has Morselli's private library.

Anna Maria Ortese

(13 June 1914 –)

S. A. Smith
Skidmore College

BOOKS: *Angelici dolori* (Milan: Bompiani, 1937);
L'infanta sepolta (Milan: Milano Sera, 1950);
Il mare non bagna Napoli (Turin: Einaudi, 1953);
translated, with three additional stories, by
Frances Frenaye as *The Bay Is Not Naples* (London: Collins, 1955);
Silenzio a Milano (Bari: Laterza, 1958);
L'Iguana (Florence: Vallecchi, 1965); translated by
Henry Martin as *The Iguana* (Kingston, N.Y.:
McPherson, 1987);
Poveri e semplici (Florence: Vallecchi, 1967);
La luna sul muro (Florence: Vallecchi, 1968);
L'alone grigio (Florence: Vallecchi, 1969);
Il porto di Toledo: Ricordi della vita irreale (Milan: Rizzoli, 1975);
Il cappello piumato (Milan: Mondadori, 1979);
Il treno russo (Catania: Pellicanolibri, 1983);
Il mormorio di Parigi (Rome & Naples: Theoria, 1986);
Estivi terrori (Catania: Pellicanolibri, 1987);
La morte del folletto (Rome: Empiria, 1987);
In sonno e in veglia (Milan: Adelphi, 1987);
La lente scura: scritti di viaggio, edited by Luca Clerici
(Milan: Marcos y Marcosa, 1991);
Il cardillo addolorato (Milan: Adelphi, 1993);
Alonso e i visionari (Milan: Adelphi, 1996);
Il paese e la notte (Rome: Empiria, 1996).
Editions in English: "A Pair of Glasses," translated
by Frances Frenaye, in *Italian Literature in
Translation,* edited by James E. Miller Jr., Robert O'Neal, and Helen M. McDonnell (Glenview, Ill.: Scott, Foresman, 1970);
"The Tree," translated by Henry Martin, in *New
Italian Women,* edited by Martha King (New
York: Italica, 1989).

Anna Maria Ortese

As Anna Maria Ortese has passed into her
eighties her career in its entirety has begun to come
into critical focus. Since the mid 1980s Ortese's
work has increasingly received the respect of Italian
critics, making up, perhaps, for the insufficient attention devoted to her work in the past. Her more
complex texts, which deserve the analyses of modern critical theorists, have only begun to receive

their due. Ortese is the antithesis of the literary personality who gathers a swarm of admirers by expressing socially correct (or incorrect) positions for
the newspapers. She is a recluse who has chosen to
live her life in work and solitude. Ortese's profound
desire to shun personal attention–for example, her
demanding that her friends *not* present her for the
1993 Campiello Prize–has no doubt contributed to

her critical neglect; nevertheless, her work has earned an important place in Italian literature. Her style is variously placed in the categories of lyrical, neorealist, fantastic, or in some combination of the above.

Anna Maria Ortese was born in Rome as next to last in a family of six children. Her father was born in the city of Caltanisetta in Sicily; his mother was from Calabria and his father from Caserta. The origin of the father's family, however, harkens back to Spain and Catalonia, where the family name was originally Ortiz. Ortese's mother, Beatrice, was born in Naples. Ortese's maternal grandfather was a well-known sculptor from Carrara, Tuscany, and her grandmother was from Rome.

Like many Italian families in the 1920s and 1930s, Ortese's parents had to struggle to survive. Her father was a civil service employee who just after her birth was drafted and left for World War I. Her mother and maternal grandmother moved the family several times but finally settled in Portici, near Naples, where survival continued to be a primary concern. The family's poverty would shape Ortese and influence her attitudes for the rest of her life, giving her a compassionate interest in the poor.

Upon the return of Ortese's father from war, the family moved to Potenza, in Lucania, and then to the colony of Libya where her father was given a plot of land. Although not on a regular basis, Ortese attended elementary school in both Italy and Libya, which at the time was home to many Italian immigrants. Sickness (at age seven she was severely ill with pneumonia) and family responsibilities often kept her at home. In 1928 the family returned to Italy and settled into poor housing near the docks in Naples, the neighborhood called Toledo, which would be the setting for her 1975 novel *Il porto di Toledo*. At age fourteen Ortese enrolled in a business secondary school but found attendance unbearable. She abandoned formal schooling that year in favor of music studies with a relative. Her intention was to obtain a diploma in music from the conservatory and teach piano for a living.

With the intensity of youth Ortese read authors such as Edgar Allan Poe and especially Katherine Mansfield, who particularly impressed her, leading her to a new vocation. In 1933 she sent three poems—including a lengthy one of more than one hundred verses inspired by the tragic death of her brother, Manuele, a sailor, in Martinique—to the prestigious review *La fiera letteraria*. Massimo Bontempelli, the editor of the journal, published them and became Ortese's first mentor. The following year her first short story, "Pellerossa" (Redskin), appeared in the same journal. Here the young Ortese

introduced for the first time a recurrent theme in her work: the spread of civilization and so-called progress that often brings destruction, consuming nature as well as human innocence.

In 1937 Ortese with Bontempelli's help published *Angelici dolori* (Angelic Pains), her first collection of short stories, containing thirteen pieces, each written in the first person. In the title story, a key for understanding the others, the first-person speaker remembers her first love from her late teenage years. A dialogue develops between her and her heart as she writes awkward and ingenuous lines of poetry about an anonymous person both worthy and unworthy of her bittersweet suffering. One afternoon at a tea party she actually finds the young man of her dreams. He seems to be unusually bright and is interested in talking to her; however, as the story progresses he develops into a sort of divinity. The young man introduces her to Aristotelian discourse on form and content, but beyond his erudition, he inspires her spiritually. By contemplating him she understands that beauty and life can only exist through art. This is one of Ortese's fundamental messages, which she will subsequently repeat and refine in her later work.

In these earliest stories the reader finds what becomes the typical Ortese form of fantasy. In "Angelici dolori" the narrative begins in the earthly realm of adolescent first love and then is elevated to spiritual and aesthetic dimensions. But Ortese does not allow the material framework to be forgotten, and the story remains firmly attached to daily physical life. The speaker's relationship with her young man begins when he asks her to pass him a biscuit. In her dialogue with her heart, she talks about matters such as straightening out the young man's tie or pulling out one of his hairs as a keepsake. She walks through a tangible but surreal stations-of-the-cross with him, lined by pale, marblelike statues of young men in thoughtful positions leading up to a grove of cypress trees. Even in the context of the Passion of Christ, Ortese keeps the parallel story line of adolescent love alive.

Other stories in the collection have similar mixtures of fantasy and reality. "Isola" (Island) begins as a young girl's fantasy, which leads her to make raids on a savage, islandlike part of the city she inhabits. One day she meets a strange man, the Spirit of Joy and Silence—tall, slim, young, and handsome. Suddenly this angelic figure is transformed into her maternal grandfather, the sculptor, whom she never knew except in her dreams. He introduces his granddaughter to the enchanted world of statues of people and animals, which live beyond the life of a person and become a part of the collective history or memory. In "Pellerossa" the poster of the Indian chief White Horse symbolically curls off the wall because of the grim reality of daily existence. "L'avventura" (Adventure), "Il sogno" (Dream), and "La penna dell'angelo" (The Angel's Feather) are linked by their common protagonist, Enrico, who is both earthly and ethereal. Enrico reappears in the Rousseau-like primordial forests of an unknown place off the coast of New Zealand in another novella, "La vita primitiva" (Primitive Life).

Virtually all critical essays on Ortese admit that her work defies categorization. In 1934 the critics reviewing the *Angelici dolori* collection generally agreed that it was a remarkable debut, marked by a distinctive writing style and a lyrical imagination. Two important critics of the late 1930s, however, violently attacked Ortese's first important publication. Enrico Falqui accused her of ultradecadent "angelism," likening her work to a confused mixture of Saint Catherine of Siena's mysticism and religious allegory, and Giancarlo Vigorelli of "magic realism." Many years later Falqui admitted personally to Ortese what was perfectly obvious to most observers: he only intended to attack through her Massimo Bontempelli, at the time a much-debated writer, for literary and political reasons.

After the publication of *Angelici dolori* Ortese spent the next three years in search of work. She traveled to Trieste, Florence, and Venice, where she found a job as copy editor. Shortly afterward she was forced to return to Naples because of the outbreak of World War II. She came to the aid of her family members. At first they were forced out of the city because their building had been bombed. Later they returned to the squalid living space graphically described in the well-known short story "Un paio di occhiali" (A Pair of Glasses), which was collected in *Il mare non bagna Napoli* (1953).

Between 1941 and 1949 Ortese traveled to Rome, Milan, Reggio di Calabria, and Palermo. Many of her travel notes from this period appear later in collections. She was slowly developing contacts in the newspaper world and began to send articles to the periodicals *Il Mondo* and *L'Europeo*. Ortese's investigative reporting was no doubt an influence in her development of a narrative style that often specified and underscored social ills, although her use of fantasy certainly mitigates any of her so-called neorealist tendencies.

In 1950 Ortese completed and published a second collection of short stories, *L'infanta sepolta* (The Buried Infant). It includes seventeen stories, several of which would reappear, some in revised form, in two subsequent collections, *I giorni del cielo* (The

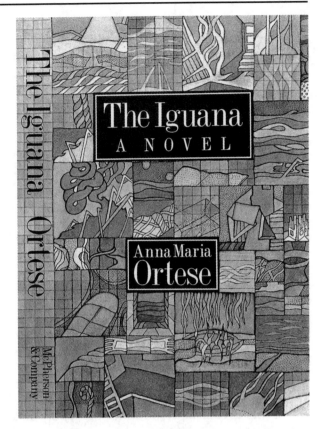

Dust jacket for the American edition of the translation of Ortese's first novel, in which a wealthy young architect encounters an iguana-girl on a mysterious island

Days of Heaven, 1958) and *L'alone grigio* (The Gray Halo, 1969). This volume has neither the depth nor literary scope of the first. The stories largely show the further development of Ortese's interest in fantasy and allegory. In "Uomo nell'isola" (Man on the Island) Ortese weaves her fantasy onto the autobiographical event of her family's journey across the Mediterranean to Libya. In the story they stop along the way to visit an old seafaring uncle who lives on the island of Malta. His housekeeper, Anna, has red eyelids and little hands that look like paws because of the red fur on the back of them. The reader soon discovers that Anna is a large monkey her uncle brought back from the faraway island of Mindanao. The uncle at the end of the story is transformed, like a prince in a fairy tale, into wind, smoke, and song. Ortese in this story explores the surreality that distinguishes her later novel, *L'Iguana* (The Iguana, 1965, translated). In both cases the story is grounded firmly in a tangible event, a journey on the sea, that is transformed into a fantastic dreamworld.

By the early 1950s Ortese had established herself as a writer. Luigi Einaudi, at the time president of the young Italian republic, complimented her on a series of articles on Naples for which she was awarded the Saint Vincent journalism prize. She was given a grant to study and write at the Einaudi Institute as a guest of the Olivetti Corporation in Ivrea (near Turin). Here she continued work on *Il mare non bagna Napoli* (1953; translated as *The Bay Is Not Naples,* 1955), a collection that includes short stories as well as journalistic sketches. It shared the prestigious Viareggio Prize with *Novelle dal ducato in fiamme* (Novellas from the Duchy in Flames, 1953), by Carlo Emilio Gadda.

Many contemporary critics praised *Il mare non bagna Napoli* in the terms of Italian post–World War II Neorealism because Ortese dealt with the subject of socioeconomic deprivation in southern Italy. One of Ortese's best-known stories "Un paio di occhiali" especially seemed to fit the concerns of neorealist critics. The nearly blind young daughter of a miserably poor family surviving in a sordid basement apartment in Naples is given a pair of glasses by her aunt. At first the world for the girl is transformed into an earthly paradise. Shortly afterward the reverse side of the metaphor is made apparent by her violent physical reaction. She can see in detail the horrifying circumstances in which her family and social class live.

The focus on poverty and the realistic depiction of its crudeness clearly fit the model of Neorealism, but Ortese's story also contains a vein of fantasy in the metaphor of looking and seeing through glasses. She uses the glasses metaphor again in her 1991 collection, *La lente scura* (The Dark Lens). In the preface to that collection Ortese explains that publishers invariably demand that authors wear rose-colored or some other clear-colored glasses. Her lens is dark to express melancholy and protest. The reader, however, quickly discovers Ortese's lens can look inward to the colorful imagination as well.

After her father's death in 1953, Ortese left Naples forever as her permanent place of residence. She established herself in Milan, which she defined in an interview with Dacia Maraini as "una città austriaca, dura, crudele" (an Austrian city, hard and cruel). At first she wrote for *L'Unità,* the official newspaper of the Communist Party. In 1954 she took two important trips: one to London and another to Moscow. The series of resulting articles on Russia was published in *L'Europeo,* and for the second time she was awarded the Saint Vincent journalism prize. The material from these journeys would be published again more than thirty years later in *Il treno russo* (The Russian Train, 1983) and in *La lente scura.*

In 1958 the publisher Laterza brought out another collection of Ortese's short stories and journalistic pieces, *Silenzio a Milano* (Silence in Milan), which is set topically and topographically around the industrial center of Lombardy. The collection begins with three examples of Ortese's blend of sociopolitical commentary and fantasy. In "Una notte alla stazione" (A Night in the Train Station) she plumbs the issue of alienation in an industrial center, but first sets up in extraordinary detail the dimensions of the metropolis as symbolized by the railroad station (including precise data on yards of frontage and the number of clocks). The sociological inquiry subsequently becomes a commentary on the mysterious and macabre, on the dark side of the "work-capital" of Italy. The same mixture of styles occurs in "I ragazzi di Arese" (The Boys in the Orphanage at Arese) and "Locali notturni" (Night Clubs).

The more traditional short stories in the collection also deal with the problem of alienation. In "Il disoccupato" (Unemployed) the social problem is the distance that separates the southern Italian immigrant from the northerner. "Lo sgombero" (Moving Out) is the story of a young working-class woman, Masa, and her brother, whose parents have died. The emotional barrenness of their existence unfolds through the ritual of packing and moving their meager belongings. The theme of leftist political disillusionment is also explored in this story. Ortese examined the same problem in "Il silenzio della ragione" (The Silence of Reason), the last piece in *Il mare non bagna Napoli.* The theme would reappear in her novels *Poveri e semplici* (1967) and *Il cappello piumato* (1979).

The generational dilemma of those who were politically or intellectually committed to social and economic change, the heirs of the Resistance movement, was expressed as impatient frustration. Italian politics were dominated by the American Marshall Aid and the Christian Democrats. The rigidity of the Communist Party seemed to have little to do with European political reality. Like many other intellectuals, Ortese lived in an internal conflict between spoken ideals and living reality. She took her leave of leftist intellectual circles shortly after her trip to Russia. She said she left the Communist Party because "volevano che io non ragionassi con la mia testa ma con la loro" (they wanted me to reason not with my own head but with theirs). Her scorn for those who stayed in or close to the party undoubtedly deepened her isolation within the left-leaning literary establishment.

Between 1959 and 1967 Ortese lived in Rome with her sister. Before leaving Milan, she published with Mondadori *I giorni del cielo,* a compilation of eight stories from *Angelici dolori* and seven tales from *L'infanta sepolta.* The one additional and previously uncollected story was the surreal "L'albero" (The Tree), in which a tree becomes a metaphor for Ortese's exploration of youth and the collective past.

In Rome, Ortese finished her first novel, *L'Iguana.* Carlo Ludovico Aleardo, nicknamed Daddo, is a wealthy young architect with royal connections. He has no particular purpose in life except to behave well, according to the canon of his breeding, and to spend his holidays combing the Mediterranean in his boat in search of any little-known site to purchase. He plans for this "locus amoenus" (pleasant place) to become an elite tourist attraction. An additional purpose of his journey is to search for a new author that his unsuccessful publisher friend can discover and launch on the stagnant and saturated Italian literary market. Daddo's quest—a motif with countless echoes in the Western literary tradition—begins as he leaves the realistic setting of the contemporary metropolis, Milan, and sets sail for the open sea.

After a few initial adventures, Daddo finds the island he is seeking, Ocaña, a name that alludes both to seventeenth-century Iberian literature and to the theme of honor. The mysterious island has a dreamlike quality, as do its people. Don Ilario Jiménez, the young, intellectual nobleman at the center of the island tale, is Daddo's foil. He has a singular love-master relationship with the iguana-girl Estrellita, his family's maidservant, who physically resembles the reptile but has the emotions of a peasant girl. Through allegory the novel explores class and gender differences. The iguana's femininity as well as her characterization as a "domestic collaborator," the contemporary Italian trade-union rubric for housemaid, lends itself to Marxist and feminist interpretations. When her use-value is surpassed, she is destined to be exchanged, like any other commodity.

Italian critics did not give Ortese's first novel the attention that it deserved. Among the brief, positive comments, it is clear that the difficult categorization of the book was the source of a sort of critical embarrassment, as many apparently wished to interpret the novel from a single perspective. While it stands together as a coherent and captivating story, *L'Iguana* is not simply a psychological allegory, a gothic novel, a fable, a lyrical romance, or a delirious dream. In his preface to the 1978 Rizzoli edition of the novel, Dario Bellezza has come closest to a full interpretation. He alludes to parallels in world literature, including Pascal and Joseph Conrad, and

relies on Ortese's own insights in his interview with her.

Ortese's second novel, *Poveri e semplici* (Poor and Simple People, 1967), was both a critical and popular success, winning the prestigious Strega Prize. She based it on the first part of a manuscript she wrote from late 1960 to early 1961. Many years later Ortese would use the second half of the same manuscript to write *Il cappello piumato* (The Plumed Hat, 1979), the sequel to *Poveri e semplici.* Both novels are grounded in her experiences in Milan during the 1950s.

Bettina, a young eighteen-year-old living in Milan in an apartment with a group of friends, is the first-person narrator of *Poveri e semplici.* She shares a beautiful fifth-floor flat in the center of town with a young couple, Andrew and Sonia, both of whom are southerners like Bettina. All three are young intellectuals who have a common desire to succeed in the new world of the North after the war; they radiate enthusiasm in the wake of the liberation of Italy from fascism at the end of World War II. The tone, optimistic and affectionate, communicates a sense of youthful freshness. The bits and pieces and the joys and sorrows of the characters' daily lives are the foundation of the story. Another important element is the tender and delicate love story between Gilliat, a young political journalist, and Bettina, which evolves against the backdrop of friendship, group solidarity, and political commitment.

The novel's positive tone contributed to its financial and critical success. The poet Alfonso Gatto makes this point in his preface to the 1974 edition: "Un lettore . . . se vuole avere ragione di questi 'poveri,' di questi 'semplici,' la Ortese gli fermerà sulle labbra le 'battute spiritose' " (A reader . . . who wishes to make fun of these "poor" and "simple" characters and situations will find that Ortese stops the ironic remarks on his or her lips).

Timing was another factor in the success of *Poveri e semplici.* The novel appeared in 1967, the birth year of the student movement. The social consciousness of Italian students in the 1960s set the mood for the country as a whole and for the literary marketplace. Ortese's work found a receptive audience because in many ways the spirit of the 1960s echoes the language and sentiments of the Italian postwar generation in the 1950s. The sense of community outside the family sphere and the desire for the accomplishment of a common good are widely articulated ideals in both periods.

Twelve years passed before Ortese published the continuation of the "poor and simple" story, *Il cappello piumato.* In the sequel Gilliat and Bettina have decided to live together, but slowly their relationship is corroded by economic difficulties, professional insecurities, and the passing of their respective political ideologies. European literature written by the politically engaged in the late 1950s, especially after the failed 1956 anti-Communist revolt in Hungary, typically reflects a loss of faith in political action. Doris Lessing's *Golden Notebook* (1962) explores the depths of this issue. Like the part of Lessing's novel that deals with the same historic moment, Ortese's tone is progressively more melancholy and nostalgic, in accordance with the mood of the story and in contrast with the earlier presentation of Bettina and her friends.

In the two Bettina novels Ortese does not depart into a dreamworld as she does in other works, but she does reiterate the existential theme of characters forced to confront the perceived meaninglessness of their lives. Bettina decides to leave Gilliat because she recognizes their loss of meaning: "Non sarà allora questo patire, questo servire per sopravvivere, la grande verità . . . una stranezza, una colpa, un non senso" (Could it be then that this suffering, this submission in order to survive, is the great truth . . . a strange thing, a fault, something which makes no sense). The perception of life as it is lived by the Iguana and by Masa in "Lo sgombero" is the same. Ortese typically resolves this conundrum by departing from a linear, realistic story into fantasy. In the unreal mode, her characters search for a collective memory that, like art, gives some meaning to or relief from current events. Though in some ways atypical, Ortese's Bettina novels show her fundamental concern with the individual's search for meaning.

Ortese's existential philosophy is evident again in *La luna sul muro* (The Moon on the Wall, 1968), a collection of six short stories. ("Masa" and "Un nuovo giorno" are retitled versions of "Lo sgombero" and "Il disoccupato," which had appeared in *Silenzio a Milano*.) The title story repeats the motif of the strangely unpredictable and fleeting nature of existence. A bourgeois young woman, while expecting her second child, makes the acquaintance of an older woman working as a waitress in a café. The young woman is fascinated by the waitress, but when her mental reflections on her own interest finally culminate in an attempt to speak to her, the concrete demonstration of human interest is thwarted. The older woman no longer works there because her adolescent son has died. When she returns, she is distant, absolutely closed in her grief. "Il cappotto rosso" (The Red Overcoat) depicts the unsatisfactory meeting in a café of two friends from school. They are now mature ladies. In "Di passaggio" (Passing Through) the lives of a middle-aged aunt and her nephew briefly cross. Although they need and could help each other both morally and physically, once again the uncontrollable flood of circumstance will not allow it. The same theme is repeated in "L'incendio" (The Fire), the story of a poor Neapolitan family and the mother's spiritual and practical need to abandon her children.

In *L'alone grigio* Ortese collects fourteen short stories, many of them from *L'infanta sepolta* and other collections, and divides them into three parts. The last three stories, "Fantasticherie" (Fanciful Thoughts), "Viaggio d'inverno" (Winter Trip), and "L'alone grigio" are new. In "Fantasticherie" Ortese uses the sounds, images, colors, and odors of the Libyan desert to evoke the mysterious and ultimately benevolent quality of Nature. "Viaggio d'inverno," which at first seems a journalistic travel account, becomes a psychological drama of travel companions in the same train compartment set against the backdrop of the pure, simple splendor of the seaside in winter. In "L'alone grigio" Ortese's dreamworld mood takes on the dimensions of a science-fiction story. A dark ring around the sun is the first sign of the beginning of dramatic natural phenomena that augur the return of the dead, who become perfectly integrated into the lives of the living when floods, tides, and volcanic eruptions cease.

Neither *La luna sul muro* nor *L'alone grigio* were as successful as *Poveri e semplici*. The cultural and political mood in Italy had changed to the point that Ortese's existential philosophy drew little interest. In the United States in 1968 Martin Luther King Jr. and Robert Kennedy were assassinated, and the following year in Italy the first terrorist bombing occurred in Piazza Fontana in Milan. Ortese subsequently withdrew into an intensely reflective period and began working on *Il porto di Toledo: ricordi della vita irreale* (The Port of Toledo: Memories of an Unreal Life, 1975), an autobiographical fantasy about her life and Naples in the 1930s.

The Toledo of the title refers to a part of Naples near the port that was originally named by the Spaniards in the sixteenth century. Ortese's title and text suggest the history of the city, especially the subtle influence of its Spanish culture. For example, she renames her Bontempelli character Giovanni Conra, Count of Orgaz, the title and subject of a resplendent sixteenth-century painting by El Greco housed in Santo Tomé, a church in the Spanish city of Toledo. The huge canvas depicts a medieval benefactor so pious that Saint Stephen and Saint Augustine miraculously appear at his funeral to lower his body into the grave.

The opening line sets the mood for Ortese's memories of this period which her large, poverty-stricken family barely survived: "Sono figlia di nessuno; nel senso che la società, quando io nacqui, non c'era" (I am daughter of no one insofar as society when I was born did not exist). As in many of her previous works, she uses fantasy in her recollections of places, people, and events, but *Il porto di Toledo: ricordi della vita irreale* is more complex structurally. She weaves poetry, parts of her earliest short stories, letters, and diary entries into a long stream of memories. The critics described it as poetic, lyrical, and fantastic, but it did not meet the taste of Italian readers of the time. In two or three months it disappeared from bookstores and catalogues.

In 1975 Ortese moved to the Ligurian seaside resort of Rapallo, near Portofino, where she lives today with her sister, Maria. Years of profound solitude and isolation followed. The practical problem of finances continues to haunt her in terms succinctly defined by Virginia Woolf in "A Room of One's Own" (1929): the space for a woman to write is insufficient without the amount of money necessary to support it and her. In 1979 *Il cappello piumato* was relatively well received, though not well enough to change Ortese's circumstances.

The decade of the 1980s was marked by a turning of the critical tide in Ortese's favor. In 1985 she received second prize in the Women Writers' section of the Premio Rapallo for *Il treno russo,* based on the articles written for the magazine *L'Europeo* after her journey to Russia in 1954. *Il mormorio di Parigi* (The Murmurs of Paris, 1986), a collection of travel notes from the 1950s, received the Fiuggi Prize for culture. New editions of *Silenzio a Milano, L'Iguana,* and *Il porto di Toledo* also appeared. Two more volumes of stories—*Estivi terrori* (Summer Terrors, 1987), a collection of travel pieces written between 1950 and 1960, and *In sonno e in veglia* (In Dream and in Wakefulness, 1987), a collection of ten fantasy-world tales—capped the decade and received largely favorable critical coverage.

Ortese has continued to be productive into the 1990s. Her 1991 nonfiction volume, *La lente scura,* is a lengthy compilation that includes many of her travel notes. In 1993 she published *Il cardillo addolorato* (The Grieving Goldfinch). Her current publisher, Adelphi, successfully distributed the novel, which occupied first place on Italian best-seller lists for months. The story, set in the late eighteenth century, follows the journey of three young men—a prince, a sculptor, and a rich merchant—who travel from Belgium to Naples along romantic trails. There, against a rose-colored sunset over the bay, they reach their preestablished goal: the elegant yet austere home of the world-famous glove maker

Dust jacket for Ortese's 1979 novel, which follows the later life of the young lovers introduced in Poveri e semplici

Monsieur Mariano Civile, who lives with his two beautiful but mute young daughters.

The older daughter, Elmina, the object of amorous proposals from two of the gentlemen, is shown to have a dark side. In a rush of envy for her ailing sister, Floridia, Elmina crushes her sister's pet goldfinch. The death of innocence and love expressed through the destruction of this tiny creature precipitates the death of Floridia and haunts her sister, the family, and her suitors. The air of magic and the fantastic images of mysterious and benevolent nature that Ortese has developed over a lifetime of work culminate in this novel.

In 1996 two more volumes by Ortese appeared. *Alonso e i visionari* (Alsonso and the Visionaries) is the story of a puma in Arizona who undergoes a radical change which ultimately brings him a human and spiritual internal dimension. The visionaries are the cast of characters who come in contact with him. The tale recounts human, political, and moral dilemmas of the terrorist chapter of contemporary Italian history. Another Ortese volume, *Il mio paese è la notte* (My Country is the Night), is a collection of poems from 1933 (dedicated to her brother who died at sea) up through the 1980s and beyond.

In her nearly sixty-year career Ortese has repeatedly explored the meaning of nature, the social commitment provoked by human suffering, and the relief to suffering provided by the search for a collective history. Each theme blends into the others in Ortese's aesthetic, which she reiterates in the final story of the collection *In sonno e in veglia.* "Piccolo drago" (Little Dragon) is a feigned interview between Ortese and an informed speaker, who probes her reasons for writing: "Non [è] soltanto la paura del denaro eterno, che comanda su chi non ne ha—non soltanto questo il motivo dell'inquietudine, nei suoi libri . . ." (It's not only the fear of eternal money, which rules over the have-nots—this isn't the only reason for the uneasiness in your books . . .).

Ortese's author-figure responds that she is afraid of force, of arms, of the rights created by arms and their authority; she is afraid of the ancient Romans and above all of Saint Michael. She recalls a childhood dream in which her grandmother says there is a dragon in the other room who wants one of the children. When the child-who-would-become-an-author climbs down from her high chair and goes into the room, the dragon comes out through the half-opened door of the closet, rolls over on its back, and looks at her with loving eyes. Thereupon the helmeted figure of Saint Michael appears and instigates the child's slaying of the dragon. Celestial order and salvation reach expression through human reason and cruelty. The young child is horrified by her action, the destruction of innocence and nature, and will be plagued by the guilt for the rest of her life. As a writer she will be consoled only by her art, her creation of meanings beyond cruelty and senseless pain.

Interview:
Dacia Maraini, "Anna Maria Ortese," in *E tu chi eri?* (Milan: Bompiani, 1973).

References:
Dario Bellezza, "Fra incanto e furore," preface to Ortese's *L'Iguana,* (Milan: Rizzoli, 1978), pp. i–xiv;

Massimo Bontempelli, "Anna Maria Ortese 'Angelici dolori,'" in *L'avventura novecentista* (Florence: Vallecchi, 1938);

Giancarlo Borri, *Invito alla lettura di Anna Maria Ortese* (Milan: Mursia, 1988);

Italo Calvino, "Il rapporto con la luna," in his *Una pietra sopra* (Turin: Einaudi, 1980), pp. 182–184;

Luca Clerici, "Anna Maria Ortese," *Belfagor,* 46 (1991): 401–417;

Clerici, "Viaggio, memoria, fantasia," *Linea d'ombra,* 19 (1987): 123–125;

Luce D'Eramo, "L'Ortese a Toledo," *Nuovi argomenti,* 49 (1976): 176–184;

Enrico Falqui, "Anna Maria Ortese 'Angelici dolori,'" in *Novecento letterario italiano,* volume 4 (Florence: Vallecchi, 1972), pp. 901–905;

Raffaele La Capria, "Il mare non bagna Napoli," in *L'armonia perduta* (Milan: Mondadori, 1986);

Claudio Marabini, "Ortese," *Nuova antologia,* 2166 (1988): 219–222;

Nico Orengo, "Anna Maria Ortese: il cielo e la tigre," in *Mormorio di Parigi* (Rome & Naples: Theoria, 1986);

Ines Scaramucci, "Una scrittrice che viene dal freddo," *Linea d'ombra,* 17 (1986): 101–107;

Claudio Varese, "Scrittori oggi," *Nuova antologia,* 1838 (1954): 266–274.

Ottiero Ottieri

(29 March 1924 -)

Emanuele Licastro
State University of New York at Buffalo

BOOKS: *Memorie dell'incoscienza* (Turin: Einaudi, 1954);

Tempi stretti (Turin: Einaudi, 1957);

Donnarumma all'assalto (Milan: Bompiani, 1959); translated by I. M. Rawson as *Men at the Gate* (Boston: Houghton Mifflin, 1962; London: Gollancz, 1962);

I venditori di Milano (Turin: Einaudi, 1960);

L'impagliatore di sedie (Milan: Bompiani, 1964);

La linea gotica: Taccuino 1948–1958 (Milan: Bompiani, 1963);

L'irrealtà quotidiana (Milan: Bompiani, 1966);

I divini mondani (Milan: Bompiani, 1968);

Il pensiero perverso (Milan: Bompiani, 1971);

Il campo di concentrazione (Milan: Bompiani, 1972);

Contessa (Milan: Bompiani, 1975);

La corda corta (Milan: Bompiani, 1978);

Di chi è la colpa (Milan: Bompiani, 1979);

I due amori (Turin: Einaudi, 1983);

Il divertimento (Milan: Bompiani, 1984);

Tutte le poesie: Il pensiero perverso, La corda corta, con ottanta nuove poesie (Venice: Marsilio, 1986);

Improvvisa la vita (Milan: Bompiani, 1987);

Vi amo (Turin: Einaudi, 1988);

L'infermiera di Pisa (Milan: Garranti, 1991);

Le confidenze di Ester, published with *La breve passione di Noemi,* by Bernardino Prella (Naples: Guida, 1992);

Il palazzo e il pazzo (Milan: Garzanti, 1993);

Storia del PSI nel centenario della nascita; e Il padre (Parma: Guanda, 1993);

Diario del seduttore passivo (Florence: Giunti, 1995);

Il poema osceno (Milan: Longanesi, 1996);

De monte (Milan: Guanda, 1997).

MOTION PICTURES: *L'eclisse,* screenplay by Ottieri and Michelanglo Antonioni, Cineriz-Paris Film, 1962.

Ottiero Ottieri

Ottiero Ottieri embraces two extremes of the narrative spectrum: the naturalistic and the psychoanalytical. He is recognized as the initiator of the literary trend known in Italy as "Literature and Industry." With his second novel, *Tempi stretti* (Hard Times, 1957), Ottieri pioneered the focus in Italian fiction on the factory and the new postwar world of industry, neocapitalism, labor problems, and social alienation. His third novel, *Donnarumma all'assalto* (1959; translated as *Men at the Gate,* 1962), is the most famous work to deal with industrialization in southern Italy. In his subsequent writing, Ottieri's interest shifts to personal relations and is marked by relentless psychological inquiry and self-analysis.

He explores existential and clinical alienation as well as the feelings of irreality, anxiety, depression, and distress.

Ottieri was born on 29 March 1924 in Rome, where his family had moved from southern Tuscany after World War I. In 1948 he graduated from the University of Rome with a degree in Italian literature, although his favorite subjects were English literature, sociology, psychology, and psychoanalysis. Ottieri would later describe the sense of alienation he felt during this period of his life. He felt pursued by what he called in *L'irrealtà quotidiana* (Everyday Unreality, 1966) his four horsemen of the Apocalypse: literature, nonliterary studies, work, and the complexity of emotions: "Questi quattro cavalieri d'ora in avanti si alterneranno con pungoli, fuochi e mazze" (From now on these four horsemen will alternate with goads, fires, and clubs).

After his university studies Ottieri moved to Milan. In an interview with Enzo Golino, he explained:

> Venivo da una famiglia d'origine nobiliare-borghese... ma volevo andare dove stava la classe operaia, per motivi di scelta ideologica, per un intimo e disperato bisogno di realtà, per uno sfrenato egotismo narcisistico: l'artista che vuol conquistare la realtà più realtà di tutte controllando su di essa l'efficacia e i limiti della propria arte. E così emigrai a Milano.

> (I came from a family of aristocratic-bourgeois origins... but I wanted to go where the working class lived for ideological reasons, to satisfy a deep and desperate yearning for reality as well as an uncontrollable narcissistic egotism: that of an artist who wants to achieve the highest degree of reality by exercising on reality the power and limits of his art. And so I immigrated to Milan.)

He worked first in the publishing industry and then was employed by the Olivetti Company as a sociopsychologist with the responsibility of interviewing and screening job applicants. This experience and a long, neurotic depression that afflicted him color all of his writings. Psychological exploration is one of Ottieri's distinctive traits as a writer.

Ottieri's first book, *Memorie dell'incoscienza* (Memories of the Unconscious, 1954), is one of many Italian novels that deal with the events of World War II. However, it is not a typical Resistance novel: neither heroic and idealistic nor disillusioned and pessimistic. His protagonist, Lorenzo, is a middle-class adolescent incapable of making any connection with the world around him. While the usual protagonist of Resistance fiction is forced by historical events to come to grips with himself and thus achieve a deeper level of awareness, Lorenzo cannot decide with whom or against whom he should fight. Although the novel takes place from June to September 1943—that is, during the fall of fascism and the start of the Resistance—Lorenzo is neither Fascist nor anti-Fascist: "Preferisco non andare da nessuna parte" (I prefer not to take sides).

In *Tempi stretti* Ottieri examines both the lives of people involved in industrial labor and the factories where they work. One of Ottieri's original contributions to Italian literature is his arresting description of a *terrain vague,* the land at the outskirts of the cities subject to the rapid growth of new factory sites that destroy the countryside. Ottieri contrasts a small printing shop managed by a paternalistic owner, Alessandri, where work is not well planned, with the large Zanini plant, which is managed by efficient personnel but where the workers are exploited: they have to do more in less time, hence Ottieri's title.

Ottieri tells the stories of Emma, a former domestic worker from a small town who is now an assembly-line worker at Zanini, and Giovanni, the production manager at Alessandri's shop. They rent rooms at the same house and eventually fall in love. Ottieri makes their relationship interesting by constantly relating it to their work. It is the reaction to their work—how work interferes with individual emotions—that lends texture to the novel. Emma is worn down by the long, monotonous tasks of factory work; her inability to adapt to her situation condemns her to frustration. The factory becomes her universe: "Per lei lo stabilimento girava come il sole, la luna..." (For her the factory was like the sun, the moon...).

Emma's only moments of spontaneity and joy occur when she is able to forget her work and literally strip off her constraining clothes: "Emma era diventata ardita nell'amore. Lo abbracciò persino, nuda, davanti allo specchio dell'armadio" (She had become daring in love. She even embraced him, naked, in front of the wardrobe mirror). Emma's defense against alienation requires a descent into a childlike, even animal, unconsciousness of the self—she is not afraid of the mirror reflecting her nakedness. Giovanni's danger, on the other hand, lies not in alienation but in full involvement with his work routine. He defends himself by being fully aware of his condition and finding ways to improve his life.

Thinking of Emma and Giovanni, Ottieri wrote in a postscript to his first novel:

> La coscienza è una faticosa conquista che gli individui e le classi sociali si guadagnano lentamente (o non si guadagnano affatto), storicamente, fin che sono al di qua

della coscienza, il loro infantilismo è tale da suscitare lo stupore, l'amore e l'insofferenza che suscitano i bambini.

(Consciousness is a difficult conquest which individuals and social classes reach slowly [or don't reach at all]: historically, until they have reached such consciousness, their infantilism is such that it arouses astonishment; it arouses the love and impatience that children arouse.)

The novel ends on a positive note. Giovanni forgoes a sure advancement in his career and becomes a member of the factory's newly formed internal committee to improve the conditions of his fellow workers.

Although *Tempi stretti* was acclaimed for its portrayal of factory life, Ottieri was criticized for his stereotypical treatment of characters. Renzo Paris notes his treatment of Emma: "Ancora una volta per lo scrittore borghese la giovane proletaria è un concentrato di istinti primitivi e violenti" (Once again for the bourgeois writer the young female proletarian is a condensation of primitive and violent instincts). This judgment seems even more justified when Emma's behavior is compared to Giovanni's, who is less sensual, more intellectual, and is not a proletarian.

A second criticism dealt with style, Ottieri's use of the old-fashioned naturalistic mode to deal with a new subject matter. In a 1969 interview with Ferdinando Camon, Ottieri explained his difficulty:

Avevo letto Marx. La conseguenza fu che non vivevo affatto i problemi della forma e del linguaggio, se non in un modo inconsapevole. Ne uscì *Tempi stretti* . . . ero completamente preso . . . [dai] nuovi contenuti . . . il *che cosa dire* assumeva una prevalenza assoluta sul *come dire*.

(I had read Marx. The consequence was that I only felt the problems of form and language unconsciously, if at all. From this *Tempi stretti* was born. I was totally taken . . . [by] the new contents . . . *what to say* took absolute precedence over *how to say it*.)

In *Donnarumma all'assalto,* his most famous novel, Ottieri seems to answer some of the complaints of his critics. He achieves more spontaneity by using his own experience to create his first-person narrator and protagonist. Characters and events are no longer invention but a directly accessible reality. When in 1954 Olivetti built a new factory near Naples with such modern comforts as an infirmary, a refectory, a garden, and a library, Ottieri was sent in to interview and help select the workers. A few hundred workers were needed, but the factory was "assaulted" by some forty thousand applicants. As Ottieri explained in his interview

Ottiero Ottieri
DONNARUMMA ALL'ASSALTO
Uno dei più significativi romanzi del dopoguerra

Romanzo

Cover for the 1995 edition of Ottieri's third novel, which is based on his experience in hiring workers for a new Olivetti factory

with Camon, "Il libro non è altro che la messa in bella copia degli appunti che io venivo stendendo giorno per giorno" (The book is but the elaboration of notes I took on a daily basis).

The novel reflects two lines of development: the personality of the narrator who reacts, comments, and explains; and the characters who desperately try to be hired. The narrator intervenes with direct comments and with contrasting sketches of life inside and outside the factory. He describes the problems that arise from the sudden introduction of industrialization into a poor farming and fishing community, the conflict between two irreconcilable ways of living and thinking. To the local residents the rationality of a modern factory appears absurd. Why should Accettura not be accepted in spite of his paralyzed arm, leg, and mouth? He protests by trying to throw himself in front of the director's car. Why should the company not hire Papaleo, a former assistant construction laborer who was injured while helping to build the factory and is now half mad since he left part of his brains inside its walls? Another character, Donnarumma, demands a monthly compensation for not being hired.

Ottieri draws unforgettable characters with a sympathetic eye. Tragic, pathetic, even grotesque, the prospective factory workers have been shaped by their pitiful economic condition. Constant hunger motivates them to act the way they do. Their circumstances distort reason and prevent the normal course of life. For example, Paola, an already-hired young woman, will call off her wedding unless her younger sister is also hired, for the sister needs the work to support the family that she will leave behind.

Donnarumma all'assalto was an enormous success. Critics discussed the validity of Ottieri's ideas with regard to the problems of industrialization in southern Italy. They noted Ottieri's trust in the rationality of the factory system and his failure to criticize its failings. Some critics argued that it requires more than the construction of ultramodern factories to bring southern Italy into the modern age and suggested Ottieri was naïve in his belief that neocapitalism could solve centuries-old problems. The debate over *Donnarumma all'assalto* increased its popularity, and in 1972 the novel was made into a television movie.

Ottieri's *La linea gotica* (The Gothic Line, 1963) is actually a notebook he kept from 1948 to 1958. Ottieri offers his views on the social and psychological problems of industrialization. His interest in the subject would soon begin to wane. In a 1973 interview with Golino he remarked: "Ripensando al dibattito sul tema letteratura e industria mi sembra molto noioso" (Thinking about the debate on literature and industry, I find it very boring).

Beginning with his fourth novel, *L'impagliatore di sedie* (The Chair Mender, 1964), Ottieri has written about deviant behavior associated with neurotic and psychotic conditions. This shift can be traced in part to his long psychic depression that led him to leave his position at Olivetti in Milan and forced him into many years of therapy. In the interview with Golino, he stated: "La scienza psicologica non è stata per me soltanto uno strumento professionale . . . è parte integrante . . . dei miei interessi culturali e mi ha aiutato a capire la mia malattia" (To me psychology was more than a professional tool . . . it is an integral part of my cultural interests and it has helped me to understand my illness).

In his introduction to *L'impagliatore di sedie* Ottieri confesses his interest in "trame . . . intime, individuali, libere da condizionamento sociologico" (intimate, personal plots, free from sociological conditioning). He prefers more "external" themes such as love, the focus of this new novel, though the existential and pathological neuroses suffered by the protagonists in a civilization dominated by technology and consumerism are obstacles to authentic relationships. Ottieri acknowledges that "accanto a una vicenda d'amore è spuntata in questo libro e si è ingrandita a danno di essa una vicenda di semifollia" (beside a love story there appeared in this book and grew at its expense a story of near madness). He concludes: "Forse la storia d'amore resta per me l'inarrivabile traguardo d'un uomo e di una società utopisticamente guariti" (To me a love story remains perhaps the unreachable goal of perfect man living in a utopian society).

The story follows Carlo, a company manager, during his short workweek in Milan and his leisurely long weekend in Rome. Longing in vain for a grand passion, Carlo is torn between the reality of his work and the eroticism of the Roman *dolce vita*. His wife, Teresa, is also in a continuously precarious state, unable to choose between the social comfort of matrimony and the romantic attraction of her lover. A third character, Luciana, a company secretary, is an extreme instance of the alienated individual; feeling separated from the world, she suffers attacks of anxiety and is on the verge of suicide.

The book recounts mental anguish, though the author, like a movie camera, remains detached. Ottieri does not explain; nor does he offer motivations. Characters are depicted through actions and gestures but mainly through words. Dialogue takes up three-quarters of the text. Critics compared Ottieri's style with the French *école du régard*. Ottieri's reliance on dialogue stems from the novel's origin as an unproduced screenplay. He also collaborated with movie director Michelangelo Antonioni on *La notte* (The Night, 1960) and *L'eclisse* (The Eclipse, 1962).

In his fifth novel, *I divini mondani* (The Divine Worldlings, 1968), Ottieri develops the long weekend of *L'impagliatore di sedie* into the whole life of the protagonist, a manufacturer of bidets who is a member of the international jet set. Orazio is a playboy without passion, yet obsessive in his pursuit of pleasure and women. Ottieri told Manlio Cancogni in an interview, "Mi affascina . . . la libertà . . . l'uomo liberato dalla struttura della settimana" (Freedom fascinates me . . . man freed from the structure of the week). Orazio is free from any constraints on his time and lives by obeying the promptings of the moment. The sequence of the events in Orazio's life—seductions, intimate dinners, cocktails, dances, skiing, hunting—could be reshuffled without altering anything. Orazio's women are interchangeable, and his acts, gestures, and words are mechanically repeated. For example, he always uses the same pickup line: Should he have on his bidets the portrait of Rudolf Valentino or the Venus by Lucas Cranach?

The meaningless sequence; the interchangeability and repetitiveness of characters, events, and words; and Orazio's lack of development seem to bring the reader into the character's unconscious, with no clear line of time, space, or concerns. These same characteristics allow Ottieri to parody his protagonist's way of life. Ottieri's development as a writer is evident in the elegance of his language, which—as Geno Pampaloni notes—is much more impressive than the content of the documentation of the jet-setters' lives.

For the next seven years Ottieri did not write fiction and devoted his attention to mental illness. He called *Il pensiero perverso* (The Perverse Thought, 1971) a "descrizione in versi della nevrosi ossessiva" (description in verse of obsessive neurosis) and *Il campo di concentrazione* (Field of Concentration, 1972) a "diario di una depressione scritto durante una depressione" (diary of a depression written during a depression). After their publication, in the interview with Golino, Ottieri said: "Oggi m'interessa solo la follia, le manifestazioni patologiche di un paesaggio mentale sconvolto" (Today I'm interested only in madness, in pathological manifestations of a perturbed mental landscape).

Ottieri returned to the novel with *Contessa* (Countess, 1975). Madness is objectified in the protagonist, Elena Miuti, a beautiful psychologist who travels almost weekly from Milan to Zurich for therapy. Ottieri called the book a psychological detective story in which Elena attempts to discover the cause of her obsessions. It is not possible for her to live a normal life, just as it is impossible for her to achieve an orgasm, her sexual pleasure being thwarted "dal ghiaccio secco di una vagina assente" (by the dry ice of an absent vagina). The book ends with Elena's failure. She rejects the cure and chooses to go on living in the unreality of the clinic.

While Elena's choice is between reality and the void, the choice of the protagonist of *I due amori* (The Two Loves, 1983), Carlo, is between normalcy and euphoria. Carlo is a middle-aged newspaperman assigned to write a series of articles on drug addiction. His visit to the "Serenissima," a clinic for rich young people, is a descent into the world of unreason. He meets his destiny when he and the twenty-year-old heroin addict Tullia fall in love with each other. Carlo must choose between his wife, Caterina, and Tullia, between sanity and sickness, normality and the excitement of youth. Loving both, he feels that choosing would destroy part of

Dust jacket for Ottieri's 1983 novel, in which a married, middle-aged newspaperman falls in love with a young heroin addict

his soul. At book's end, after Caterina has left him, Carlo is lost:

> Il baratro era interrotto da Tullia. Ma sopra questo mezzo baratro, oscillava, rioscillava il male di Carlo: non amare nessuno, amare tutte, non scegliere. Gli psicologi chiamano questo: onnipotenza.

> (The abyss was interrupted by Tullia. But above this half abyss, Carlo's sickness was oscillating again: not loving anyone, loving all women, not choosing. Psychologists call this: omnipotence.)

Carlo remains with Tullia but lies when he is asked whether he loves her. The book's last line reads, "'Sí,' mentì Carlo" ("Yes," lied Carlo). His illusion of potency and desire has changed into the delusion of postcoital powerlessness and sadness.

Ottieri shapes *I due amori* by combining Carlo and Caterina's recollections of their past love with the development of love between Carlo and Tullia. The two stories intersect each other, without change of pace or emphasis, just as Carlo's two loves are on the same level of importance. Critics praised the work as fiction, favorably noting that Ottieri had not indulged his penchant for writing essayistic or autobiographical writing.

Like Carlo, Clara, the protagonist of *Il divertimento* (Pastime, 1984), also rejects reality; accepting it would imply accepting herself for what she is, a woman with the incipient symptoms of physical decline. Clara is Ottieri's most existential character—she cannot face time, finitude, or the result of decay, death. She guards against time by diverting herself and retaining the illusion of youth by giving herself to young men. She passes her days in vain would-be acts of life.

The lives of three men suggest other possibilities for Clara. Claudio, her former husband who still loves her, represents a life to which she could return. However, Clara thinks that Claudio "non la capiva, non capiva la sua frenesia" (didn't understand her, didn't understand her frenzy). When he asks her to return to him, she answers, "No, . . . una vita con te non la concepisco più" (No, . . . I can no longer conceive of spending my life with you). She also rejects the life of useful work without metaphysical or emotional complication as symbolized by Pietro, a housepainter.

Giuliano expresses the third and worst possibility. He is experiencing a long depression and rarely gets out of bed. Clara's neurosis is his psychosis. In the last scene they are together in her car, but he wants to go back to bed because he does not want to waste time: "Il tempo è sacro, il tempo è Dio. Io passo il tempo come se pregassi. . . . Io sono ateo ma credo nel tempo. Scorre senza che noi lo vogliamo, sfugge alla nostra mancanza di senso" (Time is sacred, time is God. I pass it as if I were praying. . . . I am an atheist but I believe in time. It runs independently of our will, it eludes us because we don't understand it). Clara seems to defend herself from Giuliano's madness. With her last gesture she "fermò la macchina e lo spinse fuori. Lo vide allontanarsi tristemente per le strade del mondo prive di senso" (stopped her car and pushed him out. She saw him going away sadly through the roads of a world empty of meaning).

The ending of the novel leaves Clara's destiny uncertain. Will she succeed in exorcising chaos, in achieving what in the middle of the novel she calls the meaning of life, "imparare a invecchiare?" (learning how to grow old)? Ottieri develops *Il divertimento* through fragmentary sections, with minor details and minutiae that at times appear disconnected from the main line of the story. Some critics consider his procedure a fault. However, one can easily think of it as mirroring Clara's frantic life.

As the fading of her beauty plunges Clara into depression and makes her aware of the passage of time, so the distortion of his body—a big belly—awakens Alberto, the protagonist of Ottieri's next novel, *Improvvisa la vita* (Suddenly Life, 1987), to the realization of the distortions in his life. He believes that if he can eliminate his belly and put his arms around a woman's waist, he will be cured of his neuroses and able to relate normally to the world—"suddenly life" will spring forth.

When Alberto saves enough money, he goes to the "Casa della Respirazione" (House of Breathing), an expensive spa in Marbella, a resort town in southern Spain, where they claim to cure the body as well as the soul. Through diet, massage, acupuncture, swimming, and long walks, Alberto not only loses his belly but wins over Els, a beautiful Dutch woman. He even succeeds in realizing his dream of going to Africa on a safari. The reader soon begins to view Alberto's unusual luck in the spirit of comedy and awaits the reversal. Alberto confesses to the other guests that he came to the spa for a more important reason than his belly:

> Qui a Marbella non penso mai alla morte. Questo posto, oltre che per dimagrire . . . è stato costruito come un ariete che assalta il castello della morte e lo fa crollare. Ci sono venuto proprio per questo, a parte la mia pancia che mi infelicita, per uscire dal labirinto dell'ossessione della morte.

> (Here, in Marbella, I never think of death. Beyond losing weight, . . . this place was built like a battering ram which assaults the castle of death and makes it collapse. I came here exactly for this—apart from my belly which makes me unhappy—I came to get out of the labyrinth of death's obsession.)

The comic reversal occurs in Madrid, from whence Alberto plans to return victorious to Milan the next day. While walking back one evening to his hotel, savoring "l'inizio della prima lettera" (the start of his first letter) to Els, death, crouching, suddenly pounces on him when "la gomma pesante e dura della ruota posteriore gli schiacciò la testa" (the heavy and hard tire of a bus back wheel flattened his head).

It has been observed that Ottieri uses Alberto's death as a deus ex machina. But while in Greek tragedy the god came down to solve a premeditated impasse in the plot, in *Improvvisa la vita* there is nothing requiring solution. This whimsical, peremptory killing can be viewed as a punishment meted out to Alberto for the energy he wasted on his body. An existentialist might contend Alberto is punished because he dared to forget death; or a Greek tragedian might view his fate as the result of his hubris. Such a death bespeaks Ottieri's pessimistic view of life's precariousness. The surprise ending also suggests that Ottieri—as Claudio Marabini observes—is concerned with death, not life; with time, not the illusion of youth.

Ottieri gives his reader a telling wink with a cruel comparison found in the last scene: "La gomma . . . gli schiacciò la testa appiccicandola *come una frittata contro l'asfalto*" (The rubber . . . flattened his head, pasting it to the asphalt *like an omelette*). The playfulness of the comparison points not only to Ottieri's sarcastic distance from Alberto's past struggles and present agony but also, and more important, to his detachment from the book. By interposing himself as author so dramatically, Ottieri indicates that his creation does not have a life of its own, that its creator can do whatever he pleases with it. Ottieri upstages his story: he switches from mimesis to metamimesis. It would appear that, after his initial period of interest in industry, a second in mental illness, and a third in psychological narrative, Ottieri approached in this book a new mode of expression, metafiction.

In subsequent novels—*L'infermiera di Pisa* (The Nurse from Pisa, 1991), which takes place in a sanatorium, and the playful novel in verse, *Il palazzo e il pazzo* (The Palace and the Madman, 1993), whose protagonist is mad—Ottieri has returned to his interest in psychological narrative. Although his name is primarily linked to his classic novel *Donnarumma all'assalto*, his later books have sometimes manifested his self-analysis with such power and lucidity that his best pages will remain among the most compelling examples of psychological probing present in Italian literature.

Interviews:

Manlio Cancogni, "Da Marx a Orazio. Conversazione con Ottiero Ottieri," *La fiera letteraria,* 32 (8 August 1968): 14–15;

Ferdinando Camon, *La moglie del tiranno* (Rome: Lerici, 1969), pp. 152–166;

Enzo Golino, *Letteratura e classi sociali* (Bari: Laterza, 1976), pp. 140–144.

References:

Giuseppe Amoroso, "Ottiero Ottieri," *Letteratura italiana contemporanea,* 4, no. 2 (1987): 471–482;

Ferdinando Camon, *La moglie del tiranno* (Rome: Lerici, 1969), pp. 43–49;

Marco Forti, "Temi industriali della narrativa italiana," *Il menabò di letteratura,* 4 (1961): 213–239;

Giuseppe Iadanza, *L'esperienza meridionalistica di Ottieri* (Rome: Bulzoni, 1976);

Michele Leone, *L'industria nella letteratura italiana contemporanea* (Saratoga, Cal.: Anma Libri, 1976), pp. 35–36, 71–72, 107–119;

Claudio Marabini, "Ottieri," *Nuova antologia,* 2166 (April–June 1988): 224–226;

Geno Pampaloni, "Le lunghe ombre del liberty," *La fiera letteraria,* 33 (15 August 1968): 21–22;

Renzo Paris, *Il mito del proletario nel romanzo italiano* (Milan: Garzanti, 1977), pp. 152–156;

Walter Pedullà, *La letteratura del benessere* (Naples: Libreria Scientifica Editrice, 1968), pp. 29–33, 293–299;

Pier Aldo Rovatti, "Nota sull'ultimo Ottieri," *Aut aut,* 98 (March 1967): 85–92;

Carlo Salinari, *Preludio e fine del realismo in Italia* (Naples: Morano, 1967), pp. 347–353;

Giacinto Spagnoletti, "Ottiero Ottieri," *Letteratura italiana. I contemporanei,* volume 6 (Milan: Marzorati, 1976), pp. 1604–1624.

Goffredo Parise

(8 December 1929 – 31 August 1986)

Paolo Possiedi
Montclair State University

BOOKS: *Il ragazzo morto e le comete* (Venice: Neri Pozza, 1951); translated by Marianne Ceccone as *The Dead Boy and the Comets* (New York: Farrar, Straus & Young, 1953);

La grande vacanza (Venice: Neri Pozza, 1953);

Il prete bello (Milan: Garzanti, 1954); translated by Stuart Hood as *Don Gastone and the Ladies* (New York: Knopf, 1955) and as *The Priest Among the Pigeons* (London: Weidenfeld & Nicolson, 1955);

Il fidanzamento (Milan: Garzanti, 1956);

Amore e fervore (Milan: Garzanti, 1959); revised as *Atti impuri* (Turin: Einaudi, 1973);

Il padrone (Milan: Feltrinelli, 1965); translated by William Weaver as *The Boss* (New York: Knopf, 1966; London: Cape, 1967);

Gli Americani a Vicenza (Milan: Scheiwiller, 1966);

Cara Cina (Milan: Longanesi, 1966);

L'assoluto naturale (Milan: Feltrinelli, 1967);

Due, tre cose sul Vietnam (Milan: Feltrinelli, 1967);

Biafra (Milan: Feltrinelli, 1968);

Il crematorio di Vienna (Milan: Feltrinelli, 1969);

Sillabario n. 1 (Turin: Einaudi, 1972); translated by James Marcus as *Abecedary* (Marlboro, Vt.: Marlboro, 1990);

Guerre politiche: Vietnam, Biafra, Laos, Cile (Turin: Einaudi, 1976);

New York (Venice: Edizioni del Ruzante, 1977);

Tropici prima del motore, by Parise and Enzo Ragazzini (Milan: Touring club italiano, 1981);

L'eleganza è frigida (Milan: Mondadori, 1982);

Sillabario n. 2 (Milan: Mondadori, 1982); translated by Isabel Quigly as *Solitudes: Short Stories* (London: Dent, 1984; New York: Vintage, 1985);

Artisti (Rome: Le parole gelate, 1984);

Arsenico (Oderzo: Edizioni Becco Giallo, 1986);

Gli Americani a Vicenza e altri raccont (Milan: Mondadori, 1987).

Collections: *Sillabari* (Milan: Mondadori, 1984);

Opere, 2 volumes, edited by Bruno Callegher and Mauro Portello (Milan: Mondadori, 1987–1989).

Goffredo Parise (photograph by Antonio Sansone/Effigie)

PLAY PRODUCTIONS: *La moglie a cavallo,* Milan, Teatro Gerolamo, 17 February 1960;

L'assoluto naturale, Rome, 1968.

MOTION PICTURES: *L'ape regina,* screenplay by Parise, 1961;

La donna cannone, screenplay by Parise, 1961.

OTHER: *La moglie a cavallo, Tempo presente,* no. 11 (November 1958);

Fulvio Roiter, *Laguna,* preface by Parise (Udine: Magnus Edizioni, 1978);

Yasunari Kawabata, *La casa delle belle addormentate,* afterword by Parise (Milan: Mondadori, 1982), pp. 201–209;

Robert Louis Stevenson, *Viaggio in canoa,* preface by Parise (Milan: Mondadori, 1983).

Goffredo Parise was a significant and widely known figure in Italian culture for three decades. An accomplished author, he wrote experimental and realistic fiction as well as drama and screenplays with ease and skill. He became famous as an acute and often controversial observer of political and cultural matters, writing for newspapers and magazines of wide circulation. His reporting on international events was republished in several books.

Parise was also known for his spontaneous and unconventional demeanor. His unorthodox persona was recalled by Furio Colombo in a lively article for the 6 September 1986 *La stampa.* " Quel giorno Parise venne alla TV in maglione" (On that Day Parise Came to the TV Station Wearing a Turtleneck) draws an illuminating comparison between Parise and "the American poets of the Village."

Parise was born in Vicenza on 8 December 1929. His mother, Ida Wanda Bertoli, was unmarried, and his father was unknown. The family was not wealthy: his grandfather owned a modest garage in Vicenza. In 1937 Ida Bertoli married the journalist Osvaldo Parise. Goffredo was adopted and in 1943 assumed his stepfather's surname. He completed the secondary school and moved to Venice. He enrolled at the University of Padua where he took courses in literature, medicine, and mathematics, but he did not graduate. In 1950 Parise began his lifelong work as a journalist for the newspaper *L'Alto Adige.* Until the end of his life he contributed reports, literary and art reviews, fiction, and social criticism for several newspapers and magazines. The journals he wrote for most frequently were *Il corriere d'informazione, Il resto del Carlino, Il corriere della sera,* and *L'espresso.*

Parise's first novel, *Il ragazzo morto e le comete* (translated as *The Dead Boy and the Comets,* 1953), was published in 1951. At that time the success of Neorealism in cinema and literature was still unchallenged in Italy, and the public failed to appreciate Parise's nonrealistic work. Among the critics, however, the young author did not go unnoticed. His publisher, Neri Pozza of Vicenza, was small but influential; he was known in literary circles and was able to introduce the novel to important and discriminating readers such as Eugenio Montale, Emilio Cecchi, and Giuseppe Prezzolini, who recognized its value.

Prezzolini was instrumental in getting the novel translated and published in the United States by Farrar, Straus and Young. *The New York Times* and the *Herald Tribune* published favorable reviews.

The plot and writing technique of *Il ragazzo morto e le comete* are far from traditional. The boy's violent death is revealed at the beginning of the book, in which Parise seeks to develop a tragic tension rather than fashion a plot that moves toward a crisis as is the case with a traditional novel. The main theme is not the boy's death but his dreams and imagination; time and space are not sequentially determined. Even the narrating voice is unstable, shifting repeatedly from first to third person.

The setting is a nonspecific town in the Venetian mainland (presumably Vicenza) at the end of World War II. Parise apparently drew on his own experiences in creating the two protagonists, an unnamed fifteen-year-old boy (the *ragazzo* of the title) and Fiore, a friend of the same age. Other characters, such as the eccentric lover of animals, Squerloz; the sweet Edera; and the bizarre homosexual, Antoine, are represented in a grotesque fashion.

The novel appropriates the coming-of-age story in an unconventional manner, for though its subject is initiation as in the traditional myth, the initiation described is not to adulthood and life but to death. In a surreal twist the boys have several encounters with dead people, who for a time roam the world of the living before dissolving forever. After his death the unnamed boy too is transformed into one of the mournful and nonbenevolent wanderers. Parise does not hint at any hope for eternal life after death, and his story suggests a disenchantment with religion: "Compresi che Dio era una cometa apparsa nel cielo, bellissima e misteriosa . . . ma come tutte anch'essa aveva compiuto il suo giro, ci aveva illusi e si era spenta come una pietra, nel buio" (I came to realize that God was a splendid and mysterious comet that appeared in the sky . . . but, like all comets, it had completed its orbit, had left us deluded and now was extinguished like a stone, in the darkness). This is the conclusion of an exemplary narrative within the narrative. The speaker is an Austrian Jew who tells the boy about the centuries-old suffering of his family.

Two years after *Il ragazzo morto e le comete,* Parise brought out his second novel, *La grande vacanza* (The Great Vacation, 1953). The new novel is nonrealistic like the first and reads like an extended dream. The protagonist is once again an adolescent, the sixteen-year-old Claudio, with whom Parise establishes a loose identification through the use of some autobiographical details. Parise draws from psychoanalysis, in particular the ideas of Carl Jung, as regards archetypes and the collective unconscious. *La grande vacanza* is more traditional than the previous novel in that its narrating voice is steady and the sequence of events tighter. The historical time is the contemporaneous present, for, at the beginning of the narrative, the radio gives news about the Korean War.

Claudio goes with his grandmother, Adele Marchetti (the name of Parise's grandmother), to a spot that used to be a holiday resort in the Venetian hills; it has become a dusty, shabby home for strange-looking and senile people who are tended by nuns. Claudio's experiences with the resort's grotesque guests are furthered when he escapes only to encounter other grotesque characters, including a group of gay people living together in an uncanny apartment and a band of partisans still trying, six years after the end of the war, to round up the German invaders. His experiences are frequently interrupted by flashbacks, recollections, and fantastic digressions. The narrative ends with the grandmother's death and Claudio's return to town. The narrator remarks at the end: "E da qui cominciano gli schemi del banale" (Here the schemes of banality begin). The main themes of the novel are the loss of childhood, the initiation to maturity, and the nostalgia for a way of life that has been lost. Passage to adult life is represented as the acceptance of disorder and the grotesque.

The public gave Parise's second novel the same poor reception as it did his first, though some critics singled out his originality, contrasting it with the predictability of Neorealistic novels. Eugenio Montale spoke of his "ispirazione chagalliana" (Chagallian inspiration), rightly guessing that Parise had looked to painter Marc Chagall for inspiration. Montale appreciated Parise's fairy-tale-like atmospheres, in which autobiographical experiences appear in a distorted way in the background. He also compared Parise's attitude toward childhood to Truman Capote's: it is an attitude, he wrote, "which is devoid of all the nostalgic qualities that are typical of the Italian twilight poets (crepuscolari), qualities which, due to a long and well established tradition, we wrongly assume to be essential to childhood matters." Other critics pointed to the surrealistic quality of Parise's work. At the time Parise talked of his admiration for Fyodor Dostoyevsky, Herman Melville, Franz Kafka, and Lautréamont and described his writing as "lyrical" and "cubistic." He disliked the term *experimentalism,* which was often employed to characterize his work.

Between 1953 and 1960 Parise lived in Milan, where he worked for the Garzanti publishing house, though he traveled frequently in Italy and abroad.

During this period Parise married Maria Costanza Sperotti and established durable and important friendships with Eugenio Montale, Giovanni Comisso, and Nico Naldini. The experience of living in Milan, a large industrial and financial center as well as a notoriously "tough" city that Parise always remembered with mixed feelings, led to his developing a detachment from and a critical attitude toward his province. Parise also reflected on the cold and impersonal climate of the corporate world, which he criticized in later texts.

The first of three realistic novels Parise wrote during his stay in Milan, *Il prete bello* (1954; translated as *Don Gastone and the Ladies,* 1955), was a financial success. The narrator is a young boy named Sergio who bears a loose resemblance to the author. Through the limited perspective of the boy's voice, Parise ironically represents the provincial, bigoted, suffocating world of adults. Although Sergio's best friend, a poor rascal called Cena, dies tragically at the end, the novel is brilliantly comical, containing some of the most hilarious moments found in contemporary Italian fiction.

The setting of Vicenza, famous as one of the sturdiest citadels of Italian Catholicism, and the historical period of the late 1930s, between the end of the Spanish Civil War and the beginning of World War II, are described with great precision. The center of the novel is the courtyard of a big apartment house inhabited by members of the middle class, including well-meaning spinsters, a cobbler, a hatmaker, and a Neapolitan widower with five unmarried daughters. The sleepy provincial town comes alive with the arrival of the young, lively, pro-Fascist Don Gastone Caoduro, the "handsome priest" of the title, as well as the arrival of Fedora, young, beautiful, and easy. The novel retains the reader's attention with surprising and convincing turns of events. Parise's irony and sarcasm are pervasive, exposing the narrow-mindedness and bigotry of the middle class, the vanity and arrogance of the rich, and the ridiculous rituals of Fascism.

The success of *Il prete bello* can be traced to the social attitudes of the time. In the repressive 1950s Italy and in particular the Veneto felt the influence of the Catholic Church and the Christian Democratic Party; the memories of Fascism were still fresh, but Mussolini's regime appeared as a grotesque image of the past, worthy only of caricature. *Il prete bello* offers a satirical view of a safe target, the Fascist past, through a titillating blend of sex and scandals. At the same time, Parise reassures his readers with the final turns of events that remove the threats to the social order. After it becomes clear that Fedora is carrying the priest's child, he dies from consumption; even Cena, the street urchin, dies in an accident as he attempts to escape from a reform school.

Critical reaction to the work was divided: some reviewers saw Parise as a promising young writer; others criticized him for simplistic caricature. Not surprising, the reviewer of the Catholic journal *Civiltà cattolica* regarded the book as scandalous. The well-known critic Emilio Cecchi praised the sense of human compassion represented by the boys in the novel, but he criticized what he saw as Parise's simplistic attitude. "The very success of *Il prete bello*," he wrote, "could become a real misfortune for Parise as an artist." Other critics, such as Giorgio Pullini, registered their preference for the work's realistic vein to the obscure and at times pretentious surrealism of the previous novels.

Similar themes and the same setting appear in Parise's next novel, *Il fidanzamento* (The Engagement, 1956), also intended as a satire of provincial life. For the first time in a major work, Parise replaces his young, male, first-person narrator with an omniscient narrator. Reminiscent of a comedy of manners by the eighteenth-century playwright Carlo Goldoni, the plot is simple though a bit more sexually explicit than a Goldoni play. It is the story of an engagement, never brought to fruition, between an office clerk and the daughter of an assertive woman who, at the right moment, takes charge of the situation. The social setting is the same as in *Il prete bello* – middle-class hypocrisy and the ever-present Catholic Church form the backdrop – but Parise's satire avoids overt caricature, and, accordingly, the result is less comical. On the other hand, the ideological criticism is sharper and more explicit. Ultimately the merit of this work rests on its effective depiction of Italian provincial life in the 1950s and the sense of absurd fatalism that afflicted those who tried to question such a way of life.

After writing several short stories and novellas, including "La moglie a cavallo" (The Riding Wife), which appeared in the monthly magazine *Tempo presente,* Parise in 1959 published his third realistic novel, which completed what he called "the ideal trilogy" of life in the Veneto region. The original title was *Atti impuri* (Impure Acts), but the publisher, Livio Garzanti, deeming it too bold, changed it to *Amore e fervore* (Love and Fervor). In 1973 the novel was revised and republished by Einaudi with the original title.

The story depicts aspects of provincial life that border on perversion. Worse than mediocre and ludicrous, the characters are much more bigoted than Parise's earlier characters; they are painted as grotesque, mean, and always ready to use violence against those weaker than themselves. Their physical appearance is hideous, and they are often described as having features similar to those of animals. Young Marcello, the protagonist, works in the family-run company and is married to an unattractive woman. He is obsessed with Catholic religious practice to the point that he goes to Communion every morning and feels terribly sinful after making love to his wife without the intention of procreating. His greatest desire is to establish a personal relationship with Jesus, whom he conceives in terms of popular representations. However, Marcello falls in love with an attractive woman. After she abandons him and his family turns against him, Marcello is ruined because, rather than relying on himself, he continues to nurture his childish relationship with Jesus. The original version of the novel ended with the protagonist's death during a fatal, pseudomystical vision. In the 1973 version this ending was omitted.

The novel pleased neither the critics nor the public when it first appeared. Parise was bitter about its negative reception. Claudio Altarocca views *Amore e fervore* as a transitional work, midway between Parise's criticism of the petite bourgeoisie in the provinces and his representation of important contemporary issues, such as the abuses and greed of the corporate world.

In 1959 Parise adapted for the stage the novella "La moglie a cavallo" (The Riding Wife), which deals with the power conflict between a man and a woman. The play was produced in 1960 by Filippo Crivelli in Milan; Parise later turned the play into a script for Marco Ferreri's movie *L'ape regina* (The Queen Bee, 1961). As is the case with his other works, Parise was close to his material. *La moglie a cavallo* and *L'ape regina,* he wrote in a 15 January 1963 letter to a friend, "nascono da una osservazione naturale tra il maschio e la femmina. . . . La natura femminile quando supera o annulla gli alti spazi della ragione, ha una sua fame vorace, un suo destino riproduttore, che polverizza in poco tempo anche gli anni" (are born from observation of the natural relationship between men and women. . . . When feminine nature overcomes or nullifies the lofty spheres of reason, it develops a voracious hunger, a reproductive destiny, which in a short time destroys even the notion of time). The play surrealistically portrays the transformation of a man into a being totally submissive to his dominating wife, who harnesses him with saddle, reins, and bit and rides him like a horse. The work is a faltering drama, but it served as an important prelude to Parise's later works, such as the play *L'assoluto natu-*

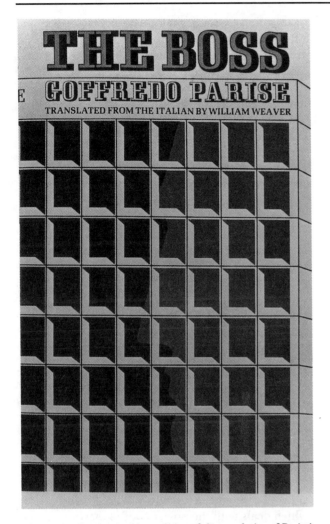

Dust jacket for the American edition of the translation of Parise's 1965 novel, in which a young corporate employee is dominated and dehumanized

rale (The Natural Absolute, 1967), which also deals with man's erotic and social bondage to women.

In 1960 Parise moved to Rome where he worked in the movie industry as a scriptwriter for several important directors, including Mauro Bolognini, for whom he adapted Alberto Moravia's novella *Agostino* (1944) and Italo Svevo's *Senilità* (1898). In the same capacity, he worked on *L'ape regina* for Marco Ferreri and *8 1/2* for Federico Fellini. In the early 1960s Parise traveled extensively and wrote various articles on the countries he visited. He also faced the ending of his marriage, a difficult experience that led to his writing *L'assoluto naturale*.

In 1965 Parise published *Il padrone* (translated as *The Boss*, 1966), which proved to be both popular and controversial. The novelist remarked in an April 1965 interview in *L'espresso* that in style and content the work represented a return to his earlier fiction. He pointed out that his most authentic writing was to be found not in the realistic, parodic novel but in the fantastic vein, and he placed the gloomy parable *Il padrone* in the fantastic vein after *Il ragazzo morto* and *La grande vacanza*. The genesis of *Il padrone* can be traced to Charles Darwin's work and Parise's travels through the United States, which he characterized as "cognitive trauma."

The novel scathingly represents the annihilation of man's personality, intelligence, and freedom under the system called at the time neocapitalism. The novel does not offer explicit Marxist criticism of capitalism, for Parise found little to admire in either system. Parise told Claudio Altarocca that "Il 'sistema' capitalistico avanzato (America) è una grande disgrazia per l'uomo . . . il 'sistema' comunista così come appare nella sua pratica (paesi socialisti, che ho visto tutti) è una grande disgrazia per l'uomo" (America's advanced capitalism is a great misfortune for human beings; on the other hand, Communism, at least as it is implemented in socialist countries, all of which I have seen, is a great misfortune for human beings).

Written in the first person in the form of a personal memoir, *Il padrone* follows a young, unnamed man coming from the Italian provinces to a big city. He goes to work for a big corporation under a boss named Max, whose task is to subdue his employees absolutely. The story does not tell what the company produces and how management is organized: Parise's main object is to depict the gradual process of subjugation that takes places in a grotesquely aseptic and quasi-religious environment. Deprived of human qualities, the characters resemble absurd, laughable zombies. They bear strange names originating in pop-culture songs and comics and display the flat mannerisms of comic-book characters. For example, the boss's fiancée, Minnie (the name of Mickey Mouse's girlfriend), utters only onomatopoeic exclamations.

The young protagonist's attempts to resist his boss are unsuccessful. After he is subdued and persuaded by Max's deceitful manner, he ends up being happily married to the mongoloid Zilietta. The parable ends at the final stage of the young fellow's development: Zilietta is pregnant and will give birth to a mentally retarded child. The father-to-be hopes, he says, that "non sia come me, uomo con qualche barlume di ragione, ma felice come sua madre nella beatitudine pura dell'esistenza. Egli non userà la parola ma nemmeno saprà mai cosa è immorale" (he will not be like me, a man with a gleam of reason left, but as happy as his mother, in the pure bliss of existence. He will not use words, but will never know the difference between what is moral and immoral).

Page from the manuscript for Cara Cina *(Goffredo Parise Collection)*

The reactions to the novel ranged from the Marxist criticism of Francois Wahl, who in a 14 April 1965 letter to Parise lamented "the total absence of trade unions" in the work, to the positive and articulate review of Guido Piovene, who interpreted the story as an apologue about capitalism as a perverse form of religion. The novel was also praised by Prezzolini and Montale, who recognized poetry in its pages. The work was immediately translated by William Weaver and published by Knopf of New York.

In 1966 Parise traveled to China to cover Mao Tse-tung's Cultural Revolution. He did so through a series of articles published in *Il corriere della sera*. The same year his entire series was published in book form by Longanesi with the title *Cara Cina* (Dear China). Parise's attitude toward reportage as a literary genre is noteworthy: "Per me reportage e romanzo nascono nello stesso modo, da un'idea, che al principio è molto semplice. . . . Il reportage è un romanzo, con una situazione di cui lo scrittore è il protagonista" (To me a reportage and a novel are born the same way, from an idea, which initially is very simple. A reportage is a novel with a situation whose protagonist is the writer himself). The "sim-ple idea" that motivated Parise's articles about China was his desire to compare and contrast the "great mass civilization" he had observed in the United States to the other "great mass civilization" of the planet. The results of that comparison are summarized at the end of the book: "I cinesi hanno urgente necessità di imparare da noi, Europa, due cose: l'analisi e la sintesi: cioè la libertà. E noi da loro altre due cose non meno importanti: lo stile della vita e l'aiuto reciproco: cioè l'amore" (The Chinese must learn from us Europeans two things: analysis and synthesis, that is, freedom. We must learn from them two equally important things: lifestyle and mutual help, that is, love).

During the spring of the following year, Parise traveled for *L'espresso* through Thailand, Cambodia, and South Vietnam. In the series of articles that he referred to as "a war diary" he described his encounters with various people, from the American GIs to the local peasants and prostitutes, involved in a conflict that at the time seemed to be under the control of the Americans. Among the most impressive exchanges are those with Gen. William Westmoreland, whom Parise portrays as a technological, antiromantic military leader. The reportages on Vietnam were published by Feltrinelli with the title *Due, tre cose sul Vietnam* (Two, or Three Things about Vietnam, 1967).

As a reporter, Parise often witnessed important events. He observed the May 1968 student insurrection in Paris. He also covered the tragic civil war and famine in Biafra. His articles were often shocking, as the ones that revealed the cynical involvement of a big Swiss corporation in Biafra's affairs.

In 1969 Feltrinelli brought out *Il crematorio di Vienna* (The Vienna Crematorium), a collection of thirty-three short stories Parise had published between 1963 and 1964 in *Il corriere della sera*. In general the tone and subject matter of these stories are similar to those of *Il padrone*. They deal with the violence that marks Western societies. The often surrealistic prose, as some enthusiastic critics suggested, exudes the power of Kafkaesque nightmares. The style is extremely cold and detached, to the point of being, as less enthusiastic critics argued, decidedly boring. The short stories have no individual titles but are designated by numbers. Story no. 9, which provides the emblematic title to the collection, is about a foreign visitor, presumably a tourist, who finds himself in a gloomy Viennese building; at the end he is surprised by a stranger, shut alive in a coffin, and cremated.

In 1971 Parise started a new narrative project, a series of short stories unified by style and general point of view. Published from 1971 to 1980 in *Il corriere della sera,* they were collected in two numbered "Primers," *Sillabario n. 1* (1972; translated as *Abecedary,* 1990) and *Sillabario n. 2* (1982; translated as *Solitudes,* 1984). These stories are different from the previous series: the tone is warm, compassionate, almost sentimental. The two collections are organized like an encyclopedia of feelings and abstract ideas. The titles of the stories, which are often conceived as diary entries, are arranged in alphabetical order. The themes range from "Amore" (Love) to "Solitudine" (Loneliness). In the introduction to *Sillabario n. 2* the author writes that he did not reach letter *Z* because his inspiration abandoned him after letter *S*: Poetry is, he says, "a bit like life and love." Parise's new work became once again the object of debate. Some critics considered it his best production; others saw it as the expression of a reactionary ideology.

Parise's new travels, to Chile after the coup d'état against Salvador Allende (1973), to New York (1975), to Saudi Arabia and the United Arab Emirates (1977), generated vivid reportages. Although his health began to deteriorate, he continued to plan new projects. He worked as a journalist, producing literary and art criticism as well as a column of correspondence with the readers under the title "Parise risponde" (Parise Answers) in *Il corriere della sera*.

His last journey of discovery took him once again through the Orient. Parise was particularly fascinated by Japanese culture. His *postfazione* (afterword) to Yasunari Kawabata's *La casa delle belle addormentate* (The House of the Sleeping Beauties, 1982) and his articles about Japan written for *Il corriere della sera* show his admiration. These articles were reprinted in 1982 with the title *L'eleganza è frigida* (Elegance is Frigid).

Goffredo Parise died in Treviso in 1986. Before his death he was awarded a *laurea honoris causa* (honorary degree) at the University of Padua. He also lived to see the publication of *Arsenico* (1986), a fascinating fragment of an autobiographical novel in poetic prose that he wrote in 1962 (the title is an allusion to a poem by Montale). His work has indeed left a mark on Italian culture, but his unconventional ideas and his complex and not always popular style have so far mainly generated ephemeral reactions in newspapers and magazines. Parise's work has yet to receive a comprehensive critical assessment.

Letters:

Goffredo Parise, *Odore d'America: Lettere all'amico Vittorio. 1961* (Milan: Mondadori, 1990).

References:

Claudio Altarocca, "Parise," *Il castoro,* 69 (September 1972);

Armando Balduino, *Messaggi e problemi della letteratura italiana contemporanea* (Venice: Marsilio, 1976);

Nico Naldini, *Il solo fratello. Ritratto di Goffredo Parise* (Milan: Rosellina Archinto, 1989);

Paolo Petroni, *Invito alla lettura di Parise* (Milan: Mursia, 1975);

Giorgio Pullini, *Il romanzo italiano del dopoguerra* (Venice: Marsilio, 1970);

Pullini, *Il teatro italiano del Novecento* (Bologna: Cappelli, 1971), pp. 188–189;

Edoardo Sanguineti, *Tra liberty e crepuscolarismo* (Milan: Mursia, 1970), pp. 164–176;

Giacinto Spagnoletti, "Goffredo Parise," in *Letteratura italiana. I contemporanei,* volume 4 (Milan: Marzorati, 1974), pp. 1873–1895;

Spagnoletti, "Goffredo Parise," in *Letteratura italiana. '900. Gli scrittori e la cultura letteraria nella società italiana,* volume 9 (Milan: Marzorati, 1979), pp. 8941–8963.

Pier Maria Pasinetti
(24 June 1913 -)

Cristina Della Coletta
University of Virginia

BOOKS: *L'ira di Dio* (Milan: Mondadori, 1942);

Rosso veneziano (Rome: Colombo, 1959; revised edition, Milan: Bompiani, 1965); translated by Pasinetti as *Venetian Red* (New York: Random House, 1960; London: Secker & Warburg, 1961);

La confusione (Milan: Bompiani, 1964); revised and enlarged as *Il sorriso del leone* (Milan: Rizzoli, 1980); translated by Pasinetti as *The Smile on the Face of the Lion* (New York: Random House, 1965);

Il ponte dell'Accademia (Milan: Bompiani, 1968); translated by Pasinetti as *From the Academy Bridge* (New York: Random House, 1970);

Domani improvvisamente (Milan: Bompiani, 1971); translated by Pasinetti as *Suddenly Tomorrow* (New York: Random House, 1972);

Dall'estrema America (Milan: Bompiani, 1974);

Il centro (Milan: Rizzoli, 1979);

Dorsoduro (Milan: Rizzoli, 1983);

Life for Art's Sake: Studies in the Literary Myth of the Romantic Artist (New York: Garland, 1985);

Melodramma (Venice: Marsilio, 1993);

Piccole veneziane complicate (Venice: Marsilio, 1996).

MOTION PICTURES: *La signora senza camelie,* screenplay by Pasinetti, Michelangelo Antonioni, Suso Cecchi d'Amico, and Francesco Maselli, E.N.I.C., 1953;

Smog, screenplay by Pasinetti, Franco Rossi, and Franco Brusati, TITANUS, 1962.

OTHER: "Storia di famiglia," translated by Pasinetti as "Family History," in *The Best Short Stories,* edited by Edward J. O'Brien (Boston: Houghton Mifflin, 1940), pp. 244–284–original Italian story first published in *L'ira di Dio*;

Great Italian Short Stories, edited by Pasinetti (New York: Dell, 1959);

Pier Maria Pasinetti (photograph by Fulvio Roiter)

"Masterpieces of the Renaissance," in *World Masterpieces,* volume 1, edited by Maynard Mack (New York: Norton, 1965), pp. 1135–1694.

SELECTED PERIODICAL PUBLICATIONS–
UNCOLLECTED: "Home-coming," *Southern Review,* 2 (Spring 1937): 736–746;

"The 'Jeanne Duval' poems in *Les Fleurs du Mal,*" *Yale French Studies,* 1 (Fall–Winter 1948): 112–118;

"Giacomo Leopardi," *Sewanee Review,* 57 (April–June 1949): 251–260;

"*Coscienza critica:* Aspects of Contemporary Italian Criticism," *Romanic Review,* 40 (October 1949): 186–197;

"The Italian Vogue," *Kenyon Review,* 12 (Autumn 1950): 677–688;

"Notes Toward a Reading of Foscolo's *Sepolcri,*" *Italian Quarterly,* 3 (Winter 1960): 3–12;

"Notes on the Poetic Image of the *Patria,*" *Italian Quarterly,* 5 (Spring–Summer 1961): 58–72;

"Fogazzaro's Little World of the Past: Program
  Notes for an Italian 'Classic,'" *Italian Quarterly,* 7 (Fall–Winter 1963): 3–14.

Novelist, professor, journalist, and screenwriter, P. M. Pasinetti has been instrumental in
promoting Italian culture in the United States
since the 1930s. At home both in Venice and Los
Angeles, Pasinetti in his work embraces the diverse
and complex experiences of life on two continents.
Without surrendering to either nostalgia or sentimental regionalism, he has written novels of intellectual breadth, filled with unique characters and
settings.

Pasinetti is the architect of a unified oeuvre.
Each succeeding novel picks up and develops situations left marginal in previous works, thus establishing a dialogue between his novels. By writing his
new work in the light of his old, Pasinetti creates a
narrative world that is neither conclusive nor definitive, that probes and questions itself and defies ideological absolutes. In *Rosso veneziano* (1959) Marco
Partibon, one of Pasinetti's most remarkable characters, observes: "Una storia non è mai finita di raccontare; tutto è vivo intorno a me e pieno di domande; scrivendo così io smuovo il terreno ma non
pretendo sistemare nulla" (The telling of a story is
never finished; everything is alive around me, and
full of questions; writing this way, I stir the ground,
but I don't pretend that I am settling anything).

Pasinetti's narrative production is essentially
dialogical. Not only do his novels echo and comple-
ment one another, they also establish a network of
intertextual references grounded in Western literary tradition. Allusions to Alessandro Manzoni,
James Joyce, and Thomas Mann, as well as to Pasinetti's own works, are made in a critical, often
ironic, manner. Pasinetti's reliance on a dialogue
with other writers also points to the open, multivo-
cal, and multifocal structures of his novels. His formal experimentalism stems from his view of reality
as being open to further interpretations and constantly asking to be interrogated and newly discovered.

The kaleidoscopic play of narrative voices and
the coexistence of contradictory perspectives that
characterize Pasinetti's work reveal his belief in the
provisional nature of all intellectual constructions
and his distrust of every form of regimentation and
authoritarianism. Pasinetti's novels, however, do
not fall into a fatalistic acquiescence of an existential
chaos. He and his characters attempt to come to
terms, cognitively and emotionally, with the historical world, and their attempts show both the limitations and the value of fiction writing. Pasinetti's

work–his blending of formal experimentation, social commitment, intellectual curiosity, and creative
enthusiasm–demonstrates his belief in literature as
a form of knowledge and as an institution with social and ideological responsibilities.

Pier Maria Pasinetti was born in Venice on 24
June 1913, the son of Maria Ciardi and Carlo Pasinetti, a prominent physician at a Venetian hospital.
Both his grandfather, Guglielmo Ciardi, and his
aunt, Emma Ciardi, were renowned painters. Pasinetti's brother, Francesco, who died at the age of
thirty-seven in 1949, wrote and directed documenta-
ries and feature films and in 1948 had become the
director of the Centro Sperimentale di Cinema-
tografia (Center for Experimental Cinema) in
Rome. Pasinetti spent his early years in Venice,
where he attended the *liceo classico,* the secondary
school that emphasizes the humanities. In his teens
he started writing for daily papers and weekly magazines. Pasinetti's vivid memories of his Venetian
youth are apparent in one of his most successful
novels, *Dorsoduro* (1983). From Oxford, which he attended in 1934–1935, and from Ireland, where he
carried out a research project on Joyce, he started
contributing to the prestigious cultural section of *La
gazzetta del popolo,* which at the time was publishing
work by important writers such as Carlo Emilio
Gadda and Eugenio Montale.

In 1935 Pasinetti earned a degree in English literature at the University of Padua, with a thesis on
Joyce; the following year he won his first scholarship to the United States. As he remarked in the interview published in 1965 in *La fiera letteraria,* the
United States provided a fundamental base for his
intellectual and moral development. At Louisiana
State University Pasinetti met Robert Penn Warren,
a friend and mentor who encouraged him to write
and contributed to his literary training.

Pasinetti arrived during a crucial period in the
development of American literary criticism; it was
at Louisiana State that Warren and Cleanth Brooks
started the influential movement known as New
Criticism. Pasinetti was thus exposed to a fresh emphasis on close literary analysis and the craft of literature. By stressing the uniqueness of poetic language, the New Critics reacted against the leveling
rhetoric of mass communication; they were troubled by the development of specialized and idiosyncratic jargon at the expense of meaning. This concern for language was to become one of Pasinetti's
chief interests, and his novels are notable for his deft
use of words.

It was Warren, a poet and novelist as well as
an academic, who invited Pasinetti to submit his
first short story, "In prossimità di casa," to *The*

Southern Review at a time when the journal was introducing such writers as Eudora Welty, Randall Jarrell, Mary McCarthy, and Katherine Anne Porter. The story appeared in English with the title "Home-coming" in the spring 1937 issue. "Home-coming" develops most of Pasinetti's early themes and reveals his ability to capture in words the complexities of a psychological situation. A third-person narrator records the protagonist's painful coming to terms with himself, his feelings, and life choices as he returns home for his sister's funeral after a long absence. *The Southern Review* also published "Family History," which as "Storia di famiglia" was included in Pasinetti's first collection of short stories, *L'ira di Dio* (The Wrath of God, 1942), together with "Un matrimonio" (A Marriage) and "Il soldato Smatek" (Smatek the Soldier).

Praised by critics such as Gianfranco Contini and Fredi Chiappelli for the narrative ease young Pasinetti demonstrated, *L'ira di Dio* appeared in Italy during the turmoil of World War II and went largely unnoticed. The earliest of the three short stories, written between 1930 and 1936, "Un matrimonio" demystifies the sound moral values of the middle class promoted by Fascist propaganda. It explores the paradox of a homecoming that reveals the characters' isolation and emptiness. Teresa, the twenty-five-year-old protagonist, returns home only to discover her deep sense of alienation from her family and hometown. For Teresa, marriage and her subsequent experiences become attempts to form deeper human relationships, soon crushed by indifference and dashed expectations.

"Storia di famiglia" reiterates the theme of the previous short story, though cast in a gloomier atmosphere, where family relationships are thwarted by misplaced feelings, estrangement, and greed. The various characters are mirror figures of one another that magnify to monumental proportions the selfishness and hatred concealed under a surface of indifference. The tale contains a scorching attack on the middle class, its conventions, and its deceptive sense of morality as well as its pervasive preoccupations with career and social advancement. Jacopo, the protagonist, is a part of this world but eventually reacts against it, thus offering a penetrating critique of his social environment. He also strives to nurture deeper feelings, which, uncompromised by false moralism and material preoccupations, constitute the redemptive, conclusive note of the story.

Written between 1936 and 1938, "Il soldato Smatek" develops the relationship between the protagonist, Antonio, and Jarmila, a young woman from Prague who travels to Italy to find the tomb of her brother, Jaroslav Smatek. The twenty-one-year-

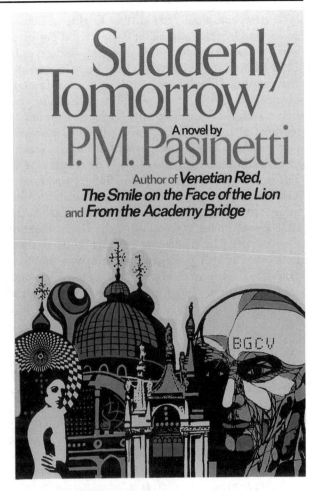

Dust jacket for the American edition of the translation of Pasinetti's 1971 novel, in which a schizophrenic former journalist resists the dehumanizing tendencies of modern society

old Jaroslav died on the Piave front in northern Italy during World War I. The narration proceeds on two levels. The first level concerns the relationship between Antonio and Jarmila, mostly from Antonio's perspective. Jarmila's otherness, both as a woman and as a foreigner with different codes of behavior, triggers Antonio's desire to overcome emotionally and rationally their differences. Their conversation makes understanding possible. It is through this dialogue that Pasinetti creates a second level of the story, in which its two absent figures, Jaroslav Smatek and Angela, Antonio's former girlfriend, are defined. As is the case with other characters created by Pasinetti, Angela and Jaroslav exist in absentia; they come to life through the characters' conversations and become part of their worlds, determining their actions and directing their choices. By sensing the strength of Jarmila's affection for her brother, Antonio is able to come to terms with himself and with his feelings for Angela.

After completing his M.A. in English at Louisiana State University in 1936, Pasinetti did graduate work at the University of California, Berkeley. In 1938 he was in Germany, where he attended the University of Berlin and witnessed the infamous events of Kristallnacht, powerfully portrayed in his first novel, *Rosso veneziano*. In 1942 he was appointed lecturer of Italian at the University of Göttingen, and from 1942 to 1946 he taught at the University of Stockholm. During this period he was trying to return to the United States. In 1946 he was finally awarded a position at Bennington College in Vermont, where he taught humanities for a year. At the time René Wellek was founding the Department of Comparative Literature at Yale University; Pasinetti enrolled in the program and was the first graduate student to receive a Ph.D. in the discipline. His dissertation, "Life for Art's Sake: Studies in the Literary Myth of the Romantic Artist," won the John Addison Porter Prize for the best literary dissertation of 1949 (it was published as a book in 1985). Pasinetti's concern with language and form represents the central issue of this study as his discussion concentrates on the aesthetic significance that life acquires for the romantic character.

In the fall of 1949 Pasinetti founded the "Humanities-World Literature Program" at the University of California, Los Angeles, and was one of the cofounders of the literary journal *Italian Quarterly*. He pursued his interest in cinema, which dated back to his work for the Italian film magazine *Cinema* in 1939–1940, contributing to the screenplay for director Michelangelo Antonioni's *La signora senza camelie* (The Lady Without Camellias, 1953). With director Franco Rossi, Pasinetti wrote the screenplay for *Smog* (1962), the story of an Italian lawyer on a flight to Mexico who is stranded in Los Angeles for twenty-four hours. Although it is generally regarded as a realistic work, *Smog* shows that Pasinetti's narrative concerns transcend realism. Pasinetti's contribution to the film is represented by the half-serious, half-ironical study of a paradoxical situation: an Italian man seeking his identity in a sprawling American metropolis.

Rosso veneziano (translated as *Venetian Red*, 1960) typifies Pasinetti's narrative in all its complexity and social diversity. The experiences of two Venetian families are chronicled from Easter 1938–just before Italy entered World War II–to the summer of 1940. The Fassolas' political ambitions and the Partibons' artistic interests set the boundaries of an eclectic fictional world where public and personal relationships develop against the background of Fascist rule. Various social and psychological realities are revealed in the interplay of narrative layers as Pasinetti skillfully merges private stories and public events.

Pasinetti neither explains nor evaluates Fascism in Italy, yet its reality emerges with dismal precision as relationships evolve, change, and deteriorate under the weight of political events. Enrico Fassola is tormented by his love for Elena Partibon and must face moral dilemmas as he is drawn both to his family's political aspirations as well as to the Partibons' unconventional spirit. Augusto Fassola's infatuation with the regime's political rhetoric crumbles when it fails to honor his pain for what he considers the heroic death of his son Massimo during an airplane's test flight. Elena's love for Ruggero Tava, which defies social conventions in the name of genuine feelings, is shattered by Ruggero's meaningless death in the war. Paolo Partibon's artistic utopia in rural Corniano contrasts with Ermete Fassola's political success in the ostentatious atmosphere of Rome under Fascism.

Rosso veneziano also tells the story of the void left by the departure of Marco Partibon, whose absence is filled by the multiple and contradictory representations that various characters provide of him. He is a mythical reincarnation of Marco Polo to his nieces, Bianca and Angelina; a rebel and social outcast to his mother; a political traitor and a spy to the regime; and a cosmopolitan traveler and man of endless adventures to his nephew Giorgio and his niece Elena. Partibon remains—in the fragmented projections of his identity—a character both requiring and defying interpretation. His openness, worldliness, and unconventionality constitute a powerful attack against Fascist mythography and the regime's obsessions with nationalism, xenophobia, and the patriarchal family. Partibon's diary entries at the end of the novel reveal a subjective, emotionally charged narrative voice that contrasts with the stereotyped, impersonal jargon of the Fascist leaders, further complicating the mystery of his identity.

Giorgio Partibon's sentimental quest for his uncle Marco is intellectually revelatory. Retracing his uncle's steps in Germany, Giorgio, a historian, discovers the value of private stories and the truth of personal feelings as ways to understand and assess larger historic events. As he witnesses the Kristallnacht of 9–10 November 1938—the night Nazi Party members demolished hundreds of synagogues and Jewish-owned businesses throughout Germany—Giorgio discovers the merciless brutality of power. As he compares his findings regarding his uncle with the current representations of him, he confronts the official view of the infamous Marco Partibon. Giorgio's experiences teach him a lesson he applies sixty years later when he returns as one of the narrators of Pasinetti's 1993 novel, *Melodramma*. He discovers that historians cannot pretend to present the past "as it really was." They have to become aware of the subjective grids, the ideological filters, and power structures that shape and construct what is presented as objective historical "reality."

Between 1953 and 1963 Pasinetti wrote *La confusione* (1964; translated as *The Smile on the Face of the Lion,* 1965), which he enlarged and republished in 1980 with the title *Il sorriso del leone*. *La confusione* retrieves, expands, and complicates the societal framework of *Rosso veneziano*. Set in the post–World War II period, the action moves from Rome to Venice and from metropolitan Los Angeles to rural Corniano. Sections of the novel are alternately written in the third person and in the first person, by three narrators—a historian, a sculptor, and a journalist—who convey different perspectives of a complex and dynamic reality.

From the impressive range of characters emerges Bernardo, a member of the rural side of the Partibon family, who returns to Italy after a twenty-year experience as an art dealer in the United States. Bernardo becomes the focus of what another character in the novel, Tito Solmi, describes as a reversed family tree that starts from its widespread branches to gradually approach its roots. Bernardo's return to Corniano is an existential quest for his origins, his self, past and present, and the meaning of his emotional ties, particularly with his sister, Maria, and his mother, Margherita. He discovers that his search can neither be linear nor easily resolved from the vantage point of the present and comes to realize that the past is still in process, that it is created and modified in the present, and that he and his relationships are in a state of flux. Even though he feels trapped in the whirlwind of an existential "confusion," Bernardo does not renounce his search for meaning, which sometimes results in epiphanies of recognition and flashes of understanding.

Il ponte dell'Accademia (1968; translated as *From the Academy Bridge,* 1970), one of Pasinetti's most successful novels, is set in Venice and southern California, where a group of international scholars research language and communication systems with the aid of modern computer technology. The Palos Rojos Institute for Language and Communication is a postmodern, air-conditioned, computer-regulated space that conceals a power struggle concerning the philosophical bases that direct the institute's research plans and orient the methods and goals of its scientific analysis. The narrative evolves in a tight progression as it shapes the two extreme groups involved in the conflict: those individuals who argue that the institute's linguistic and historical research

should be aimed at denouncing the strategies that can turn language into an instrument of control and manipulation and those who want to explore and exploit for their own advantage the potential of language to mystify and control.

The institute and its political vicissitudes provide the background for the development of a second, more introspective narrative line, involving two characters, Gilberto Rossi and Ruggero Tava Partibon. Gilberto Rossi, a "man of 1945," narrates in the first person his present and past experiences in a diary-like form. Gilberto, who emerged from World War II with a sense of political and social commitment and the idealistic hope of total renewal after the fall of Fascism, faces a personal, ideological crisis that leads him to move to California in search of a deeper understanding of his life.

Gilberto's research at the institute concentrates on the demystification of patriotic rhetoric in specific historic periods. His academic research parallels his personal quest to discover truer relationships and unearth the stories of individual characters from the sediments of fossilized historical abstractions:

Mi pareva urgente richiamare, ricaptare, interrogare le vite di questi esseri che mi si presentavano così, indicazioni senza sviluppo, soggetti amputati, oscuri, non registrabili, non percepibili dalla Storia.

(It seemed imperative that I recall, recapture and investigate the lives of these creatures, who presented themselves to me thusly—manifestations without development, mutilated subjects, obscure, not registered, not perceived by History.)

He is aided in his work by young Ruggero Tava Partibon, the son of Gilberto Rossi's best friend, the Ruggero Tava of *Rosso veneziano* who died at the beginning of World War II without knowing that Elena Partibon was pregnant with his baby.

Ruggero's scientific outlook, his obsessive need for clarity, and his noncommittal disposition contrast sharply with Gilberto's sense of loss, his problems in relating with others, his painful awareness of human existence, and his need to commit himself to specific causes. The juxtaposition of the two characters triggers the search for mutual comprehension, dialogue, and recognition. Their differences do not result in absolute and dogmatic oppositions; rather, they move the characters to communicate, question, interpret, and understand.

Venice's Academy Bridge, the allusion of the title, becomes a symbol of the epistemological stance that marks this novel and all of Pasinetti's fiction. Unlike the monumental Rialto Bridge, the

Academy Bridge is a wooden structure that looks like a temporary scaffolding ready to be altered and eventually removed: "Il suo carattere è la provvisorietà . . . la cosa importante del ponte dell'Accademia è il suo modo di durare, di durare cambiando" (This temporary appearance is its real quality . . . what is important about the Academy Bridge is the way it endures; it endures as it changes).

In *Domani improvvisamente* (1971; translated as *Suddenly Tomorrow,* 1972), written between 1968 and 1971, Pasinetti again employs a variety of narrative techniques. Through a kaleidoscopic combination of first-person diary entries, brilliant dialogue, and third-person sections, the novel offers a multifocal presentation of characters and events. *Domani improvvisamente* centers on Rodolfo Spada, a former journalist and a stubborn, eccentric defender of individualism against the leveling and depersonalizing trends of modern technological society. Rodolfo's representation varies according to the reported points of view, as he emerges both as the radical supporter of individualism and as a man unable to relate to others, obsessed with the fear of vast conspiracies. He is a schizophrenic, according to his neurologist. In the fragmentation of truths and the Pynchonian paranoia marking the novel, Pasinetti comically renders the meaningless, abstract jargon of corporate managers, contrasting it with the vernacular, often idiosyncratic language of Rodolfo's entourage. The prophetic tone of the novel implicitly asserts Rodolfo's vision: his ambiguous reason in madness translates the hope for a future revelation of authentic human relations, the "suddenly tomorrow" of the title.

Pasinetti's investigation of the power of technology, particularly the mass media and the press, and his analysis of their responsibilities in shaping public opinion is grounded in his journalistic work as well as his fiction. His journalistic interest in American culture unifies the disparate topics presented in *Dall'estrema America* (From the Far Sides of America, 1974). The volume includes pieces that Pasinetti wrote for the Milanese *Corriere della sera* from 1964 to 1974, which were aimed at acquainting Italian readers with American culture, literature, and politics. The affectionate memory of Pasinetti's experiences at the idyllic prewar Berkeley campus precedes a panorama of American society after the 1960s and a cutting view of the Nixon administration. Pasinetti's discussion of canonic authors such as William Faulkner, Ernest Hemingway, Saul Bellow, and Vladimir Nabokov are combined with an informed analysis of the literary events and marketing strategies lying behind the phenomenon of American best-sellers.

In *Il centro* (The Center, 1979) Pasinetti presents himself as the editor, P. M. P., of a set of papers drafted in the first person by three different characters. One of the narrators, Arrigo Paolotta, the executive director of a multinational publishing firm, is also the protagonist of the three accounts relating his trip to Europe in 1974 and his subsequent murder in Venice. The summer of 1974 is described from the perspective of several characters, including the highly eccentric Sven Lundquist, a mental patient. With *Il centro* Pasinetti achieves his best parodic and satiric rendition of specific languages and the ideologies that they support: the post-1968 language of the Left, the cryptic jargon of the academic world, and the abstract and impersonal idiom of the bureaucracy. The various characters offer different and often contradictory accounts of the same eventsical and thus ironically undercut the title of the novel. Pasinetti destroys the concept of universal objectivity; indeed, he lampoons all forms of cultural centralization and linguistic absolutism.

A sixty-year-old Giorgio Partibon returns as the first-person narrator of *Dorsoduro,* a novel that takes its title from one of the six districts of Venice. Giorgio recalls the city he knew as a seven-year-old boy and proves to be a perceptive and precocious observer of Venetian public and private life. The eclectic blend of different styles present in the architecture of Palazzo Bialevski illustrates, as Giorgio perceives it, the multiform makeup of the palazzo's residents and its frequent visitors. The story focuses on the Tolotta Pelzes, the Rutiglianos, the Bergs, and particularly the dentist Alvise Balmarin and his daughter Giovanna. It is the announcement of Alvise's death that triggers the Proustian recollection of a past tinged in emotional shades. The past expands beyond Giorgio's single narrative voice through the dialogues of its participants and contracts in meaningful clusters, emotional nuggets of sad, precious, and cheerful memories: young Annibale Tolotta Pelz's birthday, Alvise Balmarin's tender love for Giovanna, the fire of Palazzo Bialevski, and Giovanna's death.

By retelling the story of a distant past, Giorgio emphasizes the methods and problems involved in writing about both historical and personal realities. Like Manzoni's *I promessi sposi* (1825–1827), *Dorsoduro* reverses the traditional historical hierarchy and defends private events and individual emotions against the arid chronicles of political occurrences, epitomized by the official history of the Fascist era. Unlike Manzoni, however, Giorgio eliminates from his narration every teleological or universalizing rationale. Giorgio reminds readers that the order he shapes in *Dorsoduro* is not absolute and universal but

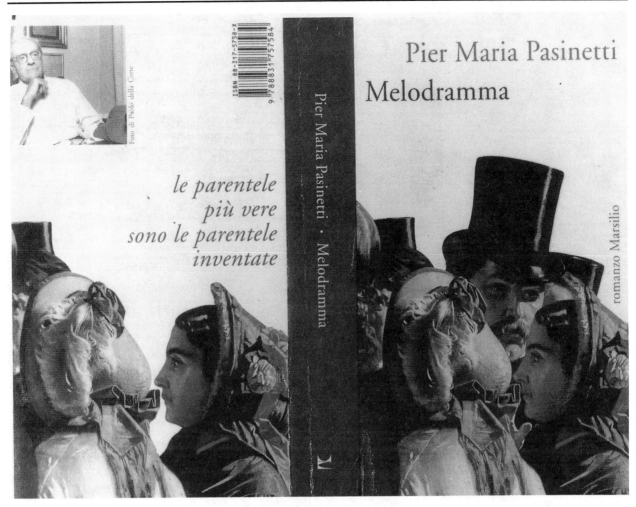

Dust jacket for Pasinetti's 1993 novel, set in nineteenth-century Venice

is the result of the varying perspectives of its participants and the narrator. The end of the novel provides an implicit connection between the private tragedy of Giovanna's death and the collapse of Italy under Fascism. The discourses of history and fiction, the political and the personal, and the official and unofficial thus relativize and illuminate each other in one of Pasinetti's best examples of critical historical fiction.

Pasinetti's *Melodramma* traces the Partibon's ancestry back to 1848, to Venice's brief independence and the return of Austrian occupation. Some of Pasinetti's characters, Giorgio Partibon, Bianca Angelone, and Amedeo Passina, shed light on an unexplored aspect of their family and their city. *Melodramma* combines historical chronicles with fictional inventions, literary borrowings with archival documents, and metanarrative allusions to the process of historical representation with references to other artistic expressions such as photography, music, painting, and the theater. Such inclusiveness complicates

the traditional tenets of historical fiction, and reproposes in a comprehensive and organic manner all the aesthetic and epistemological problems present in Pasinetti's previous work.

The possibility of historical objectivity is tested by the ironic inclusion of multiple interpretative voices; the authority of "real facts" is shattered by various texts that translate the past in different, often contradictory, narrative forms. The novel's multiple narrative voices dismantle the historian's supposed impersonality. The logic and linear sequence of traditional historiography must come to terms in *Melodramma* with plural reconstructions that stress instead the dynamic process of historical change. History, as treated here, is no longer a "given" fact; it is a multifaceted, often tentative, and always provisional construction.

Melodramma represents history as a theatrical piece, a drama, and the form is relevant to the thematic content of the novel. By choosing the closed structure of a three-act drama, Pasinetti defends its

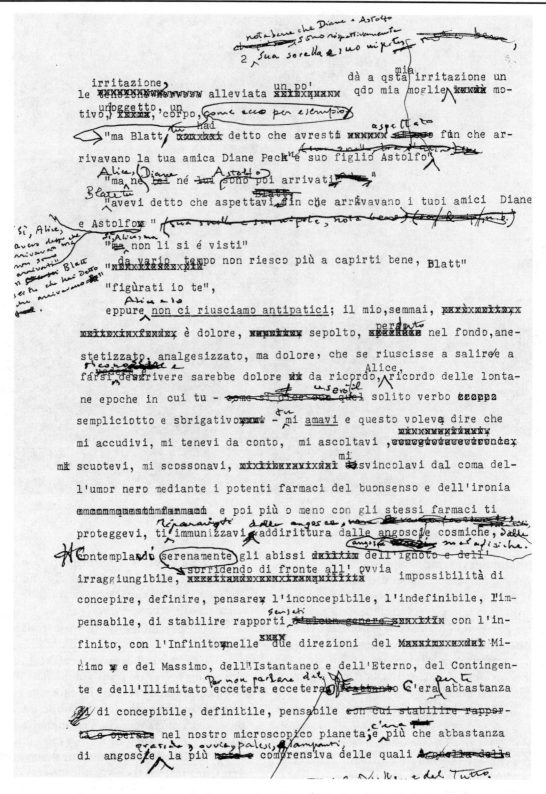

Page from revised typescript for a work in progress (Collection of Pier Maria Pasinetti)

value as a method of effectively organizing time and setting boundaries around the flux of history. At the same time, the novel implies that such a formal organization is neither natural nor universal. It is but a paradigm among others, a structuring tool incapable of exhausting the dynamics of narrative and the inclusiveness of life.

With *Melodramma* Pasinetti involves himself in the debate on intertextuality and representation, so current in postmodern historical fiction. While the structure of a three-act drama emphasizes the discursive and textual nature of all historical representations, the thematic allusions to drama, especially Giuseppe Verdi's *Rigoletto,* invalidate the common-sense argument that intertextuality stresses art's separation from the social and the political. With reference to *Rigoletto* and Verdi's problems with the Austrian censors, Pasinetti addresses the issue of censorship in art, thus emphasizing the close link between fiction, ideology, and the power structures that preside over the production and diffusion of works of literature.

According to Gore Vidal, Pasinetti is the first important Venetian novelist of the twentieth century. A master of irony, Pasinetti evokes a world that is both real and imagined, and his Venice is as vivid and complex as Proust's Paris and Joyce's Dublin. His fiction explores the nature of the relationship of human beings with their world and describes the ways in which people may come to terms with their personal and communal pasts. All of Pasinetti's characters are involved in a repeated effort to comprehend the world they inhabit. They appropriate and explain this world through reason, which erects boundaries around the incessant flow of life; they also discover and invent this world by means of emotional participation and intuitive communion. To Pasinetti, this latter element reveals the uncharted universe that Nathaniel Hawthorne called "the truth of the human heart."

Now a professor emeritus of Italian and comparative literatures at UCLA, Pasinetti divides his time between the United States and Venice. Translated into English, German, and French, Pasinetti's works have found enthusiastic reception beyond Italy and the United States, particularly in France. He is currently working on a comprehensive edition of his novels, the *opus magnum* that will gather in a multivolume edition all his fictional production. Recently Pasinetti published a new novel, *Piccole veneziane complicate* (Little Complicated Venetian Women, 1996).

Interviews:

G. A. Cibotto, "P. M. Pasinetti o della 'confusione,'" *La fiera letteraria,* 17 January 1965, pp. 1–2;

Peggy Kidney, Francesca Savoia, and Francesca Santovetti, "Intervista con Pier Maria Pasinetti," *Carte Italiane: A Journal of Italian Studies,* 5 (1983–1984): 1–18;

Laura Sanguineti-White, "Incontro con Pier Maria Pasinetti," *Italian Quarterly,* 26 (Fall 1985): 7–20.

References:

Teresa Boungiorno, " 'La confusione' di Pasinetti," *La fiera letteraria,* 8 March 1964, p. 3;

Fredi Chiappelli, "Considerazioni su Pasinetti," *Letteratura,* 94–96 (1968): 168–187;

Dante Della Terza, "Contemporary Italian Novelists: Language and Style in P. M. Pasinetti's *La confusione,*" *Italian Quarterly,* 8 (Spring 1964): 64–76;

Pier Massimo Forni, "Affetti e memoria nell'ultimo romanzo di Pier Maria Pasinetti," *Ipotesi 80: Rivista quadrimestrale di cultura,* 14 (1985): 83–88;

Forni, "*Dorsoduro* di Pier Maria Pasinetti," *Rassegna della letteratura italiana,* 88 (September–December 1984): 499–502;

M. T. Houston and S. N. Rosenberg, "The Onomastics of Pasinetti," *Italian Quarterly,* 10 (Fall 1966): 33–44;

Italian Quarterly, special issue on Pasinetti, 26 (Fall 1985);

Vincenzo Loriga, "Pasinetti, an outsider?," *Elsinore,* 3 (1966): 43–48.

Pier Paolo Pasolini

(5 March 1922 – 2 November 1975)

Joseph Francese
Michigan State University

See also the Pasolini entry in *DLB 128: Twentieth-Century Italian Poets, Second Series.*

BOOKS: *Poesie a Casarsa* (Bologna: Libreria Antiquaria Mario Landi, 1942);

Poesie (San Vito al Tagliamento: Stamperia Primon, 1945);

Diarii (Casarsa: Academiuta, 1946);

I pianti (Casarsa: Academiuta, 1946);

Dov'è la mia patria (Casarsa: Academiuta, 1946);

Tal còur di un frut, edited by L. Ciceri (Tricesimo: Edizioni di Lingua Friulana, 1953);

Il canto popolare (Milan: Edizioni della Meridiana, 1954);

Dal Diario (1945–1947) (Caltanissetta: Sciascia, 1954);

La meglio gioventù (Florence: Sansoni, 1954);

Ragazzi di vita (Milan: Garzanti, 1955); translated by Emile Capouya as *The Ragazzi* (New York: Grove, 1968);

Le ceneri di Gramsci (Milan: Garzanti, 1957); translated by David Wallace as *The Ashes of Gramsci* (Peterborough, U.K.: Spectacular Diseases, 1982);

L'usignolo della Chiesa cattolica (Milan: Longanesi, 1958);

Una vita violenta (Milan: Garzanti, 1959); translated by William Weaver as *A Violent Life* (New York: Pantheon, 1968; London: Cape, 1968);

Donne di Roma. Sette storie, edited by Sam Waagenaar (Milan: Il Saggiatore, 1960);

Passione e ideologia (Milan: Garzanti, 1960);

Roma 1950. Diario (Milan: Schweiller, 1960);

Sonetto primaverile, 1953 (Milan: Schweiller, 1960);

Accattone (Rome: F. M., 1961);

La religione del mio tempo (Milan: Garzanti, 1961);

Scrittori della realtà dall'VIII al XIX secolo, by Pasolini, Attilo Bertolucci, and Enzo Siciliano (Milan: Garzanti, 1961);

Mamma Roma (Milan: Rizzoli, 1962);

L'odore dell'India (Milan: Longanesi, 1962); translated by David Price as *The Scent of India* (London: Olive Press, 1984);

Pier Paolo Pasolini

Il sogno di una cosa (Milan: Garzanti, 1962); translated by Stuart Hood as *A Dream of Something* (London: Quartet, 1988);

Poesia in forma di rosa, 1961–1964 (Milan: Garzanti, 1964);

Il Vangelo secondo Matteo, edited by Giacomo Gambetti (Milan: Garzanti, 1964);

Poesie dimenticate, edited by Ciceri (Udine: Società Filologica Friulana, 1965);

Alì dagli occhi azzurri (Milan: Garzanti, 1965);

256

Uccellacci e uccellini (Milan: Garzanti, 1966);

Edipo re. Un film, edited by Gambetti (Milan: Garzanti, 1967); translated by John Mathews as *Oedipus Rex: A Film* (London: Lorrimer, 1971; New York: Simon & Schuster, 1971);

Teorema (Milan: Garzanti, 1968); translated by Hood as *Theorem* (London: Quartet, 1992);

Appunti per un'Orestiade africana (1970); reprinted edition, edited by A. Costa (N.p.: Edizioni Quaderni del Centro culturale di Copparo, 1983);

Medea (Milan: Garzanti, 1970);

Poesie (Milan: Garzanti, 1970);

Trasumanar e organizzar (Milan: Garzanti, 1971);

Empirismo eretico (Milan: Garzanti, 1972); translated by Ben Lawton and Louise K. Barnett as *Heretical Empiricism* (Bloomington: Indiana University Press, 1988);

Calderón (Milan: Garzanti, 1973);

La Divina Mimesis (Turin: Einaudi, 1975); translated by Thomas Erling Peterson as *The Divine Mimesis* (Berkeley: Double Dance Press, 1980);

Scritti corsari (Milan: Garzanti, 1975);

La nuova gioventù (Turin: Einaudi, 1975);

Il padre selvaggio (Turin: Einaudi, 1975);

Le poesie (Milan: Garzanti, 1975);

La trilogia della vita, edited by Giorgio Gattei (Bologna: Cappelli, 1975)–includes *Decameron, I racconti di Canterbury,* and *Il fiore delle Mille e una notte;*

Lettere luterane (Turin: Einaudi, 1976); translated by Hood as *Lutheran Letters* (Manchester: Carcanet New Press, 1983; New York: Carcanet Press, 1987);

I Turcs tal Friùl, edited by A. Ciceri and L. Ciceri (N.p.: Edizioni di "Forum Julii," 1976);

Affabulazione; Pilade (Milan: Garzanti, 1977);

San Paolo (Turin: Einaudi, 1977);

I disegni (1941–1975), edited by Giuseppe Zigaina (Milan: Scheiwiller, 1978);

Descrizioni di descrizioni, edited by Graziella Chiarcossi (Turin: Einaudi, 1979);

Il caos, edited by Gian Carlo Ferretti (Rome: Editori Riuniti, 1979);

Porcile; Orgia; Bestia da stile (Milan: Garzanti, 1979);

Poesie e pagine ritrovate, edited by Andrea Zanzotto and Nico Naldini (Rome: Lato Side, 1980);

Amado mio (Milan: Garzanti, 1982);

Dialogo con Pasolini: Scritti 1957–1984, edited by Alberto Cadioli (Rome: L'Unità, 1985);

Il Portico della morte, edited by Cesare Segre (Rome: Associazione "Fondo Pier Paolo Pasolini," 1988);

Teatro, edited by G. Davico Bonino (Milan: Garzanti, 1988);

I dialoghi, edited by Giovanni Falaschi (Rome: Editori Riuniti, 1992);

Petrolio (Turin: Einaudi, 1992);

Antologia della lirica pascoliana: introduzione e commenti, edited by Marco A. Bazzocchi (Turin: Einaudi, 1993);

Bestemmia: tutte le poesie, edited by Chiarcossi and Walter Siti (Milan: Garzanti, 1993);

Un paese di temporali e di primule, edited by Naldini (Parma: Guanda, 1993);

I film degli altri, edited by Tullio Kezich (Parma: Guanda, 1996).

Editions in English: *Poems,* selected and translated by Norman MacAfee and Luciano Martinengo (New York: Random House, 1982); revised as *Selected Poems* (London: Calder, 1984);

The First Paradise: Odetta, translated by Antonino Mazza (Kingston, Ontario: Helibox Press, 1985);

Roman Nights and Other Stories, translated by John Shepley (Marlboro, Vt.: Marlboro Press, 1986; London: Quartet, 1994);

Roman Poems, translated by Lawrence Ferlinghetti and Francesca Valente (San Francisco: City Lights Books, 1986);

Poems (N.p.: Noonday, 1996).

MOTION PICTURES: *Accattone,* screenplay by Pasolini and Sergio Citti, Cino del Duca-Arco Film, 1961;

Mamma Roma, screenplay by Pasolini and Citti, Arco Film, 1962;

La ricotta (episode in *Rogopag*), screenplay by Pasolini, Arco Film-Cineriz, 1962;

La rabbia, first part, script by Pasolini, Opus Film, 1963;

Sopraluoghi in Palestina per 'Il vangelo secondo Matteo,' commentary by Pasolini, Arco Film, 1963–1964;

The Gospel According to Matthew, screenplay by Pasolini, Arco Film, C.C.F. Lux, 1964;

Comizi d'amore, commentary by Pasolini, Arco Film, 1964;

Uccellacci e uccellini, screenplay by Pasolini, Arco Film, 1966;

La terra vista dalla luna (episode in *Le Streghe*), script by Pasolini, Dino De Laurentiis Cinematografica, 1966;

Che cosa sono le nuvole (episode in *Capriccio all'italiana*), script by Pasolini, Dino De Laurentiis Cinematografica, 1966;

Oedipus Rex, screenplay by Pasolini, Arco Film, 1967;

Teorema, screenplay by Pasolini, Aetos Film, 1968;

Medea, screenplay by Pasolini, San Marco Films/Rosima Anstaldt, Les Films Number One, and Janus Films/Fernsehen, 1969;

Appunti per un'Orestiade africana, screenplay by Pasolini, Baldi, 1969;

Pigsty, screenplay by Pasolini, Film dell'Orso/Idi Cinematografica/I.N.D.I.E.F., C.A.P.A.C., 1969;

Decameron, screenplay by Pasolini, Produzione Europee Associate, Les Produtions Artistes Associes, and Artemis Films, 1971;

The Canterbury Tales, screenplay by Pasolini, P.E.A., 1972;

The Arabian Nights, screenplay by Pasolini, United Artists Europe, 1974;

Salò, or the One Hundred and Twenty Days of Sodom, screenplay by Pasolini and Citti, P.E.A., P.A.A., 1975.

OTHER: *Poesia dialettale del Novecento,* edited by Pasolini and Mario Dell'Arco (Parma: Guanda, 1952);

Canzoniere italiano: Antologia della poesia popolare, edited by Pasolini (Parma: Guanda, 1955);

Aeschylus, *Orestiade,* translated by Pasolini (Turin: Einaudi, 1960);

La poesia popolare italiana, edited by Pasolini (Milan: Garzanti, 1960);

Titus Maccius Plautus, *Il vantone,* translated by Pasolini (Milan: Garzanti, 1963);

Pier Paolo Pasolini e "Il Setaccio" (1942–1943), edited by Mario Ricci (Bologna: Cappelli, 1977)—includes contributions by Pasolini.

Pier Paolo Pasolini was a controversial presence in Italian letters from the early 1950s until his assassination in November 1975. Deliberately provocative, his work invariably sparked debate and produced an extensive body of criticism. His novels are emblematic of the neorealist trend that dominated Italian letters and cinema during the 1940s and 1950s, and his film production continued to be at the forefront of cinematic experimentation in the decade that followed. His socially conscious essays underscored an incessant effort to undermine the status quo; they were published in the leading Italian dailies and periodicals during the final years of his life, and they stood in opposition to all contending political and social forces. His continuous search in his verse to understand the traumas afflicting contemporary Italian society earned him the appellation "civil poet." Pasolini is a rare example of an artist whose intense social and political engagement is channeled into a body of work of high caliber. His life and work provide a unique window on Italian

society in the period that begins with the reconstruction following World War II, continues through the so-called economic miracle of the 1950s and the social upheavals of the 1960s, and concludes with the political assassinations and terrorism that characterized the 1970s.

Pasolini was born in Bologna, the first child of Carlo Alberto Pasolini, an infantry lieutenant, and Susanna Colussi, an elementary-school teacher. The father's career in the military caused the family to move frequently; a second son, Guido Alberto, three years Pier Paolo's junior, was born while the father was stationed in Belluno. In 1939 Pasolini matriculated at the University of Bologna, where he wrote a thesis on Giovanni Pascoli.

During the early 1940s Pasolini was an active member of different youth organizations associated with the Fascist regime. One of his first editorial experiences was being on the board of *Il setaccio* (The Sifter), the publication of a cultural group organized by the government for university students at Bologna. In 1942 he attended an international meeting of Fascist youth in Weimar, an experience that was to mark the beginning of his reaction against the regime. The propaganda used to promote the meeting struck him as "anticultural," and in his account of the meeting for *Il setaccio* he affirmed that intellectual activity should be independent of and not subordinate to any political agenda. While in Germany, Pasolini also had occasion to meet young people from other countries living under Nazi-Fascist rule. From them he was able to form a more objective image of the Fascist rulers, and he learned of writers and artists who were hostile to Fascism.

Susanna Pasolini and her sons habitually summered with her family in Casarsa, a town located in the Friuli region, northeast of Venice. Pier Paolo came to love the peasant culture of the region, an integral part of which was the local dialect. This would be the language of Pasolini's first mature poetry: he wrote his first poems in Friulian dialect during the summer of 1941, and the following year he published them at his own expense in a book titled *Poesie a Casarsa* (Poems to Casarsa). The attraction of proletarian culture is a distinguishing characteristic of Pasolini's oeuvre, from his first, neorealist efforts in film—*Accattone* (1961), *Mamma Roma* (1962), *La ricotta* (1962), *Il Vangelo secondo San Matteo*—through his final works, the cinematic "Trilogy of Life" and, in verse, *La nuova gioventù* (The New Youth, 1975). His first book served not only to introduce Pasolini to the literary world but also to reinforce his growing distaste for the Fascist regime, which was hostile to dialects and everything that did not conform to its standardized image of what was Italian. Gian-

franco Contini, a prominent philologist, was forced
to publish his review of Pasolini's collection in a
Swiss periodical.

Pasolini was drafted into the army in 1943, but
after Italy's surrender to the Allies on 8 September
1943, he deserted. He avoided capture by the Germans by returning to his maternal homestead,
where he remained for the duration of the hostili-
ties. During the final months of the war he engaged
in clandestine subversive activity, serving as a liaison for his brother, who fought and died in combat
for the Resistance. After the war Pasolini became active in the movement for Friulian autonomy, and in
1948 he joined the Italian Communist Party.

By 1949 Pasolini was already secretary of a
Communist Party office located in a town near
Casarsa. Because of his activism, he was black-
mailed by a member of the local clergy. When he refused the demand to abandon politics, criminal
charges were brought against him for having alleg-
edly initiated an erotic encounter with a group of
teenage boys. Although he was exonerated several
years later, he lost his teaching position in the state-
run school system and was forced to look for employment elsewhere. In January 1950 he moved to
Rome. Thus, the beginning of a new decade coincided with a change of habitat.

The years in Friuli, in addition to having introduced Pasolini to the socio-economic diversity of
the peasants, was also the place where he began to
experiment with his own sexuality. The discovery
of his homosexuality, coupled with the friendships
made among the working populace, afforded Pasolini the material and inspiration for his first serious
efforts in prose. Once in Rome the experiences
gained in Friuli facilitated his discovery of an urban
subproletariat in the image of his Friulian *meglio gioventù* (best youth): the Roman *ragazzi* (street urchins) who were to inspire his two major novels, *Ragazzi di vita* (1955; translated as *The Ragazzi,* 1968)
and *Una vita violenta* (1959; translated as *A Violent
Life,* 1968), and, subsequently, his first films.

Any analysis of Pasolini as a novelist presents
difficulties of critical approach because one cannot
with justice view his writing as separate from the totality of his career. The analysis of his maturation as
a novelist must also take into account his development as thinker and artist. Pasolini considered himself first and foremost a poet. His films, which are
perhaps even more significant than his poetry, are
marked by the attempt to transpose to a different
medium the characteristics of communication in
verse. In the 1960s he theorized on a "cinema of poetry" in which the film would "narrate poetically
through images." His novels play an auxiliary role

Self-portrait by Pasolini (Garzanti Editore, Milan)

among other activities, which, in addition to those
just mentioned, include literary criticism and social
commentary.

Pasolini's first significant experiments with
prose constitute a memorial to his Friulian experience. *Atti impuri* (Impure Acts) and *Amado mio* (My
Love, 1982), unfinished novels published posthumously under the latter title, are autobiographies in
which the author unsuccessfully hides behind a thin
narrative veil. Pasolini attempts to transform the
sentimental diaries he kept in 1946 and 1947 into
impersonal, third-person accounts. In *Il sogno di una
cosa* (A Dream of Something, 1962) he recounts his
remembrances of his "best youth," the working-
class Friulians who played an integral part in his
sexual and ideological coming-of-age in the 1940s.

Pasolini's most important work as a novelist
took place in the 1950s, coincidentally the most felicitous decade of his career. In *Ragazzi di vita* and
Una vita violenta he gave literary expression to the sociological and philological research carried out
among his ragazzi, the street urchins he befriended
during his excursions through Rome's *borgate,* the

Dust jacket for the American edition of the translation of Pasolini's 1955 novel, whose frank description of the underside of Roman life led to charges of pornography

shantytowns that had mushroomed on the city outskirts in the aftermath of the war, overflowing with the unemployed workers who migrated from southern Italy to the capital. The use of dialect—in this case a hybrid of the "romanesco" spoken among the Roman working class and the dialects of the workers who inhabited the borgate—into literary Italian held for Pasolini a highly charged literary and political significance. Following his idiosyncratic reading of one of Antonio Gramsci's *Quaderni del carcere* (Prison Notebooks, 1948–1951), *Letteratura e vita nazionale* (Literature and National Life), Pasolini came to believe that the presence of nonstandard Italian in literature could serve to empower the proletarian classes, heretofore excluded or depicted paternalistically by writers of the Verismo school, such as Giovanni Verga and Luigi Capuana.

In various essays—published for the most part in *Officina* (Workshop), a literary review founded and directed by Pasolini, Francesco Leonetti, Rob-

erto Roversi, and Luciano Serra from 1955 through 1959, and later collected in *Passione e ideologia* (Passion and Ideology, 1960)—Pasolini argued that dialects were the means of expression of a marginalized class and hence their "otherness" could be made to coincide with innovative poetic forms and lexicon. In his analysis of the Italian language Pasolini also isolated two distinct forms of usage within what was considered standard Italian: the literary argot and the interregional koine used throughout the peninsula as a sort of lingua franca by the state bureaucracy. He argued that other neorealist writers, more concerned with content than stylistic questions, had uncritically coopted this koine while ignoring the regional dialects.

Although Gramsci had considered the dialects a residue of peasant culture, Pasolini believed their recuperation was a necessary element of the national popular literature Gramsci postulated in the *Quaderni del carcere*. In Pasolini's view, the interregional Italian, while suited to bureaucratic or political aims because of its ability to reach mass audiences, was too impersonal for a literary work. Generic by nature, it was incapable of representing the individual microcosm that literature necessarily depicted. At the same time, through this anti-traditionalist polemic against a centralized language, he hoped to supersede Neorealism.

Pasolini wanted to capture in his work the "soul of the times." He searched for it in the nation's linguistic fragmentation and economic stratification as well as in the conflict within the progressive bourgeois intellectual who, like Pasolini, had "betrayed his class of origin" to embrace the workers' struggle. As the decade progressed, he came to believe that a workers' party needed to encompass his country's disenfranchised subproletariat if it wished to carry forth its revolutionary goals. Pasolini would explicitly discuss this political strategy following the publication of *Una vita violenta*.

When *Ragazzi di vita* was published, the average Italian reader was shocked not by the integration of popular lexicon and speech patterns (Pasolini appended a glossary to the work) but by the graphic description of the underside of Roman life. Pasolini had introduced a new sociological stratum into the world of Italian letters: a subproletariat existing in extreme poverty on the margins of society and composed in part of pimps, thieves, prostitutes, and wealthy pederasts. This realism cost him a second criminal trial, this time for what was called the "pornographic content" of his novel. Because of the controversial nature of his art, Pasolini would be subjected over the course of his career to a psychological and economic persecution that took the form of thirty-three criminal proceedings, some of which extended in time beyond his death and all of which ended in his exculpation.

Accustomed to more risqué fare, the contemporary reader will doubtless not be shocked by the content of *Ragazzi di vita* but will note with interest its absence of a unified narration and a traditional protagonist. Rather than develop the intricacies of a main character, Pasolini presents his reader with a series of loosely related sketches that revolve around a group of adolescents as they mature into men. The narrative concentrates on what is visible, on the boys' *vitalismo* (vitality), rather than investigating the deeper, psychological motives behind their behavior. When, for example, the main character, Riccetto, spends three years in prison, the story continues uninterrupted after his release. Pasolini does not consider Riccetto's experiences in jail and the effects incarceration may have had on him.

The book opens in occupied Rome where Riccetto and his friends are in the process of looting warehouses. It then tracks the escapades of this group of young hustlers—their con games, petty burglaries, illegal gambling, impromptu soccer matches, and swimming excursions in the Tiber and its principal tributary, the Aniene River. The sum of the impressions gives the reader a more or less complete picture of life in a Roman shantytown. In order to create this effect, the narrator often leaves one character to follow the exploits of another, in a prose resembling at times cinema verité. Subtending the narrative are the parallel denouements of the opening and concluding chapters. Whereas the youthful Riccetto of 1944 is willing to dive into the Tiber to rescue a drowning swallow, in 1950 his cynicism causes him to ignore a young boy drowning in the Aniene. Despite the book's limitations, Pasolini succeeds in creating a powerful work of social condemnation.

Various factors contributed to the less than favorable reception of this first work among Pasolini's preferred interlocutors, intellectuals who were either members of or politically close to the Italian communist party. *Ragazzi di vita* was published at a time when fundamental questions regarding the nature and viability of Neorealism as a cinematic and literary trend were being asked. Neorealism had never been organized under a manifesto by any individual or group of artists. From its inception in the cinema during the early 1940s, it lacked a clear definition of its means and objectives. Nonetheless, in large part because of the popularity of Gramsci's writings, it quickly gained partisan support within progressive circles during the postwar years. By 1955, however, there was sharp disagreement as to what constituted a neorealist work and the direction neorealist art should take.

A few months before the publication of *Ragazzi di vita,* an occasionally acrimonious, protracted debate was catalyzed by the publication of the novel *Metello* by Vasco Pratolini. Those critics who were attempting to provide Neorealism with a theoretical basis considered *Metello* a proving ground for the concepts of novel and realism. While there was marked disagreement with regard to specific works, such as *Metello,* there was a consensus on the necessity of supplanting the "pseudo-objectivity" characteristic of late-nineteenth-century verismo while depicting the "organic development" of a protagonist. Pasolini was called to task for having created characters whose youthful idealism did not develop into class consciousness but instead degenerated into sundry forms of cynical individualism. Although these criteria are now alien to the contemporary reader, Pasolini took the criticisms advanced by many leftist intellectuals quite seriously.

Pasolini vehemently defended his innovations in content and form in *Ragazzi di vita;* yet his next novel, *Una vita violenta,* with its chronological narration and edifying protagonist, adhered to the unofficial tenets of Neorealism being debated in the mid 1950s. Putting aside the sweeping, "choral" depiction of life in the borgate offered in *Ragazzi di vita,* Pasolini narrowed his field of vision to concentrate on a single character who, after a series of vicissitudes, gradually attains an advanced form of class consciousness. The main character, Tommaso Puzzilli, does not instinctively adhere to socialist ideals; his conversion is not gratuitous but the result of a gradual process of maturation catalyzed by the internalization of external events.

As the novel opens, Tommaso is attending middle school in the Pietralata section of Rome, near the Rebibbia Prison. Tommaso's family had fled there when their home in the central Italian countryside was destroyed by bombs as the Allies wrested control of the peninsula from the retreating German army. Once in Rome his father found work as a trash collector and the family took possession of a shack on the banks of the Aniene. Literally and figuratively on the margins of society, Tommaso and his friends are entirely without political awareness and open to all forms of delinquent behavior. Tommaso subsequently latches on to a group of neo-Fascist youths; he finds their brand of hooliganism more to his taste because their stakes are higher than those to which his friends in the borgate aspire. Political activism for the young neo-Fascists provides a facile camouflage for auto thefts, burglaries, and assaults whose true purpose is to finance nights of drunken revelry. Little changes when Tommaso falls in love with Irene: he finances their courtship through burglaries and various acts of male prostitution. While serenading Irene, Tommaso and a group of friends are attacked by a hostile gang. Tommaso uses a knife to defend himself and is sentenced to two years in prison.

The second section of the novel takes place in 1956, with Tommaso twenty years old, and coincides with his ethical transformation. Upon returning home from his incarceration, Tommaso finds his family has been granted a low-income apartment. He decides he must adapt himself to these new lower-middle-class surroundings so he forsakes his old hustler friends and attempts to ingratiate himself with the youths in his building. More important, he believes he must marry Irene in order to conform to middle-class morality. He finds work unloading fish in the stockyards but also joins the Christian Democratic Party and asks the local priest to use his political influence so that he might find better, higher paying employment.

At this point Tommaso contracts tuberculosis and is forced to enter the state-owned Forlanini Hospital at a time when workers and patients are demanding that government provide better conditions for both. When the police intervene to suppress the protest, Tommaso, in spite of his persistent egoism, is caught up in the movement and aids the strikers. Immediately after his release from the hospital, he returns home and joins the Communist Party. His newfound social commitment comes to the fore a short while later when the Aniene overflows, submerging the shantytown he had inhabited as a child. He heroically leads rescue workers, who are unfamiliar with the landscape, through the mud and the floodwater inundating the area. Tragically, his bravery is rewarded only by the reinflammation of his tuberculosis, which causes his death a few years later.

Tommaso Puzzilli was the standard-bearer of the political strategy Pasolini was proposing to the Italian Left in the late 1950s: the valorization of the subproletariat as literary and political subject. Although Pasolini's infatuation with the Italian subproletariat would be eclipsed soon after the publication of his second novel, he invested this faith in the marginalized populations of former colonial nations in Africa and in other parts of the Third World. There he would search for a suprahistorical human essence, a prelinguistic "physical reality" to be rendered on film.

Creative expression in prose was set aside by Pasolini during the 1960s in favor of more immediate and wide-reaching media such as cinema and pe-riodicals. The relatively small audiences available to the creative writer led him to opt for an audiovisual medium that could evoke prelinguistic, primordial "images" among a much wider public. This marked a shift in Pasolini away from materialist thought. The concept of primordial images conserved in a collective unconscious is indicative of the influence on his work during these years of the writings of Carl Jung.

The decrease in Pasolini's publication of poetry during the 1960s was prompted by his subjective recognition of the advent of a historical period he would call the "Nuova Preistoria" (New Prehistory). As the decade began Pasolini experienced a personal crisis brought about by what he felt was an "anthropological change" in Italians. Italian workers had been "corrupted" by the "siren" of consumerism. Class conflict was no longer conceivable because there no longer existed, as had previously been the case, a clear separation between the proletariat and the upper classes. Pasolini no longer considered the Marxist view of history—defined as a dialectic catalyzed by an antithetical relationship between the wealthy and the working class—to be a valid interpretation of reality. With the term *Nuova Preistoria* he wished to underscore the return, at a societal level, to a nonlinear conception of time.

During the classical era, Pasolini argued, humanity had measured time not linearly but by the cycle of the agricultural seasons. Christianity, which attributed an end to time, represented a fundamental change from the classical era. Pasolini saw that his own time had come to be mired in a repetitive cycle measured in production and consumption, a "bourgeois entropy" without class conflict. This lack of class conflict had come about in the 1960s, returning humanity to what he described as the atemporal continuum of the Nuova Preistoria. He perceived Italian society of the 1960s as an amorphous mass, a sociological hybrid of popular and bourgeois strata consisting of technocrats and depoliticized consumers. The workers had "surrendered"; Italy had become a miserably petit bourgeois nation. While history could not be measured against the natural cycle, neither could it look forward, as would be the case if it were measured by Christian millenarianism or Marxist dialectic. Rather, it had become a self-sufficient and self-perpetuating cycle dominated by the upper classes.

The novel *Teorema* (1968; translated as *Theorem*, 1992) encapsulates what for Pasolini was the only social tension possible within his time: the tacit conflict between the Nuova Preistoria and the archaic prehistory surviving in peasant societies of the twentieth century. The legacy of archaic prehistory,

① Il padre di Tommasino, Torquato Puzzilli, era impie=
gato comunale, e come sempre quando si dice impiegato co=
munale, si intende dire che era spazzino. Però una volta,
al paese, suo, se da paesare un po' meglio: certamente, era
di una famiglia di lavoratori, però potevano andare a te=
sta alta, e due piatti in tavola c'erano sempre.

② Torquato possedeva una casetta di quelle tutte di
sassi, in mezzo alla campagna, a un chilometro da Isola
Liri, che gli aveva lasciato sua madre: intorno c'era il
suo orto e le sue stalle per i maiali, le pecore e le gal=
line. Per di più, Torquato era stato nominato bidello del=
le scuole di Isola Liri: così aveva potuto sposarsi con la
sora Maria, dopo un bel po' d'anni che si parlavano: nel
trentaquattro avevano avuto il primo figlio, nel trentasei
poi era nato Tommaso; poi avevano avuto una femmina, ch'e=
ra nata morta. Quando venne la guerra, Torquato andè sot=
to le armi, e l'otto settembre tornò a casa, sbandato co=
me tutti quanti. Ma dovette ripartirsene subito, però, e
stavolta con la roba e con tutto, insieme alle tante de=
gli altri profughi che scappavano su verso Roma.

③ Come arrivarono a Roma, morti di stanchezza e ridot=
ti come zingari, li misero insieme a tanti altri, di
Cassino, di Fondi, di tutti gli altri paesi della Cioia=
ria, in una scuola della Maranella, la scuola Michelazzi,
che poi, dopo il fascismo, fu chiamata Pisacane.

Su al paese il sor Torquato aveva perduto tutto: gli
areoplani gli avevano spianato la casetta di sassi, le
cannonate le stalle, e i carri armati avevano fatto spari=
re anche il ricordo. Come gli americani arrivarono a Ro=
ma, lui con la famiglia, come tutti gli altri disgrazia=
ti, furono presi e cacciati via dalla scuola, perchè
questa serviva alle truppe: per convincerli a smammare
gli diedero qualche pacco e un po' di soldarelli. Ma lo=
ro non se ne capacitavano, perchè non sapevano proprio
dove andare: allora, in una di quelle giornate d'estate

Page from the revised typescript for Una vita violenta *(Pier Paolo Pasolini Collection)*

embodied by the maid of a bourgeois family, is catalyzed by the unexpected arrival of a young, ineffably divine guest. The maid tacitly understands him and is "sanctified"; the "spiritual awakenings" of the individual family members, on the other hand, reveal to them the emptiness of their lives. Thus, the mystifications at the base of what Pasolini called "bourgeois irreality," the division of society in oppressed and oppressing classes, are cast asunder. After failing to heed the message imparted without the benefit of speech by their young guest, the family members fall from grace and "degrade" themselves. Pasolini's hope that the "age-old prehistory" of the maid might represent a possible alternative to the Nuova Preistoria quickly waned, however, and in the film *Medea* (1969) he depicts the complete annihilation of the past by the "Neo-capitalist Order."

The victory of neocapitalism first over Italy's proletariat and then over peasant culture proved to Pasolini that it was not possible to realize the Gramscian goal of national-popular art. He believed that the organic link between writer and audience had to be sacrificed to social and political incisiveness. Since society had become a "homologated" mass, the artist could no longer approach it as a collective of independent, thinking individuals. Pasolini's first efforts in the cinema had been imbued with the creative impulse of Neorealism, but as the 1960s progressed he began to make films for a more limited public. This change in strategy is a continuation of the same process that had caused him to move away from literature as a primary means of expression and turn to cinema. His films, beginning with *Uccellacci e uccellini* (1966; Hawks and Sparrows), became more arcane. His turn from the masses led him to believe that any attempt to reach a wide audience necessarily meant a lowering of artistic goals. His quest for realism coupled with social efficacy led him to restrict the intended audience for his works to a socially progressive, intellectual elite. This phase of Pasolini's career, characterized by this poetics of "unpopular realism," extends almost until the end of his life, overlapping with the elaboration of a new interpretation of history, "Dopostoria" (Posthistory), which was sparked by the student protests of 1968.

The protest movements that swept Europe that year led Pasolini to rethink his ideas regarding Nuova Preistoria. Formed intellectually in a climate of "bourgeois entropy," the rebellious students were, to use his phrasing, "neo-hedonists," "a-ideological" consumers (and therefore potentially fascistic). He concluded that those students who rebelled against the "System" did not represent the working classes but were themselves the children of the dominant class. In his view the protests constituted little more than a manifestation of bourgeois guilt, or a "purificatory rite" of "self-flagellation" necessary for the preservation of class dominion.

Pasolini conceived Dopostoria as a historical progression catalyzed by Oedipal conflicts taking place entirely within a pervasive bourgeoisie. He once again saw a dialectic pushing history forward. However, its driving force was not class conflict but the eternal tension between fathers and sons. Within this context, he believed he as an artist should adopt a defensive posture, and much of the work he produced during this period became a battlefield for the preservation of civil liberties.

In the 1970s, with the cinematic Trilogy of Life—*The Decameron* (1971), *The Canterbury Tales* (1972), and *Arabian Nights* (1974)—Pasolini returned to his youthful literary subject, the subproletariat, in an attempt to propose the sexual reality of the human body as an alternative to "bourgeois irreality," while at the same time waging an individual war against a penal code that had survived the overthrow of Fascism and severely limited the artist's freedom of expression. The cinematic trilogy constituted the bulwark of this struggle for civil rights. However, he quickly saw how a phagocytic capitalism successfully absorbed and exploited the highly lucrative Italian market for pornography he had inadvertently uncovered.

Pasolini was often forced to defend himself in court against charges of criminal pornography. Such spurious attacks, far from diminishing his will to resist, made him all the more determined. In *Salò, or the One Hundred and Twenty Days of Sodom* (1975), his final cinematic effort, sex is seen as "a metaphor for power" and domination. By exhibiting every form of sexual deviance imaginable on the screen, Pasolini hoped to avenge himself by provoking an antipornographic reaction among those who looked to the cinema for titillation. His target was the neo-hedonism he saw prevailing in Italian society. He believed that the atmosphere of "repressive tolerance" (as defined by the Marxist critic Herbert Marcuse and other members of the Frankfurt School) bred by Italian capital had corrupted his country's young and transformed their youthful idealism into a cynical quest for integration into the System.

Pasolini's final two collections of poetry also show his thinking on society. In *Trasumanar e organizzar* (To Transcend Human Nature and Organize, 1971) he underscores the ineluctable bureaucratization of all revolutionary movements and the subsequent profanation of the idealistic fervor that gave them their original impetus. This book of poetry marks his rapprochement to the Communist Party, which was possible because he had reached a tenuous balance in his own mind between faithfulness to idealistic revolutionary goals (*trasumanar*) and social incisiveness (*organizzar*). In *La nuova gioventù* (*The New Youth*), by overturning the fervor of the youthful poems of *La meglio gioventù* (The Best Youth, 1954), Pasolini underscores his profound disappointment for the changes that had overtaken Italy's young and Italian society in general, not the least of which was the conformism bred by a market economy. Nonetheless, in the final section of this volume, composed entirely of new poems, he emphasizes an invigorated *tetro entusiasmo* (bleak enthusiasm). The student movement of 1968 had shown him that the bourgeoisie was not the monolithic entity he had imagined. He felt it might be possible to provoke change by directing his discourse to the next generation, the "younger brothers" of the students with whom he had quarreled. This is the preferred interlocutor not only of tetro entusiasmo, but also of his *Lettere luterane* (1976; translated as *Lutheran Letters*, 1983).

During the 1970s Pasolini often discussed with his friends the possibility of abandoning his public career as social commentator and his work in the cinema in order to devote himself to a volume of great scope, to be titled *Petrolio* (Petroleum, 1992). Pasolini's work on the novel was halted by his murder. Even in its embryonic form (only six hundred uncorrected pages of a projected two thousand were written), the novel gives rise to various hypotheses. One might wonder, for example, at Pasolini's turn toward Sigmund Freud: while Freud is quoted several times within the text, Carl Jung's name is absent, suggesting perhaps his return to a more materialist psychoanalytical approach.

One of the striking qualities of Pasolini's writing is its *legibility,* a term he discusses in *Petrolio*. In his poetics of unpopular realism, he had shown explicitly a desire for illegibility, or making a conscious effort to produce works unsuitable for a consumer market. In the *Lettere luterane,* written in the last year of his life, Pasolini claimed to be ready to change tactics and readapt his social commitment to the needs of an "increased legibility," a renewed accessibility to a wider audience. This strategy was to coincide, on the one hand, with his uneasy reconciliation with a workers' party and, on the other, with his desire to interact pedagogically with Italian youth. Such legibility, he no doubt hoped, would spark a process among a conformist younger generation of ideological awakening similar to the one that had led Pasolini and many other contemporary idealistic intellectuals to rebel in the 1940s against Fascism and embrace Marxism.

Despite its fragmentary nature, *Petrolio* also does much to shed light on Pasolini's creative process. The work is organized into a lengthy series of *appunti,* or notes, reminiscent of film scenes. Pasolini remarks at one point that his descriptions of the landscapes inhabited by his characters seem like so many memorandums for a screenplay. In so doing, he calls to mind his often quoted essay "La sceneggiatura come 'struttura che vuol essere altra struttura' " (The screenplay as a 'structure that wants to be another structure'). In that article Pasolini depicts the screenplay as a quasigenre that, much like a theatrical script, is more than a mere intermediary between film and literature. Prior to the realization of the film, he wrote, the finished screenplay can be considered "an independent technique, a complete and self-sufficient work" of narrative. It may justifiably demand the reader's collaboration in envisioning a completed work. Inherent in the screenplay Pasolini saw the "will" of one artistic form to become another, "a movement that culminates freely and with serendipity in the writer's imagination." Much like *Petrolio,* the screenplay for Pasolini is a work in progress; both are organized into many notes—temporary forms that anticipate others.

Pasolini intended *Petrolio* to be an immense work, a summation of his entire life experience; he predicted that writing it would have occupied the rest of his creative life. Even in its unfinished state, it is extremely ambitious. Many of the themes of his journalistic essays are reiterated and developed: the conformism of the younger generation, the equivalence of "Red" and "Black" terrorism, the commercialized permissiveness derivative of consumer ideology rampant among the young, the loss of traditional values, the death of any true religious sentiment in Italy, and his desire to "recuperate" the young a-ideological Fascists" to a progressive cause.

The plot outline embraces the complexity of a society in the throes of a Pasolinian Dopostoria. The characters inhabit an environment that is itself a merciless indictment of an oppressive and self-perpetuating power structure founded on the collusion of the Italian version of multinational capitalism, the sundry center-left governments of the 1960s and 1970s, Italy's secret police, and the Vatican. The power brokers depicted in *Petrolio* constitute an unorganized but cohesive political bloc. They stage a mock struggle against neo-Fascist subversion, played out in the nation's streets and newspapers, to dupe the public and camouflage their true goal, which is to destroy Italy's erstwhile Communist Party. Those intellectuals who in Pasolini's eyes had been integrated into a morally bankrupt cul-

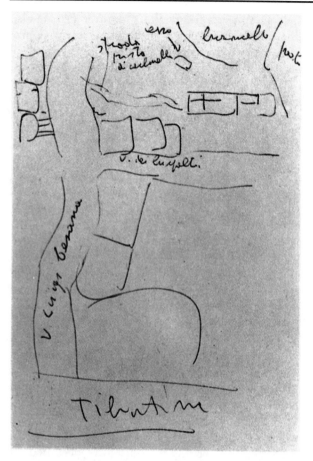

Diagram from the typescript for Una vita violenta *(Pier Paolo Pasolini Collection)*

tural mainstream were to be shown as the venal yet unwitting accomplices of a System that, through its occult ownership of the media, the literary presses, and the financing of literary prizes, had brainwashed the masses and commercialized Italian arts. This System had also fostered among the cultural elite an atmosphere of "literary restoration" that nullified the ability of literature to contest and transform the status quo. *Petrolio* is a fitting culmination of Pasolini's career because it shows his attempt to capture in its entire breadth and scope his view of the world around him.

Pasolini's premature death also cut short his contribution to contemporary Italian culture as a co-editor, along with Alberto Moravia and Alberto Carocci, of the journal *Nuovi argomenti,* a collaboration that began in 1966. Many of his editorials have been collected in *Scritti corsari* (1975). Pasolini's final works, particularly his editorial denunciations of the Italian ruling class carried forth in a scathing "trial" of the Christian Democratic Party, puts unusually sinister overtones on his murder.

Pasolini's battered corpse was found on the morning of 2 November 1975 at Ostia, a beach on the Tyrrhenian coast outside of Rome. He had met a seventeen-year-old street hustler, Giuseppe Pelosi, in front of the main Roman rail station the previous evening. Pasolini was last seen alive a short time later treating his young acquaintance to dinner near the Basilica of Saint Paul Outside the Walls. Pelosi was stopped by police early the next morning for speeding and arrested when it was discovered that the car he was driving was not his own. There were no traces of blood on Pelosi, and his clothing was in perfect order, but the same could not be said for the man he claimed to have killed. Pasolini's body was found several hours later covered in blood, with skull and fingernails crushed, face disfigured, an ear almost dissevered, and hands badly scraped.

Pelosi immediately confessed to Pasolini's murder, claiming to have acted alone and in self-defense, but the juvenile court that tried him refuted his testimony, stating that the crime could not have been committed without assistance. The police found several items of clothing in Pasolini's automobile at the moment of Pelosi's arrest that could not have belonged to Pelosi or Pasolini, and there were footprints made by neither man in the sand where the mortal scuffles occurred. The court cited as evidence that Pelosi had not acted alone the inability of the police to find the personal items Pelosi insisted he had left in Pasolini's car when he had been arrested. In addition, bloodstains not belonging to Pasolini that Pelosi could not explain were detected inside the car. Investigation showed that Pasolini was beaten, caught when he attempted to flee, kicked in the lower abdomen, and clubbed over the head with a fence pole, and that he finally died when his heart was crushed under his own sports car.

The suspicions that surrounded Pasolini's murder were intensified by the subsequent handling of the case. The court of appeals overruled the conclusions of the juvenile court and imposed a relatively lenient sentence on Pelosi, giving rise to charges of a cover-up. During Pelosi's trial, police received anonymous information that when Pasolini left the train station with Pelosi their vehicle was followed by another containing four thugs, well-known among the seedy habitués of the area near the train station.

A constant of Pasolini's career is the use of his personal situation as a synecdoche for the general human condition. Beyond its intrinsic artistic merit, his production during his Friulian period at times merits the description of "exasperated autobiography." During the 1950s, although he attempted to give his thought a Marxist patina by claiming to

Pasolini as a cleric in his 1972 film of The Canterbury Tales

place class conflict at the center of his literary investigation, the lifeblood of his creative activity centered on what he saw as the unresolved drama of the intellectual who betrayed, as had he, his own class to advocate the cause of the working people. This theme is at the core of one of his most beautiful poems, "Le ceneri di Gramsci" (The Ashes of Gramsci), a work that for many captured the spirit of his entire generation. This same spirit is reflected in the stylistic experimentation and sociological investigation of *Ragazzi di vita* and *Una vita violenta*. In the 1960s his work developed along lines that closely followed his subjective view of his role as an artist in society. In the 1970s, the years immediately preceding his brutal murder, the civil commitment characteristic of his life's work and exquisitely portrayed in the poem "Patmos" (in *Trasumanar e organizzar*) led him to assume increasingly radical stances against what had become for him "un paese orribilmente sporco" (a horribly filthy country).

The novel *Ragazzi di vita* and the poems collected in *Le ceneri di Gramsci* (1957; translated as *The Ashes of Gramsci,* 1982) firmly established Pasolini as a major writer. With the film *The Gospel According to Matthew* (1964) his reputation as an important film-maker was consolidated and spread throughout Europe and across the Atlantic. Everything he did from the mid 1950s on was the object of attention for an international public. He continues to excite vivid interest because, with the appraisal of Italian society and its political system argued in his final works, Pasolini demonstrates a vision that borders on the prophetic. His causes are not at all anachronistic but are more timely than ever.

Letters:

Le belle bandiere: dialoghi 1960–1965, edited by Gian Carlo Ferretti (Rome: Editori Riuniti, 1977);

Lettere: con una cronologia della vita e delle opere, 2 volumes, edited by Nico Naldini (Turin: Einaudi, 1986–1988); volume 1, *Lettere 1940–1954,* translated by Stuart Hood as *Letters* (London: Quartet, 1992).

Interviews:

"Dieci domande a Pasolini," edited by E. F. Accrocca, *La fiera letteraria,* 30 June 1957;

"Nove domande sul romanzo," *Nuovi argomenti* (May–August 1959);

"Otto domande sulla critica letteraria," *Nuovi argomenti* (May–August 1960);

"Sette domande sulla poesia," *Nuovi argomenti* (March–June 1962);

"Interview," *La fiera letteraria,* 14 December 1967;

Pasolini on Pasolini. Interviews with Oswald Stack (London: Thames & Hudson, 1969; Bloomington: Indiana University Press, 1969);

Ferdinando Camon, "Pier Paolo Pasolini," in *Il mestiere di scrittore, 1965* (Milan: Garzanti, 1973);

Volgar'eloguio, edited by Antonio Piromalli and Domenico Scarfoglio (Naples: Athena, 1976);

Con Pier Paolo Pasolini, edited by Enrico Magrelli (Rome: Bulzoni, 1977);

Il sogno del centauro, edited by Jean Duflot (Rome: Editori Riuniti, 1983).Bibliography: *Pasolini: una vita futura,* edited by Laura Betti (Milan: Garzanti, 1985).

Bibliography:

Pasolini: una vita futura, edited by Laura Betti (Milan: Garzanti, 1985).

Biographies:

Pasolini in Friuli, 1943–1949, prepared by Corriere del Friuli and Comune di Casarsa della Delizia (Udine: Arti Grafiche Friulane, 1976)—includes unpublished poems by Pasolini;

Laura Betti, ed., *Pasolini: cronaca giudiziaria, persecuzione, morte* (Milan: Garzanti, 1977);

Enzo Siciliano, *Vita di Pasolini* (Milan: Rizzoli, 1978); translated by John Shepley as *Pasolini* (New York: Random House, 1982);

Nico Naldini, *Pasolini, una vita* (Turin: Einaudi, 1989);

Franco Citti and C. Valentini, *Vita di un ragazzo di vita* (Varese: SugarCo, 1992);

Omicidio nella persona di Pier Paolo Pasolini. L'oscura morte di un intellettuale scandaloso: estratto dagli atti processuali (Milan: Kaos, 1992);

Barth David Schwartz, *Pasolini. Requiem* (New York: Pantheon, 1992).

References:

Beverly Allen, ed., *Pier Paolo Pasolini: The Poetics of Heresy* (Saratoga, Cal.: Anma Libri, 1982);

Tommaso Anzoino, *Pasolini* (Florence: Nuova Italia, 1971);

Giampaolo Borghello and others, *Interpretazioni di Pasolini* (Rome: Savelli, 1977);

Gian Carlo Ferretti, *Pasolini: L'universo orrendo* (Rome: Editori Riuniti, 1976);

Joseph Francese, *Il realismo impopolare di Pier Paolo Pasolini* (Foggia: Bastogi, 1991);

Pia Friedrich, *Pier Paolo Pasolini* (Boston: Twayne, 1982);

Naomi Greene, *Pier Paolo Pasolini: Cinema as Heresy* (Princeton: Princeton University Press, 1990);

Pietro Lazagna and Carla Lazagna, *Pasolini di fronte al problema religioso* (Bologna: Dehoniana, 1970);

Arcangelo Leone de Castris, *Sulle ceneri di Gramsci: Pasolini, i comunisti e il 1968* (Naples: CUEN, 1993);

Vincenzo Mannino, *Invito alla lettura di Pasolini* (Milan: Mursia, 1974);

F. Panzeri, *Guida alla lettura di Pasolini* (Milan: Mondadori, 1989);

Sandro Petraglia, *Pier Paolo Pasolini* (Florence: Nuova Italia, 1974);

Rinaldo Rinaldi, *Pier Paolo Pasolini* (Milan: Mursia, 1982);

Patrick Rumble, *Allegories of Contamination: Pier Paolo Pasolini's Trilogy of Life* (Toronto: University of Toronto Press, 1996);

Rumble and Bart Testa, eds., *Pier Paolo Pasolini: Contemporary Perspectives* (Toronto: University of Toronto Press, 1994);

Barth David Schwartz, *Requiem* (New York: Pantheon, 1992);

Testa and Rumble, eds., *Pier Paolo Pasolini* (Toronto: University of Toronto Press, 1993);

David Ward, *A Poetics of Resistance: Narrative and the Writings of Pier Paolo Pasolini* (Madison, N.J.: Fairleigh Dickinson University Press, 1996);

Paul Willemen and others, *Pier Paolo Pasolini* (London: British Film Institute, 1977);

Giuseppe Zigaina, *Pasolini tra enigma e profezia* (Padua: Marsilio, 1989).

Cesare Pavese
(9 September 1908 – 27 August 1950)

Antonino Musumeci
University of Illinois at Urbana-Champaign

See also the Pavese entry in *DLB 128: Twentieth-Century Italian Poets, Second Series.*

BOOKS: *Lavorare stanca* (Florence: Solaria, 1936; enlarged edition, Turin: Einaudi, 1943);

Paesi tuoi (Turin: Einaudi, 1941); translated by Alma E. Murch as *The Harvesters* (London: Peter Owen, 1954);

La spiaggia (Rome: Lettere d'oggi, 1941); translated by W. J. Strachan as *The Beach* (London: Peter Owen, 1963);

Feria d'agosto (Turin: Einaudi, 1946); translated by Murch as *Summer Storm* (London: Peter Owen, 1966);

Il compagno (Turin: Einaudi, 1947); translated by Strachan as *The Comrade* (London: Peter Owen, 1959);

Dialoghi con Leucò (Turin: Einaudi, 1947); translated by William Arrowsmith and D. S. Carne-Ross as *Dialogues with Leucò* (Ann Arbor: University of Michigan Press, 1965);

Prima che il gallo canti (Turin: Einaudi, 1949)—includes *Il carcere* and *La casa in collina*;

La bella estate: Tre romanzi (Turin: Einaudi, 1949)—includes *La bella estate, Il diavolo sulle colline,* and *Tra donne sole*;

La luna e i falò (Turin: Einaudi, 1950); translated by Louise Sinclair as *The Moon and the Bonfires* (London: Peter Owen, 1952); translated by Marianne Cecconi as *The Moon and the Bonfires* (New York: Farrar, Straus & Young, 1954);

Verrà la morte e avrà i tuoi occhi (Turin: Einaudi, 1951);

La letteratura americana e altri saggi, edited by Italo Calvino (Turin: Einaudi, 1951); translated by Edwin Fussell as *American Literature: Essays and Opinions* (Berkeley: University of California Press, 1970);

Il mestiere di vivere (Diario 1935–1950) (Turin: Einaudi, 1952); translated by Murch as *This Business of Living* (London: Peter Owen, 1961);

Cesare Pavese shortly after World War II

Notte di festa (Turin: Einaudi, 1953); translated by Murch as *Festival Night* (London: Peter Owen, 1964);

Fuoco grande, by Pavese and Bianca Garufi (Turin: Einaudi, 1959); translated by Strachan as *A Great Fire,* in *The Beach* (London: Peter Owen, 1963);

Racconti (Turin: Einaudi, 1960);

Poesie edite e inedite, edited by Calvino (Turin: Einaudi, 1962);

Otto poesie inedite e quattro lettere a un'amica, 1928–1929 (Milano: Scheiwiller, 1964);

Ciau Masino (Turin: Einaudi, 1968);

Poesie giovanili (1923–30) (Turin: Einaudi, 1990).

Editions in English: *Among Women Only,* translation by D. D. Paige of *Tra donne sole* (London: Peter Owen, 1953);

The Devil in the Hills, translation by Paige of *Il diavolo sulle colline* (New York: Noonday Press, 1954);

The Political Prisoner, translated by W. J. Strachan (London: Peter Owen, 1955)—includes *Il diavolo sulle colline* and *La bella estate*;

The House on the Hill, translation by Strachan of *La casa in collina* (London: Peter Owen, 1956; New York: Walker, 1959);

The Selected Works of Cesare Pavese, translated by R. W. Flint (New York: Farrar, Straus & Giroux, 1968)—includes *La spiaggia, La casa in collina,* and *Tra donne sole*;

A Mania for Solitude: Selected Poems, 1930–1950, translated by Margaret Crosland (London: Peter Owen, 1969)—includes *Lavorare stanca* and *Verrà la morte e avrà i tuoi occhi*;

Hard Labor: Poems by Cesare Pavese, translated by William Arrowsmith (New York: Grossman, 1976)—includes *Lavorare stanca* and *Verrà la morte e avrà i tuoi occhi.*

TRANSLATIONS: Sinclair Lewis, *Our Mr. Wrenn,* translated as *Il nostro signor Wrenn* (Florence: Bemporad, 1931);

Herman Melville, *Moby Dick,* translated with the same title (Turin: Frassinelli, 1932);

Sherwood Anderson, *Dark Laughter,* translated as *Riso nero* (Turin: Frassinelli, 1932);

James Joyce, *Portrait of the Artist as a Young Man,* translated as *Dedalus* (Turin: Frassinelli, 1934);

John Dos Passos, *The 42nd Parallel,* translated as *Il 42° parallelo* (Milan: Mondadori, 1935);

Dos Passos, *The Big Money,* translated as *Un mucchio di quattrini* (Milan: Mondadori, 1937);

John Steinbeck, *Of Mice and Men,* translated as *Uomini e topi* (Milano: Bompiani, 1938);

Gertrude Stein, *The Autobiography of Alice B. Toklas,* translated as *Autobiografia di Alice Toklas* (Turin: Einaudi, 1938);

Daniel Defoe, *Moll Flanders,* translated with the same title (Turin: Einaudi, 1938);

Charles Dickens, *David Copperfield,* translated with the same title (Turin: Einaudi, 1939);

Stein, *Three Lives,* translated as *Tre esistenze* (Turin: Einaudi, 1940);

Melville, *Benito Cereno,* translated with the same title (Turin: Einaudi, 1940);

George Macaulay Trevelyan, *The English Revolution 1688–1689,* translated as *La rivoluzione inglese del 1688–1689* (Turin: Einaudi, 1940);

Christopher Morley, *The Trojan Horse,* translated as *Il cavallo di Troia* (Milan: Bompiani, 1941);

William Faulkner, *The Hamlet,* translated as *Il borgo* (Milan: Mondadori, 1942);

Robert Henriques, *Captain Smith,* translated as *Capitano Smith* (Turin: Einaudi, 1947).

Few writers in Italy in the twentieth century rival Cesare Pavese for receiving the uninterrupted and undiminished attention of literary critics and the petulant curiosity of the mass media. Indeed, Pavese, who extensively theorized about myth, has assumed the significance of a myth. He stands at the threshold of the rise of the modern Italian novel and remains one of its most distinctive voices. He demonstrates the possibility of a manner of expression more consonant with the restlessness and the introspection of the age, search for authenticity and refusal to acquiesce in perceived certainties. His narrative work, which spans only the decade of the 1940s, has lost little of its cogency and none of its interest.

Cesare Pavese was born on 9 September 1908 in Santo Stefano Belbo, in that region of southern Piedmont called "le Langhe." The area is known for its wine and, according to Pavese's depiction, its barely contained violence. His family lived in Turin, where his father worked as registrar in the court system, and it is in that city that Pavese spent practically all of his life, where he completed his education and worked till his death for the Einaudi publishing house. But while Turin was the place of his existence, the countryside remained the space of his imagination and his memory.

As a student Pavese had a particular fascination for American culture, slang, and literature; he wrote his dissertation on the poetry of Walt Whitman. From 1931 to 1947 he translated many works from English into Italian, including Herman Mellville's *Moby Dick* (1932), Sherwood Anderson's *Dark Laughter* (1932), John Steinbeck's *Of Mice and Men* (1938), Daniel Defoe's *Moll Flanders* (1938), Charles Dickens's *David Copperfield* (1939), and William Faulkner's *The Hamlet* (1942). His translations, along with those of Elio Vittorini, introduced Italians to a literature different from the one canonized by a self-conscious tradition and reasserted by the Fascist regime for its own ideological purposes.

In 1935, accused of antifascist activities, Pavese was arrested and sent to Brancaleone Calabro, where he was forced to reside for ten months. By and large Pavese's maturation coincided with the suffocating dominance of the Fascist movement in Italian political and cultural life, thus imposing on him and other intellectuals the necessity of defining their own positions with regard to the regime. Torn between the perceived imperative of antifascist involvement and the demands of his own personal demons, Pavese chose the exploration of his inner voices and their resolution as a way of creating a new model of literature, thus distancing himself from the strictures of literary tradition, while continuing to be influenced by Giacomo Leopardi and Benedetto Croce.

The case has been made that Pavese's artistic endeavor is a relentless exploration of the myth of the return: the protagonist's effort to separate himself from his existential condition, symbolized by the city, and return to a privileged place, always the hill, to recuperate a mythical quality of life identified with his infancy. Each of Pavese's compositions, from the first collection of his poetry, *Lavorare stanca,* (Work is Wearing, 1936), to his last novel *La luna e i falò* (1950; translated as *The Moon and the Bonfires,* 1952), can be considered an attempt to analyze and understand that process. Pavese himself described it as his "monolith," and he termed his efforts at exploring it an "excavation."

For Pavese an artist does not discover as much as he explores; his work consists not in the attainment of a new concept or a new vision but in returning again and again to a singular vision to the point of monotonous repetition, testing the mechanism of its parts in order to evaluate what is genuinely mythical and what is merely ephemeral. His ultimate scope is not the discovery of a mythical substratum but the reduction of that substratum to clarity. His essential vision is already present in his first published poem, "Mari del Sud" (Southern Seas), which was published in 1930 and collected in *Lavorare stanca*. It marks the emergence of the archetypal myth, Pavese's first intuition, of the significance of the return. From then on the structure of the return would be subject to his persistent and "monotonous" excavation.

The first ten years of Pavese's artistic activity were dedicated to poetry, and he returned to the genre again at the end of his career. *Lavorare stanca* contains an inventory of the themes that are specific to Pavese's vision. These themes tend to form categories in binary opposition: city/countryside, idleness/commitment, man/woman, youth/maturity, nature/culture, solitude/human intercourse, self/others, familiar/foreign, quotidian/mythical, and escape/return.

Perhaps the most apparent characteristic of Pavese's poetry, particularly when it is compared to Hermeticism, the dominant poetic expression of his time in Italy, is its narrative quality: his poems tell stories about runaway boys, tramps, thieves, whores, and drunks in elongated lines that tend toward the rhythm of prose. There is a significant evo-

lution within these poems: after a first phase, which Pavese calls *poesia-racconto* (poetry as story), he begins to emphasize imagination over reality, stream of consciousness over description, and introspection over narration. In his second phase, which Pavese terms *poesia-immagine* (poetry as image), he searches for levels of meaning beyond the surface, thus granting reality a metaphoric or symbolic value. His voice becomes more lyrical and his lines shorter; the preoccupation with the story is replaced by symbolic allusiveness and a need to shed light on the inner state of the self.

Pavese returned to poetry in 1945 with *La terra e la morte* (Earth and Death), which was inspired by his love for Bianca Garufi, and in 1951 with *Verrà la morte e avrà i tuoi occhi* (Death Will Come and Its Eyes Will Be Yours), which was inspired by his encounter with the American actress Constance Dowling, to whom his last novel is dedicated. At first sight these seem to be very different poems, but in both content and form they continue the previous evolution from poesoa-racconto to poesia-immagine to *poesia-simbolo* (poetry as symbol). In a rarefied atmosphere of allusions, Pavese constantly declares the mysterious association of woman and earth and suffuses it with intimations of death.

In its historical context, Pavese's poetry exhibits an unmistakable mark of newness and diversity. Rejecting the two dominant poetic models of his age, the heroic one of Gabriele D'Annunzio's glorious musicality and the private one of the *sofferto silenzio* (painful silence) of the Hermeticists, Pavese's poetry, with its discursive narrativity, dares to speak a language of its own and to propose a vocabulary of totally fresh and original images. It has, in fact, no antecedent in the Italian poetic tradition, and it has left no immediate successor (until its rather recent rediscovery).

After 1936 Pavese's poetic creativity shows signs of hesitation and faltering. His meditation centers more and more on memory, the past, and destiny. His diary, *Il mestiere di vivere* (Diario 1935–1950) (1952; translated as *The Business of Living,* 1961), exhibits a new interest in narrative aesthetics. Eventually Pavese evidently found the formal medium of poetry to be insufficient for the task and opted for the expansion and analytical possibilities of narrative forms. He first wrote short stories (1936–1938) before turning to the novel. To excavate into the complexity of mythical reality, he felt, one needs the deep, slow rhythm of narrative discourse rather than the short, lyrical illuminations of poetry,

Pavese wrote nine novels. A tenth, *Fuoco grande* (1959; translated as *A Great Fire,* 1963), was a failed, never completed experiment in dual-gender author-

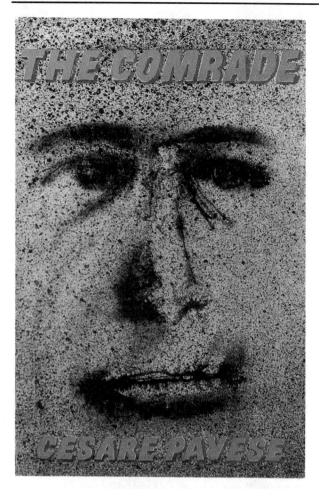

Dust jacket for the British edition of the translation of Pavese's 1947 novel, in which the protagonist joins the Communist Party

years after it was completed, as the title story in a collection also containing the short novels *Il diavolo sulle colline* and *Tra donne sole;* only *La spiaggia* was published in the same year it was finished.

They are short novels, exhibiting a remarkable thematic continuity. *Paesi tuoi* (translated as *The Harvesters,* 1961) continues the story of *Il carcere* (translated as *The Political Prisoner,* 1955), for Berto returns from incarceration only to realize that prison is not a geographical place but a persistent human condition. And if *La bella estate* is, as Pavese called it, "the story of a virginity that defends itself," one could assert that *La spiaggia* is the story of a conjugal relationship in a state of self-defense. The dominant theme of the four novels is the prison or the sense of enclosure that cannot be escaped. However, while incarceration can perhaps be perceived as a state anterior to the return, as a metaphor for human condition it denies the return. Pavese would explore later phases of the return in his future works.

These novels show an unusual degree of geographical experimentation, which is uncharacteristic of Pavese's other works. One could read the novels as telling the same story in four different settings: in *Il carcere* it is the non-Piedmontese southern countryside, whose landscape stretches from mountains to seashore; in *Paesi tuoi* the Langhe is equated to the city rather than defined in opposition to it; in *La bella estate* the setting is exclusively urban, reduced to a series of interior spaces; and in *La spiaggia* the setting is the sea in its halcyonic splendor. None of these varied settings is established as a unique polarity in the process of the return.

In terms of the myth of the return, this first group of novels seems to be a distraction: Pavese's overriding concern, his "monolith," seems to be relegated to a secondary role and at times seems almost forgotten. These novels reflect Pavese's experience of *confino* (internment) and his failed relationships, in particular with a woman known as "la donna dalla voce rauca" (the woman with the hoarse voice). Above all, they mark Pavese's apprenticeship in the art of narration, for his diary speaks of a "ricerca di stile" (a quest for style). One senses that he is experimenting with narrative, creating metaphors for his present condition. Only when he considers himself to have mastered that medium sufficiently will he go back to the treatment of the return.

In his diary from the early 1940s Pavese expresses his sense of having reached an impasse, a feeling that what he has done so far is only "raccontare immagini" (narrating images). He laments having told stories, merely stories, without reaching a deeper meaning. He found new ways of exploring

ship, in which Pavese composed a chapter and Garufi another. Pavese's narrative output was apparently the result of two distinct chronologically defined creative impulses immediately before and immediately after Italy's involvement in World War II. The publication order of his novels differs from their order of composition. To retrace the evolutionary progress of Pavese's treatment of the return, his novels must be examined according to the chronology of their composition rather than that of their publication. The novels form two distinct narrative cycles, each containing four novels, with an anomalous case falling chronologically and functionally in between.

The first cycle comprises *Il carcere* (written in 1938–1939), *Paesi tuoi* (1939), *La bella estate* (1940), *La spiaggia* (1940–1941). *Il carcere* was published ten years after it was written with *La casa in collina* in *Prima che il gallo canti* (Before the Cock Crows, 1949); *Paesi tuoi* was published two years after its composition in 1941; and *La bella estate* was published nine

meaning in his readings of anthropology and ethnology. His discovery of myth led him to the realization that images could be symbols, "realtà simbolica" (symbolic reality), that stories could point to "una più ricca realtà sotto la realtà oggettiva" (a richer reality underneath objective reality). Myth for Pavese would no longer merely be a form of expression but would become an instrument of knowledge, a means of decoding reality.

Pavese's understanding of the importance of myth enriched his artistic vision, including his appreciation of the past. The function of the past in Pavese's work is to ensure a value to the present; it is only against the pattern of the past that the image of the present becomes focused and reveals its true composition. The past event provides a meaningful substratum and determines the significance of all future activity. Pavese is the poet of the present rooted in the past. His movement toward the past is not an evasive burrowing in the comfort of unconscious certainties, an alibi that relinquishes one's pressing obligations in the present, but an effort to investigate in those certainties a paradigm that might solve the present contingency.

The relationship of the past to the present is described by Pavese in mythical terms: "Il concepire mitico dell'infanzia è insomma un sollevare alla sfera di eventi unici e assoluti le successive rivelazioni delle cose, per cui queste vivranno nella coscienza come schemi normativi dell'immaginazione affettiva" (The mythical conceptualization of infancy consists in elevating to the sphere of unique and absolute events the revelations of things that follow, so that these will live in the consciousness as normative schemes of the affective imagination). Infancy provides a cluster of fundamental experiences that determines a code of interpretation for the other experiences that follow, on the basis of which the repetition of those actions is assured mythical or symbolic significance. Thus, the past establishes a deep level of meaning for the present, serving as an archetypal model. For Pavese the past contains the original experience that alone can assure a degree of authenticity for the creative process in the present. He believes that myths are created in infancy experientially and that they are formulated rationally and poetically in the present of the artistic process.

The artist is able to define and explore the interrelatedness of past and present because the past is retrievable through memory. Like Plato, Pavese believes that to know is to remember: the poet is essentially an archaeologist. The validity of memory rests on the premise that experience is always repetitive, that events do not occur in linear progression, as unique, immediately transcendent moments of a continually progressing history, but that they reoccur in waves of reflection, reminiscent of Marcel Proust's *reverberations*. All that happens has happened before and finds its significance in its original model. To remember, then, is to be able to capture the original experience and its relatedness to the present one.

Pavese insists that the objective of these remembrances is not the salvaging of a *temps perdu* but the ontological essence that precedes awareness, the epiphany of one's being. Memories surface from the subconscious to the conscious, rational level, and their appearance imposes a continuous effort of clarification. The role of memory in the creative process is to open the artist's mythical content. The function of art is to give rational form to the chaotic experience of the subconscious. In mythological terms, it is the subjugation of the Minotaur. In the realm of knowledge, art and memory are vitally interdependent. Pavese believes that the purpose of art is to reach an understanding of the essence of reality, not through direct observation of phenomena but through the universalizing representation in memory: "Le cose si scoprono attraverso i ricordi che se ne hanno" (Things are discovered through the memories we have of them). One only knows an internalized reality.

Geography in Pavese always has a fundamental role, and it is with the mythologizing of space that his mythical categories become operative as a system. In mid September 1943 Pavese recorded in his diary his first formal affirmation of local uniqueness as a mythical category:

> Carattere, non dico della poesia, ma della fiaba mitica è la consacrazione dei luoghi unici, legati a un fatto a una gesta a un evento. A un luogo, tra tutti, si dà un significato assoluto, isolandolo nel mondo. Così sono nati i santuari. Così a ciascuno i luoghi dell'infanzia ritornano alla memoria; in essi accaddero cose che li han fatti unici e li trascelgono sul resto del mondo con questo suggello mitico.

> (Characteristic, I will not say of poetry, but of the mythical fable is the consecration of unique places, connected to a fact or to an action or to an event. To a particular place among all others we give an absolute meaning by isolating it within the world. In this manner shrines were created. In this manner to each person the places of infancy come back to memory; in them there took place things that have made them unique and purposely identify them in contrast to the rest of the world with such a mythical mark.)

In Pavese's systematization of his theory of myth, the concept of the *locus unicus* (unique place) is the premise for all his subsequent statements on mythical action, the mythical hero, mythical age, and poetry. The locus unicus is the place of infancy as it is shaped in memory and by the events that took place there. Pavese's artistic endeavor can be conceived in the following terms: given that the past is retrievable only in memory, can a physical return to the mythical place of infancy be attempted, and will it be a mythical, and thus symbolic, action? Can the mythical age of infancy be recaptured experientially through the process of the return? Pavese's subsequent work will consist of an exploration of that possibility.

The uniqueness of the place of infancy derives from its being the repository of the "selvaggio" (the wild). The statements and counterstatements in his diary show how difficult a notion this was for Pavese. His early ethnological readings, including Sir James George Frazer's *Golden Bough* (1890–1915) and Lucien Lévy-Bruhl's *Mythologie primitive* (1935), assured him of the importance of the concept in a theory of myth, but its exact role in his own system was not immediately clear. At various times he equates it with the countryside, with titanism, with a mythically qualified rusticity. From an initial identification with the forbidden, symbolized by blood and sex, the selvaggio becomes synonymous with the irrational and finally with mystery. The selvaggio suggests a reality charged with symbolism, a reality of "open possibility," or myth. Like myth, the selvaggio, too, is subject to exploration and interpretation. It is the function of art to tame the wild by resolving its mystery into an acquisition of knowledge.

Destiny is for Pavese another form of "realtà simbolica" (symbolical reality). He understands it as the repetition of the original event from infancy. The original act or event predicts the present and its meaning. Destiny is the rhythm, the cadence of returning events. Destiny, myth, and the wild, three fundamentally synonymous concepts for Pavese, ensure a symbolic significance. He spoke of "la feconda idea che destino sia il mito, il selvaggio" (the pregnant idea that destiny is myth, the savage). The artistic formulation of this theory Pavese calls a "poetica del destino" (poetics of destiny), a poetics in which "gestures, words, human existence are seen as symbol, as myth."

Myth, for Pavese, is "una norma, lo schema di un fatto avvenuto una volta per tutte, e trae il suo valore da questa unicità assoluta che lo solleva fuori del tempo e lo consacra rivelazione" (a norm, the scheme of a fact that has happened once for all times and derives its value from such an absolute uniqueness that raises it outside of time and consecrates it as a revelation). It is a concept that brings together

paradigm and symbolism. For Pavese myth eventually has to be resolved in rational terms; its symbolism has to be revealed; its savage charge has to be contained—and it is precisely the function of art to reduce myth to Logos. True art, he believed, presupposes a mythical content and aims at the same time at its destruction. To clarify one's own myths is to destroy them, to negate them as myths. Contrary to Mircea Eliade's affirmation, for Pavese the return cannot be eternal. It is conceivable that an age or a period of life could be completely devoid of myth; and what of art then? To continue to play with a demythologized myth Pavese brands as aestheticism. The conclusion therefore can be legitimately inferred that myth and Logos are not subsequent terms of a sequence but rather coexist dialectically in a state of constant tension.

At the conclusion of this crucial period of the discovery of mythical categories, Pavese published the results of his inquiry in two books. The first was *Feria d'agosto* (1946, translated as *Summer Storm*, 1966), a collection of essays and short stories suggestively combining titles borrowed from D'Annunzio and Frazer. The other was *Dialoghi con Leucò* (1947, translated as *Dialogues with Leucò*, 1965), a collection of lyrical pieces that deals with memory, infancy, locus unicus, selvaggio, art, and, especially, destiny. *Dialoghi con Leucò* is Pavese's "poetica del destino" in which human beings are characterized by having destiny (distinguishing them from the gods). Written in the form of a dialogue, it is Pavese's only work that does not have a contemporary setting. A unique experiment with non sequitur, *Dialoghi con Leucò* shows Pavese testing his newly discovered mythical categories by incorporating them into classical mythology.

Pavese's next novel, *Il compagno* (1947; translated as *The Comrade*, 1959), is surprising for its unrelatedness to his fundamental myth. It is a gesture toward political involvement in which mythical thought is replaced by an ideological thesis. The protagonist's initial state of unresolved ennui, so typical of Pavese's characters, is resolved by his affiliation to the Communist Party. After having celebrated man as the victim of destiny in *Dialoghi con Leucò,* in *Il compagno* Pavese nearly makes him one of the smiling gods, attributing to him control over his destiny through political action. Significantly, movement is not from the city to the countryside but, uncharacteristically for Pavese, from city to city.

Having paid his due to political activism, Pavese in his second cycle of four novels fully applies his newly discovered mythical categories to the subject of the return. All written between 1947 and

1949–*La casa in collina* (1949; translated as *The House on the Hill*, 1959), *Il diavolo sulle colline* (1949; translated as *The Devil in the Hills*, 1954), *Tra donne sole* (1949; translated as *Among Women Only*, 1953), and *La luna e i falò*–because of their underlying theme these novels could be called "the novels of the return." In each novel Pavese isolates one particular aspect of the process of the return and analyzes it through his mythical categories.

La casa in collina explores the return as an eventful journey during which the protagonist's true self is revealed. Paralleling the pattern of Ulysses in the *Odyssey*, Corrado, too, returns from the city (Troy-Turin) to the countryside (Ithaca-Langhe) and from war to a presumption of peace.

At the beginning of the story, Corrado lives on the hill in an effort to create his own time and space–the slow time of contemplation and the desert space of solitude–apart from the demands of society. But his intricate system of defenses gradually collapses under the menacing pressures of personal and historic events. First it is the appearance of Cate, an old girlfriend who has grown into political awareness and has accepted her own responsibilities to her son and to the present. Her reemergence from the past disturbs Corrado's peace by revealing its artificiality; she probes relentlessly into his inconsistencies. It is obvious that Corrado is the father of her son, Dino, yet he cannot accept the demanding imposition of paternity.

In addition, war is relentlessly and violently intruding on his life on the hill, which was predicated on the belief that the horrors of history could be precluded by mythical realities. But even myth apparently cannot stem the ravenous march of history. Corrado attempts to cope with his situation through depersonalization, detachment, and isolation. When all these defensive techniques fail, he embarks on a journey toward the mythical hills of his infancy: there, away from the engulfing demands of history, he is certain to find protection from its demons. His return acquires the meaning of a ritual celebration, of a religious experience.

The culminating point of that journey is a vicarious encounter with death on his native hills. Coming upon the bloody scene of an ambush in which several Fascist soldiers have been killed, Corrado interprets it as a violation of the hill, as the demythologizing of the myth. Death, as the most incontrovertible reality, is thus "celebrated" in the heart of that place that was to ensure life. Corrado is a witness to the fact that even the mythical hill has fallen victim to history. At the end Corrado, now established on his native hills, is still searching for a compromise between individuality and collectivity.

He still hopes to reestablish his isolation, but has learned that belief in a mythology does not eliminate historical necessities, that the affirmation of one's individuality in solitude still leaves the problem of one's relationship to others unresolved. Even on the hill, Corrado is part of history. The odyssey has revealed that the Ithaca of old is no longer attainable.

In *Il diavolo sulle colline* Pavese focuses on the countryside as the ultimate objective of the return. The three protagonists leave Turin for a summer vacation in the hills in quest of knowledge by direct contact with, and immersion in, the countryside. Pieretto, Oreste, and the narrator have different predispositions: one is from the city; one is from the country but definitely transplanted in the city; one is from the country and only temporarily living in the city. One is ironic; one is active; one is contemplative. The countryside they are going to explore is similarly fragmented into three qualitatively different models: the towns of Greppo and Mombello and Oreste's village are emblematic of different moral attitudes toward the countryside: the decadent that should be avoided, the pastoral that is no longer attainable, and the realistic that should be sought. The novel establishes the three types of countryside as mutually exclusive foci, thus implying the necessity of a choice between them. The story explores the three models, implicitly evaluating each as to its feasibility as the destination of a hypothetical return.

The land of Oreste's father is the land where the wild has been tamed by the work of man, where nature and man cooperate to make the land fruitful. In the description of Mombello, however, Pavese has carefully avoided all indications of work as a necessary task. The name Mombello, the italianized form of the pastoral *locus amoenus,* is significant. It is a land of oak trees and vineyards, of good food and wine. There is no mention of economic problems, and its people eat of the fruits of a generous earth. Man seems a harmonious continuation of the land; life is genuine, and it is lived in isolation, away from the strife of civic and social pressures. The Greppo, on the contrary, is a place of nongenuine life and of degenerated land. It is a land of unproductivity: the "wild" has not been tamed and made fruitful; its decadence is attributable to human abandonment. Its appearance is reminiscent of the chaotic landscape of the Decadent painters, with its suggestions of threatening hidden presences, of orgiastic entanglements, of elegant pastiche. The Greppo is a land of tension, ambiguity, and especially boredom. It is dominated by a woman, Gabriella, who is the center of the villa, sets the mood, and directs the activities. She is the typical *belle dame sans merci* (beautiful

CESARE PAVESE
The House on the Hill

*Dust jacket for the British edition of the translation of one of
Pavese's novellas in* Prima che il gallo canti

gna" (Day and night we look for the secret of the countryside). That secret is that the hill is not per se salvific, that the "devil" can infiltrate it. Mombello represents pastoralism, but pastoralism as a way of life is no longer feasible. The golden age cannot be reinstituted: it exists only as an indication of what has been lost. Significantly, Mombello is the place where the three protagonists cannot stay overnight. Greppo, on the other hand, is a decadent countryside, a corrupt mixture of the urban and the rural. There is an explicit affinity between Greppo and Gabriella's husband, Poli, the typical hero of Decadent literature who is bent on self-destruction, devoted to some sort of pseudomysticism and searching for an impossible innocence. The only acceptable form of countryside is the one symbolized by Oreste's village: a place where the need for a mythical content and the ethical imperative of work (myth and Logos) can coexist.

After the all-pervasiveness of the countryside in *Il diavolo sulle colline,* its complete absence is what makes the strongest initial impression on the reader of *Tra donne sole,* where it is replaced by the urban setting. As such absence implies, this is a novel of an abortive return, of what the return cannot be. It is the story of Clelia Oitana, a young woman of humble background, who through hard work and determination, has achieved some degree of success and is sent back to Turin from Rome to open a branch of a large clothing store. This is the crowning moment of her career, and she arrives in her native city with all the confidence and the insecurities of the self-made person. While in Turin twice she ventures into the dilapidated part of town where as a young girl she lived and struggled toward a better life. Thus this is the story of two returns: to Turin and success in the present and to the place of infancy, which signifies poverty, failure, and the abandoned past.

The variation on the usual Pavesean pattern is that Clelia's intention is not to move from one pole to the other, but to use one to enhance the other. The place of infancy is no longer a destination, but a means; it does not motivate the return but instead is a mere happenstance. It serves only as a proof of her humble beginnings, a means of glorifying the present, which remains the only true time for Clelia. Once that has been established, the protagonist will not come back again to her place of infancy. She is a creature of progress; her myth is that of the social climber.

Living "among the lonely women," Clelia has no time for memories, no inclination to relinquish her hold on the present and embark on a real return. Unwilling to abandon her success, she is still unable

woman without mercy) of Decadent literature who uses men and then discards them.

Mombello, Oreste's village, and Greppo are also differentiated in relation to the concept of the feast. At Mombello life is an uninterrupted feast; thus, every act of that existence becomes a religious action. In Oreste's village, though, there is a clear distinction between the everyday and the festive, work and celebration. The feast is only a diluted form of the original event, a commercialized version, a mixture of the sacred and the profane. At Greppo, finally, the feast occurs only when the "milanesi" (people from Milan) come to visit: it is the unnatural celebration on the hill of the corrupted rites of the city, characterized by banality and the debilitating use of alcohol and drugs. It is merely a tragicomic farce.

Pieretto, Oreste, and the narrator had set out on a quest to know the secret of the countryside. "Cerchiamo notte e giorno il segreto della campato be fully integrated into her new social circle. She stands between two worlds, alienated, an outsider to both. So she will live precariously between a lost past and a fragile present: a "lonely woman" among "lonely women." She has lost her past, and the present cannot fill the vacuum; organizing a business cannot make up for the lack of memories. She is a creature of history, unwilling to move toward myth. Clelia arrives in Turin during carnival time; and the carnival theme sets the rhythm of the whole story. In the end, devoid of mythical depth, she has successfully graduated into the life of the carnival. *Tra donne sole* is the story of the impossibility of the mythical feast to reassert itself in its genuine form.

Having explored the odyssey aspect of the return in *La casa in collina*, the quality of the countryside as its termination in *Il diavolo sulle colline*, and its requirements seen through the negative perspective of a nonreturn in *Tra donne sole*, in his last novel Pavese addresses the ultimate issue in a mythology of the return—the question of the possibility of the return as a redemptive event. Does the return satisfy the necessity that has inspired it? What does it reveal? Is the past, or the condition of the past, truly attainable? Can the mythical quality of the mythical age be salvaged by a return to its space? The answer to these questions was already present, explicitly or otherwise, throughout Pavese's work. In Pavese's first poem the cousin of "Mari del Sud" laments that "quando si torna, come me a quarant'anni, / si trova tutto nuovo" (when one comes back, as I did, at forty, / he finds that everything has changed). *La luna e i falò* is the story of a return and of the uselessness of that return.

"Mari del Sud" opens and *La luna e i falò* closes Pavese's activity as a writer. The beginning and the end are mutually reflective: the first opens with the cousin inviting the narrator for a walk on the hill, and the second closes with Nuto inviting him to repeat that experience. In both cases, the significance of the return is explored during a brief but crucial experience on the hill. The structure of the process of the return had been defined in the early poem: one returns, in search of a place and a past, and finds the first changed and the other irretrievable. But the meaning of that structure had developed significantly with the application of mythical categories to the original intuition: it had become a description of the "mestiere di vivere" (business of living) as well as of the "mestiere di scrivere" (business of writing).

La luna e i falò opens with a declaration of tension between time and space, the real protagonists of the novel. The title defines the terms of that tension: the moon, the keeper of time, tracks the sea-

sons; bonfires, mythical rites of fertility for the earth, defines the space; while the conjunction suggests their separation. The novel opens with a statement of the reason for the return of Anguilla, the protagonist:

> C'è una ragione perché sono tornato in questo paese. . . . Ho girato abbastanza il mondo da sapere che tutte le carni sono buone e si equivalgono, ma è per questo che uno si stanca e cerca di mettere radici, di farsi terra e paese, perché la sua carne valga e duri qualcosa di più che un comune giro di stagione.

> (There is a reason why I have come back here to this village. . . . I have roamed around the world enough to know that all flesh is good and is the same; but that is precisely why one gets tired and tries to put down roots, to become soil and village, so that his flesh might mean more and last longer than an average turn of the season.)

Anguilla's return is an effort to conquer time through space. The space of one's infancy determines one's identity and stands against the erosion of time: "Un paese vuol dire non essere soli, sapere che nella gente, nelle piante, nella terra c'è qualcosa di tuo, che anche quando non ci sei resta ad aspettarti" (A village means that one is never alone, one knows that in people, in the trees, in the soil there is part of you that, even when you are not there, is waiting for you). The effort to erase time through space is in essence the mythical quest; and Anguilla's return to the Langhe is a journey toward myth.

If his return to the Langhe implies an abolition of time and a mythologizing of space, then Anguilla's escape to America was an effort to find his own identity through time, for America is to time what the Langhe is to space. As a bastard, Anguilla is attracted to the United States because, as he says, in America "they are all bastards." Bastardy here is defined not in terms of illegitimate paternity (though such is evidently the case for Anguilla) but in relation to space. A bastard is one who does not have his own space, and in the novel Americans are a people on the go, committed to progress, to history, and to time, without ties to the land. America bears the scars of time and waste. In the structure of Pavese's myth of the return, it is the city grotesquely bloated to leviathan proportions.

Anguilla's return from the realm of time and history, America, to that of space and myth, though a profound need, is prompted by music. The memory of the music of his old friend Nuto's clarinet, as in the myth of Orpheus or in Grimm's legend of the piper of Hamelin, has magical power: it calls him back to the realm of myth. After his return, Nuto, as the only

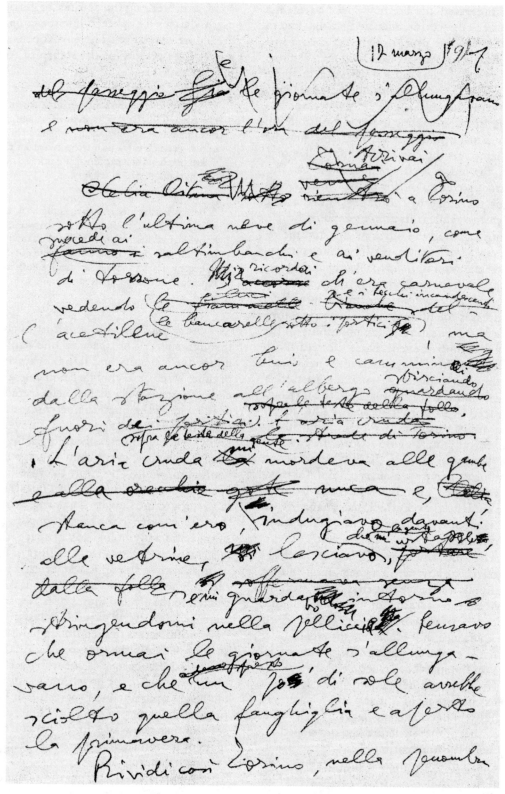

Page from the manuscript for Tra donne sole *(Einaudi Archive, Turin)*

significant survivor from his past, will guide Anguilla in the process of recovering that past.

Anguilla's infancy seems at first completely irretrievable. But the circularity of life in mythical space makes possible the rescue of the past, for it provides for the protagonist a projection of the past into the present. In the family that now has replaced his adopted one at Gaminella, Anguilla finds the small child Cinto, who becomes for the protagonist an alter ego, the repetition of the past in the present. Through the lame Cinto, Anguilla's return to the dilapidated old farmhouse becomes a true descent to original experience, during which the past is rediscovered and absorbed with the immediacy of the present. Soon after, though, Cinto's father, exasperated by poverty and a bestial existence, burns the old farmhouse down. Thus, that part of Anguilla's past ends in a *falò* (bonfire), which signifies his inability to recuperate his own past and move successfully into mythical space. Only Cinto survives, Anguilla's reincarnation in the present, the figuration of the past in the present, the possibility of a new cycle.

The other part of Anguilla's past, his experience as a laborer in the beautiful and rich farm at La Mora, has also vanished. It is again Nuto that makes to the protagonist, on the hill, that final revelation. The last survivor was Santina, the exquisite daughter of the owner. In the last episode of the novel Nuto tells Anguilla that she was killed for being a double spy by the anti-fascist Partisans and, almost reverently, burned on the top of the hill—as if in a falò.

All of Anguilla's past has been destroyed. The bonfires are no longer rites of fertilization but are means of utter destruction and human sacrifice: they declare the final, irretrievable denial of the condition of the past as an attainable goal for the present. The Golden Age, the mythical space, can no longer exist as such. Santina's death also is the result of historical pressures, of the intrusion of historical time into mythical space. Thus three of the "novels of the return" end with an actual death, and the fourth ends with an imminent one. In these novels death, though a mysterious event, assumes the function of an explicatory event, affirming the mixture of history and myth, collectivity and individuality, time and space.

Since historical time cannot be vanquished by mythical space, the return cannot accomplish its ultimate objective. Anguilla realizes this, and his new awareness is the result of his return to the hill. He may have found a home upon his return (as Nuto insists that he did), but he has not found the mythical space of his original quest: temporal, social, and historical concerns have now become associated with that space. Under the stress of time, the purely mythical space has ceased to be. Anguilla will return to Genoa, a place in between, neither America nor the Langhe, yet proximate to both. The journey was intended to go from the moon to the bonfires; but, as the title suggests, moon and bonfires have to coexist in unresolved tension. This tension is the point of arrival of all the four novels of the return and also of Pavese's meditations on myth. It constitutes the true monolith of his writing and defines at the same time the essential characteristic of his myth of the impossible return.

In 1950 Pavese received the highest literary prize in Italy, the Premio Strega, for his trilogy *La bella estate*. That same year his masterpiece, *La luna e i falò,* was published. Shortly after, before his forty-second birthday, in the early morning of 27 August, he died of an overdose of sleeping pills in a hotel in Turin. His legacy as a novelist, however, survives.

Letters:

Lettere, 2 volumes, edited by Lorenzo Mondo and Italo Calvino, (Turin: Einaudi, 1966); translated by Alma E. Murch as *Selected Letters: 1924–1950* (London: Peter Owen, 1969).

Biographies:

Davide Lajolo, *Il "vizio assurdo." Storia di Cesare Pavese* (Milan: Il Saggiatore, 1960); enlarged as *Pavese* (Milan: Rizzoli, 1984);

Dominique Fernandez, *L'échec de Pavese* (Paris: Grasset, 1967);

Lorenzo Mondo, ed., *La vita attraverso le lettere,* edited by Lorenzo Mondo (Turin: Einaudi, 1973);

Bona Alterocca, *Pavese dopo un quarto di secolo* (Turin: Società Editrice Internazionale, 1974);

Alterocca, *Cesare Pavese. Vita e opere di un grande scrittore sempre attuale* (Aosta: Musumeci, 1985).

References:

Annamaria Andreoli, *Il mestiere della letteratura: Saggio sulla poesia di Pavese* (Pisa: Pacini, 1977);

Gian-Paolo Biasin, *The Smile of the Gods: A Thematic Study of Cesare Pavese's Works* (Ithaca, N.Y.: Cornell University Press, 1968);

Giovanni Carteri, *Al confino del mito (Cesare Pavese e la Calabria)* (Catanzaro: Rubbettino, 1991);

Ettore Catalano, *Cesare Pavese fra politica e ideologia* (Bari: De Donato, 1976);

Giovanni Cillo, *La distruzione dei miti: Saggio sulla poetica di Cesare Pavese* (Florence: Vallecchi, 1972);

Cinzia Donatelli-Noble, *Cesare Pavese e la letteratura americana. Saggi e ricerche* (Pescara: Italica, 1983);

Vittoriano Esposito, *Pavese poeta e la critica* (Florence: Vallecchi, 1974);

Gilberto Finzi, *Come leggere "La luna e i falò" di Cesare Pavese* (Milan: Mursia, 1976);

Pio Fontana, *Il noviziato di Pavese e altri saggi* (Milano: Vita e Pensiero, 1968);

Elio Gioanola, *Cesare Pavese: la poetica dell'essere* (Milan: Marzorati, 1971);

Marziano Guglielminetti and Giuseppe Zaccaria, *Cesare Pavese: Introduzione e guida allo studio dell'opera pavesiana, storia e antologia della critica* (Florence: Le Monnier, 1976);

Angela Guidotti, *Tra mito e retorica: Tre saggi sulla poesia di Pavese* (Palermo: Flaccovio, 1981);

Armanda Guiducci, *Invito alla lettura di Pavese* (Milan: Mursia, 1972);

Guiducci, *Il mito Pavese* (Florence: Vallecchi, 1967);

Donald M. Heiney, "Pavese: The Geography of the Moon," *Contemporary Literature*, 9 (1968): 522–537;

Johannes Hösle, *Cesare Pavese* (Berlin: De Gruyter, 1961);

Furio Jesi, *Letteratura e mito* (Turin: Einaudi, 1968);

Erika Kanduth, *Cesare Pavese im Rahmen der pessimistichen italienischen Literatur* (Vienna: Universitäts-Verlagsbuch-Handlung, 1971);

Davide Lajolo, *Cultura e politica in Pavese e Fenoglio* (Florence: Vallecchi, 1970);

Lajolo, *Pavese* (Milan: Rizzoli, 1984);

Verena Lenzen, *Cesare Pavese: Tödlichkeit in Dasein und Dichtung* (München: Piper, 1989);

P. Lorenzi Davitti, *Cesare Pavese e la critica americana: fra mito e razionalità* (Messina-Florence: D'Anna, 1975);

Bruce Merry, "Artifice and Structure in *La luna e i falò*," *Forum Italicum,* 5 (1971): 351–358;

Franco Mollia, *Cesare Pavese. Saggio su tutte le opere* (Padua: Rebellato, 1961; enlarged edition, Florence: La Nuova Italia, 1963);

Lorenzo Mondo, *Cesare Pavese* (Milan: Mursia, 1961);

Antonino Musumeci, *L'impossibile ritorno. La fisiologia del mito in Cesare Pavese* (Ravenna: Longo, 1980);

Musumeci, "Pavese: Stylistics of a Mythology," *Symposium,* 34 (1980): 260–269;

Anco Marzio Mutterle, *L'immagine arguta. Lingua, stile e retorica di Pavese* (Turin: Einaudi, 1977);

Giuseppe Neri, *Cesare Pavese e le sue opere* (Reggio Calabria: Parallelo 38, 1977);

Pieromassimo Paloni, *Il giornalismo di Cesare Pavese.* (Legnano: Landoni, 1977);

Geno Pampaloni, *Trent'anni con Cesare Pavese: Diario contro diario* (Milan: Rusconi, 1981);

Franco Pappalardo La Rosa, *Cesare Pavese e il mito dell'adolescenza* (Milan: Laboratorio delle arti, 1973);

Sergio Pautasso, *Guida a Pavese* (Milan: Rizzoli, 1980);

Ettore Perrella, *Dittico: Pavese, Pasolini* (Milan: Sugarco, 1980);

Luigi Perrotta, *Cesare Pavese e la sua opera* (Naples: Morano, 1975);

Mauro Ponzi, *La critica e Pavese* (Bologna: Cappelli, 1977);

Alfonso Procaccini, "Pavese: On the Failure of Understanding," *Italica,* 3 (Autumn 1985): 214–229;

Procaccini, "Pavese: Tangency and Circumspection," *Lingua e stile,* 18 (July–September 1983): 457–477;

Ruggero Puletti, *La maturità impossibile: Saggio critico su Cesare Pavese* (Padua: Rebellato, 1961);

Philippe Renard, *Pavese: Prison de l'imaginaire, lieu de l'écriture* (Paris: Larousse, 1972);

Julio Manuel De La Rosa, *Cesare Pavese* (Madrid: ESPESA, 1973);

Michela Rusi, *Le malvage analisi. Sulla memoria leopardiana di Cesare Pavese* (Ravenna: Longo, 1988);

Rusi, *Il tempo-dolore. Per una fenomenologia della percezione temporale in Cesare Pavese* (Albano Terme: Francisci, 1985);

Leonard Gregory Sbrocchi, *Stilistica nella narrativa pavesiana* (Rome: Casimari, 1967);

Dietrich Schlumbohm, *Die Welt als Konstruktion: Untersuchungen zum Prosawerk Cesare Paveses* (München: Verlag, 1978);

Maria Stella, *Cesare Pavese traduttore* (Rome: Bulzoni, 1977);

Vittorio Stella, *L'elegia tragica di Cesare Pavese* (Ravenna: Longo, 1969);

Doug Thompson, *Cesare Pavese: A Study of the Major Novels and Poems* (Cambridge: Cambridge University Press, 1982);

Thompson, "Slow Rotation Suggesting Permanence: History, Symbol and Myth in Pavese's Last Novel," *Italian Studies,* 34 (1979): 105–121;

Michele Tondo, *Invito alla lettura di Pavese* (Milan: Mursia, 1984);

Tondo, *Itinerario di Cesare Pavese* (Padua: Liviana, 1965);

Giuseppe Trevisani, *Cesare Pavese* (Milan: Trevi, 1961);

Maria de la Luz Uribe, *Cesare Pavese* (Santiago, Chile: Prensas de la Ed. Universitaria, 1966);

Gianni Venturi, *Cesare Pavese* (Florence: La Nuova Italia, 1969);

Marcello Verdenelli, *La teatralità della scrittura: Castiglione, Parini, Leopardi, Campana, Pavese* (Ravenna: Longo, 1989);

Tibor Wlassics, "Nota sull'America di *La luna e i falò*," *Cenobio* (July–September 1985): 206–208;

Wlassics, *Pavese falso e vero: Vita poetica narrativa* (Turin: Centro Studi Piemontesi, 1985).

Mario Pomilio

(21 January 1921 – 3 April 1990)

Giovanna Jackson
Walsh University

BOOKS: *L'uccello nella cupola* (Milan: Bompiani, 1954);

Il testimone (Milan: Massimo, 1956); translated by Archibald Colquhoun as *The Witness* (London: Hutchinson, 1959); republished as *The Parasites* (London: New English Library, 1962);

Il nuovo corso (Milan: Bompiani, 1959); translated by Colquhoun as *The New Line* (London: Hutchinson, 1961; New York: Harper, 1961);

La fortuna del Verga (Naples: Liguori, 1963);

La compromissione (Florence: Vallecchi, 1965);

La formazione critico-estetica di Pirandello (Naples: Liguori, 1966);

Dal naturalismo al verismo (Naples: Liguori, 1966);

Contestazioni (Milan: Rizzoli, 1967);

Il quinto evangelio (Milan: Rusconi, 1975);

Il cane sull'Etna (Milan: Rusconi, 1978);

Scritti cristiani (Milan: Rusconi, 1979);

La formazione critico-estetica di Pirandello (L'Aquila: Ferri, 1980);

Preistoria di un romanzo (Naples: Guida, 1980);

Il Natale del 1833 (Milan: Rusconi, 1983);

Una lapide in via del Babuino (Milan: Rizzoli, 1991).

OTHER: "Il cimitero cinese," in *La nuova narrativa italiana,* edited by Giacinto Spagnoletti (Parma: Guanda, 1958).

PLAY PRODUCTION: *Il quinto evangelista,* September 1975.

Mario Pomilio

Il quinto evangelio (The Fifth Gospel, 1975), the work that marks Mario Pomilio's maturity as an artist, defines his lifelong experience as a man, as a writer, and as a Catholic. It is also one of the books that defines Italian literature of the twentieth century, for it attests to the clash between the existential and the metaphysical, the modern and the traditional, the malaise of a society bent on self-destruction and the yearning of the individual for salvation. It depicts the final, tremendous encounter between God and man. Since his first novel Pomilio's themes have remained constant. His work reflects the influence of other writers, including Alessandro Manzoni, Luigi Pirandello, Giovanni Verga, Ignazio Silone, and Gabriele D'Annunzio. One can even hear echoes of Elio Vittorini, Georges Bernanos, and Leonardo Sciascia. As a creative writer Pomilio received immediate critical attention, but his readers were confined to those who were drawn to his metaphysical concerns and the inner journey of the soul. He also wrote criticism and leaves a solid body of works, exemplified by *Contestazioni* (Disputes, 1967) and *Scritti cristiani* (Christian Writings, 1979).

Pomilio was born in Orsogna, a small town in the eastern part of Abruzzi. His father, Tommaso, was an elementary-school teacher and a member of the Socialist Party, which became clandestine under Fascism. He taught his son civic responsibility, the value of freedom, and empathy for human suffering. His mother, Emma Di Lorenzo, a fervent Catholic, transmitted to the boy the beliefs and traditions of the church. When Pomilio was eight years old the family moved to Avezzano, where he completed his early studies. His father's socialism continued to be a source of distress; Pomilio wrote years later that his mother lived in constant apprehension when her husband was late coming home.

Pomilio was always a private person who disliked interviews, so bits of his biography must be gathered from the recollections of friends. Giulio Butticci, one of Pomilio's professors of Latin and Greek at the lyceum in Avezzano, draws this picture of his pupil:

> Era un ragazzo simpatico dal viso aperto e cordiale; superava per intelligenza tutti i suoi compagni, ma non aveva l'albagia dei 'primi della classe.... Avendo saputo che io ero in fama di antifascista, seguiva con particolare attenzione ogni mio accenno che sapesse di filosofia, di politica e di critica più o meno scoperta, al fascismo.

> (He was a pleasant boy with an open and cordial face: he was superior to all of his classmates, but he did not have the conceit of the best of the class.... When he learned that I was antifascist ... he followed with particular attention all my references to philosophy, politics and criticism that more or less censured Fascism.)

In 1939 Pomilio was accepted at the Scuola Normale Superiore di Pisa, a highly selective college where students are admitted through a rigorous competition. He studied literature under Luigi Russo, Delio Cantimori, and Cesare Luporini. Some of his professors were members of the clandestine Partito d'Azione (Action Party). Following his military service, Pomilio returned in September 1943 to his hometown, where he lived through a difficult period amid hunger and fear of reprisal from the retreating German troops. The Allied army arrived in Avezzano in July 1944, after which Pomilio worked with others to reorganize the Partito d'Azione.

In 1945 Pomilio finished his studies, writing a thesis on Pirandello, and began to teach in various high schools in Avezzano. When the Partito d'Azione ceased to exist, he became a member of the Italian Socialist Party, to which he devoted a great deal of time and energy. He transferred to Naples in 1949 to teach in a liceo, a secondary school that stresses the study of the humanities. His withdrawal from politics was in part because of his responsibilities but mostly because of his realization that the Socialist Party was straying from its programs and ideals. A grant for advanced study took him to Brussels and Paris, where he had the twofold opportunity to see the consequences of the war and to broaden his intellectual views. Back in Naples in 1953, he devoted himself to teaching in the liceo and at the University of Naples, where he taught Italian literature. His collaboration with Michele Prisco and Rodolfo Doni led to the publication of *Le ragioni letterarie,* a critical journal of short life but of remarkable intellectual scope. The last stage of Pomilio's life was marked by serious illness. He continued to work and to lead a busy life but was aware that he was living on borrowed time. He died in Naples on 3 April 1990 and was buried at Avezzano, in his beloved Abruzzi.

Pomilio was thirty-two when he published *L'uccello nella cupola* (The Bird in the Cupola) in 1954, one year after his return from Paris. It was a difficult period for him: he was disappointed with the Socialist Party and was on the verge of a religious crisis. The story centers on Don Giacomo, a young priest who refuses to recognize that in many cases sin is not a willful choice but the result of circumstances or a series of compromises taken to avoid painful situations. Don Giacomo's life is regulated by familiar routines and events such as births, weddings, and deaths. He is accustomed to a life untouched by adversities and financial concerns. His priesthood is a buttress from which he can look down and dole out his thin formulas of forgiveness and redemption to his docile flock; he is unprepared for the test that comes to him one evening inside his cozy confessional, where moments before he felt as safe as being inside a cocoon.

Suddenly faced with Marta's illicit relationship with her lover, Don Giacomo goes to the room where the man is dying, not out of love as much as out of a sense of priestly duty: to confront the sin, not to comfort the sinner. When Marta later becomes the town's harlot, he reproaches her, ignoring the fact that a woman in her financial situation, surrounded by an unforgiving, provincial society, has few alternatives. When she tempts him, he flees, untouched by the plight of this modern Magdalen and misses the lesson of Christ completely. After he rejects her last gesture of reconciliation with God, she commits suicide; her desperate act breaks the impasse for the priest. He becomes conscious of his narrow view of virtue and sin, of repentance and confession, of his rigid service to the teaching of the church without the nurturing compassion that heals wounds made by sin. Recognizing his faults becomes the first step toward the path of healing.

The controlling metaphor and the title of the novel come from a bird being caught inside the dome of the church. Like Marta, the bird breaks Don Giacomo's comfortable routine. The bird's desperate efforts to find freedom end in its demise just as Marta's efforts prove hopeless. Repeatedly the woman is compared to the image of a bird: "simile a un uccello ferito, ad ali scese" (similar to a wounded bird, with sagging wings). While the plight of the bird is merely a distracting nuisance, Marta's tribulations test the priest's religious vocation.

This early work establishes Pomilio's constant themes and characteristics: the introverted characters given to long, agonizing, sometimes tedious self-analysis; interaction of the Christian principles of sin and redemption; the conflict between liturgical axioms and human impulses; and the tension between social forces and individual convictions. Pomilio's narrative style is marked by richly textured sentences, a precise lexicon, a wealth of images and metaphors, and a delicate humor. Even in this early work one finds that his incomparable use of landscape and interior settings underscores the dispositions of his characters. Light, wind, and rain reflect Don Giacomo's restless soul as he accompanies Marta to the bedside of her dying lover. Wind and empty streets, rain and shadows are recurring images in the novel.

Several critics have correctly related Pomilio's realism to the work of Verga and D'Annunzio. The analogy finds corroboration in the death scene of Marta's lover, with its relentless description of the dying man, his body outlined under the covers, his labored breathing, cold hands, white cheekbones splotched with red patches, the spastic concave area of the stomach, and enough details to fill an entire chapter. The scene echoes similar passages in Verga's short story "Dramma intimo" (Intimate Drama, 1891) and D'Annunzio's Le novelle della Pescara (The Pescara Novellas, 1922). The reader senses that Pomilio's realism crosses into an area that reaches the most private corners of one's being.

Pomilio can also provide a memorable public scene such as the wedding reception attended by Don Giacomo. The priest, the honored guest among his parishioners, feels a gentle benevolence for his flock; the ladies fuss dutifully after him; and a lady with a green hat sits primly next to him. In another room young couples dance. These are the protagonists in a meticulous vignette of provincial life. Pomilio subtly balances irony and tenderness, echoing the humor of Pirandello.

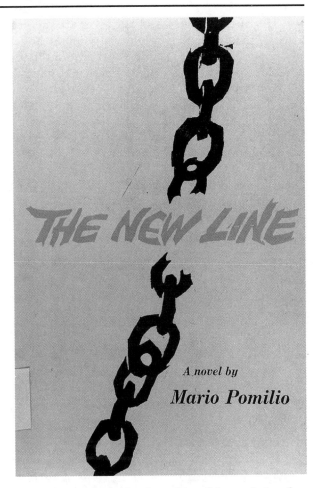

Dust jacket for the American edition of the translation of Pomilio's third novel, in which episodes are connected by the theme of freedom

In 1956 Pomilio published Il testimone (translated as The Witness, 1959), which opens with a sense of foreboding in a Paris of damp and polluted backstreets. Jeanne and her baby soon appear, gaunt, bloodless, and weak, not unlike characters in Emile Zola's Germinal (1885) or John Steinbeck's Grapes of Wrath (1939). The wretched creatures swarming through these pages are predestined by forces beyond their control to fall before they have tasted any joy or comfort. Jeanne is without free will, doomed by the structures of the industrialized, materialistic society that forces her to follow inflexible tracks. In the prison, the scene where the prostitute sucks the milk from Jeanne's engorged breasts, leaving the nipples red ringed from lipstick, calls to mind the universal condition of these sons and daughters of the earth dispossessed of their inheritance. Scenes of great pathos fill the novel, culminating in the description of Jeanne strangling her baby. In this more than any other work Pomilio follows the tenets of the nineteenth-century naturalism and its Italian derivation, called verismo.

Jeanne, her baby, and her lover are the pre-text for the drama that revolves around the police chief, Duclair. He is an able but rigid administra-tor, jaded by years of service in a system that molds all into impersonal, efficient, robotlike state offi-cers. Duclair has managed to avoid corruption but has become cynical, callous, and disillusioned. The death of his daughter several years earlier alien-ated him from his wife. Now they are careful not to disturb one another, tiptoeing around the apart-ment to avoid direct communication and adhering to a monotonous routine to save social appear-ances. Although he is constantly reflecting on death and mulling over suicide, he lacks the deter-mination to act. Once while driving to his office, he barely misses crashing his car and broods, "Potevo morire . . . bastava un attimo e potevo morire" (I could have died . . . one second and I could have died).

Duclair is also alienated from his work. Even after six years in the same office, the room lacks a personal stamp. The large room, cluttered by piles of dusty papers atop old furniture, has a window with crossed bars overlooking a grim, sunless court-yard. It is in this office-prison that he interrogates the accused brought before him. His compassion and strict adherence to regulations seem to swing ac-cording to internal impulses, and in regard to the derelicts he deals with he spins from remorse to aversion. When Duclair encounters Jeanne he is too preoccupied with his own pain to pay attention to the young woman who, through her stubborn si-lence, contributes to his misconception of her. Du-clair investigates the case in which she is a witness in the most peremptory manner, detaching himself from any human contact with her.

In his decisions or in meeting people there is always an unpredictable point that leads him off track. In a restaurant frequented by students, Du-clair meets a girl who engages him in a conversa-tion; they talk about a book she has written titled "L'École de Dieu" (God's School)—a title pregnant with irony. After months, perhaps years, of silence, Duclair feels engaged in a real conversation and be-gins to feel "una vaga disposizione alla tenerezza" (a vague inclination to tenderness). This thawing is short-lived, for he discovers that the girl has duped him for a free lunch. The scene, almost an aside, il-lustrates Duclair's vulnerability, his idealistic nature in constant conflict with the realities of life. Du-clair's invariable question, "Is it right?," emphasizes that justice has roots that are stronger and deeper than human laws. However, he suffers from a kind of moral inertia not unlike the malaise that pervades many characters in twentieth-century literature, so

cerebral and involuted that they lose all initiative. Duclair nevertheless constantly questions the appli-cation of human laws against universal justice: the former often violate the latter.

In *Scritti cristiani* Pomilio asserts that after World War II literature must go beyond ethics and must enter the arena of politics without equivoca-tion or false pleas to its autonomy. After the Holo-caust and the atomic bomb, human beings must for-ever be conscious of riding on the edge between good and evil, truth and falsehood, justice and ineq-uity. In *Il testimone* Pomilio shows through Duclair's struggle to find meaning in the law that justice re-mains blocked by the bureaucracy that dehumanizes both victims and executors.

During a sojourn in Belgium and France (1951–1952) Pomilio observed the process of recon-struction that was occurring there. From this experi-ence, he wrote the hopeful, healing story "Il cimit-ero cinese" (The Chinese Cemetery), which was published in *La fiera letteraria* on 20 April 1958 and later that year included in Giacinto Spagnoletti's an-thology *La nuova narrativa italiana*. The plot is a mere excuse for a spiritual journey that parallels a week-end trip taken by two students. The woman, Inge, is German, and the narrator is an Italian man. They are strangers in search of a common understanding, mutual reassurance, and company.

Pomilio combines the two youths' search for a romantic friendship with their search for identity within the European society in the wake of World War II. He dovetails history and story, showing how exterior forces shape the lives of individuals. He uses a simple narrative line, as the protagonist reports events, the moods of his companion, the be-havior of people they meet, the landscape around them, and their encounter with a Chinese man. The trip takes the two students from Belgium to north-ern France, on the coast near Paris-Plage, Calais, and Dunkerque. Repeatedly they encounter indis-creet people who treat them with contempt: Inge is despised for her nationality, and the narrator is scorned for his. They are in the land of the victors, and the victors resent them and humiliate them. Inge's anger explodes in the cry, "Ma finirà mai una volta?" (Will this [hatred] ever end?) Their journey takes them to the beach where they discover bun-kers built by the German army as fortifications against the Allied invasion, endless cemeteries, and ruins. On one lonely bluff, in a dilapidated farm-house, a woman tells them her son's dementia was caused by German torture.

Inge is anguished because of the guilt she is supposed to feel because of her nationality. Individ-ual responsibility for the collective sin is a theme that is common in postwar literature; here, carried in the persona of Inge, the theme takes on pathos. For the young man the experience of the war is also painful and a cause of constant reflection: "Certo, quattro anni prima qualcosa era finito; qualcosa, in quei quattro anni, l'avevamo seppellito in fondo al cuore. Ma tutti quei morti? Dove avremmo dovuto sotterrarli, per poterli dimenticare?" (Certainly something had ended four years ago; we had buried something in those four years, buried deep in our hearts. But all those dead? Where should we have buried them in order to forget them?) The defeated are ready to start anew, but the victors demand ransom from them and desire their humiliation. In this state of alienation from the human family, Inge's own feelings for her companion are numb. History—not her personal past—violates her where she is most vulnerable: in her feelings of trust and love for another human being.

The journey appears destined to remain sterile until they come upon a small cemetery for Chinese coolies who had been brought to Europe and later abandoned by the English. In a well-kept garden they meet the survivor of the group, an old man who offers words of forgiveness that transcend political ideologies. In speaking of the German soldiers, he gives this simple consolation to Inge: "In fondo, era la guerra, che volete. E poi, anche di loro ne ho visti morire tanti" (After all, it was the war, you know. I saw so many of them die also). In the consoling words of the old man the young couple finds the healing compassion and a sense of peace that liberates their feelings.

The tender story of the two students is drawn over a moving canvas of landscapes, some of breathtaking beauty, some of hideous gloom. The landscapes accompany in a subtle interplay the sentiments and moods of the two lovers. As the story opens, the couple travels through a rural countryside of green hills dotted by narrow roofs and clumps of trees. In a few deft phrases Pomilio paints a pastoral landscape that gives way to the brutal signs of the war: the skeletons of houses, disemboweled fields, trenches, dugouts, hangars, dunes spiked with barbed wire, fields of stony white crosses. The pastoral scenery and the warscapes alternate, their appearance underlining the feeling of instability and tension.

The images and atmospheric details of the wind, the milky gray of the sky, and the salt taste from the sea counterbalance the urban details of sidewalks, streets, shops, torn facades, and the dark profiles of hurried passersby. Pomilio sometimes slows the action by lingering over the landscape before refocusing on the characters. Other natural de-

Dust jacket for Pomilio's 1975 novel, in which the search for a fifth Gospel becomes a spiritual journey for many of the characters

tails, such as the tenuous sun or the flight of birds over the dunes, are synchronized almost musically with the actions and feelings of the characters. In addition to this gift, Pomilio elicits a lyrical rhythm from his words, as in his description of the seashore: "La luce saliva tutta dal mare e le dune, in quell'alone, sembravano alte su noi" (The light rose totally from the sea, and the dunes, in that halo, seemed high above us). His words often have the same soft, melodious tonality and golden-toned flow that one finds in D'Annunzio. In this novella there are many passages that attest to Pomilio's remarkable talent both as a narrator and as a poet.

Il nuovo corso (1959; translated as *The New Line*, 1961) marks a turning point in Pomilio's work in tone, content, and structure. The book consists of a series of episodes bound together by the theme of freedom. In a city the citizens wake up one morning to find freedom; they are spellbound by its presence, whether they embrace it openly or skeptically refuse it. Their actions, their reactions, their thoughts, their doubts, their folly, and their love for freedom form the various dramas within the larger boundaries of the entire tale. The impression the reader receives is the same as viewing a series of paintings in a gallery in which the individual pictures are the collective expression of a single subject.

The first and most notable among the portraits is Basilio, who by virtue of being the most popular newspaper vendor in town, shares with the intelligentsia a sort of leadership. He falls in love with the idea of freedom as soon as the newspaper *La voce della verità* (The Voice of Truth) announces freedom as the new official program of the party. Basilio is carried away by the idea that repression and censorship have been completely eradicated. For one day the whole city exults in its newfound freedom. The following morning everything is back to normal; the newspaper does not carry one hint of that freedom. Disillusioned, Basilio burns his newsstand and himself in a suicide that is a symbolic sacrifice, for only through the purifying flames can Basilio attain true freedom.

Other characters have distinct scenes. There are three workers who decide to take the good news to their nearby hometown, Chinese visitors who are hailed as the harbingers of the new freedom, and workers in a factory where no product is made who finally question the purpose of their activity. Even the old beggar-fool makes a cameo appearance and chooses death over a valueless existence. The images that accompany certain scenes are among the most haunting in all of Pomilio's work. The kite flying over the city with its message of hope is hunted down by the police as a most heinous offense against the state, and a small boy is apprehended and treated like a criminal. The kite flies away carrying its message clearly and bravely to those who yearn for freedom until it falls into a puddle and becomes a limp mess. This image is as evocative as Elio Vittorini's kite in *Conversazione in Sicilia* (1941; translated as *In Sicily,* 1947), where the kite is a symbol of the human spirit that cannot be repressed by a tyrannical government. Pomilio portrays both wise men and fools to illustrate the allegory of freedom as an unattainable but ever desirable goal.

In *Il nuovo corso* Pomilio pioneers a new structure that he will fully develop in *Il quinto evangelio.* The plot is managed through the use of loosely integrated sequences, each with its cast and subplot; but the tone, language, tension, motifs, and theme remain constant throughout. Pomilio maintains the structure by devices such as the use of a contrived time and space, which removes the event from real-

ity and relegates it to the realm of the fable and the parable. Suspense is created by the interruptions in the narrative; the sense of surrealism and the absurd are conjured up by the silences of many of the characters, the scene of empty streets, the mechanized routines of the factory workers, the sense of enormous distances, and the flatness of certain characters.

Pomilio's dialogue is always in character, and his descriptions combine colors, sensations, and rhythms that attest to his craftsmanship as a stylist. During a rally in the piazza, Basilio recognizes the many flags flying "neatly cut against the sky":

> Le une umili, le altre scontrose, le une trepidi e solerti, le altre vigili e ariose, oppure mosse e spigliate e agilmente inastate, oppure lente e pacifiche e vagamente impiegatizie; e ufficiose e commissariali quelle sporgenti dai balconi degli F. P., e azzimate e scrupolose quelle degli appartamenti degli alti gradi, e docili e discrete e indolenti quelle esposte ai terzi piani, e ossequiose e di-messe quelle delle finestre sottotetto, e trasandate come panni stesi quelle pendenti dagli abbaini.

> (Some were humble, others were high-strung, some eager and zealous, others attentive and lofty, or moving uninhibited and lightly masted, or slow and placid and vaguely clerical; those sticking out from the balconies of the party offices looked officious and autocratic; bedecked and scrupulous those from the apartments of high officials; docile, discreet, and languid those from the third floors; obsequious and subdued those from the windows under the roofs; shabby like laundry hung out to dry those from the garrets.)

The description continues, braced by the hammering rhythm of repetition, a device from which Pomilio shifts before it loses its power. Pomilio as a writer is never complacent and always controls his balance even when he plays with language.

Pomilio dramatizes his characters by the careful choice of gestures, turns of phrases, and details of the action. His skill is evident in the episode of the four Chinese visitors who cannot speak a word of the language of their host country. The hosts, for all their efforts, cannot communicate with their visitors except through emphatic gestures, which set off many misunderstandings. The four visitors are entertained, given tours, and toasted; they are bedazzled by all the festivities. They assume that the effusive parade is in their honor. The citizens, on the other hand, are under the impression that the Chinese have brought the new program of freedom, so the whole scene works on the double misunderstanding of the two groups. This makes for a twofold level of reading: on one hand, the situation is comical; on the other, noncommunication illustrates precisely the alienation that exists in a society where a political system has suppressed the exchange of ideas. The humor becomes a horrifying farce when the reader learns that shortly after its departure the plane, bedecked with streamers and signs hailing freedom and carrying the Chinese, is shot down by a military squadron. The humor in this and in other episodes takes a grim turn, reminiscent of the witty, light touch of Pirandello. The novel becomes a bitter satire, for in the end of *Il nuovo corso* Everyman's hope for freedom is destroyed.

Pomilio's early works address specific problems concerning religious, social, and historical topics. In its theme of freedom *Il nuovo corso* encompasses the realms of religion, civic ethos, and history: freedom is as much an expression of the spirit as it is the political expression of society. Written in the wake of the Hungarian uprising against Russia in 1957, *Il nuovo corso* transcends a particular historic event. This work has been called a "conte philosophique" (philosophical story) because of its treatment of freedom, but it is as enjoyable and easily understood as a parable that reveals a simple truth. For Basilio, the Everyman, freedom is a thought that dwells within oneself, nourishes the heart, and drives every action.

The human spirit with its flights into the sublime and its falls into the abyss of depravity is the underlying theme of *La compromissione* (The Compromise, 1965), where the narrator-protagonist, Marco Berardi, embodies the dilemma of modern man trying to rise from a low point in human history represented by World War II. Marco, a young, idealistic professor with leanings toward the ideology of the Left, is lured by the comfortable life of the wealthy middle class. He becomes not only a kind of a pampered parasite but a traitor to his former companions and to his own wife. That he suffers from his self-created cerebral inertia is no comfort to himself or to the reader: he is the saddest character in Pomilio's work—a man without hope. Marco unconsciously reveals to the reader his excuses, lies, rationalizations, lack of remorse, self-indulgence, and projection of guilt on others. Pomilio demonstrates Marco's unstable character, the ambiguity of his goals, his falterings and swings:

Che suo padre fosse un conservatore . . . Che io fossi socialista. . . . Essere comunisti era un modo d'essere . . . esser socialisti, una maniera di sentire. . . . E così vivevo su due piani.

(That her father was conservative . . . That I was a socialist. . . . To be communist was a way of being, to be a socialist a way to feel. . . . Thus I lived on two levels.)

The novel unfolds in a slow movement: the struggles of the Socialist Party are taken up by the professor and his companions, some of whom are veterans of the Partito d'Azione. They are eager to establish a new class of citizens who would replace rhetoric with action. But they fail in their efforts, which are undermined by lack of support, the countercampaign of the church, and the attraction of mellow provincialism with its placid routines—the café, the games of cards, the after-dinner stroll, the flirting and courting among the youths. Petty squabbles and peevish incidents reduce the effectiveness of political action. Marco and his friends often seem to pose as freethinkers, the town's intelligentsia; they like to throw insults at each other; they rabble-rouse around the table in a café but are ineffectual in organizing and in mobilizing support, especially the support of women. Their double standards are especially evident in their treatment of and attitudes toward women, both colleagues and wives.

Pomilio chooses Teramo, a small city in Abruzzi, as the setting for this novel. Teramo is the quintessential Italian provincial town: quiet, with a picturesque landscape, the hub of commercial and cultural life in the historic center, the café with its comfortable clientele, the main street for the evening stroll, the periphery dotted with the villas of the rich. Everyone here knows everyone else; life is public and care is taken to keep up appearances and adhere to unwritten rules of behavior.

In previous works Pomilio's women, with the exception of Inge in "Il cimitero cinese," have been catalysts that sparked the spiritual torment of the male protagonists. In *La compromissione* Amelia De Ritis, first Marco's girlfriend and then his wife, comes across as a woman of sensitive perceptions and strong character. Her wealth, however, dissipates Marco's political commitment. Her father, a consummate politician, gradually draws Marco into the class of the ruling party, the class that he once despised as that of the oppressors. Amelia, who was attracted to Marco because he represented a turn away from the material values of the wealthy landlords and a promise for a new Italy, tries to stand against her husband's assimilation. Every time her father proposes a compromise, Amelia reacts against it and reproaches Marco for his lack of convictions. *La compromissione* dramatizes the disillusionment that a great many Italians felt during the mid 1960s, when the social classes settled into their pre–World War II strata, consumerism invaded all aspects of life, and socialism began to lose its luster. Through his novel Pomilio recalls his own youthful enthusiasm for renewal after World War II and the failures of the postwar society. The value of the novel rests on the story of a personal failure as an allegory for the failure of Italy in the aftermath of the war to achieve equality and true democracy. *La compromissione* is Pomilio's most pessimistic novel.

Although he published critical works in the interim, a decade passed before Pomilio published his next novel, *Il quinto evangelio*. His previous works can be seen as building toward this novel, which contains spiritual and moral questions, intense introspection, highly crafted language, tongue-in-cheek humor, and a legendary, supernatural dimension. Like the architecture of buildings of which the outer and inner shells are connected and mutually supporting, *Il quinto evangelio* has a tale-within-a-tale structure, a vital form in Italian literature since Giovanni Boccaccio's *Decameron*.

Il quinto evangelio is an intricate mosaic of characters and events, which Pomilio uses to reveal the spiritual condition of Everyman. Peter Bergin, an American officer stationed in an abandoned parish house in Cologne, undertakes the search for a presumed fifth Gospel. The effort engages various individuals for many years, as the search for the legendary Gospel is revealed through manuscripts, illuminations, fragments of religious texts, inscriptions, legends, and letters spanning several centuries. The sources are as divergent as a bookish mother superior and a semivagrant, uneducated monk. The restless human spirit is embodied in both major and minor characters as they crisscross most of Europe in their search, sometimes coming close to, but never quite reaching, their objective. Occasionally someone has possession of the fifth Gospel but does not recognize it until it is too late. Such is the fate of Domenico De Lellis, who hands a copy of the apocryphal Gospel to his religious superiors, who seize the manuscript and exile him.

While the goal to find the Gospel remains the objective, the search also becomes an internalized quest for spiritual and moral values. Nowhere in modern Italian literature is the power of words—the basis of the Christian faith—better addressed than in this work. It is a written reference that sparks Peter Bergin's interest and eventually engages him and his disciples in the search for a written text that promises eternal life. The various protagonists are apostles bound by mere sounds or signs, the words that inspire a lifetime of dedication, that can conjure the vision of a utopian afterlife. Many times the encounter with the texts is casual—a curious individual shuffles through the papers left in a drawer, on a chest, on a shelf of a monastery, or in the attic of a farmhouse—but always it is the power of the word that motivates the journey.

The work ends with the play *Il quinto evangelista* (The Fifth Evangelist), supposedly written by Peter Bergin and found among his papers upon his death. The fact that the search for the fifth Gospel ends in a theatrical piece intensifies the ambiguous quality of the book. The autonomous play, which was staged in September 1975, concerns a group of people during the Nazi period who meet secretly to discuss the Gospels to better understand Christ. They find that Christ's trial is inseparable from politics; inevitably the occasion of the trial is transposed to their time, and indictments against Nazism unfold. Religion and politics are inseparable because both involve ethics, though divine and human interests often are in conflict. Like the book, the play is open-ended, and the questions remain unanswered. Pomilio refers to the Vatican Council II as the "passage of fire" because it forced the church to address pressing questions of the present era. The council caused new ferments, new dissensions. *Il quinto evangelio* depicts the conflicting interests between church and state, the individual and society, values and compromises. The church is forever renewing itself precisely because its followers struggle to find truth: Christ is reborn with each generation.

The writer Alessandro Manzoni, who lived from 1785 to 1873—the father of the modern Italian novel—is the principal character of *Il Natale del 1833* (Christmas 1833, 1983), a composite of fiction and biography. The action is minimal: Manzoni's first wife dies on Christmas Day 1833, and the terrible loss is narrated mostly by his mother, Giulia Beccaria. The intense scrutiny of Manzoni's inner self, his painful effort to resolve conflicts between faith and personal tragedy, is conducted in a tormented, unrelenting fashion. In the end Pomilio's Manzoni affirms his solidarity with a suffering humanity.

Pomilio weaves invented material with actual events and excerpts from Manzoni's writings. He invents the letter in which Giulia Beccaria relates Alessandro's suffering and the obsessive actions of a bereaved man. The reader does not know where fiction ends and reality begins; this seamlessness between invention and history is one of Pomilio's remarkable achievements. The work tests his resources as a writer, for to fictionalize Manzoni he must enter the labyrinth of that artist's mind and soul and reveal facets that are unavailable to scholars and critics. Pomilio's piece is also consistent with Manzoni's own notion of writing as a mixture of history and invention.

Mario Pomilio's last work, *Una lapide in via del Babuino* (A Tablet in Via Babuino), published posthumously in 1991, is a short piece of fifty-two pages that concerns an individual's prelude to death. The narrator-protagonist, Pomilio's alter ego, meanders through a reflective journey about things left unsaid or left undone. Aware that death is approaching, the narrator embarks on a journey that is half introspection, half reflection about a story never written. Images from his past come as "residui di sogni" (residues of dreams) and "silenzi di un personaggio non ancora nato" (the silences of a character not yet born), while "silenziose catastrofi . . . disseminano gli spazi di cimiteri stellari," (mute catastrophes . . . disperse, throughout space, cemeteries of stars). Such images leave a haunting impression on the reader.

Mario Pomilio is regarded as one of the most prominent writers of the post–World War II period, and his work has been the subject of many critical studies. *Il quinto evangelio* was awarded the Raymond Queneau Prize in Paris and the Pax Prize in Warsaw. His early works were marked by neorealistic forms that became more experimental with time. His thematic interests, which focus on ethics and modern Christianity, have remained constant. The main themes in Pomilio's work were identified as early as 1954 by Giancarlo Vigorelli, who followed the novelist's career to the end. According to Vigorelli the fundamental point of reference in Pomilio's works is human suffering. Vigorelli calls Pomilio a "Manzonian writer" analogous in discipline and sensitivity to Leonardo Sciascia. Vigorelli observes that Pomilio and Sciascia follow history as a guiding spirit and never stray from the themes of truth and justice; they diverge in that Sciascia pursues a civic direction, whereas Pomilio follows a Christian path. Both writers certainly draw from Pirandello's humor, from his *sdoppiamento,* or schizophrenic introspection, and his use of masks and pretenses.

Other critics have also written perceptively on Pomilio's career. Carmine Di Biase's *Lettura di Mario Pomilio* (1980) traces the development of Pomilio's writing from Neorealism to his experiments with style and form. Vittoriano Esposito's most perceptive commentary focuses on Pomilio's poetry, which has affinities with Eugenio Montale's work. Wanda Rupolo calls attention to the linguistic aspects of Pomilio's work and his poetic sensitivity to words. Several other critics, including Carlo Bo, Geno Pampaloni, Giorgio Barberi Squarotti, and Giuliano Manacorda, have examined Pomilio's art. Challenging and renewing himself constantly as an artist, Pomilio was a writer with an extraordinary talent in drawing modern characters and empathizing with human suffering.

Cover for a 1988 edition of Pomilio's 1983 novel, which is based on the life of the writer Alessandro Manzoni

Interviews:

Claudio Toscani, "Mario Pomilio," in his *La voce e il testo* (Milan: Istituto Propaganda Libraria, 1985);

Franco Zangrilli, "Incontro con Mario Pomilio," *Italian Quarterly,* 26 (1985): 9–31;

Zangrilli, "Mario Pomilio," in *La forza della parola* (Ravenna: Longo, 1992).

References:

Abruzzo: Rivista dell'istituto di studi abruzzesi, special issue on Pomilio, 29 (1991);

Salvatore Battaglia, *Mitografia del personaggio* (Milan: Rizzoli, 1968);

Mariapia Bonanate, *Invito alla lettura di Pomilio* (Milan: Mursia, 1977);

Ermanno Circeo, "Mario Pomilio" in *Letteratura italiana: I contemporanei* (Milan: Marzorati, 1977), pp. 1267–1285;

Carmine Di Biase, "Gratuità della parola," in his *Linea surreale in scrittori d'oggi: 1975–1980* (Naples: Società Editrice Napoletana, 1981), pp. 101–110;

Di Biase, *Lettura di Mario Pomilio* (Milan: Massimo, 1980);

Di Biase, *Mario Pomilio. L'assoluto nella storia* (Naples: Federico & Ardia, 1992);

Di Biase, "Il Natale del 1833 di Mario Pomilio," *Studium,* 79 (1983): 273–283;

Di Biase, "Il personaggio come 'confessore d'anime' in Mario Pomilio," *Cenobio,* 33 (1984): 99–114;

Vittoriano Esposito, *Mario Pomilio narratore e critico militante* (Rome: Edizioni dell'Urbe, 1978);

Silvio Guarneri, "L'esistenzialismo di Mario Pomilio," *Rassegna della letteratura italiana,* 97, no. 2 (1993): 52–61;

Italian Quarterly, special issue on Pomilio, 26 (1985);

Agata Manganaro, *Mario Pomilio* (Florence: Nuova Italia, 1983);

Maria Marchi and Carla Menotti, *Il cristianesimo come profezia in Mario Pomilio* (Rome: Libreria Ateneo Salesiano, 1984);

Antonia Mazza, "Mario Pomilio: Crisi e salvezza dell'uomo," *Libro e spettacolo,* 46 (August–September 1991): 587–604;

Leone Piccioni, "Manzoni e Pomilio: *Il Natale del 1833,*" in his *Proposte di lettura* (Milan: Rusconi, 1985);

Giorgio Pullini, "Il dramma di coscienza nella prima 'trilogia' di Mario Pomilio," *Italian Quarterly,* 26 (1985): 33–50;

Wanda Rupolo, *Umanità e stile. Studio su Mario Pomilio* (Naples: Istituto Suor Orsola Benincasa, 1991);

Ines Scaramucci, "Cultura e profezia," *Ragguaglio librario,* 6 (1980): 202–203;

Scaramucci, "Pomilio e la notte oscura di Manzoni," *Ragguaglio librario,* 1 (1983): 2–3;

Edoardo Scarfoglio, *Mario Pomilio* (Naples: Guida, 1989);

Riccardo Scrivano, "Struttura narrativa del *Quinto Vangelio* di Mario Pomilio," *Otto-Novecento,* 17, no. 1 (1993): 71–88;

Mario Socrate, "Il racconto interrotto di Mario Pomilio," *Rassegna della letteratura italiana,* 97, no. 2 (1993): 71–88;

Franco Zangrilli, "Motivi pirandelliani nel primo Pomilio," *Italian Studies,* 10 (1986): 117–131.

Vasco Pratolini
(19 October 1913 – 13 January 1991)

Anthony Costantini
California State University, Northridge

BOOKS: *Il tappeto verde* (Florence: Vallecchi, 1941);

Via de' Magazzini (Florence: Vallecchi, 1942);

Le amiche (Florence: Vallecchi, 1943);

Il quartiere (Milan: Nuova Biblioteca Editrice, 1944); translated by Peter Duncan and Pamela Duncan as *The Naked Streets* (New York: Wyn, 1952) and as *A Tale of Santa Croce* (London: Peter Owen, 1952);

Cronaca familiare (Florence: Vallecchi, 1947); translated by Barbara Kennedy as *Two Brothers* (New York: Orion, 1962); translated by Martha King as *Family Chronicle* (New York: Italica Press, 1988);

Cronache di poveri amanti (Florence: Vallecchi, 1947); translated as *A Tale of Poor Lovers* (New York: Viking, 1949; London: Hamilton, 1949);

Mestiere da vagabondo (Milan: Mondadori, 1947);

Un eroe del nostro tempo (Milan: Bompiani, 1949); translated by Eric Mosbacher as *A Hero of Our Time* (New York: Prentice-Hall, 1951) and as *A Hero of Today* (London: Hamilton, 1951);

Le ragazze di San Frediano (Florence: Vallecchi, 1949);

Gli uomini che si voltano. Diario di Villa Rosa (Rome: Atlante, 1952);

Il mio cuore a Ponte Milvio (Rome: Edizioni di Cultura Sociale, 1954);

Metello (Florence: Vallecchi, 1955); translated by Raymond Rosenthal as *Metello* (Boston: Little, Brown, 1968; London: Chatto & Windus, 1968);

Diario sentimentale (Florence: Vallecchi, 1956);

Lo scialo, 2 volumes (Milan: Mondadori, 1960); revised edition, 3 volumes (Milan: Mondadori, 1976);

La costanza della ragione (Milan: Mondadori, 1963); translated by Rosenthal as *Bruno Santini* (Boston: Little, Brown, 1964; London: Chatto & Windus, 1965);

Allegoria e derisione (Milan: Mondadori, 1966);

La mia città ha trent'anni (Milan: Scheiwiller, 1967);

Diario del '67 (Milan: Mondadori, 1975);

Calendario del '67. Lettera agli amici salernitani (Salerno: Il Catalogo, 1978);

Vasco Pratolini

Il mannello di Natascia (Salerno: Il Catalogo, 1980); republished as *Il mannello di Natascia e altre cronache in versi e in prosa (1930–1980)* (Milan: Mondadori, 1985);

Cronache dal Giro d'Italia (maggio-giugno 1947) (Milan: Lombardi, 1992).

OTHER: Mario Pratesi, *L'eredità,* edited by Pratolini (Milan: Bompiani, 1942);

Victor Hugo, *Cose viste,* introduction by Pratolini (Turin: Einaudi, 1943);

"Presento il mio libro *Cronache di poveri amanti*," *L'Italia che scrive,* 4 (April 1947): 74;

"Cronache fiorentine del ventesimo secolo, "*Il Politecnico*," 39 (December 1947): 27–29;

"Per un saggio sui rapporti tra letteratura e cinema, *Bianco e nero*," 4 (June 1948): 14–19;

Quello che scoprirai: Antologia per la scuola media, edited by Pratolini and Luigi Incoronato (Florence: Vallecchi, 1953);

"Ho ritrovato i poveri amanti nelle cronache di Lizzani," *Cinema nuovo,* 20 (1 October 1953), p. 207;

Raffaele Viviani, *Poesie,* edited by Pratolini and Paolo Ricci (Florence: Vallecchi, 1956);

"Risposte a Questioni sul neorealismo, *Tempo presente,* 7 (July 1957): 517–530;

"Dialogo con Pratolini sul romanzo," *Quaderni milanesi,* 3 (Spring 1962): 18–26;

Giandomenico Giagni, *Il confine,* edited by Pratolini and Carlo Bernari (Matera: Basilicata, 1976).

Vasco Pratolini ranks among the most important Italian fiction writers of this century. His creative activity spanned a long and difficult period in Italian history from the 1930s to the 1960s. He left a deep imprint on the literature and culture of his time by virtue of the ideological thrust of his work. Few writers in the twentieth century have provoked such intense and conflicting reactions as has Pratolini. In the case of *Metello* (1955; translated as *Metello,* 1968) the debates have gone beyond the field of literature. His narratives always deal with social and historical reality even when, as in his early works, he gives lyrical expressions to his personal life. Pratolini remained faithful to his vision of the novel as an enduring quest for truth marked by social and moral concerns.

Pratolini was born in Florence on 19 October 1913. He lost his mother as a child and was raised by his maternal grandmother. At thirteen he left school and his family and supported himself by performing odd jobs. Following the advice of friends such as the painter Ottone Rosai and the writer Elio Vittorini, he decided to continue his education by reading the works of Dante, Giovanni Boccaccio, Franco Sacchetti, Piero Jahier, and Dino Campana as well as Tuscan authors such as Aldo Palazzeschi, Frederico Tozzi, Renato Fucini, and Mario Pratesi, with whom he shared a spiritual affinity and a strong social commitment. Among foreign writers he read Charles Dickens, Jack London, Theodore Dreiser, and Fyodor Dostoyevsky. At the age of nineteen Pratolini began contributing to *Il Bargello,* a review characterized by anticonformism and populism. He wrote on various ideological and cultural topics consistent with what the Tuscan faction of the Fascist Party thought the ideals of society ought to be. His proletarian consciousness eventually led to an open break with Fascism, and his opposition to Fascism would form the base of his postwar literary career.

Pratolini's earliest works, tentative and amorphous in structure, reflect the themes, style, and even the language of the authors he was reading. He was mainly influenced by verismo, or Italian naturalism, and the style-conscious writers of the *prosa d'arte* (artistic prose). He was also receptive to *strapaese,* a cultural trend that stressed traditional Italian values in opposition to European cultural influence, which was called *stracittà.* Noteworthy among his youthful works that manifest such external forces are the short story "Prima vita di Sapienza" (Sapienza's Early Life), which was published in *Il Bargello* in 1937, and "Una giornata memorabile" (A Memorable Day), both of which he included in his first book, *Il tappeto verde* (The Green Carpet, 1941). The latter story contains social themes that would resurface in later works. His contributions to *Campo di Marte* (1938–1939), a magazine he coedited with the poet Alfonso Gatto, helped him to refine and sharpen his writing style.

In 1940 Pratolini moved to Rome to work for the Ministry of Culture. There he came in contact with a group of Marxist critics, which included Mario Alicata, Carlo Muscetta, and Carlo Salinari. He contributed to a local magazine, *La ruota,* which advocated more realism in literature. His contributions to other magazines such as *Domani, L'Ambrosiano,* and *Rivoluzione* showed his intense interest in social issues. Pratolini's social consciousness was sharpened by his active role in the Resistance against Fascism, an experience that helped shape *Il mio cuore a Ponte Milvio* (My Heart at Ponte Milvio, 1954). At this time he also developed an interest in the French "populist" writers Victor Hugo and Charles-Louis Philippe, as well as in the narrative works of Mario Pratesi.

Pratolini did not go back to Florence after the war. He decided to settle in Rome, where he lived all his life and devoted himself to writing. In a life largely devoid of salient events, his resignation in 1956 from the Italian Communist Party following the Soviet crushing of the Hungarian uprising is noteworthy.

Il tappeto verde is a work of literary apprenticeship: a collection of short prose works that lack homogeneity and artistic focus. Strongly motivated by human empathy, the pieces show a budding artist absorbed by a nostalgic recollection of his childhood. The presence of suffering, illness, and death creates a sense of human tragedy that has the ring of truth. Pratolini's writing centers on such core memories as a dying mother unable to communicate with her son, a childhood spent with grandparents, and his fear of darkness. These are among Pratolini's most personal, traumatic experiences. In "Una giornata memorabile" the evocation of painful memories leads to a sense of liberation as the protagonist discovers friendship and a sense of belonging in his neighborhood.

Adolescent memories are also at the heart of *Via de' Magazzini* (1942), a novella titled after a street in downtown Florence. The salient episodes are the narrator's loss of his mother, his life with his grandparents, and his experience of a first love. Pratolini's next work, *Le amiche* (The Girlfriends, 1943), is a collection of poems, short stories, and diary notes. He explores the world of young people whose problems, hopes, and traumatic experiences are similar to his own. Each chapter of *Le amiche* centers on the sorrowful experience of a young woman.

Il quartiere (1944; translated as *The Naked Streets,* 1952) focuses on a group of ordinary young people in their transition from adolescence to adulthood in the *quartiere* (neighborhood) of Santa Croce, at the height of Fascism's consolidation of its power (1930–1936). The neighborhood is seen as a place of social integration and of individual character development. The memories of the past unfold in a sociopolitical context, and Pratolini's moral consciousness and ideological convictions are evident. Pratolini's persona, here named Valerio, is not the protagonist – as was the case with previous works–but one of the many characters. Initially he faces emotional problems, but the Fascist regime and its colonialist adventures in Ethiopia force him to grow politically and as an individual. Pratolini structures the book as a chronicle, anticipating the narrative form adopted by writers and movie directors of the immediate postwar period.

Pratolini apparently wrote *Cronaca familiare* (1947; translated as *Two Brothers,* 1962), in one week of nearly uninterrupted writing following the death in December 1945 of his brother Ferruccio. It evokes his difficult relationship with his brother and the serious illness that led to his untimely death. The work is marked by emotional intensity and the willful exclusion of fictional elements that would diminish or falsify the relationship between the novelist and his brother. In structure the book follows the narrative rhythm found in *Il quartiere,* and, similarly, it underscores the need for ideological and political commitment in a young man's life.

In 1947 Pratolini published *Cronache di poveri amanti* (translated as *A Tale of Poor Lovers,* 1949) an original work of considerable maturity. It is widely seen as an outstanding work of Neorealism. However, Pratolini avoided the pitfalls of most neorealist writers by skirting ideological premises and opting instead to show the clash of social, political, and moral forces during the Fascist period. The book offers a powerful depiction of the plight of the common people of Florence who despite their neighborhood's downtown location live in a condition of almost self-imposed isolation from the rest of the city. Characters emerge slowly as events are chronicled to paint a full and realistic picture of the Florentine proletariat, unique in terms of culture and traditions, yet representative of the socioeconomic conditions found in other Italian cities. Everyday reality in poor neighborhoods is seen as more important than historic national events, for destitution leaves permanent scars. In this light the title of the novel brings to mind fourteenth-century chronicles such as Dino Compagni's *Cronica delle cose occorrenti* (Chronicles of Present Things) and Giovanni Villani's *Cronaca* (Chronicle) that report the struggle of common people who remain faithful to their beliefs and oppose those who are quick to find accommodation with new political masters. Pratolini's characters represent the collective spirit of a historical era: an entire neighborhood of ordinary, mostly poor people who oppose an oppressive regime. He chronicles their struggle for survival on an almost day-to-day basis.

In 1949 Pratolini published two novels, *Un eroe del nostro tempo* (translated as *A Hero of Our Time,* 1951) and *Le ragazze di San Frediano* (The Young Women of San Frediano), both of which reflect a negative outlook on life. In the first work, he deals with the resurfacing of Fascism in Italy after World War II among certain groups of young people who refused to accept the newly established democratic system. The author abandons his chronicle structure in favor of a traditional, objective representation of social and political conditions. The protagonist Sandrino is receptive to the rhetoric of violence promoted by Fascist propaganda; moreover, he confronts life with the instinctiveness of youth, unmindful of the suffering borne through the years of dictatorships and war. Indifferent to the values of the Resistance, Sandrino, whose father died in the Ethiopian campaign, embraces Fascism to gain a sense of power denied to individuals such as himself, who are confined to the lowest rungs of the socioeconomic ladder. He reflects in his emotional, erratic behavior the instability of the time. Countering this negative hero are two Communists, Faliero and Bruna, who represent reason and social consciousness. Pratolini divides his characters into two groups, representing the forces of good and evil in society – a naive and unrealistic division dictated by his political beliefs.

Some critics at the time faulted Pratolini for abandoning the chronicling of life in the quartiere; some pointed out he had mishandled the dialectical ideology implicit in the story. In retrospect *Un eroe del nostro tempo* is seen as a link between Pratolini's earlier narratives – represented by the evocation of the past and the portrait of lower-class life – and his later phase, marked by historical reconstruction and the realistic re-creation of contemporary events.

Le ragazze di San Frediano is set in Oltrarno, a lower-class section of Florence familiar to the novelist yet lacking the sentimental ties he felt for the Santa Croce neighborhood. This detachment enables him to offer a negative view of the emotional ties that bind a group of young women to a local Don Juan. In the end the women, setting aside their jealous rivalry, decide to join hands to teach him a lesson. Cloaked in the humorous vein of the Tuscan storytelling tradition well known to Pratolini, the story seeks to chastise bourgeois attitudes that survive in the working class, such as excessive attention given to one's looks, flirtation, and sexual conquest.

Il mio cuore a Ponte Milvio, included two years later in *Diario sentimentale* (Sentimental Diary, 1956) is a condensed account of the most important moments in Pratolini's life. A series of short compositions written between 1935 and 1948, it harks back to the memorialist vein of the early Pratolini. The work throws light on dramatic events that influenced his personal development, such as his experiences with a world in which death and violence become a familiar point of one's life; his initial contact with the people of the Via del Corno, the setting of *Cronache di poveri amanti;* and his partisan experience in a working-class section of Rome where he discovered the human dimension of the humble people who fought in the Resistance.

The success of *Cronache di poveri amanti* encouraged Pratolini to conceive the ambitious trilogy called "Una storia italiana" (An Italian Story), a vast historical fresco of Italian society from 1875 to 1945, in which he would illustrate the slow progress toward economic prosperity of the lower classes, the loss of freedom during Fascism, and the failure to realize the yearnings for social justice nurtured by Italians since the unification of the country in 1864.

Metello documents the country's struggle from 1875 to 1902. The presence of a proletarian protagonist, historic incidents of labor unrest, and the salient theme of social justice struck a favorable chord among those who were waiting for a realistic novel

that conformed to the ideas of the Marxist critic György Lukács. Yet those critical of Marxism, especially Catholics, took the opportunity to promote their own agendas: their reaction was so wide-ranging as to transcend literary boundaries and encompass much broader concerns. *Metello* became the cultural event of the season, generating discussions of social and political importance.

With *Metello* Pratolini sought a break with postwar Neorealism by adapting Lukács's ideas related to the novel. The action evolves around a young proletarian figure, Metello, who represents the aspirations of his social class in the struggle for unionization during the latter part of the nineteenth century. Critics differed widely on the accuracy of Pratolini's historical reconstruction. Catholic critics, such as Carlo Bo and Leone Piccioni, suggested that Pratolini should keep to the lyrical vein of his narrative and to the stories of his Florentine neighborhood. Marxist critics such as Carlo Muscetta, Cesare Cases, and Franco Fortini chastised Pratolini for his lukewarm Marxism, for diluting historic facts and not endowing the proletarian Metello with sufficient class consciousness. However, another leftist critic, Carlo Salinari, saw the work as a positive transition from Neorealism to a new form of realism. The French critic Dominique Fernandez wrote that Pratolini "è riuscito con *Metello* a fare un romanzo proletario, dotato della stessa qualità di logica e di finezza del romanzo borghese" (has succeeded with *Metello* in writing a proletarian novel endowed with the same structural and stylistic qualities of the bourgeois novel).

Pratolini created a convincing character in a historical context. Metello's ideological consciousness is consistent with the level reached by the Italian working class at the turn of the century, when it was moving from a recent anarchic past to a centralized, well-organized structure provided by the labor unions and the Socialist Party. He resisted creating a character totally committed to the aspirations of Russian socialist realism. Pratolini represents reality by capturing history in its daily making, not as an abstract class struggle, but as a concrete conflict of interests. He showed the effect of memorable historic events that marked the beginning of Italian socialism in the 1880s, when workers were fighting to improve living conditions and union leaders, rather than fomenting revolutions, were promoting class consciousness.

Metello is the story of the education of a man who makes a series of mistakes in both his private and public life. Rather than a Marxist idealist, he is a man who recognizes his limitations, tries to learn from his mistakes, and moves toward psychological maturity and class consciousness. Initially Metello is inclined to respond to the typical impulses of youth, but he learns the value of work and the needs of his social class. Recognizing his need for a family, he tries to let the private and public dimensions of his life develop together, though his actions may still prove inconsistent at times. While courting a young woman, he misses an important union meeting, which has a negative effect on a planned strike. During the strike, however, he becomes one of the leaders and spurns his boss's attempt to buy him off with a promotion. Eventually the time he spends in jail completes his maturation and solidifies his ideological convictions.

Metello is a well-knit narrative told by an omniscient narrator who neatly weaves together the protagonist's public and private lives up to the crucial episode of the strike, which he dominates even when he is not physically present. Pratolini focuses on the elaboration of Metello's character, especially through his interaction with other characters, with each relationship revealing a fresh dimension of his personality. His descriptions of the protagonist's experiences are always in tune with his state of mind.

In the next novel of the trilogy, *Lo scialo* (The Waste, 1960), Pratolini turned his attention to the crisis of the middle class, which, fearing the loss of its socioeconomic hegemony, facilitated the victory of Fascism. Faithful to his own brand of realism, Pratolini, as he stated in *Tempo presente,* avoids "ogni nomenclatura, ogni naturalismo, ogni agiografia, ogni andante veristico, come ogni e qualsiasi astrazione" (all fixed rules, stereotypical approaches, hagiography, naturalism, or any form of abstraction). Pratolini strove to give an all-encompassing view of reality by capturing even the details that make up daily life. Salvatore Battaglia has called this realism a "rivelazione delle infinite possibilità del vivere" (revelation of the infinite possibilities of living). Essentially, Pratolini sought to capture the character of the early twentieth century through a narrative account focused on the waste of life and energy through reliance on appearances and pretense, on illusions masquerading as promises, and on the enticing forces of power and violence. *Lo scialo* portrays evil under the guise of corruption, ambivalence, moral impotence, violence, and sexual perversions.

The former chronicler of the proletariat thus joins the European tradition of Thomas Mann, Robert Musil, Italo Svevo, and Alberto Moravia in his unrelenting analysis of the decadence of the middle class. Francesco P. Memmo called *Lo scialo* "un libro nel quale nessuno dice la verità, o meglio ciascuno si finge una propria (falsa) verità, e tutti ricercano un alibi per le proprie azioni attraverso la deformazi-

Cover for a 1995 edition of Pratolini's 1955 novel, in which the protagonist participates in the nineteenth-century Italian labor movement

one, in buona o mala fede, della verità" (a book in which no one tells the truth, or better, everyone fashions a false truth, and searches for alibis for his actions through distortions of the truth, made in good or bad faith). For his canvas of middle-class moral decay Pratolini chooses a group of families that reflect the distinctive aspects of Florentine society, from the Corsini-Vegni, a family willing to enrich itself by illegal means, to the Maestri-Batignani, a family eager to climb the social ladder and find access to the upper class. He offers an array of characters of diverse social background and ideological orientation, from the working class to the aristocracy. Their conflicting relationships drive a compelling narrative. As is remarked in the novel, "La forza di un romanzo consiste nel darci, della vita, non l'immagine dentro uno specchio, ma il suo inesorabile movimento" (The strength of a novel consists in rendering the inexorable movement of life, not its reflection in a mirror).

Critics were bothered by what they saw as the excessive number of characters and the sprawling nature of the work. Emilio Cecchi called *Lo scialo* "un romanzo inflazionistico" (an inflationary novel); Piero de Tommaso underlined the lack of a "principio unitario di composizione [in] un'opera le cui fila non si raccolgono in un'unità" (unifying principle of composition in a work whose plotlines do not come together). On the other hand, Claudio Varese appreciated the attention to the details of daily life. He remarked that, whereas in *Metello* history appeared as a movement of dialectical forces, in *Lo scialo* history is the life that flows in the consciousness of the characters and is captured in a series of apparently negligible events. Significantly, Pratolini chose Montale's verses as the epigraph to the text: "La vita è questo scialo di triti fatti, / vano più che crudele. / E la vita è crudele più che vana" (Life is this big waste of routine events, / useless more than cruel waste. And life is cruel more than useless).

To illustrate better the relativism and subjectivity of human perception within his grand canvas, Pratolini resorted to sophisticated narrative strategies. The egotistical self-isolation of the characters and their internal conflicts and torments are expressed through the interior monologue and the diary entries. The presence of a first-person narrator and the multiple voices afforded by the crowd scenes yield an engaging and multilayered text. In this regard *Lo scialo* foreshadowed the experimentalism of the neo-avant-garde that followed the work.

Pratolini's next novel, *La costanza della ragione* (1963; translated as *Bruno Santini*, 1964), does not belong to the trilogy, but it is connected to it since it deals with the generation that grew up immediately after World War II. Pratolini pointed out in the *Corriere della sera* of 5 May 1963 that that generation "vuole essere semmai la risposta, appunto anticipata, agli interrogativi rimasti naturalmente aperti sulle pagine di quei primi due libri della trilogia" (seeks an answer to the questions raised by the first two volumes of the trilogy). As in *Un eroe del nostro tempo,* Pratolini deals with young men who have not suffered the experience of Fascism, World War II, and the ideological persecution borne by their parents. They have, however, witnessed the crisis of the Communist Party resulting from the Soviet invasion of Hungary, the disclosure of Stalin's crimes, the decision by the Italian Communist Party to embrace European communism and to play the political game according to democratic rules. Free of the sins of their fathers, the postwar generation claims

morality and reason as the basis of their ideological convictions and political choices and accuses their elders of having committed major blunders. The falsehood of this claim becomes increasingly evident as the story of the young protagonist, Bruno Santini, unfolds.

The narrator-protagonist believes he is telling the story of a young man's emancipation from the physical and emotional protection offered by his long-widowed mother and his mentor, an old family friend and longtime Communist. But, behind his accusations of compromise, hypocrisy, and sentimentality, and the repeated boasts of his own rationality, clearmindedness, and devotion to truth, his life is replete with contradictions, sentimentality, and political compromise. He is also exploitative in sexual relationships. The novel's first-person narrator proves quite effective. Searching for the truth by recalling the past and comparing it to the present, he strives to show the fallacy of his mother's and his mentor's points of view. However, he unwittingly allows their truth to filter through to his own conscience and thus to become an unavoidable part of his own truth, no matter how hard he tries to exorcise it.

The trilogy of "Un storia italiana" was completed in 1966 with the publication of *Allegoria e derisione* (Allegory and Derision). It is a difficult book, not loved by the critics, covering the period from 1930 to 1945. The time span corresponds to Pratolini's artistic and ideological maturity and to that of his protagonist-narrator, Valerio, a character from the earlier works. Valerio is an intellectual who believes that the memory of the past has value only if it has a functional connection to the present and it is not simple nostalgia. Perennially engaged in a problematic search for reality, Valerio is subject to all the ambiguity, doubts, and uncertainty of the intellectual in the twentieth century. He believes that literature is significant only insofar as it becomes a quest and bridges the dichotomy between thought and action, between one's will and the consciousness of one's failure as a human being and a writer.

The basic theme of the book is the ambiguity that pervades love, friendship, hope, isolation, and delusion. The protagonist finds this ambiguity in his past, in his love for the family, and in his work as a writer. While the ambiguities of his emotional relationships remain within the private sphere of his life, the ambiguities that infiltrate his ideological and literary commitments generate more-complex problems. Although he belonged to the Fascist Party, he was a youthful militant in its left wing, under the illusion that Italian Fascism could take a Marxist orientation. Another ambiguity, he feels,

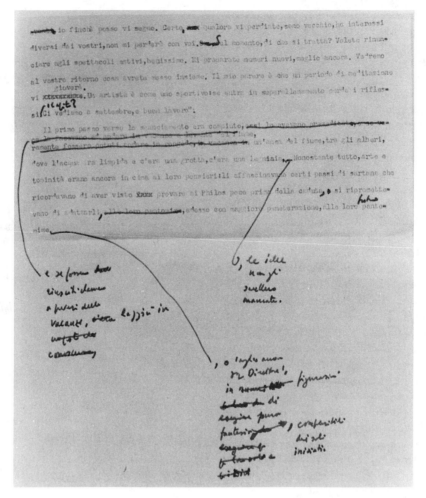

Page from the revised typescript for Allegoria e derisione *(Vasco Pratolini Collection)*

has accompanied his literary career. During the Fascist period Valerio's aspiration to write novels is curbed to the point that he succeeds only in writing a series of notes. After the Ethiopian campaign, when his faith in Fascism wanes and he embraces Marxism, he tries to overcome his intellectual crisis by identifying with the tenets of Hermetism, which stresses self-analysis and the dictates of individual conscience rather than social problems. That experience causes isolation and a deeper chasm between his actions and his convictions. Finally he joins the Communist Party, an experience that generates new ambiguities, for a writer cannot accept the dictates of an autocratic political organization if he needs to remain faithful to his role in society as an intellectual and a seeker of truth. In the early 1960s, when Italian critics were debating the crisis of the novel and the ideas of the French *nouveau roman* (new novel), *Allegoria e derisione* surprised many literati because of its adherence to the old-fashioned belief that the quest for truth should be the primary objective of the novel. In this regard it is important to note that Pratolini's structural and linguistic innovations were anchored to the search for moral and ideological values.

From 1966 to 1991, while well-known writers published novel after novel and enjoyed the financial rewards of the publishing world during the years of the economic boom, Pratolini preferred to remain virtually silent, publishing only a few books of poems, including *La mia città ha trent'anni* (My City is Thirty Years Old, 1967) and *Calendario del '67* (Calendar Year 1967, 1978). In 1989 he published the letters that he and Romano Bilenchi had exchanged for more than thirty years, *La lunga attesa. Lettere a Romano Bilenchi, 1933–1972* (The Long Wait: Letters to Romano Bilenchi).

Pratolini was an innovative writer: he did not rewrite the same book but evolved from early lyricism to his neorealistic chronicles to his own version of realism. For the most part, critics have been unwilling to recognize his process of constant renewal.

Since the 1980s a new generation of critics, less tied to partisan ideology, has attempted to reassess Pratolini's work, and his integrity as an artist has begun to be appreciated.

Letters:

La lunga attesa. Lettere a Romano Bilenchi, 1933–1972 (Milan: Bompiani, 1989);

Lettere a Sandro, edited by Alessandro Parronchi (Florence: Polistampa, 1992).

References:

Alberto Asor Rosa, *Scrittori e popolo* (Rome: Samonà e Savelli, 1965), pp. 216–230;

Asor Rosa, *Vasco Pratolini* (Rome: Edizioni Moderne, 1958);

Salvatore Battaglia, "*Lo scialo* di Vasco Partolini," *Filologia e letteratura,* 31 (1962): 246–252;

Giancarlo Bertoncini, *Vasco Pratolini* (Rome: Edizioni dell'Ateneo, 1987);

Nino Betta, *Pratolini* (Trento: Innocenti, 1972);

Mirko Bevilacqua, *Il caso Pratolini* (Bologna: Cappelli, 1982);

Carlo Bo, "L'Italia non lo sapeva," *L'Europeo,* 24 July 1960, pp. 49–53;

Italo Calvino, "Opinioni su *Metello* e il neorealismo," *Società* (February 1956): 207–211;

Emilio Cecchi, *Letteratura italiana del Novecento* (Milan: Mondadori, 1972), pp. 1102–1112;

Anthony G. Costantini, *Apprendistato e arte di Vasco Pratolini* (Longo: Ravenna, 1986);

Dominique Fernandez, *Il romanzo italiano e la crisi della coscienza contemporanea* (Milan: Lerici, 1960), pp. 201–213;

Marco Forti, *Prosatori e narratori nel Novecento italiano* (Milan: Mursia, 1984), pp. 305–321;

Franco Fortini, *Saggi italiani* (Bari: De Donato, 1974), pp. 217–228;

Olga Lombardi, *Narratori italiani del secondo 1900* (Ravenna: Longo, 1981), pp. 34–44;

Lombardi, *Narratori neorealisti* (Pisa: Nistri-Lischi, 1955), pp. 26–30;

Fulvio Longobardi, *Vasco Pratolini* (Milan: Mursia, 1964);

Romano Luperini, *Il Novecento,* volume 2 (Turin: Loescher, 1981), pp. 541–547;

Giorgio Luti, "Le giornate memorabili di Vasco Pratolini," *Nuovi argomenti,* 38 (April–June 1991): 26–44;

Giorgio Manacorda, *Storia della letteratura italiana contemporanea, 1940–1965* (Rome: Editori Riuniti, 1967), pp. 118–123, 235–241;

Francesco P. Memmo, Introduction to *Allegoria e derisione,* by Pratolini (Milan: Mondadori, 1983), pp. 5–39;

Memmo, *Pratolini* (Florence: La Nuova Italia, 1977);

Memmo, ed., *Romanzi/Vasco Pratolini* (Milan: Mondadori, 1993);

Franco Mollia, *Nostro Novecento* (Rome: Cremonese, 1961), pp. 575–582;

Rocco Montano, *Lo spirito e le lettere,* volume 4 (Milan: Marzorati, 1971): pp. 331–340;

Carlo Muscetta, "*Metello* e la crisi del neorealismo," in his *Realismo, neorealismo, controrealismo* (Milan: Garzanti, 1976), pp. 106–160;

Pietro Pancrazi, *Scrittori d'oggi,* volume 5 (Bari: Laterza, 1950), pp. 69–81;

Walter Pedullà, *La letteratura del benessere* (Rome: Bulzoni, 1973), pp. 813–818;

Luciana Pietrosi Barrow, *Dal neorealismo allo sperimentalismo* (Rome: Trevi, 1968), pp. 67–72;

Giorgio Pullini, "Vasco Pratolini," *Belfagor,* 5 (September 1953): 553–569;

Eugenio Ragni, *Letteratura italiana contemporanea* (Rome: Lucarini, 1980), pp. 667–683;

Mario Razetti, *Come leggere "Metello" di Vasco Pratolini* (Milan: Mursia, 1975);

Frank Rosengarten, *Vasco Pratolini* (Carbondale: Southern Illinois University Press, 1965);

Carlo Salinari, "Discussione e conclusioni su *Metello,*" in his *Preludio e fine del realismo in Italia* (Naples: Morano, 1967), pp. 107–127;

Salinari, "Involuzione di Pratolini," in *Preludio e fine del realismo in Italia,* pp. 271–282;

Nicola Tanda, *Realtà e memoria nella narrativa di Vasco Pratolini* (Rome: Bulzoni, 1970);

Michele Tondo, *Cronache di narrativa contemporanea* (Matera: Montemurra, 1966), pp. 114–123;

Claudio Varese, "Vasco Pratolini," in *Occasioni e valori della letteratura italiana contemporanea* (Bologna: Cappelli, 1967), pp. 305–310;

Gianfranco Venè, *Letteratura e capitalismo in Italia* (Milan: Sugar, 1963), pp. 649–678;

Giancarlo Vigorelli, "Opinioni su *Metello* e il neorealismo," *Società,* 11 (December 1955): 1139–1144;

Carlo Villa, *Vasco Pratolini* (Milan: Mursia, 1975).

Michele Prisco
(18 January 1920 –)

Carmine Di Biase
University of Salerno

Translated by Augustus Pallotta

BOOKS: *La provincia addormentata: Racconti* (Milan: Mondadori, 1949);

Gli eredi del vento (Milan: Rizzoli, 1950); translated by Violet M. Macdonald as *Heirs of the Wind: A Novel Translated from the Italian* (London: Verschoyle, 1953);

Figli difficili (Milan: Rizzoli, 1954);

Fuochi a mare (Milan: Rizzoli, 1957);

La dama di piazza (Milan: Rizzoli, 1961);

Punto franco (Milan: Rizzoli, 1961);

Una spirale di nebbia (Milan: Rizzoli, 1966); translated by Isabel Quigly as *A Spiral of Mist* (New York: Dutton, 1969; London: Chatto & Windus, 1969);

Inventario della memoria (Milan: Rizzoli, 1970);

I cieli della sera (Milan: Rizzoli, 1970);

Gli ermellini neri (Milan: Rizzoli, 1975);

Il colore del cristallo (Milan: Rizzoli, 1977);

Le parole del silenzio (Milan: Rizzoli, 1981);

Il romanzo italiano contemporaneo (Florence: Cesati, 1983);

Lo specchio cieco (Milan: Rizzoli, 1984);

Ritratti incompiuti (Rome: I.P.S., 1986);

I giorni della conchiglia (Milan: Rizzoli, 1989);

Terre basse: 25 racconti (Milan: Rizzoli, 1992);

Il cuore della vita (Turin: S.E.I., 1995);

Il pellicano di pietra (Milan: Rizzoli, 1996).

TRANSLATION: François Mauriac, *Lo scimmiottino* (Milan: Mondadori, 1959).

Michele Prisco in 1967

Since he appeared on the literary scene in 1949 with a collection of short stories, *La provincia addormentata: Raconti* (The Sleepy Province, 1949), Michele Prisco has chosen as his narrative domain the complex and mysterious world of the human conscience. At the same time, he has gained attention for his interest in the mores and values of the middle class in the large towns around Naples. In his uncharitable probing Prisco focuses on bourgeois decorum, which, on close examination, masks compromises, intrigues, and hypocrisy. In some instances evil lurks behind the appearance of respectable conduct and good intentions.

The youngest of eleven children, Prisco was born on 18 January 1920 in Torre Annunziata, a coastal town south of Naples, to Salvatore Prisco, a lawyer, and Annamaria Prisco. In 1936 the sixteen-year-old Prisco wrote in a notebook: "Scrivendo io voglio arrivare al fondo dell'uomo, voglio che gli uomini, leggendomi, imparino a conoscersi e forse, sbigottiti della loro capacità di fare del male, ad essere più buoni" (With my writing, I want to reach the depths of a human being; I want my readers to know themselves and perhaps become better individuals once they are dismayed at their capacity to do ill to others). Following a family tradition, he studied law, graduating from the University of Naples in 1942. That year he published his first short story, "Gli alianti" (The Gliders), in the journal *Lettura*. Prisco performed his military service in Scuola Allievi Ufficiali di Complemento (Reserve Officers Military School) in 1942–1943 and wrote for newspapers and journals such as *Il messaggero, Il Mattino, La fiera letteraria, Mercurio, Tempo presente, Aretusa,* and *Risorgimento.*

La provincia addormentata, which won the prestigious Strega prize, is a collection of eight stories (two more would be added in a 1969 edition) set, as most of Prisco's works would be, in the province of Naples. In the stories Prisco probes the shadowy innermost areas of individual psyches in a static and monotonous social setting; the external calm hides a subterranean emotional life of fears, unfulfilled desires, and deep anxieties. The extraordinary beauty of the physical setting is juxtaposed to the psychological misery of those who inhabit it. Prisco writes in the preface: "Allora quell'inconsueto paesaggio vesuviano, si rivela una specie d'inferno al quale sono stati condannati i personaggi delle singole vicende" (In that regard, the unusual Vesuvian landscape proves to be a sort of hell to which the characters of the individual stories have been condemned).

Family, arranged marriages, the drive to succeed, and pathological emotions – the last, primarily of the female characters – are the main elements of Prisco's second novel, *Gli eredi del vento* (1950; translated as *Heirs of the Wind,* 1953). The title is drawn from Prov. 11:29, "He that troubleth his own house shall inherit the wind." In a provincial town near Naples the police chief, Mazzu, marries a woman of means; when she dies, he marries her sister. The situation is repeated until he has married all five daughters of the prosperous family. Mazzu is greedy and opportunistic; each of the sisters accepts his proposal to fill her inner void. In the end, no one finds the happiness or tranquility that all were seeking.

On 6 October 1951 Prisco married Sarah Buonomo; they have two daughters, Annella and Caterina. In his next novel, *Figli difficili* (Difficult Children, 1954), set during and immediately after World War II, Prisco attempted, as he points out in the preface, "di scrivere il romanzo di una generazione" (to write the novel of a generation). Giuditta, unhappy in her marriage, compensates by trying too hard to make her children happy; she succeeds only

in making them "difficult." Prisco denounces those victims of a bourgeois mentality who "agonizzano nelle sabbie mobili delle loro colpe" (agonize in the quicksands of guilty feelings).

The Neapolitan review *Le ragioni narrative,* which was published in 1960–1961, championed the traditional novel while most other literary journals were announcing the death of the genre. In its first issue (January 1960) the journal affirmed its "irriducibile fiducia nella narrativa come operazione portata sull'uomo: in una narrativa cioè, che abbia l'uomo, i suoi problemi, il suo essere morale e sociale a proprio centro di interesse" (incontrovertible trust in the narrative as a cultural activity based on the individual: a narrative, that is, which has man, his social and moral being, as its central interest). In the first issue Prisco published an article, "Fuga dal romanzo" (The Flight from the Novel), which opposed avant-garde narratives such as the French "new novel" espoused by Michel Butor and Alain Robbe-Grillet as "il contrario stesso della narrativa" (the opposite of the novel). In this essay collected in *Il romanzo italiano contemporaneo* (1983) Prisco looks to such writers as Gustave Flaubert, Fyodor Dostoyevsky, Katherine Mansfield, and François Mauriac as models.

La dama di piazza (The Lady in the Limelight, 1961) is one of the high points in Prisco's fiction. In immediate postwar Naples the main character, Aurora, marries a much older man, a member of the lesser aristocracy, in order to gain social status. Aurora, whom the critic Giacinto Spagnoletti calls the Neapolitan Moll Flanders, is subjected to prejudice because of her humble background. In the end she is defeated and is left only with memories of the compromises she made along the way. Prisco's relentless probing of her aspirations, values, and desires evokes both sympathy and repulsion in the reader.

The problem of evil is a fundamental theme in Prisco's novels *Una spirale di nebbia* (1966; translated as *A Spiral of Mist,* 1969), *I cieli della sera* (Evening Skies, 1970), and *Gli ermellini neri* (The Black Ermines, 1975). The labyrinthine psychological detective novel *Una spirale di nebbia* takes place over a span of three days. Fabrizio, the main character, lives a comfortable life in a town near Naples; one day he finds his wife dead from a blow to the head. The police are unable to determine whether her death was an accident or murder. As the townspeople speculate about the case, the prosecutor uses his own unhappy marriage to assess Fabrizio's possible involvement in the death. The "mist" or "fog" of the title is a symbol of the hypocrisy and deceit that lurk in the dark recesses of consciences intent on fleeing the light of truth.

I cieli della sera is a well-crafted thriller infused with extensive psychological analysis. The narrator, David, leaves his home in northern Italy and travels to his native town in the south "per dare un senso alla violenza del mondo dopo di aver misurato la violenza che è in ciascuno di noi" (to make sense of the violence in the world after I have measured the violence that is present in each of us): his mother has died in a suspicious automobile accident, and his father has committed suicide after killing an old friend. An atmosphere of violence and crime envelops the story. David's trip to the south is also a return to his own past as he tries to find answers to nagging questions about his adolescence.

In the December 1971 issue of *Il ragguaglio librario* Prisco clarified his views regarding experimentation:

Oggi si fa un gran parlare di rinnovamento di linguaggio in narrativa, e di sperimentazione linguistica. Nei miei ultimi libri, penso che sia rintracciabile piuttosto una sperimentazione stilistica che, ritengo, ha altrettanta validità e diritto di esprimersi.

(Today there is a lot of talk about renewing narrative language and experimenting with style. I believe that in my latest books one can find a different way of experimenting with style which is equally valid and has a right to express itself.)

Among the stylistic experiments Prisco identifies in his work are variations in narrational point of view; the depth of his characters' inner life; and an emphasis on memory.

Gli ermellini neri is a search, as Prisco notes in the preface, "che non è il male quotidiano, meschino e mediocre, con le sue squallide miserie, della chiassosa volgarità della vita, ma il male in assoluto, quello che tocca le vere profondità, i veri orrori, gli atroci meandri della perdizione" (not for the everyday evil, the petty and mediocre evil of the gaudy crudeness of life with its squalid wretchedness, but absolute evil, the evil that touches the real depths, the true horrors, the atrocious meanders of damnation). The characters in this work are not the familiar bourgeois figures of the Neapolitan hinterland leading lives of passive indolence. Alvaro, emblematic of the ambiguity of contemporary society, retraces his initiation into evil even as he remains, to the end of the novel, convinced of his innocence. As a young man he was sent to a seminary, where a classmate introduced him to the ways of evil. The novel posits the question: "Da quali tenebre, da quali ferite immedicate e immedicabili zampilla a un

tratto il male dentro di noi?" (From what dark recesses, from what unmedicated or untreatable wounds does evil issue forth within us?). After leaving the seminary and experiencing years of aimless wandering, Alvaro finds himself in the deep south of Italy struggling to give meaning to his life. In retracing the tortuous path of his existence, the protagonist has to face himself.

The novel *Le parole del silenzio* (The Words of Silence, 1981) begins with the words: "Perchè voleva ricordare; perchè se il ricordo resta costante e inalterato sino a farsi continuo diventa pure un modo di rianimare il passato e ancor più la vita e adesso solo questo voleva, ricordare" (Because she wanted to remember; because if a memory remains constant and unaltered to the point of being a continuum, it becomes a way of reviving the past and even life itself; now that was all she wanted: to remember). Following the death of her husband, Cristina relives the main stages of her life in her memory in order to communicate with herself and with others through "words of silence." The novel examines the relationship of external reality to one's inner life.

In *Lo specchio cieco* (The Blind Mirror, 1984) the main character, Margherita, is shown in a double light: as the colorless girl who spent her youth in the province and as the strong and self-assured woman the narrator meets in Rome many years later. The reader is implicitly asked which is the real Margherita. The truth is revealed at the end of the book: "Bastava solo accettarla [la verità] abbandonarvisi, senza porsi problemi o perdersi nell'oscura contabilità delle interpretazioni, e allora la vita si ricongiunge con sè stessa e diventa più facile andare avanti" (One only needed to accept the truth and yield to it, without posing problems or losing oneself in the dark forest of interpretations; once that is done, life is joined to itself, and it becomes easier to go forward).

In 1986 Prisco published *Ritratti incompiuti* (Incomplete Portraits). The book is a collection of original and illuminating essays on major twentieth-century writers such as François Mauriac, Corrado Alvaro, Giuseppe Berto, and Giuseppe Ungaretti.

The novel *I giorni della conchiglia* (The Days of the Seashell, 1989) deals with a man's search for his identity. The forty-year-old Mauro was adopted at age six; in his effort to recover his past he discovers that Luca, whom he believed to be his older brother and who died tragically, was actually his father. In the end, Mauro finds that the solution lies in living in the present, with his wife and a son, rather than trying to resurrect the past: "La vita cammina, e si dimentica vivendo" (Life marches on and is forgot-

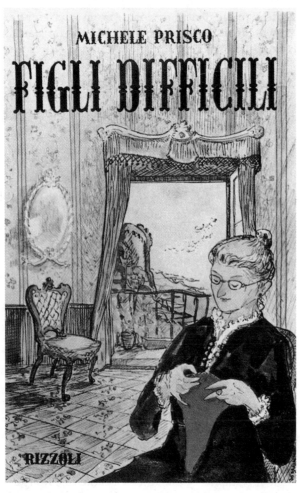

MICHELE PRISCO

FIGLI DIFFICILI

RIZZOLI

Dust jacket for Prisco's second novel, in which a devoted mother spoils her children

ten by living it). *Terre basse* (Lowlands, 1992) is a collection of Prisco's short stories, ranging from "Quando arrivano i lupi" (When the Wolves Arrive), written in 1941, to "Le fotografie" (The Pictures), written in 1991.

Prisco's novel *Il pellicano di pietra* (The Stone Pelican, 1996) deals with the rivalry between mother and daughter, and it ends in tragedy. In this work Prisco returns to the setting of *La provincia adorrmentata,* the towns around Naples "poisoned" by the lifestyle and social values of people formerly of modest means, who have become rich through steady and diligent business pursuits.

The story is dominated by the figure of Giuseppina, the mother, who is blinded by jealousy and is driven to murder by her vindictive daughter, Maddalena. A second daughter, Emilia, married young and has grown resigned to leading an ordinary life with a husband and a son. Maddalena has little to live for, other than the memories of her relationship with Alfonso, a man disliked by Giusep-

pina. Since Alfonso's body was found in a pine grove, Maddalena has lived as a recluse, a voluntary prisoner in her home in order to spite her mother.

The novel is woven with situations that give rise to feelings of repressed rancor between mother and daughter. Thus, the meaning of the title: the pelican, an image of altruism and sacrifice identified with the traditional values of a close-knit family, is transformed here into a symbol of the absurd rivalry between the two women. Since her husband committed suicide, Giuseppina has had a mediocre man for a lover. After three years of reclusion, Madalena meets a second man, Osvaldo, who is attracted to her. However, in time, she leads Giuseppina to believe that Osvalso is in love with her, the mother. When Giuseppina realizes she has been deceived, she engages the daughter in a violent altercation and kills her. As a final gesture of vindictiveness, she carries the body, hands and feet tied together, to the spot where Alfonso's body was found.

Giuseppina personifies a pitiless and unredeeming vision of the feminine condition; in the context of the novel, life is tragic and it can be coped with only by living it or doing away with it. Thus, the work casts a problematic light on human existence, reinforced by the ending of the novel as the attention again turns to Giuseppina: "Adesso si sentiva stranamente in pace, si sentiva a un tratto irrazionalmente serena, se non proprio felice" (Now she felt strangely at peace, suddenly and irrational serene, if not happy).

Interviews:

Pasquale De Orsi, "Intervista sul romanzo," *Valori umani,* 9 (September–October 1975): 16–18;

Claudio Toscani, *La voce e il testo* (Milan: I.P.L., 1985), pp. 170–186;

Luciano Luisi, *Michele Prisco: Una vita per la cultura* (Fiuggi, 1986);

Pasquale Maffeo, *Le scritture narrative: Interviste a scrittori italiani* (Marigliano: Italibri, 1992), pp. 109–118;

Franco Zangrilli, "Michele Prisco," in his *La forza della parola* (Ravenna: Longo, 1992), pp. 31–54.

References:

Carmelo Aliberto, *Michele Prisco* (Foggia: Bastogi, 1993);

Giuseppe Amoroso, *La biblioteca di Sahrazad* (Brescia: Morcelliana, 1990), pp. 148–151;

Amoroso, *Michele Prisco* (Florence: La Nuova Italia, 1980);

Aurelio Benevento, *Narrativa e fortuna di Michele Prisco* (Naples: Società Editrice Napoletana, 1983);

Cosimo Campanelli, "L'esperire della memoria: La 'poiesis' del primo Prisco," *Otto/Novecento,* 13, no. 3–4 (1989): 65–131;

Campanelli, "La provincia e il sonno: Etica, estetica e simbolica del primo Prisco," *Temponuovo,* 23, no. 47 (1989): 5–83;

Carmine Di Biase, *L'altra Napoli: Scrittori napoletani d'oggi* (Naples: Società Editrice Napoletana, 1978), pp. 73–82;

Di Biase, "Coscienza interiore e stilistica in Michele Prisco, 1977–92," in his *La letteratura come valore* (Naples: Liguori, 1993), pp. 257–292;

Italian Quarterly, special issue on Prisco, 29 (1988);

Giannantonio Pompeo, *Invito alla lettura di Michele Prisco* (Milan: Mursia, 1977);

Giorgio Pullini, *Il romanzo italiano del dopoguerra* (Padua: Marsilio, 1965), pp. 373–378;

Giacinto Spagnoletti, "Michele Prisco," in *Letteratura italiana: I contemporanei,* volume 8 (Milan: Marzorati, 1979), pp. 7313–7334;

Claudio Toscani, "Michele Prisco: Vent'anni di narrativa," *Vita e pensiero* (January–February 1971): 98–106;

Toscani, "Modi e motivi del penultimo Prisco," in his *La provincia del lettore* (Naples: Conte, 1981), pp. 121–126.

Giose Rimanelli

(28 November 1925 –)

Sante Matteo
Miami University of Ohio

BOOKS: *Tiro al piccione. Romanzo* (Milan: Mondadori, 1953); republished, with an introduction
by Sebastiano Martelli (Turin: Einaudi, 1991);
translated by Ben Johnson Jr. as *The Day of the
Lion: A Novel* (New York: Random House,
1954; London: Heinemann, 1956);

Peccato originale. Romanzo (Milan: Mondadori, 1954);
translated by Johnson as *Original Sin* (New
York: Random House, 1957; London: Heinemann, 1958);

Biglietto di terza (Milan: Mondadori, 1958);

Una posizione sociale (Florence: Vallecchi, 1959); republished as *La Stanza grande* (Cava dei Tir-
rein: Avagliano Editore, 1996);

*Il mestiere del furbo: Panorama della narrative italiana con-
temporanea* (Milan: Sugar, 1959);

Tè in casa Picasso (Turin: Il Dramma, 1961);

Il corno francese (Turin: Il Dramma, 1962);

Lares (Turin: Il Dramma, 1962);

Carmina blabla (Padua: Rebellato, 1967);

Monaci d'amore medievali (Rome: Trevi Editore,
1967);

Tragica America (Genoa: Immordino, 1968);

Poems Make Pictures; Pictures Make Poems, by Rimanelli
and Paul Pimsleur, pictures by Ronni Solbert
(New York: Pantheon, 1972);

Graffiti, edited by Titina Sardelli (Isernia: Marinelli,
1977);

Molise Molise (Isernia: Marinelli, 1979);

Antologia delle opere narrative di Giose Rimanelli, edited
by Giambattista Faralli (Isernia: Marinelli,
1982);

Il tempo nascosto fra le righe (Isernia: Marinelli,
1986);

Arcano (1970–1988) (Salerno: Edisud, 1989);

Moliseide. Ballate e canzoni in dialetto molisano, by Ri-
manelli and Benito Faraone, translated by
Luigi Bonaffini (Campobasso: Enne, 1990;
New York: Peter Lang, 1992);

Benedetta in Guysterland: A Liquid Novel, preface by
Fred L. Gardaphè (Montreal & New York:
Guernica, 1993);

Giose Rimanelli in 1992

Alien cantica: An American Journey (1964–1993), edited
and translated by Bonaffini (New York: Peter
Lang, 1995);

Dirige me Domine, Deus meus (Campobasso: Enne,
1996);

I Rascenije (Faeuza: Mobydick, 1996);

From G. to G.: 101 Sonnets, by Rimanelli and Luigi
Fortanella (New York: Peter Lang, 1996);

Detroit Blues (Welland, Ontario & Lewiston, N.Y.:
Soleil, 1996);

Accademia (Toronto & New York: Guernica, 1997);

304

Viamerica/Gli occhi, by Rimanelli and Achilli Serrao (Toronto & New York: Guernica, 1997).

MOTION PICTURE: *Suor Letizia,* script by Rimanelli, Columbia Pictures, 1956.

OTHER: *Modern Canadian Stories,* edited by Rimanelli and Roberto Ruberto (Toronto: Ryerson, 1966);
Ruta, edited by Rimanelli (Rome: De Luca, 1967);
Italian Literature: Roots and Branches. Essays in Honor of Thomas Goddard Bergin, edited by Rimanelli and Kenneth John Atchity (New Haven: Yale University Press, 1976).

UNCOLLECTED PERIODICAL PUBLICATION: "Notes on Fascist/Antifascist Politics and Culture from the Point of View of a Misfit," *Rivista di studi italiani,* 2 (December 1984): 73–80.

The popular perception is that Giose Rimanelli burst onto Italy's literary scene in the early 1950s, glowed brightly for a few years, and then dropped out of sight just as suddenly as he had arrived. In reality, he had been writing well before achieving his initial success, and he continued to publish novels, poetry, and essays after he left Italy in 1960. His powerful first novel, *Tiro al piccione* (Pigeon Shoot, 1953; translated as *The Day of the Lion,* 1954), which brought him what many considered overnight success, had been written in 1945, immediately after his return from fighting in World War II. In "Notes on Fascist/Antifascist Politics and Culture from the Point of View of a Misfit," published in the December 1984 *Rivista di studi italiani,* he observes that his books tended to be "misfits," published either too late (long after they were conceived and written) or too early (before the reading public was ready to accept them). As his novels became less conventional in language and narrative form, the major publishers and critics—particularly those who had applied the label "neorealist" to Rimanelli and *Tiro al piccione*—began to abandon him. After 1960 the Italian literary establishment, according to Rimanelli, "slammed the doors of their publishing houses and expunged my name from their literary records."

Despite the claims of the early critics and literary historians, Rimanelli was not a neorealist novelist. His novels are as distinct in style and content from each other as they are from the books of other authors. He has never belonged to a literary movement nor adhered to a political party or ideology. It was this artistic and political independence, along with his refusal to seek patronage and allies in literary circles, that led to his ostracism and eventual exile.

Rimanelli has claimed that he, like his books, is a misfit, a nomad, a perennial outsider. With other displaced writers Rimanelli shares the exile's vision, which allows him to perceive events, ideas, and conditions in greater perspective. The exiled and displaced characters in his novels are forced to recontextualize their knowledge and beliefs and to adjust their perception of reality within different linguistic, sociopolitical, and cultural frames of reference. Consequently, they are in a better position than the "native" observer to perceive and make sense of the parts of the world where they relocate. With the vantage of distance they also gain a more accurate perception of the homelands they left behind and a better understanding of how community shapes character, sensibility, beliefs, and behavior. Rimanelli's fictional characters share the exile's sense of alienation and existential concerns: the modern condition of displacement and uprootedness; the constant search for new perspectives and new truths; the desire or need to hold on to memories and traditions of the past while being supported and nourished by old roots.

Rimanelli was born on 28 November 1925 in the small hilltop town of Casacalenda in the Molise region of southern Italy to Vincenzo and Concettina Minicucci Rimanelli. His was a family of past and future emigrants. His paternal grandfather, Seppe Rimanelli, made several trips to America to labor as a sewer worker. His mother's grandfather had left Casacalenda to become a sailor, had fought in the American Civil War on the side of the Confederacy, and had subsequently become a justice of the peace in Louisiana. That grandfather's son, Tony "Dominick" Minicucci—Rimanelli's grandfather—had been born in New Orleans in 1863. In 1910 he had moved his family to Montreal, where Rimanelli's mother was born. A few years later the family had moved to Casacalenda, where Dominick had started an umbrella business. This peripatetic American grandfather, who had witnessed the lynching of eleven innocent Italian immigrants in New Orleans in 1891 and had played in Dixieland jazz bands on Mississippi riverboats, exercised a great influence on Rimanelli through his stories of those faraway places and his exotic music-making; he taught Rimanelli to play jazz and to look at life through a wanderer's eyes.

Rimanelli's family history of departures and returns produced a centrifugal pull that fueled his wanderlust and a centripetal tug that bound him to his family, community, and traditions—traditions that could be oppressive and brutalizing in a preindustrial society, where custom and the word of the father ruled despotically. The young characters in Rimanelli's fiction are aware of the value of being rooted in a self-contained, long-standing community; but they also come to perceive this community as a prison and feel the need to escape. Meanwhile, many of the older characters who have left feel the urge to return.

Rimanelli's first departure took him into another kind of closed community: in 1935 he entered the Catholic seminary at Ascoli Satriano. While there, he gave vent to his wanderlust by making plans to become a missionary to remote parts of the world. The seminary provided him with a sound classical education in Greek and Latin, patristic and medieval philosophy and literature, and music (he played the church organ) and musicology. He also studied French and Hebrew. Rimanelli abandoned the seminary before the end of his fifth year and returned, with a sense of failure and shame, to a life of despondency and futility in his hometown.

Another attempt to flee proved disastrous and provided the experiences depicted in his first novel. After the Allies invaded Italy in 1943, the Germans and the Italian Fascists retreated north, some passing through Casacalenda. Rimanelli, who had no interest in politics and had been practically oblivious to the war, agreed to head north with a fellow former seminarian who planned to join the partisans fighting the Fascists and the Germans. They were separated, and Rimanelli was arrested by the Fascists and forced to choose between being executed as a deserter or enlisting with the Brigate Nere (Black Brigades), the Fascist ragtag troops deployed after Benito Mussolini established the Fascist Social Republic of Northern Italy on 12 September 1943. Thus, Rimanelli ended up fighting against the partisans he and his friend had intended to join.

Imprisoned when the war ended in the spring of 1945, Rimanelli met the poet Ezra Pound, who was being held as a war criminal in a prison camp near Pisa. Rimanelli escaped from a train transporting war prisoners to Africa and made his way back to Casacalenda. Writing almost desperately, in a few months he completed his first two novels: *Tiro al piccione,* a semiautobiographical work based on his war experiences, and *Peccato originale* (1954; translated as *Original Sin,* 1957), the story of a family's attempts to immigrate to America. Although the two books were written practically at the same time, they are quite different in setting, style, characterization, and narrative technique.

In 1946 Rimanelli left home, alone and penniless, and traveled throughout Italy and much of the rest of Europe by hitchhiking and jumping trains. In Paris he attended the lectures of the philosopher Gaston Bachelard at the Sorbonne; met Jean-Paul Sartre and Albert Camus; and played jazz in a boîte with Boris Vian. In 1947 he settled in Rome, where he slept under bridges and spent his days in the national library, earning money by ghostwriting doctoral dissertations and books. Eventually, he started publishing articles in newspapers. When Rimanelli met the well-known Molisan writer Francesco Jovine and told him that he, too, was a writer, the older author, somewhat skeptically, asked if he had written any novels yet. Yes, two, Rimanelli answered, not counting the many adventure romances he had written in the seminary: *Tiro al piccione* and *Peccato originale.* Jovine became his friend and mentor.

In 1949 Cesare Pavese, an editor at the prestigious Einaudi publishing house and one of the most influential figures in postwar Italian letters, read the manuscript for *Tiro al piccione* and found it compelling. For Pavese it was not just a novel of Italian politics but a story of universal significance about an innocent young man sucked into a maelstrom of violence. He accepted the work for publication but committed suicide after the proofs had been printed. Without Pavese's support, Einaudi was reluctant to publish a novel written from the perspective of someone who had fought with the Fascists. Elio Vittorini, who had been an Einaudi editor before moving to the Mondadori firm in Milan, published the work in Mondadori's Medusa series in 1953. Before the novel came out, Rimanelli traveled in Argentina, Brazil, Colombia, Greece, and Israel.

At the start of the novel the narrator, Marco Laudato, in his late teens, is overwhelmed by the desire to leave his home in the fictional town of Calenda in the Molise region. He wants to escape from a closed provincial world of timeless laws and rituals, of primitive, inarticulate passions and feelings. The constant rumbling of German trucks retreating before the advancing Allied forces speaks to Marco of escape from his frustrated, futile existence. Jumping on one of the trucks, he ends up in the Piazza San Marco in Venice, the home of Marco Polo. The two Marcos associated with Venice—one the city's patron saint, the other the quintessential traveler—are two namesakes that represent the opposing impulses in Marco: San Marco suggests the safe, cloistered life; Marco Polo unbounded freedom and exploration. As Marco stands on a bridge and looks at another bridge—the Bridge of Sighs that connects the Doge's Palace to the Piombi prisons—he seems suspended in time and space, with no ground on which to stand and no destination in which to head. Venice is a liminal place, a point of transition, a porous border between the land, representing stasis and fixity, and the sea, symbolizing flux and mobility.

Marco wanders aimlessly through the labyrinthine streets of Venice. One day, seeking shelter from the rain, he is pushed into a large hall by a crowd; before he realizes what is happening, he is enlisted as an auxiliary in the Brigate Nere. Never knowing what he is supposed to be fighting for, he gets swept up in a hell of escalating violence and brutality. At first Marco and his fellow recruits shoot to defend themselves; after a while they start attacking in anger, to avenge atrocities committed against their comrades. Eventually their cruelty becomes automatic and random: they maim and kill without reflection or compunction. Marco comes to feel a sense of inebriation, instead of fear or guilt, when he fires his machine gun. He stops asking why, for those who ask that question end up dead.

Wounded, Marco is hospitalized for several months; he can think, feel, and ask himself questions again. After an intense love affair with his nurse, Anna, he returns to the front for the closing weeks of the war, when the fighting becomes even more desperate. Most of his comrades are slaughtered by the partisans, who shoot at the *piccione* (pigeon), as they call the eagle on the Fascists' berets. Imprisoned at the end of the war, Marco escapes and makes his way back to Calenda, where everyone had assumed him to be dead. In the past two years, he has experienced unspeakable, unthinkable horrors. He has lived in the midst of mutilation and death; he has wounded and killed young men like himself; he has suffered the pangs of love and loss. Yet in Molise nothing has changed. He feels more out of place than ever: how can he communicate what he has experienced? The unrepentant fascists among the townspeople insist on treating him like a hero; those who have lost their sons blame him for fighting on the wrong side or simply for surviving while their sons died; to others he is still "Marcuccio," the teenage boy he was when he left. His mother sums up the situation for him: "Tu sei stato uno che è voluto andare e ti sei perso nella guerra" (You were someone who wanted to leave and then got lost in the war). To leave home and not get lost, one must have a purpose and a destination: "Adesso sapevo che era necessario tornare in mezzo alla gente . . . e vivere finalmente per una ragione" (Now I knew that it was necessary to go back among people again . . . and to live at last for a reason).

Rimanelli's other novels would deal with many of the issues and situations raised in *Tiro al piccione:* the tension between home as a haven and as a prison; the freedom brought by being uprooted, coupled with an agonizing sense of loss and lostness; the search for a language that will allow people to understand each other; the need to acquire *coscienza,* which means both "consciousness" and "conscience." Awareness and understanding are difficult to achieve when one is either too close to one's reality to be able to perceive it objectively and question it, or so uprooted and removed from it as to have no frame of reference or context for understanding. Compelled to seek the right balance between distance from and proximity to one's community and oneself, many of Rimanelli's characters have either left or are about to leave their hometowns, while others have returned after long absences.

Rimanelli's parents and his younger brothers, Antonio and Gino, had immigrated to Montreal in 1949; his mother had two brothers who lived there with their families. Rimanelli spent ten months visiting his relatives in Canada in 1953; during his stay he served as correspondent for RAI (Italian Radio) and as editor of the Italian-language newspaper *Il cittadino canadese,* worked at odd jobs, and traveled extensively.

Tiro al piccione was an immediate success in Italy and abroad. The English translation was published in New York by Random House in 1954 and in London by Heinemann in 1956, under the title *The Day of the Lion.* In 1961 it would be made into a movie by Giuliano Montaldo, in his directorial debut. The work's critical and popular success permitted the author to publish *Peccato originale* and start making a living as a writer.

Unlike *Tiro al piccione,* which is narrated in the first person, *Peccato originale* is told in the third person and from various perspectives—primarily from that of Nicola Vietri, who is desperately trying to arrange for his family to immigrate to America. Occasionally the story is told from the point of view of his wife, Ada, who is reluctant to leave her home but allows herself to be swept up by her husband's vision of a better world for their children, a world with social justice, economic opportunity, and indoor plumbing. At other times the perspective is that of their sixteen-year-old daughter, Michela, whose preoccupations and fantasies are much more romantic. Rimanelli includes references to himself and his family in the novel: at one point Nicola reads a letter from Rimanelli's father complaining about life in Canada, where the family has immigrated without Rimanelli.

Tragedy strikes on a hot summer night, when Michela is sexually assaulted. The town's code of honor requires Nicola to seek vengeance against the perpetrators, but doing so would make it impossible for him to immigrate because he would have to stand trial. He ultimately decides to live with his

Self-portrait by Rimanelli, 1950

shame so as not to jeopardize his dream of a better life in a more tolerant and open society, where one's future is determined by one's worth and efforts and not by class or custom or superstition.

Nicola's painful renunciation of his honor proves futile when he is killed while working with people attempting to evacuate farmers from land where a new water line is to be built: his life is sacrificed for a development that may eventually take others out of the backward conditions he wanted so much to escape. Ada decides to follow her late husband's dream and build a new life in America. Before they leave the community exacts the vengeance the father had refused to seek: the women of the town, in a bloody frenzy, castrate one of the young men who abducted Michela. Order is thereby restored, and the community can again close in on itself. The Vietri women, however, leave their familiar circle for a life in an unknown "new world."

Rimanelli's second novel was not as well received as his first had been. Speaking for other Marxist readers and critics, Carlo Salinari in the 13 November 1954 *Il contemporaneo* called it too bloody, too primitive, and full of too much fascistic violence. At the end of *Tiro al piccione* Marco Laudato seemed inclined to embark on a new life and begin living for a purpose; Marxist readers tended to think that, because he had experienced the evils of Fascism, Marco was ready to become a Communist. The same was expected of Rimanelli. Jovine had told him that he should join the Communist Party; he needed to be affiliated and sponsored if he wanted to be published and appreciated. Rimanelli refused. It was not just Fascism he had learned to fear; he feared all political parties, just as he feared the seminary and the intolerant provincialism of his rural community.

Salinari and other reviewers also claimed that the novel was infused with a medieval, fatalistic mentality; that the characters had no social consciousness; and that the situation allowed no hope for their emancipation. These objections hardly seem justified: while the novel does depict the medieval conditions and customs found in rural southern Italy, its aim is to reveal and indict those conditions. Furthermore, Nicola Vietri is remarkable precisely for his social and psychological consciousness. His desperation to emigrate is based on his awareness and rejection of the injustices and dehumanizing aspects of his society, elements he recognizes in his own attitudes and behavior. He realizes that he has been shaped by those traditions and beliefs and that, as a paterfamilias, he must enforce and promulgate them. He is painfully conscious of his position as both victim and victimizer in a rigid system of class and gender roles and prejudices. That his awareness is expressed in social and existential terms, not in political terms, may have made the novel seem less relevant in the politically charged atmosphere of the 1950s.

On 6 August 1956 Rimanelli married Liliana Chiurazzi; they had two sons, Marco and Michele, before they divorced in 1962. Rimanelli's third book, *Biglietto di terza* (Third-Class Ticket, 1958), is an account of his experiences in Canada in 1953. While most of the characters and events in the book are real, others, as he says in an endnote, are fictional without being purely imaginary. Rimanelli once admitted that all of his books are autobiographical to some degree; conversely, even his most autobiographical memoirs, such as *Biglietto di terza* and *Molise Molise* (1979), are partly fictional. For him writing is a way of knowing himself and the world. Hence, nothing in his books is merely the product of his imagination without a basis in his life, while nothing in his life escapes the filter of the writer's imagination and reflection. The distinction between documentary and fiction is often blurred.

Biglietto di terza is many things at once: travel diary, sociological treatise, psychological introspection, journalism (including photographs of Canadian wilderness and town scenes), picaresque adventure story, and realistic narrative fiction. Rimanelli's Canada is a fascinating hybrid patchwork of cultures and socioeconomic conditions. There are reconstituted communities of families from Casacalenda and other parts of Italy; these familiar nuclei are scattered among foreign strands of British, French, and Native American cultures. Rimanelli finds the large, close-knit extended families in Canada as protective and oppressive as any in Molise. Beyond Montreal, which includes both the familiar and the alien, there is a limitless wilderness, both promising and prohibiting in its uninhabited vastness.

As a visitor who intends to remain an outsider, Rimanelli can be relatively detached from what he observes. He is ironic when he describes his brothers' and uncles' fixation on *bisinisse* (business) and making money. He is perceptive and compassionate in presenting the plight of unskilled immigrants who are unable to find work and whose families face much greater deprivation and suffering in this new world, which can be much less forgiving and much more punitive than the old in its social as well as its meteorological climate. He is whimsical and metaphorical about the mosaic of races and cultures he encounters and about the uneasy combination of civility and primitiveness that permeates this culture.

In Montreal Rimanelli once gets on the wrong bus; when he tries to get off he is told that the driver is deaf and that he is on the "Nowhere" bus, which goes everywhere in the city but stops nowhere until it returns to the point of departure. Later he rides another bus named "Nowhere" to a tobacco plantation. After the harvest the bus returns to pick up the migrant workers. One of the workers is shot and killed as he is about to board. The "Nowhere" bus is emblematic of Canadian and American life, which is characterized by a lack of destination or purpose and by a rat-race mentality that puts everyone on a treadmill of acquisition and consumption leading nowhere. The narrator compares the sleepy passengers on the "Nowhere" bus to "anime di condannati che il Caronte sordo portava a Dite" (souls of the damned which the deaf Charon was taking to Dis [Hell]).

At the end of the book, as the narrator prepares to return to Italy, everyone asks him why he does not want to stay in Canada with his family. His answer sums up his ambivalent feelings about this vast, savage, virginal land: it is the world's tomorrow, he says, for those who have suffered injustices and wrongs in yesterday's societies. Here they can find freedom, but only at the cost of destroying all bridges to the past. He is not ready to burn those bridges, so he must leave this land of vast horizons, where the future dwells, for the more circumscribed and past-laden landscape of ancient and eternal Rome.

Una posizione sociale (A Social Position, 1959) is a blend of fiction and autobiography, though a preliminary note claims that the characters are all imaginary. The novel is more complex stylistically than its predecessors, while its narrative content is considerably reduced. Framed by a brief prologue and epilogue, the events take place in one night, that

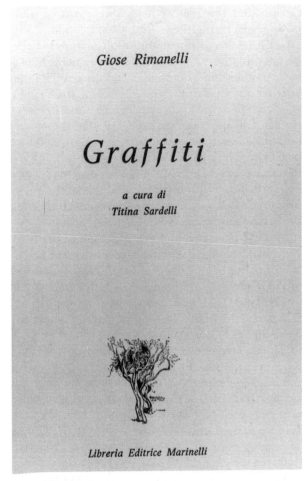

Giose Rimanelli

Graffiti

a cura di
Titina Sardelli

Libreria Editrice Marinelli

Dust jacket for Rimanelli's 1977 novel, an experimental work that was once part of a long unpublished novel written in the 1960s

of 15 January 1937. The narrator, Massimo Niro, is a melancholy, sensitive boy of ten—Rimanelli's approximate age at that time. Massimo's father, Enrico, is a surveyor, as the author's father had been; Massimo's mother, Francesca, was born in Canada, like Rimanelli's mother; Massimo's younger brothers are named Antonio and Gino, the names of Rimanelli's real brothers. The protagonist's grandfather, Tony Dominick, is clearly based on Rimanelli's real maternal grandfather: he was born in New Orleans, witnessed the 1891 lynching of Italians, played jazz trumpet on Mississippi riverboats, and immigrated to Montreal and later to Molise to find or replant his family's roots. In the novel Massimo's mother is about to give birth, and Massimo spends most of the night in a futile attempt to find someone to help her with the delivery.

When Rimanelli wrote the novel he had been away from his hometown for some years. As a result the work conveys a different vision of life in Casacalenda than the first two, which were written while he was still living there. The Casacalenda of this novel seems to be not a point of departure for emigrants but a point of arrival for foreigners: Massimo's mother and grandfather and the family's first boarder and his father, who have come from America; Stella, the traveling actress who stays to marry the scion of the town's aristocracy; and the second boarder, Cesare, an artist, jazz enthusiast, and Stella's lover. Massimo's nocturnal search through the town reveals it to be not the closed, dead-end world of repression and limited possibilities of the previous novels but a wide-open world of eccentric characters and unknown, unlimited possibilities.

Told from the double perspective of the innocent child protagonist who observes without understanding but begins to question and learn, and that of the detached adult narrator who reminisces and understands, the novel shows that extraordinary things may be hidden behind the façade of normality. While the Calenda of *Tiro al piccione* and the Cale of *Peccato originale* are closer to Giovanni Verga's Acitrezza or Ignazio Silone's Fontamara–realistic settings reminiscent of the works of Emile Zola–the Casacalenda of *Una posizione sociale,* though less fictional (as the use of the town's real name indicates), is more surreal, more allusive, closer to the Dublin of James Joyce's *Ulysses* (1922). The novel almost anticipates the magical realism of Gabriel García Márquez–not because anything magical takes place but because of the multiple perspectives and voices of the narration, which is both choral and intimate, both ironic and pathetic, both realistic and expressionistic. In this novel Rimanelli is already a "border writer," as Fred Gardaphè, borrowing the term from a book by Emily Hicks on Hispanic American "border writers," would call him in his introduction to Rimanelli's *Benedetta in Guysterland* (1993).

Possibly the most remarkable of the five books Rimanelli published in the prolific period from 1953 to 1959 is the one that led to his exile from Italy. *Il mestiere del furbo* (The Sneak's Craft, 1959), a devastating, sometimes vitriolic survey of the state of Italian letters at the time, is a collection of columns Rimanelli had been writing since 1958 for the Roman weekly *Lo Specchio* under the pseudonym A. G. Solari. The book was published by a minor Milan publishing house, Sugar.

"Solari" attacks the aestheticism and formalism, the "prosa d'arte" (artistic prose) that have characterized Italian literature since the end of World War I. He accuses writers such as Gianna Manzini and Carlo Emilio Gadda of putting stylistic and philological concerns ahead of the need to convey real emotions, real people, and real life. He

claims that the title characters of Pier Paolo Pasolini's *Ragazzi di vita* (Boys of Life, 1955; translated as *The Ragazzi,* 1968) were really "ragazzi di carta" (boys of paper). Italo Calvino, for all his verbal virtuosity and "astuzia" (narrative cleverness), is unable to create real characters or a great novel.

Solari also attacks politically engaged writing. When writing becomes propaganda, he says, art suffers. In the post–World War II period, according to him, antifascism became an end in itself and, eventually, a prison house for Italian intellectuals and artists. In this prison he places Silone, Vittorini, Vasco Pratolini, and Carlo Cassola. Not even Rimanelli's friend Jovine escapes censure for compromising his art with political propaganda.

Borrowing the term from Gertrude Stein, who applied it to artists who seem to be on the verge of meaning something but always come up short, Rimanelli labels other writers hysterical, "gli isterici." Hysterical art is reflected, filtered, distilled from artificial sources; true art is distilled from one's own character and personality. Among the hysterical writers he includes Tommaso Landolfi and Alberto Moravia. Solari saves his harshest criticism for the world of literary salons and literary prizes, a system of patronage and favoritism, media manipulation and political machinations, which promotes writers such as Giorgio Bassani and Domenico Rea regardless of their real worth. Only a few of the highly regarded writers of the time escape his invective and earn his praise; among them are Pavese, Giuseppe Berto, Corrado Alvaro, and Federigo Tozzi.

Just before the book went to press Rimanelli decided to reveal his identity. The decision instantly turned him into a pariah, shunned by writers and publishers alike; leaving his family behind, he immigrated to North America the following year. Reading *Mestiere del furbo,* however, one gets the impression that it is not really Rimanelli speaking in his own voice but an antagonistic persona he has invented, another of his semifictional alter egos, who dares to say things that Rimanelli would be reluctant to say and categorically asserts opinions that the author would deliver with more caution. One wonders how Rimanelli's career might have been different had he presented Solari's ideas in the form of Platonic dialogues, as he did in two theatrical pieces he was writing at the time: *Tè in casa Picasso* (Tea at Picasso's, 1961) and *Il corno francese* (The French Horn, 1962). In any case his marginalization in Italy served to lead Rimanelli in new and, in many ways, more fruitful directions as he started to live and write in two languages and in two cultures.

During his first few years in America, Rimanelli lectured widely and taught at various colleges

Manuscript for a sonnet by Rimanelli (Collection of Giose Rimanelli)

and universities, including Yale, Sarah Lawrence, British Columbia, and UCLA. Shortly after immigrating he published, through a firm in Milan, *Tè in casa Picasso, Il corno francese,* and *Lares.* In the summer of 1962 he married one of his students at Yale, Bettina Quatran; they had a son, David, and were divorced in 1976. In 1968 he settled at the State University of New York at Albany as a professor of Italian and comparative literature, retiring in 1990. He published a collection of essays, *Tragica America* (Tragic America, 1968).

In 1976 Rimanelli visited the Molise region to reestablish ties with his native land and went on to publish a series of books with Marinelli, a small publisher there. *Graffiti* (1977) is a novel excerpted from a much longer work, "La macchina paranoica" (The Paranoid Machine), written in the 1960s but never published. *Graffiti* is a highly experimental text with a variety of linguistic registers and narrative modes and devices from various genres, including dramatic dialogue, stream of consciousness, visionary/hallucinative associations, iconographic variations, puns, allusions, and lyric poetry. *Molise Molise* is hard to classify; it includes memoirs, reflections, and samplings of his stories and poems. It is a confession of the writer's love for the land and the people he had to abandon but now has found again. *Il tempo nascosto fra le righe* (Time Hidden Between the Lines, 1986) is a collection of fourteen stories, ranging from neorealistic works written in the late 1940s to the unconventional, experimental, and sometimes polyglot and polymorphic texts of the 1960s and 1970s. Much of Rimanelli's postexile work published in Italy has been poetry: *Carmina blabla* (1967), *Monaci d'amore medievali* (Medieval Monks of Love, 1967), *Arcano (1970–1988)* (Arcanum, 1989), *Moliseide* (1990), and *Alien cantica: An American Journey (1964–1993)* (1995).

None of Rimanelli's works has achieved the success of his first novel, *Tiro al piccione,* which is now considered a classic. In 1991 Einaudi, which was to have been the original publisher of the novel in 1950, republished the work, putting it back in the limelight and introducing it to a new generation of readers. The Einaudi edition reinstated Rimanelli on Italy's literary stage; the reviews, interviews, and articles that followed brought the attention of a new generation to the novel and the author. Though the text is unchanged, the novel is a different book in the 1990s than it was in the 1950s: the fascist/partisan dichotomy is no longer as clear-cut as it was just after the war, and readers can now better appreciate the novel's complex stylistic layers and psychological depths. It is much more subtle and sophisticated than it appeared to be to most of the early reviewers, who considered it a raw, unpolished, and therefore

more authentic account of the experience of war—particularly fascinating because it had been experienced from the "wrong," losing side. In his excellent introduction to the new edition Sebastiano Martelli points out that the book is not the crude diary of an unschooled provincial but a masterful literary construct influenced by, and comparable in content and style to, accounts of war by Pavese, Stendhal, Ernest Hemingway, Erich Maria Remarque, Louis-Ferdinand Céline, and Stephen Crane.

Rimanelli has published many scholarly articles, both in Italian and in English, and has been active in the academic profession as an author, scholar, and organizer in the field of Italian and comparative literature and more recently in the burgeoning field of Italian American literature. In 1993 he was named honorary president of the American Association for Italian Studies.

Just as Rimanelli is being rediscovered as a major writer in Italy, he is also being launched as an important American writer. His first English-language novel, *Benedetta in Guysterland,* according to Fred L. Gardaphè's illuminating preface, "occupies a pivotal position in the history of Italian/American narrative as the bridge over the border between modernism and postmodernism." A parodic novel that tells the story of the love affair of Bendetta, a beautiful Appalachian woman from Nabokov County, and the mafioso Joe Adonis, the book examines and debunks America's fascination with sex, violence, and class and ethnic stereotypes. It won the American Book Award in 1994.

In a postindustrial world where being uprooted and dislocated is a common experience and no longer the condition only of immigrants, Giose Rimanelli's writings allow readers to probe, analyze, and illuminate the dilemma of displacement and alienation: on one hand, the need to abandon restrictive mind-sets and oppressive cultural paradigms; on the other hand, the equally urgent need to be rooted somewhere and to belong to a community. His writings show how language—memories, stories, songs, and poems—can be used to build transcultural bridges that link individuals and communities across space and time, so that people's ethnic and social roots, instead of chaining them to the past, can inform their present and help shape their future. Instead of isolating individuals, their cultural "luggage" can allow them to understand and enrich each other.

As Italy itself becomes multiethnic and multiracial with the immigration of Africans and Asians, the exiled misfit author and his misfit, often polyglot books not only fit the current multicultural reality but illuminate it so that one may see it more clearly, appreciate it, and learn to live in it. His books of exile and return do not tell readers how to go back home from exile so as to hide from the present and live in the past; they show how one may make a home in exile and draw sustenance from one's roots in order to build a future.

References:

Giambattista Faralli, *Prospezione critica di un romanzo: Graffiti di Giose Rimanelli* (Campobasso: CEP, 1977);

Fred L. Gardophè, 'Giose 'The Trickster' Rimanelli's Great Italian American Parody," in his *Italian Signs, American Streets* (Durham & London: Duke University Press, 1996), pp. 107–118;

Sebastiano Martelli, "La diaspora dell'identità," in his *Il crepuscolo dell'identità* (Salerno: La Veglia, 1988), pp. 235–276;

Misure critiche, special issue on Rimanelli, 65–67 (1987–1988);

Sheryl Postman, "The Peripheral Edge in Giose Rimanelli's *Original Sin*," in *Humanitas e Poesia,* edited by Luigi Reina (Salerno: La Veglia, 1989), pp. 1089–1098;

Postman, "To Hell and Back: Marco Laudato's Journey in Rimanelli's *Tiro al piccione*," *Forum Italicum,* 27 (Spring/Fall 1993): 251–261;

Michele Ricciardelli, "Development of Giose Rimanelli's Fiction," in his *Writings on Twentieth-Century Italian Literature* (Stony Brook, N.Y.: Forum Italicum, 1992), pp. 17–25;

M. Tedeschi, *Resistenza e guerra partigiana: Testimonianze* (Bari: Laterza, 1980), pp. 205–207.

Papers:

The manuscripts for Giose Rimanelli's "La macchina paranoica," "Gli accademici/Diari di Anaconda," "Moon/Bush," and other unpublished novels and stories are in the Thomas Fisher Rare Book Library at the University of Toronto.

Lalla Romano

(11 November 1906 –)

Natalia Costa-Zalessow
San Francisco State University

BOOKS: *Fiore* (Turin: Frassinelli, 1941);
Le metamorfosi (Turin: Einaudi, 1951; revised, 1967; revised, 1983);
Maria (Turin: Einaudi, 1953);
L'autunno (Milan: Meridiana, 1955);
Tetto Murato (Turin: Einaudi, 1957);
Diario di Grecia (Padua: Rebellato, 1959; revised and enlarged edition, Turin: Einaudi, 1974);
L'uomo che parlava solo (Turin: Einaudi, 1961);
La penombra che abbiamo attraversato (Turin: Einaudi, 1964);
Le parole tra noi leggere (Turin: Einaudi, 1969);
L'ospite (Turin: Einaudi, 1973);
Giovane è il tempo (Turin: Einaudi, 1974);
Lettura di un'immagine (Turin: Einaudi, 1975); revised as *Romanzo di figure* (Turin: Einaudi, 1986);
La villeggiante (Turin: Einaudi, 1975); second section republished as *Pralève* (Turin: Einaudi, 1978);
Una giovinezza inventata (Turin: Einaudi, 1979);
Lo stregone (Turin: Stampatori, 1979);
Inseparabile (Turin: Einaudi, 1981);
La treccia di Tatiana, photographs by Antonio Ria (Turin: Einaudi, 1986);
Nei mari estremi (Milan: Mondadori, 1987; revised, Turin: Einaudi, 1996);
Un sogno del Nord (Turin: Einaudi, 1989);
Le lune di Hvar (Turin: Einaudi, 1991);
Terre di Lucchesia, photographs by Max Nobile (Lucca: Pacini Fazzi, 1991);
Un caso di coscienza (Turin: Bollati Boringhieri, 1992);
Lalla Romano pittrice [Paintings], edited by Ria (Turin: Einaudi, 1993);
Lalla Romano. Disegni [Paintings], edited by Ria (Turin: Einaudi, 1994);
L'esercizio della pittura [Paintings], edited by Ria (Turin: Einaudi, 1995);
Ho sognato l'Ospedale (Genoa: Melangolo, 1995).
Collection: *Opere,* 2 volumes, edited by Cesare Segre (Milan: Mondadori, 1991–1992).

TRANSLATIONS: Gustave Flaubert, *Tre racconti* (Turin: Einaudi, 1944);

Lalla Romano

Eugène Delacroix, *Diario (1822–1863)* (Turin: Chiantore, 1945);
Béatrix Beck, *Leone Morin, prete* (Turin: Einaudi, 1954);
Flaubert, *L'educazione sentimentale* (Turin: Einaudi, 1984).

Lalla Romano's major works evoke the past as seen through her personal experience: her childhood years in the provincial towns and mountains

314

of Piedmont, her student years in Turin in the 1920s, her marriage, the difficulties of everyday life, the relationship with her son and grandson, her husband's illness and death, and her travels and impressions of people she met. She is associated with the *letteratura della memoria* (literature of remembrance), a genre that was cultivated by many Italian authors between 1930 and 1940 when Fascism limited their possibilities of expression.

Romano's goal as a writer is to preserve the past, not to sentimentalize it. She draws from such personal experiences as domestic events and simple family affections, which she explores minutely in all their possibilities, including the fabulous. She tries to capture the moments of truth that exist in memory in a measured style, poetically evoking the moment rather than focusing on narrating a linear story. She always describes everything from a personal point of view, using various means of documentation, such as photographs, letters, drawings, and old school compositions. Romano's autobiographical material enables her to create unique novels that lie outside the mainstream of Italian narrative. Moreover, with her 1975 book *Lettura di un'immagine* (Reading an Image) she initiated a type of narrative by providing evocative commentary on a series of photographs taken by her father.

Lalla (Graziella) Romano was born on 11 November 1906 (not 1909 as most reference books indicate), in Demonte, near Cuneo (Piedmont), where her father, Roberto Romano, was employed as a land surveyor. Both of her parents were born in Cuneo. Her mother, Giuseppina Peano, was the niece of the famed mathematician Giuseppe Peano. Lalla's sister Silvia was also born in Demonte, in 1910, but in 1916 the family moved to Cuneo, where Roberto Romano joined his father-in-law's land-surveying firm. After four years of elementary school in Demonte, Lalla completed first the gymnasium and then the classical lyceum in Cuneo. She graduated in 1924, two years after the birth of her youngest sister, Luciana. Her love for mountains and her interest in poetry and painting, as well as a fascination with northern Europe, go back to these years.

In 1924 Romano enrolled at the University of Turin, where she attended classes in literature, philosophy, and art history. She was greatly influenced by her philosophy professor, Annibale Pastore, with whom she studied Immanuel Kant, Friedrich Nietzsche, and Arthur Schopenhauer and by the famous art critic Lionello Venturi. She received her degree in Italian literature in 1928, writing her thesis on the medieval poet Cino da Pistoia. But her interest in painting was as strong as her interest in literature,

and from 1925 to 1928 she had the painter Giovanni Guarlotti as her mentor. In 1928 she took lessons from Felice Casorati, in whose atelier she met many of her future friends, including Daphne Maughan, Carlo Levi, Paola Levi-Montalcini, and Mario Soldati. Still a student, Romano went to Paris to visit her friend Andrée Arnoux, with whom she had for a year in Turin shared the same room in a boardinghouse for young women run by French nuns.

In 1929, after a summer course at the University of Debrecen in Hungary, Romano worked as a substitute instructor at the Scuole Magistrali (Teachers' College) in Cuneo, but she continued to take lessons from Casorati. In 1930 she taught at the city's lyceum and subsequently became head of the local civic library. In 1932 she married Innocenzo Monti, a bank clerk, whom she had met while hiking in the mountains. He would become the president of the Banca Commerciale Italiana (Italian Commercial Bank) in 1975. Their only son, Piero, was born in 1933. In 1935 Romano moved to Turin with her husband. She continued her career as a teacher for the next twenty-five years. At the same time she continued to paint, exhibiting her paintings in various art shows in Turin. In 1941 she published her first book of poems, *Fiore* (Flower). She would return to poetry with the collections *L'autunno* (Autumn, 1955) and *Giovane è il tempo* (Young is Time, 1974).

In 1943 Romano and her son took refuge in her parents' house in Cuneo to escape the air raids that threatened the city of Turin. In Cuneo, upon invitation of the writer Cesare Pavese, then the editorial reader for the publisher Einaudi, whom she knew from her university years, she translated Gustave Flaubert's *Trois contes* (Three Tales, 1944). At this time Romano joined the anti-Fascist movement called Giustizia e Libertà (Justice and Liberty). After the war she returned to Turin.

In 1947 Romano followed her husband to Milan, where she decided to give up painting in favor of writing and established lasting contacts with the leading men of letters. She started to contribute articles to many Italian literary journals. Her first book of prose, *Le metamorfosi* (Metamorphoses), appeared in 1951 with a preface by Elio Vittorini. The work was favorably reviewed by the poet Vittorio Sereni but was otherwise generally condemned for its scandalous subject matter because it contained a series of dreams at a time when the realistic representation of life was the norm. The first-person dreams are those of five persons: a child, two young men, a mother, and a father; each represents different moments of life and reflects different preoccupations. Contemporary critics failed to notice this structure, but in the 1967 revised edition that won the Soroptimist Prize, the dreams are grouped according to subject matter under fourteen headings, and the names of the narrators are added at the end of each dream. In 1983 she again revised the work. The variations between the editions are noted in her collected works, *Opere* (1991).

Encouraged by Pavese, Vittorini, and Natalia Ginzburg, Romano published her first novel, *Maria,* in 1953. It was favorably reviewed by Eugenio Montale and was given the Veillon Prize the following year. Written in the first person by a narrator who observes her maid, it is the story of a humble and honest Piedmontese country girl who works as a maid in the city. The young woman—patterned after Romano's maid—always thinks of her duties and family, while rarely thinking of herself. Together with her relatives Maria represents the old breed of mountain people who help each other and bear hardships and illnesses with stoicism, in contrast to the violent peasants described by Pavese. Romano's originality is reflected above all in her style. She admires Maria as an equal, fusing her intellectual world with the simple world of Maria's family, with whom she visits and exchanges ideas.

Romano's next novel, *Tetto murato* (Farms within Walls, 1957), won the Pavese Prize. The title refers to a cluster of Piedmontese mountain houses where Paolo, an intellectual active in the Resistance, hides out during the final months of World War II with his wife, Ada, and their daughter. Seriously ill, he is looked after by Ada, on whose shoulders all responsibilities rest. Contrary to the contemporary literary fashion, the political theme is left in the background. Romano explores instead the complex relationship that develops between Paolo and Ada and their new friends, Giulia and her husband, Stefano. Giulia admires the active Ada and feels compassion for Paolo, while Stefano sees some of his own energies reflected in Ada. The situation offers the potential for new, ideal relationships, but that potential is never attained. Although *Tetto Murato* is not an autobiographical novel, Giulia and Stefano reflect many of the traits possessed by Romano and her husband.

Romano's literary production intensified in 1959 after her retirement from teaching. She traveled not only in Europe but all over the world. After visiting Greece in 1957 she published *Diario di Grecia* (Greek Diary, 1959), which she enlarged and revised in 1974. She found that life in Greece, marked by the country's classical heritage, provided a way of "living in eternity."

The novel *L'uomo che parlava solo* (The Man Who Spoke to Himself, 1961) is an exceptional work in Romano's canon, for it lacks autobiographical references. Written in the first person, it is the story of a man who looks back at his life and tries to discover the roots of his unhappiness. He realizes that this analysis will lead him to failure. Incapable of choosing between his wife and his young girlfriend, he loses them both; ultimately, he remains an ambiguous character, a libertine to his wife, a melancholic moralist to his free spirited lover.

La penombra che abbiamo attraversato (The Twilight We Crossed, 1964), which won the Librai Milanesi Prize, is Romano's best work. After the death of her mother, Romano visited Demonte (called Ponte Stura in the book) as a pilgrimage in her memory. The novel is constructed on two intertwining levels: the present of the visit and the past evoked by flashbacks. The author re-creates images of her parents, her sister Silvia, her grandmother, relatives, family friends, neighbors, school companions, and local inhabitants as well as places, events, objects, and even odors that she experienced in her childhood. She calls to mind a period before World War I when life was difficult but simple, so different from the world in the 1960s that it seems almost mythical.

In the eyes of the adult, former merits and events, which Romano describes in an almost lyric prose, assume the right perspective without losing any of their poetic quality. She takes her title from Marcel Proust's *Le Temps retrouvé* (1927) ("la pénombre que nous avons traversée") as an homage perhaps to the great master of the literature of remembrance, though Romano succeeds in creating her own distinctive vision of the past. Unlike Proust's *pénombra,* Romano's is not a twilight or a shadow but a diffused and faded light, similar to that of dreams. She sees herself as a little girl, a humble part of a loving family who respects the private worlds of others while isolating herself through her own contrasting tendencies—nervous restlessness, anxiety, and vivid fantasy on the one hand; serene optimism, sound reasoning, and self-irony on the other.

La penombra che abbiamo attraversato was favorably reviewed by many critics, among them Carlo Bo, who called it a poetic masterpiece. The poet Montale resigned in protest from the jury of the Viareggio Prize, who denied the prize to Romano. Anna Banti, writing about the novel in the journal *Paragone* in 1964, pointed to it as a proof that Romano had found her own authentic and courageous path.

In 1969 Romano published *Le parole tra noi leggere* (Light Words between Us), which won the Strega Prize and became a best-seller. The title is borrowed from Montale's poem "Due nel crepuscolo" (Two in Twilight). Written in the first person, the novel reflects Romano's unsentimental, almost clinical scrutiny of her son's difficult maturation, revealing the many problems and the anguish he caused himself and his parents. Mainly based on the relationship between a mother and her son, the book follows Piero from 1933 to 1966, from birth to the first four years of his marriage to Marlène.

More than a confession, *Le parole tra noi leggere* is both a self-criticism and a mother's attempt to understand her son's complex character. Romano examines what caused her son's withdrawal and what made him rebel and systematically refuse his parents' way of life. The basic problem seems to have been the inability of mother and son to understand each other, which led each to hurt the other unknowingly. There is a constant desire on the part of the mother to interpret her son's strange behavior as a sign of precocious intelligence. At the end, Romano does not come to a conclusion, but the reader realizes that mother and son, who in the novel are antagonist and protagonist, respectively, have similar personalities. They inevitably clash because each has a strong sense of personal independence and a possessive sense of love.

Romano's style is direct and dry, her prose deprived of all poetic allusions characteristic of her earlier works. Banti, discussing the novel in *Paragone* in 1969, points to this style as clearly dissociating Romano's fiction from the so-called women's style of narrative. Other critics also praised the book, although some showed reservations with regard to the content. Readers, on the other hand, saw the novel as effectively representing the generation gap, the difficulty of bringing up children, and the problems of contemporary education. The same year his mother published *Le parole tra noi leggere* Piero Monti published his first book, *Il ponte di quarta* (Fourth-Class Deck, 1969), which he followed in 1988 with *Lettera d'amore senza indirizzo* (Love-Letter without Address). The two works, published by Mondadori, seem to prove that he was not a complete failure in life, as is intimated in his mother's novel.

Also autobiographical, Romano's next book, *L'ospite* (The Guest, 1973), is a striking contrast to her previous novel—much lighter in tone, treating a short time span and dealing with simple, everyday problems. It describes the difficulties and at times the helplessness Romano faced in baby-sitting her grandson, Emiliano, born in 1970, who stayed with her and her husband for the first time when he was only a few months old while his parents were on a trip. Divided into sixty-four sketches, some of which are only one page long, the novel is a charming narration of the various situations faced by an inexperienced and not particularly practical grand-

Cover for a 1995 edition of Romano's first novel, which presents an admiring view of a country girl turned city maid

mother, who treats her charge with the respect she would accord a grown-up person. Despite having to give up her own cherished work, she becomes so attached to her grandson that she dreams of keeping him always for herself and is disappointed when he is reclaimed by his parents. The presence of the child is seen by Romano as a miraculous epiphany, a magical intrusion into daily reality.

In 1975 Romano published *Lettura di un'immagine,* which she published in a longer version as *Romanzo di figure* (Novel of Images, 1986). She groups a series of photographs taken by her father at the beginning of the twentieth century under fourteen headings, such as "The Hunters," "The Valley," "The Winter," "The Children," "The Group Portraits." She then comments briefly, trying to capture the spirit of the pictures, the sentiments hidden behind the faces of children, relatives, and simple country folk, as well as the intentions of the artist-photographer. In reading the captions and glancing at the photographs, one is reminded of Romano's *La penombra che abbiamo attraversato,* where the same characters and landscape are described with a technique obviously impressionistic in style.

Romano in 1975 also published *La villeggiante* (The Vacationer), which consists of two parts: "Avventure mancate" (Failed Adventures), containing ten short stories written mostly in the 1930s and 1940s; and "Pralève" (a locality in the Val d'Aosta region where she used to vacation in summer), consisting of twenty-two sketches of individuals. This second part, which depicts proud, hardworking local mountain people and visitors encountered in the rustic environment not yet spoiled by progress and luxury, was republished separately in 1978.

Like most Italian intellectuals in the postwar period, Romano became involved with the Italian Communist Party. In 1976 she was elected town councillor in Milan as a member of the party. A year later, however, she resigned her post because she was bored with the work, declaring herself unsuited to dealing with political, economic, or social problems.

The title of the novel *Una giovinezza inventata* (An Invented Youth, 1979) was borrowed from the aphorism "An invented youth that comes true in old age," from Elias Canetti's *The Human Province* (1978). The word *invent* should be read as meaning "enchanted" or "mythic." Romano narrates the story of her own formative years spent at the University of Turin in the 1920s. She depicts herself as a young woman interested in painting, inclined toward a contemplation of nature and ideas rather than active life. Severe yet open-minded, solitary yet joyous, rational yet full of fantasy, Romano looks with a critical eye at her professors (many of whom are mentioned by their real names), at the male and female students she befriended, at the painters whose studios she frequented, and at her relatives residing in Turin. She also examines her relationships with others, her awakening love, her attraction to the wrong person, her inability to control her feelings, and her fear of having misunderstood the sensitivity of a friend. Reflected in her experience are some basic problems faced by young women of her generation who were studying at Italian universities.

In 1981 Romano published *Inseparabile* (Inseparable), a novel dealing with the suffering of Emiliano, the grandson described as a baby in *L'ospite,* as a consequence of his parents' separation. Seen through Romano's grandmotherly eyes, the gripping story focuses on the boy's trauma as he has to adapt to his mother's new companion and to life in the country. The grandparents can only helplessly watch as the boy becomes more and more entangled in the disorder that surrounds him, for neither his mother nor her companion know anything about farming, which leads to disaster and the man's death. The return to the city brings the boy not only closer to the grandparents but also to his unforgotten father. Emiliano's touching story is one that speaks to a common experience, for many a child of divorced or separated parents leads a fragmented, irregular life.

After the death of her husband in 1984, Romano continued her life as a writer though perhaps with less zest than before. Her next project was writing the captions for the photographs taken by Antonio Ria at a garden party, which appeared under the title *La treccia di Tatiana* (Tatiana's Tresses, 1986), an allusion to Aleksandr Pushkin's *Eugene Onegin* or rather to Pyotr Tchaikovsky's opera of the work. Romano then published another autobiographical work, *Nei mari estremi* (In the Extreme Seas, 1987). Using this metaphor for eternal silence, she describes her husband's illness, death, and funeral. The clinically dry prose is interrupted by flashbacks to their close relationship and binding love. Romano's *Un sogno del Nord* (A Dream about the North, 1989) includes various articles and sketches, some of which were published previously in periodicals, about places visited or persons known. She writes about writers such as Vittorio Sereni, Pavese, Vittorini, Carlo Levi, and Riccardo Bacchelli as well as the historian Arnaldo Momigliano.

Le lune di Hvar (The Moons of Hvar, 1991) is based on the notes Romano took during four different trips to the Dalmatian island of Hvar in the company of Ria, who took pictures of the coats of arms belonging to the local nobility. There are short references to the trips—the road, hotels, and meals—but she makes no attempt to explore the local situation, past or present, even though she was there on the eve of Croatia's independence. What she records are the observations on the activities and the movements of her young companion, which read like notes for a novel on the relationship between a young man and a much older woman. In addition she includes impressions of people seen or spoken to in a fleeting way.

Above all, the book is notable for Romano's impressions of the sea, the sky, and the moon—poetic images created with rapid strokes of color. The dark, serene sea—"Il mare è tornato blu, le vele come spine bianche, sottili" (The sea has turned blue again, the sails, as fine as white fishbones)—is transformed by a rainy day: "mare bianco, metallico, liscio; cielo bianco e nero, morbido" (smooth, metallic, white sea; soft, white and black sky). Sky and sea create contrasting colors: "cielo celeste-rosa su mare turchino" (an azure-pink sky on a cobalt blue sea).

The major leitmotiv of *Le lune di Hvar,* the ever-present moon, is never the same. Its size impresses the writer: "A una svolta, improvvisa, l'apparizione. All'altezza dei nostri occhi. La luna piena, enorme." (At a turn, suddenly, the apparition. At the level of our eyes. An enormous, full moon.) It seems a companion to the sun: "Alle 6 la luna si specchia, con capigliatura leggera, bionda, mentre già le barche sono illuminate dal sole" (At 6:00 A.M. the moon, with light blond hair, mirrors herself, while the boats are already illuminated by the sun). And sometimes it is barely a line: "luna evanescente, fettina sottile tra le nuvole anch'esse sottili, diafane" (an evanescent moon, a tiny fine slice between the clouds, also fine and transparent). Such images attest to Romano's poetic inclinations and refined style, which is the strength of the book.

Romano assisted Cesare Segre when he wrote the introduction to and edited her *Opere* (Works, 1991–1992). All of her literary work is included, with the exception of the three photo album commentaries—*Lettura di un'immagine, La treccia di Tatiana,* and *Terre di Lucchesia* (The Countryside of Lucca, 1991). Segre provides a detailed biographical chronology as well as notes on the individual works and Ria adds the bibliography. In 1992 Romano produced the case history *Un caso di coscienza* (A Matter of Conscience). She describes the hypocritical accusations and the attempted disciplinary action against a colleague, a teacher who as a Christian Scientist had refused a blood transfusion for her sick child.

It is curious that none of Romano's novels has as yet been translated into English, while there have been Japanese, Romanian, French, and German translations. She is a respected writer who was recognized in 1979 by the Italian government with the Penna d'Oro Prize (Golden Pen Award) and by the mayor of Milan with the Medaglia d'Oro di Benemerenza Civica (Gold Medal of Civic Merit). She has been included in the prestigious reference work *Letteratura italiana: Novecento.* Some critics have used the word *mammismo* (the excessive attachment and interference on the part of mothers) with regard to some of her works; the criticism, however, is only true of minor moments in her literary production. Generally Romano's limpid style has a touch of magic; even when she describes daily routines or domestic problems she manages to find suggestive moments.

Cover for a 1995 edition of Romano's 1964 novel, for which she drew on memories of her childhood

In 1994 Romano was awarded the Terre del Piemonte Prize. The same year a Lalla Romano Convention was held. In 1996 her ninetieth birthday was celebrated with articles and an exhibit of her paintings (all done before 1945), which took place in Costigliole d'Asti, on the premises of the Grinzane Cavour Prize society. Romano finds artistic fulfillment through a constant interplay between the past and the present, and her achievement can be seen as a variation on the philosophical problem of time and memory. Although her novels may seem simple, they explore a complex interrelationship of the present and the past. Averse to literary trends, she has followed her own inclinations and will leave a unique legacy as a writer.

Interviews:

Sandra Petrignani, *Le signore della scrittura: interviste* (Milan: La Tartaruga, 1984), pp. 15–21;

Paola Gaglianone and Antonio Ria, eds., Conversazione con Lalla Romano. *La responsabilità della scrittura* (Rome: Òmicron, 1997).

References:

Giuseppe Amoroso, "Il 'privilegiato isolamento' di Lalla Romano," *Critica letteraria,* 6 (1978): 664-676;

Anna Banti, "Lalla Romano," *Paragone,* 15 (1964): 96-98;

Banti, "Lalla Romano," *Paragone,* 20 (1969): 104-106;

Flavia Brizio, "Memory and Time in Lalla Romano's Novels, *La penombra che abbiamo attraversato* and *Le parole tra noi leggere,*" in *Contemporary Women Writers in Italy: A Modern Renaissance,* edited by Santo L. Aricò (Amherst: University of Massachusetts Press, 1990), pp. 63-75;

Brizio, *La scrittura e la memoria (Lalla Romano)* (Milan: Selene Edizioni, 1993);

Annamaria Catalucci, *Invito alla lettura di Lalla Romano* (Milan: Mursia, 1980);

Francesco Erbani, "Passione e poesia: i novant'anni di Lalla," *La Repubblica,* 27 October 1996, pp. 28-29;

Giansiro Ferrata, "L'infanzia memorata di L. Romano," in *Letteratura italiana: Novecento,* volume 8, edited by Gianni Grana (Milan: Marzorati, 1979), pp. 7650-7655;

Giulio Ferroni, *Storia della letteratura italiana,* volume 4 (Turin: Einaudi, 1991), pp. 561-563;

Ferroni, "Postfazione," in Lalla Romano, *La penombra che abbiamo attraversato* (Turin: Einaudi tascabili, 1994), pp. 205-221;

Ferroni, "L'opera narrativa di Lalla Romano," in *Conversazione con Lalla Romano. La responsabilità della scrittura,* edited by Paola Gaglianone and Antonio Ria (Rome: Òmicron, 1997), pp. 50-63;

Marco Forti, "Lalla Romano," in his *Prosatori e narratori nel Novecento italiano* (Milan: Mursia, 1984), pp. 265-285;

Philippe Giraudon, "La musique du silence," in Lalla Romano, *Jeune est le temps* (Paris: Orphée/la Différence, 1994), pp. 7-13;

Maria Mimita Lamberti, "Sul confine," in Lalla Romano pittrice, edited by Antonio Ria (Turin: Einaudi, 1993), pp. 9-12;

Giuliano Manacorda, "Lalla Romano," in his *Storia della letteratura italiana contemporanea. 1949-1975* (Rome, Editori Riuniti, 1977), pp. 367-369;

Eugenio Miccini, "Narrativa di memoria," *Nuova Corrente,* 12 (1964): 97-114;

Massimo Onofri, "Lalla Romano: *Opere,*" *Nuovi Argomenti,* 40 (October-December 1991): 121-124;

Bruno Pischedda, "Il personaggio di se stesso," in *Tirature '94,* edited by Vittorio Spinazzola (Milan: Baldini & Castoldi, 1994), pp. 49-60;

Giorgio Pullini, *Il romanzo italiano del dopoguerra (1940-1960)* (Padua: Marsilio, 1965), pp. 327-328;

Giovanni Raboni, "Postfazione," in Lalla Romano, *Una giovenzza inventata* (Turin: Einaudi tascabili, 1995), pp. 239-245;

Raboni, "La scrittura fa 90," *Corriere della Sera/Sette,* 7 November 1996, pp. 110-115;

Antonio Ria, ed., *Intorno a Lalla Romano. Saggi critici e testimionanze* (Milan: Mondadori, 1996);

Ines Scaramucci, "Utimi romanzi di L. Romano," in *Letteratura Italiana. Novecento,* volume 9, edited by Gianni Grana (Settimo Milanese: Marzorati, 1989), pp. 508-510;

Cesare Segre, "Introduzione" and "Nota biografica," in Romano's *Opere,* volume 1, edited by Segre (Milan: Mondadori, 1991), pp. Ix-xcix;

Segre, "Varianti delle poesie di Lalla Romano," in *Le tradizioni del testo. Studi di Letteratura italiana offerti a Domenico De Robertis,* edited by Franco Gavazzeni and Guglielmo Gorni (Milan-Naples: Riccardo Ricciardi, 1993), pp. 573-589;

Segre, "Lalla Romano fra pittura e scrittura," in *Lalla Romano pittrice,* edited by Ria (Turin: Einaudi, 1993), pp. 207-209;

Vittorio Spinazzola, "L'intimismantielegiaco di Lalla Romano," in his *L'offerta letteraria* (Naples: Morano, 1990), pp. 117-126;

Giovanni Tesio, "Lalla Romano," *Belfagor,* 35 (November 1980): 671-686;

Michela Vanon Alliata, "Le immagini fra noi leggere," *Leggere,* 4 (October 1991): 10-13;

Fiora Vincenti, *Lalla Romano* (Florence: Nuova Italia, 1 74);

Vincenti, "Lalla Romano," in *Letteratura italiana: Novecento,* volume 8, pp. 7634-7650;

Giorgio Zampa, "Una perfetta definizione interiore," in *Lalla Romano pittrice,* edited by Ria (Turin: Einaudi, 1993), pp. 15-17.

Leonardo Sciascia

(8 January 1921 – 20 November 1989)

Tom O'Neill
University of Melbourne

BOOKS: *Favole della dittatura* (Rome: Bardi, 1950);
La Sicilia, il suo cuore (Rome: Bardi, 1952);
Il fiore della poesia romanesca (Caltanissetta: Salvatore Sciascia, 1952);
Pirandello e il pirandellismo. Con lettere inedite di Pirandello a Tilgher (Caltanissetta: Salvatore Sciascia, 1953);
Le parrocchie di Regalpetra (Bari: Laterza, 1956; preface added, 1967); translated by Judith Green as *Salt in the Wound* (New York: Orion, 1969);
Gli zii di Sicilia (Turin: Einaudi, 1958; enlarged, 1960); translated by N. S. Thompson as *Sicilian Uncles* (Manchester & New York: Carcanet, 1986);
Pirandello e la Sicilia (Caltanissetta: Salvatore Sciascia, 1961; enlarged edition, Milan: Adelphi, 1996)—includes "Nel cinquantenario della morte di Luigi Pirandello";
Il giorno della civetta (Turin: Einaudi, 1961); translated by Archibald Colquhoun and Arthur Oliver as *Mafia Vendetta* (London: Cape, 1963; New York: Knopf, 1964); republished as *The Day of the Owl,* in *The Day of the Owl and Equal Danger* (Manchester & New York: Carcanet, 1984);
Il consiglio d'Egitto (Turin: Einaudi, 1963); translated by Adrienne Foulke as *The Council of Egypt* (London: Cape, 1966; New York: Knopf, 1966);
Santo Marino (Caltanissetta: Salvatore Sciascia, 1963);
Morte dell'inquisitore (Bari: Laterza, 1964); translated by Green as *The Death of the Inquisitor* in *Salt in the Wound* (New York: Orion, 1969); translated by Ian Thompson as *Death of an Inquisitor and Other Stories* (Manchester & New York: Carcanet, 1990);
Feste religiose in Sicilia, with photographs by Ferdinando Scianna (Bari: Leonardo da Vinci, 1965);
Jaki (Caltanissetta & Rome: Salvatore Sciascia, 1965);
L'onorevole. Dramma in tre atti (Turin: Einaudi, 1965);

Leonardo Sciascia (photograph © Jerry Bauer)

A ciascuno il suo (Turin: Einaudi, 1966); translated by Foulke as *A Man's Blessing* (New York: Harper & Row, 1968; London: Cape, 1969); republished as *To Each His Own* (Manchester & New York: Carcanet, 1989);
Racconti siciliani (Urbino: Istituto Statale d'Arte, 1966);
Recitazione della controversia liparitana dedicata ad A[lexander] D[ubcek] (Turin: Einaudi, 1969);
La corda pazza. Scrittori e cose della Sicilia (Turin: Einaudi, 1970);

Il contesto. Una parodia (Turin: Einaudi, 1971); translated by Foulke as *Equal Danger* (New York: Harper & Row, 1973; London: Cape, 1973);

Atti relativi alla morte di Raymond Roussel (Palermo: Esse, 1971); translated by Alec Gordon as "Acts Relative to the Death of Raymond Roussel," in *Raymond Roussel: Life, Death & Works* (London: Atlas, 1987), pp. 124–146;

Il mare colore del vino (Turin: Einaudi, 1973); translated by Avril Bardoni as *The Wine-Dark Sea* (Manchester: Carcanet, 1985);

Palermo felicissima, by Sciascia and Rosario La Duca (Palermo: Punto, 1973);

Todo modo (Turin: Einaudi, 1974); translated by Foulke as *One Way or Another* (New York: Harper & Row, 1977); translated by Sacha Rabinovitch as *One Way or Another* (Manchester & New York: Carcanet, 1987);

Il fuoco nel mare (Milan: Emme, 1975);

La scomparsa di Majorana (Turin: Einaudi, 1975); translated by Rabinovitch as *The Mystery of Majorana* in *The Moro Affair; and, The Mystery of Majorana* (Manchester & New York: Carcanet, 1987);

I pugnalatori (Turin: Einaudi, 1976);

Acque di Sicilia, photographs by Lisetta Carmi (Bergamo: Dalmine, 1977);

Candido ovvero un sogno fatto in Sicilia (Turin: Einaudi, 1977); translated by Foulke as *Candido or A Dream Dreamed in Sicily* (New York & London: Harcourt Brace Jovanovich, 1979);

Sicilia, by Sciascia and Folco Quilici (Milan: Silvana, 1977);

I Siciliani, by Sciascia and Dominique Fernandez, photographs by Scianna (Turin: Einaudi, 1977);

L'affaire Moro (Palermo: Sellerio, 1978); enlarged as *L'affaire Moro. Con aggiunta la Relazione Parlamentare* (Palermo: Sellerio, 1983); translated by Rabinovitch as *The Moro Affair* in *The Moro Affair; and, The Mystery of Majorana;*

Dalle parti degli infedeli (Palermo: Sellerio, 1979);

Nero su nero (Turin: Einaudi, 1979);

Il volto sulla maschera. Mosjoukine-Mattia Pascal (Milan: Mondadori, 1980);

Il teatro della memoria (Turin: Einaudi, 1981);

La palma va a nord (Rome: Quaderni radicali, 1981);

La sentenza memorabile (Palermo: Sellerio, 1982);

Kermesse (Palermo: Sellerio, 1982);

Cruciverba (Turin: Einaudi, 1983);

La contea di Modica (Milan: Electa, 1983);

Stendhal e la Sicilia (Palermo: Sellerio, 1984);

Occhio di capra (Turin: Einaudi, 1984);

Cola Pesce (Milan: Emme, 1985);

Cronachette (Palermo: Sellerio, 1985); translated by Thompson as *Little Chronicles* (Manchester & New York: Carcanet, 1990);

Per un ritratto dello scrittore da giovane (Palermo: Sellerio, 1985);

La strega e il capitano (Milan: Bompiani, 1986); translated by Thompson as *The Captain and The Witch* (Manchester & New York: Carcanet, 1990);

1912+1 (Milan: Adelphi, 1986); translated by Rabinovitch as *1912+1* (Manchester & New York: Carcanet, 1989);

Ignoto a me stesso: ritratti di scrittori da Edgar Allan Poe a Jorge Luis Borges (Milan: Bompiani, 1987);

Porte aperte (Milan: Adelphi, 1987); translated by Marie Evans as *Open Doors* in *The Knight and Death & Other Stories* (Manchester & New York: Carcanet, 1991);

Il cavaliere e la morte (Milan: Adelphi, 1988); translated by Joseph Farrell as *The Knight and Death* in *The Knight and Death & Other Stories;*

Ore di Spagna (Marina di Patti, Messina: Pungitopo, 1988);

Una storia semplice (Milan: Adelphi, 1989); translated by Farrell as *A Straight-Forward Tale* in *The Knight and Death & Other Stories;*

Fatti diversi di storia letteraria e civile (Palermo: Sellerio, 1989);

Quaderno (Palermo: Nuova Editrice Meridionale, 1991);

Leonardo Sciascia e "Malgrado Tutto." Scritti di Leonardo Sciascia sul giornale del suo paese (Racalmuto: Editoriale "Malgrado Tutto," 1991).

Collection: *Opere,* edited by Claude Ambroise, 3 volumes (Milan: Bompiani, 1987–1991).

Edition in English: *Open Doors and Three Novellas,* translated by Marie Evans, Joseph Farrell, and Sacha Rabinovitch (New York: Knopf, 1992).

OTHER: *Narratori di Sicilia,* edited by Sciascia and Salvatore Guglielmino (Milan: Mursia, 1967);

Alberto Savinio, *Torre di guardia,* edited by Sciascia (Palermo: Sellerio, 1977);

Alberto Savinio: pittura e letteratura, edited by Sciascia and Giuliano Briganti (Milan: Ricci, 1979);

Delle cose di Sicilia: testi inediti o rari, edited by Sciascia, 3 volumes (Palermo: Sellerio, 1980–1984);

Omaggio a Pirandello, edited by Sciascia (Milan: Bompiani, 1986);

Gabriele D'Annunzio, *Alla piacente,* edited by Sciascia (Milan: Bompiani, 1988).

More than two hundred years ago Johann Wolfgang von Goethe asserted that to understand Italy one had to start with Sicily. Leonardo Sciascia, who frequently cited the German writer's aphorism, attempted through a lifelong examination of his native culture, particularly the Mafia, to uncover and account for the corrupt underbelly of this important part of Italian society. The plots of novels such as *Il contesto* or *Todo modo,* which seemed to border on the fantastic when they first appeared, can be seen in retrospect as having been only too close to reality. In the words of a minor character in *A ciascuno il suo,* reality "è sempre più ricca e imprevedibile delle nostre deduzioni" (is always richer and more unpredictable than our deductions).

Sciascia's works should continue to be indispensable reading for students of Italian society, but when the sociological interest of his writings becomes dated, they will continue to fascinate as the products of a rich imagination. Sciascia came to realize that literature was, as he noted in his miscellaneous collection *Nero su nero* (Black on Black, 1979), "un sistema di 'oggetti eterni' . . . che variamente, imprevedibilmente splendono, si eclissano, tornano a splendere e ad eclissarsi—e così via—alla luce della verità" (a system of 'eternal objects' . . . which variously, unexpectedly shine out, are eclipsed, shine out again and are eclipsed—and so on—in the light of truth).

Sciascia's origins were humble and his life essentially uneventful. He was born on 8 January 1921 in Racalmuto, near Agrigento. His mother, Genoveffa Martorelli, was a housewife; his father, Pasquale, worked in the offices of a sulfur-mining firm. Sciascia was brought up by his aunts in the house of his paternal grandfather, Leonardo Sciascia-Alfieri, who had begun life in the mines as a child laborer. After school Sciascia served as an apprentice to a tailor, but in 1935 he began his studies at the Caltanissetta teacher-training college, where the writer Vitaliano Brancati taught. Thanks to his teacher Giuseppe Granata he discovered American literature.

From 1941 to 1948 Sciascia worked in the UCSEA office, which was responsible for the collection and storing of agricultural produce. In 1944 he married Maria Andronico, who had come to Racalmuto the previous year as an elementary-school teacher. Two daughters, Laura and Annamaria, were born from the marriage. In 1948 Sciascia's brother, Giuseppe, committed suicide. In 1949 he began teaching in Racalmuto's elementary school, where he would work until 1957. He then taught school in Palermo from 1957 until 1968.

Sciascia began his work as a writer and critic in the 1950s and continued it unabated until his death. Because of his teaching he almost invariably wrote his books during the summer at Racalmuto. In 1970

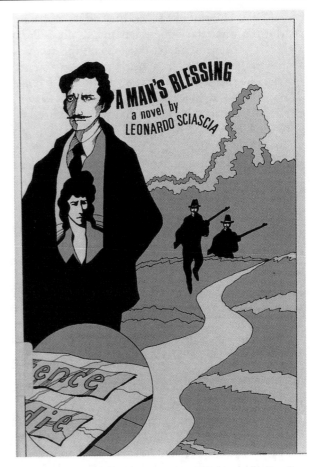

Dust jacket for the American edition of the translation of Sciascia's 1966 novel, in which a teacher's investigation of a murder leads to his death

he retired from teaching to become a full-time writer. Five years later he was elected a Palermo city counselor on the Communist Party ticket, although he was not formally a member of the party. He resigned two years later, producing an account of the experience in *Candido ouvero un sogno fatto in Sicilia* (1977; translated as *Candido or a Dream Dreamed in Sicily,* 1979). A reworking of Voltaire's philosophical tale, *Candide* (1759), Sciascia's novel gave the lie to the protagonist's assertion in *Todo modo* that all books—"Tutti. *Tranne Candide*" (All. *Except Candide*)—could be rewritten.

Subsequent to the kidnapping and murder of Italian prime minister Aldo Moro by the Italian terrorist group known as the Red Brigades, Sciascia published *L'affaire Moro* (1978; translated as *The Moro Affair,* 1987). He argued that Moro's letters to his fellow Christian Democrats were indicative of Moro's character, refuting the denials of Moro's correspondents who claimed the letters showed a different man than the honorable one they had known. In 1979, in spite of his negative political experience in Palermo, he stood for and won election to the national Parliament on the Radical Party ticket. There his main activity was on the commission into the Moro affair, which resulted in a minority report—included in the 1983 edition of *L'affaire Moro* titled *Con aggiunta la Relazione Parlamentare* (with the Parliámentary Report)—that was delivered before the elections that year. Sciascia died of a light chain disease in Palermo at the age of sixty-eight.

In 1985 Antonio Motta suggested that Sciascia's merits as a writer have been debased by excessively ideological readings of his works. Even if one were to counterbalance this assertion with Sciascia's own warning in *Porte aperte* that "la letteratura non è mai del tutto innocente. Nemmeno la piu innocente" (literature is never completely innocent. Not even the most innocent), it would be difficult to gainsay Motta's point. The prevailing Neorealism of the early 1950s certainly conditioned the perception of Sciascia's early work. It was no less a figure than fellow Sicilian Elio Vittorini, the undisputed arbiter of Italian literary taste whose ideological views on the nature and purpose of literature were well known, who chose to publish *Gli zii di Sicilia* in the Gettoni series he edited for Einaudi.

The neorealistic perspective is also evident in the marketing of *Il giorno della civetta* (1961). Its blurb asked a telling question: "Si può scrivere un racconto su un problema della nostra società che sia un'analisi chiara ed esauriente del problema . . . e—nello stesso tempo—un bel racconto?" (Is it possible to write a story on a problem in our society that is a clear and exhaustive analysis of the problem . . . and—at the same time—a fine story?). The novel was awarded the Crotone Prize because, as the citation claimed, Sciascia had given "una testuale radiografia della mafia, dei suoi armeggi e retroscena e delle allarmanti connivenze in alto e in basso" (a detailed X ray of the Mafia, of its activities and background and its alarming networks in places both high and low). From the first and throughout his career the critical emphasis has been on documentary importance, on fact at the expense of fiction. Too often critics have produced only a partial reading of Sciascia, ignoring his clear intention from the outset to be seen *as a writer.*

The earliest and clearest indication of Sciascia's distinctly literary cast of mind was his review in *La gazzetta di Parma* on 22 December 1955 of Jorge Luis Borges' *Ficciones* (Fictions, 1945), which had just appeared in translation. It was the first review to appear in Italy and clearly revealed that Sciascia was already well acquainted with Borges in the original Spanish. His influence was to increase over the years.

Sciascia's first published book, *Favole della dittatura* (Fables of the Dictatorship, 1950), was a political satire, but his other early books show an autobiographical strain that only surfaces occasionally in his later work. It appears naturally in the lyric poems of *La Sicilia, il suo cuore* (Sicily, Its Heart, 1952) but also in *Le parrocchie di Regalpetra* (1956; translated as *Salt in the Wound,* 1969), a collection of partly fictional essays that chronicles the suffering of peasants in a mythical town based on Sciascia's native Racalmuto. *Le parrocchie di Regalpetra* had as its nucleus his article "Cronache scolastiche" (School Chronicles), which had appeared in the journal *Nuovi argomenti* in 1955 and was based on his experience as an elementary-school teacher.

Gli zii di Sicilia (1958) was Sciascia's first important work of fiction. Postwar Sicily, with its hope alternating between America and Communism, provided the author with the material for two of the three short stories of the original edition of his collection: "La zia d'America" (The American Aunt) and "La motte di Stalin" (The Death of Stalin). The device of the adolescent narrator in "La zia d'America" distanced Sciascia from events and allowed him an interesting point of view to explore. It was not, however, the only distancing device that Sciascia used at this stage in his career, for he was able to step back from the reality of his own time into history in the third story, "Il quarantotto" (Forty-eight). The narrator is an old man who remembers the events of his youth, but the memories are not those of Sciascia's early years, which had provided the raw material of "La zia d'America," but the memories of a century before, covering the period from the revolution of 1848 to the landing of Giuseppe Garibaldi at Marsala in 1860.

Italo Calvino, who also worked for Einaudi, wrote to Sciascia prior to publication of *Gli zii di Sicilia*. He asserted that although "La zia d'America" was the best of the three stories, it was still "un prodotto 'di scuola' e non di prima mano, perché deriva apertamente da Brancati" (a 'school' product and not first hand, because it clearly derives from Brancati). Calvino also found fault with "La morte di Stalin," which he saw as "più pamphletistico, e un po' deludente, dato il tema" (more by way of a pamphlet, and somewhat disappointing, given its theme).

Sciascia sets "L'antimonio" (Antimony), the fourth story of *Gli zii di Sicilia,* added to its second edition (1960), in Spain during the Civil War, although its protagonist is Sicilian. The story's unnamed sources would seem to be, according to the critic Verina Jones, André Malraux's *L'espoir* (Days of Hope, 1938) and George Orwell's *Homage to Cata-*

Dust jacket for the American edition of the translation of Sciascia's 1971 novel, a detective story that is also "a fable about power"

lonia (1938). But perhaps more important than its literary sources are its references to the acts of reading and writing. Sciascia explicitly asserts what he sees as the nexus of life and literature for the first time: "lo credo nel mistero delle parole, e che le parole possano diventare vita, destino; cosí come diventano bellezza" (I believe in the mystery of words, and that words can become life, destiny; just as they become beauty). While this formulation is in terms of beauty, it would not be long before beauty became for Sciascia one with truth. Toward the end of the story, the protagonist affirms the desirability of transforming the world into a book so that it might begin to be comprehended.

In a concluding note to his novel *Il giorno della civetta* (translated as *Mafia Vendetta,* 1963) Sciascia informed his readers that he had spent a year, "da una estate all'altra" (from one summer to the next) rewriting it to "parare le eventuali e possibili intolleranze di coloro che dalla mia rappresentazione potessero ritenersi, più o meno direttamente, colpiti" (to ward off eventual and possible acts of intolerance on the part of those who by my representation might consider themselves, more or less directly, attacked). The event that probably provided Sciascia with his starting point was the murder of a well-known communist trade unionist, Accursio Miraglia. In a busy square on an early evening in January 1947 he was riddled with bullets across his chest. In the novel the union official becomes a small-time builder who is killed at dawn in a deserted square with a single bullet in the back.

While the twelve-year gap between the murder and the publication of *Il giorno della civetta* may have indicated Sciascia's concern with possible litigation, the details, regardless of modification, point up the underlying reality of the material with which he is dealing. Sciascia's concern for authenticity is plain in his explanation to non-Sicilian readers of a range of peculiarly Sicilian idioms—nicknames, proverbs, and Mafia terms. As in the actual case, the investigator in charge of the case is a non-Sicilian. Sciascia modeled his Captain Bellodi on the carabinieri commanding officer in Agrigento, Renato Candida, whom Sciascia had met after reading the manuscript of a study Candida had written on the Mafia, *Questa mafia* (This Mafia, 1956). Shortly after the publication of his study, Sciascia relates, Candida was promoted and transferred to Turin. The Mafia officially did not exist. But the captain Sciascia creates is a complex character who reflects the author as much as the model.

Like Sciascia, Bellodi reads the world through books. The possibility of a crime of passion makes him instinctively think of Giovanni Verga's short story "Cavalleria rusticana" (Rustic Chivalry) and Pietro Mascagni's musical version of it. He has read the eighteenth-century Sicilian dialect poet Giovanni Meli with the notes of the modern Sicilian writer Francesco Lanza and the contemporary Sicilian dialect poet Ignazio Buttitta with the facing translations of Salvatore Quasimodo, the Sicilian writer who won the Nobel Prize for literature in 1959. When questioning the wife of the pruner who has disappeared, the captain talks to her of nicknames but not without first having run through Sicilian literature from Verga to Giuseppe Tomasi de Lampedusa "La donna non capiva molto, e nemmeno il maresciallo . . ." (The woman did not understand much, and not even the sergeant . . .). The lack of understanding, however, apparently goes both ways, as is shown by the earlier comments of the brothers of the murdered builder on Bellodi: "I continentali sono gentili ma non capiscono niente" (People from the mainland are nice but they don't understand anything).

The risk Bellodi runs is that in his tendency to read Sicily through its literature he may end up substituting myth for reality; but on occasions his literary bent enables him to go beyond the myth to a more complex vision of reality than what on the surface seems to be the case. His earlier musical musing on crimes of passion resurfaces in his intuition—corroborated through the figure of Ciampa in Luigi Pirandello's *Berretto a sonagli* (Cap and Bells, 1917)—that in Sicily a crime of passion "non scatta dalla vera e propria passione, dalla passione del cuore; ma da una specie di passione intellettuale . . . fino a raggiungere quella trasparenza formale in cui *il merito,* cioè l'umano peso dei fatti, non conta più; e, abolita l'immagine dell'uomo, la legge nella legge si specchia" (doesn't spring from true and proper passion, from passion of the heart, but from a kind of intellectual passion . . . until it reaches that formal transparency in which *merit,* that is to say the human weight of facts, no longer counts; and, the image of man abolished, law in law reflects itself). Sciascia suggests that contrary to the commonly held view that sees the Sicilian as instinctive and passionate, he is instead the opposite: cool and logical to a fault.

Bellodi comes to recognize the family as the only institution really alive in the Sicilian's consciousness, "ma vivo più come drammatico nodo contrattuale, giuridico, che come aggregato naturale e sentimentale" (but alive more as a dramatic contractual, legally binding knot, than as a natural unit based on feelings and emotions). It alone allows a Sicilian to go beyond his "naturale e tragica solitudine" (natural and tragic solitude) and come to terms through a sophisticated web of relationships with living in society.

It is against the background of such meditations that the interview between Captain Bellodi and the local godfather takes place. The interview is memorable in part because of the two men's momentary recognition of their common humanity: "Lei, anche se mi inchioderà su queste carte come un Cristo, lei è un uomo . . . —Anche lei—disse il capitano con una certa emozione" ('But you, even if you nail me to these documents like Christ to His Cross, you're a man.' . . . 'So are you,' said the captain, not without emotion). That morally reprehensible moment of weakness is not Bellodi's only one in the novel, for earlier the captain angrily identifies with his subalterns' wishful thinking that a temporary suspension of the rule of law will enable them more quickly to resolve the crime. The anti-Fascist Bellodi corrects himself by recalling the repression of the Mafia under Fascism by the so-called Iron Prefect, Cesare Mori, who had been sent by Benito Mussolini to Sicily to eradicate the organization.

Similarly, in the interview with the godfather Bellodi recognizes that his opponents' admirable energy is tragically unredeemable because it is morally misdirected.

It is the godfather's identity as a Sicilian that Sciascia through Bellodi explores, not in order to excuse the crimes but to understand the criminal, who, like the upholder of law and order, is a product of Sicilian society. The key to understanding that Sciascia offers is literature, but he does not intend literature to be an end in itself. Literature for Sciascia is a means of widening the understanding of history, a way of embracing a range of other disciplines, particularly anthropology and its ramifications.

Although *Il giorno della civetta* is concerned with protectionism in the Sicilian building industry, the scene frequently shifts from the periphery to the center, from Sicily to Rome. The unidentified individuals of the fourth chapter are Sicilian, but it is quickly made clear that they are politicians in Rome with business connections and fear that Bellodi's investigations will involve them and their friends. They explicitly attempt to distance the murder inquiry from the political arena and to insinuate that the victim "è stato vittima in una questione di interesse o di corna" (was the victim of conflicting business interests or had been after somebody's wife). Bellodi himself muses about "quei motivi passionali . . . che per la mafia e la polizia sono, in eguale misura, una grande risorsa" (those crimes of passion . . . so useful alike to Mafia and police). The crime of passion also exists, it could be said, in order to prove that the Mafia does not, and this to the advantage of all concerned: the Mafia, for self-protection; the police and politicians, to cover up their links with criminality. But the crime of passion, of course, also exists in its own right and as such is central to *A ciascuno il suo.*

Sciascia's interest in history, which was evident in the opening chapters of *Le parrocchie di Regalpetra* as well as in the short stories "Il quarantotto" and "L'antimonio," asserted itself in *Il consiglio d'Egitto* (translated as *The Council of Egypt,* 1966), a historical novel set in eighteenth-century Palermo during the enlightened despotism of the vice-regency of the Marquis of Caracciolo. In the preface to the 1967 edition of *Le parrocchie di Regalpetra,* Sciascia suggested that all his books were in essence aspects of a single volume concerned with "la storia di una continua sconfitta della ragione e di coloro che nella sconfitta furono personalmente travolti e annientati" (the history of a never-ending defeat of reason and of those who in that defeat were personally caught up and destroyed). In *Il consiglio d'Egitto* such a fate is reserved for the noble legal reformer, Francesco Paolo Di Blasi, who in 1795 planned a republican rebellion timed for the Good Friday processions. The plot was uncovered and he was arrested, tortured, and beheaded.

Di Blasi's failure is subsumed within a more engrossing tale of the forging of a series of historical documents by the Maltese monk, Giuseppe Vella. These forgeries allow Sciascia to muse upon the nature of reality and society and its historical representation through a dazzling period re-creation. No small part of the fascination comes from Sciascia's complex attitude toward Vella, for though Vella's meticulous elaboration of the Council of Egypt is recognized as a fraud (*d'Egitto* means "of Egypt" but also "fictional"), it nevertheless "si sollevava come ondata di luce a investire la realtà, a penetrarla, a trasformarla" (surged up like a wave of light to invade, penetrate, and transform reality). Here Vella improbably joins hands with Bellodi who in *Il giorno della civetta* affirms that Sicily is "tutta una fantastica dimensione: e come ci si può star dentro senza fantasia?" (all a realm of fantasy and what can anyone do there without imagination?).

The "gagliarda fantasia" (sturdy fantasy) of Vella, however, does not prevent him from recognizing early on the limitations and power of historical discourse. That discourse is restricted because much of humanity is omitted from the record: "La storia! E mio padre? E vostro padre? E il gorgoglio delle loro viscere vuote? E la voce della loro fame? Credete che si sentirà, nella storia?" (History! What about my father? What about your father? And the rumbling of their empty bellies, the voice of their hunger? Do you believe this will be heard in history?). It is powerful because of its exclusivity, concerning only "i re, i viceré, i papi, i capitani; i grandi" (kings, viceroys, popes, generals, the great). He also recognizes that history is fiction: "Tutta un'impostura. La storia non esiste" (It's all fraud. History does not exist).

These musings clearly reflect those of Alessandro Manzoni, who in the preface to *I promessi sposi* (The Betrothed, 1827) juxtaposes the history of "principi e potentati" (princes and powers) to that of the "gente meccanica e di picciol affar" (mechanical folk and of small account). But they also are reminiscent of an anguished autobiographical page of "Cronache scolastiche" where Sciascia recognizes the still precarious status of his own recent admission to the ranks of bourgeois society: "e io che non lavoro con le braccia e leggo il mondo attraverso dei libri. Ma è tutto troppo fragile, gente del mio sangue può tornare nella miseria, tornare a vedere nei figli la sofferenza e il rancore. Finchè l'ingiustizia sarà nel mondo, sempre, per tutti, ci sarà questo nodo di paura" (and I who do not work with my hands and

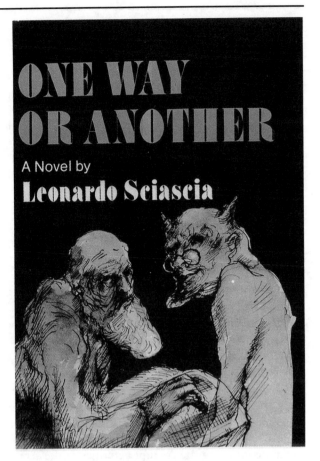

Dust jacket for the American edition of the translation of Sciascia's 1974 novel, which features a villainous intellectual priest

read the world through books. But it is all too fragile, people of my blood can find themselves yet again in misery, see again in their children suffering and bitterness. As long as there is still injustice in the world, always, for everyone, there will be this knot of fear).

That note of precariousness also surfaces in Di Blasi's consideration of Caracciolo's vice-regency: "E tuttavia . . . un uomo simile non poteva non sentirsi sconfitto. Quel che lasciava di durevole era affidato alla coscienza avvenire, alla storia: ora sarebbe bastato un tratto di penna a ricostruire quei privilegi che si era adoperato a demolire, quelle ingiustizie che aveva potuto riparare" (And yet . . . such a man could not but feel defeated. What he left of enduring achievement was entrusted to the conscience of the future, to history: tomorrow the stroke of a pen would be enough to reestablish the privileges he had worked to demolish, to restore the injustices he had been able to correct). What is perhaps most strikingly modern in *Il consiglio d'Egitto* is the recognition that it is writing that invents history.

Some argue that *Il consiglio d'Egitto* is Sciascia's best work, and time may well prove them right. He brilliantly brings to life the rich fabric of society in eighteenth-century Palermo, with its complex mixture of frivolity and seriousness, and presents a much greater range of characters than elsewhere. Moreover, the novel's protagonists, Vella and Di Blasi, are much more rounded than the protagonists of his other works, who tend to be two-dimensional, important not in themselves but as sounding boards for the ideas being debated.

Sciascia returns to his contemporary world in *A ciascuno il suo's* (1966; translated as *A Man's Blessing*, 1968), in which an unmarried, middle-aged teacher, Laurana, still living at home with his mother takes on the role of investigator. His initial interest in the threatening letter sent to the town's pharmacist is stimulated by his recognition of its source. Its words have been cut from the second page of a copy of the Vatican daily newspaper, *L'osservatore romano*, whose Latin motto "Unicuique Suum" (To Each His Own) is clearly visible.

The threat, it turns out, is merely a red herring, intended to disrupt the investigation of the murder of the pharmacist's hunting companion, who has been eliminated in order to prevent him from denouncing the corrupt activities of the secretary of the local Christian Democrats. The secretary had been discovered in compromising circumstances with the victim's wife, his cousin, both of whom as orphans had been brought up by their monsignor uncle. Here the crime of passion is no pretext but a reality, though it is inextricably linked to politics. Moreover, it is an imagined passion for the victim's widow that will lead to the death of the teacher-turned-investigator.

A series of fleeting details in its central chapters focuses on vanity and curiosity rather than a concern for justice being the compelling motives for Laurana's involvement in the investigation. A passionate commitment to the ideals of justice, rooted in his experience as a partisan, is what makes Bellodi tick. There is no such commitment on Laurana's part, only a persistent intellectual curiosity. The distance between the investigators in the two novels, which is the distance between their ideas on what constitutes justice, is astronomical. Laurana "era lontano dalla legge . . . più di quanto Marte sia lontano dalla terra" (was far from the law . . . more than Mars is from the Earth). He is a law-abiding citizen, but "l'idea che la soluzione del problema portasse . . . ad assicurare i colpevoli alla giustizia . . . non gli balenava nemmeno" (the idea that the solution of the problem might lead . . . to bringing the guilty to justice, did not even cross his mind).

There is much of Sciascia, as Massimo Onofri has recognized, in the teacher, whose gently ironic depiction makes him seem a modern Sicilian lay version of Alessandro Manzoni's Don Abbondio, the priest in *I promessi sposi*. But as in *Il giorno della civetta*, the distinctive characteristics of the individual reflect a more general behavioral code. Laurana's indifference to justice has complex historical and ethnological roots; it is conditioned by Sicily's history of conquest and oppression. The family (as Sciascia defined it in *Il giorno della civetta*), not the state, is still the only institution alive in the Sicilian consciousness, but the enduring reality is "naturale e tragica solitudine" (natural and tragic solitude). Its legal concomitant is "la vendetta della legge" (the vendetta of law) with its implications of a private, solitary, and, arguably, vengeful justice.

A shiver of sensuality runs through *A ciascuno il suo,* from the early protracted interrogation of a hapless young girl by a policeman, to clerical jokes about priests' young housekeepers, to Laurana's own increasingly morbid erotic fixation on the young widow. Calvino had singled out Brancati as an influence on Sciascia in "La zia d'America," but it is only here, in the extended treatment given to the topos of *gallismo* (an obsessive preoccupation with woman as sexual object), that Brancati's influence is evident to its fullest extent for the first—and the last—time. Laurana's discovery that the intended target was not the pharmacist but his hunting companion is revealed in the final chapter to have been common knowledge, known to everyone except him. It had already been intimated in the question asked by a member of the men's social club: "Qual è l'animale che tiene il becco sottoterra?" (What animal hides its beak underground?). The question is ambiguous, based upon the double meaning of *becco* (beak but also cuckold). The answer is not "la vedova" (the widow).

Sciascia takes his leave of Brancati in the highly sensual description of the widow as she escorts Laurana and her cousin into her husband's study. Open on the desk there is a copy of *Lettere alla signora* (Letters to Mrs. Z), an interesting volume according to Laurana, the work of Polish author Kazimierz Brandys. In an article in the 24 April 1965 Palermo daily *L'Ora* Sciascia had called the Italian translation of Brandys's book a "lucidissimo messaggio" (very lucid message). In his discussion of Albert Camus's novel *L'Étranger* (The Stranger, 1942) Brandys wrote, "Solo l'atto che tocca l'ordinamento di un sistema pone l'uomo nella cruda luce delle leggi" (Only the act that touches the ordering of a system places man in the crude light of the law). Camus's "outsider," it is clear from Brandys's analysis, is to all intents and purposes a Sicilian in the manner in which Sciascia defined him in *Il giorno della civette*. The real problem, as Laurana realizes (and in this he clearly speaks for Sciascia), is that there is no system in Sicily. There never has been a viable system and there may never be one, unless it is that perversion of a system that swallows up the innocent victims of the novel.

In the early 1970s Sciascia continued to use the detective-story genre that he had so successfully employed in the 1960s, but whereas novels such as *Il giorno della civetta* and *A ciascuno il suo* were clearly set in Sicily, *Il contesto* (1971; translated as *Equal Danger*, 1973) and *Todo modo* (1974; translated as *One Way or Another*, 1977) unfold against a more abstract background, a clear sign that the writer's concerns had moved decidedly from the local to the universal. *Il contesto* was set in a country "del tutto immaginario" (entirely imaginary) and, moreover, one "dove non avevano più corso le idee, dove i principî . . . venivano quotidianamente irrisi, . . . dove soltanto il potere per il potere contava" (where ideas no longer circulated, where principles . . . were made a daily mockery, . . . where only power for the sake of power counted). The work was intended to be, Sciascia claimed, "un apologo sul potere nel mondo, sul potere che sempre più digrada nella impenetrabile forma di una concatenazione che approssimativamente possiamo dire mafiosa" (a fable about power anywhere in the world, about power that, in the impenetrable form of a concatenation that we can roughly term *mafioso,* works steadily greater degradation).

That process of degradation is evident in the blurring of the lines between the opposition and the government in politics and the judiciary and the executive in the legislative process. But while "ideas no longer circulate" in the imaginary country, they continue to do so in the novel. They are frequently raised through paradoxes in the exchanges the investigator has with others. On the question of freedom, for example, he remarks, "E in fondo, nella vita, la più grande affermazione di libertà è quella di chi si crea una prigione" (After all, the greatest affirmation of freedom in life is made by the man who creates a prison for himself).

In the classic English detective story, epitomized by the adventures of Sherlock Holmes, both the detective and the reader are principally concerned with the resolution of the crime (hence the term *whodunit*). The genre, despite the crime that lies at its center, is essentially lighthearted, for readers know that in the end order will be restored through

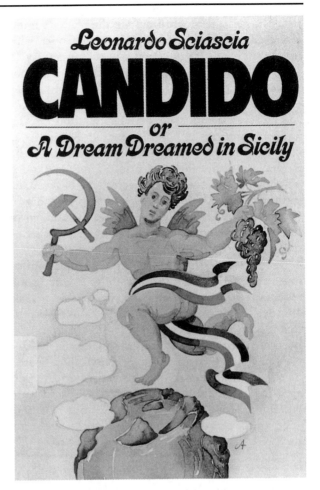

Dust jacket for the American edition of the translation of Sciascia's 1977 novel, a new version of Voltaire's Candide

the solving of the puzzle, and they read on, quickly and uninterruptedly, precisely to find out the answer. *Il contesto* and *Todo modo* both replicate this basic structure because Sciascia is aware of his readers' desire to be entertained. He amply satisfies this basic need, heightening the suspense in both novels by increasing the number of murders. In *Il contesto* judges fall to the assassin's bullet with incredible frequency, and in *Todo modo,* though the overall time span is much shorter, three killings take place in the twinkling of an eye.

But if the genre is lighthearted, Sciascia's intentions are not. He deliberately frustrates his reader's expectations in both novels by failing to provide a clear-cut solution, thereby constraining his reader to think again. This rethinking process must necessarily focus on the substance of the work rather than its structure and allows due consideration of its paradoxes, which often occur in dialogue. In general, the memorable characters are the baddies, not the goodies. For example, the character from *Il con-*

329

testo who remains disturbingly in the reader's mind is Riches, the president of the Supreme Court, with his fixation on the intrinsic guilt of humanity (a guilt, naturally, in which the judiciary does not share). No less memorable and disturbing is the character of Don Gaetano, the priest in *Todo modo,* one of Sciascia's most compelling creations. His fanatic certainty, which he shares with Riches, is as corrosive as the doubts of his antagonist, the painter-narrator. As a bad priest, Don Gaetano is willing to deconstruct the universe "ma in senso del tutto eterodosso. Alla Borges, tanto per intenderci" (but in a quite heterodox fashion. In the manner of Borges, to make myself clear).

The heretical thread running through *Il contesto* is accentuated in *Todo modo.* George Steiner defined heresy in *Real Presences* as "un-ending re-reading and revaluation." Don Gaetano, who like Mallarmé, has "lu tous les livres" (has read all the books), asserts that it is possible to rewrite everything that has ever been written with the exception of *Candide.* Sciascia's later rewriting of Voltaire's text, then, would be the ultimate heresy, but it confirmed an ever-growing belief on his part that literature and truth were one. He used literature to examine reality in such a way that orthodox views gave way to more-nuanced and consequently more-illuminating perceptions.

La scomparsa di Majorana (1975; translated as *The Mystery of Majorana,* 1987) centers on the disappearance and presumed suicide in 1938 of a precocious young Sicilian theoretical physicist, Majorana. He exemplifies the problem of moral responsibility faced by a scientist aware that the experiments in which he is involved (the splitting of the atom) may have horrendous repercussions for mankind. Rather than run such a risk, Majorana, as Sciascia imagines him, withdraws from public life to the peace and anonymity of the cloisters of a Carthusian monastery. The point Majorana makes is that not everything that can be done by science must be done. There are moral limits that should not be transgressed. The Sicilian in Sciascia's novel and German scientists in reality refused to work on atomic weapons while those in the United States went ahead. The individuals engaged in the Manhattan Project, suggests the critic Peter Hebblethwaite, were engaged in the same process as the concentration-camp guards: the industrialization of death.

Like almost all of Sciacia's works following *Todo modo, La scomparsa di Majorana* has a rich literary background, which includes allusions to the works of William Shakespeare, Luigi Pirandello, and Stendhal. *Il teatro della memoria* (The Theatre of Memory, 1981), which explores the question of loss of memory and identity provoked by the Bruneri-Canella case in Turin in 1927, includes many references to Marcel Proust, Borges, and, above all, to Pirandello's *Come tu mi vuoi* (As You Desire Me). *1912+1* (1986; translated as *1912+1,* 1989), the story of the Countess Tiepolo, who was accused of shooting her Bersagliere husband's orderly, is related against the varied backdrop of the time: the arrival of the tango from Paris, the theft of Leonardo da Vinci's *Mona Lisa* from the Louvre, guerilla warfare in Libya, and the introduction of universal suffrage. This varied backdrop is rendered even more varied through a coruscating recourse to literature, including allusions to the work of D'Annunzio, Giovanni Casanova, D. H. Lawrence, and many others, both in the body of the text as well as in a series of notes.

Centering on a triple-murder trial in Palermo in 1937, *Porte aperte* takes up the question of the death penalty that Mussolini had reintroduced after a forty-year absence. Sciascia had already broached the subject in *La sentenza memorabile* (The Memorable Sentence, 1982). Here the focus is provided by a remark by Michel Montaigne in his *Essais:* "Dopotutto, significa dare un bel peso alle proprie opinioni, se per esso si fa arrostire vivo un uomo" (After all, it means giving a lot of weight to one's own opinions, if as a result a man is burned alive). The French writer's abhorrence of extremism articulates Sciascia's feeling, which springs from a deeply rooted childhood memory of the execution of the anarchist Michele Schirru, who had wanted to but had not carried out an attempt on Mussolini's life.

The protagonist of the novel is Rosario Lavatino, the "piccolo giudice" (little judge) of the 1937 trial, who was from Sciascia's own native Racalmuto. Despite incredible pressures to seek the death sentence—one of the victims was an important member of the local branch of the Fascist Party—he persuades the jury otherwise. Lavatino in his humanity and compassion (his physical smallness is intended to highlight through contrast his moral stature) is clearly the opposite of Riches in *Il contesto,* for his warmth contrasts starkly with Riches' clinical coldness. But he is, more important, Sciascia's alter ego. Pointing out that Sciascia in his last works knows he is dying, critic Joseph Farrell is struck by "the cosmic pity and compassion with which these novels are imbued." The reluctance on Sciascia's part to speak of himself directly means that here, as in the other works in which an autobiographical strain is evident, that pity and compassion are manifested indirectly, through literary allusion though the later works take on a more somber tone than in the past.

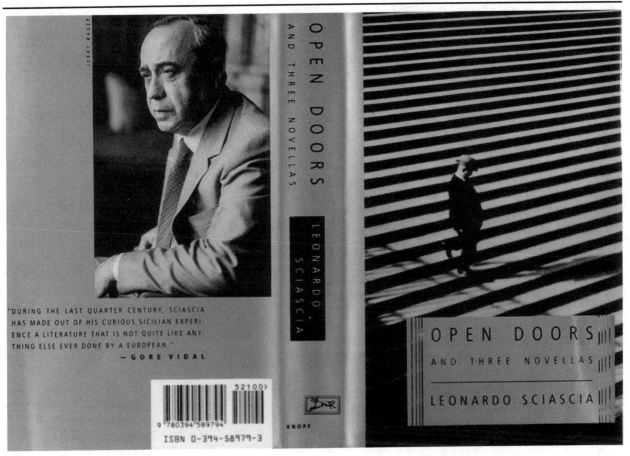

Dust jacket for the American edition of the translation of a collection of Sciascia's novellas, whose title story is about a triple-murder trial

It is not surprising that while the opening and concluding dialogues of *Porte aperte* are given over to judicial matters, a third of its extended dialogues concern books. One particular allusion, which is made in regard to the protagonist, seems especially appropriate to Sciascia: "Il nome di uno scrittore, il titolo di un libro, possono a volte, e per alcuni, suonare come una patria: e cosí accadde al giudice sentendo quello di Courier, sul cui volume delle opere complete, trovate nel solaio di un parente che non sapeva che farsene, aveva cominciato a compitare francese e ragione, francese e diritto" (The name of a writer, the title of a book, sometimes, for some people, can ring out like the name of one's homeland: this was the effect on the judge of the name of Courier, in whose *Complete Works,* found in the attic of a relative who did not know what to do with them, he had begun to spell out French and reason, French and right). Of the three hundred books he had read between the ages of eight and fourteen, Sciascia told Marcelle Padovani in *La Sicilia come metafora,* Paul Louis Courier's work was among "una

diecina che furono per me importantissimi" (ten or so that for me were extremely important).

Courier turns up as an emblematic model in Sciascia's preliminary justification for having written *Le parrocchie di Regalpetra* and was one of the writers important to his development of a strong interest in justice, which is evident when he talks to Padovani of the Italian language "come sogno di giustizia" (as a dream of justice). He spoke of another key influence in his 30 October 1987 interview in *La Repubblica* with Nello Ajello: "Nella sua opera Manzoni ha un'istanza giuridica che mi affascina" (In his work Manzoni has an insistence on justice which fascinates me). He summed it up in a reply to a question put to him by Claude Ambroise for Sciascia's *Opere* (Complete Works, 1987–1991): "Tutto è legato, per me, al problema della giustizia: in cui si involge quello della libertà, della dignità umana, del rispetto tra uomo e uomo. Un problema che si assomma nella scrittura, che nella scrittura trova strazio e riscatto" (Everything is linked, for me, to the question of justice: in which is involved that of liberty, of human dignity, of respect between individuals. A problem which is summed up in writing, which in writing finds torment and resolution).

From his first detective story and throughout his career, Sciascia's concerns are indissolubly linked to justice. His relentless and increasingly polemical defense of the integrity of those institutions, particularly the judiciary, responsible for guaranteeing the French revolutionary rights of *liberté, égalité,* and *fraternité* even against the state itself testify to his commitment to the principle. Sciascia's last fictional work, *Una storia semplice* (1989; translated as *A Straightforward Tale,* 1991), replicates much of his earlier work. It is a detective story set in Sicily with Mafia implications (drugs and stolen paintings), high-level corruption (both police and the church), and a victim who has returned from abroad to work on his family papers, consisting of letters from Garibaldi and Pirandello. Although uncharacteristic of Sciascia's later work in having only a few allusions, the story begins with an important quotation by way of preface from *Justiz* (The Execution of Justice, 1985) by the Swiss novelist Friedrich Dürrenmatt: "Ancora una volta voglio scandagliare scrupolosamente le possibilità che forse ancora restano alla giustizia" (Once again I wish scrupulously to sound out the possibilities that perhaps still exist for justice).

Sciascia is by common consent one of the most important Italian writers of the postwar era, and some believe that, given his continual concern with social justice and human dignity, his work will prove to be more important than that of Alberto Moravia or Calvino in the study of postwar Italian culture. While this may very well be true, arguably it misses the point. Although Sciacia explores a whole range of problems, he will be read above all for the imaginative manner in which he treated those problems in his fiction—for the richly allusive and quietly lyrical language in which he expressed them.

Interviews:

"Leonardo Sciascia," in *La generazione degli anni difficili,* edited by Ettore A. Albertoni, Ezio Antonini, and Renato Palmieri (Bari: Laterza, 1962);

La Sicilia come metafora: intervista di Marcelle Padovani (Milan: Mondadori, 1979); translated by James Marcus as *Sicily as Metaphor* (Marlboro, Vt.: Marlboro, 1994);

Sciascia and Davide Lajolo, *Conversazione in una stanza chiusa* (Milan: Sperling & Kupfer, 1981);

Ian Thompson, "A Conversation in Palermo with Leonardo Sciascia," *London Magazine,* 27 (April–May 1987): 39–70; republished in

1912+1, by Sciascia (Manchester & New York: Carcanet, 1989);

Sciascia, *Fuoco all'anima. Conversazioni con Domenico Porzio* (Milan: Mondadori, 1992).

Bibliography:

Donato De Vita, "Rassegna di studi critici su Leonardo Sciascia (1970–1977)," *Critica letteraria,* 16 (1977): 587–606.

Biography:

Matteo Collura, *Il Maestro di Regalpetra* (Milan: Longanesi, 1996).

References:

Liborio Adamo, *Leonardo Sciascia tra impegno e letteratura* (Enna: Paipiro Editrice, 1992);

Claude Ambroise, *Invito alla lettura di Sciascia* (Milan: Mursia, 1974; enlarged, 1983; revised, 1996);

Gillian Ania, *Fortunes of the Firefly: Sciascia's Art of Detection* (Market Harborough: University Texts, 1996);

Susan Briziarelli, "Of Valiant Knights and Labyrinths: Leonardo Sciascia's *Il cavaliere e la morte,*" *Italica,* 68 (Spring 1991): 1–12;

Aldo Budriesi, *Pigliari di lingua: temi e forme della narrativa di Leonardo Sciascia* (Rome: Effelle editrice, 1986);

Federico Campbell, *La memoria de Sciascia* (Mexico: Fondo de cultura económica, 1989);

JoAnn Cannon, "The Detective Fiction of Leonardo Sciascia," *Modern Fiction Studies,* 29 (Autumn 1983): 523–534;

Cannon, "History as a Mode of Comprehension and History as Fabulation: A Reading of Sciascia's *Morte dell'inquisitore* and *Il Consiglio d'Egitto,*" *Forum Italicum,* 19 (Spring 1985): 78–96;

Cannon, "*Todo modo* and the Enlightened Hero of Leonardo Sciascia," *Symposium,* 35 (1981/1982): 282–291;

Romana Capek-Habekovic, "Leonardo Sciascia's Socio-Political Awareness in *Le parrocchie di Regalpetra* and *Gli zii di Sicilia,*" in *Italian Echoes in the Rocky Mountains. Papers from the 1988 Annual Conference of the American Association for Italian Studies,* edited by Sante Matteo, Cinzia Donatelli Noble, and Madison U. Sowell (Provo, Utah: David M. Kennedy Center for International Studies, Brigham Young University, 1990), pp. 151–156;

Piero Carbone, *Il mio Sciascia. Tópoi e riflessioni* (Palermo: Edizioni Grifo, 1990);

Luigi Cattanei, *Leonardo Sciascia* (Florence: Le Monnier, 1978);

Mark Chu, "Le Royaume de la Folie: 'Power' and 'Reason' in Sciascia's Last Narrative Works," *Italian Studies,* 47 (1992): 68–79;

Filippo Cilluffo, *Due scrittori siciliani* (Caltanissetta & Rome: Salvatore Sciascia, 1974);

Santi Correnti, *La Sicilia di Sciascia* (Catania: Edizioni Greco, 1977);

Maurice Darmon, "Lapidaire pour Sciascia," *Critique,* 49 (June–July 1993): 421–441;

James Dauphiné, *Leonardo Sciascia. Qui êtes-vous?* (Paris: La Manufacture, 1990);

Antonio Di Grado, *Leonardo Sciascia* (Marina di Patti, Messina: Pungitopo, 1986);

Joseph Farrell, *Leonardo Sciascia* (Edinburgh: Edinburgh University Press, 1995);

Farrell, "Sciascia's Late Fiction," in *The Knight and Death & Other Stories,* by Sciascia (Manchester & New York: Carcanet, 1991), pp. 159–167;

Melo Freni, *Verso la vacanza. La morte di Sciascia* (Marina di Patti, Messina: Pungitopo, 1990);

Sara Gentile, *L'isola del potere* (Rome: Donzelli, 1995);

Fernando Gioviale, *Sciascia* (Teramo: Lisciani & Giunti, 1993);

Giovanna Jackson, "Le arti figurative come metafora negli scritti di Leonardo Sciascia," *Almanacco,* 1 (March 1991): 31–41;

Jackson, *Leonardo Sciascia: 1956–1976. A Thematic and Structural Study* (Ravenna: Longo, 1981);

Verina Jones, "*L'antimonio* and its Sources: Malraux, Orwell and Sciascia," *Italianist,* 6 (1986): 61–82;

Jones, "Leonardo Sciascia," in *Writers and Society in Contemporary Italy,* edited by Michael Caesar and Peter Hainsworth (Leamington Spa, U.K.: Berg Publishers, 1984);

Frank Kermode, Afterword to *The Day of the Owl. Equal Danger,* by Sciascia (Manchester & New York: Carcanet, 1984);

L'Arc. Revue Trimestrielle, special issue on Sciascia, 77 (1979);

Onofrio Lo Dico, *Leonardo Sciascia. Tecniche narrative e ideologia* (Caltanissetta & Rome: Salvatore Sciascia, editore, 1988); enlarged as *La fede nella scrittura. Leonardo Sciascia* (Caltanissetta & Rome: Salvatore Sciascia, 1990);

Lucrezia Lorenzini, *La "ragione" di un intellettuale livero. Leonardo Sciascia* (Cabtanzaro-Messina: Rubbettino Editore, 1992);

Luciano Luisi, ed., *Una vita per il romanzo. Leonardo Sciascia* (Taranto: Mandese, 1990);

Walter Mauro, *Leonardo Sciascia* (Florence: Nuova Italia, 1970);

Antonio Motta, *Leonardo Sciascia. La verità l'apra ventà* (Manduria: Lacaita, 1985);

Motta, *Il sereno pessimista. Omaggio a Leonardo Sciascia* (Manduria: Lacaita, 1991);

Nuove Effemeridi Rassegna trimestrale di cultura, special issue on Sciascia, 9 (1990);

Tom O'Neill, Introduction to *Il contesto,* by Sciascia (Manchester: Manchester University Press, 1986), pp. ix–xxvii;

O'Neill, "Sciascia's *Todo modo:* La Vérité en Peinture," in *Moving in Measure. Essays in Honour of Brian Moloney,* edited by Judith Bryce and Doug Thompson (Hull: Hull University Press, 1989);

O'Neill, "La scoperta dell'America ovvero Ipotesi per come componeva Sciascia," *Lettere italiane,* 47 (October–December 1995): 565–597;

O'Neill, "A Sicilian in Parma: per la preistoria di Leonardo Sciascia," in *Leonardo Sciascia. "A futura memoria." Atti del convengno. Melbourne, 25–26 aprile, 1992,* edited by O'Neill (Melbourne: Quaderni dell'Istituto italiano di cultura, 1994), pp. 3–32;

Massimo Onofri, "Il diritto impossibile: un'ipotesi su Leonardo Sciascia," *Nuovi argomenti,* 42 (1992): 29–39;

Onofri, *Storia di Sciascia* (Bari & Rome: Laterza, 1994);

Onofri, *Tutti a cena da Don Mariano* (Milan: Bompiani, 1996), pp. 193–218;

Zino Pecoraro and Enzo Scrivano, eds., *Omaggio a Leonardo Sciascia. Atti* (Agrigento: Industria grafica, 1991);

Philippe Renard, "Les lunettes de Sciascia," *Italianistica,* 6 (1977): 390–397;

Ricciarda Ricorda, "Sciascia ovvero la retorica della citazione," *Studi novecenteschi,* 6 (1977): 59–93;

Ottavio Rossani, *Leonardo Sciascia* (Rimini: Luisè, 1990);

Lea Ritter Santini, "Uno strappo nel cielo di carta," in *La scomparsa di Majorana,* by Sciascia (Turin: Einaudi, 1985), pp. 79–101;

Aldo Scimè, Nino DeVilá, and others, *La Sicilia, il suo cuore. Omaggio a Leonardo Sciascia* (Palermo: Fondazione L. Sciascia-Fondazione G. Whitaker, 1992);

Marcello Simonetta, ed., *Non faccio niente senza gioia. Leonardo Sciascia e la cultura francese* (Milan: Vita Felice, 1996);

Natale Tedesco, *La scala a chiocciola. Scrittura novecentesca in Sicilia* (Palermo: Sellerio, 1991);

Doug Thompson, " 'Per le lucciole scomparse': Observations on Sciascia's Concern with the Language of Political Bankruptcy," *Quinquereme,* 7 (July 1984): 182–198;

Tino Vittorio, *Sciascia. La storia ed altro* (Messina: Sicania, 1991).

Mario Soldati
(17 November 1906 –)

Emanuele Licastro
State University of New York at Buffalo

BOOKS: *Pilato. Tre atti* (Turin: Società Editrice Internazionale, 1924);

Salmace. Novelle (Novara: La Libra, 1929);

24 ore in uno studio cinematografico, as Franco Pallavera (Milan: Corticelli, 1935);

America primo amore (Florence: Bemporad, 1935; enlarged edition, Rome: Einaudi, 1945; enlarged edition, Milan: Mondadori, 1976);

La verità sul caso Motta. Romanzo, seguito da cinque racconti (Milan: Rizzoli, 1941);

L'amico gesuita. Racconti (Milan: Rizzoli, 1943);

Fuga in Italia. Seguito da varie poesie (Milan: Longanesi, 1947);

A cena col commendatore (Milan: Longanesi, 1950); translated anonymously as *The Commander Comes to Dine* (London: Lehmann, 1952); translated by Gwyn Morris and Henry Furst as *Dinner with the Commendatore* (New York: Knopf, 1953);

L'accalappiacani (Rome: Atlante, 1953);

Le lettere da Capri. Romanzo (Milan: Garzanti, 1954); translated by Archibald Colquhoun as *The Capri Letters* (London: Hamilton, 1955; New York: Knopf, 1956);

La confessione. Romanzo (Milan: Garzanti, 1955); translated by Raymond Rosenthal as *The Confession* (London: Deutsch, 1958; New York: Knopf, 1958);

I racconti (Milan: Garzanti, 1957);

Il vero Silvestri: Romanzo (Milan: Garzanti, 1957); translated by Colquhoun as *The Real Silvestri* (London: Deutsch, 1960; New York: Knopf, 1961);

La messa dei villeggianti (Verona: Mondadori, 1959);

I racconti 1927–1947 (Milan: Mondadori, 1961);

Storie di spettri (Milan: Mondadori, 1962);

Canzonette e viaggio televiso (Verona: Mondadori, 1962);

Le due città. Romanzo (Milan: Garzanti, 1964); translated by Morris as *The Malacca Cane* (London: Deutsch, 1973; New York: St. Martin's Press, 1973);

La busta arancione. Romanzo (Milan: Mondadori, 1966); translated by Bernard Wall as *The Or-*

Mario Soldati

ange Envelope (London: Deutsch, 1969; New York: Harcourt, Brace & World, 1969);

I racconti del maresciallo (Milan: Mondadori, 1967);

Fuori (Milan: Mondadori, 1968);

Fuga in Italia e altri racconti, edited by Mario Bonfantini (Milan: Mondadori, 1969);

Vino al vino (Milan: Mondadori, 1969);

L'attore. Romanzo (Milan: Mondadori, 1970);

I disperati del benessere; Viaggio in Svezia (Milan: Mondadori, 1970);

55 novelle per l'inverno (Milan: Mondadori, 1971);

Vino al vino. Seconda serie (Milan: Mondadori, 1971);

Viaggio nella terra dei diamanti (Bergamo: Minerva Italica, 1972);

Un prato di papaveri. Diario 1947–1964 (Milan: Mondadori, 1973);

Da spettatore (Milan: Mondadori, 1973);

Lo smeraldo. Romanzo (Milan: Mondadori, 1974); translated by William Weaver as *The Emerald: A Novel* (New York: Harcourt Brace Jovanovich, 1977);

Lo specchio inclinato. Diario 1965–1971 (Milan: Mondadori, 1975);

La sposa americana. Romanzo (Milan: Mondadori, 1977); translated by Weaver as *The American Bride* (London: Hodder & Stoughton, 1979);

Piemonte e Valle d'Aosta, by Soldati and Folco Quilici (Milan: Silvana, 1979);

Addio diletta Amelia (Milan: Mondadori, 1979);

44 novelle per l'estate (Milan: Mondadori, 1979);

La carta del cielo. Racconti, edited by Natalia Ginzburg (Turin: Einaudi, 1980);

L'incendio. Romanzo (Milan: Mondadori, 1981);

La casa del perchè (Milan: Mondadori, 1982);

Nuovi racconti del maresciallo (Milan: Rizzoli, 1984);

L'architetto (Milan: Rizzoli, 1985);

Ah! il Mundial: Storia dell'inaspettabile (Milan: Rizzoli, 1986);

L'avventura in Valtellina (Rome: Laterza, 1986);

El Paseo de Gracia (Milan: Rizzoli, 1987);

Regione regina (Rome: Laterza, 1987);

Rami secchi (Milan: Rizzoli, 1989);

Opere. Racconti autobiografici, edited by Cesare Carboli (Milan: Rizzoli, 1991);

Opere. Romanzi brevi, edited by Carboli (Milan: Rizzoli, 1992);

Le sere (Milan: Rizzoli, 1994).

MOTION PICTURES: *Gli uomini, che mascalzoni!,* screenplay by Soldati, M. Camerini, and A. De Benedetti, Cines, 1932;

Acciaio, screenplay by Soldati, E. Cecchi, and W. Ruttman, Cines, 1933;

Dora Nelson, screenplay by Soldati and L. Zampa, Urbe Film, 1940;

Piccolo mondo antico, screenplay by Soldati, Mario Bonfantini, Cecchi, and A. Lattuada, ATA, 1941;

Malombra, screenplay by Soldati, Bonfantini, R. Castellani, T. Richelmy, and E. M. Margadonna, ATA, 1942;

Le miserie del Signor Travet, screenplay by Soldati and T. Pinelli, Pan Film, 1945;

Il segno di Zorro, screenplay by Soldati ICS: Theodoli, 1951;

Un colpo di pistola, screenplay by Soldati, Bonfantini, Castellani, and C. Pavolini, Lux Film, 1952;

La provinciale, screenplay by Soldati, S. De Feo, Giorgio Bassani, and J. Ferry, Electra Copagua Cinematografica, 1952;

Guerra e pace, screenplay by Soldati, M. Camerini, E. De Concini, G. G. Napolitano, and I. Perilli, produced by Dino De Laurentis, 1955;

La donna del fiume, screenplay by Soldati, Antonio Altoviti, Bassani, Basilio Franchina, Pier Paolo Pasolini, and Florestano Vancini, Dino De Laurentis–Carlo Ponti, 1955; released in the United States as *Woman of the River,* Columbia, 1957;

Policarpo, ufficiale di scrittura, screenplay by Soldati, Titanus/Hispamex, 1959.

Mario Soldati has achieved success in various genres. As an essayist he is engaging, urbane, and provocative; in fact, he is still best known as the author of *America primo amore* (America First Love), a collection of essays that has been reprinted six times since it was first published in 1935. As host of his two-year-long television series, *Viaggio nella valle del Po alla ricerca di vini genuini* (Voyage in the Po Valley in Search of Genuine Wines, 1955–1956), he became one of Italy's most popular figures. When his other television series, *Alla ricerca del cibo genuino* (In Search of Genuine Food), ended in 1959, he was as famous as a movie star. Soldati has also been active in the motion-picture industry as a director and critic as well as a screenplay writer. His most successful movie was *Piccolo mondo antico* (Little Old-Fashioned World, 1941).

Soldati excels in narrative fiction. In *Pegaso* (September 1929) Eugenio Montale praised "Fuga in Francia" (Escape to France, 1929), one of his first stories, for its "finezza di struttura, interesse sempre vivo di narrazione, felicità descrittiva e ambientale" (subtle structure, lively narrative interest, felicitous descriptions and backgrounds). Montale added that the merits of *Salmace* (1929), the volume in which "Fuga in Francia" appeared, "bastano già a distinguere il Soldati tra i giovani narratori più solidi e intelligenti" (are enough to distinguish Soldati as one of the most solid and intelligent young writers). Most critics agree that his novella "La giacca verde" (translated as "The Green Jacket")–published with two other novellas in the volume *A cena col commendatore* (1950; translated as *The Commander Comes to Dine,* 1952)–represents Soldati's best work. He has written twelve novels; three of them were awarded major literary prizes; six were best-sellers. In his most incisive pages he investigates the self in relation to inherited social and moral values and scrutinizes those structures regarded as inherently human–identity, good and evil, honesty and dishonesty, truth and fraud–to reveal the invalidity of absolute judgments.

Soldati was born in Turin on 17 November 1906 into an old and prosperous family that had been known in the city since the eighteenth century. He was educated at the Jesuit Istituto Sociale, the most fashionable private school in Turin at the time. When he expressed a desire to join the order, he was told to think about it for a year–which was, as it turned out, time enough for him to change his mind. Although many of his characters rebel against the religious morality imparted by the Jesuits, Soldati still speaks fondly of their moral integrity and intellectual rigor and remains grateful for their introducing him to Greek, Roman, and French culture. More important is the impression that his Jesuit teachers left on Soldati: the relentless probing in which he engages in his works suggests the Jesuits' style of argumentation, epitomized by their motto *Concede parum nega saepe distingue semper* (Grant little; deny often; distinguish always).

Soldati earned a degree in art history at the University of Turin in 1927 and continued his studies at the Istituto Superiore di Storia dell'Arte (Institute for Advanced Study in Art History) in Rome. He published his first volume of short stories, *Salmace,* in 1929; the same year he left for the United States, having won a fellowship in art history at Columbia University. While there he also served as an instructor. Unable to obtain a regular university teaching appointment, he returned to Italy in January 1931. In May of that year he married a former student, Marion Rieckelman. They had three children, but the marriage ended in 1934. Soldati returned to the United States in 1932 and 1933; his experiences on these trips are related in his *America primo amore.* In 1941 Soldati began a relationship with Giuliana Kellermann. They married and had three children. From 1946 to 1960 Soldati lived in Rome. In 1960 he and his family moved to Milan, where he still lives.

In 1937 Soldati published his first novel, a psychological thriller titled *La verità sul caso Motta* (The Truth about the Motta Case), serially in the literary magazine *Omnibus;* it appeared in book form in 1941. The reader is convinced that the mystery of Motta's disappearance is about to be solved in the usual fashion of the whodunit, when the novel suddenly enters a world of fantasy, magic, and horror: the missing lawyer is living in the sea with an enormous, Felliniesque siren queen. He could not tolerate rejection by the beautiful Marisa, so he has rejected the human for the aquatic world. Reaction to

the work was ambivalent: on the one hand, while it was appearing serially the publisher of *Omnibus,* Angelo Rizzoli, felt cheated by the unexpected turn into the fantastic. On the other hand, one day when Soldati entered a restaurant the writer Tommaso Landolfi–called the Italian Jorge Luis Borges for his preference for the esoteric, the grotesque, and the metaphysical–got up from his seat and embraced the stupefied author.

Seventeen years later Soldati completed a second, more complex novel, *Le lettere da Capri* (1954; translated as *The Capri Letters,* 1955). It received the Strega Prize and became one of the first post–World War II best-sellers in Italy, though many critics found the work's intricacies, tricks, and surprises rather excessive. The critic Carlo Bo wrote in the weekly *L'Europeo* (11 July 1954): "L'errore consiste in un eccesso di vigore, in un materiale troppo ricco, in una pericolosa facilità di commento e di amplificazione. . . . Il romanzo manca di equilibrio e presenta delle parti perfette di fronte ad altre non riuscite o appena abbozzate" (The mistake consists in an excessive vigor, in the overly rich material, in a dangerous facility in commentary and elaboration. . . . The novel lacks balance and offers some parts which are perfect whereas others are not successful or barely sketched). Others admired its novelty: to the writer Anna Banti the book was a welcome change for the reader who was "stanco dei racconti di guerra e di resistenza, della scrittura sciatta, del folclore populista. La sua realtà era più complessa, più problematica, più internazionale" (tired of stories about war and the Resistance, of clumsy writing, of populist folklore. The book's reality was more complex, more problematic, more international). The American Italianist Donald Heiney called *Le lettere da Capri* "one of the best international novels about Italians and Americans since [Henry] James."

One limits the import of the novel, however, if one views it–as Heiney does–only as "the contrast of national qualities" and thinks that "all characters are chosen with absolute economy to illustrate national traits." Soldati paints a diptych in which the American husband and wife Harry and Jane Summers, spurred by their contact with Italians, discover in themselves the instinctive desires of the flesh. They begin living a double life, unable to combine sexual pleasure with love. The lovers they choose are intellectually and spiritually inferior to themselves: Harry's mistress, the Junoesque and stately Dorothea, is little more than a prostitute; Jane's lover, Aldo, a lower-class Neapolitan, is a typical Latin lover preying on American women. Harry says of his relationship with Dorothea: "L'atto dell'amore fisico con lei si riduceva a una

Soldati (fifth from left) while he was directing the 1932 movie Acciaio *(Collection of Mario Soldati)*

funzione meccanica, cui il sentimento e l'intelligenza si sovrapponevano . . . senza mai fondersi in una cosa sola con quell'atto" (The act of physical love became a mechanical function in which feeling and intelligence dominated separately . . . without ever merging into a single experience with the sexual act). Soldati vividly depicts the ecstasy of sensuality, as when Jane confesses:

> Di colpo, scoprii che fino a quel momento ero stata una ragazzina. Baciare, mi dissi, era dunque una cosa dura, una cosa forte e selvaggia. La testa girava; sembrava di svenire; il mondo intorno, . . . tutto crollava. . . . Esisteva soltanto il gusto particolare di quella bocca, ricco di infinite variazioni continuamente diverse, precise e logiche. . . .

> (Suddenly, I discovered that up to that moment I had been a little girl. Kissing, I told myself, was something hard, something strong and wild. My head was spinning; I thought I was about to faint; the world . . . everything was crumbling. . . . There was only the special taste of that mouth, rich in infinite variation, continuously different, precise, and logical. . . .)

Speaking to her lover, Jane characterizes her relationship with her husband: "Che cos'è l'amore con mio marito? Acqua fresca; e con te un liquore inebriante. Un atto volontario, voluto, forzato; e con te un irrefrenabile abbandono di tutta la mia natura"

(What's making love with my husband like? Fresh water, whereas with you it's like an inebriating liqueur. An act conscious, willed, and forced; with you, an uncontrollable abandon of all my nature).

In addition to depicting neurotic individuals, the novel searches for the truths that are hidden by cultural mystification. Dorothea and Aldo, one discovers, are more sincere and honest with themselves than are the American protagonists. On the last pages, when Harry realizes how faithful Dorothea has been to him and decides to marry her, he also realizes that "i suoi occhi verdegialli pieni di pagliuzze d'oro, i suoi occhi misteriosi . . . non racchiudevano nessun mistero. . . . Non era il male e neppure il bene, era un essere umano qualsiasi" (her green and yellow eyes full of golden specks, her mysterious eyes . . . didn't contain any mystery. . . . She was neither evil nor good; she was an ordinary human being).

Soldati had written the first part of his next novel, *La confessione* (1955; translated as *The Confession*, 1958), twenty years earlier. Encouraged by the enormous success of *Le lettere da Capri*, he added two more parts. The semi-autobiographical work depicts the distorted view of life held by a teenager whose hatred of women has been produced by his strict religious upbringing. Clemente's youthful urges grow obsessive: "Quando era solo non si sarebbe stancato mai . . . di camminare posando i piedi esattamente soltanto sulle [piastrelle] grige, oppure soltanto sulle bianche, o una volta sulle une e l'altra sulle altre, o il piede destro sulle grige e il piede sinistro sulle bianche e viceversa, e così via" (When he was alone he never grew tired . . . of walking over the tiles, placing his feet just on the gray squares, or the white ones; or at one time on the gray tiles and next on the white, or the right foot on the gray and the left foot on the white or vice versa, and so on, and on). He finally overcomes his inhibitions by substituting for the sinful women who are his actual objects of desire his young male friend Luisito. The ensuing homosexual act is "semplice, naturale: come bere un bel bicchiere d'acqua fresca quando si è lungamente giocato e corso e si ha sete" (simple, natural: like drinking a nice glass of fresh water when one has played and run for a long time and one is thirsty).

The novel, while dealing with a serious theme, does so in an ironic, indulgently witty style. Some critics faulted the work for its lightness of touch. In the 20 November *L'Espresso* Geno Pampaloni regarded *La confessione* as having been inspired "da uno schema traducibile in barzelletta" (by a scheme changeable into a joke). The best pages in the novel, however, are those that sparkle with the author's jovial and pensive winks.

Soldati's next novel, *Il vero Silvestri* (1957; translated as *The Real Silvestri*, 1960), is a retrospective inquiry into the identity of Silvestri, who is dead. The narrator, Peyrani, always thought of his friend as gentle, sensitive, innocent, even naive. But Aurora, Silvestri's mistress, describes him as malicious, a "diavolo sporco" (dirty devil), a "mostro ripugnante" (repugnant monster). Along with Peyrani, the reader at first doubts Aurora's words; later the reader starts to believe that she is at least partially telling the truth. The author does not solve the mystery, as one might expect, through a reversal of Silvestri's image; Peyrani himself finds such an ending deficient: "La conclusione, forse banale, era la seguente. Anche se Aurora aveva esagerato, non poteva aver inventato tutto" (The conclusion, perhaps banal, was as follows: even if Aurora had exaggerated, she could not have invented everything). The image of Silvestri grows more complete but, at the same time, less precise in its details. Nor does the book end with this acceptance of the insoluble complexity of Silvestri's psyche; surprisingly, the inquiry turns into a self-inquiry, an introspection. Peyrani discovers his own inadequacies and feels guilty for the limited affection he showed his friend. Rather than seeing the real Silvestri, he selfishly reduced his friend "a poco più che un fantoccio, cioè ad un essere dalle reazioni prevedibili, a un com-

pagno abituale convenzionale, dolce, riposante" (to little more than a puppet, to a being, that is, with reactions all could foresee, to a conventional, gentle, restful, and predictable companion). Peyrani's acceptance is complete: "In realtà, egli era un uomo . . . come me. Non pensavo a perdonarlo . . . ad accusarlo. Lo amavo come prima. Più di prima. Perchè ora lo conoscevo meglio" (In reality he was a man . . . like me. It did not occur to me to forgive him . . . to accuse him. I loved him as before. More than before. For now I knew him better). In the process Peyrani has also gotten to know himself better. For this subtle, final surprise, the writer Elsa Morante, who did not particularly like most of Soldati's fiction, considered *Il vero Silvestri* a small masterpiece.

Il vero Silvestri divided the critics. A few accused the author of artificiality: Bo, in his review for *La stampa* (2 July 1957), felt compelled "solvere un difficile problema di natura letteraria: fino a che punto lo scrittore è sincero con se stesso, dove comincia il giuoco?" (to solve a difficult problem of a literary nature: up to what point is the writer sincere with himself; where does the game begin?). Emilio Cecchi, however, was among those who thought that this novel was one of Soldati's most authentic works and that Aurora was one of his most genuine characters. Montale, writing in *Corriere della sera* (2 July 1957), saw *Il vero Silvestri* as a "romanzo fortemente costruito, sicuro dalla prima all'ultima pagina" (strongly constructed novel, forthright from the first to the last page), albeit invested by a realism "di una brutale raffinatezza" (of brutal refinement). He concluded that of Soldati's works it was the "più fermo e più felice" (most stable and most felicitous).

Soldati's historical novel *Le due città* (1964; translated as *The Malacca Cane*, 1973) deals with ethical and political, rather than psychological and intellectual, issues. It spans the period from before World War I to the 1960s. The moral and emotional failure of the protagonist, Emilio Viotti, represents the degeneracy of the Italian middle class, as shown by its acquiescence in the face of Fascism and political corruption. The first part of the novel is set in Turin, where Emilio passes his youth: he falls in love with the gentle and sincere Vere, and he establishes a friendship with Piero in spite of their class difference. In the second part Emilio is seduced by luxury and money in Rome. Critics agree that the most memorable pages are those that describe the dying Piedmontese upper middle class and the immorality of Fascism. *Le due città* is rich in historical detail and fine characterizations. In a 1983 interview with Davide Lajolo, Soldati said that had he not been rushed by the

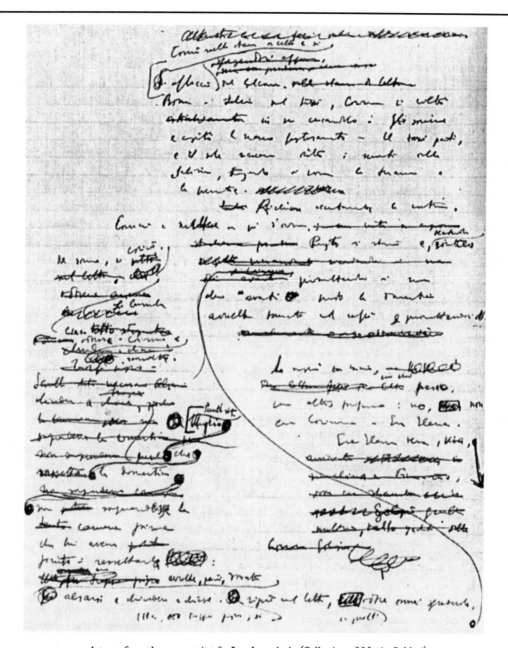

A page from the manuscript for Le due città *(Collection of Mario Soldati)*

publisher's deadline the seven-hundred-page novel could have been twelve hundred pages long.

La busta arancione (1966; translated as *The Orange Envelope,* 1969) is a semi-autobiographical novel that fictionalizes such elements as the author's mother's emasculation of her son; his father's disappearance when Soldati was seventeen; the influence of his Jesuit education; the emotional and physical aspects of homosexuality; and the author's problematic relationship with women. The protagonist, Carlo, is unable to enter into a relationship with a woman until late in his life, just as Soldati–as he admitted to Lajolo–had his first sexual encounter on

his wedding night. Soldati's description in the interview with Lajolo of his own mother, who would wait up all night for him to come home, could be applied to Carlo's mother: "Era oppressiva, dispotica, e un poco alla volta ha contribuito a stimolare in me la ricerca di una donna che somigliasse in qualche modo a lei" (She was oppressive, despotic, and slowly stimulated in me the search for a woman who might look something like her). Carlo searches for his mother image, but he is also attracted to women who are the opposite of his mother. His friend Alessandro, who, like Carlo, attends a Jesuit school, seems to have no purpose in the novel except to allow Soldati to fictionalize his own brief homosexual experience as a teenager. (Soldati's abstention from sexuality cannot be ascribed to the influence of the Jesuits; in fact, some of his schoolmates frequented prostitutes, and when the zealous young Soldati reported them to his Jesuit spiritual father he was reprimanded for being "holier than thou.")

Soldati's *L'attore* (The Actor, 1970), a bestseller that received the Campiello Prize, is a detective story. The narrator believes that his friend, the actor Enzo Melchiorri, is being financially ruined by his wife. When he visits her she appears gentle and serene; but as he is about to leave the house he begins to suspect that the maid has a mysterious power over her and Enzo. Later the maid is killed.

Lo smeraldo (1974; translated as *The Emerald*, 1977) is Soldati's most complex and intriguing novel. It concerns a journey that takes place in a long, nightmarish dream sequence framed by the daytime reality of the long first chapter and the book's last three pages. In fact, the reader is not sure whether even the events of the first chapter are real. The narrator has returned to New York after being away for forty years; he is enthralled by the fast life of the city and its advanced civilization. Yet it is here that his nightmare seems to begin. He perceives the subway as "un luogo di angoscia e di orrore" (a place of anguish and horror), and in its graffiti he observes

> enormi nudità, o vaste porzioni di nudità . . . smisurati occhi e sfinteri, colossali organi genitali . . . un caos di budella, di trippe, di viscere e bembra umane. . . . un affresco apocalittico . . . l'ultima versione del *Giudizio universale* di Michelangelo, ma . . . senza figure di speranza, soprattutto senza il dominante Cristo.

> (enormous nudities, or vast portions of nudity . . . immense eyes and sphincters, colossal genital organs . . . a chaos of bowels, of tripes, of guts and human limbs. . . . an apocalyptic fresco . . . the last version of Michelangelo's *Last Judgment,* but . . . without figures of hope, above all without the dominant Christ.)

Amid such Dantean visions the protagonist meets the repugnant but fascinating ninety-six-year-old alchemist Count Cagliani, a guardian of hell who is able to read meaning from the shape of stones. In the dream the earth's northern and southern parts are separated at the equator by an abandoned strip of land polluted by radiation from a nuclear war. The protagonist, who is aware that he is in a dream, has become the painter André Tellarini. He undertakes a forbidden journey from the northern to the southern hemisphere to take to his former mistress an enormous emerald that he has inherited from his wife. The journey is a passage from love to

instinct, from purity to sin. The desolate and horrific landscapes and cityscapes he passes through are metaphors for the changes taking place in his soul. When he finally hands the emerald to the beautiful Mariolina, it has been transformed into a synthetic stone.

The mixture of the real and the surreal, the banal and the fantastic, the quotidian and the bizarre, the pleasant and the horrific tantalizes the reader. One can understand why Italo Calvino, the creator of invisible cities and nonexistent knights, would express his appreciation of *Lo smeraldo* on the dust jacket; but even the realist Pier Paolo Pasolini, reviewing the novel in *Tempo illustrato* (29 November 1974), admired the work's language, lack of "viscosità" (viscosity), and "assoluta leggerezza" (absolute lightness).

In 1977 Soldati published *La sposa americana* (translated as *The American Bride,* 1979), which sold more than half a million copies and won the Naples Prize. It is a memoir of events that happened eight years earlier: the narrator's falling in love and marriage; his fateful attraction to another woman; his betrayal of his wife ("Anna era il male e Edith il bene e io non avevo la forza di rinunciare né all'una né all'altra" [Anna was evil and Edith was good and I didn't have the strength to renounce the one or the other]); the breakdown of the marriage ("Litigavamo come sempre, e forse di più. Quasi ogni giorno e ogni notte . . ." [We were fighting as usual, maybe more so. Almost every day and every night . . .]); and the narrator's recognition of matrimonial bliss just before it is denied him by the death of his pregnant wife.

The main interest of the novel lies in its conveying of various layers of awareness. The narrator is conscious of the different feelings that he had then and now. He frequently addresses the reader directly:

> Bisogna . . . che io metta in guardia chi mi legge. . . . Mi è difficile, l'ho già detto, ricostruire i miei stati d'animo così lungo tempo dopo. Il racconto dei fatti è fedele alla realtà, e intanto le riflessioni che accompagnano quei fatti non sono proprio le stesse che li accompagnavano allora. . . . Tuttavia sono sicuro di non falsificarle.

> (It is necessary that I warn the reader. . . . It is difficult for me, as I have already said, to reconstruct my moods after such a long time. The narration of facts is faithful to reality, but the reflections accompanying those facts are not exactly the same ones that accompanied them at that time. . . . Nevertheless, I am sure I am not falsifying them.)

L'incendio (The Fire, 1981) contrasts the normalcy of uncomplicated love and family relationships, on the one hand, with a life dominated by sub-

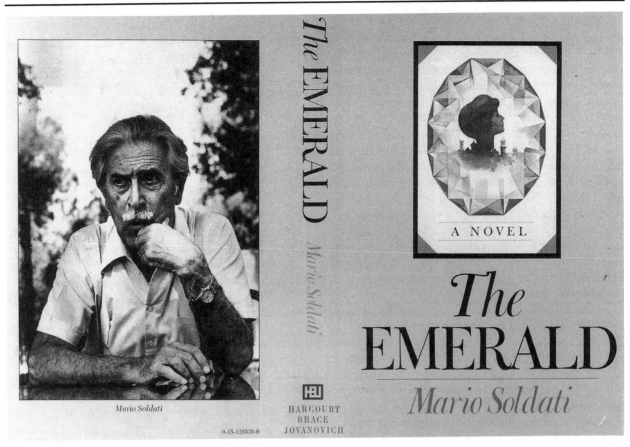

Mario Soldati

The EMERALD
Mario Soldati

The EMERALD
Mario Soldati

A NOVEL

HBJ
HARCOURT
BRACE
JOVANOVICH

0-15-128530-6

Dust jacket for the American edition of the translation of Soldati's 1974 novel, in which the narrator's return to New York City inspires his dream of an enormous emerald turning into a synthetic stone

conscious, uncivilized impulses, on the other. Being married, the narrator, Vitaliano, is forced to forgo the love of Emanuela, who symbolizes the uncomplicated life and appears only at the beginning and the end of the novel. Vitaliano exits the quotidian and enters the chaos of instincts, first, through his attraction to the beautiful and seductive painting *L'incendio* and, then, through his attraction to Mucci, the artist who created it. Vicariously, Vitaliano experiences Mucci's masochism, perversions, creativity, adventurous traveling, and faked death. Soldati originally intended to have Mucci murdered, but he could not bring himself to do so. Two years later he told Lajolo—despite the ending of *La sposa american*—that he was incapable of writing tragic endings. So the instinctual Mucci ends up as a world-famous celebrity living in California and married to Fernanda, from whom he had once run away to Africa.

Vivid lyrical moments frequently interrupt the narration; they are creative flashes inspired by paintings or by nature. Lajolo, who noticed such passages in all of Soldati's works, asked the writer about them. Soldati responded: "Quando mi fermo davanti alle montagne, quando mi innamoro di un paesaggio, dimentico i personaggi che stavo muovendo e divento poeta" (When I stop before the mountains, when I fall in love with a landscape, I forget the characters I was moving about and become a poet).

In *L'architetto* (The Architect, 1985) Vittorio, an Italian architect working in Chicago, learns from the husband of Nunzia, his mistress of forty years, that she is dead. He reflects that "Nessuna donna mi aveva fatto così felice come lei" (No woman had made me as happy as she did) but that each time he made love to her, "all[a] . . . fine di un furioso piacere . . . avven[iva] ad un tratto l'inerte gravità dei corpi, l'inanità dell'esistere, il non senso di tutto" (at the . . . end of furious pleasure . . . there befell the sudden heaviness of bodies, the emptiness of existence, the senselessness of everything). He wants to go back to his wife, Nina, "liberarmi da quella morte apparente . . . tornare alla vita" (to free myself from that seeming death . . . to return to life). Vittorio loves his wife; he does not feel the same intensity of pleasure during lovemaking with her that he did with Nunzia, but neither does he feel the anguish afterward. As he comes to understand his own experience, he understands also how Nina's infidelities had the same motivations as his: the attraction and repulsion of the flesh, alive and dying.

341

Unlike Nina, Irma—the wife of Eugenio, the protagonist of *El Paseo de Gracia* (Gracia Avenue, 1987)—is faithful. She represents the normal and the rational, while the unconscious and instinctual are symbolized by Olga, with whom Eugenio has "intermittenti, violenti, muti o quasi muti, e sempre brevi amplessi" (intermittent, violent, silent or almost silent, and always short embraces). Eugenio has a dual nature: he has two names, an Italian and an English one; he has lived in Italy and in the United States; he is an artist attracted by beauty and grace but bewitched into pain and vice; he is a loving husband, father, and grandfather but also a victimizer of the unintelligent and lower-class Olga. The novel takes an ironic view of religion, politics, business, and women. Yet, Eugenio's lucrative television series, based on Michelangelo's *Last Judgment,* is a reminder to the reader that without judgment there can be no salvation. On the Avenue of Grace in Barcelona, where, as the adage goes, everyone meets, Eugenio is relieved he has not encountered anyone he knows, since no one and nothing could bring him grace or judge him. In spite of the work's comedic elements, Soldati's vision in this novel has grown darker and more pessimistic.

Soldati's more successfully drawn characters experience a continuous tension toward a wholeness and stability that is forever denied them. They are tormented by their quest for truth and meaning, which are always distant, and they are victimized by an all-powerful Eros that mocks their illusion of freedom of action.

Letters:
Lettere di Mario Soldati (Milan: Mondadori, 1979).

Interview:
Davide Lajolo, *Conversazione in una stanza chiusa con Mario Soldati* (Milan: Frassinelli, 1983).

References:
Anna Banti, "Soldati," *Paragone,* 8 (August 1957): 94–96;

Giorgio Bassani, *Le parole preparate* (Turin: Einaudi, 1966), pp. 127–133, 189–201;

Emilio Cecchi, "La narrativa di Mario Soldati," in *Letteratura italiana del Novecento,* volume 2 (Milan: Mondadori, 1972), pp. 992–999;

Cesare Garboli, "La Fortuna critica di Soldati," in *Opere. Racconti autobiografica,* edited by Carboli (Milan: Rizzoli, 1991), pp. 883–920;

Donald Heiney, *America in Modern Italian Literature* (New Brunswick, N.J.: Rutgers University Press, 1964), pp. 29–34, 187–201;

Giovanni Raboni, Gianandrea Gavazzeni, Guido Fink, Garboli, Giacomo Magrini, and Marco Vallora, "Omaggio a Mario Soldati nei suoi ottant'anni," *Paragone,* 37 (December 1986): 47–102;

Enzo Siciliano, *Autobiografia letteraria* (Milan: Garzanti, 1970), pp. 356–360;

Piero de Tommaso, "Mario Soldati," in *Letteratura italiana, I contemporanei,* volume 3 (Milan: Marzorati, 1969), pp. 495–513;

S. Verdino, "Nel mondo di Soldati," *Nuova corrente: Rivista di letteratura,* 106 (July–December 1990): 215–248.

Saverio Strati
(16 August 1924 –   )

Anthony Costantini
California State University, Northridge

BOOKS: *La Marchesina: Racconti* (Milan: Mondadori, 1956);

La Teda (Milan: Mondadori, 1957); translated by Elizabeth Ellman as *Terrarossa: A Novel* (London & New York: Abelard-Schuman, 1962);

Tibi e Tàscia (Milan: Mondadori, 1959);

Mani vuote (Milan: Mondadori, 1960); translated by Peter Moula as *Empty Hands* (London & New York: Abelard-Schuman, 1963);

Avventure in città (Milan: Mondadori, 1962); translated by Angus Davidson as *The Lights of Reggio* (London: John Murray, 1965);

Il nodo (Milan: Mondadori, 1965);

Gente in viaggio (Milan: Mondadori, 1966);

Basilicata Calabria (Milan: Touring Club Italiano, 1968);

Il codardo (Milan: Bietti, 1970);

Noi lazzaroni (Milan: Mondadori, 1972);

È il nostro turno (Milan: Mondadori, 1975);

Terra di emigranti (Florence: Salani, 1975);

Il selvaggio di Santa Venere: Romanzo (Milan: Mondadori, 1977);

Cento bambini (Cosenza: Lerici, 1977);

Il visionario e Il ciabattino (Milan: Mondadori, 1978);

Il diavolaro (Milan: Mondadori, 1979);

Piccolo grande Sud (Florence: Salani, 1981);

I cari parenti (Milan: Mondadori, 1982);

Ascolta, Stefano (Milan: Mursia, 1985);

Miti, racconti e leggende (Rome: Gangemi, 1985);

La conca degli aranci (Milan: Mondadori, 1986);

L'uomo in fondo al pozzo (Milan: Mondadori, 1989);

Il vecchio e l'orologio (Lecce: Manni, 1994);

Melina (Milan: Manni, 1995).

Saverio Strati is a writer from southern Italy who uses that part of the country as a metaphor for the human condition. His South is not a static reality defined once and for all but is in constant ferment, a convulsion of torn passions. Although his work is rooted in his native Calabria, he avoids the folklore and other popularized forms of southern culture. Instead he directs his attention to daily events, filled with the sediment of years of frustration, humiliation, and rebellion. Strati's typical character is not resigned to living in the state of suffering and destitution experienced by his ancestors; he is a product of the proletariat who is conscious of his class identity and seeks alternatives to traditional social and political roles. Since the late 1980s Strati's attention has shifted from the workers to intellectuals who seek personal truths outside the traditional sources of ideology.

Strati was born on 16 August 1924 in Sant'-Agata di Bianco, a small town in the province of Reggio Calabria, to Paolo Strati, a mason, and Agatha Romeo Strati. He left school to work in the fields and then in construction, where he became a head mason. Until he was twenty he had little exposure to literature, but he was attracted to the oral tradition that was carried on especially by the women of his region. He told Rossana Esposito: "Per quanto mi riguarda, la vera matrice del mio narrare sta nei raccontatori di favole che da ragazzo ascoltavo senza mai saziarmene. Soprattutto le donne sapevano raccontare" (As far as I am concerned, the true matrix of my narrative is to be found in the storytellers to whom, as a boy, I never tired of listening. The women especially knew how to tell a story). His education was disrupted by World War II, but he was too young to be drafted. He went back to school at the end of the war and graduated from the *liceo* (high school) when he was twenty-five. He enrolled in medical school at the University of Messina but changed his concentration to Italian literature after he met the critic Giacomo De Benedetti. During this period he began to write short stories. He left school and in 1953 moved to Florence, where he published his first stories in *Nuovo corriere* and other magazines. These stories later appeared in his first book, *La Marchesina* (The Little Princess, 1956). In Florence he met Hildegard Fleig, a Swiss woman; in 1958 they were married and moved to Switzerland. They have a son, Giampaolo. In 1964 he moved to Scandicci, a suburb of Florence, where he still lives.

Saverio Strati in 1993

In *La Marchesina* Strati deals with his homeland in a realistic vein, pointing, often with a sense of rage and despair, to its isolation, poverty, backwardness, and lack of opportunities–themes that are common among southern Italian writers. He presents education as the way to free the South from its condition. His stories do not take a romantic view of poverty but depict a Calabria where life is intense and passionate, permeated by moral and social awareness. The pessimism of many southern writers, such as Giovanni Verga, is only partially present in the early Strati, who mitigates fatalism with Marxist revolutionary ideology.

La Marchesina was viewed by critics as a late product of neorealism. Strati, however, does not share that view. In *La fiera letteraria* of 14 July 1974 he said: "Un isolato. Anche se non ci fosse stato il neorealismo, io avrei scritto quello che ho scritto e come l'ho scritto" (I was isolated. Even if neorealism had not existed, I would have written what I have written, exactly as I wrote it). The collection includes the germs of themes and characters that are found in subsequent works. It is marked by a terse style, fresh and genuine feelings, and often by a melancholic lyricism.

The works that followed–*La Teda* (The Candle, 1957; translated as *Terrarossa,* 1962), *Tibi e Tàscia* (Tibi and Tàscia, 1959), *Mani vuote* (1960; trans-

lated as *Empty Hands,* 1963), and *Avventure in città* (Adventure in the City, 1962; translated as *The Lights of Reggio,* 1965)–feature adolescent protagonists who, like Strati and others of his generation, are forced into adulthood by external events. Strati juxtaposes the old, backward Calabria with the new generation that tries to free itself from a legacy of fear, crime, and poverty as it searches for new modes of life.

La Teda deals with a group of masons who go to work in Castellalto, an isolated village in the Calabrian hinterland. They find an environment where the Mafia has deep roots and where animals and people lead similar lives. The main characters are the young and restless Filippo and his enlightened antagonist, the more mature Costanzo. Listening to Costanzo, Filippo evolves from a womanizer into a man whose work progressively leads him to class consciousness. The *teda,* the resin candle that serves as a primitive form of lighting, is a symbol of material and cultural destitution. Costanzo is the worker-intellectual who enlightens others and articulates their unexpressed hopes for a better life.

Tibi e Tàscia is set in the rural milieu of big landowners and poor farm laborers. Tibi is a teenager living in absolute poverty that denies him the chance to finish his elementary education; but his life is enriched by his mother's love, his love for

344

Tàscia, and an unquenchable thirst for knowledge. He wants to move to the city, which his imagination transforms into an ideal place where individuals are free to develop their natural abilities.

Mani vuote is narrated by Emilio, a fatherless young man who, through a long flashback, relives his youth. Lacking the maternal love that sustained Tibi, Emilio is alone, fighting the enticements of false respect and honor offered by the Mafia. His mother looks to her son's menial jobs to restore the family's lost estate; but work, to Emilio, is a curse from which he tries to escape by immigrating to the United States. Immigration, however, does not change his life. His efforts to win his mother's affection by sending her money to regain the estate prove futile. Emilio's mother represents an oppressive society to which the individual must succumb. To Strati, the family is an institution that perpetuates the evils of southern society rather than contributing to individual growth.

The novella *Avventure in città* contrasts the city and the countryside. The latter is seen as harboring the sound moral values of family, work, and friendship, while corruption, duplicity, and underhanded dealings thrive in the city. The initial enthusiasm that sixteen-year-old Benedetto experiences in the city, where he is manipulated by people who pretend to be interested in him, disappears during his second trip, when he recognizes their falseness. He longs to return to his simple, honest life in the country. *Avventure in città* has a weak structure; its psychological portrait of the protagonist is equally weak.

Gente in viaggio (People in Transit, 1966), a collection of fourteen short stories, forms a transition to the second phase of Strati's career. Compared to *La Marchesina,* the volume offers a wider range of themes: work, poverty, exploitation, emigration, imagination, evasion, travel, and racism; an impressive variety of characters; historical settings from the 1920s through World War II; and a wider range of geographical settings, including Switzerland.

In 1965 and 1970 Strati published two novels, set in northern Italy, in which he captures the struggles of individuals who live at the margin of two cultures and belong to neither. In *Il nodo* (The Knot, 1965) an unnamed university student with literary ambitions is romantically involved with a woman from Switzerland. He cannot decide whether to leave his family in the country and move to the city, which offers better professional prospects. He finally unties "the knot" of his indecision by moving to Florence; but his anxieties about the decision he has made, and the new social setting in which he finds himself, create a state of inner turmoil that condemns him to failure. In *Il codardo* (The Coward, 1970) Michele, who has lived for many years in Milan in the North, comes to realize that northern society is as alienating as the South he left behind. Indeed, life in the North is more vexing since he feels isolated in a large, impersonal city. Both works eschew the moralistic overtones that characterize many neorealistic novels and display such innovative elements as interior monologue and the continual meshing of past and present through flashbacks—elements that would be permanent components of Strati's subsequent works.

During the 1970s Strati's work was influenced by the ideological and political climate of Italian society in general; accordingly, the experiences of his characters go beyond regional boundaries and represent a broader reality. The characters and events in these works are hardly extraordinary, but they project an epic dimension and the expectation that something important is about to emerge. Strati identifies problems in the South and offers solutions that could also relate to the rest of the country. His characters of this period refuse to accept existing class divisions as immutable; they become advocates of radical change in the organization of production and the social structure of their region. They associate work with the promotion of human dignity: through work, the proletariat may be able to break once and for all the social, economic, and political monopoly of the Mafia and the rich landowners. Strati's characters, however, are not merely vehicles of ideology: they agonize over their mistakes and uncertainties.

Strati's realism during this period is reflected in his style, which uses everyday language. In a 1986 interview he remarked:

> Ora siccome parlo di un certo tipo di uomo, ecco che quest'uomo per esprimersi ha bisogno di usare la sua lingua. Creando personaggi come quelli di *Noi lazzaroni,* del *Selvaggio di Santa Venere,* di *Il diavolaro* mi veniva spontaneo di creare una lingua popolare, presa dal parlato. Non potevo usare una lingua letteraria; non mi veniva perché il personaggio non parlava questa lingua.

> (Now, since I am talking about a certain type of individual, in order to express himself he needs to use his own language. Creating characters such as those you find in *We Poor Devils,* the *Savage of Santa Venere,* and *Possessed by the Devil,* it came spontaneously to me to create a common language reflecting daily speech. I could not use a literary language; it didn't come to me since the characters didn't speak such a language.)

Strati adopts an oral-influenced narration in which facts are juxtaposed without attention to chronological order, the syntax is uneven, and the images are

*Dust jacket for Strati's 1979 novel, about the power of
capitalism to transform Calabrian society*

crude and violent. The style reflects the characters'
frustration and inner rebellion.

In *Noi lazzaroni* (We Poor Devils, 1972) Salvatore is a mason who believes that modern consumerism has contaminated the traditional values of the
Calabria region. Young people, if they do not emigrate or join the Mafia, pursue pleasure at any cost,
drawn to the values that are promoted by popular
music, television programs, and motion pictures.
Salvatore develops the idea of rescuing the South by
making use of the experience of returning emigrants. Strati here introduces the constant overlapping of time frames, breaking the linearity of his previous works, and the interjection into the narrative
of interior monologues.

The central character of *È il nostro turno* (It Is
Our Turn, 1975) is a southern intellectual who
moves to the North. Like the protagonists of *Il
nodo* and *Il codardo,* he comes from a working-class
family; unlike them, he becomes passionately con-

cerned with the social problems of the South and
tries to devise solutions for them. The novel traces
his development through high school and college in
his hometown and several other cities, culminating
in his move to Florence. A large part of the work is
taken up by discussions of the problems facing the
South, including the incompetence of local politicians, their collusion with organized crime, the oppressive structure of southern society, and intellectuals who have immigrated to the North and forgotten the needs of their native communities in the
South.

In *Il selvaggio di Santa Venere* (1977) Strati attacks the Mafia through the experiences of three
generations: Leozzè, a self-educated, revolutionary
worker; his father, Domenic; and his grandfather,
Mico. Strati reveals the myths, behavior, and false
code of honor of the Mafia, a brutal organization
that does not hesitate to kill its own members.

In *Il diavolaro* (Possessed by the Devil, 1979),
set during the economic boom of the late 1950s,
Strati elaborates a new model of social emancipation
for Calabria, one based on private enterprise rather
than the Marxist solutions of the preceding novels.
In the conflict between Santicello, who rises from
humble origins to become a wealthy businessman,
and his son-in-law, Tonino, a union activist, Strati
seems to favor Santicello's capitalist scheme for
shaking the people of Calabria from their passivity.
Strati does not, however, fail to depict the negative
aspects of Italian private enterprise, which flour-
ishes with the support of the Mafia and political pay-
offs and leads to the destruction of agriculture, the
disintegration of the nuclear family, and the development of a superficial, materialistic society. Strati's
position is ambivalent: although he no longer believes in Marxism, he has reservations about the triumph of capitalism.

In *Terra di emigranti* (Land of Emigrants, 1975)
Giambattista, a boy of lively intelligence and natural
curiosity, comes of age in a small, isolated mountain
town. The death of his father, who had immigrated
to Germany, shows Giambattista the harsh reality
of a life of emigration. Strati demonstrates his cus-
tomary skill in combining psychological and social
themes, re-creating a youthful world where fantasies
and dreams—Giambattista dreams of being a man-
bird—do not lead to escapism and evasion but are
part of the process of acquiring a mature, though bitter, outlook on life.

The volume *Il visionario e Il ciabattino* (The Vi-
sionary and The Shoemaker, 1978) comprises two
short stories set in Florence. The title character of
"Il visionario" is a famous southern painter who
lives in Florence and confuses his hallucinations for

moments of creativity. Michele Russo, the protagonist of "Il ciabattino," is unable to free himself from the scars left by his life in Calabria, where he was exploited by his father and forced to work ten hours a day until he left for military service. In the more open society of Florence he discovers his potential and comes to view work no longer as exploitation or condemnation but as a path to freedom. His past continues to condition him, however, so that his membership in the Communist Party and his love for a young woman with strong political commitments do not lead him to the ideological clarity found by the protagonists of Strati's previous novels.

In the novels of the 1980s most of Strati's protagonists are young, belong to the petite bourgeoisie, and live in a Calabria that is more progressive than the region depicted in his earlier works. *I cari parenti* (Dear Relatives, 1982) is concerned with the disintegration of the Calabrian family unit. In this atmosphere of decay, only the grandfather, a symbol of the old Calabria of decency and honesty, stands out. The young protagonist, Antonio, grows disoriented and cannot reach an internal stability, even when his choices mirror his grandfather's values. The intertwining of interior monologue and psychological analysis, following the rhythm of oral tradition, captures the turmoil of the adolescent's world.

The protagonist of *Ascolta, Stefano* (Listen, Stefano, 1985) is an adolescent growing up in an unusual family. He is conscious of the transitional nature of the period in which he lives, with young and old generations torn apart by misunderstandings and the Mafia's illicit trafficking in illegal drugs on the rise. The protagonist's understanding is broadened by his eccentric uncle, Michelino, one of Strati's most original characters. Through him the protagonist learns about the links that tie the past to the present and the traditions that shape everyday life.

La conca degli aranci (Orange Valley, 1986) is a complex and robust narrative that stands comparison with the great novels Strati wrote in the 1970s. Thirty-year-old architect Tony, the narrator, recalls his youth in a village in Calabria. Strati again uses the institution of the family to examine the wider crisis of moral values in a society in transition. Other characters include Tony's father; his father's second wife; his brother, Giulio; his half brother, Andrea, who breaks with the family to join the Mafia; and Cicalino, another of Strati's eccentric figures. At the center of the novel is the evolution of Tony's consciousness as he observes the farmers' exploitation by the landowners and their exodus from the countryside. Strati offers the reader a vision of a backward Calabria but also of the emergence of new social classes with fresh moral and cultural values.

In *L'uomo in fondo al pozzo* (A Man at the Bottom of the Well, 1989) Strati ignores the problems of society and concentrates on the internal turmoil of the protagonist—a figure with whom the author establishes an ambiguous relationship, one that lacks the identification with the protagonists found in previous works. Strati's position is vague, betraying ambivalence toward a world that cannot be understood through the lens of ideology. The novel seems to mark the beginning of a new narrative cycle, whose scope is yet to be defined. Rocco is a nonconformist intellectual who believes in the subjectivity of truth and is convinced that the future of humanity is entrusted to a few geniuses like himself; society is a collection of meaningless individuals who are to be despised. In a final unexpected twist, however, Rocco admits that he has erred all his life and repudiates all he has tried to accomplish. *L'uomo in fondo al pozzo* is Strati's effort to portray the condition of writers and artists in today's consumer society—a society, leveled by mediocrity, in which art has become solipsistic and sterile.

Strati's most recent work is a collection of short stories titled *Melina* (1995), which reiterates familiar themes: the North-South relationship, emigration, and family concerns. What has changed is the writer's attitude toward the South, which reflects the social evolution that has occurred in Italy in the last twenty years. Educational and professional opportunities have improved for southern Italians. Emigration is no longer viewed as a curse, as it was in the novel *Mani vuote*, but as a means of bettering one's socio-economic condition.

The title story, "Melina," deals with a new relationship between northern and southern Italy based on equality and mutual respect. Melina's father, Filippo, having found success in the North, decides to return to the South to open a business. But it is Melina who symbolizes the new South, as a fully emancipated young woman who seeks an education and prepares herself for a career. Eventually she also decides to marry a local young man who was her childhood friend. Melina realizes the dreams denied to the female characters of Strati's earlier works, especially Tascia, in the novel *Tibi e Tàscia*, whose social function is limited to being a housewife and doing domestic work.

Melina marks a significant turning point in Strati's work. His characters are not created from memory and a vision of traditional southern society but rather reflect the present and the attendant freedoms and opportunities available to all Italians. One imagines that future works by Strati will likely continue to focus on the new social reality that is southern Italy at the end of this century.

In addition to short stories, novellas, and novels, Strati has published a collection of fairy tales, *Cento bambini* (One Hundred Children, 1977), and a collection of Calabrian folktales, *Miti, racconti e leggende* (Myths, Tales and Legends, 1985). His vision of life, though anchored in southern Italy, embraces universal themes and experiences. His characters, moving from near illiteracy to social consciousness, follow a trajectory that reflects the evolution of postwar Italy. A writer whose view extends beyond Italian society, Strati has also proved to be a reliable interpreter of the modern existential condition.

Interview:

Anthony Costantini, "Intervista a Saverio Strati," *Italian Quarterly,* 27 (Fall 1986): 73–81.

References:

Giuseppe Amoroso, "Saverio Strati," in *Narratori italiani del Novecento,* edited by Gaetano Mariani and Mario Petrucciani (Rome: Lucarini, 1987), pp. 697–711;

Anthony Costantini, "L'ultima opera di Saverio Strati," *Il cristallo,* 31 (1989): 75–104;

Costantini, "*L'uomo in fondo al pozzo* di Saverio Strati: Strutture narrative e linguaggio," *Campi immaginari,* 1 (1992): 67–85;

Costantini, "Saverio Strati e la funzione maturante del lavoro," *Forum Italicum,* 24 (Spring 1990): 10–24;

Pasquino Crupi, "Saverio Strati," in *Letteratura italiana: I contemporanei,* volume 7 (Milan: Marzorati, 1974), pp. 1723–1737;

Crupi, *Saverio Strati e la letteratura d'invenzione sociale* (Vibo Valentia: Quale cultura, 1971);

Rossana Esposito, *Strati* (Florence: La Nuova Italia, 1983);

Sebastiano Martelli, "Per una proposta di narrativa meridionale: La Cava e Strati," *Misure critiche,* 38/39 (July–December 1975): 35–62;

Mario B. Mignone, "Saverio Strati e il dramma dell'emigrazione," *Campi immaginari,* 1/2 (1991): 111–122;

Antonio Motta, *Invito alla lettura di Strati* (Milan: Mursia, 1984);

Persio Nesti, "Strati e l'emigrazione meridionale," *Il Ponte,* 2 (February 1967): 236–242;

Walter Pedullà, *La letteratura del benessere* (Naples: Libreria Scientifica, 1968), pp. 311–316;

Concettina Pizzuti, "Corrado Alvaro e Saverio Strati su promozione sociale e apprendistato della lingua nazionale," *Forum Italicum,* 27 (Spring 1993): 229–247;

Claudio Varese, *Occasioni e valori della letteratura contemporanea* (Bologna: Cappelli, 1967), pp. 461–465.

Giovanni Testori
(12 May 1923 – 16 March 1993)

Augustus Pallotta
Syracuse University

See also the Testori entry in *DLB 128: Twentieth-Century Italian Poets, Second Series.*

BOOKS: *La Morte. Un quadro* (Forlí: Pattuglia, 1943);

Il dio di Roserio (Turin: Einaudi, 1954);

In trigesimo (Milan: All'Insegna del Pesce d'Oro, 1956);

? Martino Spanzotti: Gli affreschi di Ivres (Ivres: Centro culturale Olivetti, 1958);

I segreti di Milano: I, Il ponte della Ghisolfa (Milan: Feltrinelli, 1958);

I segreti di Milano: II, La Gilda del Mac Mahon (Milan: Feltrinelli, 1959);

I segreti di Milano: III, La Maria Brasca. Quattro atti (Milan: Feltrinelli, 1960);

I segreti di Milano: IV, L'Arialda; due tempi (Milan: Feltrinelli, 1960);

I segreti di Milano: V, Il fabbricone (Milan: Feltrinelli, 1961); translated by Sidney Alexander as *The House in Milan* (New York: Harcourt, Brace & World, 1962; London: Collins, 1963);

Il Brianza e altri racconti (Milan: Feltrinelli, 1962);

Giovanni Paganin: Scultore dal 1952 al '63 (Milan: Milione, 1964);

Palinsesto valsesiano (Milan: All'Insegna del Pesce d'Oro, 1964);

Il gran teatro montano: Saggi su Gaudenzio Ferrari (Milan: Feltrinelli, 1965);

I trionfi (Milan: Feltrinelli, 1965);

Crocifissione (Milan: All'Insegna del Pesce d'Oro, 1966);

In trigesimo (Milan: All'Insegna del Pesce d'Oro, 1966);

Manieristi piemontesi e lombardi del '600 (Milan: Pizzi, 1967);

La Monaca di Monza (Milan: Feltrinelli, 1967);

33 opere del Seicento (Milan: La Galleria, 1967);

Giacomo Ceruti (Milan: Finarte, 1967);

Colombotto Rosso (Turin, 1967);

Gruber (Turin: Galatea, 1967);

McGarrell (Paris: Galerie Claude Bernard, 1967);

L'amore (Milan: Feltrinelli, 1968);

Giovanni Testori

James McGarrell: Opere recenti (Rome: Galleria il Fante di spade, 1968);

Erodiade (Milan: Feltrinelli, 1969);

Fra Galgario (Turin: ERI, 1969);

Vespignani: Imbarco per Citera (Milan: Finarte, 1969);

Per sempre (Milan: Feltrinelli, 1970);

Thorn Prikker (Milan: All'Insegna del Pesce d'Oro, 1970);

Nature morte di Ernesto Ornati (Milan: All'Insegna del Pesce d'Oro, 1970);

Cagnaccio di San Pietro (Turin, 1971);

Grunewald (Milan: Rizzoli, 1972);

L'Ambleto (Milan: Rizzoli, 1972);

Alain (Milan: Sciardelli, 1973);

Nel tuo sangue (Milan: Rizzoli, 1973);

Macbetto (Milan: Rizzoli, 1974);

La cattedrale (Milan: Rizzoli, 1974);

Passio Laetitiae et Felicitatis (Milan: Rizzoli, 1975);

Romanino e Moretto alla Cappella del Sacramento (Brescia: Grafo, 1975);

Paolo Vallorz (Milan, 1975);

Helmut Kolle (Milan: Galleria Trentadue, 1975);

Beniamino Simoni a Cerveno (Brescia: Grafo, 1976);

Edipus (Milan: Rizzoli, 1977);

Conversazione con la morte (Milan: Rizzoli, 1978);

Moroni in Val Seriana, edited by Giuseppe Frangi (Brescia: Grafo, 1978);

De Stefano (Milan: Galleria trentadue, 1978);

Interrogatorio a Maria (Milan: Rizzoli, 1980);

Il senso della nascita. Colloquio con Don Luigi Giussani (Milan: Rizzoli, 1980);

Factum est (Milan: Rizzoli, 1981);

La maestra della vita (Milan: Rizzoli, 1982);

Varlin: Peintures. 12 février–27 mars 1982, by Testori and Friedrich Dürrenmatt (Paris: Galerie Claude Bernard/Galerie Albert Loeb, 1982);

Eugene Bloch, 1906–1940 (Milan: Compagnia del Disegno, 1982);

Post-Hamlet (Milan: Rizzoli, 1983);

Bacon a Brera: E quaranta disegni di Grosz in sosta a Milano, by Testori and Mario de Micheli (Milan: Multipla, 1983);

Ossa mea (Milan: Mondadori, 1983);

I promessi sposi alla prova (Milan: Mondadori, 1984);

Azione teatrale in due giornate (Milan: Mondadori, 1984);

Confiteor (Milan: Mondadori, 1985);

Diadèmata (Milan: Garzanti, 1986);

Igor Mitoraj: Sculture 1987 (Milan: Compagnia del Disegno, 1987);

In exitu (Milan: Garzanti, 1988);

–et nihil: 1985–1986 (Florence: Arnaud, 1989);

Verbo (Milan: Longanesi, 1989);

Sfaust (Milan: Longanesi, 1990);

Marino Marini: Opere, by Testori and Maurizio Cecchetti (Cesena: Comune di Cesena, 1990);

Fetting (Milan: Compagnia del Disegno, 1990);

Rainer Fetting: Scultore–pittore. Comune di Cesena, Rocca Malatestiana, 15 giugno–6 ottobre 1991, by Testori and Cecchetti (Cesena: Comune di Cesena, 1991);

SdisOrè (Milan: Longanesi, 1991);

Francis Gruber 1912–1948, by Testori, Louis Aragon, and Osvaldo Pattani (Milan: Compagnia del Disegno, 1991);

Ferroni: Incisioni, 1957–1991, by Testori and Marco Goldin (Lecco/Bellinzona/Bergamo: Ceribelli, 1991);

Igor Mitoraj, by Testori and Donald Kuspit (Milan: Fabbri, 1991);

Maurino Maurini (Milan: Fabbri, 1991);

Sutherland: L'atelier dei ritratti (Milan: Fabbri, 1991);

Volte face: Cinquantanove ritratti di Sergio Vacchi (Milan: Fabbri, 1991);

Gli angeli dello sterminio (Milan: Longanesi, 1992);

Morlotti: Variazioni sopra un canto bagnanti 1991–1992; febbraio–aprile 1992 (Milan: Ruggerini & Zonca, 1992);

Nebbia al Giambellino, edited by Fulvio Panzeri (Milan: Longanesi, 1995).

Collection: *I libri di Giovanni Testori* (Milan: Mondadori, 1984).

OTHER: "Guardarti intorno e impara," in *Racconti* (Milan: Nuova Accademia, 1964), pp. 175-192;

Carlo Borromeo, *Memoriale ai Milanesi,* introduction by Testori (Milan: Giordano, 1965);

"Bestemmie e preghiere," in *Almanacco internazionale di poeti 1973,* edited by Giancarlo Vigorelli (Milan: Borletti, 1973), p. 194;

"Un uomo in una donna, anzi un Dio," preface to Michelangelo Buonarroti's *Rime* (Milan: Rizzoli, 1975), pp. i–xviii;

Disegni di Roberto Longhi, edited by Testori (Milan: Compagnia del disegno, 1980);

Luca Doninelli, *Intorno a una lettera di Santa Caterina,* introduction by Testori (Milan: Rizzoli, 1981);

Kei Mitsuuchi: Ai piedi della croce, edited by Testori (Milan: Mazzotta, 1985);

Dantale Crespi, *Nelle raccolte private,* edited by Testori (Milan: Fabbri, 1988);

Traduzione della I Lettera ai Corinti, translated by Testori (Milan: Longanesi, 1991).

SELECTED PERIODICAL PUBLICATIONS–UNCOLLECTED: "Coro della sera," *Politecino,* 6 (3 November 1945): 7;

"Stanze per la flagellazione di San Domenico Maggiore," *Paragone,* no. 226 (December 1968): 3-5;

"Dodici poesie da a te," *Almanacco dello Specchio,* 8 (1979): 175-180.

Giovanni Testori is widely known in Italy not only as a novelist and short-story writer but also as a poet, playwright, painter, and art critic. Testori never shied away from controversial social and religious questions; consequently, his writing mirrors the profound changes that have occurred in Italian society since the 1950s. His work is marked by formal experimentation; social consciousness; an intense, almost obsessive interest in sexuality; and an equally intense quest for spirituality.

Testori was born on 12 May 1923 in Novate, a suburb of Milan, to Edoardo and Lina Testori. His family owned a textile mill not far from Novate. He was educated in private Catholic schools in Milan: the Collegio Arcivescovile San Carlo and the Università Cattolic, where he studied literature, philosophy, and art history. The title of his thesis, "Forma nella pittura contemporanea" (Form in Contemporary Painting, 1947), foreshadows the interest in technical innovation that would become evident in his writings, as well as in his own paintings. A large part of Testori's professional life was devoted to painting and art criticism; as indicated by his thesis, his youthful interests were mainly in contemporary artists, among them Giacomo Manzù and Renato Guttuso, but in time his attention shifted to earlier periods. By the end of his life he was best known as an expert on seventeenth- and eighteenth-century artists from Piedmont and from his native Lombardy, and his studies led to reassessments of artists such as Giacomo Cerruti, Gaudenzio Ferrari, and Tanzio da Varallo. He organized various art exhibits, for many of which he wrote the catalogues. For his interest in art Testori credited the art historian Roberto Longhi, who was also a role model for the writer Giorgio Bassani. Testori lived in Novate all his life but had a studio in Via Brera in Milan. He held the first exhibition of his work in 1971 at Turin's Galleria Galatea.

Testori's work as a playwright generated controversy: in 1960 a judge prohibited performance of his play L'Arialda in Rome because it contained obscene language. To protest the decision, in November of that year the director of the play, Luchino Visconti, and two of the actors, Rina Morelli and Paolo Stoppa, read the text at the Teatro Eliseo in Rome before an audience made up largely of literary critics. In 1972 Testori helped to establish the theatrical group Cooperativa Franco Parenti, which staged several of his plays in the 1970s. In 1972 he became a regular contributor to the cultural section of Il corriere della sera, Italy's most prestigious newspaper.

At the beginning of his career as a writer of fiction Testori was drawn to Neorealism, the dominant force in cinema and literature of the immediate postwar period. Influenced by the Italian Marxist philosopher Antonio Gramsci, neorealist writers looked to the working class, rather than the bourgeoisie, for fresh forms of expression. In doing so, they used the language spoken by the proletariat, which more often than not was a regional dialect rather than the formal Italian used by the professional classes. Hence Testori's works, as well as those of such writers as Beppe Fenoglio, Lucio Mastronardi, and Pier Paolo Pasolini are marked by a deep social consciousness and the use of dialect.

Testori's first important work of fiction was the novella Il dio di Roserio (The God of Roserio, 1954). Testori's writing here has analogies with the cinema in its use of flashbacks and its quick-paced, visually driven narrative; furthermore, Testori's attention to tones and hues of color betrays a kinship with his interest in painting. These features did not escape the attention of Elio Vittorini, an editor for the publisher Einaudi, who recommended Il dio di Roserio for publication. Introducing the book to its readers, Vittorini wrote on the dust jacket that Testori delved into reality "con gusto preeminentemente visivo, con una sensualità che ha nell'occhio il suo uncino principale. Non per nulla egli viene alla narrativa dalla pittura" (with a style that is predominantly visual, with a sensuality that employs the eye as its main hook. It is no coincidence that the author comes to the narrative from painting). Its tense and dynamic style, arresting images, and skillful use of working-class speech caught the attention of critics and the reading public alike.

Il dio di Roserio, a work rich in descriptive and psychological rather than narrative elements, revolves around a detailed account of two bicycle races. Both are dominated by Dante Pessina, a superb athlete of humble background from the town of Roserio. Pessina is determined, at all costs, to break out of the poverty in which he was born and become a rich and famous athlete. Standing in his way is the team captain, Consonni, who has similar aspirations. In the first race Pessina deliberately causes an accident, in which Consonni suffers severe head injuries and is eliminated from the competition. In the second event Pessina races both against time and his own guilt, suppressing the latter through his indomitable desire to win. The race is a metaphor for Italian society of the mid 1950s, in which the main objective in life was material success: "Correre, correre. Per che cosa era nato se non per quello? Cosa gli importava del resto? Niente: giusto sua madre. Ma se era il caso, sarebbe disposto a passar sopra anche lei" (Racing and only racing. What else was he born for, if not to race? What else mattered? Nothing, except his mother. But, if need be, he was ready to run over her, too).

Another way of looking at Testori's novella is that it shows sports to be one of the few means available to working-class individuals to achieve economic success. This perspective led Enrico Ghidetti to remark that Il dio di Roserio betrays the crisis of

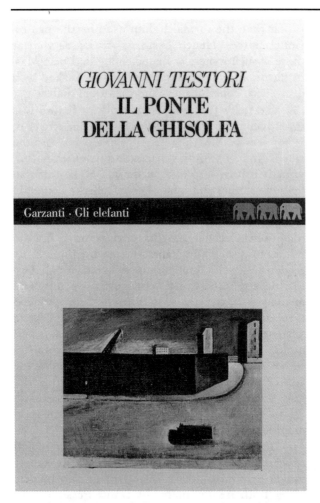

Cover for a 1985 edition of Testori's 1958 story collection, which includes a revision of his novella Il dio di Roserio

Neorealism and its governing Marxist ideology in that its attention strays from the betterment of society to the material enrichment of the individual.

After *Il dio di Roserio* Testori began working on an ambitious project, *I segreti di Milano* (The Secrets of Milan). Published from 1958 to 1961, the work consists of two volumes of short stories, two plays, and a novel, all depicting proletarian life in Italy's most industrialized city. A second novel, *Nebbia al Giambellino* (Fog at Giambellino), was published posthumously in 1995. The title echoes *Les Mystères de Paris* (The Mysteries of Paris, 1842), a serial novel by the French novelist Eugène Sue dealing with the nineteenth-century Parisian underclass; both titles point to the novelist's function of bringing to light the hidden plight of the downtrodden. Like the novels of Emile Zola, Testori's work depicts a social Darwinist society in which only the fittest succeed.

I segreti di Milano is also reminiscent of nineteenth-century Italian naturalism, or verismo—in particular, of the novels and short stories of Giovanni Verga, who portrayed the miserable lives of Sicilian peasants and fishermen. Verga relied heavily on the interior monologue to transmit the thoughts and feelings of his characters, and this device is also used by Testori.

The first volume of *I segreti di Milano* is a collection of short stories titled *Il ponte della Ghisolfa* (The Bridge on the River Ghisolfa, 1958). A good part of the book is taken up by *Il dio di Roserio,* revised to eliminate the first chapter and much of the dialect. Testori revised the novella to deemphasize its experimental character and bring it in line with is larger project. The most important theme in *Il ponte della Ghisolfa* is the role of the family as the basic unit of society; the serious crisis the Italian family is experiencing today is prefigured here with remarkable clarity. Nearly all of the stories in which the family is brought to the fore depict dissension, tension, and fracture. Often the cause of the crisis is money, but just as frequent is the breakdown of parental authority. In "Lo scopo della vita" (The Purpose of Life) an aging father who has worked all his life in a factory wants his children, Vincenzo and Piera, to marry prospects who will afford them a better future. But Vincenzo is in love with Carla, a young woman of loose morals; he tells his father: "La Carla io la sposo, la sposo anche se a te, a tua moglie, a tua figlia e a quello che sta per diventare tuo genero non fa piacere. La sposo perché piace a me. Questo è quello che conta" (I am going to marry Carla; I'll marry her even if you, your wife, your daughter and the guy who is about to become your son-in-law [Luigi, Piera's fiancé] don't like it. I am going to marry her because *I* like it. That's what counts).

In some stories the characters question the value of creating a family, either because they rationalize that the poverty of the parents would be passed on to the next generation or out of sheer selfishness. In "Lo scopo della vita," Vincenzo severs his relationship with Carla, who marries another man. At the end of the story he sees her walking down the street and notices that she is pregnant. His reaction: " 'Gelosia?' si disse. 'Macché!' rispose con una decisione che non si conosceva da tempo. 'È solo schifo; schifo per tutte queste povere dannate che non son capaci di far altro che metter al mondo altri dannati e altre dannate come loro'" ("Jealousy?" he asked himself. "Not at all!" he answered with a resolution he had not felt in a long time. "It is only disgust: disgust for such miserable wretched women who are only capable of bringing into the world other wretched men and women just like themselves.")

For Wanda in "Il ponte della Ghisolfa" having children would be a burden: "Figli? Figli no, perché rubano il pane di bocca, mettono pensieri, constringono a raddoppiare le fatiche e basta" (Children? No children, because they steal food from your mouth, cause worries, and force you to double your work, that's all). The notion that children represent a detraction from, rather than an enrichment of, life was a new development in Italian society and was given impetus by the prosperity of the postwar years—especially for women, whose role had traditionally been limited to rearing children and who, in the new economy, had the choice of working in factories. This freedom marks the genesis of the strong women's movement that would surface with full force in the widespread marches and protests of the late 1960s.

Angelica Binda in "Il ras" is a factory worker who hopes to marry the well-to-do Duilio. However what stands out in her mind is not a family but "i sogni . . . . d'uscir dalla vita misera e dannata, casa e lavoro, lavoro e casa . . . . quelli di diventar in qualche modo una signora anche lei, con una serva per se, invece che essere lei a far sempre la serva agli altri" (the dream of getting out of her damned miserable life, made up of home and work, work and home; the dream of becoming a lady, with a maid for herself, rather than her being the maid to others). Angelica is precise in defining her goal: "Lei era donna e la sua vita voleva giocarla con un uomo, con uno cioè che potesse farla ricca oltre che felice" (She was a woman, and she wanted to gamble her life on a man, someone, that is, who could make her both wealthy and happy). When Duilio rejects her, Angelica realizes that she has been "scema a illudersi che il destino per lei potesse essere meno duro di quello che era per tutti gli altri e le altre che vivevano nella sua casa in una delle tante uguali alla sua" (foolish in deluding herself that destiny would be less harsh for her than it had been for other men and women who lived in her house and so many other homes similar to hers) and falls back on her belief that she cannot change her own life. Angelica's prefeminist self-definition is not that of an individual with a potential outside the traditional role of wife but that of the hopeful candidate for a comfortable middle-class marriage.

Women like Angelica are, however, the exception in Testori's work. More often than not his women characters are strong individuals who assert themselves even in risky and unfavorable circumstances. Such is the case of Enrica, who defies her parents' wishes by marrying Michele in the title story, "Il ponte della Ghisolfa." When her parents' apprehensions prove well-founded, as Michele begins to drink and to mistreat her, Enrica seeks revenge by having an affair with Raffaele, her brother-in-law, who lives under the same roof. She thinks that Michele drinks, in part, because wine gives him "l'illusione di sentirsi uomo e uomo forte e padrone" (the illusion of being a man, a strong man, and master). Accordingly, she decides: "E tu tieni il tuo vino che io mi terrò tuo fratello per sempre" (You can have your wine, and I will keep your brother for good).

Enrica's marriage to Michele, a Sicilian immigrant to Milan, points to another theme of Testori's work: the cultural differences between North and South that were thrown into relief by the heavy immigration of southern Italians to northern industrial regions in the early 1950s. Since childhood Enrica felt what she herself regarded as a strange attraction to southerners. Her parents warned her not to date "those people": "È molto, molto più d'una questione di razza. Con quelli lí non riusciamo a parlare" (It is more, much more than a question of race. With those people we can't even communicate). Nevertheless, Enrica falls in love with Michele and marries him despite "infiniti rifiuti" (countless objections) from her parents. The marriage turns into a nightmare for Enrica when she realizes that Michele comes from a culture in which the husband "si riteneva in diritto di fare quello che voleva" (thought he had the right to do what he wanted) while she was expected to stay "a casa, a fare la buona moglie" (at home and be a good wife). Enrica's inability to accept southern mores leads to take her brother-in-law as a lover because she is attracted to him and as a spiteful action toward her husband.

Testori notes in the preface to *La Gilda del Mac Mahon* (Gilda from Mac Mahon Street, 1959), the second volume of *I segreti di Milano,* that nearly half the stories in the book are connected to stories in *Il ponte della Ghisolfa.* The love triangle of Enrica, Michele, and Raffaele, for example, is referred to in "Appena fuori Luino" (Right outside Luino) in the second volume; this story's central character, Luisa, and her brother, Romeo, initiate a cluster of five short stories in the new volume. The stories in *La Gilda del Mac Mahon* continue the portrayal of the gray lives of the individuals that make up the Milanese underclass. In *La Gilda del Mac Mahon,* however, the author's outlook is markedly more negative and pessimistic. For example, in "Cara la mia zia" (My Dear Aunt), the narrator notes that the protest of the residents of a tenement against the foul smell from nearby oil refineries will go unheeded, "come se le loro case di operai non meritassero più rispetto di una latrina o d'una fogna" (as though the homes of working-class people deserved

*Cover for a 1996 edition of Testori's 1959 book, which includes
stories that reveal the constricted lives of the poor in Milan*

no more respect than a latrine or a sewer). One of
those homes, inhabited by a young man, is given
this lapidary description: "Due stanze, padre, madre
e tre fratelli, quattro con lui" (Two rooms occupied
by his father, his mother, and three brothers—four,
counting him).

These descriptions show that the economic
boom of the late 1950s did not reach the lowest substratum of Milanese society. Unable to find work,
Raffaele, Enrica's lover, has to resort to smuggling
cigarettes from Switzerland, risking his life every
day. In addition to smugglers, the underclass that
populates Testori's stories includes domestic workers, store clerks, bartenders, prostitutes, pimps, and
pornographers. The attitudes of such characters are
marked by cynicism, pessimism, and indifference to
distinctions of right and wrong. Thus, in the story
"Fin quando ci sono io. . . ." (As Long as I Am
Here. . . .) one youngster "a vent'anni ha già schifo
di tutto e di tutti" (at twenty is already disgusted by
everything and everyone). In "Il Brianza," a story ti-

tled after an area outside of Milan, the character
called Il Brianza, who plays a central role in several
of the stories, poses for erotic pictures and then
blackmails the man who distributes the material for
a considerable sum of money, with which he buys a
motorcycle. He has no moral compunction about
his actions: "Perché, in fondo, con gli scrupoli cosa
si ottiene? Ci si rovina la vita e si resta sempre nella
miseria" (In the last analysis, what do you gain with
moral scruples? You ruin your life and continue to
live in poverty).

The stories in both *Il ponte della Ghisolfa* and *La
Gilda del Mac Mahon* are characterized by simple
plots, little action (with the exception of "Il dio di
Roserio"), and few twists or surprises. Sequential
chronology is avoided in favor of flashbacks, usually in the form of the characters' memories. The
dominant narrative mode is the interior monologue,
resulting in what Italians call *intimismo psicologico*—a
detailed probing of inner feelings and motivations
comparable to the exhaustive representation of
physical reality in works by naturalist writers. Furthermore, each action, gesture, event, or circumstance, regardless of its importance to the plot, is
broken into smaller units that are examined at great
length. Such techniques run the risk of becoming
formulaic and tiresome, and in Testori's least successful stories his writing turns into a self-indulgent,
mannerist prose concerned only with its own liter-
ariness.

In 1960 Testori published the plays *La Maria
Brasca* and *L'Arialda,* which constitue the third and
fourth volumes, respectively, of *I segreti di Milano.*
The rivalry of two women for a man ends in tragedy
in *L'Arialda* and in victory for the stronger of the
two in *La Maria Brasca.* The fifth volume of the series, *Il fabbricone* (translated as *The House in Milan,*
1962), was published in 1961. Purportedly a novel
about the factory workers Carlo Villa and Rina
Oliva, a postwar, proletarian Romeo and Juliet
whose love for one another is thwarted by the conflicting party affiliations of their families—his is
Communist, hers Christian Democrat—the work is
actually a novella inflated with ancillary characters
and events that are given greater attention and lati-
tude than would be the case in a tightly knit novel.
In fact, *Il fabbricone* is essentially an elaboration of
narrative clusters of the previous two collections of
short stories.

As in a naturalist novel, the characters here are
overshadowed by their environment. The title of
the book refers to the tenement inhabited by most of
the characters: it is called *fabbricone*—from *fabbrica*
(factory)—because its cold, impersonal design reminds the tenants of a factory. The ugliness of the

fabbricone is a synecdoche for the city of Milan, which is treated here as the antithesis of the Renaissance conception of the city as a place of social harmony, commerce, and cultivation of the arts. Testori describes modern-day Milan as physically and morally repulsive: "L'una era ormai passata e il fetore che veniva dal Pero, mescolandosi all'umidità, aveva reso l'aria irrespirabile e pesante" (It was past one o'clock and the stench coming from Pero [a suburb of Milan known for its oil refineries and chemical plants], together with the humidity, made the air heavy and unbreathable). In a typically Marxist vein, economic injustice is singled out as the root of all evil: "La miseria. Ecco cos'era la vera causa, la vera colpa di tutto. La miseria e la fame, da una parte. Il niente da fare, i soldi e i vizi, dall'altra" (Poverty. That was the real cause, responsible for everything. Poverty and hunger, on one hand; having nothing to do, money and vices, on the other).

Two of the "vices" given ample space in the work are homosexuality and male prostitution; in treating them, as well as heterosexual acts, Testori is graphic and explicit. One passage reports the feelings of a woman when she learns that her son, Sandrino, is a male prostitute:

La donna guardò il ragazzo che s'allontanava dondolando, come se non capisse niente di quel che stava facendo. Allora l'odio cominciò a salirle in corpo. Un odio per il mondo e la vita cosí com'erano. Per tutte quelle macchine. Per tutto quell'oro che brillava davanti a quei poveri disgraziati e li costringeva piano piano a perdere coscienza, dignità, onore, tutto. Lei come lei avrebbe fatto la fame. La terra avrebbe mangiato, piuttosto di scendere ai patti e alle richieste di quei maiali! Ma lei era nata e cresciuta in altri tempi. E il mondo adesso andava cosí.

(The woman watched the boy, who walked away swinging his hips, acting like he did not understand what he was doing. At that point, she felt anew a sense of visceral hatred. Hatred for the state of the world and life as such. Hatred for all those expensive cars. For all the gold that dazzled those miserable youngsters and forced them slowly to lose their moral awareness, their dignity and self-respect, everything. As far as she was concerned, she would have starved. She would have eaten dirt rather than lowering herself to deal with those pigs and satisfy their demands. But she was born and raised in a different era. And today's world was like that.)

Nebbia al Giambellino was found among Testori's papers and published posthumously in 1995. Based on narrative style and thematic content, the work was probably written in the early 1960s. Fulvio Panzeri, who edited the novel, states in the *Postfazione*, or afterword, that the date composition is

1961–1962. Accordingly, he regards it as volume six of *I segreti di Milano*.

As in all of Testori's works published in the late 1950s, *Nebbia al Giambellino* deals with the economic destitution of the underclass in the outskirts of Milan, in this case an area called Giambellino. The main character, Gina Restilli, is a happily married woman with a young daughter. She is forced by financial needs to find work as a domestic in the house of a wealthy businessman, Rinaldo Cattaneo. Determined to remain faithful to her husband, Gina resists Rinaldo's insistent advances. She is tired of what has become for her an intolerable situation, and one day she gives her employer an ultimatum: "La finisca. Io non posso più sopportare questa situazione. Ho deciso: o lei mi trova un lavoro con cui posso vivere, entro due giorni, o io la denuncio" (Stop it. I cannot put up with this situation any longer. I have made up my mind: either you find me, within two days, another job I can live on, or I will report you to the police). A heated discussion ensues, in the course of which Rinaldo, infuriated by the threat, chokes Gina to death. He runs away to escape arrest, but, unable to cope with the guilt and the legal consequences of his action, he takes his own life. *Nebbia al Giambellino* has much in common with other works, such as *Il ponte della Ghisolfa* and *Il fabbricone,* but it differs in its more intensive probing of the psychology of the characters and its juxtaposition of two social classes, the proletariat and the bourgeoisie, represented respectively by Gina and Rinaldo.

After the publication of *Il fabbricone* Testori abandoned fiction for thirteen years. To a large extent the decision was prompted by the negative reaction of literary critics, who pointed to the work's simplistic plot, deficient characterization, and excessive use of interior monologues. Testori turned to the stage, giving life to embittered, strong-willed, rebellious women struggling for self-determination. In *La Monaca di Monza* (The Nun of Monza, 1967), which treats the same historical figure immortalized by Alessandro Manzoni in *I promessi sposi* (1827; translated as *The Betrothed Lovers,* 1828), the nun is endowed with a modern consciousness and inveighs against parental authority and restrictive social codes. *Erodiade* (Herodias, 1969) offers long, overwrought monologues in which Herod's wife declares her attraction to John the Baptist. Classical dramas are rewritten to reflect modern existential themes in *L'Ambleto* (1972), *Macbetto* (1974), and *Edipus* (1977), patterned, respectively, after William Shakespeare's *Hamlet* (circa 1600–1601) and *Macbeth* (1606?) and Sophocles' *Oedipus Rex* (fifth century

B.C.). These works are among Testori's least successful efforts.

Testori published his first book of poems, *I trionfi* (The Triumphs, 1965), eleven years after the appearance of *Il dio di Roserio*. Yet in the last twenty-eight years of his life poetry, not fiction, was his preferred form of creative expression. The seven books of verse Testori wrote from 1965 to 1981 stand out as the most disturbing and moving testimony of religious crisis to appear in Italy since World War II. In the first three volumes, *I trionfi, Crocifissione* (Crucifixion, 1966) and *L'amore* (Love, 1968), Testori probes deeply and incessantly into the meaning and purpose of human existence; the quest is marked by tension, anguish, and despair. The same emotions are present, although in a milder form, in *Per sempre* (Forever, 1970), where they are attenuated by childhood memories and the comfort of loved ones. *Nel tuo sangue* (In Your Blood, 1973) marks the highest point of intensity in Testori's religious verse: here the poet's love-hate relationship with Christ is pursued with unrelenting, obsessive fervor and in language that dares to be obscene. In *Interrogatorio a Maria* (Questions for Mary, 1980), addressed to the mother of Jesus, the tone is markedly different: it is humble, devout, even inspiring. *Factum est* (It Is Done, 1981) is a sustained indictment of abortion in strong and arresting images.

Testori returned to fiction with the novel *La cattedrale* (The Cathedral, 1974). As in his other works, the story is simple: a writer with a definite physical resemblance to Testori—"il suo corpo tozzo da toro calvo e un po' folle" (his rustic body resembling a bull, bald, and a little crazy)—has a brief sexual encounter with a teenage boy that ends tragically for both. The work includes ancillary stories of a medieval goldsmith and a seventeenth-century saint. Like that of Testori's poetry, the language of *La cattedrale* is confessional and often blasphemous: "E che cieli, eh, mi risponda; che cieli non siano più inferno o più latrina dei troni e delle dominazioni?" (And what heavens, tell me, what heavens are no more a hell or a latrine than our earthly kingdoms?). In one passage the anger and despair of the homosexual writer turns into a fantasy of violent desire:

Gli sposi e gli amanti s'amavano, Lui no. Lui ne sognava un altro, d'amore: che fosse l'opposto, l'anomalo, l'inviso. Sognava che di colpo, nel pieno della notte, le campane del borgo suonassero a stormo, non per una festa del Dio, ma per una rivolta o per un incendio che divorasse in sé tutti, i boschi, i pascoli, le case, le cascine. E che, a quel suono tutti uscissero fuori e, forsennati e felici, principiassero a stringersi in un abbraccio dove niente che fosse legge, regola della natura e del Dio fosse più rispettato.

(The newly married and the lovers were making love. Not he. He was dreaming about another form of love, even though it was the opposite, anomalous, hated love. He dreamed that unexpectedly, in the middle of the night, the church bells rang a death knell, not to honor God but to signal a rebellion, or a fire that was devouring forests, grazing lands, homes, and farmhouses. And he dreamed that, on hearing those bells, everyone came out of the houses and, happy and insane, began to embrace one another in a way in which nothing pertaining to laws, the rules of nature or God, was respected.)

Testori's next novel, *Passio Laetitiae et Felicitatis* (1975), reflects a return to the experimentation with language of *Il dio di Roserio*. He fashions an artificial language that is close to baroque prose, mingling standard Italian with Milanese dialect, Latin and Latinized Italian, and words of his own coinage. The title of the novel comes from a medieval text that honors the martyrdom of the early Christians and points to suffering leading to joy and happiness in heaven. Testori transforms the Latin nouns *laetitiae* and *felicitatis* into the names of the protagonists, Letizia and Felicita. Read in the light of the novel, the Latin title can assume two possible meanings: "The Suffering of Letizia and Felicita" and "The Passionate Lesbian Love of Letizia and Felicita."

In *Passio Laetitiae et Felicitatis* Testori seeks to destroy the traditional literary form that relies on symbol and referent to convey meaning. For Testori, the work is the all-important, intrinsic signifier. In an interview with Giovanni Cappello held in 1983, Testori shunned any comparisons with avant-garde writer Carlo Emilio Gadda and affirmed instead his iconoclastic function as a writer by stating flatly, "La parola come stile non m'interessa" (The literary word as style does not concern me). He sees his work as an effort to "violate the word" ("violare la parola"), his preference being for "la parola masturbata, la parola infangata" (the word which has been masturbated, covered with mud).

As in most of Testori's fiction, the story is simple. As a teenager Felicita is introduced to sex by her brother Dorigo, who is then killed in a motorcycle accident. Shortly thereafter, Felicita is raped; the traumatic experience leads her to become a nun. In the convent she falls in love with another young novice, Letizia. The two are found in bed together and are ordered to account for their conduct before a church tribunal. To avoid the trial, Felicita persuades Letizia to escape from the convent with her. The two flee to a forest, where Felicita stabs Letizia to death and then turns the knife on herself. As in *La cattedrale*, sexual love—whether homosexual or heterosexual—is treated as a vital as well as a problematic force. Testori suggests that tradition, religion, and morality condition individuals to regard sexual acts as abhorrent forms of degradation. This duality of attraction and repulsion marks Testori's treatment of sex in all of his works. In this novel the reader often hears Felicita's assertive and angry voice celebrating the pleasures of forbidden sex, but such moments are countered by feelings of guilt and anguish that, coupled with the presence of body fluids and excrement, are clearly intended to arouse a sense of repulsion.

Testori's novel *Gli angeli dello sterminio* (The Exterminating Angels, 1992) is built around two narrative nuclei. The first is a dialogue—broken by frequent interjections and reflections by the narrator—between a young woman and the voice of her brother, who died in a motorcycle accident. (This similarity to Felicita and her brother is not coincidental, for Testori frequently links one of his works to another. As he told Filippo Elio Accrocca, "Romanzi, racconti e drammi dovrebbero, nel piano del mio lavoro, risultar legati uno all'altro in modo che l'uno trovi nell'altro la sua continuazione e il suo compimento" [In the scheme of my work, novels, short stories, and plays should be tied together so that one work will find in another its continuation and its fulfillment].) The dialogue is marked by confrontation—indeed, on the brother's part, by a strong sense of misogyny: "Troie! Le donne. Anzi le sottane. A cominciare da Eva. Fossimo stati . . ." (Whores! The women. Better, the negligees. Beginning with Eve. Had we been . . .). There is also a revulsion toward abortion: "Era uscito anch'esso [uno scarafaggio] da sotto il lavello della latrina. Tra una canna e l'altra, un pertugio vi s'era aperto esalante l'odore di feti gettativi da anni e ormai completamente marci" (A cockroach, too, had come out from under the wash basin of the latrine. Between two pipes a crack had appeared from which came the stench of fetuses thrown in it for years and now completely putrefied). The sexual act is further condemned by the presence of AIDS, which evokes biblical images of divine wrath and retribution: "Il virus! Eccolo li. Quasi invisibile, eppur enorme. Eccolo lí, all'interno del. All'interno del. Come ai tempi di, ai tempi di, ai tempi di, di, di . . ." (The virus! There it is! Almost invisible, yet enormous! There it is, inside the. Inside the. As in the days of, the days of, the days of, of, of . . .).

The second narrative nucleus is constituted by a meeting between a reporter and a mysterious upper-class woman called, interchangeably, "dame de la flûte" (the lady of the flute) and "dame au soleil couchant" (the lady of the setting sun). She is

Dust jacket for Testori's 1975 novel in which the protagonist's pleasure in forbidden sex is mixed with her feelings of guilt

the composite image of the Piped Piper and the figure of death in the guise of an attractive woman that is found in Romantic literature. The journalist interviews the woman about a fire, apparently started by disgruntled inmates in the main prison of Milan, that has virtually destroyed the city. Stark descriptions of brutality follow apocalyptic scenes of carnage and devastation. The "avenging angels" of the title are motorcycle gangs roaming the desolate streets. It is the end of the world, and, as "the lady of the setting sun" tells the reporter, it has come swiftly and unexpectedly: "Mai, le assicuro, mai avrei pensato, pur se incosciamente lo desiderassi, che la fine sarebbe coincisa con quest'ora" (Never, I assure you, never would I have thought, even if I had desired it subconsciously, that the end would come at this time).

Testori spent the final three years of his life in a Milan hospital, suffering from cancer. He died on 16 March 1993.

The half-century between *Il dio di Roserio* and *Gli angeli dello sterminio* shows that Testori never lost faith in the ability of literature to afford a revealing vision of society. Testori's short stories and novels, unlike Alberto Moravia's, do not record all of the important aspects of Italian culture during those fifty years, but it does offer valuable testimony about two of the most significant: the abject poverty and the quest for material prosperity of the 1950s and the deep social crisis of the last two decades of the twentieth century.

Interviews:

Giovanni Cappello, *Giovanni Testori* (Florence: Nuova Italia, 1983);

Luca Doninelli, *Conversazioni con Testori* (Parma: Guanda, 1993).

References:

Filippo Elio Accrocca, *Ritratti su misura* (Venice: Sodalizio del Libro, 1960), p. 408;

Giorgio Barberi-Squarotti, *La narrativa italiana del dopoguerra* (Bologna: Cappelli, 1965);

Renato Barilli, *La barriera del naturalismo* (Milan: Mursia, 1980), pp. 267–271;

G. Cascetta, *Invito alla lettura di Giovanni Testori* (Milan: Mursia, 1982);

S. Crespi, "Giovanni Testori," *Otto-Novecento,* 4 (1980): 16–24;

Piero De Tommaso, "Senso e coscienza in Giovanni Testori," *Letteratura,* 27 (March–April 1963): 52–61;

Gian Carlo Ferretti, "Naturalismo e trascendenza nell'opera di Giovanni Testori," *Il contemporaneo,* 37 (1961): 67–74;

Enrico Ghidetti, "Giovanni Testori," in *Letteratura italiana: I contemporanei,* volume 6 (Milan: Marzorati, 1974), pp. 1565–1585;

E. Greppoli, "Giovanni Testori," *Rivista italiana di drammaturgia* (1978): 125–134;

Claudio Marabini, "Testori e Milano," in his *Le città dei poeti* (Turin: Societa Editrice Italiana, 1976), pp. 35–40;

Rinaldo Rinaldi, "Testori o della profondità," in his *Il romanzo come deformazione: Autonomia ed eredità gaddiana in Mastronardi, Bianciardi, Testori, Arbasino* (Milan: Mursia, 1985), pp. 63–177;

L. Scorrano, "Uso parodico della *Commedia,* in un romanzo di Giovanni Testori," *Otto-Novecento,* 3 (1979): 37–45.

Giuseppe Tomasi di Lampedusa

(23 December 1896 – 23 July 1957)

Augustus Pallotta
Syracuse University

BOOKS: *Il Gattopardo* (Milan: Feltrinelli, 1958); translated by Archibald Colquhoun as *The Leopard* (New York: Pantheon, 1960; London: Collins, 1960);

Racconti (Milan: Feltrinelli, 1961); selected stories translated by Colquhoun as *Two Stories and a Memory* (New York: Pantheon, 1962; London: Collins, 1962);

Lezioni su Stendhal (Palermo: Sellerio, 1977);

Invito alle lettere francesi del Cinquecento (Milan: Feltrinelli, 1979);

Letteratura ingelese, 2 volumes, edited by Nicoletta Polo (Milan: Mondadori, 1990–1991).

Editions and Collections: *Il Gattopardo e i Racconti* (Milan: Feltrinelli, 1965);

Opere (Milan: Feltrinelli, 1965);

Il Gattopardo. Edizione conforme al manoscritto del 1957 (Milan: Feltrinelli, 1969).

Giuseppe Tomasi di Lampedusa, circa 1955

The British critic David Gilmour concludes his biography of Giuseppe Tomasi di Lampedusa with a sweeping assertion: "No novel in Italian literature has caused so much argument, aroused so much passion and begun so many quarrels as *The Leopard.*" The statement is certainly valid as regards literary works published in Italy in the twentieth century, though another historical novel, Alessandro Manzoni's *I promessi sposi* (1827; translated as *The Betrothed,* 1828), may be argued to fit more accurately Gilmour's assertion. Even so, there is no doubt that both novels have left indelible marks on Italian culture. The books have much in common: both are grounded in history and deal with socioeconomic distinctions; and both present memorable characters who represent essential expressions of Italian life. In Lampedusa's case, the reaction to *Il Gattopardo* (1958; translated as *The Leopard,* 1960) was complicated by the ideological factors operative in post–World War II Italy. The novel became a battleground between self-proclaimed progressive forces identified with Marxism and a much smaller community of conservative readers who were accused by Marxist critics of reactionary sentimentalism.

In large measure the controvesy over Lampedusa's novel was fueled by its unexpected focus on the aristocracy, which most Italians believed had waned as a class with World War II. In *Il Gattopardo* the centuries-old aristocracy, albeit in its fading days, is represented by the towering figure of Don Fabrizio Corbera, the proud and elitist prince of Salina. That alone disturbed socially conscious writers such as Elio Vittorini, Vasco Pratolini, and Alberto

Moravia, whose sympathies lay clearly with Marxism and the emancipation of the proletarian classes. When it became known that Giuseppe Tomasi di Lampedusa was a real prince, the tenor changed and the intensity of the critical reaction increased. Since the novel and its reception are tied to both the author's social class and family identity, it is especially important to provide an account of Lampedusa's ancestry and life.

A second biographer, Andrea Vitello, traces the origins of the Lampedusa family to Thomaso "the Leopard," commander of the imperial guard of the sixth-century Byzantine emperor Tiberias. According to legend, Thomaso married the emperor's daughter, Irene, and one of their children settled in Ancona, a port city on the Adriatic. In the twelfth century a member of what came to be known as the Tomasi family moved to Siena, where he distinguished himself in serving the church. In the course of time, a family branch settled farther south, at Capua, near Naples, and in 1580 Mario Tomasi, a military officer, married a Sicilian noblewoman who brought to the marriage large holdings of lands located on the southern coast of the island. Here the Tomasi family founded the town of Palma and became established as landed nobility.

In 1667 the dukes of Palma acquired Lampedusa, a small, barren island in the Mediterranean halfway between Sicily and the northern coast of Africa. In the eighteenth century the family purchased a palace in Palermo, where they established their main residence. It was at this time that Prince Ferdinando Lampedusa served as mayor of Palermo for three terms. In the mid nineteenth century another Lampedusa, Prince Giulio, Giuseppe's great-grandfather, sold the island of Lampedusa to the king of Naples; with the revenues he bought a second palace in Palermo, in Via Butera, and a charming villa in the town of San Lorenzo, at the outskirts of Palermo. Giulio, who was an amateur astronomer, enhanced the beauty of the villa by building an observatory. Years later, in fashioning the character of Don Fabrizio, Lampedusa was reminded of his ancestor and his interest in astronomy.

The decline of the Lampedusa family began in 1885. Prince Giulio died that year without a will, which proved disastrous to the family fortunes. The estate was to be divided among nine heirs, but they were unable to reach an agreement and turned to the courts. Placed under judicial administration, the lands and the villas languished for the next sixty years while the number of heirs increased fivefold: from nine in 1885 to thirty-eight in 1938. When the dispute was finally settled, the novelist's father, the duke of Palma, received a meager inheritance. Embittered by the reversal of his family fortunes, he nonetheless maintained a dignified lifestyle by drawing from the inheritance of his wife, Beatrice Mastrogiovanni Tasca Filangeri, a member of the wealthy aristocracy on the island.

Giuseppe Tomasi di Lampedusa was born on 23 December 1896 at the family palace in Palermo. He was schooled by a private tutor and by his mother, who taught him French. In the account of his childhood he wrote in the mid 1950s, "I luoghi della mia prima infanzia," which was translated as "Places of My Infancy" in *Racconti* (1961; selected stories translated as *Two Stories and a Memory,* 1962), Lampedusa describes with nostalgic fondness the carefree days spent at the palace. Apparently his father had little influence on his development. His mother, who was intelligent, attractive, cultured, and domineering, fashioned a relationship which Gilmour describes as "perhaps excessively close, even for Sicilian society where the bond between mother and son is usually strong." Beatrice's influence was evidently decisive and substantially negative. Gilmour writes that "she retained an overpowering, almost smothering influence over Giuseppe until long after his marriage."

From 1912 to 1914 Lampedusa attended the Liceo-Ginnasio Garibaldi in Palermo, where he excelled in philosophy, history, and Italian. For the 1914–1915 academic year he enrolled in the law school at the University of Genoa, but it is not known whether or not he attended classes. The following year he transferred to the University of Rome, where he took courses in law. In February 1916 he joined the army and was stationed in Messina. The next year he was sent to Turin to complete an officers' training course. In September 1918, during the final stage of World War I, he was sent to the front on the eastern side of the Italian Alps where the Italian army was fighting the Austrians. Two months later Lampedusa's unit was attacked; he was wounded and captured by the enemy. Twice he tried to escape, and the second time he succeeded, reaching the city of Trieste on foot.

Back in Palermo after the war, Lampedusa found the adjustment to normal life quite difficult. Gilmour records that "he spent several months in bed suffering from nervous exhaustion and from a combination of nightmares and insomnia that plagued him for the rest of his life." His parents urged him to finish law school and pursue a diplomatic career, but Lampedusa was not interested in law or a career. He traveled frequently to central and northern Italy, often accompanied by his mother. He visited Rome, Bologna, Florence,

Genoa, and Turin, calling at times on the friends he had made in the army.

The latter part of the 1920s was no doubt the most interesting and intellectually stimulating period in Lampedusa's life, marked by extensive travels throughout Europe, with extended stays in his two favorite cities, London and Paris. He arrived in London in 1925, a guest of his uncle Pietro Tomasi, Marquis of Torretta, who was Italian ambassador at the Court of St. James. He spent 1925 and most of the following year in England, traveling much of the time and visiting Scotland and Wales. He went to Oxford, Cambridge, and Newstead Abbey, where he visited George Gordon, Lord Byron's house. The long sojourn offered Lampedusa the opportunity to deepen his knowledge of English history and literature. He spent considerable time in the libraries, absorbed in assiduous reading of the back issues of eighteenth- and nineteenth-century magazines such as *The Spectator, The London Magazine, The Quarterly Review,* and *Blackwood's Magazine.* His favorite publication was *The Spectator,* of which he claimed to have read nearly half of its back numbers.

The 1920s were decisive in Lampedusa's intellectual development. He undertook a rigorous and systematic study of European history and literature, reading the major literary works pertaining to England, France, and Germany in the original languages. He seems to have held English literature in the highest esteem. Among European writers, he favored William Shakespeare, Laurence Sterne, John Keats, Stendhal, Charles-Pierre Baudelaire, and Giacomo Leopardi. His exposure to major literatures prompted a harsh, critical judgment of Italy and, in particular, of his native island, many of whose ills he attributed to its physical and intellectual insularity from the rest of Europe.

In 1925, while a guest of his uncle in London, Lampedusa met Alessandra Wolff. She was the daughter of a Latvian aristocrat, Boris Wolff, who had held a high position in the czarist government at Saint Petersburg, and an Italian noblewoman, Alice Barbi, who had married Lampedusa's uncle following Wolff's death in 1917. During his long courtship of Alessandra Wolff, Lampedusa visited her several times at the impressive Stomersee castle near Riga. On 20 August 1932 Lampedusa and Alessandra were married in a Russian Orthodox church in Riga; she was thirty-seven and he was a year younger. Fearing his parents' disapproval, Lampedusa had kept them in the dark about his marriage and informed them a few days later. From 1933 to 1939 Giuseppe and his wife, a Freudian psychiatrist, saw little of each other: he continued to live in Palermo while she lived in Riga, absorbed by her

Lampedusa (right) with his cousin Lucio Piccolo, December 1926

work. During important holidays, Lampedusa would make the exhausting train trip from Palermo to Riga to stay with her. The distance was mediated by a frequent correspondence that, in Gilmour's words, "seldom displayed feelings on either side."

Lampedusa was compensated in his separation from Alessandra by a small circle of friends in Palermo. His closest and most important friendship was with his cousin Lucio Piccolo, an erudite poet who shared Lampedusa's strong interest in English literature. The two spent a great deal of time together, usually at the Piccolos' seaside villa at Capo d'Orlando, where they engaged in long conversations dealing with history, literature, and the arts.

World War II marked a low point in Lampedusa's life. In 1943 his wife was forced to leave Riga and join her mother in Rome. She hesitated to travel to Palermo partly because the city was under attack by the Allies and partly because she did not get along with her strong-willed mother-in-law. Lampedusa and his mother sought refuge at the Piccolos' home. In April 1943 the novelist witnessed what he feared most: the beloved family palace was nearly destroyed by American air attacks. Called to the scene, Giuseppe saw his home nearly reduced to rubble. In a state of utter dejection he walked eight miles to a friend's house in Bagheria and refused to speak for three days. Gilmour's account stresses the emotional toll of the experience:

> In a life of long and frequent disappointments, this was perhaps the bleakest period of all for Giuseppe. He yearned to rebuild his palace, which might have been possible, though difficult and expensive, but eventually he abandoned the project as impractical. The destruction of his home weighed on him oppressively and continuously, and he thought about little else; after ten years, according to a close friend, he still had not recovered from the loss.

In 1945 Lampedusa bought the villa in Via Butera that had belonged to his great-grandfather. The villa befitted Lampedusa's social status, but it was far less imposing than the palace destroyed during the war. Alessandra decided to join her husband and live permanently in Palermo. Even so, they continued to lead separate lives, absorbed respectively by psychiatry and literature. To Lampedusa, literature was much more than an interest; it represented, according to Francesco Orlando, the great occupation and consolation of his life. In his diary Lampedusa wrote that he devoted ten of his sixteen hours of wakefulness each day to reading and reflection. His intellectual life was also enriched by frequent literary discussions at the Caffè Mazzara in Palermo with Piccolo and a small group of friends, which included Francesco Agnello; Gioacchino Lanza, a much younger cousin; and Orlando, whose great-uncle had served as prime minister of Italy.

In 1954 these informal conversations developed into a series of lectures on English literature that Lampedusa gave at his home three times a week. He was delighted by the opportunity to convey his great love of literature to young people; he took the course seriously and prepared more than a thousand pages of lectures. Gilmour, who has examined the manuscript, says that "they reveal an astonishing knowledge of British literature." At the end of the course Lampedusa was asked by his pupils to continue with lessons on French literature. He did, choosing to concentrate on the sixteenth century and on Stendhal, a writer he greatly admired. The lectures were eventually published in book form as *Lezioni su Stendhal* (Lessons on Stendhal, 1977) and *Invito alle lettere francesi del Cinquecento* (An Invitation to Sixteenth-Century French Literature, 1979).

A minor cultural event held in July 1954 proved to be the turning point in Lampedusa's life. The occasion was a literary conference at San Pelle-grino Terme that Lampedusa attended with his cousin Lucio Piccolo, whose book of poems, *Canti barocchi* (Baroque Songs, 1956), was introduced to the audience by the poet Eugenio Montale. Upon his return to Palermo, Lampedusa, spurred by a sense of friendly rivalry with his cousin, decided to write a historical novel. According to his wife, he had nurtured such a project since his youth.

Lampedusa worked steadily on *Il Gattopardo* for several months. In June 1955, needing a break from the novel, he began his biography. The work was to be divided into three parts (childhood, youth, maturity), but he only completed the first, "I luoghi della mia prima infanzia." As the title indicates, the emphasis in this short work is on places—the villas, the grounds, and the lands owned by the Lampedusa family, beloved points of reference in a sheltered and privileged childhood—but it is also interesting as a historical document. For instance, Lampedusa recalls the reaction of his parents to the assassination of King Umberto of Italy on 29 July 1900 at the hand of an anarchist. He also provides a vivid impression of the 1908 earthquake that devastated the city of Messina and affected some of his relatives.

While Lampedusa intended his biographical account for publication, he was writing at a time of intense ideological struggle between conservative middle-class ideology and the progressive forces allied with Marxism. The hostility Marxists felt toward Italy's shrinking nobility even exceeded their aversion for the bourgeoisie. It is noteworthy that in the midst of such social tension Lampedusa made no effort to conceal his family's inherited wealth nor the splendor of their palace at Santa Margherita, to which he remained deeply attached. The palace consisted of some one hundred rooms, and Lampedusa continued to call it his home:

> [La casa] dava l'idea di una sorta di complesso chiuso ed autosufficiente, di una specie di Vaticano, per intenderci, che racchiudeva appartamenti di rappresentanza, stanze di soggiorno, foresteria per trenta persone, stanze per domestici, tre immensi cortili, scuderie e rimesse, teatro e chiesa privati, un enorme e bellissimo giardino ed un grande orto.

> ([The house] gave the impression of an enclosed and self-sufficient entity, a kind of Vatican, as it were, that included state rooms, living rooms, quarters for thirty guests, servants' rooms, three enormous courtyards, stables and coach houses, a private theater, a church, and a great orchard.)

In its published form, "I luoghi della mia prima infanzia" is divided into eight chapters, the last of which describes the villa at Santa Margherita and its caretaker, the only one, according to Lampedusa, who was thoroughly honest in administering the estate.

With the emergence of the industrial aristocracy and a solid middle class, Lampedusa's inherited titles and eighteenth-century palaces are viewed as forgotten vestiges of a distant past. The biographical piece is notable for the author's splendid style, affording it a graceful lightness and a power of suggestion that compare favorably with salient passages in the novel:

> Qui cominciava per me la magia delle luci, che in una città a sole intenso come Palermo sono succose e variate secondo il tempo anche in strade strette. . . . Talora, specialmente in estate, i saloni erano oscuri, ma dalle persiane chiuse filtrava la sensazione della potenza luminosa che era fuori; talaltra, a seconda dell'ora, un solo raggio penetrava diritto e ben delineato come quello del Sinai, popolato da miriadi di granellini di polvere, e che andava ad eccitare il colore dei tappeti che era uniformemente rosso rubino in tutte le stanze. Un vero sortilegio di illuminazione e di colori che mi ha incatenato l'animo per sempre.

> (Here for me began the magic of light, which in a city with so intense a sun as Palermo is concentrated or variegated according to the weather even in narrow streets. . . . Sometimes, particularly in the summer, these rooms were dark, yet through the closed blinds filtered a sense of the luminous power that was outside; or sometimes at certain hours a single ray would penetrate straight and clear as that of Sinai, populated with myriads of dust particles which went on to vivify the colors of carpets, uniformily ruby red throughout all the drawing rooms: a real sorcery of illumination and color which has captivated my mind forever.)

The subdued elegance of Lampedusa's prose consistently complements the formal simplicity. In the fifth chapter he models the description of a baroque staircase of his villa on its structure. The architect devised "un sistema di possibilità di confluenze e defluenze, brusche ripugnanze ed affettuosi incontri, che conferiva alla scalinata l'atmosfera di una lite di innamorati" (possible joinings and separations, of brusque rejections and affectionate reconciliations, which imparted to the staircase the atmosphere of a lovers' tiff). The linear movement of the steps is reproduced here with short, contrasting pairings of elements that suggest the movements of two quarreling lovers.

Having set his biography aside temporarily, Lampedusa returned to *Il Gattopardo* in 1955, spending the better part of the year on the novel. By mid March 1956 he had completed four chapters and read them to several of his friends; in May he sent

Lampedusa and his wife, Alessandra, in the 1930s

the manuscript to the publisher Mondadori. During the summer two new chapters were finished and sent to the publisher, but to no avail, for by the end of the year Lampedusa was informed that Mondadori had turned the novel down. The rejection stung but did not discourage him. In the early part of 1957 he added two fresh chapters to the work, finished two short stories, and completed the first chapter of a new novel that was to be called "I gattini ciechi" (The Blind Kittens).

Lampedusa renewed his efforts to see *Il Gattopardo* in print. He sent the complete typescript to Fausto Flaccovio, a publisher in Palermo, who sent it to Elio Vittorini, the Sicilian writer who worked for the publisher Einaudi. Vittorini was familiar with the work, having read it a few months earlier when he served as editorial consultant to Mondadori. A Marxist intellectual of humble background, Vittorini was by this time an influential writer deeply committed to narrative experimentation and to the use of the novel as a mirror of socio-economic problems engendered by rapid industrialization in large urban centers. He rejected it a second time.

The ruins of the Villa Lampedusa, the model for the Villa Salina in Il Gattopardo

Toward the end of April 1957 Lampedusa was diagnosed with lung cancer. He sank to a prostrate state but agreed to travel to Rome to undergo surgery. The ensuing cobalt treatment lifted his spirits somewhat, but by July he knew that the end was near. Four days before his death he received Vittorini's letter of rejection, which, according to Gilmour, left him bitter and disappointed. To Gioacchino Lanza, whom he adopted as a son in 1956, he remarked that he would be pleased if the novel were published but not at his expense. Giuseppe Tomasi di Lampedusa died in Rome on 23 July 1957. He was sixty years old.

At the time that Lampedusa sent the typescript of *Il Gattopardo* to Fausto Flaccovio in Palermo, he consented to have a friend, Giorgio Giargia, mail a copy to Elena Croce, Benedetto Croce's daughter, who worked in Rome as a literary agent. The copy did not carry Lampedusa's name, and Elena Croce did not bother reading it until February 1958. She liked the work and sent it to the novelist Giorgio Bassani, who worked for the publisher Feltrinelli. Bassani realized immediately that it was the work of a "real writer." Through Giargia he learned of Lampedusa's identity; he traveled to Palermo, met with the novelist's widow, and secured the handwritten manuscript Lampedusa had left to Gioac-

chino Lanza before traveling to Rome for his operation. Bassani compared the manuscript received from Lanza with the typescript Elena Croce had mailed to him; since they did not differ substantially, he decided to publish a synthesis of the two. *Il Gattopardo* was finally published in November 1958.

Bassani was convinced of the book's quality, but neither he nor Feltrinelli expected the extraordinary reception by the public. Favorable reviews by Italy's leading literati, such as Eugenio Montale and Carlo Bo, were followed by many reprints of the novel as well as its translation into foreign languages. But the publication of *Il Gattopardo* also laid bare the social, political, and ideological forces that marked postwar Italy. It arrested the optimism and self-assurance of progressive-minded writers—formidable authors such as Moravia, Vittorini, Pratolini, Italo Calvino, and Pier Paolo Pasolini—who with Marxist writer Antonio Gramsci saw literature as an important tool of social change, as a means of preparing the ground for a socialist state marked by greater socio-economic equality and the blurring of social stratifications, which was regarded as essential in a country where centuries-old class distinctions had defined individual worth and identity. With its resounding popularity, *Il Gattopardo* shifted popular attention to the past, to the role of the aristocracy in Italian history, to the relationship between Sicily and the Italian peninsula, and especially to the Risorgimento movement, which began in the early 1800s and ended in 1860 with the unification of Italy. Much of the controversy had to do with the historical dimension of the novel: whether or not it offered a credible view of the newly united Italy.

Il Gattopardo covers a fifty-year span from 1860 to 1910 and follows the declining fortunes of a Sicilian family headed by Don Fabrizio Corbera, prince of Salina. The year 1860 marks the landing in Sicily of Giuseppe Garibaldi's small volunteer army and the beginning of a military campaign against the Bourbon regime that ruled southern Italy, which led to national unification. These and other events unfolding in Italian society are felt within the prince's family and occupy the first six chapters of the book. But *Il Gattopardo* is in essence an intellectual novel. The action is meager and evolves mainly around the courtship and marriage of Tancredi Falconeri, Don Fabrizio's shrewd, ambitious, and handsome nephew, and the beautiful Angelica, the daughter of Don Calogero Sedara, the aggressive and socially ambitious entrepreneur who symbolizes Italy's new ruling class. Chapter 7 is devoted to Don Fabrizio's death in 1883. The final chapter is set in 1910 and shows his daughters as old spinsters looking nostalgically back to their family. Nevertheless, they decide to rid the house of a conspicuous sign of the past: the family's stuffed Great Dane Bendicò, which was beloved by their father.

The vitality of the novel radiates from the remarkable figure of Don Fabrizio, Lampedusa's ideal projection who represents Italian and European aristocracy. Lampedusa leaves no doubt that, at least intellectually, he identifies fully with Don Fabrizio. This suggests that the unease and uncertainty that mark Don Fabrizio's character are tied less to the socio-economic problems of a nineteenth-century nobleman than to the existential crisis of a man who can relate to the searching characters of another Sicilian writer, Luigi Pirandello. In this light, one can say that Don Fabrizio is both the social emblem of the nineteenth century and the spiritual image of the twentieth—a testimonial to the strength of the work.

Il Gattopardo begins with the evening recital of the Rosary, which takes place in a large, elegant room of the palace. The paintings of mythical figures on the ceilings speak of tradition and stability and thus offer the prince a momentary sense of security. But the signs of change begin to appear with alarming frequency: a government soldier is found dead under a lemon tree in Don Fabrizio's garden; military forces around the city prepare to face Gar-

ibaldi's army; the prince receives an ominous letter about recent developments from his cousin. Don Fabrizio is finally forced to confront in his own mind the man responsible for bringing war and revolution to the shores of Sicily: "Il nome di Garibaldi lo turbò un poco. Quell'avventuriero tutto capelli e barba . . . avrebbe combinato dei guai" (The name of Garibaldi's disturbed him a little. That adventurer, all hair and beard . . . would cause a lot of trouble).

A good share of the tension and unease that afflict Don Fabrizio is social and political in nature. It boils down to his realization that the hegemony of his class, with its attendant benefits of power and privilege enjoyed through the centuries, is coming to an end. This realization weighs heavily on the members of the aristocracy, their historical role challenged by social forces they are unable to arrest. Sudden changes and uncertainties engender deep anxieties. Don Fabrizio seeks to escape reality through the all-absorbing diversion of gazing at the stars, though he is fully cognizant that astronomy is but a distraction.

Don Fabrizio's dilemma is also psychological, for the crisis affects his understanding of the intrinsic worth of life: "Il problema vero è di poter continuare a vivere questa vita dello spirito nei suoi momenti più sublimati, più simili alla morte" (The real problem is how to go on living this life of the spirit in its most sublimated moment, those moments that are most like death). Later in the work, when he feels the full brunt of historical change, Don Fabrizio experiences an almost visceral discomfort, "un acuto ribrezzo verso la congiuntura sociale nella quale era incappato" (a deep revulsion from the social circumstances in which he was so inextricably involved).

The sense of revulsion rises as he is forced to have contacts with the exponents of what will soon become the new ruling class: rich merchants, low ranking professionals, and enriched peasants who have joined the ranks of the bourgeoisie—individuals such as the accountant Ciccio Ferrara, "un ometto asciutto che nascondeva l'anima illusa e rapace di un liberale dietro occhiali rassicuranti e cravatta immacolata" (a scraggy little man who hid the deluded and rapacious mind of a liberal behind reassuring spectacles and immaculate cravats). Greed also motivates Russo, one of the prince's dependents, who eagerly awaits the changing of the guard: "svelto, con gli occhi avidi al disotto di una fronte senza rimorso, era la perfetta espressione di un ceto in ascesa" (clever, with greedy eyes below a remorseless forehead, he was the perfect specimen of a class on its way up).

Lampedusa (right) with his adopted son, Giacchino Lanza (left), the model for Tancredi, and his cousin Lucio Piccolo (center)

The major catalyst of social transformation is Don Calogero Sedara, the self-made man who through sheer willpower and hard work has amassed a small fortune. Shrewd and unscrupulous, Don Calogero has a spade up his sleeve in the form of his lovely daughter Angelica, who as a graduate of one of Florence's prestigious finishing schools is the antithesis of her hopelessly uncouth mother. Tancredi Falconeri, the prince's favorite nephew, speculates on the future nearly as much as Don Calogero: his heart tells him to marry Concetta, Don Fabrizio's daughter, who is very much in love with him, but he lets his mind prevail and marries Angelica.

Donnafugata, his country residence in the Sicilian hinterland, holds a special attraction for Don Fabrizio because there the family owns large extensions of land and the small town nearby has maintained a feudal appearance. When Don Fabrizio returns to Donnafugata in the summer of 1860 to escape the torrid heat in Palermo, he nurtures the illusion that little has changed. Much like a feudal lord, he receives the homages of the townspeople and gifts from the peasants who work his lands. But the

illusion is short-lived. At Donnafugata, Tancredi begins to court Angelica in earnest. Here, too, on a memorable evening of October 1860, the prince is told that the town had voted with near unanimity against the ancien régime represented by the Bourbon monarchy and in favor of Sicily's integration into a unified Italy. This is one of the darkest nights in Don Fabrizio's life, for the plebiscite convinces him that the winds of change have blown as far south as a remote village in Sicily. A new chapter in Italian history is beginning, one from which the prince and his social class are unceremoniously excluded:

L'Italia era nata in quell'accigliata sera a Donnafugata; nata proprio lí, in quel paese dimenticato, altrettanto quanto nella ignavia di Palermo e nella agitazione di Napoli.... Eppure questa persistente inquietudine qualcosa significava; egli sentiva che durante quei troppo enfatici discorsi, qualche cosa, qualcuno era morto.

(Italy was born in that sullen night at Donnafugata, born right there in that forgotten little town, just as much as in the sloth of Palermo and the clamor of Naples.... And yet this persistent disquiet of his must mean something; during those too emphatic speeches, he had a feeling that something, someone had died.)

Yet Don Fabrizio is hardly a reactionary nobleman. A rational, pragmatic man, he favors Tancredi's marriage to Angelica to promote "l'apporto del sangue nuovo . . . ai vecchi casati" (new blood into old families). What Don Fabrizio laments is the passing of a complex set of social and cultural values jealously guarded for centuries by his class, such as a sense of history and tradition, a way of life marked by refinement and aesthetic consciousness that values dignity, loyalty, and good manners. He makes no secret of his strong distaste for Don Calogero and his peers. He loathes their greed, their hypocrisy, and their crass materialism:

> [Don Fabrizio] cominciò ad avvedersi della rara intelligenza dell'uomo liberato. . . . Liberato com'egli era dalle cento pastoie che l'onestà, la decenza e magari la buona educazione impongono alle azioni di molti uomini, egli procedeva nella foresta della vita con sicurezza.

> ([Don Fabrizio] began to realize the man's rare intelligence. . . . Free as he was from the shackles imposed on many other men by honesty, decency, and plain good manners, he moved through the jungle of life with confidence.)

Some seminal ideas of social and political import emerge in the dialogue in the fourth chapter between Don Fabrizio and Chevalley, a Piedmontese official charged with the task of enlisting the prince and other southern noblemen to support a unified Italy governed by a constitutional monarchy. Chevalley, a northerner, believes in socio-economic progress and is optimistic about Italy's future. A southerner, Don Fabrizio is skeptical and noncommittal about his support, and cognizant of Sicily's industrial backwardness and her history of subjection to foreign rulers. Echoing Lampedusa's views, he believes in the desirability of social progress, but because his social consciousness is informed by historical pragmatism, he does not believe in the attainment of genuine equality and a classless society. His pessimism is nurtured by the realization that individuals are motivated by selfish interests, not egalitarianism or a sense of community, even as they seemingly strive for social justice. Equality, brotherhood, altruism, and justice are found in utopian literature, Lampedusa would argue, not in the pages of history.

These assertions find complementary support in the fifth chapter, where Father Pirrone, a Jesuit and resident chaplain of the Corbera family, engages Don Pietrino, a country priest, in a conversation about nobility. Like Don Fabrizio, Father Pirrone is skeptical that a new political order will bring social progress. He maintains that when the nobility yields power to the bourgeoisie, the same social hierarchies and inequities will emerge in the new social order, in a different guise and perhaps under different names, to be sure, but the same in essence nonetheless.

In declining to serve in the senate of the new state, Don Fabrizio tells Chevalley: "Sono un rappresentante della vecchia classe. . . . Appartengo ad una generazione disgraziata, a cavallo fra i vecchi tempi e i nuovi, e che si trova a disagio in tutti e due" (I am a member of the old ruling class. . . . I belong to an unfortunate generation, swung between the old world and the new, and I find myself ill at ease in both). Yet the prince's lament is less the expression of a collective historical condition than the grieving of an individual faced with a diminishing sense of his own worth in the eyes of a community he is accustomed to leading. His melancholy does not issue from the difficulties of adjusting to new realities but from the loss of an important part of his social identity. Raised in a social milieu distinguished by stability, continuity, and the hegemony of his class, he sees a long-standing structure of values crumbling under the weight of historical forces instigated by Garibaldi and the Savoy monarchy. Thus, external events are internalized as the precariousness of history is associated with the instability of the human condition. History begets alienation; social and political questions become troublesome existential concerns. It is at this point that Don Fabrizio, forgoing earthly matters, turns to the stars, to an order and permanence that history has denied him.

Once the narrative progresses from a socio-historical plane to existential concerns, *Il Gattopardo* takes on a contemporary relevance, which no doubt contributed to its remarkable popularity. It is not a coincidence that the novel gained a public at a time when the most widely read books of fiction in Europe were Jean-Paul Sartre's *La Nausée* (Nausea, 1938), Albert Camus's *L'Étranger* (The Stranger, 1942), and Samuel Beckett's *En attendant Godot* (Waiting for Godot, 1952). The currency of existential themes in Italy was evident in Pirandello's work, especially *Sei personaggi in cerca d'autore* (Six Characters in Search of an Author, 1921) and *Enrico IV* (Henry IV, 1922). The final three chapters of *Il Gattopardo* are permeated with a sense of alienation, impending death, and insistent, underlying questions about the meaning of existence. In the last analysis, it is the existential *mal de vivre,* more than external events, that darkens Don Fabrizio's spirits: "Il [suo] disagio non era di natura politica e doveva avere radici più profonde, radicate in una di quelle cagioni che chiamiamo irrazionali perché seppellite sotto cumuli di ignoranza di noi stessi" (His discomfort was not political; it had deeper roots in one of those causes we call irrational because they are buried under heaps of ignorance of ourselves).

Don Fabrizio's inner disposition at the ball in the sixth chapter, the episode that foreshadows his death, is marked by a deep sense of alienation. He willfully disengages from a world of objects and individuals he once cherished. What remains intact in the prince is a sense of compassion for human beings, their precarious existence, their pathetic struggle to enjoy a few minutes of sunshine in the dreary wintry season of life: "Il suo disgusto cedeva il posto alla compassione per tutti questi effimeri esseri che cercavano di godere dell'esiguo raggio di luce accordato loro fra le due tenebre, prima della culla, dopo gli ultimi strattoni" (His disgust gave way to compassion for all these ephemeral beings out to enjoy the tiny ray of light granted to them between two shades: before the cradle, after the last spasms).

The modernity of *Il Gattopardo* is also apparent in the absence of the traditional concern with the afterlife. Lampedusa offers instead a finite world in which the people nevertheless yearn for the transcendental and the spiritual. He purposely dissociates the spiritual from Christianity, casting it instead as a neopagan conception of immortality. A vein of pre-Christian, pagan culture is invoked at the beginning of *Il Gattopardo* and also marks the short story "Lighea" which Lampedusa wrote in January 1957 and colleded in *Racconti*. It was translated as "The Professor and the Siren."

"Lighea" deals with the friendship of two Sicilian men—a young journalist and a considerably older gentleman who turns out to be a prominent Greek scholar endowed with "il senso quasi carnale dell'antichità classica" (almost a carnal sense of classical antiquity)—who meet in Turin during the Fascist period. As the two become better acquainted, the professor confides that as a young man he had an unforgettable encounter with a mermaid. The experience lasted three weeks, but it has accompanied him for a lifetime, so much so that he has since refused to seek out other women. In "Lighea" one finds echoes of Giovanni Boccaccio, Shakespeare ("What potions have I drunk of Syren tears?"), neoclassical poetry, and many other writers, including Hans Christian Andersen, Isak Dinesen, Edgar Allan Poe, and H. G. Wells. The story may be read as Lampedusa's tribute to literature, to the cherished world of books to which he devoted his life.

The essence of the story, though, is found in the professor's sensual experiences: "Basti dire che in quegli amplessi godevo insieme delle più alte forme di voluttà spirituale e di quella elementare" (Suffice it to say that in those embraces I enjoyed both the highest forms of spiritual pleasure and that elementary one). The effort to connect so closely erotic pleasure with spiritual ecstasy suggests the sublimity of a physical act that can be called spiritual only in a pagan sense. Lampedusa's combining of the carnal and the spiritual and his further effort to portray a mythological being in a realistic vein, eschewing the manner of the fable, show that he was willfully distancing "Lighea" from traditional moral and spiritual concerns. If not pagan, the spirituality professed by La Ciura, the Greek scholar, pertains to the broad vision of a world spirit found in Jungian thought.

Beyond its content Lampedusa's writing is most notable for its style, texture, and imagery. In mid June 1955 he finished rereading Stendhal's *Vie de Henry Brulard* (1890), a work he had not liked as a young man. He records his reaction in "I luoghi della mia prima infanzia":

> Non posso dar torto a chi quasi lo giudica il capolavoro di Stendhal; vi è un'immediatezza di sensazioni, un'evidente sincerità, un ammirevole sforzo per spazzar via dei ricordi e giungere al fondo. E quale lucidità di stile! E quale ammasso di impressioni tanto piu preziose quanto più comuni! Vorrei cercare di fare lo stesso.

> (I cannot but agree with someone who judges it to be Stendhal's masterpiece; it has an immediacy of feeling, an obvious sincerity, a remarkable attempt to sweep away accumulated memories and reach the essence. And what lucidity of style! What a mass of reflections, the more precious for being common to all men! I should like to try and do the same.)

In *Il Gattopardo* and "Lighea" Lampedusa approaches and sometimes surpasses Stendhal's stylistic virtuosity. The lucidity of his style certainly accounts for some of the enthusiasm for the novel among literate readers who, tired of experimental and mostly insipid narratives, were entranced by Lampedusa's elegance, fluency, erudition, and suggestive power.

Il Gattopardo contains without doubt the most carefully crafted prose in Italian literature since Manzoni's *I promessi sposi*. Like Manzoni and other great writers, Lampedusa was naturally gifted, yet his consciousness of the full range of verbal expression came in large measure from the vast range of literary works he savored during forty years of reading. *Il Gattopardo* is the work of an inveterate reader who shortly before his death discovered that he could be a writer. He poured his energies into one work, and in it he was able to infuse all his love for language and literary diction.

Lampedusa's prose is, above all, sensorial: much of what he wishes to convey to the reader regarding characters and the milieu they inhabit is rendered through a language that carries a strong appeal to the sense. The descriptions of Sicily's vegetation and heavily scented flowers capture the exotic, the violence, and the erotic, the flavor of the culture. The prince's garden, for example, "esalava profumi untuosi, carnali e lievemente putridi" (exhaled scents that were cloying, fleshy, and slightly putrid). The roses "erano degenerate, eccitate prima e rinfrollite poi dei succhi vigorosi e indolenti della terra siciliana" (had degenerated, first stimulated and then enfeebled by the strong if languid pull of Sicilian earth). Lampedusa's prose is also remarkable for its superb treatment of light and colors, as in his memorable depiction of a lantern: "Una lanterna accesa che con l'oro incerto della sua luce accendeva il rosso delle foglie cadute dai platani" (A lighted lantern, the uncertain gold of whose gleams set alight the red of fallen plane leaves).

Lampedusa breathes life into descriptions of plants and inanimate objects, using them to resonate with the action of the plot. Sicily's imposing summer heat, "la luce autoritaria" (the domineering sunlight), is reflected in the fate of plants that may not survive the summer: "Rispuntavano trifogli e mentucce cautelose, sui volti diffidenti speranze" (From the soil cautiously sprouted clover and mint, on their faces diffident hopes). Among the cards scattered on a table in the playroom, Don Fabrizio on his way to a hunting trip notices "il cavallo di spade che gli rivolgeva un augurio virile" (a Jack of Spades waving to him a manly greeting). In the course of the hunt, the prince shoots a harmless wild rabbit. In Lampedusa's skillful hands, the incident becomes a metaphor for the hunter's social predicament and the precariousness of the human condition:

Don Fabrizio si vide fissato da grandi occhi neri che, invasi rapidamente da un velo glauco, lo guardavano senza rimprovero, ma erano carichi di un dolore attonito rivolto contro tutto l'ordinamento delle cose; le orecchie vellutate erano già fredde, le zampette vigorose si contraevano in ritmo, simbolo sopravvissuto di una inutile fuga: l'animale moriva torturato da una ansiosa speranza di salvezza, immaginando di poter ancora cavarsela quando di già era ghermito, proprio come tanti uomini.

(Don Fabrizio found himself being stared at by big black eyes soon overlaid by a glaucous veil; they were looking at him with no reproof, but full of tortured amazement at the whole order of things; the velvety ears were already cold, the vigorous paws contracting in rhythm, still-living symbol of useless flight; the animal had died tortured by anxious hopes of salvation, imagining it could still escape when it was already caught, just like so many human beings.)

Lampedusa's exacting description of Sicily's mountains yields a masterful example of cultural geography: a symbolic rendition of what he considered the complex and nearly inscrutable Sicilian character:

In cima al monte, di fra i tamerici e i sugheri radi apparve l'aspetto della vera Sicilia, quello nei cui riguardi città barocche ed aranceti non sono che fronzoli trascurabili: l'aspetto di un'aridità ondulante all'infinito in groppe sopra groppe, sconfortate e irrazionali, delle quali la mente non poteva afferrare le linee principali, concepite in un momento delirante della creazione: un mare che si fosse ad un tratto pietrificato nell'attimo in cui un cambiamento di vento avesse reso dementi le onde.

(On top of the mountain, among the tamarisks and the scattered cork trees, appeared the real Sicily; compared to that sight, baroque towns and orange groves are mere trifles: the sight of endless undulating barrenness in the shape of uneven rows of mountaintops, irrational and without comfort, the mind unable to grasp the outlines conceived in a delirious moment of creation; a sea petrified the instant that a sudden change of wind flung waves into frenzy.)

As he does elsewhere in the book, Lampedusa seeks to define essential cultural traits through topological affinities between people and their environments. Here the traits of the island that Lampedusa sees inscribed on its landscape are the barrenness of an insular culture unreceptive to outside influences, dominated by tragic and irrational forces that the mind cannot grasp."

The phenomenal success of *Il Gattopardo* in Italy, the rest of Europe, and the United States gave rise to strong, often acrimonious opposition. Vittorini, who was instrumental in preventing the publication of *Il Gattopardo* during Lampedusa's lifetime, was stung by its extraordinary popularity. He continued to object to the novel because in his view it failed to promote "una cultura capace di lottare contro la fame e le sofferenze. . . . che aiuti ad eliminare lo sfruttamento e la schiavitù, e a vincere il bisogno" (a culture apt to combat hunger and suffering. . . . apt to put an end to exploitation and subjugation, and to overcome material needs). With other critics he contended that *Il Gattopardo* had much in common with a nineteenth-century novel and, as such,

Dust jacket for the American edition of the translation of Lampedusa's only novel, which sympathetically portrays the aristocratic Don Fabrizio Corbera

shared no awareness of the structural innovations initiated by James Joyce and Marcel Proust. In a letter to Vitello dated 13 July 1962, Vittorini justified his opposition to Lampedusa in these terms: "Io da quando scrivo mi sono sempre battuto per un rinnovamento moderno della letteratura. Lei capisce dunque che non posso amare scrittori che si manifestino entro gli schemi tradizionali" (Since I started to write, I have always fought for a modern renewal of literature. You can understand then that I cannot force myself to like writers who express themselves within traditional parameters).

Other Italian writers also remained critical. The novelist Vasco Pratolini saw *Il Gattopardo* as a threat to the proletarian narrative exemplified by his *Metello* (1955). He reminded readers that he and other Marxist writers had strived for thirty years to advance the interests of the working classes. With one work, he remarked, Lampedusa "has put us back sixty years." Similarly, discussing the novel in the weekly *L'Espresso* of 7 April 1963, Alberto Moravia, reiterating what he wrote about Manzoni's

novel, asserted that it reflected the conservative ideology of the ruling class. Leonardo Sciascia, a Sicilian writer allied with the progressive ideas of the Left, wrote in 1962 that he regarded *Il Gattopardo* as a "reactionary book" because "portava alla restaurazione dei valori formali, portava a tutto quello che dal dopoguerra in poi avevamo tentato di negare" (it pointed to the restoration of traditional forms, it pointed to everything that we [writers] had attempted to negate since the end of World War II). It should be noted that six years later Sciascia retracted that statement: he pointed out that *Il Gattopardo* was a valuable book because it painted an accurate picture of the Sicilian character.

The opposition to *Il Gattopardo* received a jolt from Louis Aragon, a widely respected French Marxist. Writing in the journal *Les Lettres françaises* on 23 December 1959, Aragon called *Il Gattopardo* "one of the great novels of this century, one of the great novels of all time." He ridiculed the characterization of the book as "right wing" and "reactionary," adding that, read carefully, Lampedusa's novel offers a "merciless" view of his own class that falls well within the confines of Marxist thought. Aragon's positive assessment was echoed by other French critics, who underscored the Proustian vein of many parts of the novel. In *Le Monde* of 1 December 1959 Maurice Vassard praised the treatment of the social and historical conditions in Sicily found in the novel. Jean Blanzat, reviewing the book in *Le Figaro littéraire* of 18 November 1959, remarked that it represented the distillation of a lifetime of thought and meditation by a solitary writer.

In Britain *Il Gattopardo* was met with widespread interest. In his short introduction to the English edition of Lampedusa's *Racconti,* E. M. Forster wrote: "*The Leopard* has certainly enlarged my life—an unusual experience for a life which is well on in its eighties." Several reviewers singled out Stendhal's influence in terms of style and characterization. Writing in the *Observer* of 8 May 1960, Harold Nicolson stated that the book had "great intrinsic merit" and remarked that the figure of Don Fabrizio was drawn with "a subtlety of understanding which Stendhal would have admired."

In the United States, Lampedusa's novel was a popular success but received only modest critical attention as compared to that in France and England. William Jay Smith, reviewing the work in *The New Republic* of 20 June 1960, was taken by the portrait of Don Fabrizio, "a timeless figure caught between the past and the present, his eyes fixed on the stars." Smith found *Il Gattopardo* haunting: "It is the power of Lampedusa's visual imagination that gives the book its strange and haunting vitality: he sees everything in a panorama, complete down to the most minute detail." In his "Notes from a European Diary: 1963–64," published in the 28 May 1966 *New Yorker*, Edmund Wilson wrote at length on *Il Gattopardo*, but his most insightful remarks are reserved for Lampedusa's unfinished autobiography: "These memories are done with the brilliance and love of an unfailingly first-rate writer."

In the years since the initial controversy over *Il Gattopardo*, Italian criticism has been marked by a gradual deemphasis of ideological questions and increasing attention to literary matters. Nearly all important scholars and professional critics, including Giorgio Bàrberi-Squarotti, Giuseppe Paolo Samonà, Giacinto Spagnoletti, and Arnaldo di Benedetto, have approached the novel in a literary light without forgoing entirely the concerns that preoccupied their peers in the early 1960s.

Il Gattopardo is regarded as a work of unquestioned significance, having gained an international readership that extends beyond Western countries. Non-Italian critics have contributed—and no doubt will continue to contribute—comparative studies that examine Lampedusa's affinities with other European writers. These critics have also enriched the critical discourse by offering external views of topical matters that are central to the novel.

Among the books dealing with Lampedusa, the two literary biographies by Andrea Vitello and David Gilmour stand out for their quality and comprehensiveness. Neither is a professional man of letters: the first is a doctor; the latter, a historian. Vitello's *Giuseppe Tomasi di Lampedusa* (1987) is a massive compilation of facts pertaining to the novelist and, more broadly, to the sociohistorical settings of *Il Gattopardo*. In addition to the biographical material, Vitello offers critical evaluations of substantial merit, including a Jungian analysis of "Lighea." The wealth of information and Vitello's erudition make this a necessary reference in Lampedusa scholarship. Gilmour provides a fluent and sympathetic account of Lampedusa's life, drawn mostly from his research at the novelist's residence and his fruitful contacts with Lampedusa's adopted son. His biography offers a valuable treatment of Lampedusa's literary culture and an insightful study of his personality. Gilmour also provides a suitable assessment of the enduring significance of *Il Gattopardo:* "The principal reason for the work's success lies in its timelessness. Lampedusa once said that London would never die because Dickens had made it immortal, and to many people he has done the same for Sicily. . . . His work will survive because he wrote about the central problems of the human experience."

Letters:

Caterina Cardona, ed., *Lettere a Licy: Un matrimonio epistolare: Giuseppe Tomasi di Lampedusa e Alessandra Tomasi Wolff* (Palermo: Sellerio, 1987).

Bibliographies:

Giuseppe Paolo Samonà, "Lampedusa e la critica," in his *Il Gattopardo. I Racconti. Lampedusa* (Florence: Nuova Italia, 1974), pp. 361–426;

Andrea Vitello, *Giuseppe Tomasi di Lampedusa* (Palermo: Sellerio, 1987), pp. 442–470.

Biographies:

Andrea Vitello, *Giuseppe Tomasi di Lampedusa* (Palermo: Sellerio, 1987);

David Gilmour, *The Last Leopard. A Life of Giuseppe Tomasi di Lampedusa* (New York: Pantheon, 1988).

References:

Mario Alicata, "Il principe di Lampedusa e il Risorgimento siciliano," in his *Scritti letterari* (Milan: Mondadori, 1968), pp. 337–351;

Giorgio Bàrberi-Squarotti, "Tomasi di Lampedusa," in his *Poesia e narrativa del secondo Novecento* (Milan: Mursia, 1967), pp. 306–310;

Boris Biancheri, *L'ambra del Baltico: carteggio immaginario con Giuseppe Tomasi di Lampedusa* (Milan: Feltrinelli, 1994);

Luigi Blasucci, "*Il Gattopardo*," *Belfagor*, 14, no. 1 (1959): 117–121;

Vanni Bramanti, "Rileggendo *Il Gattopardo*," *Studi novecenteschi*, 15 (1988): 323–348;

Giancarlo Buzzi, *Invito alla lettura di Tomasi di Lampedusa* (Milan: Mursia, 1976);

Christopher Carduff, "Il caso Lampedusa," *New Criterion*, 10 (1992): 19–26;

Paola Cova, "*La Chartreuse de Parma* et *Le Guépard*," *Stendhal Club*, 33 (1991): 280–286;

Arnaldo di Benedetto, "Tomasi di Lampedusa e la letteratura," *Giornale storico della letteratura italiana*, 170 (1993): 38–65;

Antonio Dipace, *Questioni delle varianti del "Gattopardo"* (Latina: Mambra, 1971);

Rodolfo Doni, "Lo spirito religioso nel *Gattopardo* di Lampedusa," *Humanitas*, 36, no. 1 (1981): 64–78;

Derek Duncan, "Lifting the Veil: Metaphors of Exclusion in *Il Gattopardo*," *Forum for Modern Language Studies*, 29 (1993): 323–334;

Furio Felcini, "Giuseppe Tomasi di Lampedusa," in *Letteratura italiana. I contemporanei*, volume 3 (Milan: Marzorati, 1969), pp. 249–266;

Geneviève Henrot, "Le Professeur et la sirenè. Analyse thématique d'un récit de Lampedusa," *Les Lettres Romanes,* 41 (1987): 45–63;

Gregory Lucente, "Lampedusa's *Il Gattopardo:* Figure and Temporality in a Historical Novel," in his *Beautiful Fables: Self-Consciousness in Italian Narrative from Manzoni to Calvino* (Baltimore: Johns Hopkins University Press, 1986), pp. 196–221;

Ivos Margoni, "*Il Gattopardo* in Francia," *Belfagor,* 15, no. 5 (1960): 530–543;

José Ramón Monreal, "Tomasi di Lampedusa: el archivo de la memoria," *Quimera,* 87 (1989): 32–39;

Tom O'Neill, "Of Ants & Flags: Tomasi di Lampedusa's *Gattopardo,*" *Italianist,* 13 (1993): 180–208;

Francesco Orlando, *Ricordo di Lampedusa* (Milan: Schweiller, 1963);

Maria Pagliaro-Giacovazza, *Il "Gattopardo" o la metafora decadente dell'esistenza* (Lecce: Milella, 1983);

Olga Ragusa, "Comparative Perspective on Tomasi di Lampedusa: From Louis Aragon to David Gilmour," *Forum Italicum,* 26, no. 1 (1992): 201–217;

Ragusa, "Stendhal, Lampedusa, and the Novel," *Comparative Literature Studies,* 10 (1973): 195–228;

Basilio Reale, *Sirene siciliane. L'anima esiliata in "Lighea" di Tomasi di Lampedusa* (Palermo: Sellerio, 1986);

Luigi Russo, "Analisi del *Gattopardo,*" *Belfagor,* 15, no. 5 (1960): 513–530;

Eduardo Saccone, "Nobility and Literature. Questions on Tomasi di Lampedusa," *MLN,* 106 (1991): 159–178;

Simonetta Silvestroni, *Tomasi di Lampedusa* (Florence: Nuova Italia, 1979);

Arnaldo Stirati, *Il Gattopardo* (Rome: Le Muse, 1966);

Andrea Vitello, *I Gattopardi di Donnafugata* (Palermo: Flaccovio, 1963);

Nunzio Zago, *I Gattopardi e le iene. Il messaggio inattuale di Tomasi di Lampedusa* (Palermo: Sellerio, 1983);

Zago, *Giuseppe Tomasi di Lampedusa* (Marina di Patti: Pungitopo, 1987);

Sergio Zatti, *Tomasi di Lampedusa* (Milan: Cetim Bresso, 1972).

The translations of the Italian in this entry are those of Archibald Colquhoun.

Paolo Volponi

(6 February 1924 –)

Rocco Capozzi
University of Toronto

BOOKS: *Il ramarro* (Urbino: Instituto d'Arte, 1948);

L'antica moneta (Florence: Vallecchi, 1955);

Le porte dell'Appennino (Milan: Feltrinelli, 1960);

Memoriale (Milan: Garzanti, 1962); translated by Belén Severeid as *My Trouble Began* (New York: Grossman, 1964); republished as *The Memorandum* (London: Calder & Boyars, 1967);

La macchina mondiale (Milan: Garzanti, 1965); translated by Sevareid as *The Worldwide Machine* (New York: Grossman, 1967; London: Calder & Boyars, 1969);

Corporale (Turin: Einaudi, 1974);

Il sipario ducale (Turin: Einaudi, 1975); translated by Peter N. Pedroni as *Last Act in Urbino* (New York: Italica, 1995);

Il pianeta irritabile (Turin: Einaudi, 1978);

Poesie e poemetti 1946–1966, edited by Gualtiero De Santi (Turin: Einaudi, 1980);

Il lanciatore di giavellotto (Turin: Einaudi, 1981);

Con testo a fronte (Turin: Einaudi, 1986);

Le mosche del capitale (Turin: Einaudi, 1989);

Nel silenzio campale (Lecce: Manni, 1990);

La strada per Roma (Turin: Einaudi, 1991).

Paolo Volponi

Among the generation of Italian writers that emerged in Italy during the mid 1950s to the late 1960s—a period marked by experimentalism and avant-garde activity—Paolo Volponi asserted himself as both challenging and innovative. Unlike many writers who are forgotten after their first, and sometimes only, successful work, Volponi's first novel, *Memoriale* (1962), was but a milestone in a career of significant works of poetry and fiction. He established himself as an innovative writer through his contributions to the journal *Officina* (Workshop), through which he made an important contact with Pier Paolo Pasolini. Pasolini, Francesco Leonetti, and Roberto Roversi were the editors of and major contributors to the journal, which lasted about six years after it began publication in 1955. As its title implies, *Officina* provided a forum for fresh and pro-

gressive ideas, featuring writers and critics such as Franco Fortini, Gianni Scalia, and Volponi.

Volponi's first poems and essays drew the attention of Pasolini and Fortini, who noticed something original in his style and his ideas. Elio Vittorini and other Marxist writers were impressed by Volponi's progressive ideology; his rural background and employment in a large company placed him in a privileged position to address the process of industrialization that was beginning in Italy. Accordingly, Volponi, along with Lucio Mastronardi and Ottiero Ottieri, was among the first novelists to be singled out in *Il menabò,* the journal edited by Vittorini. The novelists' interest in the world of industry raised fresh hopes—and drew attention to new social and psychological problems—during the so-called economic boom of the early 1960s that saw Italy's rapid technological transformation.

Volponi's beliefs in the possibilities of modern technology and his disappointments with those who control industry were at the center of his first novel and continued to dominate most of his fiction for nearly forty years. From the beginning Volponi distinguished himself with his psychological and social realism. His main characters stood out for the unusual way in which they thought, acted, analyzed themselves, and confronted society. Afflicted by neuroses and paranoia, narrator-protagonists such as Saluggia, Crocioni, and Aspri attracted attention from both new and established critics, who came to view Volponi's work as a solid and refreshing contribution to the ailing novel of the postneorealist period.

Paolo Volponi was born in Urbino in 1924. His father ran a small family business (a plant that baked terra-cotta); his mother was the daughter of a modest landowner. Volponi was raised and educated in Urbino, a small, historical, and relatively isolated city overshadowed by the famous Palazzo Ducale. This setting and the surrounding countryside are recognizable in nearly all his work. Volponi received a law degree in 1947 and a year later published his first collection of verse, *Il ramarro* (The Green Lizard). In 1950 he was hired by the Olivetti company to join a team of social workers who were studying various socio-economic problems in regard to southern Italy. In 1955 he published his second collection of poetry, *L'antica moneta* (The Old Coin).

In Volponi's first two volumes of poetry, one notices immediately an emphasis on the personal recollections of youth and a strong sensuality in the detailed descriptions of animals, plants, countryside, and women. From the opening poem of *Il ramarro,* "Cugina volpe" (Cousin Fox), to the concluding poem of *L'antica moneta,* "L'uomo è cacciatore" (Man is a Hunter), one cannot but notice the sexual undertones that accompany the sensations associated with different seasons. This is particularly evident when such sensations are accompanied by the presence of a woman and her symbolic attributes of vitality. In an interview with Gian Carlo Ferretti in 1972, Volponi remarked that his poetry is autobiographical, going on to explain how his experiences, the sensations he felt as he began to understand nature, and his upbringing in and around Urbino constitute its foundation.

Volponi's poetry is characterized by his ability to give life, through descriptions of movement, color, and smell, to plants, animals, rivers, fields, and valleys. Some critics have suggested that Volponi's reading of Giacomo Leopardi, Giovanni Pascoli, Gabriele D'Annunzio, Eugenio Montale, and Salvatore Quasimodo influenced the development of his style, yet there is no evidence of imitation in his work, nor does it show any effort to follow a particular trend. His poetic language, style, and images—deeply rooted in his feelings about nature, other people, and his own life—usually unfold in the context of daily life in his native city.

In 1956 Volponi moved to Ivrea (in Piedmont) where he began working in the human-relations office at Olivetti, the start of what would be a long experience in the industrial world. These were the days when owner Adriano Olivetti hired young "humanists" (poets, artists, designers, psychologists, and sociologists) to help him promote his idealistic views of what modern industry should become for the workers and for society. Vittorio Sereni, Franco Fortini, Edoardo Sanguineti, Geno Pampaloni, and Ottieri are just a few of the writers who worked at Olivetti in different capacities. Volponi would work for Olivetti until 1971.

In 1960 Volponi published a third book of poems, *Le porte dell'Appennino* (The Gateway to the Appennines), which contains many poems he wrote after joining Olivetti. In a shift from his earlier poetry Volponi focuses in these poems on his ambiguous feelings toward an alienating society that does not hesitate to sacrifice the natural, the slow to change, and the simple in order to embrace the artificial and ephemeral of a rapidly changing, increasingly consumeristic industrial society. The collection offers a clear contrast between nature and the city, between Urbino and large cities such as Rome, between Volponi's desire to leave his hometown and his nostalgia for its simple life.

One can see links between some poems and the lyrical passages found in such novels as *Memoriale* and *La macchina mondiale* (1965; translated as *The Worldwide Machine,* 1967). This close connection between poetry and prose would remain true for the rest of Volponi's work, especially in his continued use of lyrical images. In the early 1960s Renato Barilli and other literary critics began to notice in Volponi's work a recurring insistence (conscious or otherwise) on the "corporeal" attributes of men, women, animals, and nature, together with an

 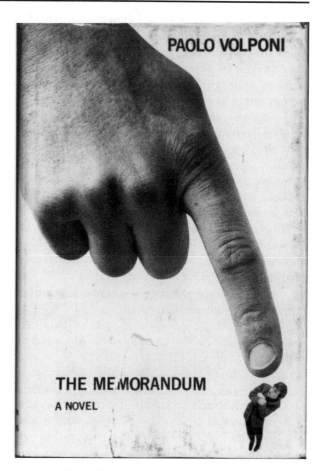

Dust jackets for Volponi's first novel and the British edition of its translation (courtesy of the Lilly Library, Indiana University)

equally noticeable emphasis on the "physical" characteristics of words. In both his poetry and prose Volponi clearly paid close attention not only to the context and sound of words but to the chain reaction of associations that each word can elicit.

Volponi's next publication, *Memoriale* (1962; translated as *My Trouble Began,* 1964), received immediate international attention. The popularity of the novel increased as critics pointed to it as a model of a new language appropriate to the representation and analysis of the effects of industrialization. The merits of the novel were debated in 1962 and 1963, mostly by Vittorini and his collaborators in *Il menabò,* but the discussion soon became widespread, as critics reacted to it as one of the leading novels, along with Ottieri's *Donnarumma all'assalto* (1959; translated as *Men at the Gate,* 1962), of a new literary trend called "letteratura e industria" (literature and industry).

As critics scrutinized the language, content, and structure of new works that focused on industrialization, they also examined, at times excessively, the ideological point of view of the authors. Marxist critics questioned the efforts of writers who sought to promote a new consciousness among people suddenly faced with socio-economic and psychological problems linked to Italy's transformation from an agricultural to a technological and industrialized nation. Both Volponi's and Ottieri's novels were used as examples of how such new works could succeed (where Neorealism had failed) in providing answers to the country's social problems, especially the socio-economic disparities that generally existed between the wealthy North and the poverty-stricken South.

Memoriale is structured as a diary account of Albino Saluggia's experiences as a factory worker from the day he is hired to the day he is fired. His first-person narration reveals a neurotic and alienated individual who feels victimized. Saluggia writes his memorandum to denounce those who made him suffer but also as a means of introducing order into his life. The act of writing is his instrument of self-therapy.

Saluggia, who is trying to forget his unhappy experiences as a prisoner of war, lives with his mother in a house by a lake. The novel begins as he is anticipating starting work in a factory in a nearby town. He has great hopes and expectations that industry and technology can improve the human condition and is confident that his new job will be the "beginning of a new life." However, from the moment he undergoes a physical examination in the factory clinic his troubles begin. When he sees his file stored in a cabinet, he feels as though a part of him has been locked away. Images of his "divided" body then become frequent. Moreover, Saluggia begins to suspect that the doctors and everyone else, including his own mother, who agrees that he needs medical attention, are trying to control him. The doctors and those close to him are concerned with his tuberculosis, but he is more preoccupied with his mental health and fears that the company doctors are trying to cure him of his neuroses, which he regards as his most private possession.

Saluggia's memorandum offers many indications that he is aware of his neuroses and that he intends to protect them because they help him to see more clearly the hidden dangers of the industrial establishment. Indeed, his neuroses do help him scrutinize the frustrating and alienating experience of competing with powerful machines on a production line. And although he is able to argue with other workers who feel no love for their jobs nor for their employer, he is not really able to communicate with any of them. Unfortunately, the system that he once praised as a new utopia suddenly proves to be too confining, too controlling, and much too different from the agricultural setting in which he grew up. Saluggia begins to equate the power of the doctors and the factory managers with the brutal actions of Sergeant Vattimo, the fierce guard who tortured him during his imprisonment.

Saluggia's illness keeps him away from the factory; thus most of the entries in his diary deal with his convalescence, his fights with doctors, his experience with a team of phony physicians in a private clinic, and his recovery in a sanatorium. Even so, his memorandum addresses such issues as workers' rights and the problem of alienation resulting from industrialization. It also includes suggestions for improving working conditions and a scale of values that places man above the machines.

The same neuroses that give Saluggia the lucidity to see the hidden dangers of industrialization also make it nearly impossible for him to interact with others at work and during his free time. He is usually alone; he either stays in his room, goes to the movies, or spends hours contemplating the differences between a country life in contact with nature and a city life working in a factory. Because of his mother's attitude toward women and sex, Saluggia develops a fear and suspicion of all women. His biggest disappointment occurs when he realizes that the factory, which at the beginning stood for order, a "beautiful cathedral," in reality is not a place in which he can find peace. Further, he senses that the company, which continued to pay for his treatment even after he was laid off, will not be defeated by anyone who challenges it and will punish anyone who tries to disrupt its operation. At the end of the novel Saluggia is fired for taking part in an illegal strike.

Volponi's main characters dare to think differently from the rest of society and thus risk being misunderstood and being considered not only insane but actually too dangerous to be left free. What makes Albino Saluggia intriguing is his self-awareness and his lucidity in detecting problems and anomalies that so-called normal people do not notice or do not consider important. Saluggia is alive to everything around him and has a particular interest in the sounds of words and the social effects of language. In the hospital he writes a long poem that illustrates his lyrical talent and his love for word associations. Saluggia's sensitivity as well as his neuroses, frustrations, and anger with a world that does not understand him earn him the label of *diverso* (different or strange). These are the traits that distinguish the Volponi protagonist.

Anteo Crocioni is the protagonist of *La macchina mondiale* (1965; translated as *The Worldwide Machine,* 1967), which won the coveted Strega Prize in 1965 and confirmed Volponi as a successful novelist. He, too, is a diverso, and like his predecessor Saluggia, Crocioni feels he is a victim and misunderstood. Again Volponi makes use of a first-person narrator-protagonist who writes as a means of therapy. Crocioni actually surpasses Saluggia in his careful use of rhyming words and of words that can set in motion chains of associations.

In *La macchina modiale* Volponi uses not a memoradum but the device of Crocioni's manuscript—a scientific treatise full of futuristic ideas on improving society—to draw the reader's attention to the metafictional and linguistic characteristics of the act of writing. Crocioni's "The Academy of Friendship for Qualified People" is based on the idea that men are "machines built by other men" and that consequently men and society, like machines, can and should be perfected. Needless to say, the treatise is not easily accepted by others, and its promoter is soon considered a threat to society. Crocioni's family members, his friends, and even a seminarian, who at first appeared to listen to him, turn their backs on him once he asks them to help promote his ideas.

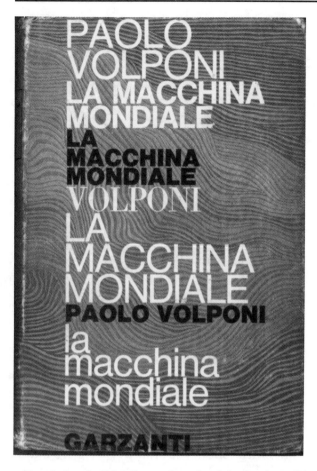 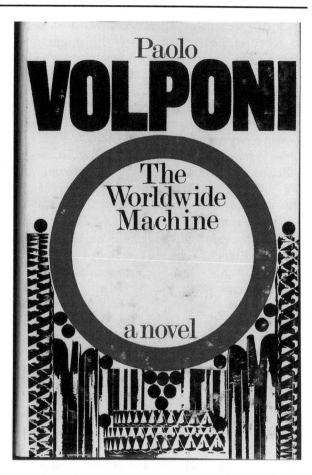

Dust jackets for Volponi's second novel and the American edition of its translation (courtesy of the Lilly Library, Indiana University)

A frustrated Crocioni leaves his narrow-minded town and moves to Rome, hoping that he will find among students and professors someone who can help him understand and promote the treatise. Unfortunately there, too, he is considered insane, and within a short time he is rejected by everyone. Crocioni is not willing to give up his utopian dream despite a series of dire consequences. He loses his wife because her family will not allow her to live with him; they then convince her to kill her newborn son because they fear he will be crazy like his father. Later Crocioni loses his house as the authorities expropriate his belongings in order to assign them to his wife. By the end of the novel Crocioni has decided to kill himself with an explosive he has developed rather than yield to authority. But before committing suicide, he resorts to robbery and vandalism as a way of rebelling against a closed-minded system that shows no tolerance for his ideas.

Volponi left Olivetti to accept a position at the Fiat plant in Turin in 1971. During his time with Fiat Volponi completed his most ambitious work,

Corporale (Corporeal, 1974)–a long novel that he had started seven years earlier. The protagonist is Gerolamo Aspri (alias Joachin Murieta), another fascinating creation in the mold of Saluggia and Crocioni. The novel is made up of four parts, with the first and third parts written in the first person, from Aspri's point of view. Like his predecessors, Aspri is obsessed with order, language, self-consciousness, and a society that appears to have lost all interest in humanistic values. The second and fourth parts are narrated in the third person and follow Joachin Murieta's adventures in a world of gambling, drugs, and prostitution, mostly in and around Milan. It is not hard to detect that Murieta (named after a famous Mexican revolutionary figure) is Aspri's split self, a mask of one of his alter egos. Overath, his loved and hated German friend, is his other major alter ego, a much-desired father figure.

In part 1 it becomes evident that Aspri is a neurotic and narcissistic character who falls victim to his many desires. He is continuously searching for a woman–first Ivana, then Imelde–or a father figure such as Overath or Trasmanati. Most of all, he searches for his true self. Aspri's difficulties in trying to come to terms with his fears, anxieties, desires, dreams, and political and religious beliefs give life to the "theatrical" second self Joachin Murieta, a man who is fearless and sure of himself and not afraid to act. In the opening pages of part 2, which is drawn from Aspri's diary and from Overath's lectures in part 1, the reader can see that Aspri is not schizophrenic. He is fully aware that through Murieta he is merely playing the "role" of a rebel, because he is unable to face his personal problems and accept his real self.

Throughout the novel Volponi draws freely from the ideas of Sigmund Freud, R. D. Laing, and Jacques Lacan, especially in the manifestations of sadomasochistic, master/slave, love/hate, I/Other relationships between Aspri and Overath, Aspri and Ivana/Imelde, and Aspri and Transmanati/Salsamiti. Several passages in *Corporale* appear to have been written specifically from a perspective of the Lacanian logic of unfulfilled desire: words such as *mirror, interlocutor, acting, theater, desire, second self, alter-ego,* and *the Other* appear frequently. Aspri's diary—basically a novel within the novel—shows that once again Volponi's narrator uses writing therapeutically in his self-analysis of psychological complexes. The novel also shows, through various references to Stalin, that Volponi is quite open in his criticism of the old-fashioned Communist Party—a party he feels needs to reassess its positions if it is to play a role in a neocapitalistic industrial society.

Volponi's attention to issues being debated at the time the novel was written can be seen in Aspri's obsession with a nuclear bomb shelter, or *arcatana* (literally "ark den"), which he builds not far from Urbino. In the 1960s and 1970s many companies took advantage of a worldwide fear of imminent nuclear war and advertised prefabricated nuclear shelters. The shelter that Aspri builds collapses on him, resulting in serious injury. The novel ends with Aspri's mysterious escape from the hospital, possibly to avoid being questioned about his true identity. He leaves behind only his "Diary of Joachin Murieta."

Corporale received limited attention in part because of the attention being lavished upon Elsa Morante's *La Storia* (*History*) and Darrigo's *Horcinus Orca.* Nonetheless, given the currency of the many debates on formalism, experimentalism, and the neoavant-garde, one can only wonder why Volponi's novel, which contained excellent examples of innovative narrative strategies, was greeted mainly by the praise of his most faithful readers.

In 1975, just four years after taking his position at Fiat, Volponi was forced to resign, partly because of his leftist political views. With his wife, Giovina, and his two children he moved to Milan. During the next two decades Volponi would move back and forth between Milan, Rome, and Urbino. In the next sixteen years he would publish five novels and three books of poems. He continued to practice his lifelong hobby as connoisseur of painting and sculpture from the sixteenth through the nineteenth centuries.

As Volponi explained in several interviews, his disappointment with the reception of *Corporale* motivated him to write a more traditional novel in language and structure. Seen by many as a departure from his previous work *Il sipario ducale,* nevertheless, treated the same issues. His reluctance to write another *Corporale* may also have been responsible for the composition of his other "well made" novel, *Il lanciatore di giavellotto.* With the exception of these two works, Volponi has continued to write in the same style and spirit for which he was known in the 1950s.

Il sipario ducale (1975; translated as *Last Act in Urbino,* 1995) was written during a period of deep social and political unrest that saw frequent incidents of terrorism carried out by both left- and right-wing extremist groups. The story revolves around the November 1969 bombing at the Piazza Fontana in Milan, one of the first terrorist acts to shock Italy. The novel was discussed for months on national television and by the press. *Il sipario ducale* goes beyond the issue of political terrorism to address various Italian sociohistorical failures—the problems associated with national unification, historical regional divisions, rigid sociopolitical structures, a conservative and decadent bourgeois class, the neglect of agriculture in the national economy, and the increasing power of television and the mass media.

Il sipario ducale appears to break from Volponi's previous novels because he employs an omniscient, third-person narration and carefully structures the two alternating parallel stories to bring them together only at the end of the novel. The anarchists Vives and Gaspare Subissoni are the main characters of one story. Vives meets Professor Subissoni during the Spanish Civil War when she helps him recover from a head wound. After the war she moves with Subissoni to Urbino where they live a secluded life until one evening they watch a terrorist act on the television news. Dissatisfied with the explanations given by the media, Vives decides to get to the bottom of the incident and goes to Milan, but she dies shortly after her arrival because of poor health. In the closing pages of the novel, Subissoni also travels to Milan. He is accompanied by Dirce, a young woman sought by Oddi Semproni, the protagonist of the other story.

Semproni is the descendant of a noble family in Urbino who lives with two unmarried aunts. He is constantly traveling around the country, visiting museums, and rapidly squandering his patrimony with the help of his opportunistic chauffeur, Giocondini. It is the chauffeur who introduces Semproni to the young prostitute, Dirce, a symbol of the oppressed proletariat. Semproni's family represents a social class that has lost its relevance in the contemporary world. When a bored Semproni finally meets Subissoni, he is understandably drawn to the professor's anarchist views. But Semproni cannot understand, nor can he accept, that Dirce, the woman whom he has decided to marry, could also be infatuated by Subissoni's ideas and lifestyle. Semproni and his chauffeur die in a car accident as they chase after Subissoni and Dirce, who are traveling toward Milan.

The apocalyptic theme of *Corporale* returns in *Il pianeta irritabile* (The Irritable Planet, 1978), an allegory of a nuclear holocaust. Volponi follows four strange survivors who had worked together in a circus before the devastation of a nuclear war: a monkey, a midget, a duck, and an elephant. As an obvious satire of the Darwinian process of evolution, Volponi presents the only human in chains, a slave of the monkey, who is in charge of the group. Hoping to reach a distant place where life may still be possible, the four must combine their individual talents and work together. The monkey is a sharpshooter; the duck knows how to count; the elephant can talk and knows by heart Dante's *Divine Comedy;* the midget remembers how things used to be and is ashamed of what his race has done. As the strange team moves across a gloomy and desolate landscape showing all the signs of death and destruction caused by war, they must face difficult moments and confront some unfriendly creatures and soldiers, who had been hiding in a submarine.

The nuclear catastrophe, which resulted from a world war and man's attempt to control nature, is presented through credible descriptions of a desolate environment and, more important, through the discussions and memories of the four survivors during their journey. One of the most original and most fascinating fictions to come out of Italy on the theme of nuclear war, *Il pianeta irritabile* is rivaled only by Guido Morselli's *Dissipatio H.G.* (The Dissolution of the Human Race, 1977) in its devastating depiction of the aftermath of a nuclear disaster. However, neither novel attracted the attention of Italian academic

Dust jacket for Volponi's 1974 novel, which alternates between first- and third-person narrative in order to present a full portrait of its protagonist, Gerolamo Aspri

critics, who have traditionally snubbed science fiction as a form of *triviallitteratur.*

Il lanciatore di giavellotto (The Javelin Thrower, 1981), Volponi's second novel in the traditional mold of a third-person narration, is the story of Damin Possanza's formative years during the Fascist era in the 1930s. The action takes place mostly in Fossembrone (near Urbino) and focuses on Damin's relationships with his beautiful and adulterous mother, Norma; her Fascist lover, Marcacci; his grandfather Damiano, a terra-cotta artisan; his younger sister, Lavinia; and his communist shoemaking friend Occhialini. Damin's psychological drama is about self-awareness, acceptance, and learning about life and the world around him.

As is the case with most novels about growing up, the experiences associated with the protagonist's sexual awakening play a key role. Unfortunately, Damin's awakening suffers a setback when he begins to spy on his beautiful mother, who has regular nocturnal meetings with the macho Fascist leader

Marcacci. Damin soon begins to hate Marcacci for his uniform, his arrogance, and his egocentrism, but he is also attracted by his strength of character, which contrasts with that of Damin's weak father, Dorino Possanza. Damin's education is enriched by his encouraging talks with his grandfather and by the frequent advice given by Occhialini, who helps the boy to become a man and to understand the political situation.

Damin sublimates his sexuality with sport activities organized by Marcacci's party, and to his own surprise at one of the track tournaments he becomes the regional champion javelin thrower. The title of the novel alludes to Damin "the javelin thrower," but other meanings of the Greek word for javelin thrower, "thrower of looks" and "thrower of himself," are relevant to the conclusion of the novel. After catching his sister Lavinia kissing a stranger, Damin kills her (perhaps to punish his mother) and then takes his own life by jumping off a bridge. Volponi again brilliantly combines psychoanalysis and sociopolitical realism, personal and social themes. The sensitive Damin, with his misdirected sexuality tending toward sadomasochism and homosexuality, is warped by Fascist society. His narcissism at times surpasses even that of Marcacci.

Moved by his strong belief that society could be changed for the better by technology and politics, Volponi at the beginning of the 1980s accepted an invitation to run as an independent Communist candidate for a seat in the Italian senate. He held the frustrating office for nearly a decade, until 1992, when he decided to leave politics and move back to Urbino. During his time in the senate Volponi continued to write. Although he was known mainly for his novels, he had not stopped writing verse. Because of the similarities between his prose and his poetry, some of the long poems in *Con testo a fronte* (With a Parallel Text, 1986) might be taken for paragraphs or pages from his novels, and vice versa. This is particularly true of the novel *Le mosche del capitale* (The Flies of the Capital, 1989), which was written shortly after *Con testo a fronte* and *Nel silenzio campale* (In the Silence of the Fields, 1990).

Le mosche del capitale (the "flies" refer to those individuals who feed on capital) is Volponi's most bitter and most personal criticism of the iniquities of capitalism and technology in a consumer society. Volponi's experiences at Olivetti and Fiat underlie this powerful postmodern allegorical satire of the failure of Italian industry to improve social conditions. In the figure of Saraccini one detects a disillusioned Volponi who once believed that intellectuals could work within the industrial establishment to democratize and humanize "progress." But Volponi

and his character have learned that the age of technocracy and multinationals, where laws are dictated by the new gods of capital and profit, does not allow for utopian dreams. The idealistic Saraccini fails as a consultant, working first as an administrator in a firm run by Nasàpeti (Olivetti) and later at a large company headed by Donna Fulgenzia (Fiat), mainly because he refuses to compromise his basic belief that workers and jobs should not be sacrificed to protect high profits.

Le mosche del capitale contains some of Volponi's best writing. Alternating first-and third-person narration, he shows a virtuosity with language, fusing poetry and prose in his philosophic monologues and his expressionistic and grotesque descriptions of characters and places, such as the descriptions of the dirty and violent ghetto where immigrant workers live. Moreover, the novel offers definite postmodern characteristics: readers will not easily forget the conversation between a computer and the moon, nor the discussions of chairs, plants and paintings (they all speak the same language) as they give different perspectives on the same issues: capital and power and the voracious flies around them. Volponi provides a powerfully ironic and disconcerting view of postmodern society, which appears to have lost sight of all human values and of what real progress could mean for the working class and society as a whole.

To be fully appreciated, *La strada per Roma* (The Road to Rome, 1991), which was published some thirty years after Volponi drafted it, should be read in the light of his poetry and fiction of the late 1950s and early 1960s. In various interviews Volponi has insisted that he did not revise this novel, which he originally had planned to publish with the title of "La repubblica borghese" (The Bourgeois Republic), and has stated repeatedly that it is a "romanzo giovanile" (a youthful novel). The work records the formative years of the first-person narrator, Guido Corsalini, who is tormented by internal anxieties and his desire to leave his loved-hated Urbino. In Guido's recollections the reader recognizes Volponi's deep anxieties as well as the frustrations, anger, and neuroses that surface regularly in his works.

The novel also depicts the experiences faced by a generation of young Italians forced to immigrate either to large cities or abroad. Volponi beautifully realizes Urbino and its surroundings; the socio-ideological debates between Guido and his friends, Ettore and Mario, about the future or Urbino and Italy as a whole; the psychological and emotional battles between parents and children of two generations; and the maturing experiences that shatter the illusions of the sensitive, idealistic protagonist. *La strada per Roma* reaffirms Volponi as one of Italy's most original contemporary authors.

Volponi's critical reception during the course of his career has been highly favorable. Although *Corporale* excited little contemporary comment, it has come to be recognized as one of his best novels. For nearly four decades Volponi's work has engaged critics and readers not only because of his remarkable literary skills but also because of his passionate clarity as a critic of contemporary Italy. His writing combines, in a most original and natural fashion, the themes and techniques of metafiction, insightful anaylsis of the human psyche, and sharp sociohistorical criticism.

Interviews:

Ferdinando Camon, "Volponi," in his *Il mestiere dello scrittore* (Milan: Garzanti, 1973), pp. 123–143;

Claudio Toscani, "Incontro con Volponi," *Il ragguaglio librario* (July–August 1974): 258–266;

Peter N. Pedroni, "Interview with P. Volponi," *Italian Quarterly*, 25 (Spring 1984): 75–89;

Paolo Volponi, "Di letteratura e industria. Paolo Volponi e la Pantera," *L'immaginazione*, 73–74 (1990): 1–11;

Rocco Capozzi, "Volponi," in his *Scrittori, critici e industria culturale* (Lecce: Manni, 1991), pp. 166–173;

Gregory Lucente, "An Interview with Paolo Volponi," *Forum Italicum*, 26 (Spring 1992): 218–235.

References:

Enrico Baldise, *Invito alla lettura di Volponi* (Milan: Mursia, 1982);

Armando Balduino, *Messaggi e problemi della letteratura contemporanea* (Venice: Marsilio, 1976), pp. 158–169;

Renato Barilli, "*Corporale* e la narrative bassa," *Il Mulino* (1974): 507–517;

Barilli, "Due romanzi simmetrici," in his *L'azione e l'estasi* (Milan: Feltrinelli), pp. 145–161;

Ferdinando Camon, *Letteratura e classi subalterne* (Padua: Marsilio, 1974), pp. 41–48;

Rocco Capozzi, "Metaromanzo e psicanalisi nella narrativa di P. Volponi," *Canadian Journal of Italian Studies*, 3 (1979): 14–33;

Capozzi, "The Narrator-Protagonist and the Divided Self in Volponi's *Corporale*," *Forum Italicum*, 10 (1976): 203–217;

Gabriella Contini, "L'ultimo Volponi: invenzione e strategia," *Allegoria*, 9 (1991): 93–101;

Gian Carlo Ferretti, *Volponi* (Florence: Nuova Italia, 1972);

Marco Forti, "La stravolta profezia di Volponi," *Nuovi argomenti* (1974): 154–170;

Forti, "Volponi romanziere: Cultura e potere industriale, allegoria, poesia," *Nuova antologia* (October–December 1989): 273–302;

Enzo Golino, *Letteratura e classi sociali* (Bari: Laterza, 1976), pp. 145–151;

Angelo Guglielmi, "La lente deformante," in *Vero e falso* (Milan: Turin, 1968), pp. 105–111;

Linda Hutcheon, *Narcissistic Narrative. The Metafictional Paradox* (Waterloo, Ont.: Wilfred Laurier University Press, 1980), pp. 104–117;

Romano Luperini, "Moderno, postmoderno e allegoria nelle *Mosche del capitale*," *Allegoria*, 5 (1990): 91–94;

Pier Paolo Pasolini, *Passione e ideologia* (Milan: Garzanti, 1960), pp. 437–442;

Walter Pedullà, *La letteratura del benessere* (Rome: Bulzoni, 1973), pp. 459–464;

Massimo Romano, *Gli stregoni della fantacultura* (Turin: Paravia, 1978), pp. 174–191;

Enzo Siciliano, "La logica della fabbrica," *Palatina*, 20 (1962): 61–66;

Siciliano, "La macchina mondiale," *Palatina*, 31–32 (1965): 112–114;

Valerio Volpini, *Pareri letterari e altro* (Verona: Fiorini, 1973), pp. 183–187.

Books for Further Reading

Accrocca, Elio Filippo. *Ritratti su misura di scrittori italiani*. Venice: Sodalizio del Libro, 1960.

Amoroso, Giuseppe. *Sull'elaborazione dei romanzi contemporanei*. Milan: Mursia, 1970.

Amoruso, Vito. *Le contraddizioni della realtà. La narrativa italiana degli anni '50 e '60*. Bari: Edizioni Dedalo, 1968.

Anceschi, Luciano. *Le poetiche del Novecento in Italia*. Turin: Paravia, 1972.

Antonielli, Sergio. *Aspetti e figure del Novecento*. Parma: Guanda, 1955.

Apollonio, Mario. *I contemporanei*. Brescia: Morcelliana, 1956.

Asor Rosa, Alberto. *Scrittori e popolo*. Rome: Samonà e Savelli, 1965.

Balduino, Armando. *Messaggi e problemi della letteratura italiana contemporanea*. Venice: Marsilio, 1976.

Bàrberi-Squarotti, Giorgio. *La narrativa dal '45 ad oggi*. Palermo: Centro Pitré, 1981.

Bàrberi-Squarotti. *La narrativa italiana del dopoguerra*. Bologna: Cappelli, 1965.

Bàrberi-Squarotti. *Poesia e narrativa del secondo Novecento*. Milan: Mursia, 1961.

Barilli, Renato. *La barriera del naturalismo. Studi sulla narrativa italiana contemporanea*. Milan: Mursia, 1964.

Battaglia, Salvatore. *Mitografia del personaggio*. Milan: Rizzoli, 1968.

Bertacchini, Renato. *Cultura e società nel romanzo del Novecento*. Turin: Società Editrice Italiana, 1974.

Bertacchini. *Figure e problemi di narrativa contemporanea*. Bologna: Cappelli, 1960.

Biondi, Marino. *Il sogno e altro: note di letteratura e psicoanalisi*. Verona: Gutenberg, 1988.

Blelloch, Paola. *Quel mondo dei guanti e delle stoffe. Profili di scrittrici italiane del '900*. Verona: Essedue, 1987.

Bo, Carlo. *Della lettura e altri saggi*. Florence: Vallecchi, 1953.

Bo. *Riflessioni critiche*. Florence: Sansoni, 1953.

Bo, ed. *Inchiesta sul neorealismo*. Turin: Edizioni Radio Italiana, 1951.

Bocelli, Arnaldo. *Giaime Pintor e la letteratura della Resistenza*. Caltanisetta & Rome: Sciascia, 1958.

Bonifazi, Neuro. *Il racconto fantastico da Tarchetti a Buzzati*. Urbino: STEU, 1971.

Camon, Ferdinando. *Letteratura e classi subalterne*. Venice: Marsilio, 1974.

Cavallini, Giorgio. *La narrativa italiana contemporanea*. Florence: Bulgarini, 1971.

Cecchi, Emilio. *Letteratura italiana del Novecento*. Milan: Mondadori, 1972.

Cecchi. *Libri nuovi e usati*. Naples: Edizioni Scientiche Italiane, 1958.

Cecchi. *Ritratti e profili*. Milan: Garzanti, 1957.

Cecchi and Natalino Sapegno, eds. *Il Novecento,* volume 9 of *Storia della letteratura italiana*. Milan: Garzanti, 1969.

Contini, Gianfranco, ed. *Storia della letteratura dell'Italia Unita, 1861–1968*. Florence: Sansoni, 1968.

David, Michel. *La psicoanalisi nella cultura italiana*. Turin: Boringhieri, 1966.

De Benedetti, Giacomo. *Il romanzo del Novecento*. Milan: Garzanti, 1971.

De Benedetti. *Saggi, 1922–1966*. Milan: Mondadori, 1982.

De Michelis, Eurialo. *Narratori antinarratori*. Florence: La Nuova Italia, 1952.

De Tommaso, Piero. *Altri scrittori e critici contemporanei*. Lanciano: Edizioni Itinerari, 1970.

De Tommaso. *Narratori italiani contemporanei*. Rome: Edizioni dell'Ateneo, 1965.

Falaschi, Giovanni. *La Resistenza armata nella narrativa italiana*. Turin: Einaudi, 1976.

Falqui, Enrico. *Novecento letterario,* series 1–10. Florence: Vallecchi, 1954–1969.

Falqui. *Prosatori e narratori del Novecento italiano*. Turin: Einaudi, 1950.

Fernandez, Dominique. *Il romanzo italiano e la crisi della coscienza moderna*. Milan: Lerici, 1960.

Ferretti, Gian Carlo. *Letteratura e ideologia*. Rome: Editori Riuniti, 1964.

Ferretti. *Il mercato delle lettere*. Turin: Einaudi, 1979.

Flora, Francesco. *Scrittori italiani contemporanei*. Pisa: Nistri-Lischi, 1952.

Forni Mizzau, Marina. *Tecniche narrative e romanzo contemporaneo*. Milan: Mursia, 1965.

Forti, Marco. *Prosatori e narratori del Novecento italiano*. Milan: Mursia, 1974.

Fortini, Franco. *Saggi italiani*. Bari: De Donato, 1974.

Frasson, Alberto. *Resoconto di letture*. Milan: Mursia, 1974.

Gianola, Elio. *Storia letteraria del Novecento in Italia*. Turin: Società Editrice Italiana, 1976.

Giuliani, Alfredo. *Autunno del Novecento. Cronache di letteratura*. Milan: Feltrinelli, 1984.

Golino, Enzo. *Cultura e mutamento sociale*. Milan: Edizioni Comunità, 1969.

Golino. *Letteratura e classi sociali*. Bari: Laterza, 1976.

Gramigna, Giuliano. *La menzogna del romanzo*. Milan: Garzanti, 1980.

Grana, Gianni, ed. *Letteratura italiana. Novecento: I contemporanei*. Milan: Marzorati, 1979.

Grisi, Francesco. *Avventura del personaggio*. Milan: Ceschina, 1968.

Guarnieri, Silvio. *Cinquant'anni di narrativa in Italia*. Florence: Parenti, 1955.

Guglielmi, Angelo. *La letteratura del risparmio*. Milan: Bompiani, 1973.

Guglielmi, Guido. *La prosa italiana del Novecento: umorismo, metafisica, grottesco*. Turin: Einaudi, 1986.

Guglielminetti, Marziano. *Il romanzo del Novecento italiano*. Rome: Editori Riuniti, 1986.

Guidorizzi, Ernesto. *La narrativa italiana e il cinema*. Florence: Sansoni, 1973.

Guidotti, Mario. *Lo scrittore disintegrato*. Florence: Vallecchi, 1961.

Heiney, Donald. *America in Modern Italian Literature*. New Brunswick, N.J.: Rutgers University Press, 1964.

Heiney. *Three Italian Novelists*. Ann Arbor: University of Michigan Press, 1968.

Iannace, Florinda, ed. *Il filone cattolico nella letteratura italiana del secondo dopoguerra*. Rome: Bulzoni, 1989.

Leone, Michele. *L'industria nella letteratura italiana contemporanea*. Saratoga, Cal.: ANMA Libri, 1976.

Lombardi, Olga. *La giovane narrativa*. Pisa: Nistri-Lischi, 1963.

Lombardi. *La narrativa italiana nelle crisi del Novecento*. Caltanisetta: Sciascia, 1971.

Lombardi. *Narratori neorealisti*. Pisa: Nistri-Lischi, 1957.

Luperini, Romano. *Il Novecento,* 2 volumes. Turin: Loescher, 1981.

Luti, Giorgio. *Narratori italiani contemporanei*. Messina: D'Anna, 1969.

Maizza, Enzo, ed. *Inchiesta sulla narrativa contemporanea*. Rome: Edizioni Cinque Lune, 1958.

Manacorda, Giuliano. *Storia della letteratura italiana contemporanea (1940–1965)*. Rome: Editori Riuniti, 1967.

Manacorda. *Vent'anni di pazienza. Saggi sulla letteratura italiana contemporanea*. Florence: La Nuova Italia, 1972.

Marabini, Claudio. *Gli anni sessanta: narrativa e storia*. Milan: Rizzoli, 1970.

Marchese, Angelo. *Officina del racconto. Semiotica della narratività*. Milan: Mondadori, 1983.

Mariani, Gaetano. *La giovane narrativa tra documento e poesia*. Florence: Le Monnier, 1962.

Mariani. *Letteratura italiana: I contemporanei*. Milan: Marzorati, 1969.

Mariani and Mario Petrucciani, eds. *Letteratura italiana contemporanea*. Rome: Lucarini, 1979.

Mauro, Walter. *Cultura e società nella narrativa meridionale*. Rome: Edizioni dell'Ateneo, 1965.

Mauro. *Letteratura sotto inchiesta*. Rome: Canesi, 1963.

Mauro. *Realtà, mito e favola nella narrativa italiana del Novecento.* Milan: Sugar, 1974.

Mazzotti, Artal. *Letteratura italiana. Orientamenti culturali: I contemporanei,* 3 volumes. Milan: Marzorati, 1963–1969.

Moretti, Vito. *Ideologia e letteratura. Saggi sulla prosa narrativa del Quarantacinque.* Bologna: Cappelli, 1986.

Muscetta, Carlo. *Letteratura militante.* Florence: Parenti, 1953.

Muscetta. *Realismo e controrealismo.* Milan: Del Duca, 1958.

Muscetta. *Realismo, neorealismo, controrealismo.* Milan: Garzanti, 1976.

Nozzoli, Anna. *La parete di carta: scritture al femminile nel Novecento italiano.* Verona: Gutenberg, 1989.

Nozzoli. *Tabù e coscienza. La condizione femminile nella letteratura italiana del Novecento.* Florence: La Nuova Italia, 1978.

Pacifici, Sergio. *A Guide to Contemporary Italian Literature: From Futurism to Neorealism.* New York: World Publishing, 1962.

Pandini, Giancarlo. *Letture critiche.* Forlí: Forum, 1978.

Paoluzzi, Angelo. *La letteratura della Resistenza.* Rome: Edizioni Cinque Lune, 1956.

Paris, Renzo. *Il mito del proletario nel romanzo italiano.* Milan: Garzanti, 1977.

Pasolini, Pier Paolo. *Passione e ideologia: 1948-1958.* Milan: Garzanti, 1960.

Passeri Pignoni, Vera. *Panorama della narrativa italiana del dopoguerra.* Bologna: Istituto Carlo Tincani, 1986.

Pautasso, Sergio. *Il laboratorio dello scrittore. Temi, idee, tecniche della letteratura del Novecento.* Florence: La Nuova Italia, 1981.

Pedullà, Walter. *La letteratura del benessere.* Rome: Bulzoni, 1973.

Pedullà. *La rivoluzione della letteratura.* Rome: Bulzoni, 1972.

Petrocchi, Giorgio. *Poesia e tecnica narrativa.* Milan: Mursia, 1962.

Piccioni, Leone. *La narrativa italiana tra romanzo e racconto.* Milan: Mondadori, 1959.

Piccioni. *Proposte di letture.* Milan: Rusconi, 1985.

Piccioni. *Sui contemporanei.* Milan: Fabbri, 1955.

Pietrosi Barrow, Luciana. *Dal neorealismo allo sperimentalismo.* Rome: Trevi, 1968.

Plebe, Armando. *Discorso semiserio sul romanzo.* Bari: Laterza, 1965.

Pullini, Giorgio. *Narratori italiani del Novecento.* Padua: Liviana, 1959.

Pullini. *Tra esistenza e coscienza: Narrativa e teatro del '900.* Milan: Mursia, 1986.

Ragusa, Olga. *Narrative and Drama. Essays in Modern Italian Literature from Verga to Pasolini.* The Hague: Mouton, 1976.

Rinaldi, Rinaldo. *Romanzo come deformazione: Autonomia ed eredità gaddiana in Mastronardi, Bianciardi, Testori, Arbasino.* Milan: Mursia, 1985.

Romano, A. *Discorso sugli anni cinquanta.* Milan: Mondadori, 1965.

Romano, Massimo. *Gli stregoni della fantacultura.* Turin: Paravia, 1978.

Salinari, Carlo. *Preludio e fine del realismo in Italia.* Naples: Morano, 1964.

Salinari. *La questione del realismo.* Florence: Parenti, 1960.

Scaramucci, Ines. *Narrativa contemporanea e condizione crepuscolare.* Milan: Istituto Propaganda Libraria, 1975.

Solari, A. G. [Pseudonym of Giose Rimanelli]. *Il mestiere del furbo. Panorama della narrativa italiana contemporanea.* Milan: Sugar, 1959.

Spagnoletti, Giacinto. *Scrittori di un secolo.* Milan: Marzorati, 1974.

Tanturri, Riccardo. *La linea del conformismo.* Padua: CEDAM, 1973.

Tartarini, Osvaldo. *L'influenza del cinema nella narrativa contemporanea.* Rome: E.R.S., 1958.

Tonda, Nicola. *Realtà e memoria nella narrativa italiana contemporanea.* Rome: Bulzoni, 1970.

Tondo, Michele. *Sondaggi e letture di contemporanei.* Lecce: Milella, 1974.

Vallone, Aldo, ed. *La condizione operaia nel romanzo italiano d'oggi.* Naples: Loffredo, 1973.

Varese, Carlo. *Cultura letteraria contemporanea.* Pisa: Nistri-Lischi, 1951.

Varese, Claudio. *Occasioni e valori della letteratura italiana contempo ranea.* Bologna: Cappelli, 1967.

Venè, Gianfranco. *Letteratura e capitalismo in Italia.* Milan: Sugar, 1963.

Volpini, Valerio. *Pareri letterari e altro.* Verona: Fiorini, 1973.

Volpini. *Prosa e narrativa dei contemporanei.* Rome: Studium, 1967.

Volpini. *Prosa e narrativa dei contemporanei. Dalla "Voce" agli anni settanta.* Rome: Studium, 1979.

Zangrilli, Franco. *Linea pirandelliana nella narrativa contemporanea.* Ravenna: Longo, 1990.

Contributors

Mario Aste..*University of Massachusetts at Lowell*
Rocco Capozzi..*University of Toronto*
Anthony Constantini..*California State University, Northridge*
Natalia Costa-Zalessow..*San Francisco State University*
Cristina Della Coletta..*University of Virginia*
Carmine Di Biase ....*University of Salerno*
Gabriele Erasmi..*McMaster University*
Charles Fantazzi ....*University of Windsor*
Giuseppe Faustini..*Skidmore College*
Joseph Francese ....*Michigan State University*
Andrea Guiati ....*State University of New York at Buffalo*
Giovanna Jackson..*Walsh University*
Louis Kibler ....*Wayne State University*
Ilona Klein..*Brigham Young University*
Emanuele Licastro ....*State University of New York at Buffalo*
Umberto Mariani..*Rutgers University*
Sante Matteo ....*Miami University of Ohio*
Claudio Mazzola ....*The College of the Holy Cross*
Giovanna Miceli-Jeffries..*University of Wisconsin — Madison*
Antonino Musumeci..*University of Illinois at Urbana-Champaign*
Cinzia Donatelli Noble ....*Brigham Young University*
Tom O'Neill..*University of Melbourne*
Augustus Pallotta ....*Syracuse University*
Mark Pietralunga ....*Florida State University*
Paolo Possiedi ....*Montclair State University*
Olga Ragusa ....*Columbia University*
Albert Sbragia ....*University of Washington*
S. A. Smith..*Skidmore College*
Giacomo Striuli ....*Providence College*
Sharon Wood ....*University of Strathclyde*

Cumulative Index

Dictionary of Literary Biography, Volumes 1-177
Dictionary of Literary Biography Yearbook, 1980-1995
Dictionary of Literary Biography Documentary Series, Volumes 1-14

Cumulative Index

DLB before number: *Dictionary of Literary Biography,* Volumes 1-177
Y before number: *Dictionary of Literary Biography Yearbook,* 1980-1995
DS before number: *Dictionary of Literary Biography Documentary Series,* Volumes 1-14

L

Cumulative Index